D0712146

HIGHER EDUCATION:
Handbook of Theory and Research

Volume III

Associate Editors

Philip G. Altbach, *State University of New York at Buffalo*
(comparative higher education)

Alan E. Bayer, *Virginia Polytechnic Institute and State University*
(faculty)

Kim S. Cameron, *University of Michigan*
(organizational theory and behavior)

Cameron Fincher, *University of Georgia*
(curriculum and instruction)

Barbara A. Lee, *Rutgers University*
(legal issues)

David W. Leslie, *Florida State University*
(institutional policy issues)

Larry L. Leslie, *University of Arizona*
(finance and resource allocations)

Kenneth P. Mortimer, *Pennsylvania State University*
(governance and planning)

Ernest T. Pascarella, *University of Illinois at Chicago*
(research methodology)

Patrick T. Terenzini, *State University of New York at Albany*
(students)

John R. Thelin, *College of William and Mary*
(history and philosophy)

William Toombs, *Pennsylvania State University*
(continuing education for the professions)

HIGHER EDUCATION:
Handbook of Theory and Research

Volume III

Edited by

John C. Smart
Virginia Polytechnic Institute and State University

Published under the sponsorship of
The Association for Institutional Research

AGATHON PRESS, INC.
New York

LB
2300
H638
v.3

LC

© 1987 Agathon Press, Inc.
111 Eighth Avenue
New York, NY 10011

All Rights Reserved

No portion of this book may be
reproduced by any process, stored
in a retrieval system, or transmitted
in any form, or by any means, without
the express written permission of
the publisher.

ISBN: 0-87586-080-X
ISSN: 0882-4126

Printed in the United States

9-8-89

Contents

The Contributors

KENNETH BETTENHAUSEN is Assistant Professor of Management in the College of Business Administration at Texas A & M University. His research investigates norm formation in ad hoc decision making groups and the role that coalitions and enactment processes play in establishing organizational strategies and the effectiveness of those strategies.

MARTHA C. BRASWELL is presently Coordinator of Undergraduate Studies in the School of Music at the University of Georgia. Recently, she graduated from the University of Georgia's Institute of Higher Education with an Ed.D. in higher education administration where she served as a research assistant for Dr. D. Parker Young. Her current research is in legal aspects of higher education and in musical sightreading.

RONALD M. CERVERO is Associate Professor of Adult Education at the University of Georgia. His publications have focused in the area of continuing professional education, particularly on the relationship of continuing education to performance, how professionals learn, and interorganizational collaboration. He is a member of the executive committee of the Commission of Professors of Adult Education and a consulting editor for *Adult Education Quarterly*.

ROBERT L. CROWSON is Associate Professor of Educational Administration in the College of Education, University of Illinois (Chicago). He has written on organizational theory and policy analysis in education, as well as on the work lives of educational administrators, from research employing qualitative methods. He is the coauthor of a recent book examining alternative theoretical approaches to educational adminstration.

CAMERON FINCHER is Regents Professor of Higher Education and Psychology at the University of Georgia where he is also Director of the Institute of Higher Education. He is the author of a chapter on "Learning Theory and Research" in Volume I and a chapter on "Trends and Issues in Curricular Development" in Volume II.

WILLIAM EDGAR MAXWELL is currently developing management research training for university and community college administrators in the doctoral program of the University of Southern California where he is an Associate Professor. He continues to study the sociology of institutional reforms in higher education whose objective has been to extend service to less privileged groups, including the innovations of the Land Grant universities, community colleges, and rural medical schools. His recent international studies involve comparisons of the impact of higher education in several developing and Third World societies.

LARRY NUCCI is Associate Professor and Chair of Educational Psychology at the University of Illinois at Chicago. His research interests include the development of moral and social knowledge, and moral education. He has published on these issues in *Child Development, Review of Educational Research, American Educational Research Journal,* and *Perspectives*.

ERNEST T. PASCARELLA is Professor of Urban Education Research at the University of Illinois at Chicago. His research interests include student persistence in postsecondary education and the impact of college on student development. He has written and published extensively in these areas over the past ten years.

JOHN R. THELIN is Professor and Director of the Higher Education Doctoral Program at The College of William and Mary. He also is a member of the American Studies Program and recipient of the university's 1986 Phi Beta Kappa Faculty Award for the Advancement of Scholarship. His research in progress includes studies of elites and access, intercollegiate athletics, and public policy in higher education.

J. FREDERICKS VOLKWEIN is Director of Institutional Research and Adjunct Professor of Educational Administration and Policy Studies, University at Albany, State University of New York. His research interests and publications include the areas of governance and administrative structure, campus-government relations, planning strategies and models, academic program evaluation, and the study of colleges and universities as complex organizations.

WILLIAM C. WEILER is Associate Director of the Management Information Division at the University of Minnesota. His publications in areas related to higher education have focused on policy issues such as student choice behavior, faculty retention, faculty retirement decision making, student loan programs, institutional costs, and institutional planning and resource allocation.

DAVID A. WHETTEN is Professor of Business Administration in the College of Commerce and Business Administration at the University of Illinois. His recent research has focused on organizational life cycle processes, and the determinants of success and failure in colleges and universities. He is the coauthor of books on organizational effectiveness, management skill development, organizational decline, and interorganizational relations. He is currently developing a Handbook of Organizational Theory. He also serves as the editor of the *Academy of Management Review,* and associate editor of *Administration and Society.*

EVERETT K. WILSON is Professor Emeritus of Sociology at the University of North Carolina, Chapel Hill. For ten years he was editor of *Social Forces.* His publications include a translation of Durkheim's *Moral Education; Sociology: Rules, Roles and Relationships;* and, with C. A. Goldsmid, *Passing on Sociology,* a book on problems of effective instruction.

JAMES YANKOVICH is Professor in the Higher Education Doctoral Program at The College of William and Mary. He also has served as Dean of Academic Affairs at the University of Michigan-Flint and Dean of the School of Education at William and Mary. His consulting and research projects include campus master planning, physical plant and facilities administration, and the study of organization and governance.

D. PARKER YOUNG is Professor of Higher Education and Graduate Coordinator in the Institute of Higher Education at the University of Georgia. He now serves as President of the National Organization on Legal Problems of Education. He has authored many books, monographs, and articles in the area of higher education law and is a contributing and consulting editor for several publications including *The College Student and the Courts, The College Administrator and the Courts, The Schools and the Courts,* and *The Computer Law Monitor.* He has been invited to address numerous higher education organizations and groups on the topic of legal issues in higher education.

WILLIAM H. YOUNG, III, is currently Dean, College of Continuing Education, and Associate Professor, within the Department of Leadership and Educational Policy Studies, College of Education, Northern Illinois University. Dr. Young has served as a continuing education administrator in higher education for 20 years. He has served in leadership positions within continuing education associations, has authored numerous articles, and has presented topics and issues of interest to educational and private sector audiences throughout the nation.

Qualitative Research Methods in Higher Education

Robert L. Crowson
University of Illinois at Chicago

Some of you may have wondered what became of our College Ghost. Because we had a ghost, and there are people in this room who saw him.

> "The Ghost Who Vanished by Degrees," in *High Spirits*,
> by Robertson Davies (1982).

Ghost tracking is certainly a bit beyond the pale of current, state-of-the-art research methods. Nevertheless, Robertson Davies's amusing account of the ghost haunting a graduate college, seeking, 'lo these many years, a chance to complete his examination for the Ph.D. ("I shall never be at peace without it"), captures well the spirit of a qualitative approach to understanding in higher education. Institutions of higher learning are filled with ghosts (even a few demons now and then). Traditions left inviolate from the Middle Ages, a system of governance that defies rational explanation, an edifice haunted by departmental rivalry and conflict, a professoriate that slips ethereally into and out of strange institutional roles and relationships, and organizational "sagas" (Clark, 1970) that live on and on in collective memory through a changing society—all of these, ghostlike, are essential elements of college and university environments.

It is only recently that scholars have recognized the productive and the definitional importance of some hard-to-measure (almost ghostly) characteristics of organizations (Peterson, 1985). Among these are the phenomena of loose coupling (Weick, 1976, 1984), organized anarchy (Cohen and March, 1974; March and Olsen, 1976); the organizational culture (Deal and Kennedy, 1982; Jelinek, Smircich, and Hirsch, 1983); organizational socialization (Van Maanen, 1976; Van Maanen and Schein, 1979); institutional myths (Martin et al., 1983; Sproull, 1981); and organizational learning (Hedberg, 1981). In the study of organizations, increased attention is being directed toward the use of research methods that probe into the above subtleties of institutional life, that seek an understanding of an environment now known to be much more complex than first imagined, and that strive for theory formation rather than theory testing and generalization. In this search for greater understanding, the use of qualitative research methodology is receiving new interest and paradigmatic development.

There are, to be sure, a number of works of a qualitative research genre that can be regarded as "classics" in the literature on higher education. Among these are such outstanding case studies as *Boys in White* (Becker et al., 1961); *The Open Door College* (Clark, 1960); *Personality and Social Change* (Newcomb, 1943); and *The Distinctive College* (Clark, 1970). Additionally, higher education is deep in essays, commentaries, and reminiscences by some of its (and the nation's) outstanding figures. While not research in a traditional sense, such contributions as Kerr's *The Uses of the University* (1964), Barzun's *The American University* (1968), and Bell's *The Reforming of General Education* (1966) all provide the from-experience-toward-theory backdrop that is a central element of the qualitative approach. Finally, some notable institutional histories and biographies have enriched the field, including Morison's *The Founding of Harvard College* (1935), Storr's *Harper's University* (1966), and James's biography of *Charles W. Eliot* (1930).

Nevertheless, the qualitative research tradition is not strong in the study of higher education. While case studies, commentaries, and histories are in evidence, investigations employing participant observation, nonfocused interviewing, disguised observation, and other techniques that are usually associated with a more ethnographic approach to data are in rather short supply (Tierney, 1985). There has been some effort to understand college student cultures through ethnographic-type methods (Bushnell, 1962; Becker, Geer, and Hughes, 1968; Cottle, 1977; Lamont, 1979). There has also been some study of the internal workings of higher education institutions in terms of their organizational cultures (Riesman and Jencks, 1962; London, 1978; Clark, 1972); their administrative dynamics (Baldridge, 1971; Miller, 1978; Hendricks, 1975; Tierney, 1983); and their efforts at curriculum reform (Grant and Riesman, 1978). The literature is not deep, however, and neither a widely shared methodology of qualitative research in higher education nor a clear delineation of the key topics and questions calling for study has yet surfaced—despite the urgency of such observations as Marvin Peterson's (1985) plea that we must "try to understand what holds together these fascinating institutions as organizations."

PURPOSE OF THE REVIEW

It is the purpose of this review to examine the literature appropriate to an improved appreciation of the role of qualitative research methods in the study of higher education. Our focus will primarily be upon the methodological traditions offered by anthropology and qualitative sociology, leaving for another reviewer the growing methodological interest in the application of historical inquiry to organizational analysis (Mattingly, 1983). The central task of our review is to highlight the key elements of and issues in qualitative research methodologies, as these methods may apply to the special institutional circumstances and conditions of work in postsecondary education in the United States. Thus, the review treats three major topics: (1) guiding principles of qualitative research methodology; (2) methodological issues in the application of qualitative research to higher education; and (3) considerations in the implementation of qualitative research in higher education.

A first key question, of course, is the definitional: Just what is qualitative research methodology? As interest in the topic has spread, it has received many labels and generated some infighting as to the most appropriate definition (Van Maanen, Dobbs, and Faulkner, 1982). To some researchers, the preferred descriptive term is *ethnography,* or with a more restrained meaning, *ethnomethodology.* Ethnography has been historically associated with anthropological method[1]; and although it has strict constructionists (e.g., Wolcott, 1984) and those who interpret loosely (e.g., LeCompte and Goetz, 1982), an emphasis upon the study of culture (usually through a lengthy period of participant observation) is the methodological focus (Spradley, 1980; Sanday, 1979). *Ethnomethodology* is a term coined by Garfinkel (1967) to represent a more sociology-based approach to understanding (e.g., using symbolic interaction theory) (Mehan and Wood, 1975; Psathas, 1979). Ethnomethodologists are less holistic than traditional ethnographers,[2] focusing intently on the meanings (and language) that individuals use to make sense of (to impute reality to) their own worlds (Geertz, 1973; Schwartz and Jacobs, 1979).

A descriptor of recent vintage is *naturalistic inquiry* (Guba, 1978; Lincoln and Guba, 1985). It is important to note that naturalistic inquiry starts its argument at the epistemological (presenting itself as an alternative philosophic paradigm), in contrast with the conventional approach to scientific inquiry (logical positivism). The basic assumptions of naturalistic inquiry are fundamentally at odds with positivism and are *not* reconcilable (Lincoln and Guba, 1985, p. 33) with the positivistic tradition. For example, while positivism assumes a discoverable reality in nature which (once known) can be predicted and controlled, the naturalist posits only "multiple constructed realities," which may not be controlled and, at best, can be understood. While positivism separates the researcher and the object of inquiry, naturalism argues that knower and known are inseparable. Positivism assumes that, through science, inquiry can proceed toward generalizable truth statements and toward a knowledge of cause-effect linkages. Alternatively, naturalism argues that working hypotheses (rather than lawlike generalizations) and "mutual simultaneous shaping" (rather than causation) are at the heart of the methodology. Using these differing philosophic assumptions as guides, the scholar would do research in the style of the naturalist paradigm—including inductive data analysis, purposive sampling, the development of grounded theory, and the use of an emergent research design (Lincoln and Guba, 1985, pp. 36–43).

Thus, within the rubric of something we'll call the *qualitative research method,* there is room for wide interpretation. Van Maanen et al. (1982) warn that a clear and concise definition of qualitative research at this time is most difficult. From a specific press toward cultural understanding (ethnography) to the larger suggestion of an alternative philosophic paradigm (e.g., naturalistic), the field encompasses a cornucopia of foci, assumptions, and techniques. Variously labeled *field research, case study research, descriptive research,* and, of course, *ethnography* and *qualitative research,* neither the method nor its key descriptors are clear. At best, it can be said that to work ''in the style'' of the qualitative researcher is to consistently employ such practices of data collection as participant observation, the discovery and use of unobtrusive measures, informal interviewing, life history construction, content analysis, and videotaping—and to seek from one's data an *understanding* of the phenomena observed rather than some generalizable knowledge or explanation, prediction, and control.

One definitional point that must be heavily emphasized, however, is that it would be wrong to conceive of research methodology as a single continuum—with conventional quantitative inquiry at one end and the qualitative approach to research (naturalism) at the other end. Smith and Heshusius (1986) have observed that despite their fundamentally different epistemological traditions, quantitative and qualitative approaches have tended of late to be treated as potentially compatible systems of investigation. Basic philosophic differences are ignored in the interest of concentrating upon *procedures* from both traditions that can be cooperatively employed to serve a line of research. The differences are ''deepistemologized,'' and the principal concern then becomes how to perform qualitative inquiry (Smith and Heshusius, 1986, p. 7).

Although this review is also focused upon the procedural, with little attention given to the underlying philosophical controversies, it is not our claim that a thorough understanding of qualitative inquiry can be left at the how-to-do-it stage. There *are* fundamental differences between the quantitative (positivist) and qualitative (phenomenological) research traditions. Qualitative research is not just another approach to ''scientific'' understanding in the conventional sense (Smith and Heshusius, 1986; Lincoln and Guba, 1985). Some of these fundamental differences become immediately apparent, below, as the review opens with a discussion of the guiding principles that surround qualitative research methodology.

PRINCIPLES OF QUALITATIVE RESEARCH

It is above all a central goal of *understanding* that forms one of the method's important procedural principles. Its other key points of departure are a norm of researcher proximity, an emphasis upon analytic induction, and an appreciation of the value-bound context of most inquiry. We will discuss each of these principles in some detail, proceeding from this discussion to the consideration of key research issues in the special context of higher education.

The Search for Understanding

Mehan and Wood (1975) use an example from a study of the Azande of Africa (Evans-Pritchard, 1937) to illustrate the central problem of understanding. When faced with important decisions in their lives, the Azande consult an oracle. This consultation consists of gathering the bark from a certain type of tree, preparing the bark in a special ceremony, and feeding it to a chicken. The decision to be made is posed in simple yes-or-no terms, and the death of the chicken signals an affirmative or negative action. For extremely important decisions, however, the Azande take the second step of feeding the substance to another chicken and reversing the meaning of the chicken's death. If the first chicken's survival indicated that the oracle had said yes, then the second chicken's death would provide the same message.

Mehan and Wood remark that our Western scientific understanding tells us that the tree bark contains a poisonous quality that kills some chickens. Our understanding stops there, however. What do the Azande do when the oracle contradicts itself? What happens to their faith in the process when the answer given by the oracle is contradicted by later events? Our Western rationalism forces us to questions such as these in the face of many mysteries and contradictions left blatantly unanswered. To the Azande, however, there are no contradictions. The Azande are not even aware of the poisonous properties of the tree. Faith in the power of the oracle is explanation enough (pp. 8–9).

To *understand* the Azande is a tall order for us. We must somehow learn to see the world in their terms, from their perspective. The contradictions that perplex us aren't theirs. To know something in their culture is a far cry from "knowing something" in ours. Of course, if one were to turn the direction of the research around, the Azande might be equally perplexed by the tendencies of our decision makers to acquire, but then ignore, stacks of number-filled computer printouts; to meet endlessly with colleagues without ever reaching "yes" or "no" conclusions; and to make a decision, only to change it immediately when "politics" intervene.

The development of understanding as a central research objective has been attributed most prominently to Max Weber (using the German term *Verstehen*).[3] The researcher who is concerned with understanding seeks to observe and interpret human behavior from the observed actor's own frame of reference—developing an appreciation of the world as others experience it, and becoming acquainted with the subjective states of mind of other people (Schwartz and

Jacobs, 1979, pp. 17–20). The search for understanding is often considered to be in direct contrast with the central goal of conventional or positivist inquiry, which purportedly seeks an objectively determined fact or causation in the study of social phenomena. The philosophic cornerstone of qualitative methodology is its effort to describe and render understandable the world of subjective experience rather than to discover its "truths" or generalizable cause-effect relationships.

An interesting illustration of this perspective is Seymour Sarason's (1982) suggestion that we indulge in a bit of fantasy—examining our educational institutions as if we were beings from outer space poised on invisible platforms above these institutions and trying to figure out "what's going on" (pp. 96–98). As observers, we might possibly start out with questions about obvious regularities—the perplexing patterns of human behavior that are noticeable down below. While Sarason's own outer-spacers were intrigued by elementary schools, the discernible regularities of colleges and universities are no less a puzzle. Poised above an urban university such as the one served by this author, our nonearthly being may ask why so many young-looking adults are in evidence during daylight hours while persons in their apparent middle years predominate in the evenings. Why do large groups of people congregate periodically in rooms with rows of seating facing one individual who talks a great deal while all others remain silent and write? Why do some of these groups appear to meet as often as five times in seven days, while others meet for longer periods as few as three times or even only once in seven days? Why does the person speaking to the large group spend so much of the rest of his or her time sitting silently alone in a small room with a desk, except when sitting around a table at irregular intervals with other speakers, all often talking at once? Why do extremely large groups of persons congregate once or twice a week in the evening without a speaker and show such enthusiasm watching the movement of a ball on a floor below them?

In short, without great sophistication or methodological elaboration, the one guiding theme of qualitative research is to assume a mantle of almost childlike curiosity, trying to understand—or even in the simple words of Baldridge (1971), trying to "find out how a situation ticks" (p. 31). This sense of curiosity (playing the role of the cultural ingenue) in the search for understanding is even conveyed clearly in the language that researchers have used to describe the purpose(s) of their work. From existing research of the qualitative genre in higher education, for example, some common descriptors have been (1) "acquiring a 'feeling' for the dynamics of the situation" (Baldridge, 1971, p. 31); (2) "discovering phenomena whose existence we were unaware of at the beginning of the research" (Becker et al., 1961, p. 18); plus (3) "discovering and investigating the unexpected" (London, 1978, p. 151). It would appear, again, that ghost tracking is not just an amusing bit of Robertson Davies; it is also a fundamental principle of the qualitative research method.

The Norm of Researcher Proximity

If understanding (in Weber's sense of *Verstehen*) is the prime goal, a norm of researcher proximity is the central procedural principle in most qualitative research. The person who is trying to understand should be there, at hand, as events occur and as behavior is exhibited. It is the researcher who is the main instrument of investigation (Burgess, 1984). Furthermore, it is the researcher as not only observer but additionally as *participant* in the events and behaviors under study that provides the foundation for *Verstehen*.

Becker and Geer (1960) explain the importance of participant observation, rather than mere observation, as follows:

> In general, the participant observer gathers data by participating in the daily life of the group or organization that he studies. He watches the people he is studying to see what situations they ordinarily meet and how they behave in them. He talks with the other participants and discovers their interpretations of the events he has observed. (p. 269)

To Becker and others (e.g., Wilson, 1977; Cusick, 1983; Dorr-Bremme, 1985), the essential value in the dual role of both observer and participant comes from an actual sharing in the events under study. By participating, and not just observing, the researcher does not simply witness and describe but, by participating, comes to the fuller understanding that belongs uniquely to the members of that culture. The result, ideally, will be a description and interpretation of phenomena that move from an outsider account toward an assessment of events that approaches *Verstehen*—for a "true understanding of the reality can be had only if one will join in the creation" (Cusick, 1983, p. 132).

There are methodological problems aplenty in this researcher role, of course, and we will discuss some of these later in this chapter. Additionally, qualitative methods do not demand that participant observation be employed as the only means of gathering data. Formal and informal interviewing, nonparticipant observation, documentary analysis, even questionnaires and paper-pencil examinations can be employed by qualitative researchers to enhance understanding. Indeed, a cornerstone of the method is the notion that wherever possible, the researcher should strive for a "thick description" of phenomena (Geertz, 1973). A thick description is a many-sided glimpse of events (using a variety of data sources), enabling the reader of a research report to form his or her own understanding of the findings (Lincoln and Guba, 1985).

Nevertheless, participant observation is a mainstay of the method. Researcher proximity is considered a necessary if not sufficient condition of meaningful inquiry. Two correlate notions that normally accompany the proximity norm, furthermore, are immersion and the study of "natural settings." Beyond proximity, the qualitative researcher must seek to examine behavior as it occurs naturally (Wilson, 1977). Individuals are influenced by their settings and are furthermore wrapped in these settings within intricate "webs of significance" (Geertz, 1973, p. 5). A strand or two removed from the web, or examined closely without a simultaneous appreciation of the structure of the entire web, could give a false impression of the observed culture. Additionally, beyond proximity, the scholar must be sufficiently immersed in the research setting to appreciate wide varieties of meaningful behavior (Naroll and Cohen, 1970; Pelto and Pelto, 1978). Face-to-face contact and verbal behavior are to be observed, to be sure, but gestures, positions, facial expressions, visual signals, and the like are also vital routes toward understanding for the fieldwork investigator, all contributing to the total message of the research setting (Dorr-Bremme, 1985).

Indeed, immersion and naturalism have been such important constructs in qualitative inquiry that for many years a "school of hard knocks approach" was considered the proper pedagogical method in the training of ethnographers (Cohen and Naroll, 1970). It was felt that a researcher would learn best if simply thrown into a culture, for technique rests ultimately on the idiosyncratic person and personality of the ethnographer. Cohen and Naroll (1970) write:

> The field worker was simply told to bring back as much material as possible documenting the way of life of the people he had lived among. To plan more rigorously would probably bias observation, it was thought; or even worse, it would prevent the collection of valuable—and often disappearing—data. (pp. 7–8)

The Emphasis upon Analytic Induction

Not only is the qualitative researcher expected to "be there," observing and bringing back whatever data seem appropriate to understanding; the method asks additionally that the inquiry seek to build understanding inductively, from the ground up (Lincoln and Guba, 1985). The point is captured best by Glaser and Strauss (1967) in the title of their influential book *The Discovery of Grounded Theory*. In place of the standard deductive activities of the scientific method, involving the formulation of hypotheses and the specification of data categories *a priori* before entering the field (Wilson, 1977), the qualitative researcher seeks to build, from the observed data, a bit of inductive knowledge. This knowledge is often in the form of tentative, working hypotheses (Lincoln & Guba, 1985, p. 38). The working hypotheses are "grounded" in the individual case and are both time- and context-bound and thus are not to be confused with data-based generalizations.

The argument in support of such an inductive emphasis is that the investigator of natural phenomena is more than likely to be abysmally ignorant of the field setting. The more precise the prior hypothesis and the more carefully structured the research design, the better the likelihood of missing meaningful behaviors and important occurrences as they fortuitously appear (Levine, 1970). The exigencies and characteristics of the research setting itself (Cohen and Naroll,

1970), and even the "feel" of the research setting (Baldridge, 1971), should direct the researcher, rather than a prior set of ideas or hypotheses. The researcher must actually enter the field and develop a sense (a feel) for what is meaningful, trusting to intuition as thoroughly as to reason. Even, strangely, in those settings that the scholar would be presumed to know well (e.g., university departments, families, and grocery stores), ignorance is abundant. To live in a setting is a far cry from being asked to study it (Psathas, 1973).

Methodological controversy has arisen as to what role any prior theorizing at all should play in qualitative research. From a purist's perspective, Psathas (1973) writes, "No presuppositions, whether they come from scientific theories or commonsense knowledge of social structures, are to influence the observer or cloud his vision" (p. 7). Researchers should set aside prior assumptions and what they think they already know about the setting, adopting the stance of completely disinterested observers (Psathas, 1973). Campbell (1975) labels such expectations naive. No culture can be observed in its entirety, and what one does "see" will surely be colored by investigator subjectivity. In recent years, fieldworkers have become more comfortable with a bit of prior focusing and sharpening in qualitative inquiry, recognizing that decisions on what to include as data and how to describe what has been observed are inevitable (Pelto and Pelto, 1978). While maintaining their flexibility and eclecticism, these fieldworkers of a more realist persuasion are willing to shape the specific themes, issues, and questions of their inquiry (Dorr-Bremme, 1985). The recognition, of course, is that the investigator's theoretical point of view does color a study and will shape the inductive vision of reality that appears in the researcher's findings. This brings us to the fourth major principle of qualitative research.

An Appreciation
of the Value-Bound Context of Inquiry

"The ethos of social science," writes Gunnar Myrdal (1969), "is the search for 'objective' truth" (p. 3). In practice, continues Myrdal, students of society are highly unlikely to be able to liberate themselves very far from the powerful hold of (1) the normative and theoretical heritage (the reigning paradigms) of their field of inquiry; (2) the influence of their own cultural milieu; and (3) the influences stemming from their own personalities. To these, Lincoln and Guba (1985) would add the problematic influence of values that reside within the research setting itself (p. 38). In short, all research, whether qualitative or quantitative, is heavily value-bound.

Persons engaged in qualitative research, particularly ethnographers, have long been aware of the colorations that ideas and beliefs place upon any interpretation of the world as it "really is." Influenced heavily by phenomenological theory (e.g., Husserl, 1952; Schutz, 1967), those who work within the ethnographic tradition have been careful not only to recognize but to try to compensate for the role that subjectivity plays in the interpretation of observed behavior (Jehenson, 1973; Rist, 1979). Ethnographic methods emphasize skills in suspending observer preconceptions (the term *bracketing* is used to describe this effort), and ethnographers seek instead to become sufficiently immersed in the culture under study to be able to take on and understand events from an insider's perspective (Wilson, 1977; Rist, 1979).

Recognizing that their efforts to suspend their own values may be far less than complete, phenomenology-minded researchers stress that one further necessary check is for observers to state their own biases clearly, hopefully to mitigate thereby some unintendedly subjective effects (Fetterman, 1984b; Dorr-Bremme, 1985). Myrdal (1969) cautions that such statements of value premises in social science research should be (1) explicit, and not concealed in implied assumptions; (2) purposefully and volitionally selected; and (3) part of a consistent and thus not mutually incompatible system of values (pp. 63–64).[4]

Interestingly, one of the principal methodological debates within the qualitative research tradition, one tied closely to the problems raised by value-boundedness, is the contrast between emic and etic approaches to ethnography. The emicist seeks to discover and describe the patterns of a culture in terms of the meanings and idea systems that natives employ *in that culture*. The eticist looks for systems, patterns, and meanings in observed behavior from the standpoint of constructs defined *by the researcher*. From the emic perspective, only statements about the single culture under study can be reported; from the etic viewpoint, cross-cultural comparisons, using the same researcher-derived concepts, are possible (Pelto and Pelto, 1978, pp. 54–66). The emic-etic debate illustrates the continuing struggle between the recognition of subjectivity (both observer and observed) and the scientific aspiration nevertheless toward objective knowledge, or at least a bit of theory building that permits some propositions about human behavior. Campbell (1970) argues that this struggle between a recognition of subjectivity and a search for objectivity can at best produce a compromise, a middle ground of "hypothetical realism"—where constructs built from observation can be only "fallibly known, through a process of hypothetical models only indirectly confirmed" (p. 69).

In brief summary, the qualitative approach to inquiry in higher education rests upon four key procedural principles. *First,* the central research objective is to understand rather than to explain, predict, or control. Procedurally, a search for understanding asks the researcher to seek to appreciate each setting through the perspectives of its natives, and to satisfy an anthropologistlike curiosity about the behaviors that have been observed ("What's going on here?"). The *second* procedural principle suggests that understanding *(Verstehen)* emerges most readily if the researcher is himself or herself the prime instrument of data collection. A norm of researcher proximity surrounds the method. Being there, on hand, as behavior occurs and/or is reported (e.g., through interviewing) assists critically in meeting the *third* procedural principle: an emphasis upon analytic induction. The method asks its adherents to build interpretive understanding from the ground up rather than, in a hypothesis-testing sense, from the top down. Whether inductive or deductive, the qualitative approach recognizes *fourth* that the search for understanding is heavily value-laden. The setting, the researcher, the larger culture, and even the intellectual assumptions one brings to the process of *Verstehen*—all color the inquiry.

METHODOLOGICAL ISSUES
IN QUALITATIVE RESEARCH IN EDUCATION

All four of the guiding procedural principles of qualitative research raise methodological questions of special importance for inquiry in higher education. Among these are issues of (1) familiarity; (2) selection; and (3) trustworthiness. Implicit in the emic-etic debate is the question of whether a person closely familiar with a culture under study (an insider) or a person less familiar but perhaps more curious (an outsider) would be the better observer of natural phenomena. Furthermore, in a method emphasizing thick description and holistic understanding, centrally important methodological decisions surround questions of what to observe, where to observe, and what to focus upon in observation (sampling and selection issues). And in a method seeking neither objective and generalizable truth nor merely subjective storytelling (but some middle ground of theory development), problems of reliability and validity (trustworthiness) must be treated carefully. We will develop each of these issues in terms of their special saliency for the qualitative study of colleges and universities.

The Issue of Familiarity

In his review of ethnographic research in higher education, Tierney (1985) finds it exceedingly strange that higher education has not been thoroughly subjected to qualitative-style inquiry. The paradox is that colleges and universities display many of the characteristics considered particularly appropriate for anthropological fieldwork. Studies of well-defined subcultures (e.g., towns, tribal villages, and communities) have been favored by ethnographers because they tend to have delimitable boundaries and populations, are relatively complete social systems, and are small enough to be covered (in transportation terms) economically by a single researcher (Pelto and Pelto, 1978, pp. 177–178). Residential colleges and universities similarly are self-contained, with definable boundaries and with their activities carried out in close member proximity. Furthermore, the researcher in higher education would have the benefit of prior intimate knowledge of the language and technology of the institution under study. Thus, he or she would also be able to enjoy the luxury of minimal acclimatization or socialization time, plus the possible benefit of full immersion "at home," where one earns a living as well as conducts inquiry (Messerschmidt, 1981; Tierney, 1985).

One of the strongest arguments for "insider research" (Aguilar, 1981) in higher education is the benefit that cultural familiarity accords any researcher who is faced with trying to understand a not-easily-illuminated and frequently arcane slice of daily life. In his ethnographic study of a Himalayan village, Berreman (1962) observed, "Every ethnographer, when he reaches the field, is faced immediately with accounting for himself before the people he proposes to learn to know. Only when this has been accomplished can he proceed to his avowed task of seeking to understand and interepret the way of life of those people" (p. 269). It was only with time, patience, and careful "impression management" that Berreman was able to unearth the purposefully concealed dark secrets of his Himalayan subjects sufficiently to provide a meaningful ethnography.

Institutions of higher education are replete with their own innumerable dark secrets (even ghosts). Masland (1985) cautions that the most informative windows upon organizational culture in higher education are often its special sagas (Clark, 1972); heroes; symbols, including metaphors (Cohen and March, 1974); and organizational rituals (providing a continuity with the past). These (usually hidden or at least masked) insights into daily life are not immediately apparent to the casual observer, nor are they likely to be shared freely with an unsocialized outsider. The university as a culture is complex, awash in contradictions (e.g., trade-offs between community and scholarship), and even flawed in places (Weick, 1984). Furthermore, Masland (1985) claims that in institutions where the culture is relatively "weak," the cultural themes will not stand out clearly and may be replete with hard-to-interpret anomalies.

An informed and culturally acceptable insider may also be better placed than an outsider to interpret observed behaviors within their appropriate institutional context. Cultures are multilayered and nested one within another (Dorr-Bremme, 1985). They involve for every person a variety of cultural attributions and a varied, lifelong chain of prior cultural experiences (Becker and Geer, 1960; Van Maanen, 1984). Indeed, in his study of differences between the graduate business schools of Harvard and MIT, Van Maanen (1984) concludes that prior socialization, the cultural impact of the business school, and the job placement and success of business school graduates all combine into a larger "culture of orientation" for individuals that cannot be easily or cleanly separated into one formative institutionalized influence versus another. Even to an insider, just what is the relevant social context of the institution under study is not readily ascertainable.

A strong argument for insider research, or at least a long period of immersion for the outsider, is fashioned additionally by Rosalie Wax (1971). Wax argues that understanding, while a desired outcome of research, is in more ways a necessary *precondition* of useful fieldwork. She writes, "A researcher cannot simply learn a few basic 'rules of fieldwork,' drop himself among an alien people like a man from Mars, and then proceed to acquire understanding. As any researcher or explorer he will fare better if he anticipates what he will confront and prepares himself accordingly" (p. 15). Furthermore, she continues:

> Perhaps the most egregious error that a fieldworker can commit is to assume that he can win the immediate regard of his hosts by telling them that he wants to "become one of them" or by implying, by word or act, that the fact that they tolerate his presence means that he *is* one of them. Indeed, this is the mistake that all experienced fieldworkers warn against. (p. 47)

While never really "one of them," the successful fieldworker must nevertheless acquire sufficient member knowledge to be able to understand shared frames of reference and to appreciate what is often covert and implicit in the social world under study. Furthermore, it helps significantly if the fieldworker is able easily to blend into the local context, thereby being less likely to alter social situations by his or her presence (Aguilar, 1981). In *Making the Grade* (1968), Howard Becker and his colleagues asked the question, "What is it like to be a college student?" They wanted to answer this question in the *students'* terms, learning about life in college through the students' eyes, and discovering in the process that this is a tough methodological job (Becker et al., 1968, p. 2).

Critics of insider research argue, however, that it is exactly the perspective of a man from Mars that *should* be emphasized in qualitative research (Stephenson and Greer, 1981). Researchers who are too much at home within a culture are apt to find little to arouse their curiosity—failing to recognize interesting, strange, or unusual patterns simply because they are too thoroughly acculturated, too familiar with the setting. Furthermore, insiders may experience member-type pressures and expectations. They may be expected by those whom they are interviewing and observing to take a stand on current issues (e.g., organizational turf battles and leader personality conflicts). They may also experience pressure to produce an advocacy-oriented report, and they may feel reluctant to ask "certain questions" known to be politically charged or personally threatening. Insiders may also not receive the openness and relaxed honesty that respondents may accord an "ignorant" outsider; and finally, they may not enjoy the allowances for mistakes (e.g., dropping in uninvited on sensitive meetings) that members often permit strangers (Aguilar, 1981; Stephenson and Greer, 1981). Stephenson and Greer (1981) conclude that fieldworkers studying the familiar must work exceptionally hard to place "stranger value" upon all that is familiar, recording as much detail as possible regardless of their sense of its relevance and adopting an "artificial naïveté" throughout the study (p. 24).

Becoming a stranger is of course exceptionally difficult for those persons (usually institutionally affiliated academics themselves) who would undertake fieldwork in higher education. The setting is familiar; moreover, the researcher is already aware of respective roles within the institution (e.g., administrator, teacher, student, and staff member) and is aware of the many norms and taboos that accompany role relationships. In a methodological appendix to his ethnographic study of a community college, for example, London (1978) discussed his difficulties in observing college classes. The instructors, used to autonomy, tended to feel evaluated and sought frequently to draw the fieldworker into class discussions as a colleague and coteacher. Fears of evaluation were also evident in postclass efforts by teachers to elicit some feedback: "What have you found out?" or "How's the study going?" (p. 162). On their part, the community college students frequently tried to turn the researcher into an informant or an adviser, sensing that the observer had developed an "in" into that mysterious world of college administration and faculty affairs that is effectively denied them within traditionally fashioned institutional relationships (London, 1978, pp. 156–164).

Realistically, the researcher, no matter how hard he or she tries, can probably never assume the mantle of a complete stranger nor be fully naive. Indeed, in his study of college reward structures, Thomas Cottle (1977) openly recognized the formative forces of his own college days in the 1950s and the guidance received from his own parents as influences upon his contemporary observation of college life. Thus, in the practice of inquiry, some advanced warning, a bit of introspection, and a knowledgeable sensitivity about the higher education setting is probably called for in understanding the responses likely among one's research subjects (e.g., faculty, students, and staff). As Wilson (1977, p. 248) points out, the subjects' cautiousness regarding the intent of the investigation, their desire to exhibit appropriate behavior, their interest in being evaluated positively, and their hope for a special personal relationship with the researcher—all these are forces that shape behavior under many research designs. Nevertheless these forces would bear special consideration in higher education—with its strange combinations of cultivation alongside suspicion of intellect, egalitarianism and elitism, avant-gardism in juxtaposition with conservatism, and freedom amidst conformity (Kerr, 1964).

The Issue of Selection

Masland (1985) suggests that to understand organizational culture in higher education, the researcher should attend most particularly to the details of daily life. But just what are these details? In answer, Masland offers four key "windows" upon an organizational culture. These are institutional sagas or stories, organizational heroes and the examples they set, organizational symbols and/or metaphors, and organizational rituals (Masland, 1985, pp. 160–163).

To other scholars, however, the details of daily life might be better observed, and more instructive, if close attention is paid to (1) the routine interactions (both verbal and nonverbal) of organizational participants (Dorr-Bremme, 1985); (2) the uses that people make of their time in organizations (Mintzberg, 1973); (3) the physical traces, episodic records, and other unobtrusive measures that pervade organizations (Webb et al., 1966); and even (4) the occasional pathologies of organizational existence (e.g., lying, stealing, or cheating) (Smircich, 1983, p. 353). In an interesting and unusual insight, for example, Abraham Maslow (1965) suggests that the level of "grumbling" in an organization is a key indicator of its state of being.

Although the fundamental goal of the qualitative-minded researcher is traditionally a holistic portrayal of a culture, recognizing that cultures are in fact integrated wholes, it is obvious that inquiry into *all* of the many details of daily life is well past the grasp of the observer. Limits must be placed upon the scope of research, a sampling of organizational behavior must occur, and a selecting and focusing of attention must take place. In a pure sense, the qualitative researcher would wish to avoid the biases that accompany a predetermined structuring of his or her observations; nevertheless, reality demands some sharpening and focusing (Cohen and Naroll, 1970). All of the people and all of the events in a social situation cannot be studied; sampling and selection are essential.

Becker et al. illustrate the problem in their now classic study, *Boys in White* (1961). Their central research interest was to discover what medical school did to medical students. While recognizing that a medical school is a social system (with relationships between participants), the researchers decided not to focus equally upon all participants, electing instead to make the student their central concern and to study other aspects of the organization (e.g., the faculty) only as these aspects affected students. Even here, not all of the students could possibly be studied. Should one group of students be observed through the four years of medical school? Should different groups be studied for shorter periods of time? Should all types of students be studied, or should high and low deviants be left alone? The decision was to observe groups of students in a variety of situations (i.e., in differing departments and stages of training), as well as at leisure, including their casual conversations, mealtimes, and get-togethers at fraternity houses. The researchers furthermore discovered that an encyclopedic recording of every event or every remark they observed was not a research possibility. They conceded:

> We did leave things out. What was included or left out of our field notes depended very much on the problems we were pursuing at the time. We carried on a running analysis of the materials we gathered and, as we became aware of certain problems, made a greater effort to include materials which bore on those problems and tended to prove or disprove provisional hypotheses we were entertaining. (Becker et al., 1961, p. 27)

Not only, then, did Becker and his colleagues have to make some critical decisions "up front" about whom to study and under what conditions, but throughout the investigation, they found themselves (while on the run as observers) refocusing, revising, selecting this, and neglecting that.

Burgess (1984) notes that its focus upon natural settings poses special problems of sampling and selection for the qualitative method. Events are complex and multidimensional; much of importance can easily escape the observant eye and ear. People seldom hold still for the ethnographer; conversations are not always recordable; and human behavior is irrepressibly immune to the logic and consistency that scholars would much prefer to impute to it.

Three key selection decisions must be made by the qualitative researcher. These are where to conduct field research (what site), whom to observe (or interview, etc.) at the field site, and what behaviors to observe. For the first of these (the research site), Spradley (1980) suggests four guidelines.

1. *Simplicity*. If at all possible, the observed situations should be simple rather than complex, for example, few people rather than many, all at once; a setting with some observable boundaries rather than one in constant flux; situations with a beginning and end, or at least some semblance of time parameters, rather than intermittent and discontinuous.

2. *Accessibility*. Qualitative research is intrusive and intensely personal. Private lives are under a microscope, organizational secrets are laid bare. While representativeness (facilitating generalizability) is a key sampling criterion in traditional research, ease of access (seldom easy) is a legitimate criterion for the ethnographer. The site to be studied is one that lets you in.

3. *Unobtrusiveness*. To study a situation "naturally," the researcher should try to blend in. In general, settings in which the observer dresses wrong, is too old or too young, speaks differently, or otherwise appears to be out of place will yield inadequate results. As Philip Cusick (1983) puts it, "The major consideration is what to do with one's own self. One has a physical presence. How will he (or she) fit it into the setting he (or she) wants to study? Often the possibility of participation in some form in the activities of the research site (with its danger of biasing the data) is to be preferred to the role of being there with nothing to do and in the process standing out like a sore thumb (p. 136).

4. *Permissibleness*. Although access is a first step, a fruitful setting should also allow the researcher free or least-restricted entry into all of its activities. Permissibleness often depends upon the real or perceived threat that the observer presents to participants—no small problem for the student of organizations, with their tradition of managers, workers, clients, overseers (e.g., trustees), suppliers, and political supporters or detractors, who are often at odds with one another.

The second key selection decision is whom to observe, and three approaches to a sampling of research subjects or informants are suggested by Burgess (1984).

1. *Theoretically directed sampling.* Originally offered by Glaser and Strauss (1967), the selection of subjects for observation can grow directly out of a developing conceptual framework. In sampling, a theoretically relevant set of events or subjects is located; and as the study proceeds, further sampling branches off or evolves into the development of a more completely grounded theory. In other words, the selection of subjects, like the evolution of the theory, proceeds from an initially vague to an increasingly well-honed state of understanding.

2. *Judgment and opportunistic sampling.* In judgment and opportunistic sampling, the focus is less upon the fit between a developing theory and a set of informants and more upon an adaptation of data collection to the special circumstances and vagaries of each research site. One makes use of informants wherever one can find them, taking advantage of opportunities that arise; and one establishes a "feel" for the research site over time, using judgment to find occasions and settings where valuable data are at hand. In his study of student culture in a community college, for example, London (1978) learned through experience which settings to avoid (e.g., being seen with certain teachers) and where rich data on student behavior were most likely to be found (e.g., the game room, the lounges, and the hallways).

3. *Snowball sampling.* Typically, in ethnographic-style research, the investigator finds that some individuals are immediately approachable, open, and accepting, while others display an obvious reluctance to be the subjects of inquiry. By finding some people (often just a few initially) with whom to associate regularly, the researcher establishes an entree, learns the ropes, and gains an opportunity to be put in touch with friends and acquaintances. Eventually, a chain of informants has been selected.

Finally, third, a key selection decision involves the determination of what behaviors or events to observe. As discussed earlier, it makes little sense to try to study "the details of daily life" without giving considerable thought to what is worth investigator attention and what is not. Qualitative inquiry can produce a rich array of data from interviews, observations, unobtrusive measures, written records, nonverbal cues, even questionnaires and other paper-and-pencil instruments. Deciding what to observe can be approached in much the same manner as the selection of a field site and the selection of subjects—in that sampling can be guided by an emerging theory—but it is also likely to build, change, and adapt as the study proceeds. Each element sampled is influenced by preceding elements, with perhaps a bit of targeting of what is most salient as the study proceeds (Lincoln and Guba, 1985).

As with the issue of familiarity, however, decisions regarding the selection of where, whom, and what to study are replete with special problems in the qualitative study of higher education. As Crane shows, in *Invisible Colleges* (1972), even the boundaries of institutions of higher learning are poorly defined in spatial terms. Many persons in the professorial ranks consider their closest colleagues—and, in fact, their institutional brethren—to be other scholars within their own disciplines across the nation, and indeed the world, rather than persons in other disciplines inhabiting next-door offices at Riveredge U., with whom they seldom interact and do not share a common vocabulary.

The extremely loosely coupled nature of higher learning, furthermore, poses inordinate problems to those who would study the daily life of an institution. Faculty and staff members come and go; much of their work is conducted in isolation and is hidden from one another. Students are of all types and proclivities and, with their wide diversity, are poorly described by such terms as the *student body*. Disciplinary distinctions, role differentiation, independence of activity and time use, disorder, and a diffusion of power and responsibility abound (Perkins, 1973). One common methodological suggestion, to illustrate the problem, is to focus upon "critical incidents" in the life of an organization (Miles and Huberman, 1984). Yet the qualitative-minded researcher in higher education would be poorly advised to focus upon the occasional student demonstration or heated debate in the faculty senate as an example of a critical incident, rather than decisions made in quiet secrecy within faculty meetings and administrative offices deep within the bowels of the institution.

The Issue of Trustworthiness

An ongoing criticism of research produced through qualitative methods is that it seldom has any truth value. With its tendency to report upon isolated, one-at-a-time case studies; to provide long, drawn out, but usually atheoretical, stories of observed phenomena; and to ignore many of the canons of representative sampling, plus reliability and validity—the method offers little opportunity for the development of confidence in its reportage and a sense of truth or generalizability in its conclusions (Filstead, 1970; Cook and Reichardt, 1979; LeCompte and Goetz, 1982). Even such widely acclaimed, enormously influential, and popularly read anthropologists as Margaret Mead and Oscar Lewis have been criticized for a tendency to reflect their own subjective assumptions and value judgments in their writing rather than the culture under study "as it really was" (Pelto and Pelto, 1978; Freeman, 1983).

In an early treatment of the problem, Howard Becker (1970b) outlined some reasons that observational methods conform poorly to traditional standards of scientific inquiry. *First,* qualitative researchers are usually more interested in a thorough understanding of an organization than in narrow relationships between specific, often abstract, variables. The essence of understanding is more enticing to the researcher than *post hoc* explanations or conclusions. *Second,* the design of qualitative research typically takes place while the research is already underway. The research site may be insufficiently understood at the beginning of the study to identify relevant data, let alone test *a priori* hypotheses. As the study continues, the analysis of data and the selection and definition of problems or foci for investigation proceed interactively, each providing direction for the other. Finally, *third*, the qualitative researcher is typically faced at the end of his or her study with the task of trying to make some sense out of an almost overwhelming complexity of information, to fashion a bit of grounded theory, and to search for a sensible model rather than to test it. In this most difficult effort, notes Becker, "observers usually view currently available statistical techniques as inadequate to express their conceptions and find it necessary to use words" (p. 196).

In his discussion, Becker used a term that has since been selected by Lincoln and Guba (1985) as a key concept in establishing the trustworthiness of qualitative inquiry (replacing the traditional notions of reliability and validity). This term is *credibility*. *Reliability* refers, of course, to the capacity of a study to be replicated—to yield the same results to a researcher who uses the same methods as a prior investigator. Because qualitative research occurs in natural settings, changes in design as the setting indicates, depends heavily upon the idiosyncrasies of each researcher, and often involves vague and intuitive insights into the setting and its data, the replicability of a piece of qualitative research is often quite problematic (LeCompte and Goetz, 1982). Qualitative research has a better claim to validity, particularly internal validity, where the researcher claims that his or her explanations match closely the actual conditions of life within the observed setting. External validity (which refers to the generalizability of a set of findings, a study's comparability and translatability) is much more difficult, however. Without acceptable reliability as a precondition, external validity is not likely (LeCompte and Goetz, 1982; Lincoln and Guba, 1985).

Lincoln and Guba (1985) argue that neither of these terms *(reliability* or *validity)* is really appropriate to the naturalistic research paradigm. They stake out a strong position, claiming that naturalistic inquiry is not just an added wrinkle upon conventional scientific methodology (positivism). Naturalistic inquiry is a new research paradigm, fundamentally different from positivism, and "*not* reconcilable with the old" (pp. 32–33). To score naturalistic inquiry as either unreliable or invalid because its methodological controls are not strong, therefore providing little chance of supporting or rejecting rival hypotheses, fails to recognize a difference between the two paradigms in their basic assumptions about the nature of reality. While positivism assumes the existence of a tangible, objectively identifiable body of facts just waiting to be discovered, the naturalistic paradigm sees no single reality or generalizable truth. There are, instead, "multiple constructed realities" that cannot be pried apart into fragments of understanding without damaging the whole. There is no ultimate benchmark of truth (or even of replicability), but numerous mental constructions that together seek not truth but a bit of *Verstehen* (Lincoln and Guba, 1985, pp. 294–296).

Furthermore, to fault naturalistic inquiry for its lack of external validity (while recognizing that it often does provide more internal validity) fails to note a basic difference between paradigms on the question of transferability. To the conventional method, the representativeness of the original sample is essential, because generalizability is the aim. The naturalist desires no generalizability (the goal rather is *Verstehen*), and the naturalist cannot know the settings for which generalizability might be sought. The burden of proof in the naturalist case rests with the person who would make a direct application of findings elsewhere rather than with the original investigator, as in the conventional method (Lincoln and Guba, 1985, pp. 296–298).

Lincoln and Guba do not, however, reject standards of careful, well-designed research. They suggest that the focus should be upon the "trustworthiness" and "confirmability" of data produced qualitatively rather than upon its adherence to conventional notions of reliability, validity, objectivity, or generalizability (p. 300). The qualitative researcher can meet a trustworthiness norm by emphasizing the following.

1. *Credibility*. The data and findings that are produced through naturalistic inquiry will more likely be credible if they are acquired through (a) prolonged engagement (e.g., with sufficient time spent to learn the culture and to build trust); (b) persistent observation (thereby uncovering that which is most relevant to a developing understanding); and (c) the use of triangulation (using multiple data sources and collection methods).

2. *Transferability*. While external validity is not the goal, the naturalist does assist the person interested in making a transfer by engaging in a thick description of the setting studied. As Lincoln and Guba (1985) summarize, it is "*not* the naturalist's task to provide an *index* of transferability; it *is* his or her responsibility to provide the *data base* that makes transferability judgments possible on the part of potential appliers" (p. 316).

3. *Dependability and confirmability*. While conventional reliability (in terms of replicability) is not applicable, the reader of a naturalistic inquiry should be confident that the process of inquiry is consistent, internally coherent, and ethically aboveboard. Furthermore, the reader should be confident that the findings are grounded in the data, logical in terms of the data, and acceptable (e.g., negative cases accounted for and an "audit" of the study carried out) (Lincoln and Guba, 1985, and 301–327).

Suggestions for methodological sophistication in qualitative research (e.g., using triangulation, thick description, and confirmability audits) will be discussed in further detail later in this chapter. As an *issue* in the study of higher education, however, trustworthiness is an especially salient concern. LeCompte and Goetz (1982) sum it up quite succinctly in noting that the researcher's central concern should be directed toward an accurate portrayal of the client's "lifeways."

But as Robertson Davies's "ghost" reminds us, an accurate rendition of the folkways, subtle nuances, shadings, and inconsistencies of college and university environments is not a simple task. The ways in which even its participants may believe budgetary resources to be distributed may be out of touch with the reality of the allocatory process (Salancik and Pfeffer, 1974). The modern image of the university as an institution rendering teaching and public service may be vital to its own self-concept and to the picture it presents to the world, but deep inside (and the cause of strain between image and reality), the demand for scholarly productivity (publish or perish) remains well intact (Caplow and McGee, 1958). Beneath a facade of gentlemanly discourse, intellectual fervor, and collegial cooperation, the internal political dynamics of the university are often rough-and-tumble—with faculty rivalries, jealousies, and "dirty deeds" flavoring mightily the institutional atmosphere (Morris, 1981).

Furthermore, beyond such contradictions between image and reality, a faithful and accurate rendition of life in higher education encounters many of the threats to internal validity first suggested by Campbell and Stanley (1963). *History,* for example, affects the nature of the data collected. Institutions of higher education present complex and mysterious histories. They are both adaptively modern and unchangeably medieval at the same time (Perkins, 1973; Clark, 1983). They are highly variable, with formative sagas from their past that create unique adaptations to changing contemporary events (Clark, 1970, 1972). They are deeply rooted in a stable and predictable time frame of student registration, class scheduling, activities calendars, and degree conferring—while being simultaneously filled institutionally with unusual freedom in the allocations that participants make of their own available time. Participants (particularly the professoriate) can sometimes even serve the institution well by being away from it for months (occasionally years) at a stretch.

Mortality, a second threat to validity, refers to the changes in groups over time as a result of losses and gains in membership. Although coming and going is a normal part of all institutional settings, institutions of higher education (even residential colleges) are laden with growth and attrition. Differences, for example, in the attitudes, motivations, and aspirations of students abound (Pascarella, 1985); thus, a set of interviews with, and observations of, one group of students at one point may yield a far different picture from the one collected six months later at the same institution but with a now-reconstituted group.

Similarly, the *selection* of study participants (whom to observe and interview) is a threat and has already been discussed as a separate issue on its own. Complex institutional environments are filled with subgroups, factions, and multihued events. An adequate inventory of subgroups is recommended (LeCompte and Gaetz, 1982) if a study's findings are not to be misleadingly underrepresentative of the variety and complexity of behaviors in the setting. However, even to an informed "insider" in a small residential college, thoroughly socialized and long at home, an adequate inventory of subgroups and factions could be a Herculean job. The range of possible events and groupings in any institution of higher education is a distinct challenge to the validity-minded researcher.

In sum, the use of qualitative methods in the study of higher education must pay special attention to three key issues. The first of these is the issue of *familiarity*. More than likely, those who study institutions of higher education will be persons with a deep insider's knowledge of the college and university culture. Such familiarity can be a benefit; it can also be handicap. Is an insider or an outsider more likely to be the better judge of what's "really going on" in an academic setting? Additionally, the *selection* of what, whom, and where to study can be an important methodological problem. With their structural looseness, their complexity and variability, their independence of individual behavior, and their diffusion of power and responsibility, institutions of higher education do not yield easily to a search for understanding. Furthermore, vital to qualitative inquiry, whatever the research setting, is the pursuit of *trustworthiness*. While traditional, scientific standards of reliability and validity should not be applied, the qualitative researcher is no less interested than the positivist-oriented scholar in as accurate and credible a rendition of institutional lifeways as possible.

USE OF QUALITATIVE RESEARCH METHODS IN HIGHER EDUCATION

All three of the key methodological issues (familiarity, selection, and trustworthiness) impact heavily upon what John Van Maanen (1979b) labels the relationship between "first-order" and "second-order" conceptions of what is going on in a fieldwork setting. First-order conceptions are informants' notions about what is happening, and second-order conceptions are the researcher's interpretations. Or in simpler terms, first-order concepts can be considered the "facts" of fieldwork, while the second order applies theory and explanation to these facts. The second-order concepts are dependent upon the fieldworker's faith in the quality and accuracy of the facts (Van Maanen, 1979b, p. 542).

This most difficult translation from qualitatively researched "fact" into grounded "theory" is the central theme of the third major section of this chapter. The practical use of qualitative research methods in higher education is explored, with special concern for analytical accuracy. With its press toward constructed reality (a search for understanding), its norm of researcher proximity, its emphasis upon analytic induction, and its appreciation of the value-bound context of most inquiry, the qualitative method faces interesting and unusual problems in the development of a *disciplined* form of inquiry, leading to confidence in the findings unearthed. In this section of the chapter, four components of the qualitative method in use are examined *vis-à-vis* research settings in higher education. The practical concern is with analytical accuracy. The components are (1) researcher entrance and rapport; (2) ethical problems in field studies in higher education; (3) data collection and design strategies; and (4) data analysis.

Entrance and Rapport

Gaining entrance to a research site and establishing rapport are often difficult and time-consuming tasks. In an ethnographic-style inquiry involving this author as part of a team observing the workaday lives of school principals within one large city school system, as many years were spent in gaining access to the schools (three years) as were spent in the observation (an additional three years) (Morris et al., 1984). Without care taken in securing entree and in the establishment of a role (rapport) that facilitates the collection of data, the accuracy or trustworthiness of the findings becomes problematic.

John Van Maanen (1979a) has noted the ''fact'' that organizational settings are full of fiction. People are prone, especially when under observation, to put forth appearances. For one thing, the researcher ''can be misled because informants want it that way. People lie, evade, and otherwise deceive the fieldworker in numerous and inventive ways''—often covering up the things that matter most to them (e.g., hidden failings, taboo-violating activities, and flagrant mistakes) (p. 544). Additionally, the researcher can be misled because the informants are themselves wrong about aspects of their own work site. Not all informants are good informants, equally knowledgeable about their own organization—as any university student knows who tries to learn ''the facts'' about course and graduation requirements from his or her faculty adviser. Finally, the researcher can be misled because informants are unaware of reasons for their own activities. People take a lot of things for granted in organizations (e.g., a categorizing or labeling of clients, or endemic rules violations), and the researcher can similarly be blinded if unquestioningly accepting the informants' own perceptual screen (Van Maanen, 1979a, pp. 544–548).

People are probably as likely to lie (either intentionally or unintentionally) in educational organizations as in any other institutional setting. Despite its apparent openness, the educational organization is typically a closed-in place. Persons sitting in college classrooms are expected to be either students (with ascribed roles of listening, responding to questions, producing effort, and discussing) or instructors (with the jobs of lecturing, asking questions, assigning work, and leading discussions). Departmental faculty meetings are typically intimate while at the same time often discursive and sometimes acrimonious affairs. Significant differences in individual ideology and perspective become apparent in crucial decisions about tenure, teaching assignments, new faculty searches, and program development or revision. Stephen Wilson (1977) observes that in every ethnographic study in education in which he has been involved, concerns have been expressed about the researcher's identity: Who is this person? What role is he or she about to play? Whose side is this person on? Perhaps most important, can I be myself while this person is around? Without care in entry and close attention to rapport on the part of the researcher, the discovery of only "appearances" is the likely research outcome.

Both Geer (1970) and Rist (1975) have talked about "the research bargain" or "the issue of reciprocity" in securing both access to and trust from the persons inhabiting a research site. In many ways, fieldworkers are at the mercy of those whom they are studying if their research is to be successful. Patterns of reciprocity are essential if interactions are to develop profitably and to achieve the stability required for deeper understanding. In his study of an urban elementary school, Rist (1975) was careful to assist teachers wherever possible (e.g., threading the film projector, moving tables, carrying heavy packages, and tacking pictures on a wall), to converse with teachers informally over coffee or at lunch and at school functions, and to listen to but maintain confidentiality in the constant flow of gossip around the school. Similarly, with school administrators, a bit of help writing a grant proposal and locating some hard-to-obtain learning materials cemented a relationship. With students, Rist was careful to avoid becoming part of the authority structure of the school and additionally attempted to be interested and supportive when children showed him their work.

With similar observations more pointedly directed toward research in higher education, Blanche Geer (1970, p. 82) warns that in studying a college, the fieldworker should start with "a cynical view of the enmities possible" in the three-level hierarchy of the organization (administrators, faculty, and students). Echoing Wax (1971) and also Richardson (1970), Geer argues that successful access requires substantial knowledge about an organization *before* the beginning of fieldwork, particularly foreknowledge of organizational structures and the distribution of power. Understanding is, at least in part, a precondition of qualitative research, as well as its outcome.

While Rist suggests reciprocity, Geer calls (in higher education) for a "period of bargaining" in the development of entry and rapport. The bargaining effort can be tricky and time-consuming. Often, the college administrator or staff member must be led to understand that the researcher is not just on a fishing expedition (despite the looseness of the design) and is not simply engaged in a bit of muckraking, looking for blemishes and bad spots that could well prove to be embarrassing to the organization. Researchers are often asked to share reports and findings with administrators before publication, cleaning up anything perceived to be harmful to the college. Furthermore, researchers are often pushed by administrators to direct their attention toward problems *they* want solved.

Similarly, bargains must be struck with faculty members, and even with students (particularly student leaders). Geer (1970) suggests paying courtesy calls on social scientists on the faculty, sharing ideas and publications, and generally engaging faculty members in repeated conversations to assure them of anonymity and confidentiality. Student leaders often tend to be a particularly suspicious lot, requiring cultivation, and proving to be not unlikely to "check with the administration and faculty to discover what sort of bargain was made with them" (p. 86).

Writing in 1970, Blanche Geer may have been overly attuned to, and full of caution following, the years of campus turmoil and dissent of the 1960s. Nevertheless, it is well recognized by qualitative methodologists that access most often requires careful researcher negotiation and is intensely personal. Researchers must often have wide latitude to choose freely where to observe and to whom to talk, but they face in the process the creation of an unusual institutional role—a role that, on the one hand, legitimizes an array of unhindered information-gathering behaviors but, on the other hand, avoids as much as possible established patterns of social expectation within the research setting (Pelto and Pelto, 1978). It is not easy; and the researcher often finds himself or herself creating and filling a new role within the organization—one with a good deal of helping behavior with simultaneously a chance to step back and watch objectively all that is going on. There is an urge to carve out a bit of usefulness, a sense that one's services are needed (Cusick, 1983). But Pelto and Pelto (1978) warn, "The local people do not forget that the anthropologists will ultimately leave them, carrying their notebooks, films, and other information-storing apparatus back to that other world from whence they came" (1978).

Thus, access and trust (and therefore analytical accuracy) often require a bit of bargaining and the negotiation of some form of jointly insider-while-at-the-same-time-outsider role for the qualitative researcher. In the process, however, the fieldworker encounters another major methodological dilemma: the Heisenberg problem. This problem was first brought to scientific attention by Werner Heisenberg, a German microphysicist, who in the 1920s enunciated his now famous principle of indeterminacy. According to this principle, there is a certain uncorrectable randomness in the behavior of subatomic particles, because there is no way for a physicist to observe and catalog their movements without simultaneously disturbing those movements. The very energy developed by electron microscopes to illuminate the target area alters the energy configuration of the particles under study. In short, the observer of phenomena disturbs and shapes the phenomena under study just by being there.[5]

While some ethnographic purists have argued that the researcher should in no way interfere with the culture under study, realism shows that, like the impact of the electron microscope, that of the fieldworker upon the setting is inevitable. Pelto and Pelto (1978) conclude, "The dilemma of the fieldworker, then, is not *whether* to interfere in the local cultural scene but *how much* to interfere" (p. 186). At what point does observer involvement intrude inordinately upon the naturalness of the setting? At what point does fieldworker involvement destroy the objectivity of the researcher, the ability to step back and analyze the events observed under a somewhat dispassionate eye? How can the fieldworker maintain balance and fairness while at the same time first establishing and then maintaining close, reciprocal interaction with his or her informants?

This dilemma is probably as acute in research into higher education as in the study of any other organizational setting. Burgess (1984), drawing heavily upon Gold (1958), describes four fieldworker roles: the complete participant, the participant as observer, the observer as participant, and the complete observer. Each role, discussed briefly below, presents a trade-off between involvement and objectivity.

First, the *complete participant* conceals the observer portion of the role from other individuals in the setting. Data are collected covertly, without the knowledge or consent of other participants. Beyond some possible ethical considerations, the difficulties are that the researcher will ''go native'' and lose the ability (and also the time) to reflect and analyze the data at hand. Complete participation in any organizational setting, furthermore, involves committee chairmanships, taking sides on policy issues, making organizational enemies as well as friends, becoming involved in difficult questions of administration (e.g., alternative usages of available resources), and engaging in some personal corporate striving or ladder-climbing. As mentioned early in the chapter, the literature in higher education is insightfully rich in a backward glance at itself by some of its major figures (e.g., Kerr, 1964; Barzun, 1968; Bell, 1966; Riesman, 1958; Perkins, 1966). Nevertheless, the complete participant will often find it difficult to be fully objective and openly critical in a look backward at an institutional setting that he or she has probably played a role in building and/or altering.

The *participant as observer*, as a second alternative, is a more common fieldworker role. The researcher does not conceal his or her research interest; indeed, it is made known that the primary reason for the fieldworker's being there is to observe, not to participate. The researcher conveys the understanding that he or she wishes considerable freedom of movement and open access to all social situations and potential informants. However, the fieldworker also contributes, as participant, to the work of the organization and establishes legitimacy with informants by assisting the institution, just as they do, with its daily work load. The dangers in this role are that the fieldworker (1) can be easily seduced into more and more participation and less observation; (2) may meet closed doors and rebuffs as observer because of his or her alliances as participant; and (3) may interfere as participant with events that as pure observer he or she would have been advised to simply record (Pelto and Pelto, 1978; Spradley, 1980; Burgess, 1984). In the study of higher education, furthermore, the role of participant in any form can place obstacles in the path of observation. Whether one chooses to participate in the guise of faculty member, student, nonacademic staff member, or administrator, some doors and interactions are likely to open to one role more than to another.

The third fieldwork role is *observer as participant*. As the reversal of the two key terms indicates, the emphasis is placed upon observation with lessened participation. The observer role is made known, and the participation that occurs is more incidental and opportunistic (e.g., building trust through reciprocity) than long-term and structured. Because the fieldworker is likely to participate over less time and only on the periphery of the organizational culture, the danger is that the research will never penetrate deeply into insider understandings (Burgess, 1984, p. 82). While there is less chance that the fieldworker will go native, he or she may be hard pressed to penetrate below the appearances and the entree offered the casual tourist. The fieldworker may be particularly susceptible to publicity release interpretations of the work of the institution rather than its operable work life.

Finally, fourth, the *complete observer* role avoids all participation and its attendant biases in favor of pure observation. Eavesdropping and data collection or event recording can occur without the knowledge of participants and without the obligations that are placed on those who become involved in institutional affairs. The central dangers are that the complete observer will learn little of the insider's world and will be barred from much activity that requires negotiated entree. Pure observation may be easily pursued in higher education at its many large-group encounters (e.g., student centers, campus comings and goings, sports contests, student registration periods, and large-group lectures). However, in its many intimate and hard-to-penetrate gatherings (e.g., a tenure review board, a college executive committee, a student dormitory bull-session, small-group instructional seminars, a Ph.D. examination, and the chancellor's advisory committee), an observer role without a participation overlay is unlikely.[6]

Thus, one key barrier to analytical accuracy and trustworthiness in qualitative research within higher education is the problem of gaining access and establishing rapport. Organizations, and the individuals serving within them, are not averse to a portrayal of appearances to those who are not yet fully accepted within the institutional culture. Acceptance often involves a bit of bargaining, reciprocity, and even active participation; the attendant danger, as the fieldworker moves back and forth between participation and observation, is that the data will be affected by researcher interference. Later, in a discussion of data analysis issues, some techniques offered by Lincoln and Guba (1985) to assist trustworthiness (e.g., member checks, peer debriefings, and independent audits) will be explained and considered.

Ethical Problems

Pelto and Pelto (1978, p. 186) write about the moral conflict that fieldworkers face whenever their values conflict with events in the community under study.

Especially poignant for ethnographers is the setting filled with human misery that could be prevented—with changes in sanitation, child rearing, crop producing, medical and dietary practices, and so on, or with changes in local power relations, governmental programs, and the like. The traditional research axiom is that the fieldworker must learn to endure the psychological tension of a hands-off approach, to observe and record but not try to change. The opposite viewpoint is expressed by Charles Valentine (1968), who argues that the fieldworker *should* become an activist on behalf of his or her subjects—"to act from the ethical position that he has major obligations to the people he is studying" (pp. 188–189).

Higher education institutions are unlikely (in most settings at least) to tax the fieldworker's conscience about unrelieved misery. However, moral conflicts of a similar type do develop. Fetterman (1984c, p. 215) reminds us that the researcher must respect informants' rights (e.g., to confidentiality and anonymity). The fieldworker must, realistically, work as well to stay on the good side of his or her subjects, maintaining, as mentioned earlier, the system of obligations and sharing and reciprocity that may have, only with difficulty and over time, provided the key to researcher access. But Fetterman observes additionally that the researcher must also be considerate of the taxpayer (ibid.). Whether the research is supported by government funds, or the agency under study is (or both), a commitment to a morality beyond the miniculture under investigation may be required.

Barnes (1970) provides additional perspective upon the dilemma. He notes that the foci of ethnographic-style studies are no longer just illiterate tribes in remote areas, but communities and institutions whose members can read, write letters, and even sue the researcher. Furthermore, the ethnographer more and more often finds himself or herself in situations where the code of values undergirding the setting is not strange or foreign, or so unusual as to warrant a fully detached (even amused at times) luxury of pure observation. Barnes concludes:

> More and more the ethnographer finds himself in situations in which he cannot avoid evaluating the actions of his informants in terms of his own moral code. If he refrains from acting on these evaluations, it is because of the way he has defined his role as a scientific investigator and not because of the cultural gulf between him and his informants. (pp. 240–241)

If reprehensible, morally wrong, even illegal activities are observed, should they be fully reported, ignored, glossed over, masked, or covered up? If reported, is damage done to the trust that was offered the fieldworker in permitting access and in opening private, institutional lives to close inspection? If not reported, can the study be considered a trustworthy portrayal of life as it really is in an institution?

Colleges and universities are not widely recognized, of course, as work settings where ethical transgressions and extralegal actions are likely to be in widespread evidence. Qualitative research has been more common in law enforcement occupations, the health professions, and social service bureaucracies, where consideration of the ethical has much day-in and day-out saliency (see, for example, Lipsky, 1980). Nevertheless, the fieldworker who penetrates student subcultures in higher education should not be surprised to find behaviors running the gamut from rule breaking to illegality. Furthermore, beneath a facade of professorial respectability, institutional life in higher education is no less immune than other types of organizations to examples of racism, sexism, favoritism, falsification, and immorality. Indeed, some would argue that modern institutional life in higher education brings inescapable ethical dilemmas to those who would administer its affairs. For example, Morris (1984) argues that college deans are imbued with a sense of service to their faculty members. Yet, as administrators, they must also work on behalf of the organization as a whole. In this larger effort, they often find themselves *using* people—their motivations, drives, and skills—to serve the corporate good. The interests of the entire organization come first, and on behalf of these interests,

> it is sometimes necessary to withhold certain kinds of information and deal it out, piece by piece, to the people who must use it, deliberately keeping it from others, especially those who may use the information in a disruptive and destructive way. The messages that flow across an administrator's desk are of a special sort. Although not literally personal, they are nevertheless privileged, an adjective which could never be applied to any sort of information in the academic marketplace. (p. 131)

Thus, using people, withholding information, bending the rules, playing favorites, and shading the facts are not at all uncommon behaviors in any organizational setting that is filled with just plain old human beings. The organization against the individual, one special interest opposing another, inequitably distributed power, purely personal motivations and needs, friends helping one another out—these are among the "stuff" of organizational life. They exist below the easily visible organizational surface or are hidden as skeletons (even ghosts) in organizational closets, but when unearthed, they can be embarrassing and even destructive.

The crunch for the qualitative researcher comes at the point of the report. Fetterman (1984c) writes:

> Fieldwork conducted in highly political settings can be more dangerous than fieldwork in the streets of the inner city. An ethnographic report rich in detail is potentially as dangerous as it may be helpful—depending on how the material is presented and who uses the information. (p. 225)

In consideration of these time-bomb qualities, a number of guidelines for reporting are typically offered.

First, it is commonly suggested that the researcher should, above all, maintain agreements concerning confidentiality or anonymity (Lincoln and Guba, 1985). By carefully masking respondent identities, one can take the edge off much disclosure that may be potentially damaging to participants. Nevertheless, a *second* guideline that is also commonly suggested goes a step further (Fetterman, 1984c; Barnes, 1970; Fichter and Kolb, 1970). The suggestion is that research findings prior to dissemination should be shared with and cleared by those most closely concerned. Informants may be asked to check the accuracy of statements and may be asked if they will agree to statements about themselves (even if identities are masked) that may appear in print (Barnes, 1970, p. 245).

Third, it is suggested that the writing of a report should not be interpretive or evaluative, except in sections explicitly intended for such purposes (e.g., a set of conclusions attempting to establish a bit of grounded theory) (Lincoln and Guba, 1985). A report that is liberally dosed with the researcher's own moral outrage, that delightedly highlights organizational or individual aberrations, and that points a finger in abhorrence at ethical transgressions can add little to the central research objective of *Verstehen.*

On the other hand, and an added part of the researcher's dilemma, those who offer guidelines on reporting suggest that (1) the inquiry has obligations to whomever supplied funds for the investigation to present the data honestly and with thoroughness, and (2) the researcher's colleagues and social scientists in general have a claim upon a serious, honest, and professionally competent report. Although assurances of anonymity, clearances, and cautious efforts to avoid moralizing are certainly in order, the fieldworker also owes a debt to his or her discipline (and even to society itself) to report thoroughly upon what was observed (warts and all) if the result is a bit of knowledge, some understanding, that has heretofore been unavailable (Fichter and Kolb, 1970). Whichever way one turns, concludes Fetterman (1984c), "guilty knowledge and dirty hands are at the heart of the fieldworker experience" (p. 231).

Data Collection and Design Strategies

Becker and Geer (1960) urge the qualitative researcher to take account of as much of an organization's complexity as time and effort will allow. Quite simply, the collection of data and the design of research strategies should be broad-based and comprehensive enough to capture maximum understanding from the natural environment. Yet, the design must simultaneously be open-ended and flexible—with an emerging structure, as the uncovered data and their analyses indicate. The trick, as Lincoln and Guba (1985) put it, is to provide an opportunity for some "hard thinking" in an open-ended way that does not come across as "sloppy inquiry (p. 225).

Lincoln and Guba contrast the conventional perspective upon research design with that of naturalistic inquiry. A bit of a paradox is encountered, in that conventional design standards require precisely what is impossible for the qualitative researcher to specify in advance. While the conventional asks for the clear statement of a research problem and the statement of an *a priori* theoretical perspective (usually with hypotheses to be tested), the naturalist merely begins with a bit of focus in the inquiry (which often changes) and a theory that emerges from the study. Convention also asks for representative sampling (in aid of generalization), operational definitions of the variables to be studied, and carefully specified data collection and analysis procedures (capable of testing the hypotheses offered). However, sampling for the naturalist is contingent and serial, data collection is opportunistic, and data analysis is open-ended and inductive. The design of a naturalistic inquiry cannot be tightly structured in advance; "it must emerge, develop, unfold" (Lincoln and Guba, 1985, p. 225).

It does not, however, unfold sloppily. Certainly, qualitative research is personalistic, with no investigator working quite as another does (LeCompte and Goetz, 1982). Nevertheless, the search for understanding (and, hopefully, some theory building) demands that careful attention be given to credibility. Two characteristics of qualitative research with important credibility overtones are (1) its provision for multiple strategies of data collection and (2) its concern for continuous checking, probing, verifying, and confirming as data collection and analysis proceed (Owens, 1982; Burgess, 1984; Lincoln and Guba, 1985).

Multiple Data Collection Strategies

Terms heard often in the discussion of field research methods are "thick description" (Geertz, 1973) and "triangulation" (Denzin, 1970, 1978). The concept of thick description suggests that it is the responsibility of the researcher to provide sufficient scope and depth in reporting to enable the reader to understand and separately interpret the study's findings. While transferability is not the central goal of qualitative research, thick description can make it possible for the reader to make his or her own applications to similar settings. In like fashion, the concept of triangulation calls for the use of multiple methods of data collection (e.g., participant observation plus interviewing, document examination, and even questionnaires). Multiple sources of (cross-referenceable) data and multiple investigators (e.g., as part of a research team) can also be modes of triangulation, as can the use of the same methods on different occasions.

As Jick (1979) points out, one fundamental assumption behind the triangulation argument is that somehow the weaknesses embedded within each single method will be compensated for by the strengths of the other(s). The direct, to-the-problem, but possibly "rehearsed" product of the interview can be balanced by the spontaneity of on-site observation (e.g., of the overheard conversation, the chance remark, the here-and-now, and the knee-jerk reaction to events). The sometimes unfathomable parade of observed events, helter-skelter, one atop another, can be clarified and rooted in time and setting through the more leisurely examination of documents and records. Nevertheless, the strengths of a counterbalancing of methods are by no means automatically ensured, and, warns Jick (1979), "Multimethods are of no use with the 'wrong' question (p. 609).[7]

In parallel with the emergent and adaptive approach to research design that is urged for qualitative inquiry, Douglas (1976) offers three principles for the use of mixed data collection strategies. *First,* the mixture should not be too tightly controlled at the outset of research. *Second,* adaptability and flexibility in the selection of method should be maintained throughout the study. And *third,* the mix should attempt to progress from natural (e.g., pure observation) to more controlled methods (e.g., focused interviews), as findings in the study accumulate. Douglas's three principles are consistent with the Becker and Geer (1960) observation that fieldwork often proceeds through a number of distinct (but overlapping and interwoven) analytical stages: (1) an initial period of focusing and selection and definition of problems; then (2) a descriptive inquiry into the existence and distribution of phenomena; and finally (3) the incorporation of observations into a bit of initial theorizing.

Amidst all of this adaptation and reshuffling, it is the researcher who is the central instrument of data collection (Lincoln and Guba, 1985). Some manner of direct observation is the mainstay of the qualitative research tradition, but the approach is rich in its variety of data collection strategies. A few of the major strategies will be discussed, briefly, as they apply to research in higher education.

Observation. The generally favored form is participant observation, despite its demand that the fieldworker play two (somewhat incompatible) roles simultaneously; observer *and* group member. The phenomenon of participation provides an intimacy with, and a sharing of, the world of the observed that is often considered essential to the central goal of understanding (Denzin, 1970). While there is a range of styles of participation (from immersion to occasional), the decided strength of the method is its opportunity to perceive reality from an insider perspective, and therefore to give the study internal validity. Observational data (and particularly participant observation data) are, of course, subject to the vagaries of time and place. The fieldworker sees what happens while he or she is there. Furthermore, as a participant, the fieldworker helps to fashion somewhat what is to be seen; and, as a participant, the fieldworker may even find it necessary to serve in a role that limits what is to be seen (e.g., a student cut off from faculty councils or a member of a humanities department having minimal communication with the hard sciences departments). London (1978) illustrates the problem clearly in his study of the culture of a community college:

> A minor difficulty of this method was the awkwardness of being seen in the company of one group by students with whom I had spent the previous day(s); moving from clique to clique, I feared being seen as having switched allegiances, although I never heard any such accusations. There were occasions, for example, when a student would see me with a student or group of students he had vilified earlier, or with a teacher for whom he had expressed a particular distaste. (pp. 164–165)

Thus, while participant observation is the much-preferred style (because of its internal validity), the study of higher education does not adapt to it easily. To be sure, persons engaged in studies of colleges and universities are likely to be uncommonly well situated (as insiders and participants) to conduct inquiry into their own professional environments. Indeed, as mentioned earlier, the literature is rich in insider essays, retrospectives, and critiques. Nevertheless, the professorial role is a strange species of organizational participation, one not unduly well placed to provide a holistic understanding. Much of one's work life is spent in isolation and, even when teaching, cut off from widespread collegial interaction. Loneliness is considered a virtue, necessary to the completion of work—and much sought after, even reveled in by many, if not most, scholars. The slice of institutional life (despite the rich variety of life forms) that is open to each role incumbent in higher education is usually quite circumscribed.

Nonparticipant observation, despite its drawbacks of access and outsider status ("What in the world is that person doing here"?) can probably be used productively to study much in higher education. Ethics aside, covert (or undercover) observation is possible in many institutional subsettings (e.g., large-group gatherings, libraries, and movements of individuals spatially around a campus). The discrete observation of nonverbal behaviors and the gathering of unobtrusive measures (e.g., of groupings of individuals, body movements, spatial relationships between people, touching, physical arrangements of buildings on the campus, and traffic patterns) in college and university settings offers a richly varied menu of data-gathering opportunities. And with careful attention given to access (properly explaining the intent of the study), the nonparticipating outsider is probably as welcome an observer in the inner councils of higher education administration as in any other organizational setting. The institutional culture understands and appreciates research, while in other organizations, the natives may wonder "why this person doesn't go out and get a real job."

Again, the central power of observation as a data collection tool is its inquiry into a natural, dynamic environment on its own terms (Guba and Lincoln, 1981). Lincoln and Guba (1985) suggest that this power can be maximized if considerate attention is given to the process of accurately recording observed phenomena. For example, observational notes can often be organized into theory-generating categories at the time of event occurrence. Time logs of events can assist data reconstruction and interpretation, as can maps of spatial arrangements and sociometric-style diagrams of the interaction patterns of individuals. "Debriefing sessions" (e.g., with other researchers), after a researcher leaves the setting, can produce observational insights that do not immediately occur to the fieldworker himself or herself (Lincoln and Guba, 1985, p. 275). There is, however, no standard operating procedure, no right or wrong methodology, in the use of observation. Settings differ in their demands and opportunities, and fieldworkers differ in their skill and creativity. Again, London (1978) provides an interesting and illustrative methodological vignette in his study of a community college:

> To remember important points from student's classes I would often take very brief notes while doodling. For example, to record the seating arrangement I would make a series of "Xs" and "Os" to designate males and females; to help reconstruct a dialog I would write key words or letters on a slip of paper or a book jacket while appearing to be nonchalantly perusing the room. Similarly, during conversations with students I would sometimes doodle and let them have a view of the doodle, yet hidden in it were symbols to help me recall as faithfully as possible what was said. (p. 165)

Interviewing. In the interest of triangulation, the interview (either structured or unstructured) provides an opportunity to gather data in the respondents' own words, to focus inquiry more pointedly toward a study's central questions, to draw data efficiently from a setting, and to seek information directly from the persons who are most in the know in a setting. A vital tool in its own right, the interview can also be a valuable complement to observation. In studies that are primarily observational, interviewing is often likely to be unfocused (or at least open-ended) and opportunistic (occurring as time and place permit). To be sure, however, qualitative research and the idea of triangulation can also be well served through the use of carefully focused interviews (and/or surveys) at prearranged times with representatively sampled informants.

The major strengths of interviewing (e.g., its opportunity to focus, its collection of the respondents' own words, and its efficiency) are also its central weaknesses. The interviewee is much more in control of the data than is the case in pure observation and knows (although some interviewing is covert) that he or she is providing data. Furthermore, the fluid (although time-consuming) nature of participant observation is stopped short in the interview. Other natural events of possible theoretical import may be flying by, unnoticed, while an interview is in progress. Nevertheless, the utility of the interview as a tool of triangulation is well recognized. An illustration of that importance, as well as of the tool's difficulties, is provided in another excerpt from the work of London (1978):

> The interviews consisted of a series of open-ended questions, some of which were modified slightly to suit the chemistry and idiosyncrasies of each interview. The chief

problem in the interviews was the sensitive nature of the questions concerning the career transition and how successfully or unsuccessfully it had been made.

As I began asking about the discrepancy between expectations and reality, I often sensed that teachers knew what I was getting at—that we were discussing or about to discuss the extent to which their careers had soured. Having seen me in their classes and having talked with me during the year, they knew I was familiar with their work problems, and many of them did reveal intimate thoughts. In three interviews I had the unverifiable feeling that teachers were not being honest and that there was nothing I could do to uncover the truth. (p. 168)

The varieties and forms of interviewing are many. Lincoln and Guba (1985) suggest that interviews can be categorized by "their degree of *structure,* their *degree of overtness,* and the *quality of the relationship* between interviewer and respondent" (p. 268). Structures range from focused to unfocused, with focused (more highly structured) interviewing more likely to be employed when time is limited, when the data to be elicited (and therefore the appropriate questions to be asked) are clear, and/or when the interview is being used to corroborate understandings that have already been established. Overtness/covertness carries some ethical overtones—with moral judgment generally weighted toward informing respondents fully of the fact of the interview, as well as of its purpose, and of how respondents' contributions will be used. Similarly, relationships between interviewer and respondent can range from hostile to empathic (Massarik, 1981), with the suggestion that effort in most qualitative research should be directed toward establishing the trust and rapport with respondents necessary to natural data collection.

One decided advantage of the interview in the study of organizations is the opportunity it provides for a glance backward as well as forward (speculatively) in time. Subjects can be asked to reconstruct past events as well as to project (from their own experience) the course of future occurrences ("What do you think is likely to happen next?"). A technique favored by sociologists some decades ago, and receiving renewed attention with the current interest in qualitative inquiry, is the development of the "life history." The life history is often a participant's glance backward at a lifetime of experience, captured in the participant's own words, with the participant's as well as the researcher's interpretations of those experiences (Denzin, 1970). Although interviewing will loom large in the life history, the compilation of documents (e.g., letters, autobiographies, diaries, and archival records) and the administration of questionnaires (e.g., attitude measures and interest inventories) can be appropriately added to the database.

The life history is a bit of contemporary organizational historiography that can be particularly useful in the study of higher education. With its structural looseness, the academic organization may be especially susceptible to the influence of an idiosyncratic personality upon its development and day-by-day work life. Certainly a Hutchins, an Eliot, or a Channing will receive marked attention, but throughout each college or university, there tend to be individuals (often little known outside the institution) whose careers leave a decided mark upon the course of intrainstitutional affairs. Furthermore, in a setting marked less by bureaucratic and hierarchic control than by the order induced through tradition and collegialism, the amalgam of beliefs, ideologies, and values embedded within the personalized life histories of its membership may be the best guide of all to the vitally important "culture" of an institution (Sproull, 1981).[8]

The importance of interviewing in the study of higher education (but bolstered by observation) is also underscored in an interesting argument by Howard Becker (1970a). Drawing upon his study of medical students, Becker argues that the values of any social group are likely to combine evidence of two polar opposites. His subjects were idealistic about their chosen profession (e.g., wanting to "help humanity" and eschewing great financial reward) and at the same time determinedly cynical about medical science and its program of professional training. In his observational data, typically gathered in group settings (e.g., at lunch and during teaching rounds), Becker found that "cynicism was the dominant language and idealism would have been laughed down" (p. 105). Consequently, he found himself systematically underestimating the idealism of his subjects—until, in interview situations, with questions asked in a sympathetic fashion, the depth of the medical ideal surfaced again and again. Conversely, notes Becker, had he relied solely upon the interview for his data, platitudes and official ideologies (mouthing the "right" slogans) might have been his sole harvest. It was only because of the acceptance emerging from his close observation of the students that informal and casual interviewing showed both cynicism *and* the admission of a deeply held (and real rather than merely voiced) idealism.

Documentation. Organizations are, of course, full of documents, in fact full of so many of varying categories (e.g., official and unofficial, draft version and final version, in-house and public, and formal and informal) that easily usable research taxonomies have not been forthcoming (Lincoln and Guba, 1985). Despite an increasing openness (under the Freedom of Information Acts) and despite the burgeoning quantity of paper produced by the photocopying machine (along with the voluminous records housed in computers), gaining access to documents and records can be a difficult and frustrating job.

Certainly an individual's right to privacy is an important ethical matter, but of even greater concern to the researcher is the presumably quite simple act of just finding appropriate and relevant documentation. Some records are readily available, of course, but many more that are filled with insights into the inner workings of an organization are deeply hidden in a committee chairperson's right-hand desk drawer, a former department head's personal papers, a secretary's unfathomable filing system, or a long-forgotten manila folder deep in the recesses of a four-drawer file. Documents, like money, tend to be "washed" as they rise from the bottom to the top of an organization, or as they proceed from inside to outside (public) view. Suitably and creatively unearthed, an organization's day-by-day flow of documentation can have important corroborative value for the qualitative researcher.

The essential research skill is a capacity for good sleuthing. Lincoln and Guba (1985) capture the essence of the document hunt well in suggesting three principles of document or record retrieval. *First,* the researcher should begin with

> the assumption that if an event happened, some record of it exists (especially in today's heavily documented society). To put it another way, every human action "leaves tracks." (p. 278)

The tracks may not always be very readable, may often disappear only to reappear in unlikely locations, and may often lead to dark caves or dead ends. Nevertheless, successful tracking can be helped by the *second* relevant principle, that is, knowing generally (perhaps through prior observation) how the institution works: "One can imagine the tracks that *must* have been left by the action." Then, *third,* by knowing one's way around, "One knows where to look for the tracks" (Lincoln and Guba, 1985, p. 278).

Thus, document hunting and ghost tracking are two not at all dissimilar endeavors. On the one hand, the search for and access to relevant documents should be somewhat easier in higher education than in other types of organizations. Colleges and universities are fond of storing much of their documentary history in their own libraries. The loose structure of governance in institutions of higher education produces large numbers of carbon (or Xerox) copies and layers of committee approval for many, many intrainstitutional decisions. The primary tasks of teaching and research (particularly funded research) are well surrounded by legalisms requiring a full documentation of steps in the degree-conferring process (from admissions records to examination decisions), the research endeavor (from human subjects' protection to expenditure audits), and the professorial role (from affirmative action in hiring to tenure protection). Furthermore, most institutions of higher learning are unusually open (as organizations) in providing for a public scrutiny of their short- and long-term plans, budgets, and staff and faculty work loads, as well as salaries, debates over institutional governance (e.g., minutes of faculty senate meetings), and even many of their institutional foibles (often gleefully highlighted in a student-run campus newspaper).

On the other hand, much of the important documentation that is produced in higher education may be accessed only with difficulty. Ethics and legality protect the records of individual students and faculty members. A Byzantine structure of committees and countervailing and overlapping approval functions typically buries many key decision-related documents in strange places. The looseness of the organization and its tradition of autonomy can lead to a wide gap between official and unofficial documentation (e.g., as a course syllabus for History 302 bears little resemblance to the catalog description of the course). And the extreme diversity of the organization (from an Office of Slavic and East European Studies, to an Integrated Systems Laboratory, to a Program in Speech Pathology) produces annually an overwhelming blizzard of paperwork—easily snowing under the researcher who, lightly clothed, sets naively out to track relevant documents.

As with the other data collection strategies, documents and records must be scrutinized carefully for their biases, inaccuracies, representativeness, and overall credibility. Interestingly, the continued ghostliness of it all is attested to in the language that Barzun and Graff (1977) use to describe the process of verification, in their book on historical method. The authors talk of ''worming secrets out of manuscripts,'' ''undoing the knots in facts,'' and ''destroying myths'' (pp. 94–97). In this subtle job of good sleuthing, the power of triangulation is again apparent. Just as ethnographers suggest the confirming assistance of the document, historians warn that good history demands the larger appreciation of a relevant culture. Barzun and Graff (1977) write:

> the investigator's original fund of knowledge must embrace even more than a well-populated chronology; it must include an understanding of how people in other eras lived and behaved, what they believed, and how they managed their institutions. This kind of mastery fills the mind with images and also with questions, which, when answered and discussed, make for what we term depth. (pp. 98–99)

Checking, Probing, Verifying, and Analyzing

Thus, quite clearly, the demands of qualitative research require a flexible and opportunistic mixture of data collection strategies. Caveats, however, are offered by Lincoln and Guba and by Yin. Lincoln and Guba (1985) warn that naturalistic inquiry tends to be particularly vulnerable to attacks that it is ''loosey-goosey.'' It is important, therefore, despite the emergent design characteristic, for researchers to plan carefully the measures to be taken to increase the credibility of their studies. Yin (1984) similarly argues the need for the development of a ''chain of evidence'' as the researcher moves through the investigation and from one stage of inquiry to another.

With detailed attention to what they label ''building trustworthiness,'' Lincoln and Guba (1985) offer the following methodological suggestions. The *first* is to give careful attention to the maintenance of at least four different types of field journals. In addition to the mandatory log of interview or observational data, the fieldworker should (1) keep careful track of his or her day-to-day activities, as a kind of calendar of appointments; (2) maintain a personal log, like a fieldwork diary, in which one reflects upon what seems to be happening in the field (e.g., initial hypotheses, introspections, and frustrations); and (3) keep a methodological log, detailing decisions made in the ongoing, emergent design of the study. Additional systematizing is offered by Miles and Huberman (1984), who suggest the use of "contact summary sheets," initial or first-level coding, and "memoing" as questions, reflections, and themes occur to the researcher.

The *second* methodological suggestion offered by Lincoln and Guba is to institute safeguards against the various forms of distortion that plague qualitative inquiry. Some of the key areas of distortion have been discussed earlier in this chapter (e.g., building rapport without going native and guarding against the Heisenberg problem). While they may not be totally eliminated, distortions can lose much of their harmful effect if they are recognized as problems (e.g., an awareness of possible fieldworker or respondent bias, and if countermeasures or checking are attempted).

Third, trustworthiness is assisted by team interaction and the use of debriefing. If a research team is engaged in the inquiry, all members of the team should meet often to share observations and to agree on the emergent design (not always easy with the heavy consumption of time in most qualitative research). Furthermore, a "debriefer" (a professional peer who is not involved in the inquiry) should have a "no holds barred conversation" with the members of the research team at periodic intervals (Lincoln and Guba, 1985, p. 283).

Fourth, trustworthiness can be helped through the accumulation of referential adequacy materials. *Referential adequacy* is a concept attributed by Lincoln and Guba to Eisner (1975). It calls for a laying aside (an "archiving") of a portion of the data that are collected in a study—not including them in the data analysis—until after tentative findings and interpretations have been reached. Then, the archived data can be retrieved (as still raw data) and tested against the conclusions already drawn. Lincoln and Guba recognize that this technique asks a lot of the fieldworker who has struggled mightily to obtain a few data, but the opportunities for comparison and corroboration are well worth the effort (Lincoln and Guba, 1985, p. 314).

Finally, *fifth,* a key suggestion and "the single most important trustworthiness technique," according to Lincoln and Guba (1985, p. 283), is the development of an "audit trail." Drawing upon the dissertation work of Halpern (1983), Lincoln and Guba urge the qualitative research team to engage an outside auditor, who will examine the records emanating from an inquiry with an eye to their confirmability, dependability, and credibility. Among the classes of records to be placed in audit would be (1) raw data (e.g., documents, field notes, and interview or survey results); (2) all data analysis efforts; (3) "process notes" (e.g., research design and trustworthiness considerations); (4) "materials relating to intentions and dispositions'' (e.g., the research proposal, personal notes); and (5) "instrument development information'' (e.g., interview schedules, questionnaires, and observation schemata). The auditor should be called in at the beginning of the study; should be given an opportunity to become thoroughly familiar with the inquiry and its records (making a determination of the study's auditability); and should be formally "locked in'' to the audit (e.g., through a contract), with conditions of timing, format, and product clearly specified. In determining the trustworthiness of an inquiry, the auditor may undertake such actions as checking the adequacy of the overall design; making sure that findings can be traced back to the raw data; looking for inquirer bias, the extent to which negative evidence was taken into account, and whether all data have reasonably been accounted for; and exploring the extent to which the study might have been unduly influenced by "practical matters'' (e.g., accommodations, subject interests, and sponsor deadlines) (Lincoln and Guba, 1985, pp. 319–327).

Data Analysis

However, despite the emphasis placed upon preparing for and planning systematically toward a defense of trustworthiness, the charge of looseness still surrounds the all-important task of *analyzing* qualitative data. In 1960, Becker and Geer observed that "the data of participant observation do not easily lend themselves to ready summary'' (p. 279). In 1982, LeCompte and Goetz were still noting that "The analytic processes from which ethnographies are constructed often are vague, intuitive, and personalistic'' (p. 40). The central difficulty lies in the need to maintain the flexibility, opportunism, idiosyncracy, and holism required to maximize the inductive potential of an inquiry, while providing the many checks that lead the skeptical reader toward a sense of confidence in the study's report.

As mentioned earlier, Miles and Huberman (1984) have helped recently in offering a variety of displays for the presentation of qualitative data. The authors note that the typical and traditional mode of display has been the narrative— usually a descriptive report, a case study, telling the "story'' of the setting under examination. The narrative, claim Miles and Huberman (1984, p. 79), is by itself a weak form of display—only vaguely ordered, often monotonous and overloading, and difficult to abstract from. As a complement to the narrative, and as an aid in data analysis, Miles and Huberman (1984) provide illustrations of numerous display formats. For example, a "context chart'' can be used to show graphically the interrelationships between the participants in a setting; a "time-ordered matrix'' provides a ready chronology of observed events; an "effects matrix'' organizes the data in terms of one or more perceived outcomes; and a "critical incidents chart'' lists the events seen to be influential or decisive during the course of some identifiable process (e.g., a period of change or an implementation phase).

As an organizing framework for understanding the treatment of qualitative (in their case, ethnographic) data, Goetz and LeCompte (1981, 1984) describe five analytic strategies that can be arrayed along a continuum of inductive-constructive-subjective to deductive-enumerative-objective dimensions of research. To the left, at the most open or inductive end of the continuum, is the technique of analytic induction—a simple scanning of the data for relationships and categories, developing out of this effort some working hypotheses and typologies. A second strategy, and a small step to the right on the continuum, is the technique of "constant comparison," offered by Glaser and Strauss (1967) and summarized carefully by Lincoln and Guba (1985). With an eye toward the development of grounded theory, the art of constant comparison calls for a coding of the incidents applicable to each category of data that emerges, an integration of categories and their properties (making category properties explicit), and then a formation of the theory. At each stage of analysis, which occurs in tandem with the period of fieldwork, there is a constant comparison of newly observed events with old, of initial categorizations with maturing, of an early feel for the data with later assignments of incidents to categories, and of early sense making with emergent theorizing. Data collection and processing, research implementation and research design, description and explanation—all occur simultaneously in a back-and-forth process of progressive understanding.

The three remaining data-analysis strategies discussed by Goetz and LeCompte are considered by Lincoln and Guba to be less typical of naturalistic inquiry. Each moves farther to the right along the subjective-objective continuum. The first strategy, "typological analysis," uses externally derived theoretical categories, which are applied to the new data. Similarly, the fourth and fifth strategies move, respectively, toward deductive and verificatory approaches—through the use of "enumerative systems" and "standardized protocols." From these perspectives, write Lincoln and Guba (1985, p. 336), data analysis tends to be predetermined, with observations coded into categories that were decided upon well before initial entry into the field.

Perhaps a more interesting and certainly clearer exemplar of data analysis in qualitative research can be provided by drawing once again upon one of the few classic observational studies in higher education: Howard Becker et al.'s *Boys in White* (1961). Becker and his research team recognized that mere anecdote and illustration, while not uncommon forms of analysis in qualitative research, do not provide sufficient power of conclusion for the skeptical reader (Becker and Geer, 1960, p. 279). Since it is impossible for a report to include all of the data that have been collected, letting the reader form his or her own sense of understanding, some form of data reduction beyond the anecdotal must be undertaken.

And here's the rub. Where does one start? What "handle" does one place upon the data? What categories does one select (e.g., ongoing relationships, patterns of interaction, time usage, or particular events)? Becker et al. chose to analyze their medical school data from the viewpoint of "perspectives"—or the ideas and actions that the students themselves gave expression to in solving their own collective problems. The perspectives, in turn, were organized by area of application (e.g., student-faculty relationships). Each perspective had to be gleaned tentatively from the data, initially from just a few incidents or a few statements, then firmed up or confirmed as it became clear that the perspective was a common conceptual framework for students in *their own* definitions of the situations they faced (Becker and Geer, 1960, p. 280).

The actual coding of their data was by observed "incidents" (often cross-coded in more than one perspective and area). In description, Becker and Geer (1960) wrote:

> If, for example, we decide that we will consider as part of our tentative formulation of the perspective that students cheat on examinations or that they believe cheating is a good way to solve their problems, then we would code separately each observation of cheating and each complete statement by a student expressing the attitude that cheating is all right. (p. 281)

As the incidents began to accumulate, it became possible to refine and describe more specifically the content of each perspective—leading toward the eventual formation of concluding statements about the attitudes and actions that, in common, gave expression to the basic perspective(s) (Becker and Geer, 1960, p. 282).

In concert with the evolving definition of each perspective, the investigators fleshed out their understanding by checking each perspective's frequency, range, and collective character. For example, a frequency check might include a tabulation of the number of positive items of a perspective in use, compared with negative instances (e.g., an alternative perspective is used in dealing with the same problem). A check of range would seek to establish how widely instances of a perspective might be distributed through the observational situations. And a check of collective character would ask how widely shared a perspective seemed to be and how legitimate (e.g., a proper way to act) students deemed the perspective.

But in concluding their methodological note, Becker and Geer (1960, p. 288) recognize, with others who puruse the qualitative genre of inquiry, that there are few formal tests of researcher judgment and few clear guides to good data analysis. Miles (1979) puts it in strong terms: "We found that the actual process of analysis during case-writing was essentially intuitive, primitive, and unmanageable in any rational sense" (p. 597). At best, one can ask for a reasoned calculation of the plausibility of a study's findings in the light of possible alternatives. Personality, subjectivity, "judgment calls" (McGrath, Martin, and Kulk, 1982), chance, opportunism, timing, motivation, intuition, structural conditions, and rapport: these enter into a complex process of observation and sense making, questioning and answering, collecting and categorizing, designing and theorizing, initiating and concluding, forging ahead and revising—all occurring at the same time. Solid technician, logician, and skeptic to be sure, but the qualitative researcher must also perform as a creative intellectual craftsman (Burgess, 1984)—flexible, aware, innovative, and responsive—ready to adapt creatively to a decidedly ghostly world. As in the creation of settings (Sarason, 1972), their analysis must be a work of art.

In sum, a review of qualitative research methods *in use* in the study of higher education has focused upon four components. These are (1) entrance and rapport; (2) the ethics of field study; (3) data collection and design strategies; and (4) data analysis. Entrance and rapport must frequently be carefully negotiated by the researcher. Furthermore, the fieldworker role often involves a bit of a trade-off between active involvement (even interference) in the setting under study and the opportunity to remain uninvolved, to step back for a more detached (perhaps more objective) appraisal of what is happening. As understanding deepens, so does the fieldworker's moral involvement. What are the ethical obligations of the researcher to her or his subjects, to the scholarly community, to the larger public? Understanding through qualitative inquiry can be deeply revealing, and therefore also ethically frustrating. Methodologically, its revelations are best achieved through an emergent research design, a strategy of data collection that remains open-ended and flexible and at the same time intensive, comprehensive, and thoughtful. Multiple data collection techniques (each with its own gains and losses) help to provide a thick description and a triangulated view of the research setting. And while not as tightly designed nor as much aimed at transferability as conventional inquiry, qualitative methods and their analyses are nevertheless thoroughly concerned with establishing the trustworthiness while preserving the creativity of their naturalism-based insights and interpretations.

CONCLUSION: THE FUTURE OF
QUALITATIVE RESEARCH IN HIGHER EDUCATION

In the end, Robertson Davies's (1982) ghost completed his Ph.D.:

"Consider it yours," said I.
"You mean that I may present myself at the next Convocation?"
"Yes. . . . "
"I shall; Oh, I shall," he cried, ecstatically, and as he faded before my eyes I heard his voice from above the skylight in the Round Room, saying, "I go to a better place than this, confident that as a Ph.D. I shall have it in my power to make it better still."
(p. 21)

There is no doubt that with the current, widespread interest in the improvement of qualitative research methods, there is an opportunity to make inquiry into the complex world of higher education "better still." In a discussion of emerging developments in postsecondary organization theory and research, Peterson (1985) urges the greater use of intensive qualitative studies but also notes that inquiry into higher education is becoming a "methodological maze"—increasingly complex and sophisticated but also confused and fragmented. A danger is that increasingly complicated research methods "may tend to make postsecondary organizational research either less useful or more difficult for administrators to comprehend" (Peterson, 1985, p. 10). It is on this note of need for usefulness and help in comprehension that this chapter ends—by examining three, final methodological issues surrounding qualitative research in higher education. These are issues in (1) the use of qualitative research in policy analysis and administration; (2) the conduct of research in a setting where one is employed; and (3) the use of multisite and multimethod research strategies.

Research and Policy

There is a developing interest in the use of qualitative inquiry to inform administrative and policy questions (Eddy and Partridge, 1978; Herriott and Firestone, 1983; Marshall, 1984; Tierney, 1985). However, it is not entirely clear just how this facilitative and practical use of fieldwork can most effectively be carried out. As Marshall (1984) puts it, two key questions are, *first*, how can qualitative researchers convince policymakers that their studies are as valuable as quantitative reports, and *second*, how can qualitative inquiry be most useful in the policymaker's search for policy-relevant information?

With its tendencies toward particularism rather than generalizability, description rather than prescription, broad rather than problem-specific study, and lengthy rather than quick-answer inquiry, qualitative research is by no means easily fit into the administrative art (Mulhauser, 1975). Nevertheless, it has been suggested that many difficult-to-measure elements in institutional life and management not only call for enhanced understanding but are potentially significant tools of organizational improvement. For example, policy- and administration-oriented qualitative research can instructively provide (1) a richer managerial appreciation of that amorphous but powerful entity we call the *organizational culture* (Clark, 1980; Dill, 1982; Smircich, 1983; Masland, 1985; Deal and Kennedy, 1982); (2) a more thoroughgoing grasp of the subtle nuances, unintended effects, and changes and resistances that are elicited in efforts at program evaluation (Fetterman, 1984a; Guba, 1978; Tierney, 1985); and (3) an improved sense of the available mechanisms for managerial control (Cohen and March, 1974; March and Olsen, 1976) plus leadership (Yukl, 1981; Pfeffer, 1977)—amidst an institutional environment known for its weak, formal controls and its ambiguous attitudes toward administrative leadership.

As a special branch of qualitative inquiry, policy-oriented research is, however, filled with hazards. Tierney (1985, p. 102) suggests that the researcher should avoid pressures toward such problem-specific questions as: How can the institution "raise a half million dollars from recently graduated alumni"? Unless such questions can be broadened (e.g., a look at the quality of life at the school with institutional giving as a component), the fieldworker should stay well out of the practical problems arena. Similarly, Everhart (1984) warns that in policy research, the fieldworker may be constrained by funding agencies or governing bodies toward results in narrowly prespecified areas or toward investigations that use only certain data sets—giving up in the process the qualitative researcher's freedom to make the most of whatever the research setting provides.

Finally, Marshall (1984) suggests that policy-oriented research may require an array of special fieldworker approaches and abilities that would not be expected in less political environments. For example, researchers may need to persuade reluctant administrators that noncooperation in the provision of information could embarrass the institution. Or they may find that overcoming barriers to access and cooperation requires that "they appear as valuable, politically knowledgeable people with important connections in high places" (p. 239). However, Marshall (1984, p. 239) also refers to the Becker and Meyers (1974) finding that by often blithely walking unannounced into a "top official's inner sanctum as if one belonged there," one can successfully produce a flow of data. And a valuable fieldworker role in a charged organizational environment may often be a conscious mask of wide-eyed, naive innocence—appearing harmless as a listener but fascinated, and amply offering such encouraging expressions as "Really?" and "No kidding!" (Marshall, 1984, p. 241).

Researching at Home

It makes good sense to assume that many qualitative researchers who wish to study institutions of higher learning will focus, at least initially, upon settings in which they are employed. The convenience that accrues, plus ease of access and the head start of institutional foreknowledge (even to the point of knowing where many "ghosts" are hiding), augurs well for a search for understanding that begins at home. The gains and losses associated with insider versus outsider research have, of course, been summarized earlier in this chapter. Assuming stranger value within a setting to gain the distance and detachment that is often associated with creative and insightful data analysis must be offset against the benefits of cultural familiarity and the understanding in depth that can accompany the insider role.

Wade (1984) and Rossman (1984) have both described their experiences as researchers in higher education settings where they are also employed. The experience of "switching hats" was particularly problematic for Wade, for she was employed as a student affairs administrator and was simultaneously engaged in the study of the world of black undergraduate students at a major university.

Understandably, many of her subjects had questions about her real place (organizational spy?) in the university community, distrusting her ability to change roles from administrator to researcher without an ongoing residue of superior-subordinate attitudes and perspectives. She found herself having to pay dues for the intrusion into her subjects' lives by providing them with special counseling, insider information, and representation (e.g., defending their interests within the university environment).

Wade (1984, p. 219) observed that persons engaged in inquiry within their place of employment can put aside any thoughts of operating as totally unaligned researchers. Indeed, both she and Rossman (who studied Ph.D. candidates) found that, to be observers, it was necessary to carve out for themselves a new *employment* role: nonjudgmental observer to be sure, but also an ombudsman, a friend in administration to be called upon, a sympathetic ear for gripes and frustrations, an information provider, a finder of bureaucratic loopholes, and even occasionally a spokesperson. As mentioned earlier, Pelto and Pelto (1978) warned that the local people do not forget that the anthropologist will ultimately leave them. However, the researcher "at home" should be warned that the local people know the researcher will *not* be leaving them.

Multisite and Multimethod Research

Herriott and Firestone (1983) observe that the last decade has "seen the emergence of a new form of qualitative research, one intended to strengthen its ability to generalize while preserving in-depth description" (p. 14). This new form is the multisite qualitative study. The multisite study is aimed at cross-site comparison without a loss of within-site understanding.

This combination of depth and breadth, of generalization along with thoroughgoing description, is not at all an easy methodological task (Cook and Reichardt, 1979; McGrath, 1982). Among the key issues are the following: *First,* to what extent do instrumentation and the focus of observation need to be standardized? Although a single researcher can conceivably study more than one setting (but not many more), the likelihood is that a team of researchers will be used. When the researcher is the central instrument of data collection, does one need to structure away idiosyncratic researcher bias and perspective, as well as the impact of within-site variability, by demanding common observer foci and an agreed sense of "just what it is we're looking for"? Similarly, *second,* does multisite qualitative research require (or at least lead to) a stress upon data reduction toward standardization and ease of comparison at the possible expense of potentially meaningful, specific detail? And, *third,* do the gains of a broader understanding using (presumably) less time in data collection per site offset the benefits of long-term immersion at a single site (Firestone and Herriott, 1984; Miles, 1979)?

One gain in multisite research is a strengthened opportunity (even a near necessity) to mix qualitative and quantitative methods (Cook and Reichardt, 1979; Jick, 1979; Yin, 1984). Jick (1979, pp. 608–609) suggests that efforts to do so can help produce greater confidence in results, elicit creativity in problem definition, discover unusual or deviant dimensions of phenomena, and lead to more inclusive theorizing. Such approaches as the case survey (Yin and Heald, 1975) and the case cluster method (McClintock, Brannan, and Maynard-Moody, 1979) are suggested as ways to create common units of analysis among separate case studies.

A Final Word

Nevertheless, as a concluding thought to this chapter, and as a concluding thought to our interest in improving the methodology (and hence the credibility) of qualitative research, it should be noted, as anthropologist Harry F. Wolcott (1985) warns us, that a careful and complete articulation of its *method* is *not* the central concern of the qualitative (specifically, the ethnographic) research tradition. Wolcott (1985) writes:

> to the ethnographer *method itself is not all that important*. It never was and never will be. What ethnographers strive for is to "get it right," and in the long run the elusive "it" of determining just what constitutes the cultural dimensions of behavior in any particular social setting creates more difficulty than the also-elusive rightness of the account. (p. 201)

Neither field technique, nor access to and rapport with subjects, nor the length and depth of site-level immersion are of the importance that is achieved in a sense of cultural understanding *(Verstehen)* that is gained from a broad observation of human behavior in its social context. Concludes Wolcott (1985): "Let educational researchers of other persuasions do the counting and measuring they do so well. Ethnographers have their commitment . . . to cultural interpretation" (p. 202). As in Robertson Davies's (1982) story of the college ghost, it is perhaps the qualitative researcher more than any other scientist who quite simply appreciates the need to take the time (sometimes very large blocks of it) necessary to perform the "act of mercy" of a bit of insight into (and an understanding of) what our strange institutions of higher learning are all about:

> "You have come at last," said the Ghost. "I have waited for you long—but of course you are busy. Every professor in this university is busy. He is talking, or he is pursuing, or he is in a journey, or peradventure he sleepeth. But none has time for an act of mercy." (p. 15).

Acknowledgments. A sincere thank you is due Yvonna S. Lincoln, Ernest T. Pascarella, and Van Cleve Morris for their forthrightly critical and extremely helpful comments on an earlier draft of this manuscript.

NOTES

1. Rist (1975) notes tht Malinowski (1922) is one of the first anthropologists to employ the term *ethnography* as a descriptor of his observation of and participation in the tribal cultures of Trobriand Islanders.
2. The oldest tradition in ethnography is the study of culture as an integrated whole (holism). Sanday (1979) shows, however, that the modern ethnographic paradigm is internally differentiated, with less emphasis upon holism in many quarters and more emphasis upon the provision of "observational data on preselected functionally relevant categories" (p. 536).
3. Weber's use of *Verstehen* is actually interpreted fully and given its modern research meaning by Talcott Parsons, in his edited volume of Weber's *Theory of Social and Economic Organization* (1947, pp. 87–88).
4. A recent approach to the problem of value-laden inquiry, which has received the philosophical label *critical theory*, asserts that research is inevitably value-determined and that all inquiry therefore serves some value agenda. Critical theorists have been active in exploring the metaphors, ideologies, and social structures (particularly socioeconomic class) that pervade our ways of thinking about the world (Lincoln and Guba, 1985; Morgan, 1980; Ortony, 1979; Schubert, 1986).
5. This is, of course, an occurrence that is by no means limited to qualitative research methods and observational studies. As Lincoln and Guba (1985, p. 95) point out, famous instances of measurement effect upon the phenomena under study are widely known (e.g., the Hawthorne effect and the Pygmalion effect).
6. Burgess (1984, pp. 83–84) makes clear that for most researchers, the adoption of *one* fieldworker role, from among these four, is less likely than the choice of different phases and places in the course of the research. Roles are seldom consistent throughout a study and may vary with differing informants and subsettings.
7. One attractive point flowing naturally out of the concept of triangulation is the argument for a mixing of both qualitative and quantitative methods (Jick, 1979; Ianni and Orr, 1979). The central difficulty, however, is that graduate training programs seldom prepare individuals adequately in more than one method, and researchers fall easily into the habit of using that one method, as it is most comfortable for them, in study after study, whatever the research problem or field setting (McGrath, Martin, and Kulka, 1982).
8. Donovan (1964) used the technique of life history informatively in an ambitious study (combining questionnaire and interview strategies) of nearly 300 faculty members at Catholic colleges and universities—assembling his data into a "social profile of the Catholic academic man" (p. 11).

REFERENCES

Adams, R. N., and Preiss, J. J. (1960). *Human Organization Research: Field Relations and Techniques*. Homewood, IL: Dorsey.

Aguilar, J. L. (1981). Insider research: an ethnography of a debate. In D. A. Messerschmidt (ed.), *Anthropologists at Home in North America: Methods and Issues in the Study of One's Own Society*, pp. 15–26. Cambridge: Cambridge University Press.

Baldridge, J. J. (1971). *Power and Conflict in the University: Research in the Sociology of Complex Organizations*. New York: Wiley.

Barnes, J. A. (1970). Some ethical problems in modern fieldwork. In W. J. Filstead, *Qualitative Methodology: Firsthand Involvement with the Social World*, pp. 235–260. Chicago: Markham.

Barzun, J. (1968). *The American University: How It Runs, Where It Is Going*. New York: Harper & Row.

Barzun, J., and Graff, H. F. (1977). *The Modern Researcher* (3rd ed.). New York: Harcourt Brace Jovanovich.

Becker, H. S. (1970a). Interviewing medical students. In Filstead, *Qualitative Methodology: Firsthand Involvement with the Social World*, pp. 103–106.

Becker, H. S. (1970b). Problems of inference and proof in participant observation. In Filstead, *Qualitative methodology: Firsthand Involvement with the Social World*, pp. 189–201. Markham.

Becker, H. S., and Geer, B. (1960). Latent culture. *Administrative Science Quarterly* 5; 303–313.

Becker, H. S., Geer, B., Hughes, E. C., and Strauss, A. L. (1961). *Boys in White: Student Cultures in Medical School*. Chicago: University of Chicago Press.

Becker, H. S., Geer, B., and Hughes, E. C. (1968). *Making the Grade: The Academic Side of College Life*. New York: Wiley.

Becker, T. M., and Meyers, P. R. (1974). Empathy and bravado: Interviewing reluctant bureaucrats. *Public Opinion Quarterly* 38; 605–613.

Bell, D. (1966). *The Reforming of General Education: The Columbia College Experience in Its Natural Setting*. New York: Columbia University Press.

Berger, P. L., and Luckman, T. (1973). *The Social Construction of Reality*. London: Penguin.

Berreman, G. D. (1962). *Behind Many Masks: Ethnography and Impression Management in a Himalayan Village*. Ithaca, NY: Society for Applied Anthropology.

Bess, J. L., ed. (1984). *College and University Organization: Insights from the Behavioral Sciences*. New York: New York University Press.

Best, J. H. (Ed.). (1983). *Historical Inquiry in Education: A Research Agenda*. Washington, DC: American Educational Research Association.

Blau, P. M. (1973). *The Organization of Academic Work*. New York: Wiley.

Bogdan, R. (1972). *Participant Observation in Organizational Settings*. Syracuse, NY: Syracuse University Press.

Bogdan, R., and Biklen, S. K. (1982). *Qualitative Research for Education*. Boston: Allyn & Bacon.

Bolman, L. G., and Deal, T. E. (1984). *Modern Approaches to Understanding and Managing Organizations*. San Francisco: Jossey-Bass.

Burgess, R. G. (1984). *In the Field: An Introduction to Field Research*. London: George Allen & Unwin.

Bushnell, J. H. (1962). Student culture at Vassar. In N. Sanford (ed.), *The American College*. New York: Wiley.

Campbell, D.T. (1975). Degrees of freedom and the case study. *Comparative Political Studies* 8; 178–193.

Campbell, D. T. (1970). Natural selection as an epistemological model. In R. Naroll and R. Cohen (eds.), *A Handbook of Cultural Anthropology*. Garden City, NY: Natural History Press.

Campbell, D. T., and Stanley, J. C. (1963). *Experimental and Quasi-Experimental Designs for Research*. Chicago: Rand McNally.

Caplow, T., and McGee, R. J. (1958). *The Academic Marketplace*. New York: Basic Books.

Clark, B. R. (1983). *The Higher Education System: Academic Organization in Cross-National Perspective*. Berkeley: University of California Press.

Clark, B. R. (1980). *Academic Culture* (Working paper, IHERG-42). New Haven, CT: Yale University, Higher Education Research Group.

Clark, B. R. (1972). The organizational saga in higher education. *Administrative Science Quarterly* 17:179–194.

Clark, B. R. (1970). *The Distinctive College: Antioch, Reed and Swarthmore*. Chicago: Aldine.

Clark, B. R. (1960). *The Open Door College: A Case Study*. New York: McGraw-Hill.

Cohen, M. D., and March, J. G. (1974). *Leadership and Ambiguity: The American College President*. New York: McGraw-Hill.

Cohen, R., and Naroll, R. (1970). Method in cultural anthropology. In R. Naroll and R. Cohen (eds.), *A Handbook of Cultural Anthropology*. Garden City, NY: Natural History Press.

Cook, T. D., and Reichardt, C. S., eds. (1979). *Qualitative and Quantitative Methods in Evaluation*. Beverly Hills, CA: Sage.

Cottle, T. J. (1977). *College—Reward and Betrayal*. Chicago: University of Chicago Press.

Crane, D. (1972). *Invisible Colleges: Diffusion of Knowledge in Scientific Communities*. Chicago: University of Chicago Press.

Cronbach, L. J., and Suppes, P. (1969). *Research for Tomorrow's Schools: Disciplined Inquiry in Education*. New York: Macmillan.

Cusick, P. A. (1983). *The Egalitarial Ideal and the American High School*. New York: Longman.

Daalder, H., and Shils, E. (1982). *Universities, Politicians, and Bureaucrats: Europe and the United States*. Cambridge: Cambridge University Press.

Davies, R. (1982). The ghost who vanished by degrees. *High Spirits*. Markham, Ontario: Penguin.

Deal, T. E., and Kennedy, A. A. (1982). *Corporate Cultures: The Rites and Rituals of Corporate Life*. Reading, MA: Addison-Wesley.

Dentler, R. A., Baltzell, C., and Sullivan, D. J. (1983). *University on Trial: The Case of the University of North Carolina*. Cambridge, MA: Abt Books.

Denzin, N. K. (1970). *The Research Act: Theoretical Introduction to Sociological Methods*. Chicago: Aldine.

Denzin, N. K. (1978). *Sociological Methods*. New York: McGraw-Hill.

Dill, D. D. (1982). The management of academic culture: Notes on the management of meaning and social integration. *Higher Education* 11:303–320.

Donovan, J. D. (1964). *The Academic Man in the Catholic College*. New York: Sheed & Ward.

Dorr-Bremme, D. W. (1985). Ethnographic evaluation: A theory and method. *Educational Evaluation and Policy Analysis* 7:65–83.

Douglas, J. D. (1976). *Investigative Social Research*. Beverly Hills, CA: Sage.

Eddy, E. M., and Partridge, W. L. (eds.). (1978). *Applied Anthropology in America*. New York: Columbia University Press.

Eisner, E. W. (1975). *The Perceptive Eye: Toward the Reformulation of Educational Evaluation*. Occasional papers of the Stanford Evaluation Consortium. Stanford, CA: Stanford University.

Ellen, R. F. (1984). *Ethnographic Research: A Guide to General Conduct*. London: Academic Press.

Evans-Pritchard, E. E. (1937). *Witchcraft, Oracles and Magic Among the Azande*. London: Oxford University Press.

Everhart, R. B. (1984). Dilemmas of fieldwork in policy research: A critique. *Anthropology and Education Quarterly* 15:252–258.

Fetterman, D. M., ed. (1984a). *Ethnography in Educational Evaluation*. Beverly Hills, CA: Sage.

Fetterman, D. M. (1984b). Ethnography in educational research: The dynamics of diffusion. In Fetterman *Ethnography in Educational Evaluation*, pp. 21–35.

Fetterman, D. M. (1984c). Guilty knowledge, dirty hands, and other ethical dilemmas: The hazards of contract research. In Fetterman, ed., *Ethnography in Educational Evaluation*, pp. 211–236.

Fichter, J. H., and Kolb, W. L. (1970). Ethical limitations on sociological reporting. In Filstead, *Qualitative Methodology: Firsthand Involvement with the Social World*, pp. 261–274. Chicago: Markham.

Filstead, W. J., ed. (1970). *Qualitative Methodology: Firsthand Involvement with the Social World*. Chicago: Markham.

Firestone, W. A., and Herriott, R. E. (1984). Multisite qualitative policy research: Some design and implementation issues. In Fetterman, *Ethnography in Educational Evaluation*, pp. 63–88.

Freeman, D. (1983). *Margaret Mead and Samoa: The Making and Unmaking of an Anthropological Myth*. Cambridge: Harvard University Press.

Garfinkel, H. (1967). *Studies in Ethnomethodology*. Englewood Cliffs, NJ: Prentice-Hall.

Geer, B. (1970). Studying a college. In R. W. Habenstein (ed.), *Pathways to Data: Field Methods for Studying Ongoing Social Organizations*. Chicago: Aldine.

Geertz, C. (ed.). (1973). *The Interpretation of Cultures*. New York: Basic Books.

Glaser, B. G., and Strauss, A. L. (1967). *The Discovery of Grounded Theory*. Chicago: Aldine.

Goetz, J. P., and LeCompte, M. D. (1984). *Ethnography and Qualitative Design in Educational Research*. Orlando, FL: Academic Press.

Goetz, J. P., and LeCompte, M. D. (1981). Ethnographic research and the problem of data reduction. *Anthropology and Education Quarterly* 12:51–70.

Gold, R. L. (1958). Roles in sociological field observations. *Social Forces* 36:217–223.

Grant, G., and Riesman, D. (1978). *The Perpetual Dream: Reform and Experiment in the American College*. Chicago: University of Chicago Press.

Guba, E. G. (1978). *Toward a Methodology of Naturalistic Inquiry in Educational Evaluation*. Los Angeles: University of California Center for the Study of Evaluation.

Guba, E. G., and Lincoln, Y. S. (1981). *Effective Evaluation*. San Francisco; Jossey-Bass.

Habenstein, R. W., ed. (1970). *Pathways to Data: Field Methods for Studying Ongoing Social Organizations*. Chicago: Aldine.

Halpern, E. S. (1983). *Auditing Naturalistic Inquiries: The Development and Application of a Model*. Unpublished doctoral dissertation, Indiana University.

Hanson, M. (1984). Exploration of mixed metaphors in educational administration research. *Issues in Education* 11:167–185.

Hedberg, B. (1981). How organizations learn and unlearn. In P. C. Nystrom and W. H. Starbuck (eds.), *Handbook of Organizational Design*, Vol. 1. Oxford: Oxford University Press.

Heisenberg, W. (1958). *Physics and Philosophy*. New York: Harper & Row.

Hendricks, G. (1975). University registration systems: A study of social process. *Human Organization* 34:173–181.

Herriott, R. E., and Firestone, W. A. (1983). Multisite qualitative policy research: Optimizing description and generalizability. *Educational Researcher* 12(February): 14–19.

Husserl, E. (1952). *Ideals: General Introduction to Pure Phenomenology.* New York: Macmillan.

Ianni, F. A. J., and Orr, M. T. (1979). Toward a rapprochement of quantitative and qualitative methodologies. In T. D. Cook and C. S. Reichardt (eds.), *Qualitative and Quantitative Methods in Evaluation Research.* Beverly Hills, CA: Sage.

James, H. (1930). *Charles W. Eliot, President of Harvard University, 1869–1909.* Boston: Houghton Mifflin.

Jehenson, R. (1973). A phenomenological approach to the study of the formal organization. In G. Psathas (ed.), *Phenomenological Sociology: Issues and Applications.* New York: Wiley.

Jelinek, M., Smircich, L., and Hirsch, P., eds. (1983). Organizational culture. *Administrative Science Quarterly* 28:331–338.

Jick, T. D. (1979). Mixing qualitative and quantitative methods: triangulation in action. *Administrative Science Quarterly* 24:602–611.

Kerr, C. (1964). *The Uses of the University.* Cambridge: Harvard University Press.

Krathwohl, D. R. (1980). The myth of value-free evaluation. *Educational Evaluation and Policy Analysis* 2:37–45.

Lamont, L. (1979). *Campus Shock: A Firsthand Report on College Life Today.* New York: E. P. Dutton.

LeCompte, M. D., and Goetz, J. P. (1982). Problems of reliability and validity in ethnographic research. *Review of Educational Research* 52:31–60.

Levine, R. A. (1970). Research design in anthropological field work. In R. Naroll and R. Cohen (eds.), *A Handbook of Method in Cultural Anthropology.* Garden City, NY: Natural History Press.

Lincoln, Y. S., and Guba, E. G. (1985). *Naturalistic Inquiry.* Beverly Hills, CA: Sage.

Lipsky, M. (1980). *Street-Level Bureaucracy: Dilemmas of the Individual in Public Services.* New York: Russell Sage.

London, H. B. (1978). *The Culture of a Community College.* New York: Praeger.

Malinowski, B. (1922). *The Argonauts of the Western Pacific.* London: Routledge & Kegan Paul.

March, J. G., and Olsen, J. P. (1976). *Ambiguity and Choice in Organizations.* Bergen, Norway: Universitetsforlaget.

Marshall, C. (1984). Elites, bureaucrats, ostriches, and pussycats: Managing research in policy settings. *Anthropology and Education Quarterly* 15:235–251.

Marshall, C. (1984). Research dilemmas in administration and policy settings: An introduction to the special issue. *Anthropology and Education Quarterly* 15:194–201.

Martin, J., Feldman, M. S., Hatch, M. J., and Sitkin, S. B. (1983). The uniqueness paradox in organizational stories. *Administrative Science Quarterly* 28:438–453.

Masland, A. T. (1985). Organizational culture in the study of higher education. *The Review of Higher Education* 8:157–168.

Maslow, A. (1965). *Eupsychian Management.* Homewood, IL: Richard Irwin.

Massarik, F. (1981). The interviewing process re-examined. In P. Reason and J. Rowan (eds.), *Human Inquiry: A Sourcebook of New Paradigm Research.* New York: Wiley.

Mattingly, P. H. (1983). Structures over time: Institutional history. In J. H. Best (ed.), *Historical Inquiry in Education: A Research Agenda.* Washington, DC: American Educational Research Association.

McCall, G. J., and Simmons, J. L., eds. (1969). *Issues in Participant Observation: A Text and Reader.* Reading, MA: Addison-Wesley.

McClintock, C. C., Brannon, D., and Maynard-Moody, S. (1979). Applying the logic of sample surveys to qualitative case studies: The case cluster method. *Administrative Science Quarterly* 24:612–629.

McDonald, S., Redlinger, L., and Edwards, W. (1980). *The Heisenberg Problem: Comments on Observer Effects in the Field Work Situation.* Paper presented at the Annual Meeting of the American Educational Research Association, Boston, April.

McGrath, J. E. (1982). Dilematics: The study of research choices and dilemmas. In J. E. McGrath, J. Martin, and R. A. Kulka (eds.), *Judgment Calls in Research.* Beverly Hills, CA: Sage.

McGrath, J. E., Martin, J., and Kulka, R. A. (1982). *Judgment Calls in Research.* Beverly Hills, CA: Sage.

McHenry, D. E., and Associates. (eds.). (1977). *Academic Departments.* San Francisco: Jossey-Bass.

Mehan, H., and Wood, H. (1975). *The Reality of Ethnomethodology.* New York: Wiley.

Messerschmidt, D. A. (ed.). (1981). *Anthropologists at Home in North America: Methods and Issues in the Study of One's Own Society.* Cambridge: Cambridge University Press.

Miles, M. (1979). Qualitative data as attractive nuisance: The problem of analysis. *Administrative Science Quarterly* 24:590–601.

Miles, M., and Huberman, A. M. (1984). *Qualitative Data Analysis: A Sourcebook of New Methods.* Beverly Hills, CA: Sage.

Miller, P. (1978). Administrative orientations from anthropology. In E. Eddy and W. Partridge (eds.), *Applied Anthropology in America.* New York: Columbia University Press.

Mintzberg, H. (1973). *The Nature of Managerial Work.* New York: Harper & Row.

Morgan, G. (1980). Paradigms, metaphors, and puzzle solving in organization theory. *Administrative Science Quarterly* 25:605–621.

Morison, S. E. (1935). *The Founding of Harvard College.* Cambridge: Harvard University Press.

Morris, V. C. (1981). *Deaning: Middle Management in Academe.* Urbana, IL: University of Illinois Press.

Morris, V. C. (1984). Plato's "philosopher-king": Position impossible. In P. A. Sala (ed.), *Ethics, Education and Administrative Decisions: A Book of Readings,* pp. 129–133. New York: Peter Lang.

Morris, V. C., Crowson, R., Porter-Gehrie, C., and Hurwitz, Jr., E. (1984). *Principals in Action: The Reality of Managing Schools.* Columbus, OH: Charles E. Merrill.

Mulhauser, F. (1975). Ethnography and educational policy. *Human Organization* 34:311–319.

Myrdal, G. (1969). *Objectivity in Social Research.* New York: Pantheon Books.

Naroll, R., and Cohen, R. (eds.). (1970). *A Handbook of Method in Cultural Anthropology.* Garden City, NY: Natural History Press.

Newcomb, T. (1943). *Personality and Social Change: Attitude Formation in a Student Community.* New York: Dryden Press.

Ortony, A., ed. (1979). *Metaphor and Thought.* Cambridge: Cambridge University Press.

Owens, R. G. (1982). Methodological rigor in naturalistic inquiry: Some issues and answers. *Educational Administration Quarterly* 18:1–21.

Pace, C. R. (1968). Methods of describing college cultures. In K. Yamamoto (ed.), *The College Student and His Culture,* pp. 193–205. Boston: Houghton Mifflin.

Pascarella, E. T. (1985). College environmental influences on learning and cognitive development: A critical review and synthesis. In J. C. Smart (ed.), *Higher Education: Handbook of Theory and Research,* Vol. I, pp. 1–61. New York: Agathon Press.

Patterson, F., and Longworth, C. R. (1966). *The Making of a College.* Cambridge, MA: MIT Press.

Pelto, P. J., and Pelto, G. H. (1978). *Anthropological Research: The Structure of Inquiry* (2nd ed.). Cambridge: Cambridge University Press.

Perkins, J. A., ed. (1973). *The University as an Organization.* New York: McGraw-Hill.

Perkins, J. A. (1966). *The University in Transition.* Princeton, NJ: Princeton University Press.

Peterson, M. W. (1985). Emerging developments in postsecondary organization theory and research: Fragmentation or integration. *Educational Researcher* 14:5–12.

Pfeffer, J. (1977). The ambiguity of leadership. *Academy of Management Review* 2:104–112.

Psathas, G. (ed.). (1979). *Everyday Language: Studies in Ethnomethodology.* New York: Irvington.

Psathas, G. (ed.). (1973). *Phenomenological Sociology: Issues and Applications.* New York: Wiley.

Reisman, D. (1958). *Constraint and Variety in American Education.* Garden City, NY: Doubleday.

Reisman, D. (1980). *On Higher Education: The Academic Enterprise in an Era of Rising Student Consumerism.* San Francisco: Jossey-Bass.

Reisman, D., and Jencks, C. (1962). The viability of the American college. In N. Sanford (ed.), *The American College.* New York: Wiley.

Richardson, S. A. (1970). Training in field relations skills. In W. J. Filstead, *Qualitative Methodology: Firsthand Involvement with the Social World,* pp. 155–163.

Rist, R. C. (1975). Ethnographic techniques and the study of an urban school. *Urban Education* 10:86–108.

Rist, R. C. (1979). On the means of knowing: Qualitative research in education. *New York Education Quarterly* (Summer), 17–21.

Rossman, G. B. (1984). "I owe you one": Considerations of role and reciprocity in a study of graduate education for school administrators. *Anthropology and Education Quarterly* 15:225–233.

Salancik, G. R., and Pfeffer, J. (1974). The bases and use of power in organizational decision making: The case of the university. *Administrative Science Quarterly* 19:453–473.

Sanday, P. R. (1979). The ethnographic paradigm(s). *Administrative Science Quarterly* 24:527–538.

Sarason, S. B. (1972). *The Creation of Settings and the Future of Societies.* San Francisco: Jossey-Bass.

Sarason, S. B. (1982). *The Culture of the School and the Problem of Change* (2nd ed.). Boston: Allyn & Bacon.

Schubert, W. H. (1986). *Curriculum: Perspective, Paradigm, and Possibility.* New York: Macmillan.

Schutz, A. (1962, 1964). *Collected Papers, Vols. 1 and 2.* The Hague: Martinus Nijhoff.

Schutz, A. (1967). *The Phenomenology of the Social World.* Evanston, IL: Northwestern University Press.

Schwartz, H., and Jacobs, J. (1979). *Qualitative Sociology: A Method to the Madness.* New York: Free Press.

Seeley, J. R. (1967). *The University in America*. Santa Barbara, CA: Center for the Study of Democratic Institutions.

Smircich, L. (1983). Concepts of culture and organizational analysis. *Administrative Science Quarterly* 28:339–358.

Smith, J. K., and Heshusius, L. (1986). Closing down the conversation: The end of the quantitative—qualitative debate among educational inquirers. *Educational Researcher* 15:4–12.

Spradley, J. P. (1980). *Participant Observation*. New York: Holt, Rinehart, & Winston.

Sproull, L. S. (1981). Beliefs in organizations. In P. C. Nystrom and W. H. Starbuck (eds.), *Handbook of Organizational Design*, Vol. 2. Oxford: University Press.

Stephenson, J. B., and Greer, L. S. (1981). Ethnographers in their own cultures: Two Appalachian cases. *Human Organization* 40:123–130.

Storr, R. (1966). *Harper's University: The Beginnings. A History of the University of Chicago*. Chicago: University of Chicago Press.

Tierney, W. G. (1985). Ethnography: An alternative evaluation methodology. *The Review of Higher Education* 8:93–105.

Tierney, W. G. (1983). Governance by conversation: An essay on the structure, function, and communicative codes of a faculty senate. *Human Organization* 43:172–177.

Valentine, C. A. (1968). *Culture and Poverty: Critique and Counterproposals*. Chicago: University of Chicago Press.

Van Maanen, J. (1976). Breaking-in: Socialization to work. In R. Dubin (ed.), *Handbook of Work, Organization, and Society*. Chicago: Rand McNally.

Van Maanen, J. (1984). Doing new things in old ways: The chains of socialization. In J. L. Bess (ed.), *College and University Organization: Insights from the Behavioral Sciences*, pp. 211–247. New York: New York University Press.

Van Maanen, J. (1979a). The fact of fiction in organizational ethnography. *Administrative Science Quarterly* 24:539–550.

Van Maanen, J., ed. (1979b). Qualitative methodology. *Administrative Science Quarterly* 24:520–526.

Van Maanen, J., and Schein, E. H. (1979). Toward a theory of organizational socialization. In B. Staw (ed.), *Research in Organizational Behavior*, Vol. 1. Greenwich, CT: JAI Press.

Van Maanen, J., Dobbs, Jr., J. M., and Faulkner, R. R. (1982). *Varieties of Qualitative Research*. Beverly Hills, CA: Sage.

Wade, J. E. (1984). Role boundaries and paying back: "Switching hats" in participant observation. *Anthropology and Education Quarterly* 15:211–224.

Wax, R. H. (1971). *Doing Fieldwork: Warnings and Advice*. Chicago: University of Chicago Press.

Webb, E. J., Campbell, D. T., Schwartz, R. D., and Sechrest, L. (1966). *Unobtrusive Measures: Nonreactive Research in the Social Sciences*. Chicago: Rand McNally.

Weber, M. (1947). *The Theory of Social and Economic Organization*, ed by T. Parsons. New York: Free Press.

Weick, K. E. (1984). Contradictions in a community of scholars: The cohesion accuracy tradeoff. In J. L. Bess (ed.), *College and University Organization: Insights from the Behavioral Sciences*, pp. 15–29. New York: New York University Press.

Weick, K. E. (1976). Educational organizations as loosely coupled systems. *Administrative Science Quarterly* 21:1–19.

Williams, G. (1958). *Some of My Best Friends Are Professors*. New York: Abelard-Schuman.

.Wilson, S. (1977). The use of ethnographic techniques in educational research. *Review of Educational Research* 47:245–265.

Wolcott, H. F. (1984). Ethnographers sans ethnography. In Fetterman, *Ethnography in Educational Evaluation,* pp. 177–210.

Wolcott, H. F. (1985). On ethnographic intent. *Educational Administration Quarterly* 21:187–203.

Yin, R. K. (1984). *Case Study Research: Design and Methods.* Beverly Hills, CA: Sage.

Yin, R. K., and Heald, K. A. (1975). Using the case survey method to analyze policy studies. *Administrative Science Quarterly* 20:371–381.

Yukl, G. A. (1981). *Leadership in Organizations.* Englewood Cliffs, NJ: Prentice-Hall.

Bricks and Mortar: Architecture and the Study of Higher Education

John R. Thelin

and

James Yankovich
The College of William and Mary

In 1953, when the President of the United States, Dwight D. Eisenhower, visited Dartmouth, he exclaimed, "Why, this is how I always thought a college should look!" (Hill, 1964). He echoed an American sentiment: we expect the campus to be a distinctive place whose architecture is at once historic and monumental— a source of pride and affiliation. For many college constituencies, it is the visual and physical legacy of the campus which seizes the imagination. This is no fleeting or peripheral matter. As one journalist observed, "The true campus symbol for the tumultuous decade of the 1960s wasn't a picket line; it was a construction crane" (Williams, 1985). The message is that bricks and mortar are central to the organizational life and shape of the American college and university.

The theme of fond recall for the campus pervades American letters and memoirs over decades. As one prominent novelist recently wrote:

> For me, there are four things that all college campuses have in common: mystery, tradition, hope and a sense of limitless possibility. I felt that way when I first set foot on the Radcliffe campus as a 16 year old freshman, and I still feel that way now, more than a quarter of a century later. . . . Part of the mystery was the hugeness of the new place, and my instinctive understanding that I would discover things there that would change my life. I went to college to have my life changed—I think in various ways we all did. (Jaffe, 1981)

Donors, prospective students, and alumni know this. The national press knows this—and responds by regularly featuring articles on the American campus as "architecture's show place" (e.g., Hamlin, 1903; *Time,* September 21, 1970, pp. 76–81; David, 1985). In 1986, the Public Broadcast System television network devoted a lengthy feature episode to celebration of the campus as a "place apart" in its nationally syndicated series on American architecture (Stern,

57

1986). Certainly architects and architectural firms have long recognized the college and university campus as central to their commissions and projects involving public design and building. But what about higher education researchers? Has this popular fascination with campus appearance sparked investigative curiosity? Our finding is that the flame flickers, but feebly.

A SAMPLER OF MAJOR RESEARCH THEMES
AND THREADS FROM 1960 TO 1975

Since the late 1950s, numerous prominent higher education researchers have made brief yet specific note that architecture ought be given serious attention as an important and underappreciated dimension in the study of colleges and universities. The following summaries illustrate these research themes and threads from 1960 to 1975 within such higher education topics as organization and governance, finance, curriculum, and student development.

Organization and Governance

In grafting the methods and concepts of political science to research on higher education, one key argument in the early 1960s was that study of the campus as a complex organization ought include analysis of such physical features as architectural styles (Lazarsfeld, 1961). A decade later, this was expanded and refined to advance the notion of an "environmental code" for both understanding and creating a "sense of place" associated with the college campus; central to the code were the following tenets (Sturner, 1972):

1. The university is a total environment, a system of exploratory activities occurring in various forms of order and disorder which take place in a particular setting.
2. The physical environment, that which houses the formal learning component, simultaneously reflects and shapes, is both a response to and a cause of, the values and practices of an educational institution.
3. The physical environment of a given campus should not only mirror and support the learning process in general, but it also should reflect the distinctive values and aspirations of those who actually live at and use a particular college or university.

In the 1970s, expertise in higher education planning had come to include explicit attention to campus building and construction (Halstead, 1974), and organizational theory had matured to include the concepts of behavioral settings and ecological environments. Here was recognition that "The sizes and shapes of buildings are important" and that the "style, color, and arrangement of the architecture and landscaping give a campus a physiognomy, a set of traits which communicate the personality of the institution and its inhabitants'' (Sturner, 1973).

For the study of organization and governance in higher education, this meant particular attention to the so-called ''edifice complex'' as a priority for college and university presidents. Architecture was cited as a key element in studies of presidential leadership and administrative reorganization of the American campus. For example, at the State University of New York at Buffalo in the mid-1960s, a bold campaign to transform an ''existing, mediocre campus'' into the ''Berkeley of the East'' was predicated in large part on the construction of an ''academic New Jerusalem of unlimited money'' (Bennis, 1977). Its brand-new futuristic $650-million campus was to be the architectural magnet which would attract numerous high-caliber faculty and administrators. It was heralded as offering thirty small colleges, along with a massive administrative building which one observer said would ''dwarf the pentagon'' (Goldman, 1969). If architecture was integral to recruitment and to soaring expectations of institutional transformation, the subsequent finding was that the absence (or failure) of grand architecture was equally potent as a source of organizational disenchantment and declining morale; that is, the proposed SUNY Buffalo campus was not fully realized, leaving recruited faculty and administrators to face overcrowding into ''drab'' prefabricated structures and leased industrial buildings.

Construction became central to higher education budgets and finance. From 1965 to 1970, an average of seventy-six new institutions were established each year, a rate of three campuses completed every two weeks. Capital outlay expenditures during the five-year period 1968 to 1972 averaged $3.8 billion per year—and an estimated 53 million square feet of new architectural space each year (Halstead, 1974, p. 468).

Therein was the mixed legacy of campus architecture in the post–World War II decades: the paradox of abundance and disappointment. The unprecedented amount of college and university construction included some high points in architectural style and innovation (*Time,* September 21, 1970, pp. 76–81). Yet hasty and uninspired design characterized the bulk of campus building in this era. In the wake of the campus construction boom of the 1960s and 1970s, both administrators and researchers in higher education grappled to make sense of the tendency toward overbuilding. There was, as noted above, the familiar notion of architecture as the ''magnet'' to *attract* new constituents and supporters. A second and newer insight was the administrative impulse toward endurance (even immortality). Political scientist Bruce Vladeck's (1978) analysis of buildings and budgets attributes overconstruction to the peculiar ambiguities of being a university president: the relative absence of data on job performance tends to prompt presidents to build heroic campus structures:

The competition for students and faculty is closely interwoven with the general drive for institutional prestige. Like most people, administrators and trustees are generally eager to do a good job and to appear to be doing a good job. But in higher education, as in most nonprofit services, it is extremely difficult to tell what a good job is, since it is so extraordinarily difficult to evalute the quality of the "product." (p. 39)

One predictable response is for presidents to leave behind tangible evidence of accomplishments, namely, monuments. Hence, there has been an irresistible impulse to build. And the unfortunate consequence is that subsequent presidents and other administrators inherit the inglorious burden of paying for the maintenance of these monuments—a syndrome which left many colleges and universities strapped for funds in the late 1960s and the 1970s. Vladeck's proposed solution was that in the future, all monies and donations for campus building include a minimum percentage set aside as a maintenance endowment.

Failure to consider the long-run costs of the "edifice complex" has consequences both for institutional operation and state-federal policy. First, during a period of extended inflation (e.g., 1973 to 1981), university financial officers often tend to delay maintenance of buildings and grounds as an obvious way to balance budgets and reduce operating expenses. This short-run strategy ultimately backfires and "costs" an institution: deferred maintenance will be expensive because of increased prices *when* the institution does finally get around to making repairs; furthermore, quite apart from inflation, the extended and increased erosion of facilities will make ultimate replacement costs escalate. Presidents and deans then are caught in a no-win downward spiral: buildings in disrepair and unkempt grounds may cause a loss of tuition dollars by repelling prospective students and their parents. And in the Frost Belt region of the United States, unprecedented oil prices and fuel costs often meant that monumental buildings became "white elephants" which were expensive to keep open and, if closed, were a source of embarrassment.

In matters of government policy toward higher education, the conspicuous feature is that monies are often restricted so as not to be allowed for certain kinds of campus construction (e.g., dormitories), in favor of funding for such programs as student loans. This has had a two-fold consequence for colleges. First, a disproportionate amount of private philanthropy is channeled toward new construction (in part because donors share with college presidents a desire for testimonial monuments). Second, it tended to shape public policy away from a residential model of undergraduate education.

Campus and Community: External Relations

Colleges and universities have long enjoyed stature as landmarks and symbols of civic and local pride—stature which helps directly and indirectly in fund raising, tax exemptions, and other salubrious relations with community and government. Implicit in this relationship is the notion that a campus shall be a *historic* and *dignified* architectural environment. A good illustration of this popular expectation and regional pride is the following commentary about a "Walk Through History on Campus" in the South:

> The South's varied college campuses speak individually of time and place and of generations who have walked the quadrangles. Fall is a fine time to read their storied facades. . . . When the South goes to campus in fall, to visit college students, or attend special events, the campus itself is part of the draw. Whether a revered landmark, a quiet oak-lined quadrangle, or the historic disarray of fraternity row, the images evoke lives lived and years passed. We want them to remain, and, indeed college campuses have been good repositories of memory.
>
> Southern campuses vary greatly in size, physical setting, and period of development. They are expected to be beautiful, and you will often hear people comparing one campus to another like paintings seen in a museum. The older parts, like much else in our towns, cities, and countryside, tend to be more graceful and refined, though age may have something to do with it.
>
> Whatever the age or setting or spread, college campuses tell the history and settlement of the region, a sequence of distinctive places with buildings that can be read like books. An autumn stroll through a campus—especially with a good guide—can be suffused with history as light through coloring leaves, as stirring to the spirit as it is to the senses. (Morris, 1983, p. 82)

In many instances, the architectural and environmental presence of the campus is so commanding that it dominates the community, giving rise to the generic "college town" as a distinctive part of American life (Canby, 1936; Jaffe, 1981). A half century ago, Henry Seidel Canby recalled the "Gothic Age" of the American campus and college town of the 1890s—a memoir shaped by architectural allusions:

> As trading or industrial centers their life might be indistinguishable from towns or cities of a like size, but in their social consciousness there was always some recognition of peculiarity. For the heart of the community was a college. Its subtle influences were as pervasive if less noticeable than the quite unsubtle symbols of college life—playing fields, cafés, and collegiate clothing. . . . The campus and the college buildings dominated its architecture like the temple and citadel of a Greek city-state, a difficult relationship since there was always some doubt in the minds of the town folk whether the college was an asset or a parasite. The town with its college was like a woman's club committee with a celebrity in tow, a credit to them but also an embarrassment and sometimes a nuisance. (Canby, 1936, p. 4)

The underside of this popularity is a curse of bigness, that is, recognition of the college or university as a large and sprawling employer and landlord. Hence, apart from the nostalgia for and the local booster pride in the historic campus, recent research signals public concern about collisions between campus and community. Ironically, colleges and universities now are sometimes criticized for having destroyed historic structures and neighborhoods in order to gain urban space for construction of new facilities and buildings (Russell, 1983). This latter dimension complicates the benign and historic image of campus architecture as a sanctuary for historic preservation. Thus, if one accepts from organizational theory the notion that a campus has a "corporate personality," one must entertain the corollary that it can be a "split personality," which at one time salvages and at another time destroys the heritage of the physical environment.

The Curriculum in Higher Education

Over twenty years ago, sociologist Martin Trow's (1963) article on administrative implications of analyses of campus cultures made the point that an "area where research on student culture may make a much larger contribution to the life of the college is in connection with the design and layout of the physical plant." His concern was that in an era of rapid expansion in higher education, campus constituents—students, faculty, and administrators—had an unprecedented opportunity to shape the so-called learning environment. However, research about living and learning on a campus would have to be fused with the work of architects and engineers. The breakthrough was that analysis of campus architecture shifted to concern and conjecture about its consequences for studying, teaching, and learning, a marked shift from the days of simplistic efficiency. As one higher education researcher noted:

> Many campus buildings seem to be designed with the janitor and maintenance staff in mind rather than the student. The simplest building for a janitor is one built on the model of a hospital or a bathroom—tile floors and walls tiled two or three feet up make it possible for janitors to approach their task with a hose and mop. Too many classrooms have this sanitary quality. (Bask, 1965, pp. 308–309)

Higher education researchers warned about the adverse effects of buildings which were sterile, authoritarian, and cold; they concluded that campus design ought respond to questions of aesthetics and impact and that "good educational design" allowed for variation in size, shape, color, decoration, and furniture (Bask, 1965, p. 309).

The caveat was that academics were wrong to blame wholly external groups—architects, engineers, and government officials—for uninspired campus design. Much of the fault could be attributed to indifference among academics themselves:

> The reasons why many campuses are unexciting and drab are easy to understand. Most members of the university community—faculty, staff and students alike—are insensitive or simply don't care, unconsciously tolerating arid environments because such austerity complements the rational, visual and linear thrust of their book-oriented lives. (Sturner, 1973, p. 75)

For "curriculum," architecture was essential to the notion of the distinctive (and expensive) residential quadrangles of the 1930s, as personified by the "house plan" at Harvard and "colleges" at Yale (Jencks and Riesman, 1967). Elsewhere, starting in the late 1920s, the Claremont Colleges in California resisted the temptation toward undifferentiated growth, opting instead for expansion via a unique organizational model: a federation of small, interdependent institutions which shared some human and physical resources.

In the 1960s, interest in the crucial connections between architecture and curriculum blossomed in the form and ethos of the so-called cluster college innovations (Grant and Riesman, 1978; Riesman, 1980, pp. 208–209). Indeed, the architectural environment of the cluster college was the concept which would organize and animate formal learning and living in a conscious effort to break down the infamous "impersonality of the multiversity." As an antidote and alternative to mass education and large lecture halls, the honeycombed cluster college arrangement was intended to "make the university seem smaller as it grew larger":

> Since its opening in 1965 the most luminous illustration of the subcollege option in public higher education has been the University of California at Santa Cruz. Its original design, developed when Clark Kerr was president of the University of California system, contemplated building a series of colleges of about 600 students each. The college would be residentially self-contained under the leadership of a provost; a group of a few senior faculty members would develop collegewide curricula with different foci, which would in turn be compatible with different styles of noncollegiate life in each campus. One college was to be built every year until the campus reached the ceiling of 27,500 students that President Kerr had succeeded in imposing on both Berkeley and UCLA—already well beyond what he regarded as the optimal scale for a good research university between 10,000 and 15,000 students. . . . It is hard to think of any university constructed with such close attention to the relation between architectural forms and collegiate life, whether in the dining facilities of the colleges or in their residential arrangements. (Riesman, 1980, pp. 208–209)

Related themes surfaced in the sociology of higher education, where David Riesman, Christopher Jencks, Burton Clark, and Martin Trow looked closely at residential patterns and house systems in order to understand institutional ethnography and student subcultures.

Student Development and the Campus Setting

Closely related to concerns over architecture and curriculum is the issue of campus environment as a factor in changes in student attitudes, values, and beliefs. Leaders for over thirty years in the study of colleges as social and psychological environments which shape student attitudes and values have each alerted colleagues to the importance of the kind of dormitories and campus arrangements as a factor in the differential impact of the college experience (e.g., Pace and Stern, 1958; Elton and Bates, 1966; Astin, 1968). On the one hand this research could take the form of microanalysis, in which social scientists probed the consequences of *where* on campus a student lounge ought be located, or *how* freshmen ought be housed in relation to juniors and seniors (Trow, 1963). On the other hand, perhaps the most essential research strand dealt with the large and fundamental policy question of whether or not a college ought build dormitories at all.

Astin's *Four Critical Years* (1978), a monumental study of the differential impact of kinds of campuses on changes in students' values indicated that the single most important factor was the residential campus: "The student's ratings of the undergraduate college experience and environment are strongly influenced by various forms of involvement. The greater satisfaction associated with being a resident rather than a commuter has been reported by several other investigators. . . . Students are also much more likely to be satisfied with virtually all aspects of their undergraduate experience if they live in a dormitory or private room rather than at home" (p. 186).

Astin's research finding led directly to an important policy implication for higher education. Since World War II, the unprecedented bulk of expansion in access and enrollments had taken place in the public community colleges or in state-supported commuter colleges—institutions which seldom provided a residential undergraduate education. And as Astin emphasized, these were precisely the institutions which had *relatively* little impact on changing the attitudes and values of commuting students. One message was that if one wants the college experience to be consequential, one cannot afford *not* to invest in architecture, especially campus dormitories and residence halls:

> Results of this and other empirical studies . . . suggest that, from an educational viewpoint, cessation of dormitory construction and expansion of places for commuters was a poor idea. In almost every respect, residents benefit more than commuters from their undergraduate experience. Residents not only show greater changes in personality and attitudes but also become more involved in campus life. Most important is the increased chance of persistence, which in turn maximizes the chance of implementing career plans. Residents are much more satisfied with their undergraduate experience than are commuters. (Astin, 1978, p. 249)

The implication for facilities construction policy and practice is thus:

> Since living in a campus residence rather than commuting from home enhances the impact of college across a wide range of affective and behavioral outcomes, legislators and policy makers—particularly at the federal level—might reexamine the current moratorium on support for construction of residential facilities. While such a decision necessarily involves political considerations and possible tradeoffs with other sources of support for education, the potential benefits are substantial. In particular, the fact

that the residential experience significantly reduces student attrition offers the possibility that some of the resources currently used for other purposes—student loans, for
example—could be more profitably diverted to support dormitory construction. (Astin,
1978, p. 255)

Summary and Synthesis

Perhaps the manifesto which best illustrates the rationale for including architecture as an element in higher education organizational behavior comes from Allan
Nevins's 1962 study of state universities:

> One of the more difficult obligations of these new institutions has been the creation of
> an atmosphere, a tradition, a sense of the past which might play as important part in the
> education of sensitive students as any other influence. This requires time, sustained
> attention to cultural values, and the special beauties of landscape and architecture. . . .
> This spiritual grace the state universities cannot quickly acquire, but they have been
> gaining it. (p. 82)

These scattered works were invitations. As Lewis Mayhew wrote in 1969,
"Until recently an overlooked strand of institutional influence was the campus
itself and the buildings and space it comprises. Gradually, however, has come an
awareness of the idea of [architect Richard] Neutra that 'The shapes on a campus
are not extracurricular . . . ' " (pp. 131–133). The disappointing finding is that
in the past decade, relatively few higher education researchers have accepted the
invitations. There is no lack of articles on college and university architecture.
But on close inspection, one finds that these are largely confined to journals in
which architects write for one another. Our concern is incorporation of campus
architecture into the interdisciplinary and multidisciplinary study of higher
education.

Here the signs are not especially promising. For example, a search of over
7,900 journal articles dealing with "colleges" and "universities" published
since 1965 and registered in the ERIC clearinghouse database yielded 158 titles
which dealt with architecture and building design; the majority of these 158
articles were technical and specific reports on construction of particular buildings
on particular campuses, with little connection to overriding themes in higher
education research. Another graphic anecdotal datum is that review of the
national conference programs sponsored by the Association for the Study of
Higher Education from 1978 through 1985 showed no papers or sessions devoted
primarily to the issue of campus architecture.

There is an intellectual and conceptual imbalance of trade between academics
and architects. Our impression is that although architects often write for fellow
architects, they also make great effort to exchange ideas and materials with
college and university officials. A good example is the periodic forum between

college presidents and architects in the journal of the American Institute of Architects (AIA) and since 1963 the establishment of the AIA Committee on School and College Architecture.

RECENT RESEARCH INTEREST
IN CAMPUS ARCHITECTURE

A ray of hope is that in the past year, there has been a definite groundswell of interest in campus architecture. One noteworthy recent definitive work which might stimulate interest in architecture as central to the study of higher education is Paul Venable Turner's *Campus* (1984). The book presents a massive compendium of architectural plans and projects for American colleges and universities since the seventeenth century. Turner, an architectural historian, sought a national and historical context for a case study of his home campus (Stanford). In so doing, he found that "There had been no attempt to look at the overall picture of the campus, at its evolution as a building form and its relation to educational principles." To remedy this situation, he read widely in the history of American education, conducted a survey of more than 350 colleges and universities, and visited numerous campus sites. The result was a study of how the form of the campus has reflected educational reforms and social and historical forces. Turner's major thesis is that "the American campus is one of the most distinctively American forms that has ever been created. The desire for a special place where scholars study and live together is ingrained in the American sense of what a college is" (Turner, quoted in Biemiller, 1984).

Turner's work does not stand alone. Another intriguing work which comes to mind is Helen Horowitz's *Alma Mater* (1984), a study of connections between architecture, curriculum, and mission at women's colleges from 1830 to 1930. This study of ten leading women's colleges shows convincingly that in each era, when a new college was founded, a distinctive architectural arrangement was consciously intended to fulfill an academic and a social mission, built "not only to improve women's minds but also to shelter their femininity" (Horowitz, 1984). It is the historical *change* which stands out; Mount Holyoke, built in 1837, advanced the notion of a "seminary model." This would be altered elsewhere over the years; for example, Smith College would introduce in 1875 a campus comprised of small cottages. Innovation and advocacy would continue in the architectural and curricular founding of Wellesley and, in the 1920s and 1930s, Scripps College and Bennington. The residual point is that architecture was not accidental.

The University of Chicago's 1982 library exhibit on that university's architectural evolution between 1890 and 1930 was so popular among alumni and citizens that the research staff, led by Jean Block, were prompted to write and publish *The Uses of Gothic* (1983), a work which stands as a model of archival research and documentary analysis. How was it that medieval motifs, gargoyles, quadrangles, and spires were fused with I-beam girders and reinforced concrete on a grand scale to provide a home for the modern American university? Answering this question via a case study of the University of Chicago is the heart of this story. *The Uses of Gothic* meticulously reconstructs and narrates forty years of campus planning, organized around two heroic architectural events in the city's history: the 1892 Columbian Exposition and the 1932 "Century of Progress" World's Fair.

The author's premise is that the neighboring University of Chicago was aware of both great civic events, but with a markedly different attitude in 1932 than in 1892. Important to note is that the "Collegiate Gothic" was neither a static nor stagnant form. It was amazingly well suited to accommodating university growth over several decades while harmoniously housing a range of unprecedented functions and activities in the large buildings which the modern university would demand. The contribution of the new University of Chicago at the turn of the century was to develop a true sense of an urban campus—not merely a haphazard accumulation of uncoordinated structures (Thelin, 1985, pp. 22–26).

Will such scholarship spread to foster interest among leaders and decision makers in higher education? One promising sign is that in Spring 1985, *Change* magazine featured a lengthy cover article on the "Architecture of the Academy" (Williams, 1985). And *The Chronicle of Higher Education* now features a regular column on issues and trends in campus architecture. Such recent studies and signs are heartening, but they are exceptional islands in the sea of higher education research. The conclusion is that we all like to look at campus architecture; we just do not want to analyze it. Why might this be so?

RESEARCH CONSTRAINTS AND QUALMS

As social and behavioral scientists, we are wary of a topic which invites vague impressions and subjective views of aesthetics and taste. We are sensitive to the charge that discussion of the visual impact of Alma Mater makes one feel sentimental or nostalgic. This is fine for personal memories, but out of bounds for serious professional research.

Even if we did wish to pursue systematic inquiry into campus architecture, we face methodological constraints: How does one capture the highly graphic and visual character of architecture when the primary research tool is analysis of the attitudinal survey and the statistical database? Sociologist Martin Trow (1963) expressed this aversion and research dilemma over twenty years ago:

> The kind of research most needed in this area would, in large part, take the form of systematic observations of existing spaces and the uses made of them. Incidentally, I suspect that one of the reasons more research of this kind is not done is that anthropological observations do not appear to most administrators to be really

scientific. He can see the results of a sociological questionnaire or an instrument to measure aspects of personality; the hard figures are there as visible proof that somebody was working. But to ask a man to loaf around in student lounges or coffee shops for a few months seems to be frivolous and indefensible. Somehow, the very large contributions to our knowledge of social processes made by trained observers in medical schools and mental hospitals, not to speak of primitive tribes, are not thought to be relevant to the "real" problems of building a new residence hall or a student union or a science lab. Needless to say, I think this is a great error, both in practical terms and in its conception of the nature of science. (p. 108)

Serious architectural analysis also would require higher education researchers to gain familiarity with at least the essential technical concepts and vocabulary of that discipline (Halstead, 1974, pp. 467–518; Blumenson, 1981). And, cost-conscious publishers probably cannot afford to produce journals and books based on manuscripts which depend on large numbers of photographs of buildings and physical plant.

Finally, many of the existing articles about campus architecture are precious—indulgent accounts about one particular place which have limited interest beyond an immediate circle of old grads. In short, such articles suffer because they fail to connect architecture with the overriding questions and hypotheses which constitute significant and coherent research on higher education.

RESEARCH ANTIDOTES AND STRATEGIES

These limits and reservations are fair, but not insurmountable. The following commentary provides some counterstrategies and resolutions.

Reliance on Archival Records for Data

First, there are antidotes to casual and sloppy generalizations about campus appearance and imagery. In fact, the topic of campus architecture has abundant records and sources for documenting motives, plans, ideals, processes, and outcomes. It is one of the most fertile areas for connecting ideas and institutions because architects, donors, planners, and their college clients must correspond and negotiate with each other to determine what is to be built, for what purpose, and for what ideals. The styles, innovations, and restorations we see in a particular campus at a particular time may be complex, but they usually are associated with some intentional decisions and actions—and often can be reconstructed and explained. Apart from correspondence, there are such tangible records as blue prints, artists' renderings, photographs, discussions in minutes of board meetings, contracts, and specifications. And there are records of speeches at ground-breaking ceremonies and grand opening events.

One reason for the healthy prospects for ascertaining connections between building and planning styles and institutional mission is that often we know who was responsible for designing and ultimately building a famous campus. And what stands out is that the American campus in each era has tended to attract prominent architects and major architectural and construction firms. The names of McKim, Mead, and White; Gideon Shylock; John Galen Howard; Bernard Maybeck; Julia Morgan; Thomas Jefferson; Frederick Olmstead; Ralph Adams Cram; Henry Ives Cobb; William Burgess; William Peirera; and Richard Neutra—to cite a few—stand as a pantheon of American architects. They were thoughtful, influential, and prolific. Their campus projects were usually among the most grand and celebrated public architectural projects of their respective eras.

Beyond Buildings: Campus Landscape

Along with building design and construction, we also can systematically study another important dimension of campus appearance: landscaping. Note how we often assume that the foliage and lawns of a beautiful campus are both natural and inevitable. They are not; they are the product of conscious design and even sharp debate. To illustrate this, we resurrect the biography and work of one Beatrix Farrand—hardly a familiar name in the cosmos of higher education, but influential nonetheless. Between 1910 and 1940, she was principal consultant and designer for campus landscaping at Princeton, Yale, Oberlin, Chicago, Occidental, and Cal Tech. During her decades of professional influence, one finds her university and college clients heeding her advice to establish permanent, elaborate greenhouses, horticulture services, and grounds maintenance departments.

Beatrix Farrand made explicit decisions about which plants to use—and which to avoid—in sculpting the college grounds into the "campus beautiful." Most American campuses today have few evergreens—an omission which bears the influence of Beatrix Farrand's resolute plans from the 1920s and 1930s. The results of her decisions on campus details are taken for granted today. For example, she devoted months to convincing university officials at Chicago to have benches throughout the campus; this was not all—she spent weeks designing appropriate campus benches. And even though she personally created the landscaped atmosphere of several Ivy League colleges, her diaries, letters, and journals indicate that she had reservations about ivy—a plant best used to obscure existing, ugly buildings. Often, at Yale and Princeton, what we think is ivy on walls is, in fact, another plant—Virginia creeper, grape vines, or climbing hydrangea—carefully selected by Beatrix Farrand (Balmori, 1985).

Tracking and Tracing Architectural Styles: The Ethnography of Design

The important residual from such cases of construction and landscaping is that researchers can track and trace architectural and aesthetic styles. And one can follow diffusion of style as one campus emulates another. Reliance on a variety of records can rescue campus architectural commentary from the uninformed conjecture which makes empirical researchers groan. Above all, this research vein reminds us tht there was no imperative to cause campus design to evolve as it did; it was the result of deliberate ideas and actions.

This is not to say that campus plans always come true. Rather, one major finding in looking at the American campus until the late nineteenth century is that: the greatest architects were commissioned—and they usually delivered fascinating plans. One study which made imaginative use of campus lithographs and sketches does, in fact, show that the American college consciously evolved from an Oxbridge quadrangle to an open-sided "E" shape and, eventually, to a row arrangement of primary structures (Tolles, 1973). But for the most part, grand campus plans were seldom realized in total, usually because of lack of funds. The result was that by the 1870s, most American colleges were a small hodgepodge of false starts, incompleted dreams, and expedient structures. Surprisingly, although the old-time small college is depicted as cohesive, undergraduates usually fended for themselves to find lodgings and meals in the local community, since many of these colleges could not afford to build dormitories or dining halls to accommodate all their students.

Distinction between proposals and actual practices provides a careful reminder which separates higher education researchers from counterparts who write for architectural journals. Architects and architectural historians tend to deal with the proposals and award-winning competitions, whereas research in higher education ought pay attention to what was actually built and what actually occurs in the campus environment. The task is to decode the process whose end products are the landmarks and buildings—not only in their origins and construction but, equally important, in their subsequent use.

This task calls in part for sociological analysis. One needs, for example, to consider the changing functions and dysfunctions of buildings in the life of an institution. A few dramatic examples illustrate this general caveat.

Recycled Forms and Changing Functions

For years, the University of Chicago's handsome football stadium was a popular structure, the home of winning teams and large crowds. After the University of Chicago dropped football in 1939, the stadium fell into disrepair and was overgrown with weeds and plants. Appearance was deceiving, for the structure enjoyed a life after death: in the 1940s the space underneath the stands became the secret site of a high-caliber physics laboratory where a team of researchers worked on the atom bomb—an unlikely and inconspicuous landmark in the history of large-scale university research and development (Jensen, 1974).

Campus architecture illustrates not only educational ideals, but also curious compromises and combinations. A good example is the 1929 "Tower of

Learning'' of the University of Pittsburgh. Its ''girder Gothic'' style was an American Dream which fused the inspiration of medieval universities with I-beam construction and the insatiable need for offices and classroom space in an urban setting (Biemiller, 1985a, p. 3; Thelin, 1982, p. 25).

Construction problems can lead to interesting educational explanations by faculty and administrators. As noted in the earlier discussion of architecture and curriculum, the proposed University of California at Santa Cruz received a great deal of publicity as the campus whose unique ''cluster college'' design and ''scholarly villages'' would ''make the university seem smaller as it grew larger.'' Unfortunately, construction was far behind schedule for the arrival of the first group of entering freshmen. The solution in 1965 was that brochures told prospective students that enrollment at the new campus was an opportunity to be an ''educational pioneer . . . in a journey of educational discovery'' while living in ''twentieth century covered wagons.'' This was a euphemism for bracing freshmen for the news that their temporary quarters would be mobile trailers.

Restoration Versus Revivalism in Campus Architecture

Today we readily accept the proposition that restoration of historic buildings on campus is a ''good thing,'' and that such restorations are a source of prestige. This is a fairly new trend (e.g., *Chronicle of Higher Education,* April 12, 1971, p. 6). As late as the 1930s, the oldest standing buildings from the colonial era at such historic institutions as William and Mary, Princeton, and Brown were in bad repair, often cluttered with layers of haphazard additions and jerry-built porches. Neglect followed by demolition of old buildings was an accepted part of organizational life. Only in the last fifty years have colleges undertaken careful and expensive renovation of historic structures to recapture an approximation of their original style and grandeur. Usually *revivalism*—the construction of new buildings with historical motifs—had surpassed preservation as the standard academic practice (Patton, 1967).

Social Functions and Dysfunctions of Architecture

Plans do not always go as expected. The monumental plans for residential quadrangles of the 1930s and 1940s were widely praised by architects, donors, and university presidents. These groups failed to take into account student response. Often overlooked today is that at the time of construction, student groups (supported by alumni) complained loudly and bitterly that the Harvard ''house plan,'' the ''residential colleges'' at Yale, and the quadrangles at Princeton and Brown were intrusions into the traditional student life; the grandiose residential plans were denounced in student editorials as ''model villages'' and ''expensive dog kennels.'' Fondness for historic motifs of Gothic and Georgian revival led students to call the quadrangles "mausoleum architecture." Only later would the residential units be accepted and absorbed into the student culture.

BEYOND ARCHITECTURAL ANECDOTES: ADVANCING SIGNIFICANT HYPOTHESES

One might argue that these episodes are intriguing but limited and anecdotal. What is needed to bring campus architecture to maturity as a part of the study of higher education is to connect with significant themes and hypotheses. How might this be done? Drawing from the various preceding anecdotes, one might advance the hypothesis "The organizational revolution which characterized the American university between 1880 and 1910 was followed closely by an architectural transformation."

The aim is to test the proposition that organizational structure and purpose were consciously associated with architectural forms. Our primary evidence is the preponderance of highly publicized architectural competitions between 1890 and 1940 which ushered in a definite era of the "campus beautiful and the greater university." In contrast to the eighteenth- and nineteenth-century colleges, this time around commissions for plans by great architects were usually followed by contracts and construction, largely because of the coincidence of large-scale philanthropy combined with the changing role of the president as literally a "campus builder" and tireless fund-raiser. It also was a phenomenon well covered in the national press and followed enthusaistically by the American public.

The institutional appetite for elaborate architecture and landscaping was necessary, in part, to house new and numerous unprecedented services and functions; laboratories, museums, gymnasia, and libraries each represented a scale of activity virtually unknown prior to 1890. The convergence of so many ascending activities called for architectural and planning solutions beyond growth by accretion. The exciting twist to the organizational behavior of the American college and university is that the campus construction boom cannot be wholly explained as a manifestation of the "form follows function" principle. The campus looked older as it became newer and larger. As journalist Edwin Slosson observed about the young University of Chicago in 1910:

> The University of Chicago does not look its age. It looks much older. This is because it has been put through an artificial aging process, reminding one of the way furniture is given an "antique oak finish" while you wait by simply rubbing a little grime into the grain of it. (p. 429)

Connecting expanded and new functions to an inspired past became a discernible strand in the academy's image and identity in its architectural style and in its public ceremonies and rituals. Bigness and complexity, combined with institutional strategy and public pride, provided the proper chemistry to attract and pay for monumental campus planning and construction by prominent architects. Internationally famous architects spent great time and effort entering competitions for the honor of designing a university! Laurence Veysey describes the academic strategy as follows:

> These leaders, in conjunction with trustees, undergraduates, and alumni, spoke for goals with which a large American audience could readily sympathize: moral soundness, fidelity to the local group, and the implicit promise of enhanced social position. The external face of an American campus reflected these familiar values in its ornate buildings, its efficient and burgeoning business staff, its athletic stadiums, its renewed facilities for student supervision (often again including dormitories), and its annual commencement pageantry. When most Americans visited a college or university, these were the things they saw; these for the most part were the items included in casual academic boasts. (1965, p. 443)

This was the atmosphere which fostered an era of heroic campus building across the nation. As one architectural historian noted about the competition just prior to the emergence of "American collegiate Gothic" and the comprehensive campus plans of the 1890s,

> In the field of architecture, the nineteenth century was one of much confusion and uncertainty. A whole series of stylistic fashions swept across the country in rapid and apparently accelerating order. During the first fifty years there was a revival of the Classic and the Gothic, and between 1850 and 1890 Second Empire, Victorian Gothic, Queen Anne, Richardsonian Romanesque, and Beaux Arts were in vogue. The practicing proponents of each style quite naturally wished to demonstrate its virtues in the most striking fashion. Each wanted to make his building stand out among its fellows, and the best means of doing so was by strength of statement and contrast. The effect of this competition on centers of learning was to make the campuses battle-grounds for architectural prima donnas. (Patton, 1967, p. 4)

The result was that by the turn of the century, "The leaders of reform in higher education were well aware that all the aspects of the desired transformation were interrelated. They realized that campus planning and architectural developments would have to accompany or precede revisions in the administration, curriculum, educational methods, and general life of the college. One kind of planning would make other kinds possible" (Patton, 1967, p. 4)

Important to note is that this phenomenon had a start and a finish. It is not necessarily a universal or perennial truth for colleges and universities—but might explain a phase in their organizational evolution. To flesh out and complicate the variations in campus building, it is useful to contrast the "campus beautiful" procedures, circa 1890 to 1930, with an archetype of campus building in our own era.

THE ANATOMY OF ARCHITECTURE:
CONSTRUCTING THE CONTEMPORARY CAMPUS

German poet Bertold Brecht raised a fundamental puzzle in the study of architecture. Writing from the perspective of a workman reading history, he asked:

> Who built the seven towers of Thebes?
> The books are filled with the names of kings.
> Was it kings who hauled the craggy blocks of stone? . . .
> In the evenings when the Chinese wall was finished
> Where did the masons go? . . .

Equally puzzling today is "Who builds the American college campus?" Specifically, what is the process from conceptualization to construction? Case studies give good insight into the combination of philanthropy, civic involvement, and academic planning in such significant universities as the University of Chicago (Block, 1983), the University of California at Berkeley (Brechin, 1978), and other famous campuses (Turner, 1984). Yet the participants and process have become less clear in recent decades, especially in light of the proliferation of new or expanded institutions. One important and underexamined topic is the contemporary process for building colleges and universities in the public sector.

In contrast to the attention to details and embellishments circa 1890 to 1930, careful review of campus construction in the 1950s and 1960s marks a new approach with a whole new set of ground rules: low-bid state construction and an elaborate official procedure in which the campus is interdependent with numerous state agencies. It is characterized by centralization, rationalization, and standardization of the building and planning liturgy in the public sector. And given that regulatory and authorizing agencies within a state may have been responsible for processing numerous project requests from public colleges and universities, state decisions often were made on the basis of quantitative data, ratios, and formulas.

Again, there is the paradox of austerity amid abundance. Certainly the amount of dollars and numbers of projects for public higher education construction were unprecedented. Yet, after World War II, this generous public funding also included a streak of severity. A public campus was no longer assumed to be inherently "special." Each building proposal faced hurdles of justification. Whereas the Berkeley campus from 1900 to 1940 might have been the unchallenged "jewel" in the state crown, by the 1950s the historic, monumental campus had forfeited much of its autonomy and embellishment. For example, in California during the 1960s, memoranda and guidelines from the state's department of finance scolded the university administrators for having submitted architectural plans which included provisions for sculpture on buildings and for lounges for students—both explicitly defined as "unnecessary" by state officials (Brechin, 1978). An era had ended—or, at least, subsided—and in the post–World War II period, the heroic tradition of the "campus beautiful" would coexist precariously with new criteria and standards for institutional design and construction.

One excellent overview on the 1960s and early 1970s is provided by Halstead (1974, pp. 467–518). He introduces contemporary campus building and planning with the following perspective:

> Amid the growth and ferment, one might expect that at least the physical structure of campuses—the buildings and the land—would remain fixed in form and function. But changes are occurring here, too. Buildings are being erected in new places and in new arrangements and for different and variable functions. Examples are the communications-lecture-hall-center and the modular library. What is newer than the flight-deck principle of laboratory research space? How old is the cluster concept of grouping colleges? It is probably not too great a generalization to say that much of the growth and innovation taking place in higher education is being accurately embodied and permanently recorded in the new kinds of buildings and campuses that are being created. (p. 467)

Halstead's survey, however, stimulates rather than closes questions about the complexities of the process. We present here the anatomy of campus planning and building, pieced together from Halstead's work, from a case study of one state (Virginia), and from interviews with a prominent architectural firm committed to building schools and colleges.

This is, in effect, a first step toward writing an ethnography of college planning and building. Its summary suggests the myriad details, interactions, and state agencies with which a college or university president and board must work in the 1980s. Certainly this is a markedly different climate and process than characterized the heroic days of the "university builders," circa 1880 to 1910. Ironically, it is largely an invisible process, unknown and ignored by most in higher education—that is, until one wishes to have a new building. Architecture, then, becomes an interesting litmus for understanding the current character of state government and campus relations *writ large*.

State colleges and universities are state agencies and, therefore, are required to comply with bureaucratic rules and regulations that apply to other (and all) state agencies. In the case of a capital project or building construction in Virginia, state universities and colleges connect with the state's Department of General Services, which contains the Division of Engineering and Buildings as well as of Architecture and Engineering; and with the State Council of Higher Education, the Secretary of Education, the Department of Planning and Budget, the governor's office, the House Appropriations Committee, and the Senate Finance Committee, among others. The process from start to the award of a construction contract typically takes six to eight months.

The first step in any capital project procedure is to have the *master site plan* approved by the governor. The governor's office will approve the project on the advice of the Secretary of Education, the State Council for Higher Education, the Division of Engineering and Buildings, and the Art and Architecture Review Board.

The second step is considered *preplanning justification,* which is done on campus by in-house personnel. To grasp the detail and complexity of this phase, one has only to glean the criteria which must be addressed in the preplanning study. The study must include a statement of need, the background and description of the proposed project, data on the number and characteristics of the clients, an analysis of the existing facilities, a review of space guidelines, a description of deficiencies, and the alternatives, as well as documentation on the size and scope of the building, its owning and operating costs, and a cost-benefit analysis. Specific criteria include the following:

Location proximity	Value/cost of property
Available services	Privacy and aesthetic setting
Flood plan	Topography
Water	Vegetation
Community accredibility	Mineral rights
Local zoning	Evaluation of at least three sites
Environmental impact	Expansion capability
Uniform building code	State handicapped standards
Source of funding	Maintenance and operation costs
Energy conservation standards	Future construction
Heating and cooling	Life expectancy of buildings
Internal features	Acquisition costs
Type of construction	Access
Aesthetic requirements	Architectural style
Loading	Parking

The justification is submitted to the Department of General Services, the Department of Planning and Budgeting, the State Council for Higher Education, the House Appropriations Committee, and the Senate Finance Committee. The Department of General Services sends the recommendation of approval to the Secretary of Education.

If the Secretary of Education approves the justifications, the *planning study* then constitutes the third step. This phase requires the utilization of outside professional assistance. Therefore, the college prepares the study with its own funds from the General Assembly. The House Appropriations Committee and the Senate Finance Committee are notified of the status of planning throughout the ensuing process.

After the planning studies have been approved by the governor and the General Assembly, a *Request for Authority to Initiate Capital Outlay Project* is submitted to the director of the Division of Engineering and Buildings. The Department of Planning and Budget receives an informative copy. In addition, a *status of approval* by the Council on the Environment is forwarded to the Division of Engineerings and Buildings. After approval by Engineering and Buildings and the governor, the college or university may employ and enter into a contract with an architect and/or an engineer.

State law stipulates that a *building advisory committee* on the campus have the responsibility for employing the architect or engineer. The committee has two permanent members: the campus planner and the director of maintenance and operation. Also, a representative of the primary area (e.g., the department in the school) and any others appointed by the board of visitors or the president. The state office of the attorney general provides legal advice; and the Division of Engineering and Buildings provides technical advice. In short, the building advisory committee acts on behalf of the college in dealing with the architect or engineer and notifies the college president.

Schematic (project criteria), preliminary, and working drawings are prepared by the architects or engineers. A number of other agencies and boards are notified and render advice and approval when appropriate (e.g., the Art and Architecture Review Board and the state fire marshall).

Plans for state buildings (including colleges and universities) must be approved by the Division of Engineering and Buildings before submission to the governor's office for final approval. Furthermore, in a few states, there is a less known but important participant: the state's art and architectural board reviews and prepares recommendations for the governor's office on building projects, landscaping, art, frames, and sculpture that are under consideration for state ownership. This independent board, appointed by the governor, typically consists of five members: an architect, an art historian, an artist, a representative of the state's museum of fine arts, and a member-at-large. The board meets once per month and is primarily concerned with aesthetics, that is, the exterior of buildings, their context with other campus buildings, color, texture, and appropriateness. Since the board members are all well-trained professionals and experts in art and architecture, there usually is consensus among the board.

Architects commissioned by colleges and universities usually work well with the state's art and architectural review board. For architects, delays and disagreements and major constraints usually come in discussions with and review by other state agencies, for example, the department of budget, where criteria and decisions are made less by peers of architects talking with architects (or architects talking with clients and users) than, by an analysis of the proposed costs and finances. For example, an established architectural firm may indicate that excellence in design and construction for a college or university building will cost about $110.00 per square foot; a state budgeting agency (and/or the host college) may authorize only $75.00 per square foot. Hence, the perennial dilemma is "What price aesthetics or design?"

The conventional wisdom is that building costs have escalated—thus providing one explanation for the proliferation of drab campus buildings in recent years as compared to the distinctive and ornate college buildings of the 1920s and 1930s. In fact, this is not wholly accurate; building costs per se have not risen beyond the general inflation rate. The extraordinary costs have cropped up in dimensions associated with the support system of the building, for example, electrical wiring systems, air conditioning, acoustics, security systems, and heating.

Another potential source of constraint for architects who accept contracts with public colleges and universities is the state's interpretation of codes. Certainly the addition of new codes in such areas as handicapped access make a campus more suitable to more clients. Problems arise in making official decisions based on the codes. Codes are usually written by architects as guidelines, with allowance for interpretation by architects. However, often, within the state building and design procedures, code interpretation by architects gives way to specific and inflexible rulings by a member of the state bureaucracy who is not an architect.

Finally, architects who build for the public sector today face an added complexity and burden: liability insurance costs. Architects contend that they are close behind obstetricians in the high charges they must pay for professional liability insurance.

Often, then, one net result of the hurdles and labyrinth of agencies, cost constraints, fear of liability, and so on is that public campus buildings tend to be bland. Avoidance of conflict and compromise with numerous groups accumulate to discourage distinctive approaches to architectural and educational situations. The lamentable feature of this era of campus planning and building is the tendency toward reductionism, that is, reducing campus design to formula. Perhaps the solution to or escape route out of this quagmire of blandness rests in Halstead's 1974 overview of campus planning, namely, the reminder that comprehensive planning does include careful attention to aesthetic and normative dimensions of higher education as well as to compliance with technical requirements. By this logic, a balanced approach to campus building and design embraces both responsible stewardship and accountability for spending public monies and recognizes that the inspirational and enduring aspects of a college and university have a proper and conspicuous place. As Halstead (1974) notes as a premise for building and planning, "Every campus needs a symbol":

> Northwestern has Lake Michigan; Cornell has rolling hills overlooking Lake Cayuga. Wisconsin University, too, has a lake. M.I.T. has the Charles River. Colorado University has magnificent mountains as a backdrop. A college in western Colorado has its own natural pedestal: a dramatic mesa. These God-given symbols do a better job than any man-made symbols can ever do. But man-made symbols are also necessary. Texas University has a library tower. Washington University in St. Louis has a sallyport, and Duke has a magnificent chapel.

> But these are more than symbols. They serve as unifying elements and give a certain visual order to the hodge podge of buildings. Lakes, rivers, and mountains give personality to campuses. Unquestionably, the campus planner should capitalize on the uniqueness of the natural environment. (p. 483)

A careful and important aside is that this broad concept of campus planning is not simply (nor simplistically) a mandate to return to the heroic days of unregulated organizational founding and expansion. Fair state guidelines and procedures can provide a necessary hedge against financial and architectural abuses in the public sector. The more subtle message from Halstead et al. is that the rationalized planning and construction procedure can also be reasonable. Failure to acknowledge the importance of symbols, landmarks, student lounges, and bas-relief sculpture for a college campus is a false sense of economy which belittles architects and educators alike. The intriguing challenge in building and maintaining colleges and universities is to save the present and future campus from the blandness and unevocative doldrums which has been called the "folly of modern architecture" (Blake, 1974).

CONCLUSION

Exploration of the preceding hypothesis about and trends in the evolution of the American campus is hardly the final word in explaining organizational development in higher education. But it does illustrate that the architecture and campus design we inherit can often be understood and explained as the result of conscious decisions and policy changes—developments which are undergirded by discernible criteria, values, and circumstances. This is the necessary counter against careless impressions and subjective observations about the visual dimension of higher education.

Most of the cases and periods discussed in this chapter deal with established, well-known institutions. Some neglected areas which warrant fresh research might include analysis of the origins and use of student union buildings or the plans and realities of commuter-campus and community-college design. Do these newer institutions have a planning tradition? If so, did the architectural plans work as intended?

In closing, consider a staple of academic oratory: At commencement ceremonies, presidents often give the perpetual reminder that a college is "more than bricks and mortar." Perhaps the college presidents protest too much! The social fact that parents, students, and alumni must be continually reminded about this attests to the importance of architecture. But perhaps those of us who study the impact of the college and university on various constituencies ought not to take the president's reminder literally. On the contrary, we might heed the reminder that higher education *does* include "bricks and mortar" as the interesting setting in which the organizational drama of higher education is played out in a changing, complex, and unfinished script.

Acknowledgments. Research for this project was made possible in part by a faculty grant from The College of William and Mary. The authors owe special thanks to Professor Robert L. Vickery, AIA of the University of Virginia and VMDO Architects for his commentary on college and school design. We also wish to thank the following individuals for their research and editorial assistance: A. S. T. Blackburn, especially in the area of campus landscape design; and Marsha V. Krotseng, doctoral student in the higher education program at The College of William and Mary.

REFERENCES

Andrews, W. (1964). *Architecture, Ambition and Americans: A Social History of American Architecture.* New York: Free Press.

Architecture and college presidents (1964). *AIA Journal* 41:73–76.

Astin, A. W. (1968). *The College Environment.* Washington, DC: American Council on Education.

Astin, A. W. (1978). *Four Critical Years.* San Francisco: Jossey-Bass.

Balmori, D. (1985). Campus work and public landscapes. In D. Balmori, D. K. McGuire, and E. M. McPeck (eds.), *Beatrix Farrand's American Landscapes: Her Gardens and Campuses.* Sagaponack, NY: Sagapress.

Baskiw, S. (1965). The campus climate: A reminder. In *Higher Education: Some New Developments.* New York: McGraw-Hill.

Bennis, W. G. (1973). *The Leaning Ivory Tower.* San Francisco: Jossey-Bass.

Bennis, W. G. (1977). Who sank the yellow submarine? Eleven ways to avoid major mistakes in taking over a university campus and making great changes. In G. L. Riley and J. V. Baldridge (eds.), *Governing Academic Organization.* Berkeley, Ca: McCutchan.

Biemiller, L. (1986). Beneath a Carnegie Hall's soot and ivy, lines from an era of lesser sensitivities. *Chronicle of Higher Education* (March 5): 3.

Biemiller, L. (1985a). Pittsburgh's collegiate skyscraper mixes Gothic tracery and deco forms. *Chronicle of Higher Education* (May 29): 3.

Biemiller, L. (1985b). A vain attempt at second-guessing Jefferson. *Chronicle of Higher Education* (October 23): 3.

Biemiller, L. (1984). Planning the college campus: The evolution of a "Distinctively American Form." *Chronicle of Higher Education* (May 30): 5–7.

Blake, P. (1974). The folly of modern architecture. *Atlantic Monthly* 234:59–66.

Block, J. F. (1983). *The Uses of Gothic: Planning and Building the Campus of the University of Chicago, 1892–1932.* Chicago: University of Chicago Library.

Blodgett, G. (1985). *Oberlin Architecture: College and Town.* Oberlin, OH: Oberlin College.

Blumenson, J. J. G. (1981). *Identifying American Architecture: A Pictorial Guide to Styles and Terms, 1600–1945.* Nashville, TE: American Association for State and Local History.

Brechin, G. (1978). Classical dreams, concrete realities. *California Monthly* (March 1978):12–15.

Building Harvard: Architecture of Three Centuries. (1971). Cambridge: Harvard University Information Center.

Campus Americana (1985). *Newsweek on Campus* (April):22–27.

The campus: Architecture's show place (1970). *Time* (September 21):76–82.

Campus architecture: The architect's view, the president's view. (1964). *AIA Journal* 41:68–72.

Canby, H. S. (1936). *Alma Mater: The Gothic Age of the American College.* New York: Farrar & Rinehart.

Cardwell, K. H. (1983). *Bernard Maybeck: Artisan, Architect, Artist.* Salt Lake City, UT: Peregrine Smith Books.

Community College Planning Center. (1965). *Planners and Planning* Stanford, CA: Stanford University Community College Planning Center.

Corson, J. J. (1960). *Governance of Colleges and Universities.* New York: McGraw-Hill.

David, D. (1985). Campus Americana. *Newsweek on Campus* (April):22–27.

Dober, R. P. (1963). *Campus Planning.* New York: Reinhold.

Elton, C. W., and Bate, W. (1966). The effect of housing policy on grade point average. *Journal of College Student Personnel* 7:73–77.

Goldman, M. (1969). Architecture and social control: The story behind the design of the new campus at the State University of New York at Buffalo. Unpublished paper.

Gores, H. B. (1963). Bricks and mortarboards. In G. K. Smith (Ed.) *Current Issues in Higher Education, 1963.* Washington, DC: Association for Higher Education.

Grant, G., and Riesman, D. (1978). *The Perpetual Dream: Reform and Experiment in the American College.* Chicago: University of Chicago Press.

Groves, J. R., Jr. (1985). An examination of architecture and planning at the University of Kentucky and its precursors: An annotated bibliography. Unpublished paper, University of Kentucky.

Halstead, D. K. (1974). Campus building planning. In *Statewide Planning in Higher Education.* Washington, DC: U.S. Office of Education.

Hamlin, A. D. F. (1903). Recent American college architecture. *The Outlook*, August, 357–366.

Hill, R. N. (ed.). (1964). *The College on the Hill: A Dartmouth Chronicle.* Hanover, NH: Dartmouth College.

Horowitz, H. L. (1984). *Alma Mater: Design and Experience in the Women's Colleges from Their Nineteenth Century Beginnings to the 1930s.* New York: Knopf.

Jaffe, R. (1981). College towns, U.S.A.: The dream revisited. *Travel and Leisure* 11:34–50.

Jencks, C., and Riesman, D. (1967). Patterns of residential education. In Sanford, N., *The American College.* New York: Wiley.

Jensen, O. (1974). *A Campus Album.* New York: American Heritage Books and McGraw-Hill.

Kauffman, J. (1980). *At the Pleasure of the Board.* Washington, DC: American Council on Education.

Klose, K., and Kalmanson, L. (1985). A canopy that's not to be. *The Washington Post* (September 12). C1, C9.

Lazarsfeld, P. (1961). Introduction. In A. H. Barton, *Organizational Measurement and Its Bearing on the Study of College Environments.* New York: College Entrance Examination Board.

Maddex, D. (Ed.). (1985). *All About Old Buildings: The Whole Preservation Catalog.* Washington, DC: Preservation Press.

Mayhew, L. B. (1969). *Colleges Today and Tomorrow.* San Francisco: Jossey-Bass.

Mayhew, L. B. (1966). The learning environment. In L. Dennis and J. Kauffman (eds.), *The College and the Student.* Washington, DC: American Council on Education.

Morris, G. P. (1903). The Harvard Stadium. *Overland Monthly,* May, 344–355.

Morris, P. (1983). Walk through history on campus. *Southern Living* 18:82–87.

Neutra, R. B. (1957). In G. K. Smith (ed.), *Current Issues in Higher Education, 1957.* Washington, DC: Association for Higher Education.

Nevins, A. (1962). *The State Universities and Democracy.* Urbana: University of Illinois Press.

New Canopy for Illinois Institute of Technology Library Removed After Charges It Violated Campus Heritage. (1985). *Chronicle of Higher Education,* (September 18): p. 2.

Pace, C. R., and Stern, G. (1958). An approach to the measurement of psychological characteristics of college environments. *Journal of Educational Psychology* 49:269–277.

Pascarella, E. T. (1985). College environmental influences on learning and cognitive development. In J. C. Smart (ed.), *Higher Education: Handbook of Theory and Research,* Vol. I, pp 1–62. New York: Agathon Press, 1985.

Patton, G. (1967). American collegiate Gothic: A phase of university architectural development. *Journal of Higher Education* 38:1–8.

Physical and Psychological Environments Polluted by Colleges, Health Group Is Told. (1971). *Chronicle of Higher Education* (May 17):5.

Planning for a Community of Scholars. (1982). *University of Chicago Magazine* 74:3–13.

Remodeling. (1971). *College and University Business* 50:43–48.

Renovating old buildings often called wiser for colleges than erecting new ones. (1971). *Chronicle of Higher Education,* April 12, p. 6.

Riesman, D. (1980). *On Higher Education.* San Francisco: Jossey-Bass.

Riesman, D., and Jencks, C. (1967). The viability of the American college. In Sanford, *The American College.*

Russell, S. (1983). When campus and community collide. *Historic Preservation* 35:36–42.

Sanford, N. (Ed.). (1967). *The American College.* New York: Wiley.

Schlereth, T. J. (1985). Schools of architecture. *Preservation News,* p. 15.

Slosson, E. E. (1910). *Great American Universities.* New York: Macmillan, 1910.

Stern, R. A. M. (1986). Academic villages: places apart. *Pride of Place.* New York: Houghton-Mifflin.

Sturner, W. F. (1973). The college environment. In D. W. Vermilye (ed.), *The Future in the Making.* San Francisco: Jossey-Bass.

Sturner, W. F. (1972). Environmental code: Creating a sense of place on the college campus. *Journal of Higher Education* 43:97–109.

Thelin, J. R. (1977). California and the colleges. *California Historical Quarterly* 56:140–163.

Thelin, J. R. (1982). *Higher Education and Its Useful Past.* Cambridge, MA: Schenkman.

Thelin, J. R. (1985). Essay review on the uses of Gothic. *Educational Studies* 16(Spring): 22–26.

Tolles, B. F., Jr. (1973). College architecture in New England before 1860 in printed and sketched views. *Antiques* 103: 502–509.

Trow, M. A. (1963). Administrative implications of analyses of campus cultures. In T. Lunsford (ed.), *The Study of Campus Cultures.* Boulder, CO: WICHE.

Turner, P. V. (1984). *Campus: An American Planning Tradition.* Cambridge, MA: MIT Press.

Varley, P. (1985). Bricks and mortar get a Herculean face-lift. *Harvard Magazine,* Jan–Feb., 70–75.

Veysey, L. R. (1965). *The Emergence of the American University.* Chicago: University of Chicago Press.

Vickery, R. L., Jr. (1983). *Sharing Architecture.* Charlottesville: University Press of Virginia.

Vladeck, B. C. (1978). Buildings and budgets: The overinvestment crisis. *Change* 10:36–40.

Williams, S. (1985). The architecture of the academy. *Change* 17 (March–April): 14–30, 50–55.

Wolfe, T. (1981). *From Bauhaus to Our House.* New York: Farrar, Strauss, & Giroux.

Enrollment Demand Models
and their Policy
Uses in Institutional Decision Making

William C. Weiler
University of Minnesota

The estimation of the demand for attendance in higher education institutions has a long history; the first widely cited study was that of Richard Ostheimer in 1953. Many of the early studies were not addressed specifically to institutional policy issues, but were concerned with the sign and magnitude of the effects of family income and attendance costs on student demand behavior. While it is, of course, true that the effects of attendance costs on enrollment demand behavior are of concern to institutions, the estimates were not interpreted in that context in these studies. Reviews (see, for example, Jackson and Weathersby, 1975; Weinschrott, 1977; Hyde, 1978) also tended to focus on statistical or specification issues and to compare studies on the basis of their reported income and price elasticities. The potential importance of these types of studies to informing policymakers in individual institutions was typically not a subject that was addressed.

The focus of enrollment demand studies and the interpretation of their results in a policy context began to change with the growth of federal financial aid programs in the early 1970s. However, most of these studies were concerned with the effects of financial aid on attendance behavior nationally; of special interest was the effect on potential students from low-income households (again, see Hyde, 1978). The results of these studies generally showed that students from poorer families were not very responsive to attendance cost changes and that federal financial aid formulas as constituted were ineffective in providing access to large numbers of these students. The policy prescriptions were either to reallocate the available funds from other students to the economically disadvantaged or to increase financial aid to the latter students through additional federal expenditures.

This shift in focus in the use of enrollment demand studies, while of interest to institutional policymakers, still did not inform them about the impact of these issues on their own institutions. In fact, from the perspective of an individual institution, increasing federal financial aid or changing the rules for its distribution changes the relative price of attending all schools and might have a negative impact on that institution even as it might increase access generally. This result would be of most interest to the institutional policymakers and is the type of issue that they would like to see addressed with enrollment demand studies that concentrate on their own individual institutions. The purpose of this chapter is to describe how enrollment demand studies can be specified and the estimated results used to inform decision makers on these types of issues.

What must be discussed first is how to specify enrollment demand models for analyzing student demand for a single institution. Relevant points emphasized here include an analysis of the variables that should be included in these models, the interpretation of the effects of these variables, the types of data that can be used, and the different categories of students for which separate models should be specified.

The next question is to determine the institutional policy issues that can be addressed with estimated enrollment-demand equations. Policy issues discussed in this chapter include tuition policy, "environmental scanning," budget forecasting, faculty staffing, institutional closure or consolidation, and optimizing objectives related to the size and composition of enrollment.

SPECIFYING ENROLLMENT DEMAND MODELS

The basic model that underlies all economic studies of student decision-making is the human capital model (e.g., Becker, 1962; Schultz, 1963), which implies that potential students view education as investment in the same terms as an investment in stocks, bonds, or physical capital. Educational investments are undertaken to increase future monetary incomes and to increase the utility of future consumption activities. As with most investment decisions, the investor, in this case the potential student and possibly his or her family, is theoretically expected to compare the benefit of each alternative investment option with its cost and select the option that maximizes the present value of benefits less costs.

In the context of higher education, the investor first computes the benefits of each attendance option, primarily the difference between postschooling income and the income expected if the nonattendance option were selected, although to the extent that they could be measured, this calculation could also include the increased utility values gained as a result of more effective and efficient use of time for future consumption activities. The potential investor also computes the costs of each option, primarily the cash outlays for attendance, although the income "lost" through giving up the opportunity to work rather than be enrolled in school is often cited as an important cost of attendance. The criterion that determines the most attractive of the available options is then the one for any investment: choose the option that maximizes the difference between benefits and costs where both components are appropriately discounted to reflect the fact that the benefits are generally received over a long period of time, while the costs are incurred only in the period while enrolled. A common way of comparing the benefits and costs of such investments is the rate of return. For each option, this is the implicit interest rate that equates the discounted values of benefits and costs. For an extensive review of the literature on rate-of-return studies in higher education, see Leslie and Brinkman (1986).

Given this model of behavior, an individual student's attendance choice proceeds as follows. The student first selects a set of institutions for which he or she is eligible and to which he or she wishes to apply. (The option of nonattendance is always in this choice set.) Since the particular choice made, given the circumstances of the individual, is the one that maximizes the difference between benefits and costs, the variables that influence the choice are obviously those that influence either the costs or the benefits of each option. The variables that influence the costs of each option include out-of-pocket expenses (e.g., tuition, fees, room and board, and books) less any financial aid. The expected benefit is primarily the difference between income with and without attendance. These benefits are therefore influenced by labor market conditions that can affect the two income streams. In addition, other variables related to the student's particular socioeconomic circumstances can affect either the ability to pay the costs or the probability that the benefits will be realized, or both. Obvious variables of this type include family income and student ability as measured by high school rank or standardized test score, but psychological factors related to goals or motivation may also be important influences on attendance choice.

The direction of the effects of changes in some of these variables on attendance choices is straightforwardly predicted from their effects on discounted costs or benefits. For example, an increase in any of the components of attendance costs for a given option will reduce the difference between the benefits and costs for that option. Hence, the increase will reduce the likelihood that the student will select that option. An increase in the financial aid available if a given institution is chosen will reduce the costs of that option, increase the difference between benefits and costs of that option, and therefore increase the probability that a student will select that institution.

The situation is somewhat different with an increase in financial aid directly awarded to the student irrespective of the specific institution the student attends. This aid will reduce the costs of attending any option. It therefore increases the probability of attendance versus nonattendance, but its effect on attendance at any particular institution is uncertain. We shall return to this point below. A student with higher ability and/or family income should also be more likely to select some attendance option versus the option of not attending, although the direction of the change in the probability that this student will attend a particular institution is again unclear.

The effects of labor market variables on attendance choice are more difficult to interpret because they have ambiguous effects both on choice of attendance versus nonattendance and, given attendance, on the choice of institution. With regard to the first of these problems, we noted above that the opportunity costs of attendance are often considered one of the costs of attending a higher education institution. Suppose that potential students consider the wage of non-college-graduates as an appropriate measure of the wage they could currently earn given their level of education. It is generally argued that an increase in this wage unambiguously reduces the probability of attendance for a given student because it increases the opportunity costs of attendance. However, this wage actually has three separate effects on the choice between attendance and nonattendance (see Hoenack and Weiler, 1979, pp. 94–95). First, this wage may act as a proxy for students' estimates of their future earnings if they do not attend college. This reduces the benefits of attendance and therefore acts to reduce the probability of attendance. Second, this wage can influence the students' values of the time they spend in college. This is the common interpretation of this variable as a measure of the income forgone from attendance or the opportunity cost of attendance, and increases in it would again reduce the probability of attendance. Third, this wage may act as a proxy for the income a student could earn working part-time while enrolled and during vacations. In this instance, an increase in this wage reduces the costs of attendance and therefore increases the probability of attendance.

The last of these effects has an impact opposite to the impact of the first two. Although the first two effects are usually the only ones thought of when considering the effect of labor market conditions on attendance choice, there is no reason to automatically assume that these two effects dominate the third. Thus, there is no basis for asserting that an increased opportunity cost of attendance, as measured by an increase in the noncollege wage, unambiguously increases the probability of selecting the nonattendance option.

Labor market conditions can also effect the choice of which school to attend, given attendance. Consider, for example, the effect of a reduction in the earnings of college graduates. This decline will reduce attendance, but it will also cause some students who would otherwise have enrolled in one institution to enroll instead in another institution that enhances the students' ability to compete with other college graduates in the labor market. Hence, the expected sign of the estimated effect of this variable on attendance at a particular institution is ambiguous.

The fact that some variables can have effects on which institution the student selects, given attendance, as well as on the choice of attendance versus nonattendance, is probably the most difficult problem involved in specifying enrollment demand models for individual institutions for two reasons, one conceptual and one empirical. The conceptual problem is that little is known about how students compare the benefits of one institution to those of another.

If students rationally select the institution that yields the largest difference between benefits and costs, then there must be some perception of differences in the benefits the institutions confer; otherwise, students would always select the least cost option that offered the type of program they wanted. However, we know little about how students perform the benefit calculation. For example, students certainly value the prestige, however measured, of an institution, but whether it is the prestige itself that is valued or whether students make some individual calculations about how a more prestigious school will enhance their earning power is unknown.

The empirical problem is that analysts studying the choice of a given institution must also consider variables that alter the choice among institutions as well as the choice of whether to attend. This presents two problems. First, the list of variables that can influence choice among institutions includes more than the variables that influence the choice between attendance and nonattendance. In particular, choice among institutions is influenced by variables that measure the degree of substitution among institutions. The human capital model sketched above, for example, predicts that a student will be more likely to attend a given institution if the costs of attending that institution fall. However, this decline in the cost of attending the given school makes attending that school more likely both for students who would otherwise not have attended any school and for those who would otherwise have selected another school. Thus, in analyzing the demand for attendance at a particular school, we need to include variables measuring the costs of attending all competing schools, not just some index of cost of attendance. (In studies concerned with attendance versus nonattendance, the value of the least-cost option is often used in this context.) More generally, we must consider all aspects that measure the degree of substitution among institutions in the analysis. These include both cash outlays and proximity costs, the time and travel costs to alternative institutions.

Second, the interpretation of the effects of variables on attendance at a given school are sometimes confounded by the presence of substitutes; we alluded to some of these difficulties above in discussing financial aid and labor market variables. Suppose a student orders the institutions according to the rate-of-return criteria discussed above. Then suppose that the student's federal financial aid award is increased by a fixed dollar amount irrespective of the institution attended. This changes the computed rate of return attending each option and could easily change the preferred option, most likely to a more costly institution. Aggregating these effects over a large number of potential students certainly suggests that, while more students may attend some institution, those institutions in the middle of the cost spectrum will probably gain some students who would otherwise have attended lower-cost institutions, or who would not have attended, and will lose some students they otherwise would have had to more costly institutions. Whether the net change in enrollment for these schools will be positive or negative is an empirical matter. However, it is clear that the effect of the change in aid on attendance at these schools cannot be inferred from a national study of the effects of financial aid on access in general. The measured effect at individual schools will almost certainly be smaller than that for the national study and may even be "perverse" in the sense that increased aid may reduce attendance. Similar examples could also be constructed for the effects of other variables, particularly labor market variables, on attendance at specific institutions.

A summary of all of these considerations suggests that the symbolic representation of the enrollment demand for a particular school, based on the aggregation of the choices of the individuals eligible to attend the institution, can be written as follows:

$$E = f(COST, COSTOTHER, LABOR, PROXIMITY, FINANCIALAID, \qquad (1)$$
$$FAOTHER, SES)$$

where

E	= enrollment;
$COST$	= cash outlays for attendance at the institution;
$COSTOTHER$	= cash outlays for attendance at substitute institutions;
$LABOR$	= labor market conditions;
$PROXIMITY$	= proximity costs of all institutions;
$FINANCIALAID$	= financial aid at the institution;
$FAOTHER$	= financial aid at substitute institutions;
SES	= other socioeconomic variables, such as ability, family income, or sex.

In this formulation f represents an unknown mathematical function specified by the analyst. The fact that enrollment is on the left of the equals sign implies that enrollment results from the levels of the other variables. Therefore, E is called the dependent variable, and the other variables are called the causal or independent variables. Note that the constructs referring to other institutions are really vectors of length equal to the number of substitute institutions, and that SES also has several elements in it.

The list of independent variables in Equation (1) is long and difficult to define. In particular, when specifying the variables related to competing institutions, we have to define the full set of competing institutions. In principle, this set consists of all schools that any of the potential students considers a substitute for the institution whose demand we are analyzing. Without extensive data on each potential student, including information on the student's perception of the institutions that are substitutes, we cannot precisely specify all of the causal variables in Equation (1).

Fortunately, many of the variables that might be included in Equation (1) do not need to be included in the enrollment demand equation(s) actually statistically estimated. One reason is that some variables do not vary within the data samples commonly used for estimation. For example, living expenses are unlikely to differ systematically across the institutional options in the choice set, or even with nonattendance. The same is true of the cost of books, at least for the attendance options. If a possible independent variable does not vary across the data sample used to estimate Equation (1), then that variable cannot influence the attendance demand behavior of the students in that sample.

Another reason that the number of variables in the equation actually estimated may be less than the number implicitly included in (1) is that particular variables may not vary across the sample, depending on the nature of the sample itself. Data samples, in this or any statistical analysis, can be characterized as samples of individuals or groups of individuals gathered at a point in time (a cross-sectional sample) or grouped data gathered over a number of specific time periods (time series), and the particular variables that vary with enrollment and must be included in the analysis will differ depending on which type of sample is used. For instance, in a grouped time-series sample, student ability varies only with the average aggregate ability of potential students over time and is likely to vary only modestly within the sample. Cash costs of attendance at both the institution under study and the competing institutions are the same for each individual in a cross-sectional sample, but proximity costs are not; hence, the latter can be included in the estimated equation when using that type of sample, but the former cannot.

Labor market conditions, especially wages, present a rather complex case. These variables do vary across time series samples and should be included in those analyses based on the work of Richard Freeman (1971), who developed the basic model of enrollment demand that incorporates current labor market conditions, particularly wage rates. (Using national time-series data samples, he has also done most of the studies in which the effect of current wages on attendance has been estimated. Several of these studies are referenced and discussed in Freeman, 1976.) Measured labor-force conditions such as those gathered from government statistics, however, are unlikely to vary for individuals at a point in time, and these measures, at least, should not be included in a cross-sectional sample. It may be possible, though, to impute estimated wages for both the attendance and nonattendance options to each individual in the sample based on his or her socioeconomic characteristics (Schwartz, 1985).

There is also an artifact of time-series data samples in particular that can limit the number of variables in the analysis. The problem is that some variables may be highly correlated with each other. This situation, called the problem of multicollinearity in descriptions of the multiple regression estimating procedure, means that it is hard to statistically discern the separate effects of each variable in the analysis. The best example of this phenomenon is that while cash attendance costs at different institutions all vary across a time series sample, these costs are often so highly correlated that it may be impossible to estimate the separate influences of each on enrollment at the institution under study. In this particular instance, it is possible to include only the institution's own tuition in the model. However, the interpretation of its estimated effect is now as the effect of a concomitant change in tuition at all institutions, an effect we still expect to be negative since a concomitant reduction in the costs of attending all institutions should increase attendance at our institution by more than the enrollments we lose to competing institutions if our institution is what economists call a "normal" good. It should be emphasized, though, that this is a statistical problem, as opposed to a problem in obtaining data on a particular set of variables. More precisely, it is a problem with the particular data sample rather than with the specification of the model. Nevertheless, it is a common problem in most time-series data samples that are used to analyze enrollment demand.

We should also note that the specification of the dependent variable in Equation (1) also varies with the type of data sample. With grouped data, the essential point is that enrollment depends on the number of prospective students that compose the group as well as the other dependent variables we have discussed. In specifying the equation to be estimated, we can either include the variable measuring the number of potential students as an additional independent variable or, what is more common, specify the dependent variable as the ratio of enrollment to this variable. For example, if we are using a time series sample to study the attendance choice behavior of new freshmen in a region, the choices of the potential student variable are recent high-school graduates or possibly the number of persons in the region in a particular age group, such as 18–21 or 18–24. Assuming we select recent high-school graduates as our measure of the number of potential students, we have the option of using the number of new freshmen as the dependent variable in our model and the number of recent high-school graduates as one of the independent variables or of using the ratio of new freshmen to recent high-school graduates as the dependent variable. As noted, the latter formulation is more frequently employed.

When the data sample consists of observations on individuals, the dependent variable can best be thought of as representing the choice among two or more mutually exclusive and exhaustive institutional options. (Hence, nonattendance is always one of the options in the choice set.) Each individual either does or does not select each option but must select exactly one of the options. It is standard in this type of problem to represent the dependent variable as a vector with as many elements as there are options in the choice set, and to let each element in the vector be either a zero (did not choose the option) or a one (did choose the option). For instance, if there are five options, then each individual's choice can be represented by the vector $(p_1, p_2, p_3, p_4, p_5)$, where each p_i is *either zero or one, depending on the option that individual selects; that is, the vector is (0, 0, 1, 0, 0) for an individual selecting the third option, and so on.*

Enrollment demand models estimated with either individual or grouped data samples can provide useful information to policymakers at a particular institution, although the interpretation of the estimated coefficients (i.e., the estimated effect of each independent variable on the dependent variable) is different. If the data are grouped, the estimated coefficient of a particular independent variable shows the effect on the enrollment rate of a one-unit change in the variable (assuming that the more common formulation of the dependent variable is employed). Multiple-regression analysis is almost always employed in estimating the coefficients of the equations when using grouped data.

If individual data are used, it is natural to think that we can interpret the effects in terms of the specific option that each individual will select. However, it turns out that the information obtained in this context is sufficient to estimate only the change in the probability or the likelihood that the individual will select each option. Hence, the estimated coefficient of a variable is an estimate of the effect of a one-unit change in the variable on these probabilities, not on the specific option selected. There are several ways of statistically estimating models that use individual data. The most common are the logit and probit techniques. These are discussed in Pindyck and Rubinfeld (1981, Chapter 10).

Another difficulty with using data on individuals has to do with the measurement of the financial aid variable. When using grouped time-series data, the financial aid variable is usually measured by the average aid awarded to those in the group. The value of this variable for any particular observation is almost certainly not the amount that would be awarded to a particular individual in the group if that person attended the institution under study, but it does fairly represent the expected per student amount for the group. However, when using individual data, we observe the financial aid awarded to each individual who did attend a higher education institution for the school he or she attended, but we do not observe a value of financial aid for attendees for the schools they did not attend, nor do we observe any financial aid figures at all for nonattendees. To obtain these unobserved values of the financial aid variables, we must undertake an auxillary analysis that produces a predicted value of financial aid for each individual for each institution he or she did not attend. See Fuller, Manski, and Wise (1982), Manski and Wise (1983), and Schwartz (1985) for these types of analyses.

The sample selected for a particular analysis depends in large part on how the results are to be used. The most important consideration in this regard is to select the sample so that variables important to the policy discussion at hand vary across the sample. In fact, it is tempting to include only those variables, or possibly those variables plus any others under the control of institutional administrators, in the analysis. However, all variables that theoretically influence attendance behavior and vary across the data sample must be included in the estimated equation to ensure that the estimated effects of all of the variables are unbiased. Only variables that have small, random influences on enrollments can be safely omitted.

In general this consideration suggests that time series samples should be used whenever the analysis is to be used for future-oriented activities such as enrollment forecasting or tuition policy studies. In these instances variables such as labor market conditions, as well as tuition itself, will vary over the time interval to which the analysis will be applied. Hence, we need samples that include the requisite variation in these variables. Samples of individuals, on the other hand, are best when studying the effects of variables which vary more substantially across individuals than the aggregates of these variables vary over time within a group or when undertaking policy studies in which options that treat individuals differently are to be investigated. These include policy studies of financial aid or the differences in attendance behavior of students classified by socioeconomic characteristics such as income or ability. Note that variables like financial aid and income will almost certainly vary over time for a grouped time-series sample, but the important point is that evaluation of policies that, for example, increase financial aid for some students while lowering it for others will require an analysis developed from a cross-sectional sample of individuals.

To this point, the discussion and examples have either explicitly or implicitly considered attendance from the perspective of behavior of choosing to attend while not now attending. However, the basic theory and methodologies described can also be used to analyze the behavior of students already enrolled in the institution under study or in other institutions. In the latter case, policymakers are often concerned with the propensity of students enrolled elsewhere to transfer to their school. This, of course, is particularly true in situations in which community college transfers constitute a substantial fraction of the upper-division students at the policymakers' institutions.

In studying transfer behavior to four-year schools, the important points are to determine the particular institutions that a potential transfer student might select and to specify the pool of potential transfer students. The former problem is analogous to the specification of the initial attendance options for a set of high school graduates, with the equivalent of nonattendance being the choice not to transfer. The specification of the pool of potential transfer students is somewhat more difficult than in the case of new freshmen because the pool of potential transfer students is not as well defined as the pool of potential new freshmen. The recent graduates of nearby community colleges are obvious candidates, but many community college students transfer to four-year schools before they obtain a community college degree. Further, students from a four-year school can often transfer to other four-year schools, especially to schools that offer programs not offered at the source institutions. The question of how to define the sample of potential transfer students arises whether we use individual or grouped data. One possible way to reduce the difficulty that this issue may pose is to estimate separate equations for transfers from each different source institution or possibly from different groups of institutions. This method also has the advantage of allowing the data to determine if transfer behavior differs across different source institutions. It is important to note that this same point could be made about the attendance choices of new freshmen. It might be best, for example, to estimate separate equations for high school graduates living within and beyond commuting distance to the institution being analyzed. Not only might behavior be different for the two sets of potential students, but it is also possible that the universe of competing institutions will differ for the two sets. The choice of how many separate equations to estimate will largely rest on these issues and the extent to which detailed data are available for individuals or groups.

For students already enrolled in the institution being studied, the analytical question is whether they will continue to be enrolled the following term or year or will drop out. This simplifies the consideration of "alternatives" since there are only two, and it also presents no problem in defining the pool of potential continuing students; they are simply the ones enrolled the previous period who did not graduate. The most important issue in studying this behavior is that previous analyses of continuation—or persistence, as it often called—indicate that individuals' social and psychological characteristics are important determinants of their behavior in this regard. In particular, much of the research in this area has been concerned with the congruence between students' characteristics and what is generally called the institutional environment. Not surprisingly, the probability of the persistence of an individual student is directly related to the degree of congruence thus defined. (See, for example, Pascarella and Chapman, 1983; Bean, 1982; and the references in those papers.)

Studies using grouped data are not common in this area, and studies of individuals must control for these factors, plus the effect that these same factors have on students' use of institutional programs and resources that can independently influence their probability of persistence. The latter issue is especially important from an institutional policy perspective. If the persistence of a student with given socioeconomic and psychological characteristics is affected only by those factors and not by institutional factors such as financial aid, cultural centers, or special advising, then the only policy option that increases persistence rates is the reduction of the proportion of students with "poor anticipated persistence" through admission decisions. Hence, it is necessary in continuation studies using individual data to specify the model in such a way as to separately estimate the effects of student characteristics and institutional-policy-controllable characteristics on persistence. It is generally not sufficient simply to include the institutional policy variables, however measured, and student characteristics separately in a single equation that explains persistence because this specification ignores the fact that students themselves may self-select various types of institutional assistance. Recent advances in statistical modeling can be used to provide unbiased estimates in this type of problem; see the chapters in Maddala (1983) that deal with models estimated in the presence of self-selection. See also Pascarella, Terenzini, and Wolfe (1986) for an example of this type of study.

INSTITUTIONAL POLICY ISSUES

Enrollment Forecasting

Probably the most obvious use of enrollment demand equations in institutional policy decision-making at an individual institution is in forecasting the institution's enrollments. (This discussion of the use of enrollment demand models for forecasting draws heavily on Hoenack and Weiler, 1979.) As noted above, this usually requires equations estimated from time series samples because the factors that influence enrollment demand over time must be entered in the model if it is to be used for this purpose.

In general, we conceive of the enrollment-forecasting model as three sets of estimated enrollment-demand equations. Each set consists of at least one equation, but most will have more than one. The first set is equations for new freshmen, the second is equations for transfer students, and the third is equations for continuing students. We noted in discussing continuing students that it was uncommon to use time series samples to estimate persistence behavior, except possibly for the use of Markov or cohort survival models. This issue is discussed in Hopkins and Massy (1981, Chapter 8). However, we do so in enrollment forecasting without worrying about the factors that influence individual persistence decisions because these factors will vary only slightly over time using aggregated data. The estimates of the effects of variables included in the resulting continuation equations will not have the same policy uses as estimates from individual persistence studies. Their only uses will be in enrollment forecasting and in analyzing the effects of tuition policy, a subject discussed below.

The complete enrollment forecasting model is as follows. The set of equations for new freshmen can be represented as

$$A_i = a_0 + a_1 X_1 + \ldots + a_n X_n \qquad i = 1, k \qquad (2)$$

There are k equations, one for each enrollment category. The X_j's denote the particular independent variables from Equation (1) that belong in the equations estimated with a time series sample. The a_j's are estimated multiple regression coefficients. A_i is the dependent variable, assumed to be the ratio of enrollment, E_i, to the number of eligible recent high-school graduates, H_i. Two additional sets of similar equations are specified and estimated for transfer and continuation enrollments. The equations for transfer students are

$$T_i = b_0 + b_1 X_1 + \ldots + b_n X_n \qquad i = 1, t \qquad (3)$$

and those for continuing students are

$$C_i = c_0 + c_1 X_1 + \ldots + c_n X_n \qquad i = 1, p \qquad (4)$$

The full model then consists of $k + t + p$ estimated enrollment demand equations. Each set of equations is shown as containing the same independent variables as the equations for new freshmen, but this is only for ease of exposition. In most cases, the variables will differ even for different equations in the same set. The dependent variables in the transfer equations are assumed to be the ratios of transfer students to the number of students who are potential transfer students. The dependent variables in the continuation equations are ratios of continuing students to students enrolled one period earlier at the institution. One can envision this set consisting of separate equations that represent the progression from freshman to sophomore, from sophomore to junior, and so on. The alternative is a single equation in which the numerator of the dependent variable is the sum of all students continuing to the next year, and the denominator is the total number enrolled in the institution in the previous year. The choice depends on data availability and whether the effects of the independent variables are expected to differ across the cohorts.

Given the values of the estimated multiple-regression coefficients for each equation, the calculation of an enrollment forecast proceeds as follows. The initial problem is to determine values of the X_j's and values of the denominators of the ratios of the various dependent variables for the forecast period, that is, the year(s) for which we want a forecast. The latter, of course, are the eligible high-school graduates, H_i, for the initial attendance equations, students enrolled the previous year in the relevant source institutions for transfer students, and students enrolled the previous year in the institution being studied for the continuation equations.

The forecast itself is then computed in three steps. The first step is computing the forecast values of each of the $k + t + p$ dependent variables. For one of the equations, this is simply the process of multiplying each forecast X_j by its estimated coefficient and summing over the values. The second step is multiplying each of the forecast A_i's, T_i's, and C_i's by the forecast values of their denominators. This is just calculating each E_i from the product of A_i and H_i in the case of the set of initial attendance equations plus similar calculations for transfer and continuing students. The last step is to sum the resulting enrollments to get a total enrollment for the institution. Note that since the denominators of the T_i's are themselves enrollments at other institutions, developing this model for a single school could have spillover benefits for other institutions. A state with large numbers of transfers between institutions might even have a statewide model encompassing most of the schools in the state.

One component of institutional enrollments at universities is missing from this model: the postbaccalaureate students. These students are not included because Equations (2)–(4) represent enrollments that are determined by student demand behavior. Thus, we are implicitly assuming that the institution will admit all students in these catagories who meet the institution's admissions standards, or in economic terms, that the supply of places in the institution is infinitely elastic at the prevailing tuition schedule.

This assumption would seldom hold for postbaccalaureate graduate and professional programs. While individual students will still use the human capital model to make their decisions on the particular fields in which they hope to continue their studies, and also on the particular institution they will attend given that they are accepted (Alexander and Frey, 1984; McClain, Vance, and Wood, 1984; Punj and Staelin, 1978), the number who apply to a program at any one institution is typically larger than the number who are admitted. The level of enrollment in these programs is thus determined by the institution or, probably more accurately, by the departments within the institution. Hence, these enrollments are determined by institutional supply behavior rather than student demand behavior. Forecast values of enrollments in these programs should be based on departmental decisions as to how many students they plan to admit in the forecast period. Variation between the forecasts and actual enrollment will presumably be due to student decisions to enroll once admitted. It is possible to analyze this process of matriculation with statistical models, but the conceptual framework is somewhat different from the one discussed above.

It is also clear that while the assumption of infinitely elastic supply accurately depicts what happens in public institutions at the undergraduate level (e.g., open admissions and admitting all state residents with a high school diploma), it is not an accurate description of reality at most private institutions. The level of undergraduate enrollments at these institutions is determined by a process much like that just described for graduate and professional enrollments at public universities. The important decision on the student side in this context is the decision to matriculate once admitted. Again, this decision is somewhat different conceptually from the demand decisions explained above. In particular, it is difficult to conceive of using equations estimated using grouped data to model this decision. We will discuss models of private decision-making below that include matriculation decision equations. While we will not emphasize the point, similar models could conceivably be used to estimate the determinants of matriculation into graduate and professional schools in public (or private) institutions.

What we actually have in Equations (2)–(4), then, is a model for forecasting undergraduate enrollments at a public institution. A question that then could easily arise about this model is how it compares with other models that might be used in this context. Specifically, it appears to be a complex approach that may be hard to explain to policymakers. It also requires a lot of data for estimation and even more data for forecasting. To deal with this question, we will first describe its advantages over other models of forecasting and then discuss the manner in which the requisite data, especially the forecast period data, might be obtained.

Other formal enrollment forecasting models are trend techniques of one type or another (Wing, 1974). (We do not consider idiosyncratic "finger in the wind" approaches.) They range from simply using last year's progression rates and high-school-graduate yields to statistically sophisticated Box-Jenkins techniques. The advantage of these techniques is that they are simple to explain, at least in principle, and require few data beyond historical institutional enrollments. The first disadvantage of using them is that they do not provide ready answers to the typical "what if" questions of institutional policymakers. In particular, questions about such items as changing tuition can be answered only on an *ad hoc* basis or through a side analysis. The approach described here explicitly incorporates variables influencing enrollment directly into the analysis and, further, provides estimates of the effects of each variable on enrollment. This enables the analyst to easily answer these "what if" questions and, in addition, means that the assumptions inherent in the forecast must be stated explicitly before the forecast is made. A corollary is that a number of forecasts based on alternative assumptions can easily be made. Trend techniques produce a single forecast unless estimated parameters are arbitrarily changed ("This time trend is a little strong") or unless an *ad hoc* change is made in the forecast itself.

A second advantage of the model presented here is that it yields unbiased estimates of the effect of each independent variable on enrollment. Further, the standard errors of these estimates are obtained. Both the trend approaches and the model here produce forecasts that are centered within the statistical distribution of the estimated forecast errors, but with the model based on enrollment demand equations, the analyst can determine which variables significantly affect enrollment and can also calculate the contribution of the variance of each coefficient estimate and the standard error of the residuals to the estimated forecast error.

Whatever type of model is used, the size of the forecast error determines the degree of flexibility that institutional administrators should maintain in decisions that depend on the level of enrollment. In any statistical model, the deviation eventually observed between the forecast and actual values of the dependent variable is the result of four factors: misspecification of the underlying behavior that generated the data, the variances of the coefficient estimates, the variance of the residuals (the cumulative effect of variables that are excluded from the model and of behavior that is inherently unpredictable), and incorrect values of the independent variables predicted for the forecast period. It is not possible to determine what the first and last of these contributes until after the actual values of the dependent variables are known. However, the model presented here sheds much more light on the expected error from the second and third of these components and also enables the analyst to estimate the likely error associated with forecasts of some of the independent variables.

With regard to the second and third components, the minimum forecast error for an equation, given that the values of the independent variables are known exactly, is the standard error of the residuals. Hence, the knowledge of these separate variances shows the proportion of the forecast error that cannot be reduced and allows institutional administrators to evaluate the uncertainty of the coefficient estimates relative to the uncertainty inherent in student demand behavior that is not captured by the variables in the model. The latter component is particularly useful in preserving flexibility in administrative decision making.

A final advantage of this model is that the magnitudes of its estimated coefficients enable administrators to determine the relative effects on enrollments of variables they can and cannot control. Specifically, administrators can observe the potential control they have over enrollments through the use of tuition policy to influence enrollment decisions or to counteract demographic trends. Trend forecasts, which do not yield estimates of the effect of individual variables by definition, do not allow this type of analysis.

As we noted, the forecast and actual values of a dependent variable may also differ because of incorrect forecasts of the independent variables in its equation. In trend models, there is no problem in "forecasting" the value of the independent variable because it is known exactly from knowing the date of the forecast period. This appears to be an advantage in trend techniques, and it is, to the extent that the data required to compute a forecast are reduced, often considerably. However, it is not true that trend forecasts have smaller forecast errors because there is no "error" in forecasting the value of the independent variable. The deviation of historical enrollments from the particular way trends are incorporated into the estimated equations will be picked up by the variance of the residuals or the variances of the coefficient estimates; these variances will therefore include any errors that result from the fact that variables theoretically influencing enrollments that may vary over the estimation period independently from the trend included in the model are not included in its estimated equations.

This does, however, bring up the issue of how forecasts of the X_j's and the denominators of the A_i's, T_i's, and C_i's can be developed for a forecasting model that is based on estimated demand equations. Values of these variables can be estimated using trend techniques or multiple-regression equations with these as dependent variables or, if they are controlled by institutional policy, can be specified by institutional administrators. The choice between trend techniques and additional regression equations depends on whether a theory relating other variables to the independent variables is available. For example, there are many theoretical analyses relating labor market variables such as wages and unemployment rates to aggregate economic conditions. These can be used to provide estimated regression equations for predicting labor market variables for the forecast period. Trend techniques can be used when no theory is available or when the requisite data for any additional regressions are not available.

Note that the use of additional regression equations for generating values of the X_j's in the forecast period requires the determination of the values of the independent variables in these additional equations for this same forecast period before an enrollment forecast can be made. It is also the case that these auxilliary regressions—and, for that matter, auxilliary regressions that simply include time trends—contribute to errors expected in forecasting enrollments because of the potential errors that they produce in the forecast values of the X_j's. However, these errors can be calculated and their contribution to the expected forecast error in enrollments quantified. In this sense, we can calculate the expected error of having the "wrong" values of these particular independent variables, which is the fourth forecast error component mentioned above.

In our work at Minnesota, we have found it useful to provide policymakers with three separate measures of the standard error of the enrollment forecast. These are the minimum error discussed above, a second error computed assuming the X_j's are known exactly (an unconditional forecast), and a third error computed by additionally incorporating the errors in the auxilliary regressions (a conditional forecast). These estimated forecast errors obviously become larger as additional components of uncertainty are introduced. In fact, the second error is usually about 50% larger than the first, and the last is usually much larger (two to three times larger) than the second and grows much more rapidly in both absolute size and as a percentage of the forecast level of enrollment as the forecast period is extended further into the future. (See, for example, Hoenack and Weiler, 1979, Table 4, p. 109.)

Environmental Scanning

An interesting aspect of this description of the process of how the enrollment forecast is developed and used is how closely it is related, at least in its basic framework, to the currently popular concept of environmental scanning. Although there are many issues involved in this concept, not the least of which is exactly what it is, it seems that the core of the concept includes the notion of systematically relating the institution's external environment to its internal decision-making (see, e.g., Hearn and Heydinger, 1985).

This is almost precisely what is done using the enrollment forecasting model. First, the analyst creates a model to describe the historical relationship between enrollments and the variables that influence them. In addition to its advantages vis-à-vis trend techniques, it thus appears that formulating this model defines a set of "environmental variables" that influence an important element of the institution's planning. Second, the analyst estimates the equations in the model. These provide estimates of the practical and statistical significance of the interactions between the external variables and enrollments. Finally, enrollment forecasting itself requires a systematic determination of future values of the environmental variables and the processes that generate them, enables the institution's administrators to determine how the external environment will influence its enrollment under alternative scenarios, and possibly most important, allows institutional decision-makers to observe the degree to which they can mitigate the environmental effects through the use of variables they can control, such as tuition.

While the emphasis in this short discussion is on the symbiosis between environmental scanning and enrollment forecasting, it is also true that other uses of enrollment demand models provide the same type of close relationship to environmental scanning. This is especially true of the budget-planning and forecasting model that we discuss below.

Tuition Policy

Another area in which enrollment demand analyses for institutions can inform institutional policymakers is in providing estimates of the effects of tuition policy. Since the primary concern in this context is usually the effect of tuition on total enrollments, the same demand equations estimated with grouped data that are used for enrollment forecasting can be used to analyze tuition policy. However, if the concern is over which particular students—say, by income or ability level—are most affected by tuition policy, then the analyst must estimate enrollment demand equations with individual cross-sectional data. The difficulty in that analysis is that tuition at the institution—or at competing institutions, for that matter—does not vary across the sample. As a result, the estimated effects of proximity costs must be used as proxies for the effects of out-of-pocket costs (see, for example, Hoenack and Weiler, 1975).

We also again include the caveat that the model of Equations (2)–(4) holds for public institutions but probably does not accurately represent behavior in determining the effects of tuition on attendance at private institutions. The concerns there are not with the effects of tuition on total enrollment, but more likely with the effects on the socioeconomic composition of the student body. The model of matriculation discussed above is more likely to be useful in this regard. We discuss the approach in more detail later in this chapter.

The procedure for computing the effect of tuition on enrollment using an estimated enrollment-demand equation is straightforward. If we let X_1 in Equation (2) be tuition at our institution, then the estimated coefficient a_1, which we expect to be negative, is the effect of a one-dollar change in tuition on the attendance rate A_i. Hence, if the proposed tuition is X_1^* and the current tuition is X_1, then the new attendance rate A_i^* is equal to $A_i + a_1(X_1^* - X_1)$. Since we expect $a_1 < 0$, this means that A_i^* is below A_i if tuition increases, and conversely. Clearly, the new enrollment, E_i^*, is simply the product of H_i and A_i^*, while the old enrollment, E_i, is the product of H_i and A_i. Thus, we can rewrite the above relation in terms of enrollment as

$$E_i^* = E_i + a_1(X_1^* - X_1)H_i \qquad (5)$$

Similar calculations yield the transfer and continuing student enrollments expected as a result of the new tuition policy. Note that while we have written Equations (2)–(4) to provide a linear relation between attendance rates and the level of tuition along with the other independent variables in order to simplify both the exposition and this calculation, analogous calculations can be performed if either or both A_i and X_1 are expressed in logarithms. The form of Equation (5) would change, but we still could write a relationship expressing the new enrollment as the sum of the old enrollment and a factor that depends on the change in tuition and the coefficient of the tuition variable.

The effect of the tuition policy on graduate and professional enrollments is again a special case. Some research has indicated that these students do respond to differences in attendance costs in their choice of which institution they attend among the set to which they apply (Punj and Staelin, 1978; McClain et al., 1984). However, since most graduate and professional programs have substantial excesses of applications over admissions, it is not clear that a tuition increase in a particular institution necessarily leads to reduced enrollments in these programs, since the institution can alter its admissions policy.

For these types of students, the most obvious assumption to make is that enrollment in programs with an excess of applications for admission will not change in response to a tuition change, although the particular students who enroll will obviously change. As noted above, the important issues in this context are related to institutional or departmental admissions policies and the change in the quality of the students who enroll. It is potentially possible, of course, for tuition increases to result in enrollment declines in these programs if the admitting unit is unwilling to accept a sufficient number of lower quality students, but it is highly unlikely that total applications will fall below the department's enrollment target.

The two most important issues in the evaluation of the effect of tuition policy on the institution's undergraduate enrollment can be derived from an examination of Equation (5). First, the size of the coefficient a_1 determines the magnitude of the effect of tuition on enrollment. Second, the variance of this estimate determines the size of the statistical forecast error associated with the expected change in enrollment resulting from the change in tuition policy.

With regard to the size of the effect, the responses to tuition changes are likely to be different for eligible high-school graduates deciding on their initial attendance choice, for already-enrolled undergraduates deciding to continue in the institution, and for students enrolled elsewhere deciding whether to transfer to the institution under study (Hoenack and Weiler, 1979). Specifically, a given percentage change in the level of tuition will produce much larger percentage changes in enrollment of initial attendees and transfer students, at least for four-year schools, than in enrollment of continuing students, or in economic terms, the former two groups of students have larger tuition elasticities than the latter group. The reason this happens is that initial attendees and transfer students are choosing among a larger number of institutional choices, some of which are likely to be only slightly different from each other in the minds of the students. Hence, just like consumers of closely related products who choose according to small price differences, we expect that a relatively large number of these educational "consumers" will change their institutional choices in response to the change in tuition at our institution. Continuing students, on the other hand, have already invested time and effort at the institution. While some of them may have focused educational objectives that induce them to drop out or transfer elsewhere, the cost of leaving to most will include some loss on this investment. In terms of the human capital model, the additional benefits of continuing are likely to outweigh the additional costs of a tuition increase plus the loss of the time already invested for most students now enrolled.

With regard to the forecast error associated with these coefficients, we expect that most institutions will be able to obtain accurate estimates of the effect of tuition on initial attendance. The most likely difficulty is that mentioned above: an inability to include separate tuition variables for each competing institution in the analysis. In that case, the problem is not the accuracy of the estimate, but its interpretation as representing the effect of tuition at the analyzed institution alone. It may be possible in this context to use the results of a separate set of equations estimated with cross-sectional data to adjust the time series estimates; in this regard, see Hoenack and Weiler (1979, p. 95, especially footnote 9).

We also believe that most institutions will be able to obtain good estimates of the effect of tuition on aggregate continuation rates. As noted above, we do expect the effects to be smaller, but this is an issue related to the practical significance of the estimates, not to their statistical significance. However, the estimates are also likely to be of practical significance because the number of continuing students, at least at four-year schools, greatly exceeds the number of freshman and transfer students. Thus, even a small demand elasticity creates a relatively large change in aggregate institutional enrollment.

It is not as likely that all institutions will be able to obtain statistically precise estimates of the effect of tuition on transfer attendance rates. The difficulty is in determining the correct denominator of the dependent variable T_i in Equation (3). To the extent that this denominator does not accurately measure the potential transfer student population, it produces what is called measurement error in the dependent variable. Measurement error in the dependent variable of a multiple-regression equation does not produce biased estimates of the coefficients, but it does increase their estimated standard deviations and thus lowers their statistical precision. Experimentation with various ways of defining this denominator or with separate regressions using different groups of source institutions will allow the analyst to determine the extent of this problem.

One area in tuition policy in which the estimated enrollment demand equations are unlikely to provide much help is in estimating the effects of changes in tuition by program within the institution. It is difficult to estimate the effects of these types of changes, which are likely to encourage some students already enrolled to transfer to other programs in the institution, because most institutions have not had sufficient variation in tuition in different programs over time to provide a data sample to estimate these effects. However, these effects may be relatively small in that most schools that have differentiated tuition by program have a single rate for freshmen and other lower-division students regardless of program, and it is this group of students that has the largest enrollment response to a tuition change. Further, continuing students have much lower tuition elasticities, so that even fairly large tuition changes across upper-division programs are not likely to have much enrollment impact.

Given that an institution will be able to obtain statistically precise estimates from the enrollment demand equations that show that tuition elasticities are larger for initial attendees and transfer students than for continuing students, the next question is whether those results imply anything about the tuition policy that the institution should follow. It is not the purpose of this chapter to discuss all of the factors that enter the institutional policy deliberations with respect to tuition (see Gilmour and Suttle, 1984, in that regard), but the results are suggestive in at least one respect.

This suggestion comes from the fact that in most institutions, instructional costs are lowest for lower-division instruction, increase for upper-division undergraduate programs, and are highest, perhaps much higher, for graduate and professional programs. In addition, tuitions tend not to fully reflect these differences in costs, so that there is an inverse relationship between instructional costs and the tuition paid by each level of student as a percentage of instructional costs. Hence, if the tuition policy were altered in the direction of having individual students pay more equal percentages of their instructional costs, holding constant total tuition revenue as a percentage of total instructional costs, tuitions would fall, perhaps significantly, for lower-division students, would be changed only slightly for upper-division students, and would increase, perhaps substantially, for graduate and professional students.

Such a change in policy would mean increased numbers of lower-division students (i.e., initial attendees), along with only a small reduction in the total tuition revenue collected from these students, or perhaps even a revenue increase depending on the absolute sizes of the tuition elasticities. There would be little change in both enrollment of and tuition revenue collected from upper-division students (i.e., transfer and continuing students), both because tuition rates would not change much and because tuition elasticities are low for most of these students. Under the assumption that the level of enrollment in graduate and professional programs is determined by institutional policy rather than student demand, there would be no change in graduate and professional enrollments, along with a potentially large increase in the total tuition revenue collected from them. In total, then, the institution's enrollment would increase with little, if any, loss of tuition revenue, even in the first year under such a policy, and the results would be magnified over time as the larger number of initial attendees continued to flow into the institution in the future. This idea of a cost-related tuition policy has already been implemented in some schools, and others are considering it. Berg and Hoenack (1987) describe the issues involved and the results to date of the implementation of such a plan at the University of Minnesota.

Institutional Budgets

Of course, public institutions would consider the scenario described above under a cost-related tuition policy a substantial boon even if they gained no additional tuition revenue. The reason is that many public institutions receive funds from their state legislatures through a formula that directly relates their budgets to their enrollments. Even those public schools whose legislative allocations are not directly tied to a formula have probably historically observed a high correlation between their allocations and their enrollments.

At first glance, then, the role of enrollment demand analysis in a model of institutional budget determination looks very simple. One just uses an enrollment-forecasting model of the type we have already discussed to produce a forecast value of enrollment and then inserts that value into the formula that the legislature uses to calculate the legislative subsidy. At worst, we might have to add an additional estimated regression equation that explains the legislative allocation as a function of institutional enrollment. This estimated equation, along with an enrollment forecast, could then be used to forecast the subsidy. The calculation of the forecast of the other major source of instructional revenue for a public school, tuition revenue, would simply fall out as the product of the forecast enrollment and the per student tuition rate.

However, the relationship between the institution's enrollment and its budget is not quite so simply explained as this story suggests. We can illustrate the complexity with two examples. First, suppose that the state's tax revenue fluctuates along with enrollments. It has been altogether too clear to many of us in the last few years that such a situation, particularly a case in which there is an unexpected shortfall in tax revenues, leads to "retrenchment," or at least to a reduced institutional budget. Even in cases in which the institution is ostensibly subsidized strictly on a formula basis, the legislature can change or not fully comply with the formula. In any case, it seems clear that the legislative subsidy, and thus the institution's budget, depends on something in addition to enrollment.

But this situation seems fairly easy to overcome in a model of the determination of the institutional budget. We need only to include some measure of state revenue—state tax revenue per capita might be an obvious choice—as another independent variable in the legislative allocation determination equation. We still have a simple budget-forecasting process that flows from institutional tuition policy to the level of enrollment to the institution's instructional budget. But now the second example: Suppose the institution substantially reduced its tuition for all undergraduate students. From the enrollment-forecasting model, we know that enrollments would increase, and from the simple budget determination process we have postulated to this point, so would the legislative allocation. In fact, the subsidy would increase by a larger percentage than enrollments because in many instances, the legislative allocation is the difference between the institution's expected costs and its tuition revenue. In this circumstance, the legislative subsidy would also have to pick up any tuition revenue lost as a result of the reduction in tuition rates.

What is most interesting about this example, though, is why an institution would not try to lower its tuition even if the subsidy were allocated net of tuition revenue. After all, if the institution received its overall average cost per student on a formula basis from its legislature, all additional enrollments would be funded at this overall per student amount. However, most of the additional enrollments produced by reducing tuition would be by students taking lower-division instruction, where average instructional costs per student are almost surely less than the institution's overall average costs. On top of that, the marginal costs of the additional lower-division instruction are almost certainly less than the average costs. Hence, the institution could receive an increase in its legislative appropriation that substantially exceeds its actual additional costs, even if it were not reimbursed for any decline in tuition revenue. Note that even an institution funded on a formula that provided for reimbursement below the institution's overall average costs for lower-division instruction would still gain the difference between average and marginal costs under such an arrangement.

Clearly, the reason that institutions do not pursue such a policy en masse, beyond the fact that it might be prohibited by their legislatures, is that they know full well that the legislature would not fully fund the additional instruction at any amount near the funding implied by a formula or a historical relationship between enrollment and the legislative appropriation. The reason that the legislature would not pay, irrespective of its income, is that the per student price that it would have to pay as a result of this policy would be too high. In essence, even though it may be expressed through what at first glance appears to be a strict formula, an institution's legislative appropriation is derived from the demand of legislators for the provision of higher education opportunities for their constituents. Even though they may not express it in terms of a legislature's demand, higher education administrators know that the legislature can change a formula or not fully fund it whenever the formula allocation exceeds the amount they would pay based on their desire or demand for higher education.

Like the consumer demand for any product, legislative demand for higher education is a function of the price the legislature must pay and the income it has to spend. (The analysis in the rest of this section closely follows Hoenack and Pierro, 1986.) We can symbolically express this relationship determining the legislative allocation to a given institution in terms of an unknown functional form, g, as

$$L = g(P, INCOME, V) \tag{6}$$

where

L	=	the legislature's per student appropriation to the institution;
P	=	the net price the legislature must pay per student;
$INCOME$	=	the income the legislature has to spend;
V	=	other variables that influence legislative demand for higher education, especially constituent demand for higher education as opposed to other services supplied by government.

Even including Equation (6) still does not appear to cause substantial problems because this equation, at least superficially, still appears to be just another regression equation to be estimated as part of the budget-forecasting model. However, the net per student price of attendance faced by the legislature is the institution's cost per student less the tuition collected from each student. Hence, we can define P as $P = C - T$, where C is the institution's total instructional costs per student and T is the average tuition paid per student. Note, though, that C is the sum of the legislative appropriation (the variable L in Equation 6), tuition revenue, and other instructional revenue the institution may obtain from sources such as investment income and indirect costs recovered from research contracts and is just the budget variable we have discussed above. This variable clearly depends on enrollments as well as on other variables through a cost function. We can write this cost function, which represents the behavior of the institution in supplying instruction, as

$$C = h(E, Y) \tag{7}$$

where h is a functional form, E is total enrollment at the institution, and Y is a vector of other variables influencing institutional costs. The variables in Y include input prices such as faculty salaries and technological factors that might have some effect on the relationship between instructional expenditures and enrollment (see, e.g., Brinkman, 1985).

The complete model of the determination of the institution's budget therefore consists of Equations (6) and (7) and the enrollment demand relations (2)–(4) that determine E. The most important feature of this model is that enrollment, the legislative appropriation, and the institution's instructional budget are determined simultaneously by these relationships. Thus, the simple model described above in which the institution sets its tuition policy to produce its desired enrollment level and then sits back to wait for a legislative appropriation that produces its desired budget to instruct the students is not valid. In particular, if it sets its tuition too low relative to the price that the legislature, as represented by its demand, is willing to pay for the resulting enrollments, the institution will not receive an appropriation sufficient in its eyes to instruct the students. Hence, this model captures the essence of why the legislature would not fully fund or would change a formula that appears at first glance to provide an institution with strong incentives to enroll as many students as possible.

Statistical estimation of this model must utilize a technique that takes into account the simultaneous determination of enrollment, the institution's instructional budget, and the legislative appropriation. There are a number of estimation methods that can be used in this context (see Pindyck and Rubinfeld, 1981, Chapters 7 and 11), but the most important consideration with a simultaneous equations model is the concept of identification. Identification of the unknown coefficients of the equations making up a set of simultaneously determined relationships is a property that logically precedes estimation of the coefficients. Identification of the coefficients of one equation in the system is determined by the answer to the question: Could the observed data sample have been generated by only one set of values of the unknown coefficients, by just a few sets of values, or by an infinite set of values? The coefficients of the equation are called just identified (or exactly identified), overidentified, or not identified, respectively. In the latter case, the coefficients of that equation cannot be estimated with any data sample. For a discussion of identification, see Pindyck and Rubinfeld (1981, especially Sections 7.5 and 11.2).

Hoenack and Pierro (1986) discuss a model much along the lines of Equations (2)–(4), (6), (7). They show that with the proper specification of the variables V and Y in Equations (6) and (7), respectively, the coefficients of each equation in this model satisfy a condition that is necessary for identification. They then estimate the model using time series data for Minnesota. Probably their most interesting conclusion is that institutional funding from the legislature depends crucially on the institutional provision of services that the legislature wants, particularly access to constituents. Although this seems obvious at first blush, it is often the case that institutions base their legislative requests on activities they value rather than on what the legislature desires. Hoenack and Pierro's results, however, suggest that a strategy of providing what the legislature wants can yield an appropriation that is sufficient to perform the tasks the legislature wants with resources left over to undertake the activities the institution and its faculty consider important. That an institution takes such actions in its internal allocation of instructional resources is supported by the results in Hoenack et al. (1986), who show that an institution allocates much more per student to graduate instruction even in a case in which the institution's legislative allocation is hardly affected at all by the mix of students by level for a given enrollment.

The use of this model for forecasting the institution's legislative appropriation and tuition revenue proceeds in much the same way as using the enrollment-forecasting model. The only difference is that because the relationships in the model simultaneously determine the values of several of the variables, we must first create what are called the reduced-form equations of the model. These are simply a set of equations, equal in number to the number of simultaneously determined variables (the endogenous variables). Each reduced-form equation has one of the endogenous variables on the left-hand side of the equals sign and only variables whose values are determined outside the model (the exogenous variables) on the right-hand side. Once we have the reduced-form equations, forecasting proceeds just as with the enrollment-forecasting model, beginning with the estimation of the values of the exogenous variables for the forecast period.

Staffing

Along with their role in determining and forecasting a public institution's budget, estimated enrollment equations can also play a role in analyzing the size and composition of the institution's faculty. This role is often overlooked in institutional analyses concerned with this issue. The focus in these studies is usually on the effects of faculty personnel policies related to hiring, promotion, retention, and retirement on the faculty composition by age, rank, sex, race, tenure status, and other characteristics (Bleau, 1985, is a good example).

The faculty flow models that are used in these studies require the analyst to estimate the total size of the faculty each year in the forecast period to produce their results. The analyst also needs to incorporate estimates of the institution's personnel policies: promotion rates; retention rates; hiring by race, sex, tenure status, and so on; retirement rates; and the like. These are then varied systematically to provide forecasts of faculty composition, given the assumed size of the faculty each year, under alternative assumptions. (Hopkins and Massy, 1981; Chapter 8, provide an overview of the development of faculty flow models.)

The focus on personnel policies tends to lead analysts to overlook the fact that their models could also be used if they reversed the order of things and varied the faculty size over time holding constant a personnel policy, or more generally, if they considered policies that would change the institution's faculty size in addition to just personnel policies. The question raised by this suggestion is just what policies the institution can pursue in order to change faculty size.

It is here that enrollment demand analysis becomes relevant. While there may not be a stable known relationship between faculty size and enrollment in the institution, available evidence suggests that the student-faculty ratio in United States higher education has remained nearly constant since the 1930s, and that short-run deviations from this fixed long-run value appear to have been due to the inability of institutions to immediately adjust the number of faculty to changes in enrollments (Freeman, 1971, Chapter 9). In this context, most institutions could probably estimate a simple trend relationship between enrollment and faculty size in order to forecast their total faculty size in the forecast period.

Hence, the institution can estimate both the direct effects of personnel policies and the indirect effects of policies related to enrollment on faculty size and composition. The basic model for this task consists of a faculty flow model, the enrollment-forecasting model of Equations (2)–(4), and an equation or equations that explain either faculty size or the faculty-student ratio as a function of enrollments (see Hoenack and Weiler, 1977). Of special interest is the use of this approach to informing policymakers about the degree of potential control they have over the size and composition of their faculty without resorting to personnel policies that can create fear and uncertainty in the faculty. For example, Hoenack and Weiler (1977) found that a cost-related tuition policy would produce a larger faculty size, more new hires, and a lower fraction of tenured faculty for the University of Minnesota than policies reducing the probability of achieving tenure or encouraging additional early retirements.

Matriculation Decisions and Policy
in Selective Private Institutions

Private institutions, especially those modified by the adjective *selective*, face a somewhat different sort of problem when dealing with enrollments from that of the public schools we have discussed above. In particular, administrators in a private institution must decide which applicants to admit and how to encourage the ones they admit to subsequently enroll in their school. It is this latter problem of matriculation that most closely corresponds to the enrollment demand analyses with which we are concerned and on which we will concentrate here under the assumption that the institution has enough applicants with each set of desirable characteristics—ability, sex, race, family income, and so on—so that policymakers can choose among the applicants. If the school also wishes to attract more applicants with particular characteristics, it must also study the potential students' application process, a separate topic not addressed here. An econometric analysis of application decisions is presented in Manski and Wise (1983).

To influence the proportion of accepted students with a given set of characteristics that eventually enrolls, a proportion often called the yield, the institution can offer financial aid from its own funds to augment any financial aid the student may receive from noninstitutional sources, particularly, of course, the federal government. It is this substantial ability to change the attendance costs for individual students, which the institution determines simultaneously with its admissions decisions, that makes the modeling of the matriculation decision different from the modeling of enrollment demand, although it is the student who makes the eventual decision to enroll in both instances. Most public institutions, of course, offer scholarships from their own funds, but the proportion of students aided is much smaller in the typical public institution as opposed to the typical private institution.

As part of its analysis of policy issues, then, a private institution needs to estimate its yield from pools of admitted applicants with various characteristics. Just as with demand, the student bases his or her matriculation on the human capital model. Hence, the same variables that appear in Equation (1) would appear in the usual matriculation equation. It is also clear by the basic nature of the results it wants to estimate that the school needs to use a cross-sectional data-sample of individuals in this task. In that case, the variables in Equation (1) that vary only over a cross-sectional sample need to be included in the estimated equation. Given the degree of competition among private schools for many students, it is especially important in this regard to include variables that describe the other schools to which the student has applied, especially the financial aid the student would obtain if he or she attended the other schools.

The probability, F, that a given student will eventually enroll in the institution can be symbolically written as

$$F = f(AUS, AOTHER, X)$$ (8)

where AUS is the cost of attending the institution under study, $AOTHER$ is a vector of costs of attending other institutions, and X is a vector of the student's characteristics. We could estimate this equation for all applicants or estimate separate equations for applicants having particular characteristics. It is also the case that in practice, the variables in $AOTHER$ are usually restricted to those for only one of the other institutions to which the student applied, simply because this type of information is difficult to obtain. Good examples of the specification and estimation of yield equations for a single institution can be found in Ehrenberg and Sherman (1984).

The most obvious way that these estimated equations can be used by policymakers is in decisions on how to award financial aid. If we assume AUS is the difference between the institution's posted tuition and the student's financial aid, then reducing AUS through increasing financial aid will increase the probability that the student will attend. An institution with substantial resources to devote to financial aid could therefore use these equations to produce both a level and a socioeconomic composition of enrollment to its liking.

However, in reality, most private institutions have limits on financial aid budgets, categories of students they value more than others, and limits on how many undergraduate students they can accommodate. It is more likely, then, that a private institution will use these estimated equations as part of a larger model in which it attempts to achieve the best configuration of enrollments subject to these limits.

This is a classic example of a situation in which the institution wants to optimize (in this case, maximize) goals related to the types of students it wishes to enroll subject to the resources it has to achieve these goals. Specification of this kind of model requires that we derive functional relationships for both the goals, or what is called an objective function, and the constraints, as well as that we specify the variables under the institution's control that appear in these relationships. Hopkins and Massy (1981, especially Chapter 9) describe this type of model in very general terms. They argue that the most difficult aspects of this exercise are to specify the objective function and to determine the functional forms and values of the fixed parameters (what would be coefficients in a regression equation) in the constraints. They note that an option to trying to specify the exact objective function is to provide several outcomes that satisfy the constraints and to have policymakers choose the most preferred. Even better, they suggest, would be to design an interactive computer program that somehow "leads" the policymaker from his or her current solution to a more preferred solution. However, as they point out, such a program is difficult to write, but more importantly, it is often *very* difficult to make the individual decision maker sit down at a computer terminal and actually go through the exercise.

Specific examples of optimization models developed for use in individual private institutions that incorporate yield equations like Equation (8) in their constraints are discussed by Ehrenberg and Sherman (1984) and by Elliot (1980). Ehrenberg and Sherman assume that the policy objective is to maximize the quality of the enrolled student body subject to a constraint that limits the total amount of financial aid to the sum of tuition revenue plus revenue available from other sources less instructional costs, the estimated yield equations, and equations that estimate the average quality of each category of applicants as functions of the number of applicants in that category who eventually enroll. They point out that an analyst could also maximize this same objective function subject to the yield equations, the quality equations, a constraint that total enrollment not exceed a specified capacity, and the same constraint on the institution's financial aid. In general, however, the solution to the two problems would not be the same, although they would be if the optimal enrollment were below the capacity limit. This example shows that it is important for policymakers to carefully spell out the constraints under which they are operating as well as the objective they wish to maximize or minimize.

Of course, it is also true that the optimal solution will also differ if the objective function changes. Elliot (1980), for example, specifies a model in which the objective is to maximize the difference between the institution's tuition revenue and its financial aid expenditures subject to yield equations, a constraint on the total amount of financial aid available, and a constraint limiting the financial aid awarded to each student. Note that in this model, the objective function is just that: objective. It does not include any variables that reflect the values of the policymakers such as the quality weights attached to each category of applicants in the Ehrenberg and Sherman model. Thus, it may not reflect actual policymaking, or more to the point, the optimal solution may not be accepted by policymakers.

In addition to these specific examples of optimization models that incorporate objectives and constraints strictly related to enrollment and student characteristics, we can envision such models on a much larger scale for private institutions. This scale expands in two directions. First, we can significantly expand the number of institutionally controllable variables beyond financial aid to include faculty size and characteristics, endowment and the management of it, and other financial and staffing variables. Second, we can extend the model to incorporate time so that decisions now affect the future. Hence, the objective function includes variables for several time periods, and the optimal solution is a set of yearly results that maximizes this function. In general, this optimal solution is not the same as the one that would be obtained if each year's optimal solution were generated separately without consideration of past or future periods. These models will still include some type of yield equations among their fundamental constraints. The interested reader should consult Hopkins and Massy (1981), certainly the most comprehensive and best written book on the topic of planning models for higher education institutions.

While this section focuses on the use of optimization models for private schools and the use of yield equations in them, it should also be observed that public institutions can utilize optimization models that incorporate enrollment demand functions. Probably the best example of this approach applied to a single institution is discussed by Hoenack (1971). He estimates separate enrollment-demand equations for different groups of students stratified by family income and incorporates them as constraints in an optimization model that has some function of enrollment—for example, total enrollment or equal enrollment in each income category—as its objective function. The variable controlled by the institution is tuition, and in addition to the enrollment demand equations, there is a constraint that essentially provides an upper limit on the difference between total instructional costs and the tuition revenue that the institution must collect. While this might not appear at first glance to be a useful analysis because institutions are unlikely to vary tuition by the income of the student, its relevance becomes clearer if we replace the idea of tuition with the student's attendance costs net of financial aid. In that context the model can inform policymakers how need-based financial aid can be distributed to optimize objectives related to the size and socioeconomic composition of the student body.

Institutional Closure

In the current era of budget retrenchments and an expected continuation of enrollment declines fueled by declining numbers of high school graduates, there has been some consideration of closure of institutions. An essential part of the analysis of this issue is estimating the enrollment effects, that is, the estimation of the alternative attendance choices of those students who would otherwise have attended the closed institution(s). This analysis, of course, is of particular interest to regional or state policymakers, but institutional closure also has obvious impacts on the individual institutions that might get most of the affected students. Another important issue is the extent to which the affected students would not attend—or in the vernacular, would be "denied access"—as a result of the closure. All of these issues can be investigated using estimated enrollment equations (see Weiler and Wilson, 1984, and Weiler, 1986).

The basic way we can use enrollment demand equations to estimate the impacts of closing an institution is by assuming that closing an institution is equivalent to increasing the costs of attending it to the point where no one attends. To illustrate, consider a "system" of two institutions so that potential students have the choice of attending Institution 1 or Institution 2 or not attending. Ignoring for a moment all of the variables that influence students' attendance choice except the costs of attending the two institutions, we can write enrollment demand equations for them as

$$E_1 = a_1 T_1 + a_2 T_2$$
$$E_2 = b_1 T_1 + b_2 T_2$$

where E_1 and E_2 are enrollments and T_1 and T_2 are attendance costs at Institutions 1 and 2, respectively, and the a's and b's are estimated coefficients. We expect a_1 and b_2 to be negative and a_2 and b_1 to be positive; that is, we expect an increase in the costs of attending Institution 1 to reduce attendance at 1 and to increase attendance at Institution 2 and conversely for an increase in the costs of attending 2. Note also that we expect enrollment at 2 to increase by no more than the decrease at 1 as a result of the increase in the cost of attending 1. Hence, we assume that b_1 is no larger than a_1 in absolute value, and similarly for a_2 and b_2.

Now suppose Institution 1 is closed. Under our assumption that this closure is equivalent to raising T_1 to a value T_1^* so that $E_1^* = 0$, the value T_1^* is defined by the relation

$$E_1 = a_1(T_1 - T_1^*) \tag{9}$$

This equation follows from the analysis we used to obtain Equation (5) in our discussion of the effect of tuition policy; the only difference is that what we called the new enrollment there is zero here.

We can solve for the effect that this hypothesized change in the costs of attending Institution 1 has on enrollment at Institution 2 analogously:

$$E_2 - E_2^* = b_1(T_1 - T_1^*) \tag{10}$$

If we now solve Equation (9) for $T_1 - T_1^*$, substitute the solution in Equation (10), and rearrange the terms, we get

$$E_2^* = E_2 - (b_1/a_1)E_1 \tag{11}$$

Equation (11) shows that the new enrollment at Institution 2 is the enrollment at 2 before the closure plus a fraction of the enrollment that otherwise would have been at Institution 1. This fraction is the ratio of the effect of a one-dollar change in T_1 on attendance at 2 to the effect of the same cost change on attendance at 1. E_2^* is larger than E_2 because b_1 and a_1 have opposite signs. Further, the ratio of these coefficients is bounded by -1 based on the discussion above, so that only a fraction of the affected students attend 2, and since the only other attendance option in this simple example is nonattendance, those who do not alternatively attend Institution 2 when 1 is closed will not attend.

There are two important points about this example that carry over to the general case of more than two institutions. First, we had estimated enrollment demand equations for two of the three assumed attendance options. In the general case with n attendance options, we must have equations for $n-1$ of them; normally, of course, these will be for the schooling options. Second, attendance costs at the closed school had to be included as a variable in both of the equations. The extension to the general case is the same; this variable has to appear in each of the $n-1$ equations. More precisely, it has to appear in equations that represent the enrollment demand for schools that students regard as significant alternatives to the closed school. It is obviously possible that some schools in, for example, a large state will not attract significant numbers of new students when another institution is closed. These points, along with other issues regarding the specification and estimation of the enrollment demand equations in this context, are discussed in Weiler and Wilson (1984).

The example given implicitly assumes estimation with grouped data, either time-series or cross-sectional. However, we previously observed that attendance costs at different institutions are likely to be highly correlated in a time series sample and that the separate effects of each of these cost variables may not be estimable in an enrollment demand equation. Hence, given the crucial role the estimated coefficients play in this use of enrollment demand equations, it may be best to use cross-sectional data. In that case, proximity costs, but not out-of-pocket costs, will vary across the sample. This may even be an advantage in that it is precisely the proximity costs that change when an institution is closed.

Another question is whether individual cross-sectional data can be used in this type of analysis. They can, but with some reservations regarding interpretation of the estimate coefficients and the method used to estimate the equations. These are rather technical issues; see Weiler and Wilson (1984) for a discussion of the interpretation questions and Weiler (1986) for a discussion of the estimation methods.

Hoenack and Roemer (1981) present the results of applying this technique to the hypothetical closure of some institutions. Their analysis also includes the resulting effects on a state's costs of providing higher education, including the costs of providing access to the affected students who would otherwise not attend if an institution were closed; these access costs were also estimated using the estimated enrollment demand equations. Of particular interest is the fact that they found that the net savings to the state were substantially less than the expenditures at the closed institution.

The final issue regarding this analysis of the enrollment effects of institutional closure is whether alternative estimation methods could be used, especially less complex ones. One alternative is simply to ask students now attending an institution what they would do if the institution were closed. While I know of no published work in this area, my perception is that such a survey would cause unnecessary consternation on the part of the surveyed students. Further, the students' answers to the hypothetical question would probably not reflect their actual behavior if they were truly faced with the choice. Students at my institution are surveyed periodically about what they would do in response to tuition increases, and the proportion saying that they would no longer be able to attend is invariably larger than estimated tuition elasticities based on their actual behavior would suggest. In addition a survey on the expected post-high-school plans of most of the high school juniors in Minnesota done about 10 years ago revealed that about half of the respondents did not subsequently choose the option they selected as juniors.

A second alternative would be to assume that students would redistribute themselves among the remaining institutions in proportion to total enrollments in the remaining institutions (with or without assuming nonattendance as an option). However, a method based on the actual behavior of students is likely to produce better results than this alternative as well. For the assumed redistribution to actually occur, it is necessary that the second choices of those attending the closed institution be distributed identically to the first choices of those who chose other options. This is unlikely because the characteristics of the students attending the closed school, including their proximity to the remaining schools, are not likely to be identical to the characteristics of the students who chose the other options before the institution was closed. Using enrollment demand analysis explicitly considers relative substitutability because the resulting coefficient estimates reflect actual attendance choices when students were faced with all of the alternatives, including the closed school.

CONCLUSION

While there is an extensive literature on enrollment demand analysis, very little of it addresses issues at the level of the individual institution. The basic purpose of this chapter is to illustrate the usefulness of enrollment demand studies, estimated for a single institution, in policy deliberations within the institution. Of course, this is not equivalent to saying that more broad-based studies are inevitably irrelevant or ineffective in this regard. It is just that studies of individual schools have substantial advantages, especially with regard to policy choices that involve specific variables controlled by the institution.

There are two different types of problems that must be addressed in using enrollment demand analyses in this manner. First, there are issues of model specification and interpretation that are different from those faced in analyses that use national data. Nearly all of these issues follow from the fact that the analyst must take into account the choice of students to attend a specific institution when close substitutes are available. This changes the variables that should be included as part of the analysis, the interpretation of the effects of some of these variables, and the expected signs and magnitudes of these effects relative to expectations when analyzing just "go-no go" decisions. The first major section of the chapter is concerned with these problems.

The second problem is to show how the estimated enrollment-demand equations can be part of the policy analyses undertaken at an institution. Some uses of the equations, such as for enrollment forecasting, are obvious. In those situations, it is important to consider both how the equations can be used and why their use is an improvement over alternative approaches. In other cases, such as budget determination and forecasting at a public institution, the complexity of the analysis is of greater concern; that is, the question of "how" is of more importance than the question of "why." Both types of policy uses were discussed in the second major section of the chapter, which, I suspect is of more interest to most readers of this volume. However, the level of confidence that can be placed in the results that are estimated to follow from the specific policy choices is only as high as the quality of the analyses that are used to produce the estimates.

Acknowledgments. This is a revised and expanded version of an earlier publication (Weiler, 1984). I wish to thank Colleen Davidson for comments on earlier drafts.

REFERENCES

Alexander, E. R., and Frey, D. E. (1984). An econometric estimate of the demand for MBA enrollment. *Economics of Education Review* 3: 97–104.

Bean, J. P. (1982). Student attrition, intentions, and confidence: Interactive effects in a path model. *Research in Higher Education* 17:291–320.

Becker, G. S. (1962). Investment in human capital: A theoretical analysis. *Journal of Political Economy* 70(Part 2):9–45.

Berg, D. J., and Hoenack, S. A. (1987). The concept of cost-related tuition and its implementation at the University of Minnesota. *Journal of Higher Education* 58 (May/June), in press.

Bleau, B. L., (1985). Faculty contract configurations: Probable impact. *Research in Higher Education* 23:293–306.

Brinkman, P. T. (1985). The financial impact of part-time enrollments on two-year colleges: A marginal cost perspective. *Journal of Higher Education* 56:338–353.

Ehrenberg, R. G., and Sherman, D. R. (1984). Optimal financial aid policies for a selective university. *Journal of Human Resources* 19:202–230.

Elliot, W. F. (1980). Financial aid decisions and implications of market management. In J. B. Henry (ed.), *The Impact of Student Financial Aid on Institutions*. New Directions for Institutional Research, No. 25. San Francisco: Jossey-Bass.

Freeman, R. B. (1971). *The Market for College Trained Manpower*. Cambridge: Harvard University Press.

Freeman, R. B. (1976). *The Overeducated American*. New York: Academic Press.

Fuller, W. C., Manski, C. F., and Wise, D. A. (1982). New evidence on the economic determinants of postsecondary schooling choices." *Journal of Human Resources* 17:477–498.

Gilmour, J. E., Jr., and Suttle, J. L. (1984). The politics and practicalities of pricing in academe. In L. H. Litten (ed.), *Issues in Pricing Undergraduate Education*. New Directions for Institutional Research, No. 42. San Francisco: Jossey-Bass.

Hearn, J. C., and Heydinger, R. B. (1985). Scanning the university's external environment. *Journal of Higher Education* 56:419–445.

Hoenack, S. A. (1971). The efficient allocation of subsidies to college students. *American Economic Review* 61:302–311.

Hoenack, S. A., and Pierro, D. J. (1986). *An Econometric Model of a Public University's Income and Enrollments*. Minneapolis: Management Information Division, University of Minnesota.

Hoenack, S. A., and Roemer, J. K. (1981). Evaluating campus closings in the 1980's: A case application of an optimization model. *Research in Higher Education* 15:49–68.

Hoenack, S. A., and Weiler, W. C. (1975). Cost-related tuition policies and university enrollments. *Journal of Human Resources* 10:332–360.

Hoenack, S. A., and Weiler, W. C. (1977). A comparison of the effects of personnel and enrollment policies on the size and composition of a university's faculty. *Journal of Higher Education* 48:432–452.

Hoenack, S. A., and Weiler, W. C. (1979). The demand for higher education and institutional enrollment forecasting. *Economic Inquiry* 17:89–113.

Hoenack, S. A., Weiler, W. C., Goodman, R. D., and Pierro, D. J. (1986). The marginal costs of instruction. *Research in Higher Education* 24:335–418.

Hopkins, D. S. P., and Massy, W. F. (1981). *Planning Models for Colleges and Universities*. Stanford, CA: Stanford University Press.

Hyde, W. D., Jr. (1978). *The Effect of Tuition and Financial Aid on Access and Choice in Postsecondary Education*. Denver: Education Commission of the States.

Jackson, G. A., and Weathersby, G. B. (1975). Individual demand for higher education: A review and analysis of recent empirical studies. *Journal of Higher Education* 46:623–652.

Leslie, L. L., and Brinkman, P. (1986). Rates of return to higher education. In J. C. Smart (ed.), *Higher Education: Handbook of Theory and Research*, Vol. II, pp. 207–234. New York: Agathon Press.

Maddala, G. S. (1983). *Limited-Dependent and Quantitative Variables in Econometrics*. New York: Cambridge University Press.

Manski, C. F., and Wise, D. A. (1983). *College Choice in America*. Cambridge: Harvard University Press.

McClain, D., Vance, B., and Wood, E. (1984). Understanding and predicting the yield in the MBA admissions process. *Research in Higher Education* 20:55–76.

Ostheimer, R. H. (1953). *Student Charges and Financing Higher Education.* New York: Columbia University Press.

Pascarella, E. T., and Chapman, D. W. (1983). Validation of a theoretical model of college withdrawal: Interactive effects in a multi-institutional sample. *Research in Higher Education* 19:25–48.

Pascarella, E. T., Terenzini, P. T., and Wolfe, L. M. (1986). Orientation to college and freshman year persistence/withdrawal decisions. *Journal of Higher Education* 57:155–175.

Pindyck, R. S., and Rubinfeld, D. L. (1981). *Econometric Models and Economic Forecasts* (2nd ed). New York: McGraw-Hill.

Punj, G. N., and Staelin, R. (1978). The choice process for graduate business schools. *Journal of Marketing Research* 15:588–598.

Schultz, T. W. (1963). *The Economic Value of Education.* New York: Columbia University Press.

Schwartz, J. B. (1985). Student financial aid and the college enrollment decision: The effects of public and private grants and interest subsidies. *Economics of Education Review* 4:129–144.

Weiler, W. C. (1984). Using enrollment demand models in institutional pricing decisions. In L. H. Litten (ed.), *Issues in Pricing Undergraduate Education.* New Directions for Institutional Research, No. 42. San Francisco: Jossey-Bass.

Weiler, W. C. (1986). A sequential logit model of the access effects of higher education institutions. *Economics of Education Review* 5:49–55.

Weiler, W. C., and Wilson, F. S. (1984). Prediction of the enrollment effects of institutional closure. *Research in Higher Education* 20:23–33.

Weinschrott, D. (1977). *Demand for Higher Education in the United States: A Critical Review of the Empirical Literature.* Santa Monica, CA: Rand Corporation.

Wing, P. (1974). *Higher Education Enrollment Forecasting: A Manual for State-Level Agencies.* Boulder, CO: National Center for Higher Education Management Systems.

State Regulation and Campus Autonomy

J. Fredericks Volkwein
University at Albany
State University of New York

At a time when decentralized management is gaining favor in the business world, many public institutions of higher education and state governments are examining the wisdom of current oversight practices. To what extent should organizational authority be decentralized, and what are the appropriate mechanisms of accountability and control? These questions have become important issues in the 1980s and are under active review by corporations, governments, and multicampus systems alike. This chapter examines the dimensions of government regulation and summarizes what we know about current state practices across the country. Finally, some areas for further research are outlined.

Contemporary organizational theory stresses the important role of the organization's environment. Contingency theory (Lawrence and Lorsch, 1967), the natural selection model (Aldrich, 1979), and the resource dependence model (Pfeffer and Salancik, 1978) focus on the external environment as a crucial influence on the life of an organization, its structure, and its activities. If public universities are viewed as complex, loosely coupled organizations, their regulatory relationships with state governments form a critical component of the external climate within which these institutions pursue their goals.

It is possible, of course, to identify different dimensions of state regulation. Berdahl (1971) drew a distinction between procedural and substantive autonomy: *Procedural* controls dealing largely with administrative accountability do not have much impact on academic or *substantive* matters. However, more recent writers have raised the possibility that the cumulative effects of procedural accountability and regulatory practices have shifted effective authority beyond the campus for many substantive matters as well (Glenny and Bowen, 1977). "Priorities are shifted as faculty and administrators spend more time on paperwork than on academic planning" (Carnegie Foundation, 1982, p. 66). By requiring state approval for purchases of research equipment, out-of-state travel, salary adjustments, and the like, state officials intrude into academic decision-making. Freedom from controls is not limited to universities with constitutional autonomy. Some universities with statutory status report being relatively free of constrictive state controls, and others with constitutional autonomy find themselves being treated like state agencies (Glenny and Dalglish, 1973; Volkwein, 1986c).

The Carnegie Foundation (1982) and Levy (1980) are among those who have identified three important areas of university autonomy: financial or budgetary, personnel or appointive, and academic. *Academic autonomy* refers to a university's ability to chart its own mission, to offer academic programs compatible with its mission, to control the instructional and research activities of the campus, and to set its own standards for admission and degree requirements. *Financial flexibility* is possessed by universities which control the preparation and allocation of their budgets, and which are relatively free to manage revenues and expenditures with few external restrictions beyond those associated with postaudit accountability. *Appointive powers* govern such activities as the hiring and promotion of personnel and their conditions of employment. State personnel controls typically restrict the number and type of employees, as well as the salaries they may receive.

THE CLIMATE OF REGULATION

A variety of factors have led to the climate of regulation which exists in many states today. The rapid growth in the number of colleges and students in the 1950s, 1960s, and 1970s has been well documented in the literature, including various Carnegie reports. The number of students in public colleges and universities has increased almost tenfold since 1950, and financial support from taxpayers has grown at an even greater rate, even after adjusting for inflation. Such a rapidly increasing investment in higher education has inevitably attracted public attention.

The governance structure of higher education has increased in both size and complexity. The need for greater coordination, particularly at the state level, has spawned a number of multicampus systems, consolidated governing boards, and coordinating bodies. Before World War II, very few states had coordinating bodies, whereas by 1960, twenty-three states had formal coordinating agencies for higher education, and by 1980 all fifty states, several territories, and the District of Columbia had some formal structure: a consolidated governing board, a coordinating board, or a planning agency (Hines and Hartmark, 1980). These bodies fill the need in each state to engage in some form of planning, to formulate or review campus budgets, and, more recently, to undertake academic program reviews.

During this same period (after 1950), another development occurred throughout government in general. An emphasis on sound management practices caused the public sector in some areas to embrace PPBS and to apply systems theory and "generally accepted accounting principles" to the management of state agencies, including public higher education. Governors and legislators became self-conscious about the need for efficiency and accountability in government, and they hired analysts and other professional staff to oversee higher education and other operations which receive the benefits of public financing. State fiscal audits were expanded to include review of institutional and administrative performance. Since expertise was needed, many of the people filling these positions came from universities, from system offices, and from state coordinating agencies. With such backgrounds, they were unlikely to view campuses as untouchable.

If institutions of higher education lost their "mystique" in the eyes of state officials during these years, campuses certainly lost the confidence of the average taxpayer during the late 1960s when television news broadcasts brought scenes of unruly, unkempt, and ungrateful college students into American homes. Campus protest against the Vietnam War and government policy was followed by some public discontent with higher education, which was sometimes reflected in legislative enactments.

Beginning about 1972, state budgets began to suffer from the twin effects of inflation and recession. State funds for higher education began to be accompanied by regulations aimed at cost containment, and state governments introduced controls to keep expenditures in line with revenues.

In addition, states like West Virginia appear to have implemented control practices in response to incidents of scandal involving misuse of public funds. Once introduced, control practices tend to become embedded in the bureaucracy even though the particular conditions which led to their creation were highly localized or have changed entirely. "Government officials have a tendency to generalize policy from isolated 'worst cases,' and then impose that cautious standard on all" (Carnegie Foundation, 1982, p. 65).

These events and trends, of course, did not have consistent impacts across all the states. Many public colleges and universities operate with relative autonomy, while others experience substantial executive and legislative oversight (Volkwein, 1984). Some campus leaders have considerable academic and financial discretion, while others are treated like managers of a local branch bank.

Whatever the reason for the growth, there is an overwhelming consensus that the degree and scope of regulation have increased in a good many states and that this regulation is both costly and unproductive.

The Carnegie Commission on Higher Education, in its 1973 report titled *Governance of Higher Education*, concluded that campus autonomy had declined substantially since the end of World War II. The commission presented an analysis of and recommendations for the proper distribution of authority between public control and institutional autonomy. Recognizing the legitimate interests of both state government and academic governance, the Carnegie analysis recommended a balance of authority between campus and state in academic and intellectual affairs, in financial and business affairs, and in governance.

In a 1975 study sponsored by the American Association of State Colleges and Universities, almost two out of three presidents reported an increase in external administrative control practices in the previous five years (Harcleroad, 1975).

In 1976, the Carnegie Foundation for the Advancement of Teaching published a report entitled *The States and Higher Education*, which identified five major concerns; two of them were the increasingly centralized control of public higher education and the erosion of campus autonomy. In arguing for institutional independence from "centralizers and regulators," the Carnegie report made the undocumented claim that the states which allowed their public universities the greatest freedom were the ones with the strongest universities.

An important study of state budgeting was conducted in the mid-1970s by L. Glenny and the Center for Research and Development in Higher Education at the University of California, Berkeley (Glenny, 1976). Glenny reviewed the budget formulation practices in seventeen states and reported that extensive and complex, even redundant, budget reviews tended to occur in the larger industrial states, which are characterized by strong governors, effective, well-staffed legislatures, and regulatory coordinating agencies.

The Sloan Commission on Government and Higher Education (1980) urged state governments to protect institutional autonomy in academic affairs, personnel matters, and planning decisions. The commission also was critical of the regulatory and reporting burdens imposed by state procedures dealing with central purchasing, financial audits, personnel administration, and control of campus-generated funds, among others.

In its final report, the Carnegie Council on Policy Studies (1980) concluded with a checklist of "imperatives" which urged federal and state governments to avoid excessive regulation and other encroachments on campus autonomy, including preaudit of expenditures, unnecessary reporting requirements, and infringements on admissions policies (pp. 131–133).

The 1982 study by the Carnegie Foundation surveyed decision-making practices in each state, pointed out the limitations of government regulation of higher education, and defended campus self-regulation. Using the strongest language of the various reports, the foundation reported that state officials "Often fail to reward efficient leaders" (p. 43), and that campus managers "feel caught in a confusing bureaucratic web that demands accountability, but provides few incentives for responsible decision making" (p. 67). Organizational behaviorists believe that an increase in monitoring activity increases operating costs, both for those doing the monitoring and for those being monitored (Downs, 1967). "An ambitious range of bureaucratic oversight generates a workload that government itself cannot handle." (Carnegie Foundation, 1982, p. 66).

In a study of state government coordination of higher education in twenty-five states, John Millett and his associates (1984) found that while "the reconciliation of public control with institutional autonomy is not a simple problem," institutional independence in many states is "under substantial threat" (Millett, 1984). After analyzing the situation within each state and looking especially at the roles of statewide governing, coordinating, and advisory boards, Millett concludes that "State government departments of administration, governor's offices, state legislatures, and state legislative agencies were far more evident as enemies of institutional independence than were coordinating boards" (ibid., p. 233).

A variety of indicators reflect the increased public control which states have exerted in recent years. If the volume of legislative enactments can be used as a crude indicator, state governments have grown enormously in the statutory authority which they exercise. In the past three decades, state legislative enactments have increased from roughly 15,000 to 50,000 annually. While the number of these bills affecting higher education is unknown, Fisher (1986), in a study of postsecondary laws passed during this century in four representative states, found that nearly half of the higher education laws had been enacted in the most recent two decades. Of the laws passed in the most recent decade, 124 were classified as "control laws," compared to 82 "flexibility laws." However, she also found that the number of flexibility laws had grown proportionately, and that the ratio of control to flexibility had not changed significantly over the eight-decade study.

An indirect measure of bureaucratic, if not regulatory, growth is apparent in the size of the state work force. According to figures available from the U.S. Census Bureau, the number of state employees had grown from about one million in 1952 to over three million in 1982. The number of state government workers per 10,000 of population had increased from about 50 to 130 in the same period.

In some states, a consulting contract or the purchase of a computer, for example, may undergo multiple approvals by system administrators, by state auditors, by the attorney general's office, by the department of general services, and by the governor's budget staff. The State University's Independent Commission in New York (1985) cited numerous examples of frustrating and costly delays of routine purchases and repairs which were produced by the "archaic public policy" in that state (pp. 32–38).

In more than a few states, an annual budget request may receive redundant scrutiny by a statewide coordinating board, legislative committees, and executive staff, after it leaves the central system offices. In addition, there are now a myriad of other reporting and oversight mechanisms associated with specific issues such as affirmative action, energy policy, research involving human subjects and warm-blooded animals, radiation safety, student financial aid, and privacy rights, among others. "Taken by itself, any single action may not be unbearably intrusive, but the combined impact of many actions can nearly suffocate an institution" (Carnegie Foundation, 1982, p. 65).

Budgetary and personnel issues appear to lie at the heart of the debate in most states, but the struggle goes beyond financial and bureaucratic matters. There are in higher education deeply held convictions about autonomy and effectiveness: "Most of us believe that the great colleges and universities have been those that were the least managed'' (Atwell, 1985). Such views are widespread on college campuses but are probably less prevalent among those occupying positions in state offices across the nation, thus forming the basis for a conflict rooted in differing values.

Of course, there is the danger that some of the claims for flexibility may be exaggerated. Most writers in the field would agree with Millett that "Campus autonomy in an absolute sense is an unreasonable expectation" (1984, p. xiv). Every campus has a natural interest in reducing external constraints, and every state has a natural interest in ensuring an appropriate level of efficiency and effectiveness from recipients of state revenues. The challenge is to find the right balance between these competing interests.

Of the many kinds of controls imposed by the state, the postaudit of funds is perhaps the most justifiable, for it is an essential responsibility of the state to determine that the funds it has appropriated have been properly expended. But at what points do state oversight practices become unnecessarily restrictive, if not destructive? Which managerial constraints dampen motivation and initiative, rather than encourage efficiency? Many business organizations advertise the greater customer service and profitability which results from managers who have "local authority," but there is no equivalent performance measure in higher education. Increasing attention is being given to the identification of incentives and disincentives for effective management in higher education (Mingle, 1983; Hyatt and Santiago, 1984). "States are faced with this choice: they can try to force productivity improvements through regulation and control, or they can try to encourage efficiency by providing incentives and delegating authority and responsibility to institutional officers and board members" (Mingle, 1983).

Based on their study of the changing relationships between the State of Washington and its public institutions of higher education, Curry and Fischer (1986) developed a conceptual framework for describing the alternative relationships between campus and state. They identified four models: the *state agency model*, the *state-controlled model*, the *state-aided model*, and the *corporate model*. These four models lie along a continuum from almost complete state control over financial and personnel transactions to almost complete independence.

Under the Curry and Fischer description, the state agency model is a university which is treated as a branch of state government. All revenues are deposited in the state treasury and are subject to appropriation control. Student tuition and fees are usually prescribed by the legislature, and allotment is often specified by both function and object of expenditure. Under this model, prior approval must normally be obtained (in the form of a preaudit) for most purchasing and personnel transactions, and unexpended appropriations are returned to the state general fund at the end of the fiscal year. In short, oversight is directed at process, with little consideration given to effectiveness.

The state-controlled model has many of the same features but is not quite so extreme. While appropriations and expenditures are still managed by the state, the appropriations are not as detailed nor the expenditures as tightly controlled as under the state agency model. State appropriations are likely to be on the basis of a funding or enrollment formula, and many of the revenues generated locally are retained and managed by the campus.

Under the state-aided model, the state grants funds to the university which the institution is generally free to spend within certain guidelines. Budget requests are keyed to base appropriations and contain less expenditure detail. A greater proportional emphasis on plans and objectives is reflected in the requests. Generalized formulas are used to ensure stability of funding, and consideration is given to special-purpose requests. Tuition and fees and other student fees and charges for services are usually set by institutional governing boards. All funds raised by the institution are retained locally and are not subject to state controls. Fiduciary accountability for state tax funds appropriated is accomplished through periodic postaudits. Local fund balances, including revenues from tuition and fees, normally carry forward at the end of the fiscal year and do not affect the extent of state appropriations. In addition, limited carryover of state funds is sometimes allowed.

In the Curry and Fischer conceptualization, the corporate model features total institutional control of all revenues, as well as of all matters of personnel and payroll. Using a third-party board or agency, the state contracts with institutions for particular services, including a designated number of student spaces in particular kinds of institutions, but the state assumes no responsibility for program or finances. Access is ensured through substantial state student financial aid funding, and accountability provisions focus on effectiveness rather than on process.

Most campuses lie somewhere in between the two extremes. The corporate model, in particular, is a pure type which rarely exists outside of independent universities and colleges. Curry and Fischer also provide a checklist to be used as a tool for developing a description of the campus/state relationship. The checklist descriptors cover such areas as the nature of the budget process, transfer of funds, disposition of year-end balances, expenditure oversight practices, methods of accountability, requirements for reporting and record keeping, pricing policies for tuition and fees, control of revenue funds, the nature of salary and personnel controls, the control of admissions policies and enrollment levels, and finally, the approval/review/elimination of academic programs.

A similar conceptualization exists in the community college literature. Garms (1977) analyzed the arrangements in thirty-six states for financing community colleges and proposed a series of models ranging from private free markets to centralized planned economies. Between these extremes, he described a variety of decentralized and mixed models. Most states had mixed patterns, and very few states exhibited a pure form of any one model. The Garms models, although more numerous, are to some extent congruent with the Curry and Fischer models. However, Garms placed more emphasis on the source of funds as the primary criterion for classifying states and their community colleges and gave less attention to the regulatory strings that might be attached to the funds.

Another useful systems model has been proposed by Crossen (1984), based upon her study of the state policy-making process in the state of Pennsylvania. Her input-process-output model, shown in Figure 1, summarizes the complex interactions which take place at the state level among key components of the educational and political system: the governor and executive agencies, the legislature and various interest groups, and the campuses and statewide governing and coordinating bodies. Recognizing that regulatory practices in each state are a policy outcome, the model provides a conceptual map for analyzing the policy process.

REGULATORY PRACTICES

In a national study of state financial and personnel control practices in higher education, Volkwein (1984, 1986a) gathered data on a variety of academic, financial, and personnel transactions. Developing measures for each of the three types of university autonomy discussed by Levy (1980) and by the Carnegie Foundation (1982), Volkwein collected data from public, doctoral-granting universities in forty-nine states and constructed separate scales for each of the three types of regulation. His survey and data collection, by happenstance, included information about almost all the items contained in the Curry and Fischer checklist. At any rate, he ranked states along a continuum of practices ranging from states which retain a great deal of control and authority in these matters to states within which universities have a great deal of flexibility.

The Carnegie survey reported the perceived locus of "effective authority" for various academic, personnel, and financial decisions in each state. Volkwein used the Carnegie data for academic decisions in "flagship institutions" to form a scale measuring academic regulation (1986c). Table 1 shows the number and percentage of states for which "effective authority" lies beyond the campus in the six academic areas. In about one-third of the states, the effective authority to add new graduate or undergraduate programs rests with state officials. Only seven or fewer states effectively involve state officials in defining campus mission and reviewing or discontinuing programs and departments.

Financial and personnel regulation are measured by a set of questions derived from the Volkwein survey of states and campuses (1985, 1986a, 1986c). These questions gathered information about the nature of the budget allocation and expenditure process, the management of tuition and other revenues, the disposition of year-end balances, the employee appointment and payroll process, the management of both positions and funds, and the existence of position classifications and salary schedules. While survey information was obtained

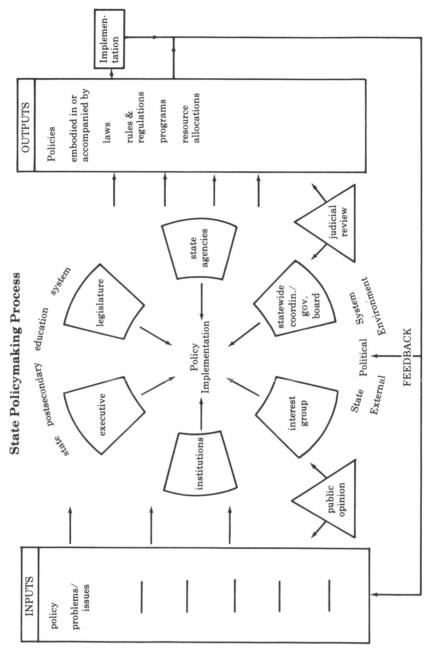

State Policymaking Process

INPUTS

policy problems/ issues

state postsecondary education system

executive

legislature

state agencies

institutions

interest group

statewide coordin./ gov. board

judicial review

public opinion

Policy Implementation

OUTPUTS

Policies embodied in or accompanied by

laws

rules & regulations

programs

resource allocations

Implemen- tation

State Political System External Environment

FEEDBACK

FIG 1. A state postsecondary education policy model adapted to the policy of state support for independent institutions in Pennsylvania.

TABLE 1. Data on State Academic Authority[a]

Area of authority	Number and percent of states having effective authority with state agency/legislature/executive	
	Number	Percent
Define campus mission	7	14
Add new undergraduate program	15	31
Add new graduate program	16	33
Review/discontinue undergraduate program	6	12
Review/discontinue graduate program	7	14
Add/discontinue department	4	8

[a]$N = 49$ states.

about a wide array of transactions which reflect generally on state university "financial" and "appointive" autonomy, the items in Table 2 exhibit the most reliable indicators of state financial regulation, and the items in Table 3 tend to reflect regulatory practices in personnel matters in 1983.

As shown in Table 2, 15 states allocated funds in "lump sum" fashion to their public universities, whereas 14 specified both dollars and positions within object or function or both. After allocation, 38 states gave their universities considerable flexibility to shift funds among budget categories without state approval. While the majority of states (57%) in 1983 did not go to the trouble of "preauditing" university expenditures, 11 states had elaborate procedures involving two or more state agencies. The majority of universities also retained and managed tuition and other revenues generated by the campus and its students and cut their own checks for payroll and purchases. Only 8 states considered most types of revenue to be treated as state income. Twenty states gave their universities the incentive to good management which accompanies the retention of unspent funds, but the majority of states exercised a policy of reclaiming unspent state funds on an annual basis, thus forcing campus managers to spend them.

Table 3 shows the 1983 data on state personnel controls. About one-third of the states imposed a cap on faculty and nonfaculty positions, and six other states limited the total number of positions without distinguishing among the various employee groups. While few states had a classification system or salary schedule for faculty, close to half had personnel systems and pay schedules for other types of employees.

Table 4 shows the intercorrelations among the three scales. The financial and personnel scales show a strong relationship ($r = .57$), but the academic scale appears to measure something very different from the other two. Although

TABLE 2. Data on State Financial Regulation

Type of financial control	States	
	Number	Percent
Lump sum vs. itemized budget allocation		
Dollars allocated lump sum	15	31
Dollars allocated by object/function	20	41
Dollars and positions by object/function	14	29
State control over expenditures after allocation		
Advance state approval to shift funds	11	22
Univ. can shift within function or within object	18	37
Great univ. flexibility to shift	20	41
State preaudit requirements		
Elaborate (two or more state agencies)	11	22
Moderate (one state agency)	10	20
None	28	57
Checks issued by		
State cuts checks: both payroll and purchases	14	29
State cuts checks: either payroll OR purchases	6	12
Univ. cuts checks for both payroll and purchases	29	59
State control over revenues		
Tuition treated as state income	18	37
Tuition retained and managed by univ.	31	63
Most nontuition revenues treated as state income	8	16
Several categories of nontuition revenue retained by campus or system	16	33
All nontuition revenues retained and managed by campus of origin	25	51
State policy on year-end budget balances		
Recovered by state annually	25	51
Recovered by state biennially	4	8
Retained by university	20	41

TABLE 3. Date on State Personnel Regulation[a]

	States	
State-imposed regulation/control	Number	Percent
Ceiling on faculty positions	18	37
Ceiling on other positions	16	3
Ceiling on total positions only	6	12
Classification system for faculty	4	8
Classification system for other employees	25	51
Salary schedule for faculty	5	10
Salary schedule for other employees	21	43

[a]$N = 49$ states.

TABLE 4. Intercorrelations Among the Three Types of
State Regulation

	Academic	Financial
Financial	.13	
Personnel	−.16	.57

financial and personnel control practices are conceptually distinct, the most reliable items in each scale form a single factor which can be used as a combined regulation measure (Volkwein, 1986c).

Using these twin notions of academic regulation, on the one hand, and a combination of financial and personnel regulation, on the other, states can be classified according to their higher education regulatory practices.

Table 5 groups the states according to their centralized versus decentralized tendencies in academic and financial matters in 1982 and 1983. As described by Garms (1977) and by Curry and Fischer (1986), some state governments treat their public institutions of higher education as state-owned and -regulated agencies, while in other states, public colleges and universities are treated as state-assisted but privately controlled. In still other states, the pattern is mixed. Seven states, like Massachusetts and West Virginia, have fiscal and academic practices which are placed on the more centralized or regulated ends of both continua. At the extreme, these seven states behave in academic matters like European ministries of education and, in financial affairs, treat their universities like state agencies. At the other ends of the continua, twelve states, like Delaware and Vermont, tend

**TABLE 5. Classification of States According to Their Regulatory Practices
toward Public Universities**

| | Financial authority (1983) | | | |
| | Centralized | Decentralized | | Independent |
Academic authority (1982)	State agency	State controlled	State aided	Corporate model
Centralized (European ministry)	Mass. Mont. N.Car. N.Y. S.Dak. Vir. W.Va.	Ga. La. N.J. Okla. Tenn. Tex. Wis.	Ala. Ind. Ken. Miss. Mo. Utah	
Decentralized (campus control)	Conn. Fla. Hawaii Ill. Kansas Maryl. S.Car.	Ariz. Ark. Calif. Col. Neb. Nev. Ore. R.I. Wash. Wyo.	Del. Idaho Iowa Maine Mich. Minn. N.Hamp. N.Mex. N.Dak. Ohio Penn. Ver.	
Independent (Free market)				

more toward decentralized authority in both academic matters and financial transactions, at least as far as public, doctoral-granting universities are concerned. In most respects, these twelve states adopt an approach which resembles a state-aided model, rather than a state-controlled one. Seven other states, like Connecticut and South Carolina, tend to treat their universities financially like state agencies but adopt a more decentralized approach academically. Conversely, six states, like Alabama and Utah, have a more state-aided or decentralized approach to fiscal affairs but are more controlling in matters of academic program.

Such a classification of states should be interpreted with the knowledge that the measures were developed using a population of research universities and that the practices in some states are changing. Other two- and four-year public colleges may not necessarily receive the same treatment by their state governments, and the nature of regulatory practices may be undergoing adjustment. For example, Table 6 summarizes the recent changes reported in the literature in the states of Colorado, Connecticut, Idaho, Kentucky, Maryland, Massachusetts, New York, Washington, and Wisconsin. Except for the State of Washington, all the changes described in Table 6 are in the direction of deregulation. This suggests that the various Carnegie reports and their recommendations (discussed above) may be having an impact.

Except for New York, the changes in these states are already reflected in Table 5, and they suggest a rather fluid regulatory environment. In spite of this apparent fluidity, the Volkwein surveys reported that (with the exception of a handful of states) the dominant features of the regulatory atmosphere for most universities have been in place for decades. The relative stability of regulation from state to state is also suggested by two other studies. McGuinness (1986) notes that the basic patterns of state-level governance and organization today were in place in the early 1970s, and Fisher (1986) found that the four states in her study retain the same relative position regarding institutional autonomy now that they held early in the century.

At any rate, the relationship between state government and higher education is under review in many states, although it is not clear what changes, if any, will result. McGuinness (1986) recently summarized the various special studies and blue ribbon commissions which were organized in 1985 and 1986. His review indicates that twenty-one states in these two years undertook various initiatives ranging from reorganization of governance structures to program improvement. DiBiasio (1986) analyzed six of these statewide reports and found that the recommendations fell into eighteen categories ranging from finance and governance to economic development and qualitative program review. McGuinness is quick to point out that not all these efforts have resulted in changes. Recent adjustments at the state level have been considered but *not* adopted in West Virginia, Idaho, and Mississippi, among other states. Nevertheless, significant higher education restructuring has occurred in a few states and appears to be a matter of active concern and discussion in a good many others.

Summary of What is Known
about Current Regulatory Practices

In summarizing the literature discussed thus far, it is possible to draw several conclusions about our knowledge of regulatory practices in higher education. First, there is a consensus that the amount of regulation has grown in the past forty years. Second, there is wide variation from state to state in the nature of academic, financial, and personnel control practices. Third, many of the more

TABLE 6. Recent Changes in State Regulatory Practices for Higher Education

State	Description of regulatory changes	Campuses effected	Refs.
Colorado	1981 transfer of responsibility for financial management to institutional governing boards, including lump sum budgeting, local management of revenues, local authority to set tuition and other prices.	All public institutions	McCoy (1983)
Connecticut	Given authority in 1981 to set tuition and locally manage tuition revenues.	University of Connecticut	Hyatt and Santiago (1984)
Idaho	1979 conversion to lump sum appropriations, local management of all revenues, and carryover of year-end balances.	All public institutions	Hyatt and Santiago (1984)
Kentucky	1982 freedom from broad array of state management oversight in purchasing, budgeting, accounting, capital construction, auditing, payroll, disposition of real estate, and operation of affiliated foundations and corporations.	All public institutions	Carter and Blanton (1983) Hyatt and Santiago (1984)
Maryland	1984 adoption of budgeting flexibility on transfers of funds, carryover of unexpended balances, crediting of interest income to campus, overhead cost recovery, computer purchases, and using gifts according to donor's wishes.	All public institutions	Meisinger and Mingle (1983) Hyatt and Santiago (1984)

TABLE 6. *(Continued)*

State	Description of regulatory changes	Campuses effected	Refs.
Massachusetts	1983 conversion from a line item budget by campus to one of five categories submitted by reorganized governing board on behalf of all higher education in state.	All public institutions	Hyatt and Santiago (1984)
New York	1985–1986 implementation of flexibility measures for purchasing and contract procedures, for personnel and salary classification, for certain budgetary matters such as transfer of funds, and for dormitory self-sufficiency.	State University of New York System	Wharton (1986)
Washington	Erosion of some financial and budgetary flexibility during late 1970s and early 1980s: loss of lump sum budgeting and ability to transfer some funds among program categories, stipulation of enrollment caps, campuses no longer set tuition/fees and retain the income, state now controls indirect cost revenues.	All public institutions	Hyatt and Santiago (1984) Curry and Fischer (1986)
Wisconsin	1982 reduction in some state preaudit controls for purchases under $10,000, printing, and employee classification.	University of Wisconsin system	Lorenz (1983)

centralized state control practices are widely believed by the higher education community to provide disincentives to good campus management. Fourth, because of this belief, state regulatory practices are under attack, especially in those states which tend to treat their universities like state agencies. Fifth, the dominant aspects of each university's relationship with state government have been relatively enduring over the years, even though there have been minor adjustments in nearly every state. Sixth, the recent changes which have been introduced in a few states tend to be deregulatory in nature.

CONTRIBUTORS TO REGULATORY CLIMATE

What, then, are the causes of regulation? How do states which are highly regulatory differ from states which are not? Is there concrete evidence for the belief that regulation is costly? Are the "best" universities the ones that are the least regulated? These are some of the questions addressed in the remaining pages of this chapter.

Literature on the topic has pointed to a number of factors which appear to contribute to a state's regulatory climate. Various studies have examined the role of strong governors, legislatures, and state higher education boards and agencies. There is also evidence that underlying socioeconomic and political variables are important contributors to the regulatory climate in states.

Socioeconomic Factors

Dye (1966) examined the relationships among state politics, socioeconomic characteristics, and various state policy outcomes. In his review of the literature and analysis of available data, he concluded that "Political system characteristics are much less important than socioeconomic inputs in determining policy outcomes." Under his model, economic development shapes both political systems and policy. Lindeen and Willis (1975) examined state patterns of support for public higher education in relation to a wide range of political, socioeconomic, and demographic variables. They found that population characteristics, such as density and magnitude, accounted for the greatest variance in support levels. To the extent, then, that state regulation of public universities is a "policy outcome," the relative amounts of tax capacity and effort, urbanization, industrialization, population characteristics, and education levels in each state should be associated with university fiscal and academic autonomy.

Political Factors

The governor is increasingly viewed as a dominant figure in public higher education. As the head of state government and the leader in policy making, the governor occupies a strategic position of influence. Gubernatorial formal authority was analyzed by Schlesinger (1971), who identified four major factors and developed a widely used index of the governor's formal powers in each state. He found, in general, that large states with urban populations were more apt to have strong governors. More recently, Abney and Lauth (1983) have developed a measure of relative gubernatorial influence in each state, but their measure has not yet been used as a tool to explain policy-making phenomena.

Glenny (1976), Hines (1974), Wirt (1976), and Zollinger (1985) are among those who have studied gubernatorial involvement in educational policy-making. In a national study, Glenny (1976) used Schlesinger's index of governors' power and observed a tendency for strong governors to be found in the larger industrial states, thus reinforcing the Dye model (1966).

Hines (1974), in his study of twelve states, rated each governor's involvement in four categories from issue definition, through policy formulation, to enactment and implementation. He found positive relationships between his index of gubernatorial involvement and state size, industrialization, and the Schlesinger index of governors' power. However, he found an even stronger relationship with legislative technical effectiveness and with the state's political culture.

Using the Lowi typology of policy intervention, Zollinger (1985) found that governors rarely intervene in regulatory policy issues but, instead, are likely to allow them to be handled by other state officers. On the other hand, he found that governors were likely to intervene directly when there was a strong relationship between an institution's programs and the political interests of the governor. Supporting this finding, Fisher (1986) reports, in her analysis of legislation in four states, that governors, rather than legislators, instigated the most extensive intrusions on campus autonomy. There appears to be little doubt in the literature, then, about the key role of the governor in higher education. Governors Edmund Brown in California and Nelson Rockefeller in New York are prominent examples of those who exerted strong influence, and who expanded their state's public higher education in the 1960s.

Several authors have examined the role of the legislature and party politics in higher education. As noted earlier, Fisher (1986) found a growth in intrusive legislation enacted, but she questioned whether the governor or the legislature was more responsible for its initiation. Glenny (1976) identified not only state legislatures but their staffs as sources of oversight activity. Hines (1974), Patterson (1976), and Wirt (1976) are also among those who have noted a relationship between legislative effectiveness and educational policy development. The Citizens Conference on State Legislatures, which rated several dimensions of legislative effectiveness in each state, has provided an analytical tool which has been used in many studies (Burns, 1971).

Another useful legislative tool has been provided by Walker (1969), who has measured the extent to which some states tend to be among the first to adopt new legislation and programs, while others tend to be among the last. His "innovation index" separates the pioneering states from the laggards based on an analysis of eighty-eight different programs enacted prior to 1965.

Some of these same authors have also noted a correlation between policy activism and the strength of the Democratic Party in elections, and the size of the government bureaucracy. The more a state is characterized by a pattern of elected Democrats and by a large number of government employees, the more likely it is to be active in educational policy. For example, Zollinger (1985) found that Democratic governors (as distinct from Republicans) were three times more likely to make a significant investment of their time in higher education issues.

The influence of political culture and tradition has also received attention. The link between the central versus the local traditions of states and educational policy was made by Elazar (1972). He developed a four-part typology that has been shown to be related to school finance and to gubernatorial power (Wirt, 1976). A different measure of discretionary authority of local government in each state was constructed by Zimmerman (1981). In a project for the Advisory Commission on Intergovernmental Relations, he rated the various governmental units in each state on a variety of measures and then ranked the states according to the composite score of local authority.

The relationship between state government and higher education is exercised most vividly through its statewide governance structure or coordinating body. State governments have found it necessary to establish some kind of governing board or coordinating agency in order to control the competition for state funds, the proliferation of costly programs, the spread of branch campuses, and the rivalry for students. While the provisions of Section 1202 of the Higher Education Act of 1965, as amended in 1972, stimulated state higher education structure, most states now desire to have a statewide structure for administering federal funds, as well as for comprehensive planning.

In his study for the American Council on Education, Berdahl (1971) classified the arrangements in each state into voluntary associations, advisory boards, regulatory boards, and consolidated governing boards. This typology has served as a model which others have utilized. For example, Millett (1984) employed categories called advisory boards, coordinating boards, and statewide governing boards and used criteria that cause some states to be placed in different categories from those in the Berdahl framework. The fourth chapter of Millett's book gives an analysis of the advantages and disadvantages of the various types of structures.

The Education Commission of the States has another useful classification scheme which attempts to describe the complexities of higher education structures among the states (McGuinness, 1986). This classification is based upon the varying nature of authority possessed by the different boards, as well as upon the types of institutions over which they have responsibility. Table 7 is

TABLE 7. Authority of State Boards of Higher Education, 1986[a]

	Consolidated Governing Board		Coordinating board	Planning agencies
	All public institutions	Senior institutions only		
Authority over both budget and program	Alaska Georgia Hawaii Idaho[b] Maine[c] Massachusetts Montana Nevada[b] N. Dakota Rhode Island S. Dakota Utah West Virginia	Arizona Florida[b] Iowa Kansas Mississippi New Hampshire N. Carolina Oregon Wyoming Wisconsin	Alabama Connecticut Illinois Maryland New Jersey Ohio Oklahoma S. Carolina	
Authority over budget with program review/recommendation			Arkansas Florida[b,d]	
Authority over Program with budget review/recommendation[e]			Colorado Indiana Kentucky Louisiana Missouri Pennsylvania[b] Tennessee Texas Virginia Washington New York[b] (no budget role)	
Authority limited to review/recommendation for both budget and program			Alaska[d] California Michigan[b] Minnesota New Mexico Oregon[d]	
No statutory budget or program role			New Hampshire[d]	Delaware Nebraska Vermont

[a]Source: Education Commission of the States.
[b]States with agency responsible for all levels of education.
[c]Maine Maritime Academy and Vocational-Technical Institutes are under other boards.
[d]Statutory coordinating agency separate from and in addition to governing board.
[e]Some boards develop the budget formula which forms the basis for institutional allocations.

139

adapted from information obtained from the Education Commission of the States and shows the levels of authority and structure from state to state. In summarizing the various structural and policy concerns in statewide governance across the nation, McGuinness identified decentralization, deregulation, and management flexibility as tendencies countervailing the trend toward strong state policy leadership.

The United States is characterized by diversity, excellence, and access in postsecondary education. Higher education politics at the state level includes both cooperation and conflict. The nature of the relationship between the public and the independent institutions has been recently examined by Berdahl in five case studies (1985). He summarized the areas of cooperation and conflict in each state and identified the crucial role of statewide associations in determining the prevailing conditions and policies. The balance between public and private institutions in each state is highly variable, in terms of the numbers of campuses, their enrollments, and their cross-sector relations. These differences may bear some relationship to the regulatory climate experienced by public institutions.

THE CORRELATES OF STATE
REGULATION AND CAMPUS AUTONOMY

The literature discussed thus far would lead us to expect fairly strong associations between the amounts of state regulation and the characteristics of states. To what extent, then, are the three types of state regulation associated with the various economic, social/demographic, and political/bureaucratic variables?

Table 8, which draws on data collected by Volkwein (1984, 1986a,b), shows the zero-order correlations valued at plus or minus .20 or higher and reveals partial support for some expectations but not for others.

The data suggest that certain types of regulation may be products of certain state characteristics: a heavy tax burden, a highly concentrated and well-educated population, a well-staffed and well-organized legislature, elected officials who are Democrats, a large state bureaucracy, a high proportion of private universities, and state boards with authority over both budget and program. On the other hand, other variables are associated with campus autonomy rather than regulation: a relatively large population between ages five and seventeen, large per capita expenditures for public higher education, and large public enrollments. However, the data in Table 8 reveal neither consistent nor strong correlations between the amount of state regulation, on the one hand, and the major economic, social, and political variables, on the other. The low relationships suggest that regulatory controls may perhaps be more idiosyncratic, and therefore more easily changed, than commonly believed by many in higher education.

Many of the expected correlations did not appear. For example, the measures of political culture, local authority, and innovation proved to be generally

TABLE 8. State Characteristics and Their Correlations with Three Types of State Regulation of Universities[a]

State characteristics	State regulation		
	Academic	Financial	Personnel
Economic			
Tax capacity			
Tax effort		.27**	
Expenditures per capita for H.E.	−.32**		
Social-demographic			
Total state population			
Population density	.26*	.25*	.20
Metropolitan area population		.21	
Population change (1970–80)	−.23		
Percent population age 5–17		−.33**	−.36**
Percent population age 65 +			
Percent with 4 years of college		.39**	
Private Enrollment per thousand			
Public enrollment per thousand	−.25*		
Political-bureaucratic			
Governor's power (Schlesinger, 1971)			
Governor's influence (Abney/Lauth, 1983)			
Legislative professionalism		.29**	.21
Democratic party strength	.26*	.22	
Political culture (Elazar, 1972)	.21		
Local authority (Zimmerman, 1981)			
Innovation index (Walker, 1969)			
Number of gov't employees	.25*		
Proportion of gov't employees			
State private-public funding			
Private/public univ. ratio	.39**		
Type H.E. agency (Berdahl, 1971)			.22
Type H.E. agency (Millett, 1984)		.23	
Authority of H.E. agency (McGuinness, 1986)		.30**	.32**

[a]$N = 49$ states.
*$p < .10$; **$p < .05$.

unrelated to the regulation measures. This is an unexpected finding in view of the predictions and observation of other authors. The lack of a significant relationship with the Schlesinger and Abney-Lauth measures of the governor's power and influence is particularly inconsistent with the expectations produced by earlier studies (Hines, 1974; Glenny, 1976). It may be that the governor, as suggested by Zollinger (1985), has relatively little to do with the academic and financial control practices which have evolved in each state.

If certain state characteristics tend to produce a regulatory climate, do universities develop measurable resistances to state regulation? The variables in Table 9 were judged to be among those qualities which made a university less likely to be heavily regulated. Again, only those values exceeding plus or minus .20 are shown. Constitutional status is the only variable significantly associated with more than one type of regulation. Constitutional autonomy does appear to provide protection from financial and personnel restrictions. A high level of research grants and of endowments, as well as the existence of a medical school or hospital, are negatively correlated with the academic scale. Less dependence on state funds appears to accompany campus autonomy in academic matters.

Assumptions about causal sequence are risky in research of this kind. It is tempting to assert that all environmental variables precede all university variables, but this assertion probably ignores important interactions. For example, the resource-dependence model of organization, as described by Aldrich and Pfeffer (1976) and by Pfeffer and Salancik (1978), and as modified by Hall (1982), seems especially fruitful for understanding the interaction between a university and its environment. Organizations require resources and must interact with those who control those resources. The model emphasizes the role of managers both in analyzing the external demands on the organization and in actively attempting to alleviate the constraints of the setting in which the organization is embedded. Over time, organizations and their managers attempt to manipulate their environments and to structure themselves to acquire sufficient resources for accomplishing their major goals. The amount of regulation and control by state government constitutes an important force which imposes constraints and which shapes the strategic choices made by university management.

It is probable, therefore, that within the interactions between public universities and state governments, there are forces operating both for greater regulation and for deregulation. For example, by improving its quality and becoming less dependent on the state for funds, a university can instill a feeling of pride and confidence among state officials and citizens. This, in turn, reduces the pressure for regulatory control.

At any rate, the data in Table 8 indicate that regulatory controls are most common in states with a heavy tax burden; a high population density; a low proportion of school-aged children; a college-educated population; an effective, well-staffed legislature; a high proportion of private universities; and a higher

TABLE 9. University Organizational Characteristics and Their Correlations with Three Types of State Regulation[a]

University variables	Type of regulation		
	Academic	Financial	Personnel
Age			
Size			−.21
Constitutional status		−.25*	−.36***
Flagship status			
Faculty quality			
Undergraduate quality			
Government grants	−.35***		
Endowments and gifts	−.36***		
Medical school-hospital	−.29**		
Number of doctoral programs			

[a]$N = 49$.
*$p < .10$; **$p < .05$; ***$p < .01$.

education agency with authority for both budget and program. Table 9, on the other hand, suggests that an institution's constitutional status and external funding success provide at least some immunity from some types of regulation.

THE IMPACT OF REGULATION ON INSTITUTIONAL COST AND QUALITY

The discussion thus far has described the nature of state regulatory practices in higher education and the characteristics of states which differ in their approaches. We noted earlier that some states give their campuses considerable autonomy to manage their own academic and financial affairs, while others are heavily controlling. There is also considerable literature suggesting that a great deal of external oversight is both costly and unproductive. Most administrators and faculty, as well as the authors of numerous national reports, believe that less regulated universities operate with less administrative cost and with greater effectiveness than do institutions which are treated like state agencies. For example, a 1984 study found that officials at sixty-three of eighty-eight public universities believed that moderate or great savings would result from state deregulation (Volkwein, 1984). The more heavily controlled the campus, the more frequently the predicted cost reduction was characterized as "great."

On the other hand, state officials often have legitimate concerns about keeping expenditures in line with revenues, avoiding salary inflation, ensuring economical purchasing practices, and protecting against fraud and corruption. In many states, there is political and bureaucratic tension between those who want incentives for good management and those responsible for protecting the state and its taxpayers. The Carnegie Commission recognized these competing interests in its 1973 report when it recommended a distribution of authority between public control and institutional independence.

Does heavy regulation tend to increase costs or save the taxpayers money? Unfortunately, there is little empirical evidence to settle the issue. Most of the literature on the topic is based on informed opinion rather than on empirical research. One exception is a study by Van Alstyne and Coldren (1976) which focused on the administrative expense of mandated federal programs and found sizable cost increases on each of the six different types and sizes of campuses which were examined.

The only other empirical studies of the impact of regulation on administrative cost were conducted by Volkwein (1984, 1986b). Table 10 is constructed from the data gathered for those studies. When relevant control variables are entered into a regression analysis, there are virtually no differences in administrative expenditures, administrative salaries, or administrative elaborateness among universities that enjoy a great deal of autonomy and those that are subjected to relatively heavy oversight. Administrative expenditures are most strongly associated with the level of state appropriations and the level of unionization. Campus administrative salaries are most strongly associated with the size of the student body and the level of state appropriations. Administrative elaborateness appears to be a function of the size and age of the institution. The possession of flexibility or freedom from state control explains an insignificant amount of the variance. The right-hand column in Table 10 does provide evidence of more cost-effective management under conditions of deregulation. Even accounting for important control variables, the two measures of flexibility are significantly associated with a high proportion of revenue from nonstate sources. This suggests that universities which are less hampered by state control become less dependent on state appropriations.

Thus, there is no evidence among public doctoral-granting universities in the early 1980s that freedom from regulation is associated with lower or higher administrative expenditures, nor with lower or higher administrative salaries, nor with more or less elaborate administrative structures. While these data do not suggest that freedom from the burdens of state control produces a reduction in administrative overhead, they also provide no evidence that a heavy dose of state fiscal or academic control forces universities to operate more efficiently. Universities which possess a great deal of autonomy apparently behave no differently, at least on these gross measures, from institutions which are treated like state agencies. These findings raise questions about the value of spending state resources and energy on centralized control practices.

TABLE 10. Regression Beta Weights for Measures of University Efficiency
$(N - 86)$

Variables	Admin. expenditures		Admin. salaries (Pres & VPs)	Admin. elaborateness (# VPs & Deans)	% Revenue from nonstate sources
	Per FTE student	% of budget			
Economic					
State approp. per FTE[a]	.54***	−.14	.32*	.12	−.37***
Cost of living	−.06	−.20	.06	.06	.19*
Unionization	.25*	.41**	−.16	.07	−.14
Organizational characteristics					
Size: FTE students	−.01	−.05	.51***	.56***	−.02
Age	−.10	−.21	.03	.25**	.09
Constitutional status	.07	.03	.17	−.03	−.02
Flagship campus	−.01	.01	−.18	.10	.09
Medical/agric./engin.	.09	−.13	.08	.10	.31**
Autonomy					
Financial	.13	.13	.13	.01	.19*
Academic	.12	.06	.02	−.15	.20*
$R^2 = (d/f = 10,75)$	.43***	.24*	.50***	.58***	.45***

$*p < .05; **p < .01; ***p < .001.$

Institutions which are relatively free of state controls are less dependent on state appropriations and raise a larger portion of their funds from nonstate sources. The data suggest that universities which are encumbered by heavy state fiscal control are less likely to develop alternative sources of revenue, or that they do so less effectively. Freedom from the burdens of external oversight may encourage universities to shift administrative resources away from coping with the state bureaucracy and into more cost-effective activities, such as alumni development, fund raising, and research grantsmanship. One possible explanation, then, for the lack of a significant relationship between flexibility and administrative cost and elaborateness is that highly regulated campuses devote more of their administrative operations to activities which interact with state government. The configuration of administrative resources for less regulated campuses, while being no smaller, may be more adaptively oriented. These data

TABLE 11. Regression Beta Weights for Measures of University Effectiveness[a]

Variables	Faculty quality	Undergrad quality	Gov't grants per FTE	Endowment and gifts per FTE	Combined measures (alpha = .77)
Economic					
State approp. per FTE	.45***	.47***	.52***	.51***	.61***
Cost of living	.18*	.14	.11	.13	.17
Unionization	.02	.02	−.09	−.17	−.09
Organizational characteristics					
Size: FTE students	.67***	.27*	−.05	.11	.23**
Age	.15	.13	.01	.09	.10
Constitutional status	−.07	−.20	−.06	.15	−.03
Flagship campus	.06	.11	.05	.09	.09
Medical/agric./engin.	−.27*	−.27*	.21*	.10	.02
Autonomy					
Financial	−.12	.00	.07	.05	.02
Academic	.07	−.05	.12	.23**	.14
R^2 = (d/f = 10,75)	.67***	.31***	.42***	.52***	.54***

[a]$N = 86$.
*$p < .05$; **$p < .01$; ***$p < .001$.
Source: Journal of Higher Education (September–October 1986).

suggest that the impact of regulation is less a matter of administrative cost than a matter of resource deployment, at least at the campus level.

If there is no evidence of a strong association between autonomy and campus efficiency, is there an association with effectiveness? Are less regulated, more autonomous universities more effective in academic activities, which are more central to their mission than administrative operations? We noted in the earlier discussion that many in higher education are convinced of the benefits of deregulation. Do campuses that are relatively unhampered by state regulation demonstrate higher levels of academic quality and success?

This question was addressed by Volkwein (1986c), and Table 11 is reprinted from that study. Faculty reputational quality appears to be highest in universities which are large, are generously funded, and are located in relatively expensive areas of the country. Academic and financial autonomy do not make significant, unique contributions to the explained variance.

Regarding the second measure, undergraduate quality, it appears that a high level of state support for a university helps it attract good students as well as good faculty. The presence or absence of state regulation has virtually no relationship to the quality of the student body, at least as measured by the Barrons, the Cass and Birnbaum, and the Fiske ratings (Volkwein, 1986c).

Table 11 also indicates that the two measures of flexibility are not significantly associated with a high level of government grants per FTE. Apparently, those universities which receive greater support from their states and which have expensive professional schools are relatively more successful in the grants competition process.

Turning to the fourth measure, endowment and gifts per student, we see that the variable most strongly associated with this measure of university success, once again, is state appropriations. However, one other variable makes a significant unique contribution, and that is the scale of academic flexibility. Those campuses which have the most freedom from constraints on their academic programs, and which are funded generously by the state, are most successful in raising funds from alumni.

The last column of Table 11 shows the results of a regression which combines the four measures to form a single measure of university quality and success. The resulting regression beta weights reflect a pattern similar to those noted for several of the separate criterion measures, namely, a strong association with state funding and campus size. The other variables, including the two measures of flexibility, are not strongly associated with the variance in the combined measures.

Thus, the data do not support the popular belief of a strong relationship between freedom from state academic and financial constraints, on the one hand, and measures of campus effectiveness, on the other. Rather, it appears that the significant differences in quality and success among public, research universities are explained, for the most part, by differences in state generosity and campus size. The exception appears to be in the fund-raising area, where academic flexibility is significantly associated with a high level of endowment and gifts and is positively, but not quite significantly, associated with the combined measures.

CONCLUSION AND AREAS FOR FURTHER RESEARCH

The data in Tables 10 and 11 can be interpreted as supporting the resource-dependency model of organizations. Within the environmental conditions perceived by the organization, its top executives make strategic choices designed to acquire sufficient resources to attain the major institutional goals. If faculty reputation, student selectivity, and success in raising external funds are considered proxies for effectiveness, the most effective public universities appear to be those that have also been the most successful in eliciting superior levels of state funding. Stated differently, those universities that compete successfully in their environments for one type of resource tend to compete successfully for other types of resources as well. Attracting the strongest faculty and students appears to be the goal, and ample financial support and large enrollments appear to supply the means.

The dynamic interaction between state governments and the institutions which they support represents an important and fruitful area for further research. Figure 2 presents a conceptual guide. In the model, the state policy process is influenced by underlying socioeconomic forces, by institutional characteristics, and by external influences in each state. The solid lines suggest direct influences, while the dotted lines indicate indirect impact on the policy process. The process produces a number of policy outcomes, including regulatory controls.

Various economic, social, and demographic factors constitute the basic realities which are faced by policy makers. In an already heavily taxed state with a declining population, the policy outcomes are potentially very different from those in a wealthy state with a high proportion of school-aged children. Regulation is one of several types of policy outcomes, but socioeconomic forces promote conditions which either favor regulation or reduce the need for it.

The policy process in Figure 2 is also influenced by institutional characteristics and actions. By possessing constitutional status and by raising considerable resources from nonstate sources, a university has an effect on policy outcomes. In its environmental interactions, a campus influences the way it is supported and regulated. Presumably, a state which is proud of its public university, and which perceives it to be important and useful, is less likely to constrain its management. On the other hand, a record of mismanagement or scandal is likely to increase the degree of regulation.

The amount of regulation evolving from the policy process is additionally influenced by a variety of external factors. For example, state policy depends in part on the public attitude toward higher education in general and toward the university in particular. Obviously, the university can have some impact on the public support it enjoys. The regulatory relationship is also influenced by national academic customs and by the regulatory practices in other states. For example, recent changes in the regulatory practices of several states suggest that the numerous Carnegie and other national reports are being felt. The policy process itself includes many participants (the governor, the legislature, and state boards for higher education, among others) and several types of outcomes (the size and scope of public institutions, the level of degree programs offered, resources, and regulations). This model represents an initial attempt to provide a framework for examining the regulatory relationships between public universities and the state governments which support them.

Many areas of research on this topic remain unexplored. In the first place, no studies have yet examined the financial costs of the various regulatory practices in each state. The resource implications for the responding institution constitutes only part of the picture. Some states require an enormous work force to carry out their centralized oversight practices, and these have not been studied. It would be

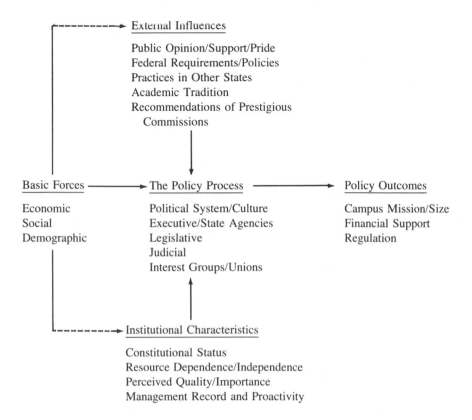

FIG. 2. Policy formation flowchart.

useful to compare the relative amounts of efficiency and waste in the bureaucratic structures of states with differing philosophies of regulation and control.

Second, it may well be that the benefits of flexibility and the organizational impact of regulation need to be measured over a longer period of time. We noted earlier that the dominant aspects of each university's relationship with state government have been relatively enduring over the past several years. In only a handful of states has there been significant change, even though there have been relatively minor adjustments in every state. Nevertheless, universities are at different developmental stages with respect to their academic development, their faculty and student quality, and their external fund-raising. A longitudinal methodology, which would take into account the different "starting points" of each university and would monitor the differential progress of heavily regulated and less regulated campuses, would be more enlightening.

The benefits of flexibility may be visible elsewhere in the organization, and they may have their impact on variables not yet studied. Although the data summarized here represent a broad array of defensible criteria, it is not possible for them to reflect completely the excellence of academic performance, the intellectual growth of the students, the instructional skills of the faculty, nor the educational "value added" of student attendance at each university, among others. How does external regulation effect administrator performance and satisfaction? Are more autonomous universities more adaptable to their environments? Are their managers able to devote more attention to educational matters? Is their work force more satisfied and responsive? These questions must be the focus of other studies.

Could it be that campus managers who have a great deal of freedom from state control do not necessarily use it to enhance the quality and effectiveness of their universities? Conversely, do those universities that are treated as state agencies "try harder," like Avis? If so, sound campus management may be relatively independent of the state's regulatory climate. This possibility must be taken seriously in view of the data in Tables 10 and 11. These data suggest that academic and financial flexibility are statistically overwhelmed by the level of state funding and the size of the institution. The level of state appropriations, in particular, is consistently and significantly associated with each of the separate and combined criterion measures.

A resource-dependence model suggests that universities as organizations interact with their environments in order to maximize the needed resources. Campus management seeks to acquire these resources in order to accomplish major institutional objectives—objectives which probably include the enhancement of the institution's quality and reputation. Within the model, then, the successful acquisition of both state and nonstate funding by public universities provides a form of flexibility, for it supplies the means for universities to improve themselves. In fact, freedom from academic and financial regulation may be most important under conditions of financial stringency and could be relatively unnecessary if funding is adequate. On the other hand, it may be that only adequately funded campuses can take advantage of what autonomy they enjoy. If this is so, it substantially explains the generally low relationships found thus far between campus flexibility and the measures of efficiency and effectiveness. Viewed in this light, generous state funding provides the most important form of flexibility and is strongly associated with each of the separate and combined measures of university quality and success.

This discussion, then, suggests several research questions for further investigation on the topic:

1. Do states with comparatively heavy regulatory practices devote relatively more resources to those oversight activities?

2. What is the proper balance between the competing interests of state accountability and campus autonomy? Is there a measurable point where state policies and control practices become disincentives to effective management?

3. Will those campuses that are less regulated show greater gains over time in measures of quality and success than campuses which are more heavily regulated?

4. Does external regulation of academic organizations have impacts on the satisfaction and performance of individual administrators, the amounts of student growth, the quality of campus life, and the responsiveness of administrative services, among other variables not yet studied?

5. Is effective academic management in public universities relatively independent of the state's regulatory practices?

6. Does flexibility have the greatest benefit for campuses which are poorly funded?

7. Must a campus be adequately funded before it can take advantage of flexibility?

At the very least, the empirical studies to date suggest that the connections between campus autonomy and cost and quality are not so clear as some higher education authors and Carnegie reports have claimed. Can the benefits of centralized versus decentralized management and control be demonstrated in academic organizations, which, by nature, have few quantifiable goals and instead have educational objectives which are difficult to measure? This problem offers a challenge to researchers in higher education.

REFERENCES

Abney, G., and Lauth, T. P. (1983). The governor as chief administrator. *Public Administration Review* (January/February):40–49.

Aldrich, H. E. (1979). *Organizations and Environments.* Englewood Cliffs, N.J.: Prentice-Hall.

Aldrich, H. E., and Pfeffer, J. (1976). Environments of organizations. *Annual Review of Sociology*, Vol. 2. Palo Alto, Calif.: Annual Review Inc.

Anthony, R. N., and Herzlinger, R. E. (1980). *Management Control in Nonprofit Organizations.* Homewood, Ill.: Richard D. Irwin.

Atwell, R. H. (1985). A View from Washington. In Gardner et al., *Cooperation and Conflict.*

Berdahl, R. O. (1971). *Statewide Coordination of Higher Education.* Washington, D.C.: American Council on Education.

Berdahl, R. O. (1985). Examining Intersector Issues. In Gardner et al., *Cooperation and Conflict.*

Bowen, H. (1980). *The Costs of Higher Education.* San Francisco: Jossey-Bass.

Burns, J. (1971). *The Sometimes Governments: A Critical Study of 50 American Legislatures by the Citizens Conference on State Legislatures.* New York: Bantam.

Carnegie Commission on Higher Education. (1973). *Governance of Higher Education*. New York: McGraw-Hill.

Carnegie Council on Policy Studies in Higher Education. (1976). *The States and Higher Education: A Proud Past and a Vital Future*. San Francisco: Jossey-Bass.

Carnegie Council on Policy Studies in Higher Education. (1980). *Three Thousand Futures: The Next Twenty Years for Higher Education*. San Francisco: Jossey-Bass.

Carnegie Foundation for the Advancement of Teaching. (1982). *The Control of the Campus: A Report on the Governance of Higher Education*. Princeton, N.J.: Princeton University Press.

Carter, E. A., and Blanton, J. C. (1983). Management flexibility in Kentucky: the passage of House Bill 622. In Mingle, *Management Flexibility and State Regulation in Higher Education*.

Crossen, P. H. (1984). State postsecondary education policy systems. *The Review of Higher Education* (Winter) 7: 125–142.

Curry, D. J., and Fischer, N. M. (1986). Public higher education and the state: Models for financing, budgeting and accountability. Paper presented at annual meeting of ASHE, San Antonio, February.

DiBiasio, D. A. (1986). Higher education under study: a comparative analysis of six statewide reports. Paper presented at annual meeting of ASHE, San Antonio, February.

Downs, A. *Inside Bureaucracy*. (1967). Boston: Little, Brown.

Dressel, P. (ed.). (1980). *The Autonomy of Public Colleges*, New Directions for Institutional Research, No. 26. San Francisco: Jossey-Bass.

Dye, T. R. (1966). *Politics Economics and the Public*. Chicago: Rand McNally.

Elazar, D. J. (1972). *American Federalism: A View from the States*. New York: Thomas V. Crowell.

Fisher, L. A. (1986). State legislatures and the autonomy of colleges and universities: a comparative study of legislation in four states, 1900–1979. Paper presented to ASHE. San Antonio, February. (Forthcoming in *Journal of Higher Education*.)

Folger, J., ed. *Increasing the public accountability of higher education*. New Directions for Institutional Research, No. 16. San Francisco: Jossey-Bass.

Gardner, J. W., Atwell, R. H., and Berdahl, R. O., eds. (1985). *Cooperation and Conflict*. Washington, D.C.: Association of Governing Boards.

Garms, W. I. (1977). *Financing Community Colleges*. New York: Teachers College Press.

Glenny, L. (1976). *State Budgeting for Higher Education: Interagency Conflict and Consensus*. Berkeley: University of California.

Glenny, L. A., and Bowen, F. M. (1977). *State Intervention in Higher Education: A Report for the Sloan Commission on Government and Higher Education*, November. (ED 184 427).

Glenny, L. A., and Dalglish, T. (1973). *Public Universities, State Agencies and the Law: Constitutional Autonomy in Decline*. Berkeley: University of California.

Hall, R. H. (1982). *Organizations: Structure and Process*. Englewood Cliffs, N.J.: Prentice-Hall.

Harcleroad, F. F. (1975). *Institutional Efficiency in State Systems of Public Higher Education*. Tucson: College of Education, University of Arizona.

Hines, E. R. (1974). Governors and educational policy making. In R. Campbell and T. Mazzoni (eds.), *State Policy Making for the Public Schools: A Comparative Analysis*. Columbus: Ohio State University.

Hines, E. R., and Hartmark, L. S. (1980). *Politics of Higher Education*, AAHE-ERIC Higher Education Report No. 7.

Hyatt, J. A., and Santiago, A. A. (1984). *Incentives and Disincentives for Effective Management*. Washington, D.C.: NACUBO.

Jacob, H., and Vines, K., eds. (1976). *Politics in the American States*. Boston: Little, Brown.

Lawrence, P. R., and Lorsch, J. W. (1967). *Organization and Environment*. Cambridge, MA: Harvard University Press.

Levy, D. C. (1980). *University and Government in Mexico: Autonomy in an Authoritarian System*, New York: Praeger.

Lindeen, J. W., and Willis, G. L. (1975). Political, socioeconomic and demographic patterns of support for public higher education. *Western Political Quarterly* 28:528–541.

Lorenz, R. H. (1983). Improved efficiency through decreased government regulation: the case of Wisconsin. In Mingle, *Management Flexibility and State Regulation in Higher Education*.

McCoy, M. (1983). The adoption of budget flexibility in Colorado: its consequences for the University of Colorado. In Mingle, *Management Flexibility and State Regulation in Higher Education*.

McCoy, M., and Halstead, D. K. (1982). *Higher Education Financing in the Fifty States: Interstate Comparisons for Fiscal Year 1979* (2nd ed.). Boulder, Colo.: National Center for Higher Education Management Systems.

McGuinness, A. (1986). Recent trends in state policy related to higher education. *Grapevine* 327 (April): 2054–2060.

Meisinger, R. J., Jr., and Mingle, J. R. (1983). The extent of state controls in Maryland public higher education. In Mingle, *Management Flexibility and State Regulation in Higher Education*.

Millett, J. D. (1984). *Conflict in Higher Education*. San Francisco: Jossey-Bass.

Mingle, J. R., ed. (1983). *Management Flexibility and State Regulation in Higher Education*. Atlanta: Southern Regional Education Board.

Morehouse, S. S. (1976). The governor as political leader. In Jacob and Vines, *Politics in the American States*.

Patterson, S. C. (1976). American state legislatures and public policy. In Jacob and Vines, *Politics in the American States*.

Pfeffer, J., and Salancik, G. R. (1978). *The External Control of Organizations: A Resource Dependence Perspective*. New York: Harper & Row.

Schlesinger, J. A. (1971). The politics of the executive. In Jacob and Vines, *Politics in the American States*.

Sloan Commission on Government and Higher Education. (1980). *A Program for Renewed Partnership: An Overview*. Cambridge, MA: Ballinger.

State University of New York. (1985). The Challenge and the Choice: Report of the Independent Commission on the Future of the State University, January 16.

Van Alstyne, C., and Coldren, S. L. (1976). The cost of implementing federally mandated social programs at colleges and universities. Washington, D.C.: American Council on Education.

Volkwein, J. F. (1984). State financial control practices and public universities: results of a national study. Research paper presented at the Annual Meeting of the Association for the Study of Higher Education, Chicago, March 1984. Reprinted as a Working Paper, Rockefeller Institute of Government, State University of New York, Number 18, Spring 1985.

Volkwein, J. F. (1986a). The correlates of state regulation and university autonomy. A paper presented to the Annual Meeting of ASHE, San Antonio, February.

Volkwein, J. F. (1986b). State financial control of public universities and its relationship to campus administrative elaborateness and cost. *Review of Higher Education* 9(3): 267–286.

Volkwein, J. F. (1986c). Campus autonomy and its relationship to measures of university quality. *Journal of Higher Education* (Sept./Oct.): 510–528.

Walker, J. L. (1969). The diffusion of innovations among the American states. *American Political Science Review* 63:880–899.

Wharton, C. R. (1986). Implementation of flexibility legislation: status report to the board of trustees. State University of New York, Feb. 12, 1986.

Wirt, F. N. (1976). Education, politics and policies. In Jacob and Vines, *Politics in the American States.*

Zimmerman, J. (1981). *Measuring Local Discretionary Authority.* Washington, D.C.: Advisory Commission on Intergovernmental Relations.

Zollinger, R. A. (1985). Governors and higher education: an unstudied relationship. Paper presented at annual meeting of ASHE, Chicago, March.

Administrative Leadership in Higher Education

Cameron Fincher
University of Georgia

The research literature on leadership is voluminous—and mostly ignored. Thus the purpose of this chapter is to review the published literature and to relate the major findings and implications of theory and research to the academic administration of American colleges and universities. Efforts are made (1) to examine critically the theoretical assumptions and implications of research findings; (2) to consider the practical and potential implications of leadership theory and research for the administration and governance of institutions of higher education; and (3) to clarify the implied and/or inferred applications of theory and research to the various administrative decisions and actions required for effective leadership.

In reviewing the research literature, leadership is considered as a sociocultural phenomenon that is personally and situationally determined. In relating research findings and implications to higher education, administration is regarded as the various decisions and actions of persons in positions of leadership. Administrative leadership, a term that many academicians believe contradictory, is viewed as the role behavior of academic administrators who initiate, encourage, review, or otherwise influence the programs and performance of institutions of higher education. A value premise of the chapter is the belief that administrative leadership is the source of most constructive, substantive, and enduring changes in higher education. American colleges and universities are often subjected to intense outside pressures and to pervasive internal stimulation. To such pressures and stimulation, however, institutions make a remarkable accommodation, and most enduring changes are attributable to administrative and governance processes that are endowed with their own forms of leadership.

Another value premise involved in the review of research is the belief that research findings and their implications are dependent, in various ways, on the methods of inquiry and analysis that are used by knowledgeable and experienced researchers. Research methods are frequently guided by the theoretical assumptions (or suppositions) of researchers and their sponsors—and by the sophistication or expertise of researchers in using specific methods, techniques, or skills in systematic, objective studies. Empirical research on leadership is particularly difficult when theoretical and methodological preferences obscure findings and results that others could appreciate and use more effectively. A similar blindness is evident when researchers believe their methods to establish relations that are independent of situation, society, and culture. If the research literature on leadership has established any lasting insight into the nature and complexities of leadership, it must surely be the viewpoint that leadership is relative to the situations and conditions in which it is studied. The extent to which research findings can be generalized to other situations and conditions is itself a matter to study systematically and objectively.

THEORIES AND TYPOLOGIES

Leadership is often identified as a concept that lacks adequate definition. In similar manner, leaders are regarded as individuals who are, in unexplained ways, recognizable by their appearance and actions. And as many writers on leadership are fond of pointing out, leadership is a learnable pattern of behavior, but no one should be so presumptuous as to train leaders for specific positions of leadership. All three points of view are vestiges of the mystique that has customarily surrounded leaders, their selection, and their effectiveness. Whatever leadership is, it is presumed to emerge within groups, organizations, and societies in times of crisis. As an emergent event, leadership is thus seen as unpredictable but somewhat inevitable. An organizational or national crisis evidently produces just exactly the kind of leadership needed to cope successfully with uncertain and hostile events or forces.

The term *leadership* evidently did not enter the English language until quite late, and Williams (1976) does not include the term in his historical dictionary of key words in Western society and culture. All societies have suitable terms for chiefs, heads of tribal councils, rulers, nobles, and others with recognized authority over common members of tribe or society, but such terms refer to leaders as individuals and not to the special status, role, or function that is denoted by leadership. The problems of definition are therefore regarded by some researchers as overwhelming. Fortunately, the difficulties of definition do not prevent researchers from distinguishing, in many informative ways, leaders from other group members and from investigating the many interesting patterns of thought, feeling, and action that are often perceived as leadership.

To study leadership with some semblance of objectivity, researchers have rejected mythological or romantic notions of leaders who were endowed with mystical powers and whose control over groups was supernatural. Support for some hypotheses could occasionally be found in anecdotal, commonsense, or literary conceptions of a leader's personality or character, but neither traditional, bureaucratic, nor charismatic forms of leadership was amenable to the research methods at the empirical researcher's disposal. The earliest years of interest in leadership are characterized, therefore, by theories that displayed a penchant for observation and classification but not controlled inquiry and analysis. The sole outcome in many cases was a typology of leaders that explained most of their behavior by descriptively labeling the style or manner in which they presumably led others.

Types of Leaders

Leadership typologies no doubt date from Plato and his distinction between those who know and those who do. His notion of philosopher-kings who would know what others should do and instruct them accordingly has long served to set leaders apart and to give them a special status in society. Niccolò Machiavelli's "prince" and Thomas Carlyle's "hero" have had much greater influence in Western civilization, however, and greatmen theories of leadership are likely to surface at any moment. Jennings (1960) analyzed the nation's need for leadership in terms of princes, heroes, and supermen. In his analysis, princes were power-directed, heroes were purpose-directed, and supermen (Friedrich Nietzsche's term) were self-directed. In industry and business, Jennings found a cult of human relations, the domination of organization or team men, and a dearth of independent and creative leadership in most American organizations and institutions. A national faith in personal, conspicuous leadership was threatened by a loss of control over personal destinies. The solution, as seen by Jennings, was a rebirth of leaders and a revival of their unique powers of innovation and their courage to accept great risks.

A similar picture for college students was painted by Levine (1981) following an era of student dissent, faculty restiveness, and campus disruptions triggered by the national tragedies of Vietnam and Watergate. Levine found many similarities in national mood and receptivity to leadership between the post–World War II period and the late 1970s. Unlike Jennings, however, Levine did not see a solution in a rebirth of leadership.

A more informative classification of historical leaders has been made by Hook (1955) in his distinction between eventful men and event-making men. An eventful man is one who influences the course of historical events because of the position he occupies at the time. An event-making man alters the course of events by sheer dint of his intelligence, character, or other outstanding characteristics. Such influence is not an accident of history, and the event-making man is not a creation of his particular time and place in history. In brief, event-making leaders make a difference in outcomes and consequences by virtue of the leadership qualities they bring to the challenges and opportunities of their particular generation or period in history. In Hook's assessment, the Russian Revolution was not inevitable, and it could not have succeeded without Lenin's leadership; thus, Lenin was a leader who made events and did much more than just ride the waves of historical inevitability.

The popularity of typologies was given a substantial boost by Burns's (1978) definitions of transactional and transformational leadership. Burns proposes that leadership is best understood within a framework of power and purpose, and he draws heavily from humanistic psychology in his formulation of transformational leadership as guiding and directing intellectual and revolutionary change. Transactional leadership, by contrast, is discussed as opinion leadership of groups, parties, and legislative or executive branches of government. Charles de Gaulle is believed by Burns to be the best example of transactional leadership, while Lenin, again, may be cited as an obvious example of transformational leadership. Burns's uses of the behavioral and social sciences had been demonstrated earlier in his biography of Franklin Delano Roosevelt and the entitlement of the first volume as *Roosevelt: The Lion and the Fox*.

Typologies of interest to researchers have been supplied in the form of autocratic, democratic, and laissez-faire leadership (Lewin, Lippett, and White, 1939); bureaucratic, patrimonial, and charismatic leadership (Weber, 1947); organizational leadership as Theory X and Theory Y (McGregor, 1960); bureaucratic leaders who are climbers, conservers, zealots, advocates, and statesmen (Downs, 1967); nomothetic, idiographic, and synthetic leadership (Getzels and Guba, 1957); and exploitive-authoritative, benevolent-authoritative, consultative, and participative systems of management (Likert, 1961).

An appealing typology has been provided by Maccoby (1976) in his identification of craftsmen, jungle fighters, company men, and gamesmen. Craftsmen are seen by Maccoby as deriving their sense of personal worth from their knowledge, skill, and self-reliance; their productivity and inventiveness supply the resources and technology that other managers develop and exploit. Jungle fighters are the entrepreneurs or robber barons of another era; they are Machiavellian foxes, cunning and aggressive, and having inordinate needs to dominate others. Company men perceive themselves as individualistic, self-reliant, and loyal to the firm; they are essential to large corporations and equate their own development with the company's long-range success.

Gamesmen are competitive, innovative, and flexible and are team players. They are fascinated by technique, new methods, change, and risk. They see a new project as a personal challenge to be approached in terms of its options, possibilities, and payoffs—and are compulsively driven to succeed. The gamesman of corporate industry and business is thus engaged in activities and functions where his desire is to be known as a winner; he is playing for fame, glory, and the exhilaration of winning, as well as the financial rewards his triumphs bring.

In summary, the development of leadership typologies is an interesting and often enlightening enterprise. Insights can be gained and points of view can be appreciated. The limitations, of course, are the limitations of all typologies. More leaders will be found outside the designated types than inside, and more than a few will be found straddling the categories that theorists and researchers have so carefully devised. There is further disadvantage in the various roles and responsibilities that come with positions of leadership in pluralistic and multi-dimensional organizations and societies. Few leaders are representative of any one type at all times in all places with all people. Table 1 provides a potpourri of leadership types that can be found in the literature on leadership. As given, however, each pair should be regarded as a continuum of leadership and not as dichotomous or opposed types.

Types of Theories

Leadership theories are as diversified as typologies of leaders. It's a bit trite to say that everyone who writes about leadership has his or her own theory, but the variety of theories is impressive, and a typology of theories has been suggested by more than one researcher trying to make sense of voluminous research studies. Leaders at the various levels of state, society, and nation; in the many associations, organizations, and institutions that characterize the American people; in the political, social, and technological sectors of the American economy; in the intellectual and cultural dimensions of western civilization; and in our seemingly infinite social and interest groups, occupations, professions, and civic organizations—all strongly imply that different theoretical explanations are needed. And an adequate conceptual grasp of leadership as a culturally bounded phenomenon would more than dictate some kind of grouping, clustering, or classification of the many explanations and interpretations that continue to be offered.

The grouping of leadership theories presented here (see Table 2) is a provisional effort only. No contention is made that the groups of theories are consistent, mutually exclusive, or exhaustive. As a rough classification of theories, however, the following theories and models should have one or two appealing features, and they should provide some degree of insight into the various efforts of theorists and researchers.

Fate and Destiny

Theories of leaders that deal with fate and destiny are better known as "great man" theories. As such, they reflect traditional or conventional notions of leadership and the mind, character, or personality of leaders. The source of fate and destiny theories is myths, legends, folklore, biographies, and other forms of literature, such as personal memoirs. Leadership is perceived as a special characteristic that manifests itself early in the life of outstanding leaders. Home

TABLE 1. Types of Leaders

Symbolic	Substantive
Supportive	Strong
Transactional	Transformational
Event-made men	Event-making men
Mystics and prophets	Priests and theologians
Craftsmen	Gamesmen
Bureaucratic	Charismatic
Democratic	Autocratic
Idiographic	Nomothetic
Exploitive-authoritative	Participative
Group-oriented	Goal-oriented
Laissez-faire	Authoritarian
Other-directed	Inner-directed
Climbers	Statesmen
Lieutenants	Field marshals
Caretakers	Founding fathers

and family are important features of the leader's development, and the leader's potential for greatness is usually detected in early life by parents, relatives, and/or teachers. Indeed, once greatness is achieved, at least one former teacher can be found who will verify the leader's early promise. Biographies and memoirs of such leaders customarily include their genealogical lineage, with sometimes obvious and sometimes subtle implications that greatness is a part of the leader's inheritance. Classic examples of fate-and-destiny theories, of course, are found in Galton's (1869) studies of hereditary genius and Carlyle's (1841) adoration of heroes. An analysis of leadership among the classical Greeks (Sarachek, 1968) identified justice and judgment (Agammemnon), wisdom and counsel (Nestor), shrewdness and cunning (Odysseus), and valor and action (Achilles) as the qualities needed to fulfill one's destiny. Later examples are found throughout the literature on leadership, but most notably in studies of leadership traits that lean in the direction of heredity. Jennings (1960) can be read as a more recent interpretation of the "great man" as prince, hero, or superman. Mills (1956), Hunter (1959), and Presthus (1964) give elitist explanations of leadership that suggest the continuing presence of great men.

Time and Place

Theories of leadership often include situational or environmentalistic conceptions of leaders who emerge or step forward in times of crisis. If not an inherent

TABLE 2. Types of Theories

Fate-and-destiny theories:

Traditional or conventional notions of human mind, character, and heritage as the source of leadership, with special characteristics that are manifest in early life; leaders are born, and history is the biography of great men.

Time-and-place theories:

The emergence of leadership in a time of need; given the opportunities, threats, or risks of the occasion, leaders will be found; history is the saga of persons who appeared at the right time, and situational demands usually determine who will lead.

Group-and-organization theories:

Often a matter of size, complexity, and perceived challenges of the group or organization; personal qualities and interpersonal skills are secondary to, if not determined by, group demands and expectations.

System-and-process theories:

Leadership as a minor factor in a context larger than leaders, groups, and organizations; roles, norms, expectations, and values are submerged in the systemic features of an ongoing process.

Selection-and-training theories:

May have begun with Plato's philosopher-kings and statesmen who were carefully groomed and did not ascend to leadership until they were 50; . . . often seen in the assessment of talent and managerial, executive, and administrative development programs.

Here-and-now theories:

Have many vestiges of great-man theories and hero worship; successful or popular leadership is more often depicted than effective leadership, and the power of positive thinking is overestimated.

Interaction-and-effectiveness theories:

Recognize the nonlinear effects of personal characteristics, situational variables, and group or organizational complexities; the effectiveness of leadership is an outcome of person-situation-group-goal interactions that are often difficult to ferret out.

---

characteristic of outstanding individuals, leadership is at least an inherent property of society and its confrontation with challenge. If leadership, of a particular kind, is what the occasion demands, leadership is optimistically believed to be what the occasion will bring forth. Environmentalism is a component of many theories of human behavior, however, and its influence can be seen in most theories that regard behavior as contingent upon the opportunities, threats, or risks of the moment. Many heroes obviously have their time and place in history, and time-and-place theories can incorporate much that is suggested by fate-and-destiny theories, as well as by those concerned with the group and organizational origins of leadership. In brief, there are hints of time and place in virtually all historical accounts of leadership and great leaders. Burns's transactional and transformational leaders are obviously influenced by time and place. And a study of college and university presidents (Kerr and Gade, 1986) strongly implies that institutional leadership is often dependent upon being in the right place at the right time.

Group and Organization

The influence of environment, situation, and current conditions is also seen in group-and-organization theories. The size, composition, and perceived tasks of a group have much to do with the kind of leader they will choose, if permitted to choose freely. In much the same manner, the qualities and characteristics of chosen leaders are often related to the level and complexity of organization in business and industrial firms, government agencies, professional societies, and social institutions. Leaders believed to be effective at one level of organization may *not* be effective at a higher *or* lower level. The distinctive feature of group-and-organization theories, nonetheless, can be understood best when organizational and group characteristics are seen as dominating personal and interpersonal qualities that leaders might bring to their responsibilities. Many sociological theories treat leadership as a function of the group, organization, or society in which a leader's role or status becomes a matter of attention. Leader behavior is explained in terms of the leader's success in meeting group norms, needs, and expectations. Tannenbaum, Weschler, and Massarik (1961), Hollander (1964), Stogdill (1959), Argyris (1957), Cartwright and Zander (1960), Thibaut and Kelley (1959), Beckhard (1969), Bennis (1969), and others provide interpretations of leadership, as influenced by group and organizational characteristics and conditions.

System and Process

In the application of many theories to leadership, there is usually a concern for a larger significance or meaning than the personal qualities of leaders, their behavior, and the effects of leader behavior on group or organizational productivity. The social, political, or economic system for which leaders are ostensibly needed is dominant, and the process by which leaders enter, perform in, and exit the system is an overriding matter of attention. Getzels et al. (1968) provide an excellent model of educational administration as a social process in which individual personality and needs are interrelated with institutional roles and expectations. The former dimension of the social system is identified as nomothetic because of its normative or lawlike features, while the latter dimension is known as the personal or idiographic dimension. There is much about Getzels, Lipham, and Campbell's education as social system that would apply equally well to the employment and performance of lawyers in legal systems; accountants, economists, and bank workers in financial systems; and even engineers in certain kinds of technological systems. The gist of system-and-process theories, nonetheless, is the accommodation of leader characteristics, performance, and effectiveness within a larger, more complex structure of interrelated parts. Other examples of system-and-process concepts of leadership can be found in Likert (1961, 1967); Katz and Kahn (1966); March and Simon (1958); Cohen and March (1974); and selected volumes in the literature on organization development (Blake and Mouton, 1969; Lawrence and Lorsch, 1969; Schein, 1969).

Selection and Training

Various models of leadership are related to the trait-and-factor theories that have been greatly discredited by many researchers. Yet the military services and corporate business still give appreciable credence to such models, if their numerous attempts to measure, assess, or otherwise identify personal qualities of potential leaders are considered and if their innumerable training and development programs are taken into account. The military services, in particular, maintain firm and consistent ideas about the nature of military leadership, the kinds of service personnel who are trainable as leaders, and the means by which leadership may be trained and/or developed. Corporate industry also maintains such ideas with respect to many middle-management positions, and moderate-sized business firms still seek more suitable means of personnel selection as a means of reducing training costs. Colleges and universities, on the contrary, have accepted few features of selection-and-training models, as applied in business, industry, and some government agencies. Virtually no one takes a test in application to an administrative position, and universities have been most reluctant to accept any responsibility for the in-service development of their presidents, deans, and department heads.

Here and Now

Many studies of leadership seize upon the specifics of the occasion and state observations and conclusions in general terms. There are no sound reasons that researchers should not be permitted to theorize from particular studies, and quite often the inductive beginnings of a good theory are forgotten as it generates good hypotheses for further testing. The criticism that *ad hoc* theories are seldom productive should be heard, however, and the appealing phrases and catchwords of here-and-now explanations of leadership should not encourage careless generalizations of concepts, findings, and conclusions to other situations and conditions. In particular, the datedness of many specific conclusions should be remembered. On the other hand, there is sometimes a tendency for *ad hoc* theories to remain both innocent and silent about time-and-place theories that are obviously relevant. The popular literature on business management and/or leadership is particularly subject to here-and-now theorizing, and many of the concepts and principles of leadership often border on the specious. (See Peters and Waterman, 1982; Bennis and Nanus, 1985; and *many* others).

Interaction and Effectiveness

The systematic, objective studies of leadership in the past 40 years have been much concerned with interaction and leader effectiveness. The research dimensions of leadership are often defined as (1) leader behavior (or characteristics); (2) group or organizational characteristics; (3) goals, objectives, tasks, or other desired ends and outcomes; and (4) interactions among leaders and groups, leaders and group performance, groups and tasks, and so on as these conditions relate to the effectiveness of leaders in contributing to or facilitating group or organizational outcomes. The emphasis in such theories is thus placed on the inner relations of leaders, groups, tasks, and outcomes with varying efforts to partial out the specific contribution of leaders. In most research related to these theories, the criteria are measures of group performance, productivity, satisfaction, or other outcomes. The results of such research are often discussed as conditional, dependent, or contingent upon the interactions of leadership, group characteristics, and situational variables. Bass (1960, 1981), Fiedler (1967), Hunt and Larson (1977), and Stogdill (1974) should be consulted for the many interesting examples that could be cited.

THE OHIO STATE LEADERSHIP STUDIES

The research on leadership cannot be fully appreciated without familiarity with the Ohio State Leadership Studies conducted during the 1940s and 1950s, and continuing into the 1960s. Leadership in military, business, industrial, governmental, and educational organizations was studied by a diverse group of researchers and resulted in a remarkable list of published reports, journal articles, and books. The findings, conclusions, and implications of the OSU studies were instrumental in the greater portion of research, development, and training efforts in the 1960s and 1970s. The influence of the studies continues in the 1980s with Bass's (1981) revision and expansion of Stogdill's (1974) handbook of theory and research.

Directed by Carroll Shartle, the OSU studies were funded by the U.S. Office of Naval Research, the U.S. Air Force, the Rockefeller Foundation, and various business and industrial corporations. The diversity of the studies is exemplified by Shartle's (1956) studies of executive performance and by Stogdill's (1959) research-based theory of group and organization achievement. Shartle's book underscored the importance of executive leadership in the nation's business and industrial corporations, while Stogdill gave the more comprehensive summary of theory and research related to group structure, performance, and outcomes.

The beginning of the studies may be dated from Stogdill's (1949) review of personal factors associated with leadership. His survey of the research literature included all studies (up to 1947) in which an effort was made to determine the traits and characteristics of leaders. Discussed in his article were all traits and factors studied by three or more researchers. Stogdill concluded from his research review that the personal factors most often associated with leadership are (1) intelligence; (2) scholarship; (3) dependability; (4) active participation; and (5) socioeconomic status. Other factors associated with leadership were (6) sociability; (7) initiative; (8) persistence; (9) know-how; (10) self-confidence; (11) alertness and insight; (12) cooperativeness; (13) popularity; (14) adaptability; and (15) verbal facility. Low positive correlations were found between leadership and physical characteristics such as age, height, weight, physique, energy, and appearance.

Stogdill classified the personal factors associated with leadership under the headings of capacity, achievement, responsibility, participation, and status. Also related to leadership, however, was another significant factor, which he identified as situation (i.e., group characteristics, objectives, and so on). Stogdill concluded that leadership was not a function of any particular combination of factors, but that patterns of personal factors were related to the characteristics, activities, and goals of followers. Leadership thus should be studied as an interaction of leadership and group variables. However leadership might be defined, it is a relationship between people in social situations.

A later review of research by Stogdill (1974) gave emphasis to the fact that research findings are dependent upon the kinds of research conducted. Where the earlier studies had been conducted on groups available to researchers at the time, later studies conducted on other groups displayed the varying influence of characteristics such as age, height, weight, and physical appearance. Levels of activity or energy, personal ascendancy or dominance, and desire to excel were indicative of personal characteristics associated with leadership in the later groups. In the 1970s, leaders could be characterized by vigor and persistence in their pursuit of goals, originality in problem solving, social initiative, sense of personal identity, toleration of frustration and failure, and ability to influence the behavior of others. These were the kind of research variables that differentiated leaders from followers, effective from ineffective leaders, and higher-level leaders from those at lower levels. In brief, the personal characteristics associated with leadership were not unrelated to the ways in which researchers defined and assessed their research variables.

An understanding of the methods of inquiry, analysis, and verification used in the OSU leadership studies is essential to their findings, conclusions, and implications. An appreciation of the studies, therefore, is obtained best from the series of research monographs issued as the OSU studies progressed. Researchers in the studies accepted leaders as identified by the organizations with which they worked. This meant, in most studies, that the leadership actually studied was the status or position leadership of persons employed within the organization. Research methods included interviews, questionnaires, and rating scales constructed and developed for the specific purposes of the studies. Factor analysis, as used in the studies, proved to be an invaluable aid to data reduction—and to the identification of the underlying dimensions of leader behavior.

Situational Factors

Among the earlier research questions raised in the OSU studies were the requirements for leadership in different situations. A group dimensions questionnaire was constructed to describe group situations in terms of their specific characteristics (Hemphill, 1956). Results were then analyzed in terms of their usefulness in understanding what behavior was required of successful leaders. The 15 dimensions identified in developing the questionnaire were (1) size; (2) viscidity, or the degree to which the group functioned as a unit; (3) homogeneity, or similarity of relevant characteristics; (4) flexibility, or freedom from rules, customs, and so on; (5) permeability, or the ease with which new members joined; (6) polarization, or orientation to a single goal; (7) stability; (8) intimacy, or mutual acquaintance and familiarity; (9) autonomy, or group determination of activities; (10) control, or the regulation of member behavior; (11) position (of individual members), a dimension later discarded from the questionnaire; (12) potency, or the significance of the group to its members; (13) hedonic tone, or general feelings of pleasure; (14) participation; and (15) dependence (of members on leaders), another dimension later discarded. Scores on the group dimensions provided a profile of the individual's perceptions of and attitudes toward the group and thus a basis for the comparison of different groups.

A measure of leadership adequacy was obtained by ratings of the leader's overall quality (of leadership) and the individual judgments of the group's overall quality. Other indicators of leadership adequacy were ratings of group morale, effectiveness, the degree to which the leader was liked, and a composite score for all variables rated. Having decided an index of leadership, Hemphill then turned to an analysis of leadership adequacy, as related to group dimensions and to more specific characteristics of leader behavior. The adequate leader was defined as:

1. Exhibiting behavior that was indicative of his or her ability to advance the purposes of the group,
2. Indicating competence in administrative functions,
3. Inspiring members to greater activity,
4. Augmenting members' feelings of security, and
5. *Not* necessarily making decisions quickly.

Hemphill concludes from his study that the leader's most important function may be that of maintaining membership as a satisfying experience *and* facilitating their group's actions as a unit. In studying the interactions of leadership adequacy and group characteristics, Hemphill derives several interesting hypotheses that more-or-less capture the flavor of interaction-and-effectiveness research:

1. If leaders make decisions quickly, their adequacy may be judged low by large, closely knit, and unstable groups, whereas quick decisions may net a high rating in informal groups;
2. If leaders do not create the impression of confidence in their decisions, their adequacy *and* hedonic tone may be judged low;
3. If leaders lose prestige, unstable groups may give low ratings on adequacy; if leaders lose emotional control, groups low in flexibility and hedonic tone may rate leaders low;
4. If leaders are unwilling to risk their personal welfare, they will be judged low by polarized and restricted groups;
5. If leaders prefer the company of superiors, they will be judged low by large, cohesive, and formal groups; and
6. If leaders reverse their decisions frequently, their adequacy will be judged low by cohesive, inflexible, permeable, polarized, and disagreeable groups.

Group Dimensions

Hemphill's efforts to define situational factors in the form of group dimensions were refined into the Group Dimensions Descriptions questionnaire, for which a technical manual was published (Hemphill, 1956). Stanine scores for the scales were developed from raw scores describing 950 groups, and a standard population was defined from five subsamples of (1) 100 miscellaneous groups, such as sororities and other campus organizations; (2) 130 members of a liberal arts faculty; (3) 185 women office workers; (4) 215 student members of nine religious associations or clubs; and (5) 320 public school teachers. In each case, respondents described the agency, association, department, organization, or school system to which they belonged.

The reliability coefficients of the scales ranged from + .28 for hedonic tone to + .92 for autonomy and give good evidence of the consistency with which group characteristics can be rated by relatively naive observers. A factor analysis of the intercorrelations among the 13 scales disclosed factors that were identified as (I) behavioral regulation appearing as social structure; (II) effective synergy; and (III) primary personal interaction. The validity of the questionnaire was examined by comparing the pattern of individual member responses to the averaged responses of total groups and by correlating scale scores with job satisfaction ratings and group productivity.

Leader Behavior

An early decision in the Ohio State Leadership Studies led to the development of measures of behavior and/or performance, as opposed to personality or leadership traits. Thus, one principal objective of the studies was to test hypotheses concerning situational determinants of leader behavior, and reliable indications of leader behavior were needed in the formulation and testing of hypotheses. Efforts to develop measures of leader behavior were predicated on the belief that leadership per se should not be equated with "good leadership." Also involved was the premise that the description of leader behavior and the evaluation of leader behavior were separate operations. Consequently, adequate description should precede efforts to evaluate.

The development of the Ohio State Leader Behavior Description Questionnaire (LBDQ) also involved an option to describe *how* leaders carry out their various activities and to avoid entanglements in *what* they did. Items for the questionnaire were selected to describe specific behaviors instead of general traits, to restrict their content to one kind of activity, and to apply specifically to a single behavioral dimension. Emotional or evaluative terms were avoided in writing the items, and they were worded in terms believed to be meaningful to potential respondents. Items were written in the present tense and used the third person, as one means of making the instrument applicable to various groups and situations.

The tentative behavioral dimensions identified in the development process were (1) integration; (2) communication; (3) production emphasis; (4) initiation; and (5) domination. The assumptions of the researchers are now obvious in their choice of relevant dimensions, and it is not surprising that their chosen dimensions were found to be interdependent. Initial results with the LBDQ led its creators to the tentative conclusion that the various scales were a relatively expansive overall rating stemming from the respondents' judgments of individual leadership qualities.

Factorial study of the LBDQ (Halpin and Winer, 1957) resulted in the extraction of two factors: consideration for others and the initiation of structure in situations involving leaders and followers. For B-50 bomber crews, consideration of others was found to correlate negatively with technical competence, conformity to standardized operating procedures (SOP), performance under stress, attitude and motivation, and overall effectiveness—as these criteria were rated independently by supervisors. The initiation of structure, however, correlated positively with all such indices, and consideration of others correlated + .64 with a crew satisfaction index. The two factors of consideration and structure were extracted in other factor analyses with other groups, and the correlation of consideration with satisfaction proved to be a harbinger of later, and consistent, findings.

Such experiences with the LBDQ apparently convinced the OSU researchers that leaders could accomplish their task in at least three different ways. They could concentrate on being socially acceptable individuals in their interactions with group members, *or* emphasize the importance of group production, *or* seek ways in which members of a group or organization could work together more effectively. In brief, leaders could work well with individual members or help them work well with each other; if neither of these efforts worked, leaders could stress ''getting the job done.''

The independence of consideration and initiating structure, as behavioral dimensions in leadership, was further confirmed in early studies by Halpin (1957). The aircraft commanders rated highest in overall effectiveness by their superiors tended to score higher on structure than consideration. The commanders who were rated high by subordinates on friendship and cooperation were perceived as most considerate. And commanders satisfying both superiors and subordinates were above average in both consideration and structure. Low correlations resulted, however, from initial studies of actual leader behavior and ideal leader behavior. When aircraft commanders and school superintendents were asked how they should behave, and subordinates were asked to rate their actual behavior, correlation coefficients were not impressive.

An industrial version of the Leadership Behavior Description Questionnaire was developed by Fleishman (1957). Industry and business, like the military services and education, were suitable fields for the study of leadership because leaders were identifiable by position, were aware of the importance of leadership, and were familiar with the research methods employed in studies of leader behavior. Leaders in the armed forces, public education, and private industry also had much in common and had seen in the past a hesitancy to study administrative positions because of their complexity.

A study conducted by Fleishman, Harris, and Burtt (1955) at International Harvester was designed to meet the company's objective of reducing conflict and promoting greater worker satisfaction, as a means of obtaining great efficiency. Pretraining and posttraining differences in the scores of front-line supervisors showed a significant decrease in structure and a corresponding increase in consideration. Trained foremen, however, scored lower in consideration and higher in structure than untrained foremen, an outcome raising several questions about the differences between verbal behavior, as ostensibly reflected in the leadership scales, and actual performance on the job.

Further studies in supervisory leadership disclosed the importance of leadership climate by suggesting that foremen who worked under considerate leadership were more likely to be considerate of the workers they supervised. Considerate supervision was related to employee morale in most industrial divisions, but structure evidently had a differential effect for productive and nonproductive divisions. In the former, it was found that foremen with high proficiency ratings showed more initiation of structure, where in the latter, the reverse was found. Neither accident rate nor turnover was related to the two forms of supervisory leadership, but absenteeism was positively related to structure and negatively related to consideration. And unfortunately for the leadership climate of industrial firms, some evidence was obtained that training in human relations could result in poorer human relations on the job.

The continued development of leader behavior scales resulted in relatively short, easily completed instruments with appreciable internal consistency. The intercorrelations of items on particular scales ranged from $+.70$ to $+.80$ or higher (Schriesheim and Kerr, 1974), and reliability coefficients were often found to be $+.81$ or higher. Stogdill (1963a) eventually reduced the LBDQ to 10 items, in the revised LBDQ-XII, as a measure of structure only—the efforts of leaders to define their own role and to let followers know what was expected of them. From a psychometric standpoint, however, the scales were often suspect because they suffered from halo effect and were subject to errors of leniency in rating. As research on the LBDQ was publicized, consideration and structure became socially desirable characteristics in firms and corporations that regarded their leadership as enlightened. In some respects, the popularization of the scales (and their many imitators) contributed to a stereotypical view of leadership, in which leaders were expected to score high on both scales *or* to give justifiable reasons why they didn't.

As early as 1959, Stogdill proposed additional scales for the LBDQ in hopes of establishing conceptually distinct patterns of leader behavior—other than consideration of others and initiation of structure. LBDQ-XII eventually yielded 10 factors, which were identified as (1) general persuasive leadership; (2) tolerance of uncertainty; (3) tolerance of freedom of action by followers; (4) representation of the group; (5) influence with superiors; (6) production emphasis; (7) structuring expectations; (8) consideration [I]; (9) consideration [II], and (10) retention of the leadership role. Most of the factors, however, were only confirmation that leader behavior is complex, a fact that most researchers have never doubted. When subjected to higher-order analysis, the factors derived from LBDQ-XII were amenable to a two-factor theory of leader behavior in which structure and production emphasis could be seen as one factor—and tolerance (both of uncertainty and of followers) could be seen as the other. Consideration made a contribution to the second higher-order factor, and it could still be regarded as a form of supportive leadership, but its lines and features were no longer distinct. Research findings became dependent upon which form of the OSU leadership scales the researcher used: the LBDQ, the Supervisory Behavior Description Questionnaire (SBDQ), the Leadership Opinion Questionnaire (LOQ), or the LBDQ-XII. In particular, the differences between the LBDQ and the LBDQ-XII appeared to be a matter of the way in which the two instruments were developed, the specific content of items, and the groups in which they were used (Bass, 1981).

Group Effects

Other studies conducted in the OSU Leadership Studies were effective in other ways. The studies clearly established leadership as a group effect and an aspect of organization. The minimal conditions for leadership were identified, from the beginning, as a group, a common task or goal, and a differentiation of roles for leaders and followers. Leadership was increasingly viewed as a process of interaction with defined groups, their members, their designated tasks or goals, and their accomplishments. In discussing social psychological theory and its practical applications, Campbell (1956) was of the opinion that important ''payoffs'' should still be sought in the relationships between leadership criteria and the psychological attributes of leaders. Self-descriptions and descriptive ratings by subordinates were subject to error, but descriptions by subordinates were at least informative of the leadership values, beliefs, and ideologies held by subordinates. Self-descriptions tended to be favorable, but they were more discriminating (and more useful) than the ratings of subordinates. Furthermore, there were reasons to believe that the bias of self-descriptions was less systematic than that of descriptions by others.

In working with departments of instruction in a moderately large university, Hemphill (1957) found that older faculty members could rate consistently the administrative reputations of academic departments, and that faculty members could rate consistently the leader behavior of department heads. When correlated, a significant relationship was found between administrative reputations of departments and ratings of departmental heads who were above average on both consideration and structure, as seen by their respective faculties. Administrative reputations were apparently influenced by departmental size, but no relationship was established between faculty characteristics and administrative reputations.

In his effort to bring theoretical structure to leader behavior and group achievement, Stogdill (1959) identified achievement as the totality of the outcomes experienced by groups. Added to this definition, however, were the outputs resulting from the input variables of performance, interaction, and expectations, as mediated by group structures and operations. Effectiveness in group production was inadequate to account for the totality of group outcomes, and the essential dimensions were identified as (1) productivity—the direct outcome of task performance; (2) morale—freedom from restraint; and (3) integration—the ability of the group to maintain its structure and to function under stress.

Among Stogdill's sometimes surprising premises was his definition of morale as the goal direction of activity and its freedom from restraint (not the subjective feelings that members might have about effective actions). Successful outcomes evidently reinforced expectations for further success and brought prestige and higher status, but member satisfaction, contrary to other theories, was not as closely related to morale or productivity as it was to the group unity and loyalty that are evident in routine operations. Morale, as defined by Stogdill, was a function of structure and control, two group characteristics closely related to group leadership. When group efforts are fragmented and there are subgroup activities unrelated to group goals, the group is not goal-directed and it is not free from restraint; thus, the group suffers a loss in morale.

Every group must devote some of its productive energies to the internal development of its structure and to maintaining itself. Member satisfaction may be negatively related (at times) to productivity, but it was believed by Stogdill to be at a maximum when individual goals and group goals were identical. Productivity is apparently at its maximum when the role structure of the group is clearly defined and members in high-status positions can maintain group structure and goal direction. Leadership evidently is at its best when the responsibility and authority of subordinates for controlling operations can be enlarged. More-or-less implied by all this is the probability that productivity, group morale, and group integration must be obtained at a cost to the group. Outcomes that confirm expectations, however, will tend to increase group expectations, and not to decrease them.

Administrative Patterns

Included among the studies at Ohio State were several efforts to identify and analyze patterns of administrative behavior. The administrative leadership of naval officers was studied (Stogdill and Shartle, 1955) by (1) interviews with officers in administrative positions; (2) analysis of organization charts and manuals; (3) review of the mission and objectives of the total organization and its respective departments and divisions; (4) sociometric studies of working relationships; (5) responsibility-authority-delegation scales to assess the status of administrative functions; (6) job analyses of administrative performance; (7) measures of leader behavior, as described by the officer administrators and other members of the organization; and (8) ratings of individual and unit effectiveness.

In conducting these studies, the researchers sought an integrated approach to research on administrative performance and leadership, the development of measures that could be used in diagnosis and eventual selection, and other systematic means of describing administrative behavior in terms of what exists at a particular time and place.

Stogdill and Shartle established that executives could estimate, with reasonable accuracy, the time they spent on directly observable and frequent activities. When activities were infrequent, there was less correlation between logged time and estimated time. Executive performance, they believed, was related to the position held, the position level within the organization, and the type of organization. Time spent on various activities, however, was regarded as the most quantifiable aspect of administrative performance, and appreciable similarity of time use was reported in a study of 470 navy officers and 66 business executives. Both kinds of executives spent more time with subordinates than with superiors, spent an appreciable amount of their time in reading and writing reports, and spent less time on planning than on other reported activities.

Factor analyses of administrative time on task disclosed eight factors, which were identified as (1) high-level policymaking; (2) administrative coordination; (3) methods planning; (4) representation of group interests to others; (5) personnel services; (6) professional consultation; (7) maintenance services; and (8) inspection. By relating the uses of time to position held, the researchers were able to document the specialization of administration and identify functional specialties, such as public relations, personnel administration, technical supervision, planning, and directing. Further analyses revealed level differences between junior and senior officers and occasional disagreement between self-descriptions of what the officers did and self-expectations as to what they thought they should do (Stogdill et al., 1955).

In a study of executive positions, Hemphill (1960) isolated 10 factors, which he identified as (1) providing a staff service; (2) supervising the work of subordinates; (3) business control; (4) technical (pertaining to markets and products); (5) community and social affairs; (6) long-range planning; (7) exercise of broad power and authority; (8) business reputation; (9) personnel demands; and (10) preservation of assets. The implications of the research on administrative patterns were taken up by other researchers, and administration, like leadership, was extensively studied in terms of its differentiated roles and responsibilities.

Residual Effects

In retrospect, the impact of the Ohio State Leadership Studies may be seen as a commendable initiation of structure in leadership theory and research. The studies were most effective in their redirection of research questions to situational, group, and organization variables and their interactions with leader behavior, as perceived by observers (superiors, subordinates, and others) and leaders themselves. Methods of measuring and/or assessing group characteristics, leader behavior, and administrative functions such as authority, responsibility, and delegation were developed and effectively applied in a remarkable diversity of experimental and field studies. Factor-analytic methods, as a means of identifying underlying dimensions of complex phenomenon, were employed with increasing sophistication and were successful in yielding factors that proved to be highly useful in research, theory construction and development, leadership training, and management development. The two-factor theory of structure and consideration was, in itself, a boost to leadership research, training, and development—and to administrative practices in corporate industry and business. To no small extent, management training and development became a thriving industry in its own right, and the commercialized versions of structure and consideration scales became a mainstay in innumerable management and supervisory training programs.

The theoretical implications and the research methods of the OSU studies were most instrumental in clarifying leadership concepts, situational variables, and the many interesting ways in which leader behavior, groups, and organization interact. Diverse and innovative approaches to the study of leadership were fostered, and research following the work of Shartle, Stogdill, Hemphill, and many others was significantly different from the studies dealing with leadership during the pre–World War II years. The many imitators, and others who have borrowed freely without acknowledging any debts, are perhaps the most visible sign of the effectiveness of the OSU studies in addressing a highly significant and interesting issue in meaningful ways.

CONTINUITY AND CHANGE

The status of leadership theory and research, 40 years after the initiation of the Ohio State Leadership Studies, must be regarded as interesting and robust. James MacGregor Burns's (1978) historical analysis of transactional and transformational leadership has given theorists and researchers another two-factor theory of leadership, and a bandwagon effect is much in evidence. Organizational theorists have discovered, through their contacts with managers and organizations in other cultures, that cultural differences are indeed relevant dimensions in the study of leadership, management, and organizational effectiveness. Organizational culture is now studied instead of organizational climates (Schein, 1985), and an incredible interest in charismatic leadership suggests that theoretical and research interests are returning to earlier fascinations with personality traits and their cultural origins.

Where research on interactive effects and leader effectiveness continues, it is most likely to be concerned with the dyadic interactions of leaders and one or two followers. Researchers have shown substantial interest in the needs and expectations of followers, as well as those of leaders, and the interactions of mutual needs and expectations are the object of various research efforts. Both theory and research have been inclined to focus sharply on highly specific acts or events of leadership, and there is an appreciable tendency to analyze increasingly abstract variables, such as power relations, legitimacy, empathy, social insight, and charisma. In less rigorous fields of research, there is an active concern with leadership styles, as opposed to techniques, and on another plane, contrasts are made between leadership style and substance. One research interest shows a continuing concern with *how* leaders lead, as opposed to what they do, and the other implies a dissatisfaction with observed leader behavior *and* a preference for ideal leadership. In both approaches to leadership styles, there is often a remarkable indifference to situational differences and an optimistic assumption that leadership styles, once delineated, can be consciously adopted.

As the research interest in transactional and transformational leadership shows, however, there is a continuing interest in dichotomous, or two-factor, theories of leadership. Leadership, in the western world, is apparently better understood when it can be viewed as opposing tendencies in human nature, and when a choice of leadership is evidently permissible. Forms of democratic leadership are still contrasted with authoritarian forms, and person-oriented supervisors and managers are still preferred in many business and industrial firms to production-oriented leadership. *And* researchers in the field of leadership continue to be divided in their choice of organizational criteria by which to judge leader effectiveness. Productivity (and its many variations) is the criterion preferred by researchers interested in strong leaders, and it is usually the criterion preferred by corporate executives and stockholders. Individual satisfaction is a criterion preferred by advocates of supportive leadership (and most workers). Group productivity and group satisfaction are criteria that are employed with varying preferment and with varying results.

Changing Implications

The implications of leadership theory and research are more pronounced in the 1980s than they were in the 1970s. A generation of young adults with individualistic values, needs, and expectations gave little credence to conceptions of leadership as the initiation and maintenance of structure in group expectations and interactions. If not actually preferring to "do their own thing," members of the generation were nonetheless explicit in rejecting traditional notions of authority and conventional role models in leadership. As a consequence of such conflict in cultural values, research in the 1970s cannot, from the vantage point of the 1980s, be regarded as brilliant or creative. Social, economic, and technological developments in the 1960s and 1970s apparently altered public beliefs and attitudes concerning leadership and, in their rejection of traditional leadership, gave credence to Maccoby's (1979) views of the gamesman. The increasing presence of women and blacks in higher education (and other paths to positions of leadership) suggested a new or emerging national character torn between self-development and self-centeredness, a more critical attitude toward authority and a lingering sense of rebellion, and polarized lifestyles—careerism and social detachment (see Maccoby, 1979).

Stogdill (1974), in reviewing the research on leadership, identified intelligence, ability, task motivation, task performance, and social competence as variables that were usually higher among chosen leaders—but of varying importance. Insight into group member behavior or feelings, or an ability to size up situations, was not a characteristic that was particularly astute in most leaders. In much the same manner, a leader's esteem or respect among group members was more likely to be a function of his or her perceived influence with superiors than a function of personal and interpersonal competence. Yet persuasiveness might well be the most common characteristic of leaders, and their effectiveness in representing group interests to superiors and outsiders was an expected part of their role behavior.

Bass (1981), in revising and expanding Stogdill's handbook, concluded that personal traits and characteristics continue to be an important factor in the emergence of leaders and in their maintenance of role behavior. Active participation in group activities is one indication of which member of a group will emerge as its leader, and possession of information or knowledge relevant to the group's problems can contribute significantly to a leader's emergence. Social insight and empathy are still not distinctive characteristics of group leaders, but spontaneity of action in experimental groups (and in other groups) often identifies members who tend to emerge as leaders.

Leadership could still be viewed in 1974 and in 1981 as a focus of group process, as a differentiated role, and as an effect of group interactions, but the leader's powers of persuasion and the exercise of those powers in the group's behalf were more pronounced in 1981 than in 1974. Such conclusions are related, no doubt, to the emergence and the occasional domination of special-issue groups in the nation's public policymaking process; the growing influence of voluntary associations, professional societies, and similar organizations; and voluntary enlistment in the armed services. Each is further evidence of group tendencies to structure roles and relations as a means of (1) ensuring member welfare or morale; (2) fulfilling individual roles; (3) tolerating frustration; and (4) tolerating divergence in membership.

Persisting Patterns

The consistent finding that leaders tend to emerge in groups and the limited value of tests of personality, ability, and social skills in selecting effective leaders are indicative of the difficulties in identifying, recruiting, and selecting leaders for complex organizations and institutions. It is true that no single pattern of traits and characteristics has been verified for leaders, irrespective of group and situational variables. But it is also true that patterns of traits vary from situation to situation—and from time to time. Thus, there are always possibilities that specific patterns can be identified for particular situations and groups. Such patterns can be of considerable help in the early identification of potential leaders, and in the continuing selection process that is usually seen in many groups, associations, and organizations.

There is much in the recent literature on leadership to suggest that personal traits and/or qualities might call the group's attention to an individual and thereby become instrumental in that individual's selection. The particular pattern of personal traits used in selection, however, might not be the qualities, traits, or characteristics needed for effective performance. Whatever leader qualifications might be, they are apparently related to the stages of development evidenced by groups, associations, and organizations. Leaders who can maintain adequate role structure and goal direction at one level are not necessarily the leaders who are needed at higher or more complex levels of group development. In brief, there are reasons to believe that leader-group interactions are relative ''in time'' as well as for particular situations.

Much the same can be said about the group's identification with its chosen leaders. There are stages in which group members presumably identify strongly with leaders, and there are stages in which identification is minimal. Group satisfaction is apparently highest when leader behavior is both predictable and effective. In turn, leader behavior is believed by group members to be more effective when it is adaptive to the conditions and circumstances in which the group finds itself. Thus, it is often possible for leaders to initiate structure when the situation is regarded by members as either easy or difficult. Consideration is a more appropriate form of leader behavior when the situation is moderately favorable. The implications for leaders are related to whether they are primarily oriented to initiation of structure or to consideration of group members. When situational demands increase, leaders oriented to the initiation of structure should reduce their emphasis on structure and increase their concern for consideration. In the same situation, leaders oriented to consideration should increase the pressure for structure and decrease their concern for group member welfare. Once again, these conclusions and implications are indicative of results that can be derived only from studies of interactive effects.

Another consistent research finding with broad implications is the dependency of leader effectiveness on the criterion chosen for group performance. Many leadership studies suffer from the choice of a single criterion and from a failure to specify the properties of that criterion in ways that are significant and meaningful. Research findings are more clearly communicated when measures of group productivity, satisfaction, or cohesiveness are used as criteria. Leader efforts to structure group expectations are the *one* behavior pattern contributing positively to productivity, satisfaction, and cohesiveness, but other leader behavior can be effective, depending on the situation. Considerate leadership, of course, is often conducive to group satisfaction, and it is often a relevant factor in promoting group cohesiveness. No consistent relationship has been established between consideration and productivity, however, and when the two are positively related, the relationship is evidently dependent upon other factors, conditions, or situations.

The OSU studies and virtually all other research have been consistent in their rejection of leadership as a general or unitary trait. Many studies, however, have suggested that group productivity, morale, satisfaction, cohesiveness, and reputation may suffer from *poor* leadership, as defined by defects in leader personality, character, competence, or public image. The repetition of this suggestion implies that personal traits of leaders are *not* positively and uniformly correlated with desirable group outcomes—but negative traits and characteristics *can* affect group performance in adverse ways. Also suggested is the possibility that poor leadership might be a general or unitary trait. A direct implication of such a view is that groups should seek first *not* to select poor leaders—and, secondarily, to try to pick good ones.

Another administrative implication of the research on leadership follows from studies of persistence and transfer. There is appreciable evidence that effectiveness as a leader is not solely dependent upon the situation or leader-group interactions. Some personal qualities, such as self-concept, values, beliefs, and personal habits, display an obvious persistence, and leaders who have been successful in one situation are likely to lead in other situations, unless rejected. The best prediction, therefore, of effective leadership is prior success in serving as a leader.

Sociocultural Issues

Recent research on leadership may be interpreted as an effort to move on to other concerns and issues in society and culture. Societal problems influence, in many ways, a researcher's choice of leadership variables, conditions, and situations— and cultural pluralism in a democratic society undoubtedly influences public thought and discussion concerning leaders, how they are chosen, and what they are expected to do. The complexity of society, its diverse institutions, and its innumerable associations and organizations imply an inexorable specialization of leader behavior and leadership roles. Also implied is an inevitable separation of leaders from their followers as they must deal more and more with leaders from other societal agencies and sectors. Distinctly possible is a power elite of elected and appointed leaders who meet separately and collectively with each other in various coalitions, for various purposes, and with continuously changing agendas. Unlike the leaders studied by Stogdill and Shartle (1955), who spent more time meeting with subordinates, future leaders may spend no time with followers and constituencies—because they must spend more and more time representing group and organizational interests to other group and organizational representatives.

The multinational dimensions of business corporations, government agencies, and other organizations imply an increasing concern with cultural differences and their implications for leadership. As business corporations have become more complex, there have been many reallocations of managerial and leadership roles (with many accompanying shifts in responsibilities). An all-volunteer armed forces is indeed essential to national defense, and different concepts and methods of leadership and military command are inevitable. And as the personal qualities and role behavior of leaders are increasingly revealed by the news media, public needs and expectations for leadership change in subtle *and* complex ways.

Personal Styles

Each of the societal and cultural issues mentioned previously are reflected in efforts to study transformational (and charismatic) leadership in the mid-1980s. Some theorists and researchers regard transactional leadership as an obsolete model that must give way to more viable and more effective forms of leadership in a world of international tension and cultural conflict. Instead of exchanging wages for work, privileges for votes, entertainment for adulation, and approbation for orderly conduct, transformational leaders are seeking ways in which to motivate followers to higher-level organizational or societal goals. Charisma, as a leadership style, is much admired when it succeeds in making groups and organizations productive—and Number One!

Bennis and Nanus (1985) are among those calling for a new theory of leadership. The beginnings of this new theory may be found in history and social science, and in the reflective observations of those who have transformed society and culture throughout the ages. They undoubtedly agree with Robert Reich (1983), who argued persuasively that the American era of management came to an end in 1970. As a result, new leaders must emerge in a time and place of "commitment gaps," "increasingly complex organizations," and losses in "credibility." In short, the well-established transactions (interactions) of leaders and followers have gone awry.

The solution, according to Bennis and Nanus, is leaders who will take charge. These leaders, no doubt, are transformational leaders, but Bennis and Nanus prefer to call them transformative leaders. Such leaders must (1) have a vision of organizational futures—as a target that beckons; (2) communicate that vision to followers—and capture their imaginations; (3) establish trust—by knowing what is right and necessary; and (4) develop a positive self-regard (or image)—which can be used as a major instrument of change. The exemplars of transformative and personalistic leadership are found in history, biography, and memoirs (and in the reflective observations of Bennis and Nanus's 60 chief executive officers whose organizational accomplishments exceeded expectations).

Charismatic leadership is placed on a more solid footing by House (1977). Defined as a form of leadership that is capable of profound and extraordinary effects, charismatic leadership is verified by the ways in which followers emulate the leader's goals, values, and behavior. Thus, leadership is still perceived as a group effect that is the result of interactions among leader behavior or personal qualities and group needs, expectations, and behavior. The charismatic leader does not possess special gifts as much as he or she possesses unusual self-confidence, domination of others, and a firmly entrenched conviction of moral, social, or political righteousness. Such leaders induce others to follow by serving as a role model, by personifying the values and beliefs that followers should adopt, and by articulating in transcendent terms the mission or cause that followers should serve. The determinants of charismatic leadership are undoubtedly social and/or cultural. There must be opportunities for charismatic leadership to emerge—and there must be group needs that call for highly personal and inspirational forms of leadership. Some groups apparently insist on such leadership (Alse and Jessner, 1961).

In an effort to describe transactional and transformational leadership in behavioral terms, Bass (1985) developed a leadership questionnaire in which scales for transformational, transactional, and inspirational behavior were included. Also included was a rating scale for the extra effort that leaders might foster or encourage. Factor analysis of the scales revealed five factors which were retained by Bass and were labeled (I) charismatic leadership; (II) contingent reward; (III) individualized consideration; (IV) management by exception; and (V) intellectual stimulation. The scales for charismatic leadership, individualized consideration, and intellectual stimulation were designated by Bass as transformational factors, while contingent reward and management by exception were designated transactional factors. A higher-order factor analysis reduced the five factors to (I') active-proactive leadership and (II') passive-reactive leadership.

The gist of several exploratory studies with the scales was evidence that transactional and transformational leadership, when described and rated behaviorally, are not independent or opposing forms of leadership. Both are present in situations calling for active and supportive leadership, and both are apparently needed for leader effectiveness in many situations. For example, both the transactional and the transformational scales make significant contributions to the prediction of scores on the extra effort scale. In other studies, both were related in varying ways to leader effectiveness and group satisfaction with the leader. In summary, transactional and transformational efforts are ways in which effective leader behavior might be appropriately described; it is most doubtful that they are separate and distinct forms (or styles) of leadership.

PRESIDENTIAL LEADERSHIP

Administrative leadership in American colleges and universities is a direct function of presidential leadership, the personal qualities of presidents, and their interpersonal effectiveness with other administrators and leaders within the academic community. Until recently, however, the college or university presidency has been a fallow field for the cultivation of internally consistent hypotheses, systematic inquiry, and objective verification. Much of what was known about the personal qualities and interpersonal effectiveness of college and university presidents was embedded in carefully guarded memoirs and in biographies written for captive audiences by admiring spouses, relatives, and disciples. Any explanations of leadership that might be gleaned from such publications were undeniably great man or fate-and-destiny theories, and the institutions portrayed were indeed lengthening shadows. Dodds (1962), Lowell (1938/1969), and Stoke (1959) were presidents who wrote for other presidents in the genre of presidential memoirs, but who managed to include useful points of view and advice.

Glimpses of presidential leadership can be gained from institutional histories and their celebration of institutional greatness. It is a rare institutional history that does not pay homage to the transformational leadership of founding presidents or those who presided in periods of momentous change. The autocratic styles of many presidents are clearly delineated, however, and benevolent autocracy may be the leadership style most frequently associated with the rise of modern American universities. Veysey's (1965) history of the American university's emergence gives insight into administration and governance almost as much as it does into the new structures and functions of higher education. Rudolph's histories of the American college and university (1962) and their undergraduate curriculum (1977) provide a historical perspective that is essential to presidential roles and responsibilities in the development of higher education. Gray's (1951) history of the University of Minnesota may be mentioned as one of many interesting institutional histories that place presidential leadership in perspective.

It is most unfortunate for an understanding of leadership that college presidents have not been studied as systematically as business managers, corporate executives, governmental officials, military officers, civic leaders, industrial supervisors, and school superintendents. In many respects, the college presidency is an *ideal* leadership position to investigate. Authority and responsibility for institutional leadership are clearly delegated to presidents by most governing or coordinating boards. The constituencies of a college president are multiple and diverse, but they are usually identifiable as specific and finite groups: alumni, faculty, trustees, students, and other institutional clientele. The communities served by colleges cut across the social, political, and economic sectors of society, and no societal or cultural institution in the 20th century has acquired a more diversified *and* important mission or role.

Research on the college presidency is appreciable, nonetheless, and despite a paucity of theoretical guidance, recent studies are directed to the leadership exercised by the nation's 3,000 + presidents and/or chancellors. Research findings are dependent on methods of inquiry, of course, and much of what we know about presidential leadership is derived from personal interviews and survey questionnaires, and not from systematic observation under controlled conditions. Responses in personal interviews are especially dependent upon recall and candor, and as research in the behavioral and social sciences has often demonstrated, those engaged in complex activities are not necessarily the ones to explain what they are doing. None of this denies, however, the potential hypothetical richness of many research findings.

The value of research on college presidents was demonstrated in delightful ways by Bolman (1965). In a survey conducted by the American Council on Education (ACE), 135 newly appointed presidents were asked to complete a questionnaire detailing their professional and personal qualifications and asking selected questions about the selection process they had recently experienced. In addition, 100 personal interviews with board members, faculty, alumni, or other administrators or educational officials provided insight into the nature of presidential selection and its general effectiveness. In writing his report, Bolman makes excellent use of interview quotations to document the lack of clear-cut objectives with which search committees begin their work, the shopping lists of personal qualifications they are likely to prepare, and the seemingly haphazard ways in which they might select a president.

At least 15 of the 116 responding presidents were appointed without benefit of a selection committee, and 97 newly appointed presidents were interviewed by no alumni other than those on the board or faculty. Over a third of the presidents had no opportunity to discuss long-range fiscal or academic plans. Most presidents were informed about the various problems confronting their institution, but a fifth of the responding presidents were not adequately informed about presidential limits on dealing with the problems. Bolman attributed such confusions to an absence of rules and a lack of planned procedures. In making recommendations for a more orderly process, he included nothing that should not have been common sense in 1959–1962, the years in which the surveyed presidents were appointed.

A later study conducted by Brown (1979) provides unusual insight into the self-perceptions of presidents as institutional leaders. Using other presidents and administrators as interviewers, Brown believed that presidents and chief academic officers could learn best from each other and that confidential interviews between colleagues can supply valuable information about academic administration. The portrait of leadership resulting from such interviews is one in which leaders provide a sense of institutional direction, project a sense of enthusiasm, and furnish a structure for implementation. The most crucial talent that academic leaders must have is "to know, to shape, and to articulate what the college or university is becoming" (p. 53). Under his three umbrella hypotheses of direction, enthusiasm, and structure, Brown provides 12 hypotheses on effective academic leadership. Effective leaders might well be those who understand the ethos of their institution, recognize its present momentum, and proceed by incremental implementation; who possess interpersonal skills, educational convictions, and respect for the expertise of others; who think positively and about future possibilities, higher principles, and broader generalities—and the relation of personal values to decision making; and who act with energy while recognizing that different situations call for different actions.

Presidential Styles and Effectiveness

The leadership of college presidents is given a more critical examination by Benezet, Katz, and Magnusson (1981), who conclude that presidents do make a difference in institutional effectiveness. College presidencies obviously require an expenditure of time and energy, and many features of a president's public and private life may be blurred by daily routines. And although presidents must deal with economic, financial, or budgetary matters, they rarely concentrate on such matters. The one undeniable responsibility of a college president is that he or she must make decisions. Presidents make decisions in different ways, however, and their decision-making styles are related to their working relations with staff members or others who may be involved in decisions. Thus, the administrative styles of presidents vary and may reflect the inner structure of presidential relationships more than a president's lack of experience or personal qualifications for the position.

Benezet et al. are of the opinion that most candidates appointed to a college presidency have the requisite personal characteristics but become isolated because of the nature of the job. They believe also that presidential style and accomplishments are reflected in institutional image or reputation, and that presidents' desires to leave their mark are a source of presidential motivation. Presidential styles observed and delineated in this particular study include (1) presidents who take charge—in a highly visible way; (2) presidents who are standard bearers—for institutions that have arrived; (3) presidents who are preoccupied with organization—and the gears of complex machinery; (4) presidents who are moderators—in what they believe to be an egalitarian society; and (5) presidents who are explorers—in quest of new challenges. Also described as a presidential style (or role) is that of a founding president, a style that is becoming rare.

In a national survey of former college and university presidents Carbone's (1981) findings were much as conventional wisdom would have predicted. Respondents had been chosen for their respective presidencies on the basis of prior experience and, as a group, came from a diversity of backgrounds. A substantial number entered the college presidency from the ministry, the armed forces, and from other nonpostsecondary education positions such as government and the public schools. Most of these, however, were presidents of smaller, specialized colleges for which their backgrounds were a suitable stepping-stone. Most respondents held a doctoral degree of some kind, but the Ph.D. (48%) was not the doctoral degree held by a majority. For those ascending to a presidency on an academic career ladder, a college deanship appeared to be the previous rung. When he examined four subsets of his 1,406 institutions, Carbone found other patterns of ascent and performance. The selection of presidents was a function of institutional status as a two-year college, a four-year state college, a state university or land-grant institution, *or* a private, independent institution.

The primary focus of Carbone's study was the postpresidential careers of the respondents. The strength of his findings, however, is the clarification he brings to popular notions concerning the college presidency. Much to Carbone's credit, he establishes that college presidencies differ widely from campus to campus and differ according to size, type, control, and traditions. The college presidency has no "commonly accepted role" (p. 80) and is often what the incumbent makes it. Most presidential decisions and actions are responses to pressure or to circumstances; as Carbone points out, presidents must deal with constituencies that are "informed, organized, and aware of the power they can wield" (p. 81). Instead of being in charge of their institutions, most college presidents are "external agents" (p. 81) and must deal continuously with governing boards, alumni, legislators, and others for whom the focus of attention is community, state, or nation—and not the institution.

Few presidents are blessed with governing boards who fully understand their policymaking responsibilities. Most members of most governing boards "have no special qualifications" (p. 82) and are appointed because they have political connections or can make financial contributions. Fortunately, shared governance is not a problem for many presidents; they have governing power and they know how to use it. Few presidents have the impact they envisioned when appointed; and most of them do not leave their mark on the institution. Presidential teams, cabinets, or councils are not carefully crafted by skilled hands; more often than not, new presidents inherit their administrative colleagues, and the best they can do, in many situations, is to hire one or two key staff members.

Old presidents do not return to the classroom as frequently as they take up professional lives in the nonacademic world. The college presidency apparently prepares its incumbents for other responsibilities as well as institutional leadership. And finally, most candidates are actively seeking a presidency rather than waiting patiently for the right presidency to find them.

Kauffman (1980), a president who *did* return to teaching (and research), deals with the expectations and realities of college presidencies in a more convincing way. Most college presidents receive no formal training for their presidential duties and often succeed or fail because of "on-the-job training." Preservice training, development, and educational programs have not been attractive to potential presidents because the college presidency is still perceived as a temporary position in academic careers. Useful concepts can be found, however, in role theory, and Kauffman believes that role expectations are an important facet of college presidencies. The role expectations of others are essential to the presidential selection process and have a direct bearing on a committee's choice. The role of a new president's predecessor has a bearing on the organizational structure and staff assistance that the new president inherits. In situations where a new president is expected to assume a role as "heroic leader," the difficulties become obvious. New presidents, he finds, must often scale down their role expectations and gain a more realistic appraisal of the influence they have as presidents. In particular, it may be necessary for them to recognize that they will have "the least influence" in college classrooms, where most teaching and learning takes place.

In his research on newly appointed presidents, Kauffman found an erosion of authority and a removal of many decisions from presidential leadership. Uniform policies, rules, regulations, and procedures have replaced presidential discretion in many institutional matters, often leaving presidents with little more than approval-and-referral powers. Given the loss in presidential status, authority, and leadership, Kauffman, like many others, is concerned about the development of leadership for the future. The problems of identifying and developing that leadership are directly related to those encountered in the presidential search-and-screening process. Individuals with promise for presidential leadership may not be attracted to presidential positions, and when they are, they may be screened out in favor of safer, less independent candidates. In higher education's need for more visible presidential leadership, Kauffman finds Burns's views on transformational leadership germane.

Presidential Roles

The most scathing look at the college presidency has been taken by Cohen and March (1974). In a study for the Carnegie Commission on Higher Education, these two researchers reconsider the assumptions underlying presidential effectiveness and draw the iconoclastic conclusion that college presidents are passive, reactive leaders who seek primarily to reconcile conflicting pressures on their time—and their institutions. Career pathways to a presidency, which must be traced retrospectively, are mostly a series of socially conservative filters and assure that presidential leadership will be responsive and not proactive. Colleges and universities are relegated to a class of organizations called "organized anarchies." Thus, they are characterized as (1) having inconsistent or ill-defined goals; (2) not understanding their own internal processes or functions; and (3) having too many participants who come and go, without clear-cut commitments.

Unfortunately for college and universities presidents, Cohen and March's theoretical preferences and their penchant for terms like "organized anarchy" and "garbage can models of decision making" override their research methods and initial findings. Between their disastrous selection of a stratified sample of colleges *and* their *non sequitur* interpretations of their data, Cohen and March provide some fairly accurate information about college presidencies. A close examination of the 42 institutions drawn as a study sample should explain some of the marvelous leaps the researchers take with their data. The sample is stratified by size (large, medium, and small institutions) and resources (rich or poor), and as a stratified sample, the 42 institutions are representative of the population of institutions ($n = 1,235$) from which the sample is drawn. The only problem with the sample is that it is unrepresentative of most institutional characteristics relevant to higher education. The sample is not stratified according to type of control (public-private), and no midwestern state university is included in the sample. Neither does the sample include an adequate number of the state universities and land-grant colleges that educate a majority of students majoring in professional and applied fields. In brief, the sample is representative only of colleges, as sampled for the purpose of the survey, and generalizations across the six cells of rich/poor–large/medium/small matrix are more misleading than informative.

Cohen and March's study draws heavily from previous studies and makes good use of selected findings. Too much importance is attached to presidential age and tenure, however, and insufficient attention is given other personal or social characteristics for which age is a poor indication. The substantive contribution of the study is found in chapters dealing with governance and leadership, presidential images, and presidential use of time. Cohen and March needed assistance in their classification of governance models as (1) competitive market; (2) administrative; (3) collective bargaining; (4) democratic; (5) consensus; (6) anarchy; (7) independent judiciary; and (8) plebiscitary autocracy. And they made an inexcusable mistake in linking each governance model to a specific presidential role. Nonetheless, there is appreciable insight in the identification of the entrepreneurial, administrative, mediative, political, managerial, catalytic, judicial, and legislative roles that most university presidents play at one time or another in providing institutional leadership. But again, it is unfortunate that Cohen and March could not describe each role in better (behavioral) terms and explore the frequency and effectiveness with which presidents resorted to such roles.

Insight can also be gained from Cohen and March's efforts to identify the dimensions of presidential success. From interviews with presidents, chief academic officers, business officers, and assistants to the president (at the 42 institutions), the following indicators of successful leadership were identified: (1) fiscal status; (2) range or quality of programs; (3) institutional growth; (4) absence of student disruptions; (5) quality of students; (6) quality of faculty; (7) respect of faculty; and (8) respect of students. From interviewee judgments of role similarity, Cohen and March infer that a college president's role is more like that of a mayor or a business executive than a cleric or a military commander.

In closing out the discussion of Cohen and March's study, it is well to mention that undue attention has been given their "theory" and not enough consideration has been given to their research. It is most difficult for other researchers to draw Cohen and March's conclusions from Cohen and March's data. And nowhere in the book is an "organized anarchy" adequately defined—or other organized anarchies identified. If *organized anarchy* is defined by the contention that "Teachers decide if, when, and what to teach. Students decide if, when, and what to learn" (p. 33), higher education, as known to most other theorists and researchers, is obviously *not* an organized anarchy.

Time and Place

In a study for the Association of Governing Boards (AGB) and sponsored by the Carnegie Corporation, Kerr and Gade (1986) refute all lingering notions that college presidencies are unitary positions occupied by universal types of presidents. Their study is a sequel to an earlier report (*Presidents Make a Difference,* 1984) and is based on 800 or more interviews with presidents, former presidents, presidential spouses, and others in a position to observe and/or study presidents in action. As a study of American college and university presidents, Kerr and Gade's report becomes the best single source of information and knowledge about presidential leadership and effectiveness. It is also an interesting testament to the belief that time, place, and circumstance do indeed influence presidential selection, performance, and impact.

From the 800 interviews conducted by themselves and 17 members of the National Commission on Strengthening Presidential Leadership—and from related research on governance and administration—Kerr and Gade give a knowledgeable overview of presidential differences, origins, roles, and competencies. They underscore these characteristics by pointing out that by 1990, 5,000 individuals will have served (during the 1980s) as a president of an American college or university. Collectively, they will have been appointed by 50,000 persons serving as trustees, and they will have worked with 750,000 faculty members.

The source of presidents continues to be the academic and administrative ranks of colleges and universities. At least 85% come from the corridors of academe, and an additional 7.5% have had prior experience as faculty members or administrators. As newly appointed presidents, however, they are not likely to be appointed from within their own institutions. Almost 80% of recent presidential appointees have come from other institutions, a matter that is apparently preferred by faculty members (who may be jealous of their own kind) and board members (who believe strangers to be more dependent). New presidents do come from similar institutions, however, and the compartmentalization of presidential career patterns may be one of the strongest points made by Kerr and Gade. Public and private institutions obviously prefer their own, and career ladders are further divided by levels: research universities, comprehensive universities and colleges, and community colleges in the public sector; and research universities, highly selective liberal arts colleges, comprehensive universities and colleges, and less selective liberal arts colleges in the private sector. Among the less selective, private liberal arts colleges, there are further compartments for religiously affiliated colleges and for historically black institutions.

The average length of office for presidents is calculated as seven years, and at least 312 presidents are expected to leave office in any given year. Upon leaving office, only 20% of the former presidents will return to teaching; 25% of them will enter the ranks of the retired, and another 25% will find employment outside higher education. The remaining 30% will remain in academic administration—at least 15% of them in another presidency. All of this is relevant because it gives an appreciation of presidential pathways that research has been slow to provide.

An important finding of the AGB study is the role-defining opportunities that come with most presidential positions. Viewed in their broader features, the duties and responsibilities of presidents are similar to executive functions in industry and business. Within the various functions, however, presidents are often able to write their own job descriptions. A common pattern of administrative functions among presidents is identified as (1) identifying and analyzing problems; (2) deciding priorities; (3) developing solutions; (4) organizing support; (5) obtaining the resources needed; and (6) taking action. Such a pattern does not differ greatly from logical problem solving (Dewey, 1910) and from the orderly procedures implicit in most management textbooks.

Presidents apparently define their leadership roles by the manner in which they assume executive or administrative responsibilities. Setting goals, establishing priorities, and organizing (or initiating) a structure for goal-priority accomplishment are responsibilities that many presidents reserve (or should reserve) for themselves. Assembling an effective group of assistants is another presidential function that is difficult to delegate. Allocating resources, ensuring their effective use, handling unprogrammed problems, maintaining relations (with board, faculty, students, staff, alumni, and others), and administering sundry personnel and program policies are identified in the report as functions and/or responsibilities that might be carried out through others. An essential feature of presidential role-definition, however, is to build in strategies and tactics for self-protection.

In their identification of presidential strategies, Kerr and Gade make a less-than-substantive contribution. Presidents who take charge are evidently pathbreaking leaders. Those who are primarily concerned with the efficient pursuit of ongoing programs and activities are managerial leaders, while those who seek only to survive are survivors. A fourth type of leadership and/or presidential strategy is identified (for presidents who evidently cannot avoid it) as scapegoating. Royal personages (or titular heads), climbers, and caretakers are other presidential roles or strategies which are occasionally observed in presidential offices.

Kerr and Gade present in much better detail a hierarchical model, a collegial consensus model, a polycentric model, and a limited-power (or organized-anarchy) model of presidential leadership, but none of these have particular appeal or give significant insight into presidential influence, power, effectiveness, or impact. Recently appointed presidents and members of selection committees will prefer to read, no doubt, the distillations of presidential wisdom that are given in an appendix. Much to the potential distress of readers, however, there is much in presidential wisdom (and in the selected annotated bibliography) that does not support a basic premise of time, place, and character.

Experiential Benefits

Millett (1980) is among several presidents who bring presidential experience and scholarly tools to bear on the study of leadership and its relevance for academic administration. Millett believes that no part of the selection process is more important than the selection committee's determination of the personal qualities or characteristics that their institution should be seeking in a president. He is convinced that presidents must (1) understand and be committed to the values of the academic community; (2) demonstrate the planning and management competence that would permit them to exercise leadership in the development of academic programs and policies; (3) demonstrate the planning and governance competence that would permit them to deal with their various internal constituencies; and (4) demonstrate an appropriate leadership style by delegating authority, making decisions on a timely basis, and committing themselves (and their institutions) to academic excellence.

Leadership, according to Walker (1979), must be exercised in an environment that is active-reactive. Universities are not inert masses, but active, bubbling places. They also have many organismic features, such as unified (or defensive) reactions and self-correcting mechanisms. The presidential role, as Walker sees it, suffers from an absence of realistic theories and from concepts of the heroic president. Often, presidents cannot be the long-range planners or the decision makers depicted in management theory because of conditions and situations beyond their control. A democratic style of leadership, placing a premium on teamwork, coalitions, and negotiation, is explicit in Walker's views of the academic presidency.

W. H. Cowley's (1980) views of academic governance and administration are among the most insightful to be found in print. Presidential responsibilities are overburdened, he wrote, with fundraising and institutional development, and the day has long passed since presidents can continue as scholars in their chosen academic fields. He believed too many presidents serve as "headmen" and not as leaders. Yet leadership in policymaking is a major function of presidential leadership, and no college or university has become great without such a leader. Cowley's appraisal of presidential leadership might have been revealed by his decision *not* to accept the presidency of the University of Minnesota—but to devote his career to scholarship.

Other insights and viewpoints on leadership and academic administration may be found in Balderston (1975); Baldridge et al. (1978); Bennis (1973); Brown (1984); Demerath, Stephens, and Taylor (1967); Dolan et al. (1976); Dressel (1981); Fisher (1984); Gould (1964); Keller (1983); McCorkle and Archibald (1982); McLean (1974); Millett (1968); Ralston (1980); Raub (1969); Richman and Farmer (1974); Rourke and Brooks (1966); Perkins (1973); and Vroom (1984).

PERSONAL QUALITIES AND ROLE BEHAVIOR

The extensive literature on leadership and the growing literature on academic administration have significant implications for administrative leadership. The selection each year of over 300 new institutional leaders and the untold number of other administrative appointments imply that a major effort in contemporary higher education is directed to the selection and placement of academic administrators who are expected to exercise varying kinds and degrees of leadership (Kerr and Gade, 1986; Nason, 1984b). The emphasis placed upon administrative performance, evaluation, and development further implies that effectiveness in administration is expected and that ineffective administration or leadership will no longer be concealed or excused (Farmer, 1979; Shtogren, 1978; Nason, 1984a).

Research in leadership should greatly assist governing boards, search-and-screening committees, performance review committees, and others who are concerned with or who have delegated authority for selecting, appointing, reviewing, and evaluating administrative performance and effectiveness. Forty years of research have clearly demonstrated that effective leadership is a function of personal qualities, group and organizational characteristics, situational demands, and societal or cultural values. No leader or administrator behaves in a social, political, economic, or technological vacuum. And no leader or administrator is completely devoid of some degree of administrative discretion at one time or another. Decisions must be made, problems must be solved, issues must be considered, and conflict must be resolved—and the personal qualities of institutional leaders *do* make a difference.

Research on leadership has consistently underscored the value of looking at *what* leaders do. Leadership styles are fascinating, and there are no doubt many situations in which style is as important as substance, occasions on which style will carry the day when substance fails. *How* leaders respond to particular challenges, nonetheless, is a more difficult form of behavior to observe and assess than *what* leaders do when confronted with a challenge. Style is especially difficult to assess (in terms of effectiveness) when observers (and followers) do not have informed expectations as to what leaders should do first. In brief, the behavior of leaders and administrators is what we should observe, and leader or administrative behavior is what we should evaluate or judge. Ineffective leaders with style are still ineffective leaders, and institutional costs are just as high.

Research in leadership also underscores the value of looking at leader behavior in terms of the many (and varied) roles that leaders must play. Two-factor (and polarized) theories of leadership should be relegated to theoretical scrap heaps, and no theorist, researcher, or practicing administrator should cast leadership roles or models in an either/or form. The size and complexity of contemporary organizations and institutions are sufficient evidence of the many constituencies that leaders must serve. For each constituency, there may be different demands and expectations that call for a different leadership role. This does not imply that institutions would be wise to hire actors as presidents, but it does signify the importance of "stage presence" and "a sense of timing." Speakers who do not "know" their audiences are not invited back. And academic roles that are unsuitable for the occasion can be disastrous performances.

To initiate more intelligible structure, the personal qualities and role behavior of administrative leadership are presented in Table 3 as functions of the stages at which personal qualities or role behavior should be the focus of assessment or evaluation attention. The qualities and behavior that should be assessed or evaluated in the selection and screening process are *not* the qualities and behavior that should be evaluated in performance review. Indeed, a strong value premise of the proposed structure is that role behavior, as such, should be the sole focus of performance review, while personal qualities should receive primary attention in the identification, screening, and appointment of administrative development.

Personal qualities are shown in the table as ascribed or attributed characteristics (Being) and as achieved or attained characteristics (Becoming). The

**TABLE 3. A Provisional Theoretical Structure for
Administrative Leadership**

Emergence and Selection		Performance and Effectiveness
Role Behavior	•	Planning skills and methods
		Organizing capabilities
		Guidance and direction
		Staff selection and development
		Communication and rapport
		Effectiveness in:
		Interpersonal relations
		Cooperative efforts
		Delegating authority
		Assessing results
		Rewarding performance
Becoming	Continuing development	
	Administrative competence	
	Commitment/dedication	
	Interpersonal skills	
	Effectiveness with groups	
	Professional reputation	
	Experience/expertise	
	Social/emotional maturity	
Being	Age/sex/race	
	Physical Appearance	
	Socioeconomic status	
	Intelligence	
	Emotional stability	
	Ease of expression	
	Social poise	
	Family background	
	Formal education	

personal qualities of family background, physical size and appearance, formal schooling, and so on are status variables over which most individuals have little personal control. Yet they are variables that often serve as surrogates for other variables in the initial identification and screening of administrative candidates. Age, sex, and race—as obvious examples—are related in various ways to virtually every aspect of later performance, but they are not strong predictors of future performance, and under affirmative action procedures, they should be irrelevant. Nonetheless, age, sex, and race will be considered in the selection process, and such variables will exclude many candidates.

Personal qualities that are more directly the function of personal experience are shown as achieved or developing characteristics. Experiential learning is the means by which interpersonal skills, effectiveness in working with others, and administrative competence are evidently developed. As qualities still in a state of becoming, they are shown in the table as overlapping attributed qualities and role behavior.

Role behavior, of course, pertains to the performance variables that are observable, assessable—and relevant to effectiveness in administrative behavior. As behavioral variables, they should be distinguished from the competence and reputational variables that must be inferred from other sources and at other times. Implicit in the proposed structure is the value premise that the evaluation of competence, reputation, and professional experience should be of secondary or minimal importance in reviewing the performance of administrative leaders. Performance and effectiveness should be the primary focus, and administrative leaders should not be judged by qualities or characteristics that should have been assessed at the time of selection and appointment. It should be needless to add that all personal qualities and role behavior shown in Table 3 are suggestive only; by no means are they exhaustive or mutually exclusive.

In closing, it is well to emphasize that administrative leadership may be one of the genuinely urgent needs of higher education in the closing years of the 20th century. This chapter has been written with that possibility in mind, and the research literature on leadership has been reviewed with expectations that administrative development will receive increasing attention in the years ahead. Theory and research in leadership are relevant to the administration and governance of American colleges and universities. *And* administrative leadership is *not* a contradiction in terms.

REFERENCES

Alse, D. Wilfred, and Jessner, Lucie. (1961). The psychodynamic aspects of leadership. *Daedalus* 90(4): 693–710.
Argyris, Chris. (1957). *Personality and Organization.* New York: Harper & Row.
Balderston, Frederick E. (1975). *Managing Today's University.* San Francisco: Jossey-Bass.
Baldridge, J. Victor, Curtis, David V., Ecker, George, and Riley, Gary L. (1978). *Policy Making and Effective Leadership: A National Study of Academic Management.* San Francisco: Jossey-Bass.
Bass, Bernard M. (1960). *Leadership, Psychology, and Organizational Behavior.* New York: Harper & Row.

Bass, Bernard M. (1981). *Stogdill's Handbook of Leadership: A Survey of Theory and Research*. New York: Free Press.

Bass, Bernard M. (1985). *Leadership and Performance Beyond Expectations*. New York: Free Press.

Beckhard, Richard. (1969). *Organization Development: Strategies and Models*. Reading, MA.: Addison-Wesley.

Benezet, Louis T., Katz, Joseph, and Magnusson, Frances W. (1981). *Style and Substance: Leadership and the College Presidency*. Washington, DC: American Council on Education.

Bennis, Warren G. (1969). *Organization Development: Its Nature, Origins, and Prospects*. Reading, MA: Addison-Wesley.

Bennis, Warren G. (1973): *The Leaning Ivory Tower*. San Francisco: Jossey-Bass.

Bennis, Warren, and Nanus, Burt. (1985). *Leaders: The Strategies for Taking Charge*. New York: Harper & Row.

Bess, James L., ed. (1984). *College and University Organization*. New York: New York University Press.

Blake, Robert R., and Mouton, Jane S. (1969). *Building a Dynamic Corporation Through Grid Organization Development*. Reading, MA: Addison-Wesley.

Bolman, Frederick deW. (1965). *How College Presidents are Chosen*. Washington, DC: American Council on Education.

Brown, David G. (1979). *Leadership Vitality: A Workshop for Academic Administrators*. Washington, DC: American Council on Education.

Brown, David G., ed. (1984). *Leadership Roles of Chief Academic Officers*. New Directions for Higher Education Series, No. 47. San Francisco: Jossey-Bass.

Burns, James MacGregor. (1956). *Roosevelt: The Lion and the Fox*. New York: Harcourt, Brace.

Burns, James MacGregor. (1978). *Leadership*. New York: Harper & Row.

Campbell, Donald T. (1956). *Leadership and Its Effects upon the Group*. Columbus: Bureau of Business Research, Ohio State University.

Carbone, Robert F. (1981). *Presidential Passages*. Washington, DC: American Council on Education.

Carlyle, Thomas (1841). *On Heroes, Hero-Worship, and the Heroic in History*. Cited by Eric Bentley, *A Century of Hero-Worship* (2nd ed.). Boston: Beacon Press, 1957.

Cartwright, Dorwin, and Zander, Alvin (eds.). (1960). *Group Dynamics: Research and Theory* (2nd ed.). New York: Harper & Row.

Clark, Walter H. (1958). *The Psychology of Religion*. New York: Macmillan.

Cohen, M. D., and March, J. G. (1974). *Leadership and Ambiguity*. New York: McGraw-Hill.

Cowley, W. H. (1980). *Presidents, Professors, and Trustees* (ed by Donald T. Williams, Jr.). San Francisco: Jossey-Bass.

Demerath, Nicholas, Stephens, Richard W., and Taylor, R. Robb (1967). *Power, Presidents, and Professors*. New York: Basic Books.

Dewey, John. (1910). *How We Think*. Boston: D. C. Heath.

Dodds, H. W. (1962). *The Academic President: Educator or Caretaker?* New York: McGraw-Hill.

Dolan, W. P., Gallagher, B. G., Maguire, J. D., Perelman, L. J., and Schwab, J. J. (1976). *The President as Educational Leader*. Washington, DC: American Association of State Colleges and Universities.

Downs, Anthony. (1967). *Inside Bureaucracy*. Boston: Little, Brown.

Dressel, Paul L. (1981). *Administrative Leadership: Effective and Responsive Decision Making in Higher Education*. San Francisco: Jossey-Bass.

Farmer, Charles. (1979). *Administrator Evaluation: Concepts, Methods, Cases in Higher Education*. Richmond, VA: Dietz Press.

Fiedler, Fred E. (1967). *A Theory of Leadership Effectiveness*. New York: McGraw-Hill.

Fisher, C. F., ed. (1978). *Developing and Evaluating Administrative Leadership*. New Direction Series in Higher Education, No. 22. San Francisco: Jossey-Bass.

Fisher, James L. (1984). *Power of the Presidency*. New York: American Council on Education and Macmillan.

Fleishman, Edwin A. (1957). A Leader behavior description for industry. In Ralph M. Stogdill and Alvin E. Coons (eds.) *Leader Behavior: Its Description and Measurement*. Columbus: Bureau of Business Research, Ohio State University.

Fleishman, Edwin A., Harris, Edwin F., and Burtt, Harold E. (1955). *Leadership and Supervision in Industry: An Evaluation of a Supervisory Training Program*. Columbus: Bureau of Educational Research, Ohio State University.

Galton, Francis. (1869). *Hereditary Genius*. New York: Appleton.

Getzels, Jacob W., Lipham, James M., and Campbell, Ronald F. (1968). *Educational Administration as a Social Process*. New York: Harper & Row.

Getzels, J. W., and Guba, E. G. (1957). Social behavior and the administrative process, *School Review* 55; 423–441.

Gordon, Thomas. (1955). *Group-Centered Leadership*. Boston: Houghton Mifflin.

Gould, J. (1964). *The Academic Deanship*. New York: Teachers College Press.

Gray, James. (1951). *The University of Minnesota: 1851–1951*. Minneapolis: University of Minnesota Press.

Halpin, Andrew W. (1957). The leader behavior and effectiveness of aircraft commanders. In Ralph M. Stogdill and Alvin E. Coons, (eds.), *Leader Behavior: Its Description and Measurement*. Columbus: Ohio State University, Bureau of Business Research.

Halpin, Andrew W. (1966). *Theory and Research in Administration*. New York: Macmillan.

Halpin, Andrew W., and Winer, B. James. (1957). A factorial study of the leader behavior descriptions. In Ralph M. Stogdill and Alvin E. Coons (eds.), *Leader Behavior: Its Description and Measurement*. Columbus: Bureau of Business Research, Ohio State Unversity.

Hemphill, John K. (1949). *Situational Factors in Leadership*. Columbus: Bureau of Educational Research, Ohio State University.

Hemphill, John K. (1956). *Group Dimensions: A Manual for Their Measurement*. Columbus: Bureau of Business Research, Ohio State University.

Hemphill, John K. (1957). Leader behavior associated with the administrative reputations of college departments. In Ralph M. Stogdill and Alvin E. Coons (eds.) *Leader Behavior: Its Description and Measurement*. Columbus: Bureau of Business Research, Ohio State University.

Hemphill, John K. (1960). *Dimensions of Executive Positions: A Study of the Basic Characteristics of the Positions of Ninety-Three Business Executives*. Columbus: Bureau of Business Research, Ohio State University.

Hollander, E. P. (1964). *Leaders, Groups, and Influence*. New York: Oxford University Press.

Hook, Sidney. (1955). *The Hero in History: A Study in Limitation and Possibility*. Boston: Beacon Press.

House, Robert J. (1977). A 1976 theory of charismatic leadership. In James G. Hunt, and

Lars L. Larson (eds.), *Leadership: The Cutting Edge*. Carbondale: Southern Illinois University Press.

Hunt, James G., and Larson, Lars L. (eds.). (1977). *Leadership: The Cutting Edge*. Carbondale: Southern Illinois University Press.

Hunter, Floyd. (1959). *Top Leadership, U.S.A.* Chapel Hill: University of North Carolina Press.

Jennings, Eugene E. (1960). *An Anatomy of Leadership: Princes, Heroes, and Supermen.* New York: Harper & Row.

Katz, Daniel, and Kahn, Robert L. (1966). *The Social Psychology of Organizations*. New York: Wiley.

Kauffman, Joseph F. (1974). *The Selection of College and University Presidents.* Washington, DC: Association of American Colleges.

Kauffman, Joseph F. (1980). *At the Pleasure of the Board: The Service of the College and University President*. Washington, DC: American Council on Education.

Keller, George. (1983). *Academic Strategy: The Management Revolution in American Higher Education*. Baltimore: Johns Hopkins University Press.

Kerr, Clark, and Gade, Marian L. (1986). *The Many Lives of Academic Presidents: Time, Place and Character*. Washington, DC: Association of Governing Boards of Universities and Colleges.

Lawrence, Paul R., and Lorsch, Jay W. (1969). *Developing Organizations: Diagnosis and Action*. Reading, MA: Addison-Wesley.

Levine, Arthur. (1981). *When Dreams and Heroes Died: A Portrait of Today's College Student*. San Francisco: Jossey-Bass.

Lewin, K., Lippitt R., and White, R. K. (1939). Patterns of aggressive behavior in experimentally created "Social Climates." *Journal of Social Psychology 10;* 271–299.

Likert, Rensis. (1961). *The Patterns of Management*. New York: McGraw-Hill.

Likert, Rensis. (1967). *The Human Organization: Its Management and Value*. New York: McGraw-Hill.

Lowell, Abbott L. (1969). *What a University President Has Learned*. Freeport, NY: Books for Libraries Press. (Originally published, 1938.)

Maccoby, Michael. (1976). *The Gamesman*. New York: Simon & Schuster.

Maccoby, Michael. (1979). Leadership needs of the 1980's. *Current Issues in Higher Education: Perspectives on Leadership*. Washington, DC: AAHE.

Machiavelli, Niccolo. *The Prince*. Mentor ed., 1962.

March, J. G., and Simon, H. A. (1958). *Organizations*. New York: Wiley.

McCorkle, Chester O., Jr., and Archibald, Sandra Orr. (1982). *Management and Leadership in Higher Education*. San Francisco: Jossey-Bass.

McGregor, D. M. (1960). *The Human Side of Enterprise*. New York: McGraw-Hill.

McLean, Sandi, ed. (1974). *The Changing Role of the College Presidency: Essays on Governance*. Washington, DC: American Association of State Colleges and Universities.

Millett, John D. (1968). *Decision Making and Administration in Higher Education*. Kent, Ohio: Kent State University Press.

Millett, John D. (1978). *New Structures of Campus Power*. San Francisco: Jossey-Bass.

Millett, John D. (1980). *Management, Governance, and Leadership: A Guide for College and University Administrators*. New York: AMACOM.

Mills, C. Wright. (1956). *The Power Elite*. New York: Oxford University Press.

Nason, John W. (1984a). *Presidental Assessment: A Guide to the Periodic Review of the Performance of Chief Executives*. Washington, DC: Association of Governing Boards of Universities and Colleges.

Nason, John W. (1984b). *Presidential Search: A Guide to the Process of Selecting and Appointing College and University Presidents*. Washington, DC: Association of Governing Boards of Universities and Colleges.

Perkins, J. A. (1973). *The University as an Organization*. New York: McGraw-Hill.

Peters, Thomas J., and Waterman, Robert H., Jr. (1982). *In Search of Excellence*. New York: Warner Books.

Petrullo, Luigi, and Bass, Bernard M. (eds.). (1961). *Leadership and Interpersonal Behavior*. New York: Holt, Rinehart & Winston.

Presthus, Robert. (1964). *Men at the Top: A Study in Community Power*. New York: Oxford University Press.

Presidents Make a Difference: Strengthening Leadership in Colleges and Universities (1984). Washington, D.C.: Association of Governing Boards.

Ralston, Sandra K., ed. (1980). *Defining Leadership*. Washington, DC: American Association of State Colleges and Universities.

Raub, Morton A. (1969). *The Trusteeship of Colleges and Universities*. New York: McGraw-Hill.

Reich, Robert B. (1983). *The Next American Frontier*. New York: Times Books.

Richman, Barry M., and Farmer, Richard M. (1974). *Leadership, Goals, and Power in Higher Education: A Contingency and Open System Approach to Effective Management*. San Francisco: Jossey-Bass.

Rourke, F. E., and Brooks, G. E. (1966). *The Managerial Revolution in Higher Education*. Baltimore: Johns Hopkins University Press.

Rudolph, Frederick. (1962). *The American College and University: A History*. New York: Vintage Books.

Rudolph, Frederick (1977). *Curriculum, A History of the American Undergraduate Course of Study Since 1636*. San Francisco: Jossey-Bass.

Rush, Carl H., Jr. (1957). Leader behavior and group characteristics. In Ralph M. Stogdill and Alvin E. Coons, (eds.), *Leader Behavior: Its Description and Measurement*. Columbus: Ohio State University, Bureau of Business Research.

Sarachek, B. (1968). Greek concepts of leadership. *Academic Management Journal* 11; 39–48.

Schein, Edgar H. (1969). *Process Consultation: Its Role in Organization Development*. Reading, MA: Addison-Wesley.

Schein, Edgar H. (1985). *Organizational Culture and Leadership*. San Francisco: Jossey-Bass.

Schriesheim, Chester A., and Kerr, Stephen. (1974). Psychometric properties of the Ohio State Leadership Scales. *Psychological Bulletin* 81; 756–765.

Schriesheim, Chester A., and Kerr, Stephen. (1977). Theories and measures of leadership: A critical appraisal of current and future directions. In James G. Hunt and Lars L. Larson (eds.), *Leadership: The Cutting Edge*. Carbondale: Southern Illinois University Press.

Scott, Ellis L. (1956). *Leadership and Perceptions of Organization*. Columbus: Bureau of Business Research, Ohio State University.

Shartle, Carroll L. (1956). *Executive Performance and Leadership*. Englewood Cliffs, NJ: Prentice Hall.

Shartle, Carroll. (1961). Leadership and organizational behavior. In Luigi Petrullo and Bernard M. Bass (eds.), *Leadership and Interpersonal Behavior*. New York: Holt, Rinehart, & Winston.

Shtogren, John A., ed. (1978). *Administrative Development in Higher Education—The State of the Art;* Volume 1. Richmond, VA: Dietz Press.

Stogdill, Ralph M. (1949). The sociometry of working relations in formal organizations. *Sociometry* 12; 276–286.

Stogdill, Ralph M. (1957a). *Leadership and Structures of Personal Interaction*. Columbus: Bureau of Business Research, Ohio State University.

Stogdill, Ralph M. (1957b). *The RAD Scales: Manual*. Columbus: Ohio State University, Bureau of Business Research.

Stogdill, Ralph M. (1959). *Individual Behavior and Group Achievement: A Theory, the Experimental Evidence*. New York: Oxford University Press.

Stogdill, Ralph M. (1963a). *Manual for the Leader Behavior Description Questionnaire—Form XII*. Columbus: Ohio State University, Bureau of Business Research.

Stogdill, Ralph M. (1963b). *Team Achievement Under High Motivation*. Columbus: Bureau of Business Research, Ohio State University.

Stogdill, Ralph M. (1965a). *Manager, Employees, Organizations*. Columbus: Ohio State University, Bureau of Business Research.

Stogdill, Ralph M. (1965b). *Manual for Job Satisfaction and Expectation Scales*. Columbus: Ohio State University, Bureau of Business Research.

Stogdill, Ralph M. (1974). *Handbook of Leadership: A Survey of Theory and Research*. New York: The Free Press.

Stogdill, Ralph M., and Coons, Alvin E. (1957). *Leader Behavior: Its Description and Measurement*. Columbus: Bureau of Business Research, Ohio State University.

Stogdill, Ralph M., Scott, Ellis L., and Jaynes, William E. (1956). *Leadership and Role Expectations*. Columbus: Bureau of Business Research, Ohio State University.

Stogdill, Ralph M., and Shartle, C. L. (1955). *Methods in the Study of Administrative Leadership*. Columbus: Ohio State University, Bureau of Business Research.

Stogdill, Ralph M., Shartle, Carroll L., Wherry, Robert J., and Jaynes, William E. (1955). A factorial study of administrative behavior. *Personnel Psychology* 8; 165–180.

Stogdill, Ralph M., Shartle, Carroll L., and Scott, Ellis L., and Coons, Alvin E., and Jaynes, William E. (1956). *A Predictive Study of Administrative Work Patterns*. Columbus: Bureau of Business Research, Ohio State University.

Stogdill, Ralph M., Shartle, Carroll L., and Associates (1956). *Patterns of Administrative Performance*. Columbus: Bureau of Business Research, Ohio State University.

Stoke, H. W. (1959). *The American College President*. New York: Macmillan.

Tannenbaum, Robert, Weschler, Irving R., and Massarik, Fred. (1961). *Leadership and Organization: A Behavioral Science Approach*. New York: McGraw-Hill.

Thibaut, John W., and Kelley, Harold H. (1959). *The Social Psychology of Groups*. New York: Wiley.

Van Creveld, Martin. (1985). *Command in War*. Cambridge: Harvard University Press.

Veysey, L. R. (1965). *The Emergence of the American University*. Chicago: University of Chicago Press.

Vroom, Victor H. (1984). Leaders and leadership in academe. In James L. Bess (ed.), *College and University Organization: Insights From the Behavioral Sciences*. New York: New York University Press.

Walker, Donald. (1979). *The Effective Administrator*. San Francisco: Jossey-Bass.

Weber, Max. (1947). *The Theory of Social and Economic Organizations*. New York: Free Press.

Williams, Raymond. (1976). *Keywords: A Vocabulary of Culture and Society*. New York: Oxford University Press.

Department Reviews for Product Improvement in Higher Education

Everett K. Wilson
University of North Carolina at Chapel Hill

Not long ago, department reviews in higher education institutions were exceptional, marking two sorts of organizations: those in trouble, and the very good departments alert to the need to make fair good, and good better. These reviews have now become common procedure, typically employing the services of several outside consultants who enjoy some prominence in the discipline that defines a department's work. Consultants interview faculty, administrators, and students, either singly or in conferences. They visit classes, laboratories, and libraries. Since the task is formidable, they often divide their labors while periodically conferring with one another. All this occupies two or three days, after which review team members write a report, either separately or collectively. This report is submitted to the department chair and to dean, provost, chancellor, or president. It is assumed that the report is open to all department faculty. Such reviews are often rotated among a school's departments so that each department will be evaluated, say, every fifth year.

Department reviews are assessments that can best be considered in context. In time and scope, they are intermediate between the decennial evaluations of regional accrediting societies and the annual appraisal of teaching by students—or the periodic appraisals of instructors at points of hiring, reappointment, and promotion. Along with reviews of student work (grades) and a parallel evaluation of faculty work (reviews of manuscripts submitted to professional journals together with published reviews of their books and articles), we discover a wide range of methods of evaluation. And this is to disregard the ephemeral external appraisals by the Senator McCarthys or the House Un-American Activities Committee; the sporadic indignations of those like Jesse Helms, who found Marvell's words to a coy mistress dangerous fare; or the more recent organization to monitor classroom work in order to spot departures from truth in teaching. Whatever the reason, it is clear that evaluation of and accountability for the links between purpose, procedures, and product are increasingly favored and warily practiced. Indeed, Conrad and Wilson report (1985, p. 1) that "higher education agencies in all 50 states now conduct state-level reviews; 28 of those agencies have authority to discontinue programs. Moreover, a majority of the multi-campus systems have introduced program reviews, and over three-fourths of the nation's colleges and universities employ some type of program review" (p. 1).

So we see scattered signs of a movement in higher education to develop more accurate measures of worker performance. This is attributed, in public colleges and universities, to the leverage of legislatures and governing boards. Thus the relationship between professional and client is mediated—monitored and modified—not by the third party called administration but by public representatives controlling funding. Such assessments serve to measure certain student achievements and to signal preparedness for succeeding work; to provide indicators for weighing the value added to the student's knowledge through the instructor's intervention; and to provide some basis for the differential allocation of scarce resources. "Value-added tests compare students' achievement in academic subjects and in such [skills] as analyzing a newspaper column, a mathematical table, or a television advertisement before and after certain set periods of college study, typically by using standardized examinations" (Jaschik, 1985, p. 1). At the University of Tennessee, entrance and exit tests are used to try to measure effects of instruction. Some such program of instructor- and organization-evaluation is required by the state's Higher Education Commission if a school is to qualify for "performance-based funding" (Jaschik, 1985, p. 16). South Dakota followed the lead of Northeast Missouri State University in instituting tests for freshmen (ACT) and again at the end of the sophomore year, with seniors revealing degree of competence in their major field by scores on a national standardized test. New Jersey, Maryland, Colorado, and other states are pushing in the same direction. Some colleges and universities use similar tests to gauge whether students are prepared to advance to the next level of instruction (*New York Times,* Nov. 5, 1985, pp. 15, 16). About such efforts, President Anrig of the Educational Testing Service says (ibid., p. 15) "It was a natural progression for the reform movement to look at higher education the way it has looked at elementary and secondary schools. Now colleges and universities are devising their own means of testing before others are imposed on them" (p. 15).

If it was, indeed, a natural progression, it is not clear why nature moved so slowly; or whether influences outside the schools—business, industry, professional athletics, and the military—increasingly justified systematic evaluation. Justification often occurs after the fact as practice dulls apprehensions of strangeness and time turns up a series of legitimations. As Hill (1982) writes of another profession, "It surprised the doctors to start with, but as usual with their kind, they rapidly developed explanations which eventually devolved into foreknowledge" (p. 274). After the fact, it is often hard to understand why a given development should have been so long delayed. But to grasp the meaning of assessment, one has to appreciate the conditions that hindered the evaluation of role performance. Such obstacles reside both in the social and cultural surround and in the organization itself.

OUTSIDE THE ORGANIZATION: SOCIAL AND CULTURAL FACTORS MILITATING AGAINST EVALUATION OF PERFORMANCE

Fifty years ago, in an essay reflecting Simmel's influence, Louis Wirth (1938) described the city, the dominating form of human settlement, by these demographic features: great size, density, mobility, and heterogeneity. Wirth saw these features as generating and embodying quintessential characteristics of modern culture: vast extension of knowledge (and at an increasing rate), sophistication, callousness (a celebration of the head rather than the heart), great increase of power at these centers of control, and enormous diversity in conceptions of the good, true, and beautiful. There follows, then, increased uncertainty about the valued ends of life and, necessarily, the ends of higher education. Comfortable, provincial views face challenges. Andrew Carnegie, an orthodox rabbi, Henry Thoreau, and the deprived black see purpose and product quite differently. But with a wider range of knowing, appreciating, and believing, not only do the ends differ, so also do the means. The linkage of cause and effect becomes more varied and complicated. Hence it becomes harder to evaluate new roles—and adequacy of performance in them for attaining professed goals.

Refined Knowledge, Complexity, and the Impossibility of Evaluation

One aspect of this change in culture is that the larger and simpler terms used to deal with our worlds are revealed as increasingly inadequate. Larger wholes are found to have ever smaller parts. We move, always and irreversibly, toward more refined scales, from discrete to continuous ones, from nominal to ordinal to interval and ratio scales. Black and white, right and wrong, male and female, yin and yang become much too crude for adequate understanding, appreciation, and control of our circumstances. The scales of knowledge (and of the justifications for acting) become infinitely divisible. It is likely that we err more often in our readings of reality, although the gravity of the error will not be so great as when the phenomena of an earlier world were simply dichotomized. Thus evaluation becomes more difficult—and perhaps shunned on that account. Complexity justifies the contention of impossibility. Complexity may also lead to the agnostic position that there is no better and worse, that all is relative.

The notion of relativity (deriving from the spread of populations and contact among heterogeneous peoples) has been invoked to condemn the inclination to evaluate. Pluralism wins the field; judgment points to bigotry. But the extension of this view to academic evaluation may be a non sequitur; for here the question is usually one of improving the *means* for achieving agreed-upon ends.

The diversity that accompanies population growth and contact, creating both the complexities and the relativism that discourage evaluation, produces a similar outcome by a different path. People adapt to limited resources by carving out new niches, new activities that respond to particular needs. The process is seen in the extreme subdivision of the labor force. In several ways, this specialization is not compatible with objective evaluation of performance.

Specialties: Estimated Promise
Rather Than Demonstrated Performance

Like the artist, a specialist remystifies a world which habit has rendered simple and certain. "There are more things in heaven and earth" than the constraints of custom permit us to see. Specialists, in remystifying the world, devise a new vocabulary to suit the novelties they unfold. This is daunting to the ordinary person, who does not discriminate between quirks and quarks, and who is quite unable to judge the specialist's work. Thus while they endlessly complicate our worlds, specialists' esoteric skills and neologisms militate against ready assessment by outsiders.

The specialist's self-interest may work toward the same end. It is pleasant to be free of the school's testing and a supervisor's periodic appraisal. If there must be some evaluation, we seem to say, let it be *ante facto* certification, the blessing bestowed *in advance* by the Bar Association, the College of Medical Examiners, or the department conferring Ph.D. or baccalaureate. Thus we arrive at the practice of estimating promise rather than evaluating performance.

Were the estimate of promise accurate, both public and the specialist could enjoy the best of two worlds: freedom from evaluation and assurance of skilled production. But this is unlikely for several reasons. Measures of future performance are less than perfect. Furthermore, the work situation may differ markedly from that on which certification was based. (Newly certified Ph.D.'s may be required to teach courses on subjects in which they have scanty background—perhaps no training at all.) In any case, the world changes, and knowledge and skills become obsolete. Hence later performances may fall far short of the standards that the *ante facto* certification would lead one to expect.

Service Occupations:
Ambiguous Product, Uncertain Assessment

A particular class of specialties has burgeoned in this century. These are the service occupations, one of five features which, Bell suggests (1975), mark postindustrial society. In general, ambiguity of cause and effect—uncertainty of ends, means, and outcomes—is increased as a larger proportion of the labor force is employed in service occupations. When Americans were chiefly engaged in extractive industry—agriculture, mining, forestry, and fishing—the obvious transformation of raw materials made objective assessment of performance quite possible. But over time, the transformation of things has been superseded as the dominant activity by other sorts of work. In 1820, agriculture claimed 72% of our gainful workers. As a percentage of employees in the civilian labor force, workers in agriculture were, in 1940, 1950, 1960, 1970, and 1980, 18.6%, 12.4%, 6.7%, 3.5%, and 2.9%. While the proportion of farm workers declined fourfold in the first 70 years of this century, service workers increased fourfold (Census, 1975). In the span of a lifetime (1900–1970), while the number of people producing goods tripled, those in service occupations increased sixfold. The 12-fold growth in number of employees in finance, insurance, and real estate was greatest—308,000 to 3,690,000—followed by government employees, whose numbers grew 11.5 times—1,094,000 to 12,535,000. Of these, in 1980, 2.3 million were employees of the federal government (Census, 1985).

Different sorts of service workers do not equally present problems of assessing performance. Some services have clear-cut outcomes, contributions to which are readily measured. A trucker delivers desired goods from manufacturer to merchant, producer to consumer. The skill, timeliness, and reliability of this service can be evaluated. But services entailing changes in people are another, and more difficult, matter. The teacher's product is a transformation of selected student traits. The lawyer's product is a change in the condition of the defendant and the plaintiff. The psychiatrist, the social worker, the priest or rabbi, the sales representative, the advertiser, and others may profess muddily specified purposes, may employ means whose efficacy is unknown, or both.

A century ago, Herber Spencer justified *The Study of Sociology* (1891) with the promise that it would achieve more accuracy in describing the facts of social life, and in revealing their connections. This is desirable since ignorance and error are common and costly. "Nearly every parliamentary proceeding is a tacit confession of incompetence. There is scarcely a bill introduced but is entitled 'An Act to amend an Act.' The 'Whereas' of almost every preamble heralds an account of the miscarriage of previous legislation" (Spencer, 1892b, p. 13). We are in a like position, especially in those occupations that aim to change people's attitudes, knowledge, and behaviors. For example, widely variant views of what constitutes good child-rearing (or effective instruction) displace and succeed one another endlessly. This occurs, in part, owing to the lack of three things. We often lack clear-cut specifications of purpose, that is, purposes operationally defined. (We are sometimes told by academic administrators that we strive for excellence!) Nor have we determinedly set out to develop the social homologues of professed purpose, the procedures that might realize desired ends. To the extent that these assertions are true, it follows that we cannot have developed ways of scrupulously appraising the adequacy of the means-ends connection: we are poor in research and development—in the service occupations generally, but particularly in higher education. Planning the future—and shaping it, through research and development—is another feature that Bell invokes (1975) to describe postindustrial society. But only belatedly is a like view being taken in the service occupations. In the meantime, many such occupations, and especially teaching, are marked by ambiguity of purpose, procedures, and product.

Conglomerates, Finance Capitalism, and Structural Alienation from Product

Two features of our society put a distance between workers and product. In such large, complex organizations as universities, workers' tasks so differ that they may be unable to speak the same language on job-related matters. Now it is seldom the case that the life course of one worker progressively replicates that of his or her precursors, providing a community of experience. Nor is it the case that differences in power are congruent with differences in knowledge or commitment. It is, then, hard to hold to purpose, articulated from the top and affirmed through lower echelons. And a preoccupation with symbols rather than the substance of production, the activities represented in finance capitalism, has a similar effect of alienating workers from purpose or product. The upshot, then, is the impossibility of specifying appropriate means, which are the social homologue of purpose, and, therefore, the impossibility of evaluation.

> "Cheshire-Puss . . . would you tell me, please, which way I ought to go from here?"
>
> "That depends a good deal on where you want to get to," said the cat.
>
> "I don't much care where . . . ," said Alice.
>
> "Then it doesn't matter which way you go," said the cat. (*Alice in Wonderland*, pp. 89–90)

Lewis Carroll places his tale in Wonderland. But it is no longer Wonderland, but the mundane experience that purpose and procedures are disconnected.

Conglomerate Structures Obscure Purpose, Making Evaluation Difficult

If the disjuncture between ends and means is old—perhaps as old as organized societies—there is today a stronger, structurally rooted indifference to product than has been the case before in American society. The alienation from product is, in part, a function of the structure we call conglomerate. The university is a case in point, with its schools (law, medicine, education, journalism, library science, social work, and the like); its tens of departments, curricula, institutes, and programs; its museums and its entertainment business (music, theater, sports, and miscellaneous celebrations); and its multimillion-dollar programs of research. In such an organization, it is obvious that the leaders—presidents, chancellors, and provosts—cannot know what the product is. (Perhaps the clearest conception of product is the winning team, a goal that makes evaluation easy and points to the necessary means of its achievement.) Six CEOs, like the six blind men of Hindustan, will have at best but a very limited conception of the elephant's anatomy.

In the past, when the table of organization resembled a pyramid, the person at the apex was able to do whatever the subordinates could do. One can envisage a kind of Guttman scale revealed in the table of organization, each level representing a known increment of skill and knowledge, beyond but including all lower levels. No longer pyramidal, the large academic organization is better represented by an elongated rectangle having manifold subdivisions peopled by the technically trained, each of whom, in academic organizations, regards herself or himself as *primus inter pares*. It becomes increasingly hard to celebrate a particular organization purpose or product. For the substance of an organization goal—getting oil out of the ground, producing books or cars or enhanced skill in critical thinking—we are likely to equivocate with such Rorschach abstractions as profit or excellence. Then, to reiterate, the murky statement of ends to be achieved makes impossible the specification of appropriate means; and without a clear-cut statement of means and ends, evaluation becomes, in turn, impossible. The indifference to the destination means, as with Alice, "it doesn't matter which way you go."

Finance Capitalism Obscures Purpose, Making Evaluation Difficult

We know what happens with blacks of deprived backgrounds when the means are lacking to achieve the goals celebrated in white middle-class culture. Such destinations are beyond the ken and reach of poor blacks, so it doesn't much matter which way they go. Unemployment becomes intolerably high, families are vulnerable, and illicit means short-circuit the route between need and its satisfaction. We are not so aware that the disjuncture between ends and means is found among some of the privileged. Here is Professor Robert Reich (1985) describing an alienation from their products that characterizes some of his students:

> "What would you like to do when you graduate?" I ask one of my best students.
> "I want to make deals," he says instantly.
> "But what do you want to *do?*" I ask again. "What do you want to make deals *about?*"

> The deal makers . . . are the armies of lawyers, investment bankers, accountants and financial consultants who profit whenever corporate ownership changes hands—or even looks like it might. Legal and financial thrusts and parries are their stock in trade. . . . As each major corporation seeks to maintain a deal-making edge over every other, it hires ever more (and more costly) legal and financial mercenaries, which causes other corporations to reinforce their own troops, and so on. . . . These people thrive on instability (*New York Times,* Dec. 29, 1985, p. E15)

These activities are crowding to the forefront in our day. Financial manipulation enables short-run profit (independent of marketplace competition) to supersede the goal of a high-quality, cost-efficient product. Finance capitalism produces the intermediaries who block the view to the horizon, the destination that an organization is created to reach. Years ago in *The New Yorker,* E. B. White wrote in his wry fashion about the sad case of a man who in one day profited to the tune of $100,000 on the Chicago grain exchange. But alas, he was not interested in grain or food: his sole interest lay in a change of price. He was impoverished, for he had no vision of a green-gold field of wheat ruffled by the wind. He had never smelled the inside of a barn. He had never known the sensation of corn or wheat or barley grains running through the fingers of one's cupped hands. The point, of course, is that product and production are obscured when interest is restricted to a change in price.

Ignorance and Affluence

This insouciant neglect of product may result both from ignorance and wealth. Although it stretches credence, it is possible to contend that all is for the best in the world of teaching and other service occupations, since the evidence on desired and unwanted outcomes, and their sources, is spotty and uncertain. Under these conditions, affirmation is as justified as denial.

But the suspicion insinuates itself that laboring mountains of money and good intentions may be producing a ridiculous mouse. And this suggests a further reason for an indifference to evaluation: Riches enable us to disregard the costs of disconnected ends and means. We are probably the only nation which can afford to keep 57 million young people in school under the tutelage of 2.4 million teachers, at a total cost of $184.7 billion ($3,230 per student and 6% of the GNP) (Census, 1985, pp.126, 140, 224).

These costs may become too great. Employers have objected that new cohorts of workers are un- or miseducated and are, therefore, too costly to their businesses. The military may complain that beyond lack of skills, their recruits lack the habit of discipline. And it may be that the sum of our resources is diminishing: resources no longer infinitely exploitable (even air and water become more precious commodities with their pollution, and with more drinkers and breathers); and a market not so surely expanding as in the past through population growth at home and uncontested demand from abroad. As these changes press upon our habits and our hopes, we can expect stronger support for more rigorous evaluation.

Technical Difficulties

There are other impediments. Accurate assessment of means-ends connections is not a simple matter. How does one identify, much less measure, certain subtle learnings in the humanities? How does one avoid—if it is desirable to avoid—gearing instruction to satisfactory test performance? Assuming one has adequate before-and-after measurements of knowledge or proficiency, how can such changes be attributed to a particular influence, that of an instructor, a course, a book, peers, parents, and others? Assessment implies both measurable outcomes and the ability to identify, disentangle, and weigh a number of factors that might affect learning. Newcomb speaks to the problem of influences on learning commonly overlooked:

> Not long ago a group of social scientists met to consider a set of problems which might be summarized in the question: "How can we find out what happens to students in American colleges and universities and why it happens?" Being social scientists, we soon found ourselves categorizing the sources of variance in institutional output. . . . We guessed that graduating students are different because they were different on first coming to college, because they have met different kinds of faculty-administration influence, and because they have done different kinds of things to each other while in college. We may label them *selection, tutelage,* and *peer influence.* [Italics added]
>   . . . We then went on to rank them in terms of estimated importance. Somewhat to our own surprise, we found ourselves virtually unanimous. We believed that selection (i.e., all the things that students bring with them on arriving at college) more fully accounts for the final product than does either of the other sets of factors. (Newcomb and Wilson, 1966, p. 2)

In the same volume, Wilson writes that

> the entering college student is a congeries of characteristics, many of which are about to be altered in some degree—by his own design, by experiences contrived for him (as in the classroom) and by means unplanned and even unwittingly experienced. . . . If higher education is to be something more than a holding operation or an ill-considered act of faith, we need to know with what traits a student enters and leaves, and what accounts for any change. (p. 71)

In this study, a sample of seniors reported 1,412 changes they thought significant, occurring in the course of their college careers: development of new viewpoints and interests, altered worldview and personal philosophy, personal and social developmental changes, and shifts in career plans and choices and in attitude toward the college. These seniors were asked what or who the agent of change was, in each case. Aside from the "don't know or not ascertained" and "miscellaneous" categories, respondents identified 13 change agents, among which a course figured in 17% of the cases and the teaching faculty in 10%. (Newcomb and Wilson, 1966, Table 3.4, p. 88).

So the difficulty of the task adds to the impediments, cultural and societal, that work against a program of evaluating teacher intervention. Still, these general, ambient influences do not exhaust the roster of obstacles to effective assessment of collegiate instruction. Some impediments are not only matters of the social and cultural surround; they are attributes of the organization—college or university—itself.

WITHIN THE ORGANIZATION, OBSTACLES TO EVALUATING EXTENT OF GOAL ACHIEVEMENT

Specialization

Specialization has already been identified as posing problems for assessing the degree of achievement of liberal arts goals. Esoteric knowledge justifies the claim to an exclusive right to internal appraisal on matters in the specialist's domain. But in addition, knowledge deep and narrow propels students toward the realm of work. Other elements of life, other marks of the liberal arts product are displaced. The aim of enriching a person's life beyond the 40 hours spent in the workplace becomes peripheral. Other institutional spheres—family life, religion and philosophy, performance in the civic role, and the productive use of leisure—are progressively minimized. There is a tendency, then, for the priority accorded professional preparation to render other goals less urgent, their evaluation less justified. At its worst, the corollary is a narrowness that shrinks the world and its wonders, leading to the false certainties that are the inevitable concomitants of isolation. Evaluation then shifts to the auspices of the American Medical Association or the American Bar Association and other such agencies whose members command special knowledge. In parallel fashion, the concern shifts from an academic community to an association representing a discipline. Evaluation surely becomes both more precise and easier under these circumstances. But the organization product has been changed, along with the procedures used to achieve the outcome.

Parochialism and Obsolescence

Sometimes departments cannot evaluate students' achievements properly because new knowledge and altered circumstances have made both product and procedures obsolete. The effects of an ever faster rate of increase in knowledge is exacerbated by the tenure system, which locks in a number of people who were once active intellectual contributors but who are now out of touch with the range of new developments.

Departments of small size suffer like outcomes, since their offerings must be an inadequate sample of rapidly developing disciplines. Assessing change in the student then yields a false conception of growth, for low expectations, or erroneous ones, lead to complacency about achievements which, on an adequate scale, would be seen as unsatisfactory. It is as though physical growth were evaluated in a setting where geophagy was an accepted part of the diet, or where moral and religious achievement were judged by a fundamentalism that strips religion of depth, beauty, and pertinence. Parochialism and obsolescence distort measures of achievement.

Asymmetry of Power in the Teaching Relationship

"One must be struck by the arrangement that locks [teachers] for the duration of a career into a relationship with the innocent, uninformed, and powerless young. It is a frightening thought, not only as it may lead to subtle forms of miseducational dominance; but also as it distorts, by inflating, our conceptions of ourselves. [Furthermore] the disparity of power represented in our customary testing-grading practices creates an adversary diad . . . [a relationship that] perpetuates a compliant dependence, engenders higher levels of deception, subverts the goals of learning, and ultimately has the effect on the master that slavery always has." (Wilson, 1985a, pp. 33, 35)

What is the effect on evaluation? The validity of measures is put in question. For the learning which we seek to measure, we may get instead what is thought to be the instructor's pleasure. The primary evaluator, the instructor, may be hearing an echo, more or less distorted. The secondary evaluator—the department chair or an outside evaluator—may be hearing an echo of an echo. In sum, pleasing the powerful does not yield results equivalent to the revealed mastery of facts, skill in critical thinking, or new ideas generated through experiences devised by the change agent. Asymmetry of power tends to distort measures of achievement.

Innocence and Transience of Administrators

As we have noted before, organization leaders—presidents, deans, and vice-chancellors for business and finance—are no longer knowledgeable about the product or about the various means by which the desired output is achieved (in this case, the transformation of student traits). The hierarchy of power and rewards is no longer congruent with the hierarchy of knowledge. This is the case with all kinds of complex organizations: industry, business, government, research, and philanthropic groups as well as colleges and universities. Hence the ever-increasing use of technical staff and consultants. But recourse to such specialists entails the problems for evaluation hitherto noted. New, vocationally oriented goals are substituted for the quite different aims of a liberal arts education. Then, with a change in purpose, there must be a concomitant change in procedures, together with new and different tasks for a different breed of discipline-oriented evaluator.

There is yet another difficulty owing to the nature of administration in higher education. This is the transience of university officers. The CEOs—particularly second-echelon personnel—may follow one another in rapid succession. This tendency reflects the value assigned to collegiality, the insistence on participating in policy decisions, and the view that, after doing one's administrative chores, it is de rigueur to return to the more respected work of research and teaching. To the extent that these values promote a revolving-door pattern of administration, they make continuity of purpose and product more difficult. This, in turn, complicates the task of evaluation, a task that is defined by declared ends and the means currently employed to attain them.

The Innocence of Workers

College and university faculty in the United States are typically well trained in their several disciplines, but they are not trained in its transmission. Indeed, matters of education are matters of indifference, if not to be deplored. The assumption seems to be that having been on the receiving end for 20-odd years, the former students must, by osmosis, have acquired all the talent needed for work on the giving end. There is every reason to believe that this is an erroneous assumption. But its error is seldom uncovered, owing to the disparity in power, which defends the powerful against negative imputations, and which enables them to assign responsibility for defective transmission to the stupidity or obduracy of the powerless. The victim is culpable.

Student traits, cultivated or ascribed, may indeed contribute to the product, sometimes lowering its quality. But the social scientist can scarcely be at ease with this glib and self-serving explanation as the whole word, or the last. One needs to inquire further into the assumptions disclosed by common practice. Does talking to (or at) students constitute effective instruction? Is the professor the sole or the most important agent in so altering student attributes as to achieve desired ends? Are there adverse side effects from the instructor's intervention—or favorable ones, for that matter? Is a final examination an adequate probability sample of the attributes it was the purpose of the course to change? Is the evidence on such points as these selective? A matter of hearsay? Or of intuition? Faculty are often unprepared, by inclination or training, to answer such questions—or even to pose them. The result is that they preempt evaluation by explaining the product as being due to some combination of student sloth and instructor acuity. The inevitable upshot is that such innocence distorts the process of evaluation.

The Peculiar Product

Finally, one must recognize that the product of the organization we call a liberal arts college is hard to define. If the ends are unclear, then the means of producing them must be uncertain. It follows that evaluation must necessarily be difficult—and inaccurate. The general goal is learning; but at that level of abstraction, we are not much advanced. It is not helpful to say that our product must be learning beyond what marked the person at point of entry. What sorts of learning? And how much change must there be? Perhaps the product should be marked by some skill in solving problems. Moral problems? Aesthetic problems? Scientific problems? Perhaps one purpose is to achieve a product displaying some epistomological sophistication. The person can answer the questions: How do I know what I think or say I know? And in what ways is this method of knowing superior to other ways of approximating the truth? Or perhaps the aim is to sharpen humane sensibilities, to savor the variety of lives, beliefs, and talents and the implication in one another's lives of even the most remotely situated, to understand in concrete fashion the interdigitation of people's fates.

Walking such very general purposes down the abstraction ladder is hard enough—as the social scientist knows who must transmute abstract concepts and propositions into operational terms. But beyond this, there remains the task of inventing social mechanisms for learning that are homologous with the professed purpose. If the purpose is to reinforce a creed, then authoritative instruction, selective use of evidence, and careful selection of raw material (student traits) and processors (faculty) together with isolation from corrupting influences will be indicated. If critical thinking and self-dependence are among the hoped-for attributes of the product, then highly participative learning will be indicated, with emphasis more on the interrogative than on the declaratory, and a hospitality to the data that, being exceptions, test (prove) the rule. Then readings, fieldwork, laboratory exercises, and examinations must be devised so that the concrete means to be used are consistent with the ends pursued.

Then, with purposes and procedures sharply specified, there is some chance of assessing the extent to which the means are adequate to the ends, or of speculating, on the basis of theory and empirical research, what other means might better serve.

THE STRAIN TOWARD ASSESSMENT

Nonetheless, despite all the difficulties, there remains a strong impulse to improve and extend the poor modes of evaluation that we now employ to advance the cause of a liberal arts education. The problem with professional education is much less urgent for a number of reasons. The chair of a distinguished department of sociology once said, "if our [graduate] students need us, they shouldn't be here." To the extent that this is true, it is because such students, like those in law or medicine or journalism or any other graduate program, are, in effect, in trade school training. The purpose is to achieve vocational competence. The purpose is clear and can be readily operationalized. The students are self-selected. Their aims are at one with those of their faculty: command of a discipline. They have both the motivation and the talent to drive toward the organization (department) goal. Evaluation can be frequent and reasonably precise. None of these characteristics applies in like degree to the undergraduate. And yet the importance assigned a liberal arts education, the perennial problems with which it deals, and the dissatisfaction inevitably felt with the indeterminate efficacy of instruction impel efforts to evaluate the link between organization goals and procedures.

Integration and Discovery:
Hallmarks of a Liberal Education

Vocational training was once associated with the crafts. Increasingly it is linked with the professions, a term now used to designate a wider sector of the labor force. But beyond training for work, there remains a nebulous realm of learning that is presumably pertinent to the 64% of our waking hours *not* spent at work. What sort of education bears on this realm? It is learning that enlightens other institutional spheres, the family, religion, education itself, the polity, and the organization of health and welfare, together with various skills—the logic of problem solving, good reading and writing and speaking—and the gaining of some identity through an appreciation of one's location in social time and space. These realms of life and hoped-for skills point to clusters of problems: What cryptic combination of dependence and autonomy will make a marriage work? How rear a child composed, self-sufficient, wise and courageous? What are the ethical imperatives for a responsible and fulfilling life in this world in the last decade of the twentieth century? What makes for a cultivated human being, and to what extent does education empower the young with the resources of our culture? What do I owe fellow nationals? And they, me? And we, together, those who are gratuitously deprived? Who is the enemy? On what grounds, what evidence? Referring as they do to broad, institutional domains in which all people are implicated, these questions are not answered through the lore of any single discipline. They are not, as is schooling in a discipline, to be answered through vocational training. They are cross-disciplinary in their reach. Not excluding the skills, they all entail problems of the good, the true, and the beautiful—problems of ethics, knowledge, and aesthetics.

A liberal arts education, then, occurs not within a discipline, not within a course, and not within a major field of concentration. Such an education occurs *between,* at the interstices of conventional disciplines. The process of education is one of building bridges, of integrating knowledge and insights that bridge the parochialisms of disciplines and courses. With luck, the crossing back and forth engenders a stimulating dialectic, an awareness of differences which, combined in new ways, enables discovery and integration. These complex and different goals exert a strain toward evaluation *as the necessary means of gradually devising those procedures that are homologous with avowed purpose,* in their indirect as well as their direct effects.

Integration

The impulse toward assessment is strengthened whenever organization goals are in conflict, are ambiguous—perhaps owing to complexity—and are desirable. On occasion, integration of knowledge is recognized as desirable. The writer Louis Auchincloss (1964) expressed the need for fructifying exchange across intellectual boundaries when he had his rector of Justin say, "An equation, a Keats ode, a Gothic cathedral, a Mozart aria, the explosion of gases in a laboratory, they should be seen as *related*—and divine" (pp. 285–286; italics added). Such a laudable impulse toward intellectual integration does not confer carte blanche on the dabbling dilettante. Mastery of the field of instruction is a sine qua non for the instructor (and, in lesser degree, for the student). When Goldsmid, Gruber, and Wilson (1977) analyzed 2,900 student statements in support of nominations for distinguished teaching awards at the University of North Carolina, they found that professional competence was highly salient in students' minds, among the qualities imputed to superior teachers. But command of a specialty does not exhaust the meaning of mastery for the undergraduate instructor. Such mastery means the ability to cultivate a synoptic view of a complex field, bridging specialties within a discipline. But further, it means that the instructor's education should be sufficiently rich to be able to link his or her field with other realms of inquiry in a liberal arts education—with mathematics, language, and history; with the biological and physical sciences; and with philosophy and the social sciences.

Even within a field of study, one may find undesirable isolation among specialties, an apartheid the more serious when it separates generic realms of inquiry such as empirical and theoretical approaches to problems. Zetterberg (1965) speaks to the point in the field of sociology, which has, he says,

> already bridged the gulf between theory and research; this is true both in principle and in the work of several gifted scholars. . . . The question now is to teach students to run back and forth across this bridge. Our compartmentalized instruction in theory and research might obscure the connection between the two for the students, and we need to establish a better pedagogical tradition at this critical juncture. (p. viii)

This is not a sentimental yearning for the renaissance mind. The effective teaching performance responds to the fact that learning is some function of context; it occurs within a gestalt. Contrarily, the more the learning situation approximates a randomly ordered set of discrete cafeteria items, the lower the level of comprehension and retention. Some integration of ideas and skills across subfields and disciplines multiplies the instructor's points of purchase across varied student backgrounds. It also anticipates the impact of ideas and skills across a broad range of life experiences that students must inevitably encounter: love, death, military service, ethical issues, drugs and other forms of illicit behavior, work and the ideologies connected with it, the meaning of patriotism or civic duty, and the like.

The goal of integration in a liberal arts education is well served by the heuristic yield of cross-disciplinary analogy, or by the bridging of different intellectual realms in a more abstract construction that embraces the commonly separated domains. Forced and rigid parallels or unions may mislead. But carefully used, they can move the mind beyond a necessary command of facts to implications worth pursuing. The organic analogy, bridging the realms of biology, sociology, and psychology, is a case in point. What is society? "Society is an Organism" (Spencer, 1892a, pp. 435, 437). And Durkheim, pursuing the organic analogy writes (1938, pp. xvii et seq.) that

> Whenever certain elements combine and thereby produce, by the fact of their combination, new phenomena, it is plain that these new phenomena reside not in the original elements but in the totality formed by their union. The living cell contains nothing but mineral particles, as society contains nothing but individuals. Yet it is patently impossible for the phenomena characteristic of life to reside in the atoms of hydrogen, oxygen, carbon, and nitrogen. . . .
>
> What we say of life could be repeated for all possible compounds. The hardness of bronze is not in the copper, the tin, or the lead, which are its ingredients and which are soft and malleable bodies; it is in their mixture. The fluidity of water and its nutritional and other properties are not to be found in the two gases of which it is composed but in the complex substance which they form by their association.

Here are two illustrations of the way certain conceptualizations can bridge, in a stimulating fashion, different levels and realms of thought. Stuart Dodd (1955) does it inductively, producing in the end a simple mathematical assertion that applies under stipulated conditions—so he claims—to molecules, mice, or men, that is, to the domain of the inorganic, the organic, or the superorganic. This assertion grew out of work at the Public Opinion Laboratories at the University of Washington, where he and his colleagues were trying to shape a generalization about the way propaganda leaflets dropped from U.S. Air Force planes were diffused in a given population. In his words:

> Here in the logistic model for simple group behavior the preconditions—random, steady, pairing—are stated in reliably observable, perfectly predictive, universal, and culture-free terms. . . . Whatever the behavior; whoever the group; whenever and

wherever they act, however the motivations, stimuli or physical causes may affect them; an S-shaped logistic growth curve will invariably occur insofar as the attribute spreads solely by random, steady, pairings. This principle applies to fruit flies in bottles, or to populations of nations, or to molecules of a gas, or to people telling a news item or communicating any new culture trait. (pp. 499, 394).

Moving to a high level of abstraction, Miller et al. (1953, pp. 2–10, passim) bridge the realms of biology, psychology, and various social sciences:

All behavior can be conceived of as energy exchange within a real system, or from one such system to another. A system is a bounded region of space-time in which component parts are associated in functional relationships. Any exchange of energy across a boundary results in some alteration or distortion of the energy form. Those specific functions of systems which we can stipulate and whose magnitude we can measure in a relative scale we will call "variables" if they are within the system and "parameters" if they are in its environment. Every system has its environment, and all living systems are open systems with inputs and outputs, and tend to maintain steady states. . . . Inputs and outputs may be either coded or uncoded. Coding is a time-binding process of subsystems, whereby input "A" is coupled with input "A_1" so that either will elicit the other in the future. Coding involves conditioning, learning, or pairing of two processes in a system and the memory or retention of this union over a period of time. Any action is non-coded unless—like speech or gesture—it has some added significance as a result of such a bond.

There is a range of stability for any parameter or variable in any system. It is that range within which the rate of correction is minimal or zero, and beyond which correction does occur. Inputs, either coded or uncoded which, by lack or excess, force the variables beyond the range of stability, constitute stresses . . . within the system.

In individual psychology the system has generally been known as an organism; the input, as the stimulus; and the output, as the response. Uncoded inputs . . . can result in strains or disequilibria within the organism [and] are known as primary or somagenic drives. Coded inputs result in secondary, learned, acquired, or psychogenic drives. . . . When stresses create strains great enough to call into play complex sub-systems to restore equilibrium, we sometimes refer to such processes as "defense mechanisms." [Around such notions Freud built his whole theory of the frustrated libido suffering coercive coding which then leads to the use of various defense mechanisms, displacement, projection, sublimation and the like.] When these mechanisms fail, severe disruption of the steady state of the organism, known as mental or physical illness, or ultimately death, occurs. The total of the strains within the individual resulting from his environment is often referred to as his values. The relative urgency of reducing these individual strains determines his hierarchy of values.

Quantitative similarities may be discovered between the characteristics of an input of impulses into the axon of a neuron; an input of words to a jury; and an input of raw materials into the economy of an isolated community.

Department reviews—and other forms of assessment—provide a chance to estimate whether the integrating purpose of the liberal arts education is being served by the use of such devices as analogy and bridging abstractions.

Discovery

Intellectual integrity implies exposure to complementary—sometimes conflicting—knowledge and values. So does discovery or invention. Beyond the integrating effect of interdigitating ideas drawn from other fields, there is a higher probability of discovery and invention. For new ideas are generated at the crossroads where contraries and complementaries meet. Such intersections are places of coerced—situationally coerced—problem solving. This is often uncomfortable. Such indeterminate situations imply uncertainty, a loss of control—disconcerting even though temporary. The contrary situation is that of the comfortably familiar. Human beings have a neurological conservatism built into their systems. And there are various mechanisms through which the familiar is reinforced and extended into the future. Many of these ensure isolation from the strange and unsettling. Specialization is one such device: the assured and the conservative are linked with the deeper, surer knowledge enabled by mastery of a narrowly defined domain, isolated by its esoteric knowledge from other realms. There are other mechanisms that promote isolation: language does it, and so do religious affirmation of the traditional, class identity, and nationalism, together with the threat of the enemy and alien ways.

Effective learning requires a challenge to the comforting isolation of the habitual. Critical thinking—and therefore more reliable knowledge—occurs only when the smooth, ongoing tenor of our lives runs afoul of some unanticipated barrier. This is the point Dewey (1922/1930) is making when he writes that ''Deliberation has its beginning in troubled activity and its conclusion in a course of action which straightens it out'' (p. 199). And it is for this reason that Goldsmid and Wilson (1980, p. 80) link the teacher's goal of enhanced skill in critical thinking to a pattern of instruction they call *benign disruption.*

But if effective instruction is a disruptive process, we are warned that there can be too much of a good thing. One can conceive of a degree of disruption that could be disabling. For successful instruction, then, the trick must be to engender enough disruption to stimulate but not so much as to disable. Technically put, learning is a curvilinear function of disruptive events. Or as Portia's discerning maid says (in the *Merchant of Venice,* I, ii, 5), ''they are as sick that surfeit with too much as they that starve with nothing.''

A liberal arts education can be thought of as a mind-opening business, the seeing of things unperceived before, the thinking of thoughts hitherto inconceivable. But it is unsatisfactory to view higher education's task as that of pouring pearls into a cerebral vacuum. If one thinks of college or university as a social system with inputs and outputs, the former include traits, generated outside the system, that affect outcomes. The unique set of attributes characterizing the learner join with novel and disruptive new experience in discovery and, sometimes, in the novel combination of ideas that we call invention.

Both discovery and integration, the joining of many, disparate learnings by a few ideas that illuminate them all—both of these products are desired and difficult of achievement. But however difficult, there are persons and agencies who push beyond desire to the demand for demonstrable achievement.

The Demand for Accountability

Both practical and ethical imperatives move workers to account for their stewardship. The practical imperatives are registered among those who believe they have a legitimate claim to certain outcomes from higher education. For example, professional societies and accrediting associations are invited to check the college's technical competence in linking purpose to procedures to product. Parents (and students) think it proper that the college demonstrate its capacity to cultivate students' skills, knowledge, and judgment. The college must demonstrate the production of enhanced knowledge in the civic role to those who demand political purity of the college product, and to those who seek in the product—that is, in student traits—command of pertinent knowledge and a careful weighing of the data as requisites of a free and responsible polity. Schools, and their products, must demonstrate to employers the production of enhanced skill and responsibility in the work role. For employers will seek in the product some combination of competence, conscientiousness, and creativity. Parents and alumni, those old enough to wish what might have been, will hope that the college can demonstrate the production of skills and understanding pertinent to other institutional spheres—to family, religion, education, government, philanthropy, and the creative pursuit of leisure.

And of course, there is variable pressure from the workers (faculty), who need to know the extent to which they are doing what they think (and hope) they are doing. Beyond the coercion expressed as commissions and legislators press for accountability, faculty members need to know how their work helps in promoting the ends of a liberal arts education, "to clarify our ever changing present and to inform the future with wisdom" (Bliss, n.d.). This need is very real, although it may be unwittingly suppressed in the relentless pressures of the daily chores of teaching or may be relegated to a trivial concern when classroom work is superseded by the demands of research or service to professional societies or consulting work for business and industry. The need of the worker to know something reliable about his or her contribution to the product is the obverse of the disquieting alienation from product that marks the unevaluated task. Underlying the inclination to know what one is doing, there is the quite fundamental need to tie cause and effect together, to gain a degree of predictability—and therefore some control over one's world.

The Practice of Evaluation Responds to a Need for Predictability

It is often useful and desirable to know what we are doing. Perhaps the statement should be qualified: The lack of adequate appraisal of our efforts can be a useful, protective device. But if we have a commitment to a discipline and to students (or customers or clients or patients or parishioners), it is disconcerting to discover that we are not accomplishing what we set out to do or *are* accomplishing what we would not have wished. We have, it seems, a quite fundamental aversion to the discontinuous and unpredictable. ("The characteristic of incalculability," Weber [1947] wrote, "is the privilege of the insane.") In small doses the unanticipated can be mentally stimulating. But both laboratory experience and daily life reveal preference for the familiar, the habitual, the predictable. (Gilbert and Sullivan [1882/1941] were wrong in writing that we are born either little conservatives or little liberals. This is no either-or business: We are all conservatives in this fundamental sense.) One result is a degree of stability in our personal and professional lives. This is the basic reason for more-or-less reliable assessment. In it lies the apology for our lives. Nor should we overlook a second possible outcome, quite different from that suggested by stable cause-effect linkages. A degree of dependability may enable a degree of freedom: a minimal determinacy may be a requisite of freely indeterminate action. With some assurance about means-ends connections, it becomes possible to digress, to detour, to take sorties into unknown country, knowing the while that one can return to assured competence. And of course, freedom is enhanced by knowing how to achieve, more surely and efficaciously, a desired end.

In sum, despite resistances to evaluation, obstacles thrown up by the larger society as well as those often marking the organization, there is a strong strain toward improved assessment in higher education. This stems not only from the fact that buyers want assured or improved quality, or that it disconcerts the producer to be poorly informed about—alienated from—the product. Instructors themselves feel an urge for evaluation both because the outcomes are subtle and difficult, and therefore challenging, and because they are so eminently desirable. Teachers find joy in the learner who begins to build a coherent (integrated) structure of knowledge, one who takes pleasure in discovery, even attempting invention. It is likely that such discoveries are mostly the repeated revelations experienced by successive cohorts of the innocent. All the same, that is "a consummation devoutly to be wished." And on occasion, when the means of instruction are well adapted to the end, the discoveries may actually be inventions—ideas or insights that enrich our cultural legacy.

In discussing the work of a department, or the larger organization it is part of, we find ourselves speaking of goals or ends or purposes; of means or procedures; and of outcomes or product. These provide useful nodes of analysis in the ensuing discussion of department reviews.

PURPOSE, PROCEDURES, AND PRODUCT

There is a simple view of the link between purpose and product. It is the view of person or group as rational. Rationality entails a clear statement of purpose, a desired end or product to be achieved; a persuasive justification for seeking that end; the careful design of the course of action which experience tells us is best suited to gaining the desired end; and a series of actions described as quality control (or research and development) so contrived as to improve the connection between purpose and product. In shorthand, we have purpose, procedures, and product, in that sequence, along with evaluation procedures.

This conception of rationality does not correspond with the actual course of events in many organizations, and certainly not in the larger conglomerates of higher education. Purposes are many, and discovering some common denominator is difficult. One might find two animating goals: the creation and transmission of knowledge. But even so simplified, there are such variations within the practices of teaching and research that purpose defined by operations departs markedly from purpose expressed in leaders' rhetoric.

In business conglomerates—United Technologies or General Dynamics, for example—the task is easier. The undebatable purpose is profit. Other outcomes—employment levels and contributions to national welfare—are secondary. If such secondary purposes come in conflict with the primary end, they are subordinated. Unprofitable sectors of a conglomerate are dropped, despite impact on employment. Patriotic sentiments do not reduce profit margins even though the contract is with the U.S. Department of Defense. Furthermore, business and industry have effective means of determining whether extant procedures are, in fact, promoting declared purpose. Accounting procedures are elaborate and reasonably precise. The situation is quite otherwise in the conglomerates of higher education.

As in other organizations ("systems of continuous, purposive activity of a specified kind," Weber, 1947, p. 151), the identity and persistence of a university depends on professed purpose in the short run and, in the long run, on procedures and product. Early on, a college or university must devise the means for realizing its purpose. To retain its identity, to endure, it must create various social arrangements that are effectively geared to the purpose for which the organization was formed. These include replacement of personnel—students, faculty, and administrators—committed to organization goals; decision making and rule making consonant with purpose; an early-warning system and mechanisms to hold deviance within tolerable limits; a division of labor; and means of assessing performance in support of group purpose.

Since ends, means, and outcomes are linked, any change in the procedures threatens a change in purpose, a change in the identity of the organization. Thus a change in the material to be processed (student traits) or in the processors (faculty) can lead to a different product—and to the need to change the methods of processing, if that is indeed possible. Ultimately it may lead to a restatement of purpose. For example, one of the characteristics of the open admissions policy at CCNY was high volume and the rapid input of a new type of student. Values on all three variables—volume, rapidity, and type—were so high, so incompatible with extant methods of processing student traits, that Dean Theodore Gross (1978) wrote about CCNY under the title "How to Kill a College." A change in admissions policy meant, in turn, student and faculty populations whose sources, backgrounds and destinations differed from those of earlier cohorts. These differences then required different modes of instruction, tutorial and other compensatory devices, and changes in the evaluation yardsticks. There followed, then, a selective loss of faculty (processors), revealing the antitheses between two sorts of workers: those responding to movements of the times and those transcending the times, the populists and the elitists, those willing to tackle elementary instruction and those who felt incompetent and unwilling to do so, those sympathetic to immediate social reform through political means and those relying on delayed change through the intermediation of the well educated, those fixing on *categories* of persons defined by class and ethnicity and those whose work fixed on the superior *individual*. The final product was quite unlike that of earlier times at CCNY. After the fact, the college's purpose adapted to the change already effected.

The treatment of students by administrators and faculty can alter procedures entailing a post facto change in purpose. An administrator writes, "the purpose of [the college] is to evoke a high degree of learning and growth compatible with [students'] own increasing self-determination and their own aspirations" (Keeton, 1971). Except as such individual purposes are embraced by and are compatible with organization purpose, the organization is put in jeopardy. There is a limited range beyond which the diversity of raw materials to be transformed by an organization will change the character of the organization, if, indeed, it survives.

Faculty procedures can change product and purpose. We sometimes find that faculty let students shape their evaluations, the grades given, by relying on the distribution of scores that students provide (grading on the normal curve). In doing so, these faculty forgo the right—or neglect the obligation—to set and sustain their own standards or those of their department.

Administrators are particularly apt to bend purpose by changing curriculum and instructional patterns because of one characteristic of the leader's role. CEOs in colleges and universities "can be expected to have less interest in perfecting programs initiated by their precursors than in devising new departures that will carry their stamp. The primary reference group of executive officers is likely to be their counterparts in similar organizations; and their standing among such peers will depend on distinctive changes they have wrought in the organizations they administer" (Wilson, 1985b, p. 22).

Every organization feels the impact of forces from its social surround. Colleges and universities are no exception, and inevitably these environing influences affect purpose. This effect is usually indirect, the impact on procedures and product working its way back to a reformulation of purpose supported by a post facto justification. Money from external sources may fund campus papers or magazines to serve some political or ideological position. Young Republicans and young Democrats are nurtured and supported by the national parties. Professional sports, along with the entertainment industry, coopt the college or university which serves as a farm camp for talented athletes. In some instances, the athletic program becomes vulnerable to criminal activity, as gambling and illicit drug traffic capitalize on sports. The military attach themselves to colleges and universities through reserve-officer training programs, and scores of government agencies, from the CIA through every major department, subsidize faculty research. Beer and junk food companies thrive on this special population. Newman student centers, the Hillel Foundation, and various Protestant centers ring the campus, taking advantage of a critical sector of the population assembled by a school. Business and industry may command—perhaps coopt—the service of faculty members as consultants.

Private research centers emerge in the environs of the school, the better to tap the knowledge, skills, and renown offered by the university. Expansion of physical plant and personnel has made a bonanza for the real estate business in academic communities. Inflated residential prices have driven younger faculty and staff farther from the work place, altering teaching schedules, reducing informal teacher-student contact, and hindering the committee work of department and university. Foundations have had a heavy influence on the work of colleges and universities. About one school, Wilson (1985b) writes "that, from their offices in New York City, [foundations] may have had more influence on the College's destiny than the faculty or governing agencies of the College. The three programs which most altered the course [and by implication, the purpose] of the organization were Foundation supported" (pp. 270–271). Various sorts of social movements may capture the time and commitment of some faculty and students. The impulse to promote needed reform can lead to a passionate commitment that drives out the creation and transmission of knowledge as the prime aim—may even drive out the criteria by which scientific adequacy is judged. (Few academicians are as successful as was Marx in devising the fruitful interplay of outer and inner worlds, the world of action, on the one hand, and the reflective formulations that illuminate that world, on the other hand.) Publishers, through their textbooks, may shape—indeed, dominate—some courses. This is doubtless one of the reasons that Dubin and Taveggia (1968) found that differences in teaching techniques appeared to have little effect on teaching: it is plausible that the course bible, the textbook, can override the effects of different patterns of instruction.

Like John Donne's everyman, no organization is an island, entire of itself. Thus a review of a department's work must raise the question: How, and to what extent, do these myriad influences challenge or reinforce the purposes of the organization?

The Department Review:
Points of Inquiry As to Purpose

Purpose is so intimately linked with procedures more-or-less wittingly contrived, and to external forces which modify internal practices, that it becomes impossible to think of purpose in isolation. But the triad purpose-procedure-product may be useful as a mnemonic device, and in following the rational sequence (inevitably altered in practice), we can simply use each term, in succession, as a point of departure. Let us ask first about the extent to which purpose is transmuted into procedures consistent with a department's aims.

In a department review, this is a question of some urgency: How do department and university officers define the mission? How does purpose differ for different categories of students? Above all, are leaders sensitive to the continuous transformation of purpose under the influence of changed procedures which are, in turn, the outcomes of constantly changing social and cultural conditions in the organization's environment? Is there evidence of a discriminating use of these influences which, owing to the character of higher education—its hospitality to fresh ideas and new departures—flood through the organization's permeable boundaries? Are those influences that advance the school's purpose successfully exploited? Government and foundation bounty? The computer revolution? The movement to monitor truth in teaching? Are these and other influences assessed for their unintended impact on the school, the side effects of every new procedure? Are there instances in which new departures have been rejected on the grounds that their acceptance would jeopardize purpose?

How, and how frequently, are organization goals reinforced? In contrast to the things processed in a factory, the raw material processed in college or university is constantly changing. So, indeed, are the processors, the faculty. With such inconstancy, steadfastness of purpose becomes more difficult. If given purposes are still affirmed, or taken for granted, the department review must look for the mechanisms that, despite change, sustain that purpose. The obvious related question is whether the processes of selecting students, faculty, and administrators are consonant with the declared purpose, and whether on-the-job training reinforces commitment to that purpose.

Can the assertion of purpose be so stated as to help workers devise a social template (for example, schemes of instruction) that will produce outcomes consistent with that purpose? Obviously, this must depend very much on the specificity and clarity with which the purpose is expressed. This is not easy to achieve—the translation of abstract goals into concrete operations. As a case in point, Logan (1976) found that, although virtually all his instructors averred that skill in critical thinking was a goal of theirs, none appeared to achieve it, with this exception: Instructors in those sections which specifically aimed at teaching such skills did produce some of the desired outcomes. These instructors had come out of the stratosphere of abstract pieties to create experiences that enhanced the chances of achieving their purpose.

This is a hard task, and it may not even be recognized. So a careful review of a department's work must ask whether officers, faculty, and staff recognize the continuing need to try to create the optimum social homologue of their professed purposes.

To put it another way, we can ask: Are procedures consistent with purpose? Purpose can be betrayed by preference or habit. If the rewards come from publishing in one's field, if the orientation is intradisciplinary, if the aims of a liberal arts education are not salient, then instructors will follow their interests and preferences by designing a set of courses geared to subfields within a discipline. This approach may fly in the face of the central purpose and may run contrary to the academic marketplace. For, first, vocational training distorts the vision of a liberal education. The questions posed are narrow and are confined to the department's field. They will not treat the perennial problems confronting students and their world, questions that must be tackled with the resources of several disciplines. And second, in some instances, at any rate, the larger number of students are those who will not become majors in the department. In the case of sociology, Stauffer (1985) speaks to this point when he notes that "we irrationally persist in thinking that one of our central responsibilities is to represent the discipline, so that students can decide if it is for them. We deceive ourselves again when constructing the introductory course as a foundation for subsequent courses, since most students won't take any" (p. 127).

Habit also leads us astray. Especially at the graduate level, the purpose of training keen-witted, independent thinkers able to augment our stock of reliable knowledge is compromised by hoary conventions of instruction. Course work often follows a pattern familiar since elementary school: The knowledgeable tell the ignorant, who record, memorize, and reassert on demand. A pattern inculcating passivity, compliance, and deferential acceptance of truth by authority is inconsistent with generative research. Where factual material is to be mastered, this pattern is inefficient; it can be better handled in written form, individually, permitting the student-instructor relationship to be fixed on significant problems of theory, epistemology, the search for negative cases that promise to test the rule, the extension of findings to issues of policy and practice, and the like. We must ask, then, whether the process of graduate instruction is consistent with its purpose—and the desired product.

Purpose confers identity on an organization. It is exemplified in a distinctive product. It is sometimes said that colleges in the United States do not have a distinctive product; the bachelor's degree is becoming a universal and undiscriminating badge. This does not mean that, if training and product are universal, they are undesirable. Universal literacy is properly esteemed, as is— or would be—universal appreciation of our cultural legacy or universal skills in problem solving. What might follow, if schools were not distinctive, is that purpose and the assessment of product would shift from the level of organizations to the institution of education, generally (in contrast to outcomes of other institutions). And for organizations to escape the anonymity of sameness, identity would rest on distinctive quality of product, on a different sort of raw material, on innovations in processing, or on all three.

This is indeed the case. The significance of purpose as a feature of a college or university persists because the product differs in quality, or because the scheme of education differs. Bob Jones University and Wheaton College (Illinois) have distinctive purposes, and their methods of transforming student traits differ in various ways from those of other schools. Harvard College, Wesleyan University, Reed and Oberlin, Amherst, Williams, and Swarthmore are distinctive schools owing to their serious intellectual purpose. (Doubtless, procedures of instruction, formal and informal, count for a good deal, although it is hard to separate processing from recruiting, i.e., self-selection and selection by the organization.)

Purpose comes into play in another, important way as schools and curricula aim at vocational proficiency or an informed wisdom across the spectrum of life's problems. The contrast in purpose might be represented by a course in business administration and one in philosophy. Each has its own apology. For some, the bachelor's degree is a pretty decoration, a dilettante's self-indulgence. It gets one nowhere in the central business of earning a living. And certainly food, clothing, and shelter—even a certain standard of living—may be critical. And it is true that for the modern labor force, old patterns of in-service or on-the-job training are inadequate. The old teachers, our parents who farmed and fished and felled forests or mined, or the master artisan who trained the apprentice—these are rarely available because we extract raw material with great economy of labor.

On the other hand, much of the world's work changes rapidly, so that today's preparation is outmoded tomorrow. And the rapidity of change is likely to quicken. Some contend that the broader, liberal arts education is most needed in managerial and other roles, and that specific occupational skills should come only later, in professional schools or through in-service training. And some would add that there is no demonstrable correlation between vocational prowess, on the one hand, and either happiness or virtue, on the other.

We find, then, major differences in orientation and purpose, and if a school is to have its own identity—a necessity in recruiting and in seeking support—its purpose must be clearly declared. A task of the department review team is to look into the clarity and persuasiveness of the organization's declared purpose.

Like creeds and other commitments, purposes do not sustain themselves without appropriate social mechanisms. The Doxology, the Boy Scout oath, the national anthem, selective recruitment and dismissal, and assessment at points of promotion—these are only a few instances of such devices.

In this respect, there is a marked difference between people-processing organizations and those that transform things. In schools, the traits to be altered or achieved are carried by people who participate in their transformation. It becomes imperative, then, that they share the views of the principal processors, the teachers, as to ends and means. This can become a severe problem in public colleges and universities, especially if they have something like an open admissions policy. To a degree, this problem may be solved by sorting people into different fields of concentration, curricula pursued with different methods and differing in the rigor of that pursuit. In any case, the department review team will wish to discover the extent to which purpose is shared by faculty and students, as well as the mechanisms used—or those which might be used—to reinforce common commitments.

For example, it becomes important to ask how clearly purpose is projected in catalogs and other public statements by the school. If high school counselors and parents and students pick up a clear and accurate message as to purpose (and procedures), then shared expectations will smooth the way for the desired product. This will not, by itself, be sufficient, for every prospective student will get a somewhat different message. (Each has a unique filter of experience though which the message is read.) It becomes necessary, then, to provide some systematic means of straightening out misconceptions. Hence the indoctrination of newcomers, early on. Such orientation sessions again speak to organization purpose, and to the means of actualizing that purpose. In doing so, the school's identity is affirmed. What that identity is, what image is conveyed, must affect task performance—by allaying anxiety, reducing disappointment from unmet expectations, reducing friction, and enhancing morale. So it is well for the review team to inquire into the department's statement of purpose, and into its means of gaining commitment to that purpose.

The Department Review:
Points of Inquiry As to Procedures

In the logical sequence, procedures are intermediate between purpose and product. They are crucial since they are the operational definition of purpose, the template shaped by purpose and, in their turn, shaping the product. If the template is a faithful homologue of purpose, the product will not be far from the mark. But this is not always the case; indeed, it may be seldom so. For it requires a pedagogical sensitivity and inventiveness that is often betrayed by an unquestioning acceptance of conventional instruction which relies on the simple supposition that telling is teaching. The question is not raised as to how different ends require appropriately differing means. The result is that methods of instruction may be at odds with intentions.

If, for example, the integration of differing experiences is seen as a purpose, then instruction that limits exposures becomes counter-productive. So, too, if the aim is to strengthen political and religious commitments, isolation from contending views will strengthen the heart but weaken the mind. In a college operating a work-study program, parietal rules restricting hours and woman-man visiting are inconsistent with the autonomy of life on the job. The imposition of a language requirement may be felt as irrelevant and arbitrary if its implied usefulness is not confirmed beyond language classes in foreign travel, or in readings in other courses. If one goal is to nurture curiosity and the habit of inquiry, instruction requiring the passive ingestion of others' ideas will scarcely produce the desired outcomes. If enhanced skill in critical thinking is a purpose, then instructors will need to create learning experiences that confront students with the unfamiliar, the disconcerting, the exceptions that prove (meaning test) the rule. The instructor will be cast in the role of benign disrupter. If, instead of a vocational orientation with training chiefly within a discipline, a liberal arts education is the aim, then procedures will be developed that generate ideas at the interstices of two or more fields. And the curriculum may be different. In the case of sociology, Smelser (1973) offers these suggestions as examples. Instead of a course in social organization and one in political sociology, the undergraduate would be offered a course on ''The Implications of Bureaucracy for Human Freedom.'' Rather than taking a course on stratification or social class and mobility, the student would register for ''The Costs and Benefits of Social Inequality.''

The differences in procedures appropriate to graduate and undergraduate work merit emphasis. I have argued that vocational training and liberal arts education differ, the former being intradisciplinary, the latter interdisciplinary in its arrangements for learning. This is because the problems dealt within in a liberal arts program are intractable except as we tap the resources of several bodies of knowledge. For example, there is no hope of understanding extraordinary rates of unemployment among blacks without exploiting such knowledge as we have about economics, politics, family, religion, law, crime and delinquency, public education, commercial sports, and the like. In contrast, professional training requires command of a few subfields *within* a discipline, together with an apology for this commitment developed through professional socialization. Liberal arts education entails sharpened skills in communication and problem solving, an attack on problems (and their tentative solutions) that persist across time and space, having their particular manifestations in our own back yards. The one is an answer to the question: How do I earn a living that serves me and my values? The other is an answer to the question: How do I live a life that exercises my wit and taps my experience in a satisfying way? The quintessence of the one is seen in the role of the engineer, the professional soldier, the physician specialist, or the research professor. The other is seen in the role of the polymath, whose rewards are found in diverse activities, especially those beyond the hours of formal work.

Not only is the liberal arts education by the nature of its problems interdisciplinary; but the pursuit of the liberal arts is necessarily comparative. One does not arrive at plausible solutions without some answer to the questions: What would happen in the absence of the alleged causal influence? Or, to shift from an either-or analysis, what would happen if values on the independent variable(s) were higher or lower than in the case we observe? What if, for example, the percentage of women in the labor force were higher (or lower) than now obtains here and elsewhere? We are then driven to compare our society with others—or with ours in the past. Such procedures—comparative strategies—"make accounting for differences an intriguing exercise and . . . lend particular relevance to the question whether there are more successful ways of responding to similar problems of structuring similar experiences" (Stauffer, 1985, p. 42).

Curriculum

How does the curriculum describe the means of achieving a desired product? Is it an accurate description—or prescription? The curriculum is central in the clarification of purpose. In spelling out its requirements, we begin to understand what the organization is about, and what manner of product it hopes to turn out. But a department review will go astray if the visiting assessors accept course labels as the description of a curriculum. Such a review can, indeed, be an exercise in self-deception. In past days, the department will have been smaller in faculty and students, and the content of a course will have been fairly well-known. In time, and across a succession of instructors, course content becomes obscured as labels come to stand for substance, and numbers finally come to stand for labels. If, for example, the curriculum for an undergraduate major or for a graduate degree includes courses in theory and courses in methods of research, what can we infer about content? Is it a matter of laying great thinkers head to foot across the years? Or of identifying major schools of thought? Or of pitting one's preferred social philosophy against that of the philistines? Or of building theory as part of the process of inquiry? And what of the methods requirement? Is it defined by a knowledge of elementary statistics? Does it include philosophy of science? Structural equations? Skill in handling computer programs? Qualitative methods? Should it enable students to understand the methods used (and the methodological issues at stake) in current issues of the major professional journals?

As to substantive courses, the problem is similar. Courses traveling under the same label may differ widely from one time to another—and from place to place. The review team can best inform itself of the adequacy of such courses by discovering desired output as indicated in the final examination. (Even that approach is not adequate if effects of instructor intervention are at issue, for it is quite conceivable that competence revealed in a final examination is owing to factors other than the professor's influence. The efficacy of the procedures used depends on the extent to which the students will be able to do after a course experience what they were not able to do before. But what they were able to do before is, more often than not, unknown.)

Who should specify procedures—courses, curriculum, and miscellaneous hurdles? It seems reasonable to suggest that those who require are those who should specify, and that those who specify (or their surrogates who know the specifications) are those who should evaluate the extent of achievement attributable to the required experience. Those who require are many and various. Professional associations—the American Chemical Society, for example—impose requirements that must be met if a department is to be accredited by the society. Whole faculties may stipulate requirements. So may departments. The faculty member is ultimately the person who sets course requirements, specifies their content and meaning, and in some fashion appraises the extent of their achievement.

The clear statement—that is, the operational specification of program requirements—has several distinct advantages. It reduces levels of uncertainty and anxiety. It allows one to identify appropriate means more readily. It helps reveal redundance: courses differently labeled may unwittingly treat the same matters of content. It enables a department to build a cumulative experience for undergraduate majors and for graduate students, so conveying a gratifying sense of growth. Such a cumulative experience will include known points of repetition and reinforcement. And it may suggest a useful variety of means to achieve the specified end. For example, a colloquium series might emerge as a better means of achieving certain ends than the treatment of the same problems in a course context.

Requirements imposed by the department pose a special problem. The realization of the goals for which they are imposed is necessarily delegated to an instructor who serves as agent for the department. Because this is a collective mandate, it implies that, however differing the approaches of faculty members, and despite the inevitable (and desirable) idiosyncracies, there are minimum essential learnings which must be specified and which are to be achieved regardless of the agent's penchants. In fulfilling their responsibilities, administrators will take soundings to ensure that the faculty agent will respond to the mandate, as registered in students' achievements. A department review provides the chance to identify those who impose requirements, their justification for doing so, and the extent to which they invest the requirement with meaning by the specification and evaluation of outcomes.

A related question bears on the legitimation of a requirement. Does a requirement have clear justification in the way it contributes to the student's development? Are the outcomes of the requirement—skills and knowledge—put to work so as to help realize a declared purpose? In some graduate departments, the ability to use a foreign language has been displaced, as a requirement, by competence in mathematics or computer science. In sociology, to take an example, this has occurred precisely at the time when a larger part of the world's work is being done in a foreign language. Thus this strange circumstance: As the need for it increases, the learning of language decreases. In some instances, the language requirement remains on the books but without any obvious reason for its retention.

If one purpose is to define an advanced degree, in part, by an exemplary awareness of the work currently being done by foreign colleagues, certain procedures consistent with that purpose are needed. The language requirement will be retained. Foreign language resources will be used in the work assigned students. Dissertation work will take into account pertinent contributions in foreign tongues. Syllabi will refer students to foreign language research bearing on the course subject matter. Thus graduate students will be prepared to exploit current work by scholars who write in a different language, so reducing the time lag of years between the publication of research findings and their translation into English.

One aspect of the curriculum, too little attended to, merits inquiry by the department review team. This is the question of sequence and cumulation. For department majors, this is a particularly serious issue, for the assumption that students are experiencing cumulative growth from the introductory course to their time of graduation may not be accurate. Although it may be too rigid a model, some approximation of successive learning experiences to a Guttman scale would increase both yield in learning and greater satisfaction. It would also provide faculty with useful information. Instructors would be more accurately informed as to what students do and do not know at each point in a sequence of courses. Thus unwanted redundance would be avoided, and earlier learning would be reinforced and built on. This is impossible without some design for cumulative learning. It is clearly impossible with a miscellany of course offerings from which students pick at will, at any time.

If the department has such a sequence, one must ask whether some minimum set of learnings is clearly stated for each course in the sequence, learnings on which instructors can build in succeeding courses. Such minima might constitute a tenth, or a fourth, or a half of the learnings the instructor hopes to achieve in a given course in the sequence.

Teaching through the Informal Curriculum

What sort of informal curriculum supports the department's goals? Are there ways, systematically employed, to promote exchange among faculty and students? To disclose the range of scholarly interests? To open up possibilities for collaborative work? Are there colloquia, an informal part of the curriculum that helps to break down the isolation of the parts and to reinforce the distinctive nature of the whole? Are there presentations which, together with ensuing discussion, can touch all the work of a department—problems of teaching, research, publication, application to policy issues, and everyday practice?

Every department turns up a few gifted students with talent and appetite for advanced work. Is there an honors program that attends to the needs of such students? Is there also a general, schoolwide honors program, such as the cum laude in general studies at Harvard?

Restricted time and proliferation of course offerings lead easily to a situation in which, for convenience or by necessity, intellectual realms are divided and subdivided. It may be useful for a department review to consider how students are encouraged to join what is artificially put asunder. What means are employed to articulate, or integrate, aspects of inquiry commonly separated in the curriculum?

For example, ontological and epistemological questions may be separated from the tactics of inquiry and from the discovery or application of knowledge in specific substantive research. In sociology, courses labeled "theory and methods" embody generic problems that cut across all realms of content. This accounts both for the universality of their requirement and for their separation from particular content. Yet such a separation may convey a false conception of intellectual activity. One possible outcome is aridity or irrelevance of theory unconnected with concrete research problems. Or it may make for a naive empiricism in which the broader implications of a piece of empirical research are lost for lack of theory. To the extent that this is so, the review team will wish to ask about the means employed to overcome a specious separation of aspects of inquiry. How are big ideas (theory and abstract explanatory propositions) and the means of their testing bound together in students' minds with the extension and application of knowledge?

This question is related to the problem of the general, in contrast to the specialized, orientation of students and faculty. The question a review team may pose is this: How does the department reconcile the preemptive dispositions of depth and breadth? For graduate students, this entails some inquiry as to how subfields of special competence, together with the dissertation work, are linked—and contribute—to the larger field synoptically viewed. For the undergraduate the question is: By what means are the discoveries, presumably achieved through distribution requirements, made to feed one another, and to build into a coherent structure of knowledge? And how is this knowledge brought to bear on the perennial problems faced by people in American society?

A further related question is this: Are there arrangements for ensuring that students will get some experience in extending ideas and abstract propositions to the concrete circumstances of everyday life? And of enlarging ideas and so getting an intellectual purchase on the mysterious melange of human experience? One must look, then, to the ways a department seeks to make knowledge useful—and to refine and rectify knowledge—by creating an interplay between reason and experience, between theory and empirical reality, between big ideas and their testing. How does the department emphasize that this reciprocity, built into course and program, mirrors the active intellectual life? What devices are regularly employed to show that ideas, otherwise disembodied, can be put to the test, and that, so refined, or refuted, or confirmed, they feed back to enrich the original conceptions?

For undergraduates, the review team will wish to ask whether students are actively involved and sufficiently challenged. A scanning of syllabi may reveal that students do not read or write enough, or have enough lab work. Assigned reading from a text with, perhaps, some supplementary readings may reveal an anemic intellectual diet. Perhaps they do not take an informed and responsible part in planning their work. It is worth asking whether students are expected to chart and keep a record, regularly revised, of their academic plans. This is not to absolve the registrar but to involve the student. There are at least three reasons for stressing the extension of such responsibility to the student. First, it is an occasion for the faculty to show their concern for the student's intellectual growth and, in so doing, to underline the central purpose of the organization. Second, having a major share in the planning process is a way of engendering commitment to the planned tasks. (Reducing the sense of external imposition is a necessary prelude to an internalized desire and sense of obligation.) And third, students will gain a better understanding of whatever wisdom there is behind department requirements, options, and sequences.

For graduate students, different aspects of the informal curriculum become important. The review team will wish to know about means of support, the emotional, financial, and physical resources for sustaining good spirits and effective work. Do the students get regular and accurate estimates of the quality of their work to date? Are they aware of the guidelines for distributing financial assistance—why some get more, others less? Is extent of financial support predictable so that graduate students can know what to expect over a period of, say, five years? Are there opportunities to exchange ideas among themselves, outside class sessions? Do they collaborate in preparation for exams? May they, and do they, write papers as joint authors? Is there a sense of community among graduate students? Do they participate, with or without voting privilege, in certain of the department's committees? Is their orientation to the department, its history, and its contributions to the discipline adequate? Do they get the counsel, help, or encouragement they think they need?

Graduate students commonly complain on all these grounds. This is understandable. They are in a program that will give direction to the rest of their lives. Much hinges on their success in graduate work, and decisions about their competence and prospects are almost wholly in the hands of omnipotent elders. Graduate work is trying. What is needed is a set of useful common experiences, formal and informal, that provide support, both intellectual and, as a side effect, emotional. These are critical matters meriting inquiry and evaluation by the department's review team.

Elements of the informal or collateral curriculum that advance the process of professional socialization are such as the following. The department review will check on the presence or absence of these and other mechanisms that move the tyro from the status of student to that of junior colleague:

1. An apprenticeship to a faculty member:
   a. In teaching.
   b. In research.
2. Formal instruction and laboratory work on problems of instruction in the discipline represented by the department.
3. The experience of independent instruction in a department course.
4. Some exposure to the realm of applied sociology through, for example, analysis of the changing social structure of a hospital or a business, or a civic organization.
5. Participation in selected aspects of department work.
6. Presentation of papers to fellow graduate students and faculty in anticipation of their presentation:
   a. at regional or national meetings of the professional association; or
   b. in anticipation of job interviews.
7. Discussion of research papers presented by faculty and visitors at department colloquia.

The Faculty: Procedures in Support

No procedures are more important for an academic organization than those in support of its front-line workers, the faculty. Any review team must invest much of its time in evaluating the faculty role and the way the department nurtures teaching, research, and service activities. Obviously, the review will include an appraisal of the adequacy of salaries (with the AAUP annual summaries as a point of reference); of sabbaticals and leaves of absence and the requirements attached to these periodic assignments for scholarly work; and of the adequacy of research support, equipment, library resources, staff assistants, and financial aid. There are many other matters to be considered. Among them, the following are a few examples.

The makeup of the faculty: Does its composition by rank, age, or minority status pose problems for the department? There are problems of succession in any organization, but in academic ones, the practice of tenure, together with rapid change in the information base and the methods of acquiring it, raise special problems of obsolescence. Persons at the instructor and assistant professor level offer some protection against outdated instruction, but if such younger workers become a miniscule part of the department faculty one has to ask: What arrangements are there for professional development in support of research and of teaching? One looks, then, for sabbaticals (how they are determined and used), heightened use of colloquia to present recent developments in the field, the extent of collaboration between older faculty and colleagues more recently trained, the level of participation at professional meetings, and the like.

The drive to hire minority faculty poses special problems for any department as ascriptive criteria supersede achievement criteria. Insofar as minority group faculty have suffered a second-rate education, as is often the case from elementary school through college, the sins of the fathers will indeed be visited upon the children for many academic generations. The unhappy irony is that minority group faculty, thought to serve as role models for minority group students, may serve as inferior, sometimes embarrassing models. And there is always the demeaning intimation that must cloud any such appointment, that the minority group member has been hired despite the limited experience that would otherwise make him or her ineligible. Here again, as with the handicap of age, a review team must inquire into the mechanisms devised to offset such hazards: in-service training and faculty development programs, collaboration with other colleagues, catch-up and refresher periods to compensate for past deprivations, and the like.

Such remedial work is not the need of minority group faculty alone. Because all faculty start their careers with little thought or preparation for a major task, teaching, departments need to devise ways of helping newcomers. And so the review team will ask such questions as these: Does the department help new, relatively inexperienced instructors improve their teaching? Does it go beyond the casual evaluation of instruction which exploits only students' subjective evaluations of their instructors? Does the department consider, in faculty meetings once or twice a year, issues of curriculum (requirements and especially prerequisites operationally specified), current evaluation techniques, and innovative teaching procedures? Does it make available time, and other resources, for planning a new course to be added to the curriculum? Do members of the department contribute to the journal on teaching sponsored by their professional society? Does participation in the constructive assessment of colleagues' work at the time of promotion or tenure decisions clarify expectations and standards for members of the department—and especially for newcomers?

The review team will also pose the question: Who teaches what? How does the allocation of work fit the needs of the department and the school? Does the department assign the most difficult courses to the most transient and the least prepared? Graduate students are best prepared to teach their specialties. They are likely to have most competence and confidence in one carefully defined subfield of a discipline. And general service courses, introductory courses, are the hardest to teach. They require breadth of experience; a capacity for artful integration; an ability to tap mundane happenings familiar to the student; facility in exploiting large ideas while subjecting them to careful analysis; an ability to tap the humanities and the biological and physical sciences, so building bridges between fields and lending integrity to the student's intellectual experience; and an easy delight in exploring unanticipated questions that surface during a class session. These are the skills most likely to mark the more experienced and ablest faculty, people probably in mid-career.

Faculty load will necessarily be another point of inquiry. A high but desirable standard would require an hour in preparing for a class, another hour in conducting it, and a third hour in post facto reflection. (This is the same as the rule of thumb for student investment in a course: two hours' outside work for each class hour.) Time spent by the faculty member, preparing and reflecting, will entail the review of questions posed during the just completed class session and a consideration of how they might be more instructively fielded in future; the extent of class participation at selected points; the examples employed, their pertinence, and the possibility of more telling ones; the extent to which allusions are made or bridges are built to other course work the students are concurrently engaged in; and new or further extensions or applications of propositions to extend their leverage and impact.

This kind of investment, for a three course load, would mean (at nine hours per course) 27 hours devoted to class work, apart from office conferences, reading and grading of papers and examinations, tutorials, and supervision of independent study. This sums to a minimum of 30 hours devoted to teaching chores, independent of the instructor's background study. There remains, of course, the faculty member's own scholarly work—research and writing— together with service on college or university committees and to professional groups and, in some cases, consulting.

A most important feature of a productive department is a degree of intellectual yeastiness—without falling into divisiveness or dissension. One would not minimize the open airing of disagreements or vigorous debates as hallmarks of a healthy department, nor would one endorse the view of some administrators for whom the quiet department is the good one. Nonetheless, conflict requires constructive venting of views. And certainly a department needs enough administrative stability and procedural specificity to allow most energies to be channeled into the primary tasks of teaching and research. It is probably accurate to suggest that department morale and productivity are curvilinear functions of intellectual and other sorts of disagreement. The review team will wish to know whether this is a matter taken into account in the recruiting process. Sometimes a department will emphasize replication, each newcomer being expected to approach perfection in each of three domains: research, teaching, and service. But it may be useful, in recruiting newcomers, to consider the need for complementarity as a way of introducing productive differences in talent and interests.

In this sampler of procedural matters bearing on the faculty, one more matter merits the review team's reflection. It is a problem that affects most faculties, yet one that is seldom articulated. It can be expressed in this question: What is the balance between individual and group? Between personal distinction and collective renown?

The strength of a department, its success in recruiting first-rate students and faculty, its visibility across the nation and beyond, and its standing in its own academic community—these things depend on some cryptic combination of individual distinction and collective repute. Some departments seem to be visible as they reflect the light of a few stars. In others, there are integral characteristics, such as distinctive programs, that lend an identity to the department and reflect advantageously on its members. In some cases, the department seems less, in others more, than the sum, or product, of its parts.

Where the stress is very largely on advancing the work of the stars, centrifugal forces may be generated with some damage to the department. Luminaries may contend for students, creating cliques of the like-minded who revolve in smaller orbits eccentric to others and to the common planet of department needs. Sometimes differing intellectual interests are amplified by incompatible ideological positions. Internal communication suffers, as do joint research and department service. Should this policy reinforce the isolation of the parts, it will fail to capitalize on the department's diversity. If a reasonable range of interests is, as one might suppose, an esteemed quality, then that diversity should be revealed and defended in a public forum. If this is done, students will move toward a fuller vision of the field, and freedom of choice will be enhanced as options are multiplied.

On the other hand, heavy teaching loads and the demand for local commitments may lead to internal ties at the expense of the scholarship that engenders individual eminence (together with the reflected glory gained by the stars' national visibility). There is, then, the dilemma of Marys versus Marthas, of cosmopolitans versus locals. (See Merton, 1968, pp. 441–474, and Gouldner, 1958, pp. 281–306, 444–480.) It is not easy to reconcile these sometimes antithetical orientations, but since the welfare of a department depends on such a reconciliation, it behooves the review team to raise questions such as these: What are the means by which the department promotes distinguished scholarship? And what are the means by which it strengthens internal bonds among faculty and students to advance the work of teaching and service? By what means is an appreciation of both research and teaching sustained? How does the department protect itself against the emergence of second-class citizens in the role of locals?

Research and Development: Procedures in Support of Department Purpose

A peculiarity of the key role in higher education is its privacy. Teaching, as T. H. Marshall has said, is "practiced as a secret rite behind closed doors and not mentioned in polite academic society" (see Layton, 1968, p. vii). The result is a degree of pluralistic ignorance peculiar in an organization whose product is so important and, indeed, so well supported from the public coffers. Not only may each be ignorant of colleagues' concurrent work, many will be ignorant of the past, even including those policies established in the past which may, or may not, shape present practice. Some departments, that is to say, have no history. This may be a result of a revolving-door pattern of department administration which itself is related to a lack of data—the records, easily accessible, that could reveal where the department stands on a number of measures.

So it is not unusual to find that procedures go full cycle, returning to practices discarded in the past as undesirable: Comprehensive examinations are instituted, rejected, and reestablished. Alternate introductions to a field displace a single mode of entry and are themselves displaced to return to a common introduction. One is reminded of Spencer's comment on the British Parliament, earlier cited in this chapter. It may very well be that the reasons for the changing procedures are as sound as those for returning to the discarded practice, but whether sound or not, we are unlikely to know. Such shifts commonly occur with very poor evidence. Since faculty members are likely to see themselves, each of them, as *primus inter pares,* wide latitude is given to personal preference and conviction despite the paucity of supporting data.

What is clearly needed in academic departments is some agency for research and development, evaluation research providing data useful in assessing current practices in research and teaching. Certainly members of a review team will wish to inquire whether the department has a memory, and to ask a number of questions: How are data from the past exploited to inform current decisions? Are there records of curricular decisions, changes, and requirements—and the underlying arguments in support of these decisions? Are there records of alumni and their work affiliations? Their publications? Are there records of the research and the published scholarly work of department faculty? And of the value to colleagues of such research as indicated in the Social Science Citation Index?

In the best of circumstances, the review team will find a department resource center including tools for teaching as well as for research. Such a resource center would include books and periodicals, for example, the *Chronicle of Higher Education,* the professional journal devoted to problems of instruction in a given discipline, the periodically issued pamphlets from the Center for Research on Learning and Teaching at the University of Michigan, and, on matters of substance, the principal journals of the discipline. Here one would find audiovisual equipment, files of the most recent course syllabi, examinations (preferably with analyses of level of difficulty and discriminating power of items), copies of projects, exercises, reading guides, reviews of films and their uses for instruction, descriptions and evaluations of field projects, and the like. Such resources would be especially useful for graduate students, who, anticipating their first appointment, would be in the process of preparing their courses for the first time.

The Department Review:
Points of Inquiry as to Product

Disconcerting as it may be, a department review can scarcely escape the question: What is the product? Or less delicately put: What are you doing? Insofar as the question is answered at all, the response is likely to be based on the subjective estimates of partisans, referring to very short-term evidence on the least significant among the hoped-for outcomes. Infrequently the estimator may be a third party, a colleague from another school, the Educational Testing Service, or the department itself, represented by a committee. Ordinarily it is the instructor, basing estimates of product on a midterm or final examination. Examination items may be poor indicators of the intended learnings—low in validity. Invariably the more complex outcomes—enhanced skill in critical thinking, or an appreciation of the systemic character of human groups, or an ability to transmute abstractions into valid variables which can then be manipulated to test the higher-level conceptualization—will be harder to test for than the simple command of a few facts. Thus, in a tester's version of Gresham's law, the poorer (simpler) items will drive out the better ones. Although the attainment of important purposes may be checked through essay examinations, responses in this form are notoriously hard to evaluate, and blind comparisons of estimates can be expected to reveal discouragingly low levels of reliability. In any case, these are estimates of very short-range outcomes. Seldom do we have anything more, after a period of years, than the unrepresentative testimony of an alumnus encountered by chance.

Yet the strain toward assessment in higher education presses for attention to the product on several grounds—practical, ethical, and perhaps even neurological, if there is, indeed, a feeling of unease when means are not clearly linked to desired ends. Evaluation research is difficult, but even short of omniscient appraisal—learnings indisputably attributable to specified agents in specified degree—first steps are possible. Half loaves are edible while searching for a bigger bread pan.

One such a half loaf is the simple scheme of before-and-after testing. The obvious difficulty is that we cannot tell what would have happened in the absence of the supposed causal influence—either as to overall change or as to changes by sectors of the course and the type of instruction employed. All the same, it might be a comfort to learn that some change had, indeed, occurred, and carefully wrought instruments would inform the instructor (and the department) which among the desired goals had been most nearly achieved, and which require more effort and imagination.

Shortcomings of the before-and-after way of estimating the impact of course and instructor are largely met in the classical research design, which adds a control or comparison group whose members are differently treated or who are simply *un*treated. The random assignment of students to experimental and control groups works to eliminate otherwise confounding variables. With a large enough population of students and the assurance of several course sections, this scheme promises a realistic estimate of the course product measured in the change of student responses from Time 1 to Time 2.

Another mode of estimating would employ an analysis of variance to determine whether differences between experimental subjects and a number of controls were greater between than within the several groups. If the former, it might be a reasonable inference that course influence accounted for the differences.

The estimate of product is crucial. It is not merely a matter of accountability, nor alone a matter of knowing what the department and its faculty members are achieving. It is the necessary basis for doing the job better. It is a matter, as one would say of a physical product, of quality control. It is the *R*, in *R and D,* the provision of the data needed if there is to be development. It is probably the only means by which teaching can approach research in respect and rewards. For these reasons, any department review must inquire into the matter of product assessment.

IN SUM

This discussion may have conveyed the impression of department reviews as heralds of a brave new world. This would not be quite accurate. Although such reviews have become more common over the last twenty years, they have not been much thought about or analyzed until quite recently (see Wilson, 1982). Pick-up teams of department reviewers will operate quite differently. There is no codification of points of inquiry and no guidelines, therefore, apart from the spotty, unrepresentative experience of team members. They are costly— moderately so. (A three-person team doing a three-day site visit will cost the department $1,500 to $2,000, i.e., .02% of a million-dollar budget.) More to the point, they are necessarily intrusive, disrupting the routines of a department, demanding the collection of many data, and, on occasion, raising critical issues that may leave disturbances and divisions in their wake. In some instances, the requirement is universitywide and is, therefore, imposed from outside. The department itself, while acknowledging in principle the desirability of such periodic stock-taking, may be unenthusiastic about the actual operation. Perhaps it is not paradoxical that it is the better departments that view such an effort as worth the candle and exert themselves to bring it off.

But that raises the question whether such departments could not themselves perform the evaluation quite adequately. The obvious response is that distance makes for objectivity, fewer conflicts of interest, and fresh points of view. The rebuttal would have it that scholars are trained in objectivity, that they are more fully committed than any outsider to the improvement of their department's work, and that the very nature of their profession requires their acquaintance with the newest research and orientations in their discipline. Furthermore, it may be that evaluation under internal auspices would be more likely to generate remedial action than would the recommendation of a hit-and-run team of outsiders. (We are, in fact, quite ignorant of the actual effects induced by the department review process.)

Quite possibly one could make the case for an improved design for department reviews. One such scheme would substitute a yearly stock-taking for the current quinquennial evaluation seizures. Each year the department might fix on a limited problem: the quality of the graduate program, so likewise for the undergraduate program, the meaning of professional service (to national, regional, and state associations; to the college or university; and to civic groups and social movements in the local community and beyond), to the scholar's practice—and to the links between all of these. Indeed, the roster might include all the issues raised in this chapter, taken singly or in related clusters.

In the meantime, we might regard the department review by a visiting team as a transitional device, inferior in many ways, but the only formal, widely used mechanism we have now to work with. And for the time being, it may be helpful to think about department purpose, procedures, and product, touching such points of inquiry as those suggested in the preceding pages. Many features of our society work against these evaluations. Yet the importance of the task and the very subtlety and complexity of its goals make assessment compelling for those who commit themselves to higher education. The realization of their fondest hopes lies in creating procedures that are valid templates for generating products consistent with formidable purposes.

REFERENCES

Auchincloss, L. (1964). *The Rector of Justin*. Boston: Houghton-Mifflin.
Barak, R. J. (1982). *Program Review in Higher Education: Within and Without*. Boulder, CO: National Center for Higher Education Management Systems.

Bell, D. (1975). *The Coming of Post-Industrial Society*. New York: Pantheon.

Bliss, R. W. Inscription on the Robert Woods Bliss Medieval Museum, Dumbarton Oaks, Washington, DC.

Bureau of the Census (1975). *Historical Statistics of the United States, Colonial Times to . . .* Washington, DC: U.S. Government Printing Office, Series D 75–77.

Bureau of the Census. (1980). *Historical Statistics of* the United States, Colonial Times to . . . Washington, DC: U.S. Government Printing Office, Series D 15, 16.

Bureau of the Census (1986). (1986). *Statistical Abstract of the United States, 1985*. Washington, DC: U.S. Government Printing Office.

Carroll, L. (1885). *Alice in Wonderland*. New York: Macmillan ed.

Conrad, C. F., and Wilson, R. W. (1985). Academic Program Reviews: Institutional Approaches, Expectations and Controversies. Executive Summary of Report #5 prepared by the ERIC Clearinghouse on Higher Education. Washington, DC: Association for the Study of Higher Education.

Dewey, J. (1930). *Human Nature and Conduct: An Introduction to Social Psychology*. New York: Henry Holt. (Originally published 1922.)

Dodd, S. (1955). Diffusion is predictable. *American Sociological Review* 20: 392–401.

Dubin, R., and Taveggia, T. C. (1968). *The Teaching-Learning Paradox: A Comparative Study of College Teaching Methods*. Eugene, OR: Center for the Advanced Study of Educational Administration.

Durkheim, E. (1938). *The Roles of Sociological Method*. Chicago: University of Chicago Press. (Originally published 1895.)

Gilbert, W. S., and Sullivan, A. S. (1941). *Iolanthe*, Act 2. New York: Simon & Schuster. (Originally published 1882.)

Goldsmid, C. A., Gruber, J. E., and Wilson, E. K. (1977). Perceived attributes of superior teachers: An inquiry into the giving of teacher awards. *American Educational Research Journal* 14: 423–440.

Goldsmid, G. A. and Wilson, E. K. (1980). *Passing on Sociology*. Belmont, CA: Wadsworth.

Gouldner, A. (1958). Cosmopolitans and locals: Toward an analysis of latent social roles. *Administrative Science Quarterly*, 2: 281–306, 444–480.

Gross, T. (1978). How to kill a college: The private papers of a college dean. *Saturday Review of Literature* (February 4): 13–21.

Hill, R. (1982). *Who Guards the Prince?* New York: Pantheon.

Jaschik, S. (1985). Public universities trying tests and surveys to measure what students learn. *Chronicle of Higher Education*, (18 September): 1, 16.

Keeton, M. T. (ed.). (1971). A Study of Antioch College, 1971. Prepared for the North Central Association of Colleges and Secondary Schools. Yellow Springs, OH and Columbia, MD, College Offices.

Layton, Donald (ed.). (1968). *University Teaching in Transition*. Edinburgh: Oliver & Boyd.

Logan, C. H. (1976). Do sociologists teach students to think more critically? *Teaching Sociology*, 4 (October): 29–48.

Merton, Robert K. (1968). Patterns of influence: Local and cosmopolitan influentials. In *Social Theory and Social Structure*, pp. 441–474. New York: Free Press.

Miller, J. G., et al. (1953). *Symposium: Profits and Problems of Homeostatic Models in the Behavioral Sciences*. Chicago: University of Chicago Press.

Newcomb, T. M., and Wilson E. K. (eds.). (1966). *College Peer Groups: Problems and Prospects for Research*. Chicago: Aldine.

Reich, L. (1985). *The Making of American Industrial Research*. New York: Cambridge University Press.

Simmel, Georg. (1903). The Metropolis and intellectual life. Trans. by H. H. Gerth and C. Wright Mills, in *The Sociology of Georg Simmel*, ed. and trans. with an introduction by Kurt H. Wolff. Glencoe, IL: Free Press. (Originally published 1903.)

Smelser, Neil. (1973). The social sciences. In Carl Kaysen (ed.), *Content and Context: Essays on College Education*. New York: McGraw-Hill.

Spencer, H. (1891). *The Study of Sociology*. New York: D. Appleton.

Spencer, H. (1892a). *The Principles of Sociology*. New York: D. Appleton.

Spencer, H. (1892b) *Social Statics*. New York: D. Appleton.

Stauffer, R. E. (1985). Making comparative sense of America: Reflections on liberal education and the initial sociology course. In Frederick L. Campbell, Hubert M. Blalock, Jr., and Reece McGee (eds.), *Teaching Sociology: The Quest for Excellence*. Chicago: Nelson-Hall.

Weber, Max. (1947). *Max Weber: The Theory of Social and Economic Organization*, trans. by A. M. Henderson and T. Parsons, ed. with an introduction by T. Parsons. New York: Oxford University Press.

Wilson, E. K. (1985a). Apartheid and the pathology of sociology instruction. In *Teaching Sociology: The Quest for Excellence*, Frederick L. Campbell, Hubert M. Blalock, Jr., and Reece McGee (eds.). Chicago: Nelson-Hall.

Wilson, E. K. (1985b). What counts in the death or transformation of an organization? *Social Forces* 64: 259–280.

Wilson, R. F. (ed.) (1982). *Designing Academic Program Reviews*. San Francisco: Jossey-Bass.

Wirth, L. (1938). Urbanism as a way of life. *American Journal of Sociology* 44: 1–24.

Zetterberg, H. L. (1965). *On Theory and Verification in Sociology*. Totowa, NJ: Bedminster Press.

Diversity in University Governance: Attitudes, Structure, and Satisfaction

David A. Whetten
University of Illinois
and
Kenneth Bettenhausen
Texas A&M University

Organizational scholars have described the modern university as a loosely coupled system (Weick, 1976), an organized anarchy (Cohen and March, 1974), a battlefield (Bennis, 1973), and an urban renewal project (Pondy, 1983). Each of these characterizations emphasizes the diversity inherent in American universities. Among other things, university departments differ in the subjects they study, the methodologies they employ, the scope of their research, the ways they organize, and the role administrators play. In order to understand universities as organizations, it is important to investigate the causes and consequences of this diversity across academic departments.

This is particularly critical during this "era of retrenchment," in which the conflicting interests embedded in our colleges and universities have surfaced to dominate discourse. In the context of what one administrator has referred to as a "mean mood on campus," it is vital that all parties involved in intense debates over funding priorities, ideological preferences, and strategic directions understand the root elements underlying the misunderstanding and acrimony within the contemporary research university. In the course of a broader study of academic governance processes, we have observed numerous discussions involving department heads and deans. Many of these have been marred by a superficial understanding of the competing parties' perspectives. Stereotypical labels and unsubstantiated attributions were commonly invoked as explanations for failure to resolve disagreements.

This study is the product of our desire to better understand the underlying causes responsible for these observed differences in administrative style and decision-making processes. We began our investigation by interviewing faculty and administrators across a wide variety of disciplines. In the process, we became increasingly dissatisfied with the prevailing theoretical explanation in the organizational literature for these differences: level of paradigm development. As a result, we developed a more comprehensive model incorporating our observations as well as findings from previous research on a variety of related subjects. This paper describes that model and reports an initial test of its ability, versus paradigm development alone, to explain differences in the governance structures across academic departments.

MODEL OF DIFFERENCES
BETWEEN ACADEMIC DISCIPLINES

To date, paradigm development has been the principal explanatory variable used in the organizational literature to explore differences among university disciplines (Lodahl and Gordon, 1972; Beyer, 1982; Salancik, Staw, and Pondy, 1980; Pfeffer, Salancik, and Leblebici, 1976; Pfeffer and Moore, 1980a, b).

Paradigm development was popularized by Thomas Kuhn (1962) in describing the evolutionary-revolutionary nature of scientific development. A scientific paradigm (i.e., the values, beliefs, and techniques shared by members of a scientific community) provides a coherent way of seeing the world. Disciplines with highly developed paradigms display strong consensus regarding the topics that ought to be investigated, as well as the methods for investigation.

Paradigm development was introduced to the organizational literature by Lodahl and Gordon (1972). They found empirical support for Kuhn's conceptualization of paradigm development: physicists expressed general agreement while sociologists and political scientists displayed little agreement concerning the content of undergraduate survey courses and graduate degree requirements and course content. In addition, physicists and chemists utilized greater numbers of research assistants than sociologists and political scientists. Chemists also used a greater number of teaching assistants and expressed a greater interest in working with graduate students, while sociologists, political scientists, and physicists (unexpectedly) used fewer teaching assistants and were less interested in working with students. Lodahl and Gordon argue that the ease of communication in highly developed disciplines facilitates both the teaching and the research activities.

Additional research has uncovered several other differences between academic departments. Beyer (1982) reports that physical science departments (physics and chemistry) generally had less frequent personnel changes and more frequent structural changes than social science departments (sociology and political science). Physical science departments rated their department head's authority and central administrative interference higher than did social science departments, except when departments were dependent on relatively independent faculty. Using the same sample plus data from two English universities, Beyer and Lodahl (1976) report that in both England and the United States, the central administration has greater influence in social science departments than in physical science departments and that social science departments are more collegial but less decentralized than physical science departments.

Exploring a related aspect of administrative governance, Pfeffer and Moore (1980a) discovered that the average department head's tenure was positively related to the department's level of paradigm development. Salancik et al. (1980) also explored administrative turnover in academic departments using paradigm development to indicate the extent to which members share operating beliefs. They found that during turbulent times, highly interdependent departments from low-paradigm fields had less stable administrations than departments from high-paradigm fields.

Several studies have linked paradigm development and level of uncertainty. Pfeffer and Moore (1980b) found that greater predictability within high-paradigm fields reduced internal conflict and increased coalition formation, thus strengthening the department's ability to obtain external funding. Cheng and McKinley (1983) reported that external bureaucratic control, exercised via national science policy, increased research productivity for high-paradigm fields but reduced it for fields experiencing high uncertainty because it dampened their information-processing capacity.

Level of paradigm development has served as a useful conceptual framework for illuminating numerous organizational patterns in academic life. We do not fault what it has uncovered, only what research in this area has left unexplored. We believe, therefore, that its utility as an organizational construct is limited, for a number of reasons.

First, paradigm development is a philosophy-of-science concept that has been stretched to accommodate the conceptual interests of a broad range of organizational researchers. Consequently, it has become a catch-all term representing a diverse set of organizational properties, including ease of communication, level of uncertainty, and degree of consensus.

Second, several of the studies cited above didn't measure level of paradigm development directly. Instead, they merely contrasted those disciplines which had previously been identified as typical of high and low levels of paradigm development in the literature and then attributed any observed differences between the contrasted disciplines to level of paradigm development. Consequently, in many cases, we are simply not sure why the diversity between academic departments reported in these studies exists.

Third, research using paradigm development has frequently ignored other important explanations. This literature as a whole can be characterized as an independent variable searching for dependent variables. As a result, a single component of faculty ideology (agreement on scientific means and ends) has been overemphasized at the expense of exploring other ideological and structural aspects of academic institutions. Paradigm development is clearly a key construct in investigations of differences in forms of scientific exposition, and in the review procedures of professional journals and research foundations, across disciplines (Beyer and Snipper, 1974; Pfeffer et al., 1976; Beyer, 1978). However, the paradigm development literature's fixation on a single explanation has produced a truncated analysis in studies of diversity in administrative practices, governance structure, and turnover rates of department heads (Pfeffer and Moore, 1980a; Salancik et al., 1980).

These reservations suggest the following conclusion about the paradigm development research. Although it is obvious that there are systematic differences between disciplines, particularly between the physical and biological sciences and the social sciences and humanities, it is unclear how much of the reported diversity in organizational structure and process across academic departments can properly be attributed to the "level of agreement on the goals and methods within a discipline."

This conclusion suggests the need for a more systematic and complex predictive model of diversity within universities encompassing a broader range of individual and organizational constructs. Specifically, we will argue that studies of internal diversity in universities must incorporate three additional key variables.

1. Previous research has identified a broad spectrum of political values among academics. This is of interest to us because of evidence suggesting that political ideology is linked to beliefs about acceptable forms of institutionalized control, including academic governance.

2. The literature on value formation argues that the rudimentary elements of a person's ideology are in place early in life. However, these are clearly strengthened and refined by early on-the-job-professional experiences, especially those related to the design of work and the structure of work groups.

3. Previous research has also shown that the source of funding for research and teaching, as well as the overall level of funding required, also accentuates divergent belief systems and structural arrangements across departments.

Before proceeding to describe our model of organizational diversity within academic institutions, it is important to point out that while finer distinctions between disciplines can and ought to be made, to simplify our initial description of this model we will focus only on the difference between the humanities and science (physical and biological). We have chosen this extreme contrast because it represents the most intuitively obvious comparison, it is consistent with the distinctions typically used in the paradigm development literature, and it has received considerable attention in the philosophy-of-science and science-policy literatures (Snow, 1959; Rabi, 1956; Trilling, 1962). The posited distinctions are summarized in Figure 1 (see below).

Political and Institutional Ideology

Ideology has been frequently invoked as an explanation of worker attitudes (Gouldner, 1954; Bendix, 1956). Ideology is a set of fundamental beliefs (sometimes called a doctrine) that order the world in which we live. All that we know to be right or wrong is encompassed in our ideology. In addition, ideology provides the basis for rational action by allowing certain behaviors to be seen as normal and contradictory behaviors as irrational. These beliefs are grounded in early family, religious, educational, and social experiences and remain fairly stable throughout adult life (Alport, Vernon, and Lindzey, 1960; Kohlberg, 1969).

In their study of political beliefs within the academic community, Ladd and Lipsett (1971, 1972a, b, 1973) found that scientists typically held more conservative political views than humanists, that professors who viewed themselves primarily as researchers tended to be more liberal than those who emphasized teaching, and that the elite members of all disciplines tended to be the most liberal. They also report that undergraduates, graduate students, and faculty in a given discipline all tend to have similar political views, but that these views tend to become more extreme at each successive level. This suggests that higher education represents a radicalizing experience: students are socialized to hold progressively more extreme views, and the less extreme students tend to drop out along the academic career path.

We are interested in political ideology primarily because it appears to be linked to scientific ideology (paradigm development) and to what we call institutional ideology. There is some evidence to suggest that individuals end up in academic disciplines which are compatible with their political views (Lipsett and Ladd, 1972; Ladd and Lipsett, 1972b). Scientists seek to discover the causal relationships which explain phenomena in the natural world. But this knowledge has a strong instrumental focus: it is used to improve one's ability to make accurate predictions and ultimately to solve problems. This orientation is best reflected in the applied-research component of all the natural sciences (e.g., various forms of engineering). The principal funders of, as well as beneficiaries of, problem-solving research in science are the major institutions within our society (e.g., government, military, and business). Science's close ties to the current institutional structure in our society is consistent with a conservative, status-quo-oriented political ideology (Ladd and Lipsett, 1972b). This form of research is also facilitated by a highly developed paradigm in which research projects are not encumbered by debates over scientific priorities, research methods, or measures of quality.

In contrast, academics in the humanities tend to have a more expressive view of knowledge. It is valued for its own sake and therefore tends to be more descriptive, seeking only for more insightful understanding. In addition, humanists not only don't see their work contributing directly to the support of existing institutions, they are deeply suspicious of contemporary institutionalized forms of power and status (Ladd and Lipsett, 1972b). One of the most enduring themes in literature is the demands of institutions, including their "need" for improved technology, being met at the expense of the rights of individuals (Burden et al., 1977). Whereas scientists are inclined to view institutions like the military, the government, and industry as solutions to societal problems, humanists tend to view these social and political structures as the cause of many of society's problems. Indeed, humanities professors in general view social criticism as an integral component of scholarship (Ladd and Lipsett, 1972b).

These values are not only more likely to be linked to a liberal voting record, they are also consistent with a low degree of agreement about research methods. Inasmuch as a scientific paradigm represents an institutionalized system of rules and conventions, one would expect strong resistance within the humanities to increased paradigmatic control. Being able to make relatively unfettered choices regarding forms of discourse, modes of inquiry, and topics for investigation is consistent with the broad ideological values of the humanist.

It is important to point out that this polarization of political values is not unique to our society. Research encompassing 19 countries has shown that, "on the whole, students in the social sciences, law and the humanities are more likely to be politicized and leftist than their colleagues in the natural and applied sciences" (Emmerson, 1968). It is also important to note that this pattern has not always existed. In earlier eras, the natural sciences served as the principal centers for social criticism and political dissent. The reason for this shift over time is summarized effectively by Ladd and Lipsett: "A field of study becomes highly ideological when, under a given set of circumstances, it offers a fulcrum for the rejection of established social arrangements; and throughout much of the West in the 18th and 19th centuries, natural science occupied this position" (1972b, p. 1095). They further point out that this is still the case in many authoritarian societies today, where the voice of social dissent has been muted in most fields of scholarship, except the natural sciences.

We expect that this highly interrelated value system will be reflected in the attitudes of scientists and humanists regarding the legitimate role of administration within their academic institution. Specifically, we believe that humanists are likely to prefer a decentralized and generally weak form of departmental administration. They are likely to have a frequently rotating chair, rather than a long-term head, presiding over their department. Furthermore, the chairmanship is likely to rotate between established members of the immediate department (so as to assuage inherent feelings of distrust toward administrators). In addition, there is likely to be a strong system of checks and balances in the form of heavy faculty involvement in committees and required faculty votes on matters of long-term interest to the department. It follows that full-time administrators in the humanities would tend to personally identify less with this role. Instead, they would continue to view themselves primarily as scholars in their area of specialization, and to treat their current duties as an unseemly, unfortunate, and certainly temporary imposition.

In contrast, we expect that scientists will be willing to place considerably more trust in a strong, central department administrator. Therefore, science departments are more likely to be presided over by an executive head, who will serve for an indefinite term, and whose successor will be selected following a national search process. We would also expect that a higher percentage of first-time department heads in the sciences would move on to a higher-level administrative position (e.g., dean, director of a research laboratory, or vice-chancellor.

Work Structure

Research reveals a strong connection between the nature of one's work relationships and the values and attitudes one holds on a more general level (Schein, 1978). In a series of laboratory experiments, Breer and Locke (1965) found that individuals, while working on a task, develop beliefs, values, and preferences which are consistent with the forms of behavior that are most successful in that situation. Over time, successful behavioral patterns are defined as legitimate and morally right. The values and beliefs which support those behaviors are then generalized to other areas of life.

In universities, the research act can be characterized in terms of the extent to which it is technology-dependent and group-centered. We have already cited evidence that students selected degree programs compatible with their personal values, and that these values are substantially strengthened and refined through the early professional socialization experience. We believe that these imprinting processes are particularly critical in solidifying budding academics' views of the legitimate role of administration. Specifically, we believe that the manner in which research work activities are organized in the humanities and the sciences reinforces an apprentice's nascent views of the harm or benefit to be expected from university administrators.

Comparisons of the early professional experiences of scientists and humanists help clarify this line of reasoning. Students expressing interest in becoming chemists might begin their laboratory research career as undergraduate hourly employees performing menial chores. Next, as graduate students, they would gradually become integrated into an ongoing research project, generally under the supervision of a postdoctoral fellow. The move to postdoctoral status is marked by a significant increase in administrative duties, in many cases encompassing responsibility for the day-to-day activities of a large research project. Finally, the step up to professor means assuming full responsibility for sustaining an uninterrupted flow of outside resources, complying with regulations and restrictions from funding agencies, effectively matching project tasks with the abilities and interests of team members, aggressively protecting the physical boundaries of the lab space from encroaching competitors, and efficiently coordinating experiment schedules with student program deadlines, equipment availability, and so forth. Through this series of professional stages, the young scientist comes to understand the need for coordination, rules, and authority structures.

This description suggests that scientific research activities are both group-centered and technologically dependent. There is daily contact between most team members and frequent contact with the supervising professor. Articles from projects are seldom single-authored, and most dissertations represent a small piece of a larger study. The research activities of the project members are closely coordinated to efficiently utilize space and equipment resources. In this milieu, researchers gain personal experience performing various administrative responsibilities as they progress from lab assistant to professor. Along the way, they see ample evidence that research scientists' productivity is affected by their management prowess. Having been socialized to view effective administration as a necessary component of good science, faculty members in the sciences should prefer department heads and deans who are capable administrators and should be willing to give them a freer hand in running the department or college. They should also feel less personal aversion to moving into a full-time administrative position.

In contrast, the early professional socialization experiences in the humanities are quite different, due to a radically different mode of organizing scholarly work activities. A student's initial interest in a specific aspect of the humanities often stems from a strong identification with a single professor and is nurtured through a highly individualized mentoring process. Students are seldom incorporated into an ongoing formal research group under the supervision of the mentor. Consequently, they are not likely to measure their professional progress according to their expanding responsibilities in a research team. In fact, they are seldom given responsibility for supervising other students (outside the classroom), nor are they likely to be involved in any research-related administrative duties performed by their major professor.

In practice, the role model for most graduate students in the humanities is a professor with a relatively heavy teaching load performing his or her research in an autonomous setting (e.g., a library carrel or a single-occupant office). Consequently, students are not likely to associate a mentor's scholarly productivity with his or her administrative interest or acumen. Following this example, humanities graduates typically adopt the work regimen of an isolated scholar—working alone on their dissertation with only minimal contact with other students and faculty members.

This work-activity pattern reinforces the importance of individual autonomy and encourages new assistant professors to defend the principle of self-governance against the threat of centralized administration. Because they see only a relatively modest instrumental linkage between administrative activities of any sort and personal research productivity, or excellence in teaching, there is no reason for them to temper their inherent negative attitudes about institutionalized authority structures.

Resource Dependence

In addition to personal ideology and work structure factors, resource dependencies resulting from research requirements should have a major impact on faculty attitudes about university governance processes. During the past decade considerable attention has focused on the consequences of resource dependence (Pfeffer and Salancik, 1978; Pfeffer, 1977). Particular emphasis has been placed on examining its role in the university budgeting process (Salancik and Pfeffer, 1974; Lodahl and Gordon, 1973). A basic axiom of the resource-dependence perspective is that the more resources are concentrated in a single source, the greater the recipient's dependence. Under conditions of high dependence, therefore, we can expect to observe a high degree of relationship maintenance activity (Salancik, 1977). This might include currying the favor of the dominant party, bargaining to improve the terms of exchange, monitoring the performance of the resource allocator to insure against violations of implicit or explicit agreements, and lobbying against policies or priorities that might erode one's competitive position.

This perspective is particularly well suited to our discussion of the differences between humanists and scientists, because the funding needs and resource allocation mechanisms for the two groups are strikingly dissimilar (Lodahl and Gordon, 1973). As we discussed earlier, laboratory science research is very resource-intensive. It requires the use of expensive equipment that is housed in laboratories and is operated and maintained by a staff of professionals and paraprofessionals. In contrast, faculty in the humanities have relatively modest research-related resource needs. They are heavily dependent on the size and quality of the university's library, but the financial support for this "shared good" comes from sources only indirectly linked to the size of personal research grants and department budgets. While the failure to obtain funding for a specific research request may be equally crippling to the success of a specific research project in the sciences and the humanities, the magnitude of the overall resource requirements needed to sustain quality research in the sciences dwarfs the funding needs for a comparable level of research in the humanities.

One outcome of this significant disparity in funding requirements is that scientists must seek multiple sources of support. They generally cannot rely on a single outside source, and they certainly cannot exist on the support they receive from internal university sources. In contrast, researchers in the humanities are heavily dependent on internal resource support because there are fewer external funding opportunities. Also, most major research universities have established internal research budgets large enough to fund a substantial number of modest-sized projects. In addition, because humanities professors tend to have significantly heavier teaching responsibilities than their counterparts in science departments, their dependence on internal resources is further intensified (especially when the definition of resources is enlarged to encompass space and time).

There is an additional reason that the humanities tend to have a greater dependence on internal sources of funding. Lodahl and Gordon (1973) and Pinner (1962) have argued that academic fields differ in terms of the public-at-large's support, reflected in their views regarding the competence of their scholars, the truth of their findings, and the values that inform their work. Pinner divided disciplines into dissensual and consensual categories, reflecting this general level of social support. The natural sciences are categorized as consensual, while the social sciences and the humanities are dissensual. According to Pinner, this distinction partly accounts for the disparity in research support made available to scholars in these fields by sources external to the university. The common practice of creating a pool of internal research money from a portion of the indirect costs recovered from external grants reflects the pressures placed on central administrations to provide internal funds for departments with few external funding opportunities.

As a result of this heavy dependence on internal resources, it follows that faculty in the humanities will be very concerned about their level of influence over the administrative processes governing these allocation decisions. Their acute sense of vulnerability to unfavorable outcomes from these processes should intensify their underlying distrust of powerful administrators. They should therefore have a strong preference for weak department chairs whose authority is circumscribed by an elaborate faculty committee system. This increases the individual professor's opportunities to influence any given allocation process and reduces his or her chances of being disadvantaged by a single unsupportive administrator.

In contrast, we have argued that scientists share neither their humanities colleagues' strong ideological preference for broadly shared decision-making power nor their very pragmatic concerns about losing control over the local resource-allocation processes. Instead, they see the advantages of a strong department head who can buffer them from the numerous distractions and irritants attendant on being a faculty member at any large university. Rather than jealously protecting their rights of self-governance, they are willing to invest considerable discretionary authority in their department head in exchange for minimizing their non-research-related responsibilities.

Professional Status

The final component of our model focuses on a related aspect of power and dependence. Just as few external options for obtaining needed research resources increase a faculty member's dependence on internal allocation processes, in like manner, faculty with low external visibility and limited mobility tend to be more dependent on their current university for employment. In contrast, faculty members with high external visibility tend to bring prestige to the department (which increases the university's dependence on them), and they do not lack for job alternatives since they are in demand in the job market (which reduces their dependence on the university).

Beyer (1982) has argued that professional status is primarily a function of research reputation. Reputation is, in turn, largely based on publication productivity. Although publication quality is obviously an important ingredient in establishing one's reputation, investigators have found strong correlations between total publications and other indices of quality of publications, for example, citations (Lightfield, 1971).

The characteristics of this elite cadre of high-status, extremely mobile research scholars have been described by Ladd and Lipset (1972b). The composite picture suggested by their analysis portrays this group as more vocal, more liberal, and more sensitive to governance issues. However, because of their emphasis on research productivity, these research scholars also place a premium on living in a "hassle-free" academic environment. That is, they value effective administrators who aren't continually making demands on their time for involvement in routine decision-making activities. They want to be kept informed, and they are very concerned about the priorities and values embodied in the administrative decisions, but they don't want to spend a lot of "unproductive" time in meetings. Therefore, given the fact that high-status, highly productive scholars appreciate the contribution made by an effective administration to the success of their scholarly ambitions, as long as administrative decisions are consistent with their values, they will allow administrators considerable latitude in structuring the administrative process.

Based on this composite picture of high-status faculty, it appears that they have characteristics typical of both humanists and scientists. On the one hand, they are extremely liberal ideologically, like humanities faculty members. The accompanying inherent distrust of institutionalized authority structures should cause them to favor highly decentralized, weak academic administrative structures. However, like scientists, their work history and habits suggest greater appreciation of, and less inclination to meddle in, the administrative process. On balance, we expect that the views regarding the legitimate role of administrators in the university governance process held by high-status faculty will be more similar to those expressed by scientists, as a group. This is because their high mobility possibilities decrease their dependence on the actions of any particular administrator. Given the option of being able to move to another institution readily, and their confidence in being able to influence the administrative process (at the very highest levels, if necessary), they will accord local administrative leaders considerable autonomy. In contrast, the low-status faculty will have greater dependence on their current university and will therefore, like the humanists, be more concerned about insuring broad access to the governance process in that institution.

APPLICATION OF MODEL TO PREDICT GOVERNANCE STRUCTURE, SATISFACTION, AND PRODUCTIVITY

Thus far, we have described a model of diversity within institutions of higher education based on extensive interviews and review of the literature. We have argued that members of different disciplines (notably scientists versus humanists) hold divergent political views, which are related to beliefs about the benefits versus the liabilities of institutionalized work and authority relationships. We further proposed that the nascent ideological views present early in one's academic career are reinforced (made more extreme) by participation in the socializing processes of the respective disciplines. At the core of this experience are the social patterns, the authority relationships, and the work responsibilities associated with the manner in which research is conducted in the sciences versus the humanities. Finally, we drew attention to the vital role that resource dependencies play in accentuating these fundamental differences between internally and externally funded disciplines. The contrasting characteristics of the humanities and sciences are summarized in Figure 1.

We turn now to a partial test of this model using data from a national survey of faculty attitudes and activities. We will do this in three stages: First, we will determine whether there is a difference in the mean responses between humanists and scientists on the key variables shown in Figure 1. This represents a simple, but necessary, test of the assumption underlying our model that humanists and scientists operate within distinctiy different realms of academe. Second, we will examine whether these variables explain a significantly greater percentage of the variance in department governance structure than level of paradigm development alone. Finally, we will address the "so what" question. That is, "Assuming that ideology, work structure, and resource dependencies are, in fact, related to departmental governance structures, what difference does that make?" As a partial answer to this question, we will examine the extent to which faculty whose attitudes, work activities, or existing departmental governance structures are inconsistent with the norm for their discipline report lower research productivity and less satisfaction with their collegial relations, their research and

FIG. 1. Model of diversity in faculty characteristics and relationship between faculty characteristics and congruent governance structures.

Faculty discipline	Political ideology of faculty	Institutional ideology of faculty	Structure of research work activity	Resource dependencies	Congruent departmental governance structure
Humanities	Liberal	Anti-institutional	Autonomous scholar	Minimal resource needs are internally funded	Weak chair serving short term
	Strong social critics	High distrust of authority	Administrative abilities have little instrumental value	Moderate dependence on local resource allocations	Strong faculty committees
Laboratory sciences	Conservative	Pro-institutional	Research team coordinator	Extensive resource needs; chiefly funded externally	Strong head serving long term
	Support status quo	Low distrust of authority	Strong link between administrative acumen and research productivity	Low dependence on local resource allocators	Weak faculty committees

teaching activities, the performance of their administrators, or their overall university experience.

This third stage of the analysis is guided by a congruence model of organizations (e.g., Nadler and Tushman, 1977). This perspective argues that key components of an organization need to be in balance with one another. Failure to maintain minimal levels of congruence, or fit, between these components impairs organizational performance. In the case of universities, we are positing that the faculty characteristics depicted in Figure 1 should be congruent with the corresponding departmental governance structure, shown in the right-hand column. If our model is accurate, then in cases where these components are "out of synch," we should find evidence of diminished faculty satisfaction and research productivity. These predictions are summarized in Figure 2.

FIG. 2. Model of the relationship between faculty characteristics, departmental governance, and faculty satisfaction.

A: Faculty characteristics	B: Administrative structure		C: Faculty satisfaction

Political
ideology

Institutional
ideology   Departmental
                            governance   "Fit" of A and B
Research work   structure
structure

Resource
dependence

Faculty satisfaction
with:

Collegial relations
Research activities
Teaching activities
Performance of
  administrators
Career success
Overall university
  experience

Research productivity

METHOD

The Sample

Data from the Carnegie Commission Survey of Faculty and Student Opinion were used to test the proposed model. There are 20,008 respondents and 391 variables. The data consist of a random one-third sample subsetted from a total of 60,028 mail questionnaires returned by a national sample of college and university faculty.[1]

The initial sample consisted of the schools that were part of the 1966 ongoing survey of first-time students done by the American Council on Education (ACE). The ACE sample was stratified by institutional type (two-year colleges, four-year colleges, and universities); the size of enrollment (two-year colleges only); and per student expenditures (four-year colleges and universities only). In 1967, approximately 115,000 faculty were employed in 303 participating ACE sample institutions. Six sevenths (100,290) of these were polled regarding their backgrounds, attitudes, and beliefs regarding a wide-ranging number of topics.

The survey questionnaires were mailed during the second week of March 1969. Follow-up postcards were mailed approximately one week later. Two weeks after the postcards, letters were sent to all nonrespondents. Six weeks after the initial mailing, a second questionnaire was sent to the remaining nonrespondents. Most people (52%) responded to the initial questionnaire. Approximately 8% responded as a result of the three additional mailings. A random sample of 2,000 faculty drawn from the original sample were interviewed by telephone to explore possible response bias in the available sample.

The only discrepancy uncovered was a 5% lower response rate from faculty whose primary interest was "very heavily in teaching." Thus, the achieved sample somewhat overrepresents individuals interested in research or research and teaching. Additional details concerning the study's design, questionnaire development, data collection, respondent bias, and nonrespondent bias are reported in Martin Trow's *Teachers and Students* (1975).

Our analyses were confined to the 14,957 respondents employed at universities, as opposed to four-year or two-year colleges, where the differences between departments is most pronounced. Of those, 8,229 indicated that their "present primary field of research, scholarship, or creativity" was one of the natural sciences or the humanities and social sciences. The 4,441 scientists included all the faculty in any of the biological or physical science disciplines (e.g., bacteriology, biochemistry, botany, zoology, chemistry, physics, and geology), as well as any of the engineering disciplines and medicine. The second group included 3,788 faculty in the humanities (e.g., English and foreign languages and literature, history, and philosophy), the social sciences (e.g., anthropology, archaeology, economics, political science, and sociology), and the various psychology disciplines.[2] Faculty in the fine arts (e.g., art, music, dramatics, and architecture and design) and professional fields (e.g., business, law, journalism, nursing, agriculture, and social work) were excluded from the present analysis so that our groupings would correspond to the disciplinary distinctions commonly used in the paradigm development literature.

Operationalizations

One of the obvious disadvantages of using secondary data for testing a model is lack of control over the choice of variables and operationalizations. Fortunately, this particular survey contains questions pertaining to most of the key variables in our model (a more recent survey conducted by the Carnegie Foundation in 1975 could not be used because it had very few questions on university governance). To partially overcome the inherent problems of developing measures of the model variables using existing survey questions, we have, whenever possible, used multiple-item indices. These indices were either constructed by Ladd and Lipsett in their original data analysis or developed through our own factor analysis of potentially relevant survey items. In general, although we regret having to rely on existing data, we feel that most of our variables are adequately measured for this initial test of the model. A summary of the items used to construct each variable index follows.

Political ideology (IDEOL. Politics) was measured with the survey's liberal-conservative index. It reflects the faculty's position on the major political issues of the time. Items include: (1) "How do you characterize yourself politically?" (2) "What is your position on the Vietnam war?" (3) "Should marijuana be legalized?'' (4) ''Should busing be used to integrate schools?'' And (5) ''Is white racism the main cause of Negro riots in the cities?'' Scores could range from −12 (most liberal) to 12 (most conservative).

Institutional ideology was measured with two indices which reflect faculty attitudes toward institutional and administrative arrangements at the university level. These were based on a factor analysis of seemingly related survey items (see Appendix A). Institutionalized scholarship attitudes (IDEOL. AmHiEd) captures the respondents' faith in, or cynicism toward, institutionalized scholarship as practiced in American higher education. It includes their agreement or disagreement with five statements: (1) ''Most Ph.D. holders in my field get their degrees without showing much real scholarly ability''; (2) ''Many of the best graduate students can no longer find meaning in science and scholarship''; (3) ''Graduate education in my subject is doing a good job training students (reverse scored)''; (4) ''Some of the best graduate students drop out because they do not want to 'play the game' or 'beat the system' ''; and (5) ''Most American colleges reward conformity and crush student creativity.'' Responses to each item were combined into a single scale; low scores are most cynical and high scores most supportive.

The second measure of institutional ideology, administrative attitudes (IDEOL. AttAdm), reflects the respondents' attitudes toward their institution's administrators. The three items included in this index are (1) ''This institution would be better off with fewer administrators''; (2) ''There should be faculty representation on the governing board of this institution''; and (3) ''Trustees' only responsibilities should be to raise money and gain community support.'' A low score (1) indicates strong agreement with these statements: administrators are not trusted and should have a limited role. A high score (4) indicates confidence in and trust of the administration and a willingness to allow administrators wider influence.

Few questions in this survey dealt with the issue of work structure. No information was collected regarding the respondent's dependence on technology. Nor were any questions directed toward the socialization practices experienced by respondents during the various stages of their professional training and development. The one measure available asked whether, on their current major piece of research or scholarship, they were (1) essentially working alone; (2) working with one or two colleagues; or, (3) working as a member of a larger group.

A precise measure of resource dependence was not available from our data set because neither the size of the respondent's research budget nor the size or number of research grants received was reported. However, two measures of resource dependence (DEPEND. NSources and DEPEND. IntExt) were developed. Respondents indicated whether research support during the last 12 months came from (1) institutional or department funds; (2) federal agencies; (3) state or local government agencies; (4) private foundations; (5) private industry; or (6) other sources. DEPEND. NSources consists of the number of different sources for research support and ranges from 0 to 6. DEPEND. IntExt used the same information but classified the source of research funding along a continuum based on the respondent's dependence on the local institution. The 1,622 faculty who received no research support were considered most dependent on their local institution. They were coded 1. Also highly dependent were the 1,459 faculty who received only institutional or department funds. They were coded 2. Less dependent on their institutions were the 2,379 faculty, coded 3, who received some external research funding. Least dependent were the 1,818 faculty, coded 4, who received all of their research support from external sources.

The status of the faculty (STATUS. Prod) was measured using a question in the survey regarding the number of publications (books, papers, chapters, and so on) produced in the previous two years. Responses were scored on a five-point scale from 1 = zero publications, to 5 = more than 10 publications during this period. As noted earlier, the number of publications produced by a scholar has been shown to correlate highly with the quality of those publications, using measures such as number of citations (Lightfield, 1971). Preliminary analysis indicated that this measure of status is highly correlated with the distinction between humanists and scientists. To examine the unique effect of status, we standardized each score by subtracting it from the mean of the appropriate group (scientists: 2.70; humanists: 2.28).

The second stage of the model (see Figure 2) focuses on how authority relationships are institutionalized in university departments. The extent of faculty involvement in, and control over, departmental decision-making (DEPT. Participation) was determined from faculty response to three items: (1) "Do you feel that the administration of your department is: (very autocratic, somewhat autocratic, somewhat democratic, very democratic)?" (2) "How much opportunity do you feel you have to influence the policies of your department (a great deal, quite a bit, some, none)?" And (3) "In your department, are decisions other than personnel matters normally made by the vote of the whole department, including junior members?" Items 2 and 3 were reverse-scored, so low scores indicate less faculty participation in department administrative matters.

The third stage of the model deals with the faculty's satisfaction. We chose to examine faculty satisfaction with their university experience both "in general," and along five specific dimensions of professional activity. In every case, lower scores indicate greater levels of satisfaction. General satisfaction levels were determined by whether respondents thought their university was "a very good place," "a fairly good place," or "not the place" for them. Satisfaction with the administration was also determined by a single item: Respondents were asked to "rate the administration at your institution: excellent, good, fair, or poor."

Satisfaction with the support available for research was tapped with ratings for the "general research resources (e.g., library, labs, computers, space, etc.)" and

TABLE 1. Tests of Differences Between Scientists and Humanists[a]

Faculty characteristics (variable)	Mean for scientists	Mean for humanists	t value	2-tail probability
IDEOL. Politics	−.629	2.797	−30.18	.000
IDEOL. AmHiEd	3.003	2.662	26.58	.000
IDEOL. AttAdm	2.264	2.063	12.96	.000
Work structure	1.579	1.198	28.27	.000
DEPEND. IntExt	3.015	2.099	39.04	.000
DEPEND. NSource	1.849	1.496	12.83	.000

[a]Low scores indicate more conservative; more cynical; less supportive; smaller research teams; more highly dependent; or fewer sources of funding.

the "availability of research funds from all sources" at the respondent's university. Satisfaction with collegial relations was determined from ratings of "the intellectual environment," "personal relations among faculty," and "faculty/student relations" in the respondent's department. Satisfaction with the teaching environment was indicated by ratings of the "teaching load" and the "ratio of teaching faculty to students" at the respondent's university.

RESULTS

The results will be presented in three sections. The first section examines whether scientists and humanists actually differ in the ways summarized in Figure 1. The second section addresses the issue of whether our model (summarized in Figure 2) substantially increases our ability to explain the differences in the ways academic departments are governed. Finally, we will present our findings regarding the implications of our model in understanding faculty satisfaction.

Differences Between Scientists and Humanists

Table 1 reports the differences in mean scores between scientists and humanists in our sample. Scientists and humanists differ in the predicted directions on each of the dimensions deemed relevant in our model. Faculty in scientific and engineering disciplines are significantly more conservative in their political views than faculty in the social sciences and humanities. In addition, scientists view large-scale institutionalized research in a more positive light and express greater confidence in the quality of American higher education. Finally, scientists have greater confidence in and view the role of university administrators less narrowly than humanists.

Although the sample did not allow much discrimination in the size of one's research work group, scientists report conducting more joint research and working in larger groups than humanists. Scientists and humanists also differ significantly on both measures of research dependence. Scientists received funds from more sources and were less dependent on funding from within the university than faculty in the social sciences and humanities. In fact, while 77.8% of the scientists sampled received at least some research support from outside their universities (and 33.5% received all their research support from external sources), only 33.2% of faculty in the social sciences and humanities received any external funding at all.

Predicting Department Governance Structures

Having determined that the basic predictive variables in our model do, in fact, discriminate between humanists and scientists, we now must examine their ability to explain a significantly larger share of the variance in departmental governance structures than level of paradigm development alone.

This proposition was tested by conducting a hierarchical regression using the level of faculty participation in departmental administration. To provide a conservative test of our model, paradigm development (as it is typically operationalized in the literature) was entered into the regression equation first. Once all the variance attributable solely to paradigm development, (i.e., whether one is a scientist or a humanist) was accounted for, the faculty characteristic variables from our model, work structure, and resource dependence were introduced to determine what additional variance they could explain. Because our two measures of resource dependence are highly related, only one (whether research support came from internal or external sources) was used in the regression equation. We felt that this variable more closely captured the concept of resource dependence presented in the model.

The amount of variance explained by paradigm development alone, compared with the additional variance explained by the variables in our model, are reported in Table 2. Paradigm development by itself explained only .29% of the variance in level of participation. Faculty views on institutionalized scholarship (IDEOL. AmHiEd) and the role of administration (IDEOL. AttAdm) explain considerably more variance (2.97 and 3.65%, respectively). The faculty's political orientation (IDEOL. Politics) and professional status (STATUS. Prod) are also significant predictors of participation in the department's administration. Surprisingly, work structure and dependence on the university for research support (DEPEND. IntExt) both failed to account for a significant amount of variance. Together, the variables from our model account for an additional 8.03% of the explained variance. Although this percentage is not large, it is substantially larger than the .29% explained by paradigm development alone. In addition, other factors not

TABLE 2. Predicting Departmental Governance Structures

	Variance explained in participation in department governance[a]
Paradigm development	.29[b]
IDEOL. Politics	.59
IDEOL. AmHiEd	2.97
IDEOL. AttAdm	3.65
Work structure	-NS-
DEPEND. IntExt	-NS-
STATUS. Prod	.81
Total variance explained (R squared)	8.32%
Variance explained using paradigm development only	.29%
Additional variance explained by proposed model	8.03%

[a]Except for paradigm development, which entered the regression equation first, the variance reported is the marginal variance explained by each variable after all other variables were considered.
[b]Explained variance is reported only for variables whose standardized beta weights are significant at $p < .001$.

tested in the model obviously impact departmental structure, for example, the size and type of university and university-specific norms.

Tests of a Congruence View of Organizational Outcomes

One practical implication of our model is that faculty whose political and/or institutional ideologies, work structure, and/or resource dependence are inconsistent with the norm for their discipline should be less satisfied and productive than faculty who are "in synch" with the task demands of their discipline and the political views of their peers. Referring to Figure 2, one notes that it is the "fit" between Faculty Characteristics (A) and Departmental Governance Structure (B) that is predicted to affect Faculty Satisfaction and Productivity (C). To test this model, we needed to know how "far away," or discrepant, each respondent's personal characteristics were from the norm for his or her disciplinary peers. This norm is represented by the solution to the multiple-regression equation reported above. The residuals from this regression represent the distance between the predicted and observed values of the dependent variable for each respondent.

The larger the residual, the greater the discrepancy between an individual and his or her disciplinary peers. Since low responses indicate greater satisfaction, a congruence model would predict positive correlations between the residual scores and measures of satisfaction and productivity. As Table 3 reports, all the correlations were positive and significant. Correlations were greatest between the respondents' discrepancy scores and their satisfaction with the collegial nature of the department $(r = .324)$, the institution in general $(r = .225)$, and the administration's performance $(r = .131)$.

As a final measure of the impact of governance structures, we examined the relationship between the respondents' overall satisfaction with their university experience and their satisfaction with four specific aspects of academic life (research support, teaching responsibility, colleagues, and administration). To the extent the faculty feel that the outcomes of the governance process are vital to their interests, we should find that satisfaction with administration is an important component of overall satisfaction with the university. The results of our regression analysis, shown in Table 4, indicate that after satisfaction with colleagues, satisfaction with administration had the largest impact on overall satisfaction (with standardized beta weights of .351 and .236, respectively).

DISCUSSION AND CONCLUSIONS

The purpose of this paper has been to present a model explaining observed differences in the governance process across academic departments in major research universities. The prevailing explanation, level of paradigm development, has been used extensively in previous research, even though it provides relatively little insight into the organizational processes accounting for reported differences in administrative practices between disciplines. To broaden our understanding of these differences, we have argued that departmental governance structures reflect faculty political and institutional values, organization of research work activities, and relative dependence on intrauniversity research support.

Using data collected in a national study of faculty attitudes during the late 1960s, we conducted an initial test of our model. First, we found that the predictive variables in our model do, in fact, discriminate between the humanities and the natural sciences. As predicted, scientists were more conservative politically, less cynical about the negative impact of institutionalized control over graduate education and research in general, and more positive about the value of the administrative component of higher education. In addition, their research activities are more technology-dependent and group-centered—giving them greater appreciation for, and experience with, administration. Finally, they were less dependent on internal funding sources.

We then examined the extent to which these differences between disciplines added significantly to our ability to explain differences in departmental gover-

TABLE 3. Effects of Congruence on Satisfaction

Satisfaction variables	Correlation with residuals from department governance regression
Collegial relations	.324[a]
Research activities	.034
Teaching activities	.054
Administrators' performance	.131
Institution in general	.225

[a]All correlations are significant at .001.

TABLE 4. Regression of General Satisfaction with University with Other Measures of Satisfaction

Satisfaction with	Standardized beta
Administration	.236
Colleagues and intellectual environment	.351
Research support	.087
Teaching responsibilities	.030
Total variance explained (R squared)	28.03%

nance practices. Although our model explained only a modest amount of variance in the level of faculty participation, half of these variables individually accounted for more variance than level of paradigm development. We suspect that one reason for our low overall R^2 is the small amount of variance in our dependent variable (participation in department governance). Unfortunately, for this study, scientists and humanists alike reported a high level of faculty participation in departmental administration. Access to data on a broader set of characteristics of the governance process would have provided a more robust test of our model. In addition, the fact that some of the independent variables did not perform as well as predicted can be attributed to similar limitations in our choice of measures. Specifically, we had little information on the characteristics of the work structure, other than the number of members on the research team. Unfortunately, this taps only a small aspect of this important distinction between the humanities and the sciences.

Given these limitations, one must be cautious in extrapolating conclusions from this study. However, it does appear that the best predictors of differences in departmental governance are faculty attitudes about the legitimate role of administration in higher education, the relative status of the faculty member, and the impact of institutionalization on scholarship. Those who distrusted administrators and decried the negative side effects of large institutions were most likely to be in departments with high faculty participation in the governance process. Political values were only moderately linked to administrative practice, possibly because the logical link is more indirect. That is, attitudes about social policies appear to be related to department governance via their link to attitudes about institutionalized scholarship and the legitimate role of administration.

To assess the impact of different levels of faculty participation in departmental governance processes, we adopted the logic of congruence models of organizational effectiveness. Specifically, we postulated that the fit of faculty ideology, work structure, and resource dependence with the form of departmental administration would have an impact on faculty satisfaction. We expected that faculty in departments where there was a "good fit" of personal attitudes, work structure, and level of resource dependence with the preferred departmental governance structure for their discipline would report high levels of satisfaction.

The residual analysis reported in Table 3 suggests that this congruence approach to effectiveness is useful, at least for some measures of satisfaction (with collegial relations, with the performance of administrators, and with the institution as a whole). These results suggest that faculty have definite expectations regarding how administrative actions, particularly those affecting personnel policies and staffing decisions, as well as the overall intellectual climate in the department, should be handled within their discipline. Furthermore, when observed practice is congruent with these expectations regarding appropriate administrative practice in the humanities or the sciences, faculty members report high levels of satisfaction. We suspect that the satisfaction with administration would have been even higher if the survey question had been less ambiguously worded and had been focused specifically on department level administration. The relatively low correlations with satisfaction with teaching and research activities is to be expected, since these are affected by a wide range of individual, organizational, and external factors, only a few of which are directly related to the department governance process.

As a final test of the impact of the governance process on faculty members, we examined the relationship between individuals' overall satisfaction with the university and their satisfaction with specific components of academic life. We expected that the factors most directly affected by the departmental administrative practice would be the best predictors of overall satisfaction. This is reflected in the results shown in Table 4. The pattern is similar to the results in Table 3: satisfaction with administration and satisfaction with colleagues and intellectual climate are better predictors of overall satisfaction than are satisfaction with teaching activities and satisfaction with research support. This suggests that overall loyalty and commitment to a university are affected more by the performance of its administration and by the satisfaction derived from intellectually stimulating colleagues than by the quality of a faculty member's experience in the research lab or classroom. This conclusion clearly underscores the need for further investigations of the impacts of the governance process in universities.

Although we feel that the results of this study demonstrate the utility of key aspects of our model of academic governance, there are several obvious reasons for being cautious at this point. First of all, since our primary objective was to suggest a broader conception of differences in governance structures across academic disciplines, we viewed the empirical portion of this paper as only illustrative. Therefore, we have used less than optimal measures of several of the variables, and we were unable to explore some aspects of the model, for example, the propensity of humanists versus scientists to pursue an academic career path. A more definitive test of the model must, therefore, await further investigation. Second, we are concerned about generalizing from data collected during the 1960s. It is not just that nearly 20 years have lapsed since this survey was conducted. More important, campuses today are very different from those in this radical, strife-ridden era. It is hard to know how that general climate might have affected these data, but one suspects that many of the attitudes and values measured were more polarized during the 1960s. This possibility further reinforces the need for further investigation of this subject.

In conclusion, independent of the merits of this particular empirical investigation, our model of university governance suggests some important avenues for future research on this topic. For example, organizational research on the university resource-allocation process has explained discrepancies in funding for the humanities versus the sciences in one of two ways. Salancik and Pfeffer (1974) argued that the larger budgets in science departments reflect their superior bargaining position. Because the sciences generate much larger amounts of external funding for the institution, they are in a stronger position to get internal funding, relative to the humanities. Pfeffer and Moore (1980b) argued that the difference in funding levels across departments reflects their relative degree of paradigm development. That is, because fields with a higher level of paradigm development should be able to generate more consensus among members on critical issues, they are in a better position to bargain for university resources.

While both of these explanations are consistent with our model, it suggests additional hypotheses that were not considered in previous studies. For example, the preference for relatively weak department chairs in the humanities also reduces their ability to bargain for scarce university resources. Department administrators in the humanities turn over more rapidly than their counterparts in the sciences (Pfeffer and Moore, 1980a) and have less authority to make commitments and trade-offs in the negotiation process. Furthermore, in general, department heads in the sciences have had more experience with budget making, fund raising, and negotiating activities, due to the larger administrative component in their research projects. Also, their greater ease in shifting from managing their lab to administering a department increases their ability to understand and relate to central campus administrators. Their higher level of comfort with the administrative role and their greater familiarity with the administrative process should significantly enhance their effectiveness at the bargaining table.

One of the values of this broader view of the governance process in the humanities and sciences, therefore, is that it highlights a basic paradox confronting humanities departments. During this era of shifting priorities and overall retrenchment in many large universities, the humanities on many campuses are seeing their already meager financial base eroded further. The analysis above suggests that one remedy for this situation is to alter their internal governance process by, for example, installing stronger department heads for longer periods of time. However, this runs counter to their deeply ingrained distrust of administration and institutionalized activities, in general. Tracking the tension between these competing priorities in humanities departments is one of the challenging possibilities for future research on the governance process in universities suggested by our model.

Acknowledgment. We would like to express appreciation to Janice Beyer for her helpful comments on a earlier draft.

NOTES

1. The data were collected by Martin Trow through the Survey Research Center at the University of California at Berkeley and subsetted by Everett Ladd and S. M. Lipsett through the Social Science Data Center at the University of Connecticut. The current data set was made available by the Inter-university Consortium for Political and Social Research (ICPSR 7501). Neither the original collectors of the data, the producers of the data, nor the consortium bear any responsibility for the analyses or interpretations presented here.

2. Categorizing departments and disciplines into two broad groups, such as humanities and sciences, is obviously a challenging and risky task. We have taken as our guidance previous research on paradigm development which has tended to lump the humanities and the social sciences together as low-paradigm fields (Salancik et al., 1980; Lodahl and Gordon, 1972). Although there are several important differences between the humanities and the social sciences, previous research has shown that their similarities are considerable, when compared with the physical and biological sciences.

REFERENCES

Alport, G., Vernon, P., and Lindzey, G. (1960). *Study of Values*. Boston: Houghton Mifflin.

Bendix, Reinhard. (1956). *Work and Authority in Industry.* New York: Wiley.

Bennis, Warren G. (1973). *The Leaning Ivory Tower.* San Francisco: Jossey-Bass.

Beyer, Janice M. (1978). Editorial policies and practices among leading journals in four scientific fields. *Sociological Quarterly* 19: 68–88.

Beyer, Janice M. (1982). Power dependencies and the distribution of influence in universities. In S. B. Bacharach (ed.), *Research in the Sociology of Organizations,* Vol. 1. Greenwich, CN: JAI Press.

Beyer, Janice M., and Lodahl, Thomas M. (1976). A comparative study of patterns of influence in United States and English universities. *Administrative Science Quarterly* 27: 104–129.

Beyer, Janice M., and Snipper, Rueben. (1974). Objective versus subjective indicators of quality in graduate education. *Sociology of Education* 47: 541–557.

Breer, Paul E. and Locke, Edwin. (1965). *Task Experiences as a Source of Attitudes.* Homewood, IL: Dorsey Press.

Burden, Charles, Burden, Elke, Eisiminger, Sterling, and Ganim, Lynn (1977). *Business in Literature.* New York: David McKay.

Cheng, Joseph L. C., and McKinley, William. (1983). Toward an integration of organization research and practice: A contingency study of bureaucratic control and performance in scientific settings. *Administrative Science Quarterly* 28: 85–100.

Cohen, M. D., and March, James G. (1974). *Leadership and Ambiguity: The American College President.* New York: McGraw-Hill.

Emmerson, D. K. (1968). Conclusion. In D. K. Emmerson (ed.), *Students and Politics in Developing Nations.* New York: Praeger.

Gouldner, Alvin W. (1954). *Patterns of Industrial Bureaucracy.* New York: Free Press.

Kohlberg, L. (1969). The cognitive-developmental approach to socialization. In D. A. Goslin (ed.), *Handbook of Socialization Theory and Research.* Chicago: Rand McNally.

Kuhn, Thomas. (1962). *The Structure of Scientific Revolutions.* Chicago: University of Chicago Press.

Ladd, Everett C., and Lipsett, Seymour M. (1971). The politics of American political scientists. *PS* 4: 135–144.

Ladd, Everett C., and Lipsett, Seymour M. (1972a). Contours of academic politics: 1972. *New York* 5 (Oct. 16).

Ladd, Everett C., and Lipsett, Seymour M. (1972b). Politics of academic natural scientists and engineers. *Science* 176: 1091–1100.

Ladd, Everett C., and Lipsett, Seymour M. (1973). *Professors, Unions, and American Higher Education.* Berkeley, CA: Carnegie Commission on Higher Education.

Ladd, Everett C., and Lipsett, Seymour M. (1975). *The Divided Academy.* New York: McGraw-Hill.

Lightfield, E. T. (1971). Output and recognition of sociologists. *American Sociologist* 6: 128–133.

Lipsett, Seymour M., and Ladd Everett C. (1972). The politics of American sociologists. *American Journal of Sociology* 78: 67–104.

Lodahl, Janice Beyer, and Gordon, Gerald (1972). The structure of scientific fields and the functioning of university graduate departments. *American Sociological Review* 37: 57–62.

Lodahl, Janice Beyer, and Gordon, Gerald (1973). Differences between physical and social sciences in university graduate departments. *Research in Higher Education* 1: 191–222.

Nadler, David A., and Tushman, Michael L. (1977). A diagnostic model for organizational behavior. In J. R. Hackman, E. E. Lawler III, and L. W. Porter (eds.), *Perspectives in Behavior in Organizations*. New York: McGraw-Hill.

Pfeffer, Jeffrey. (1977). Power and resource allocation in organizations. In B. M. Staw and G. R. Salancik (eds.), *New Directions in Organizational Behavior*. Chicago: St. Clair Press.

Pfeffer, Jeffrey, and Moore, William L. (1980a). Average tenure of academic department heads: The effects of paradigm development, size, and departmental demography. *Administrative Science Quarterly* 25: 637–653.

Pfeffer, Jeffrey, and Moore, William L. (1980b). Power in university budgeting: A replication and extension. *Administrative Science Quarterly* 25: 387–406.

Pfeffer, Jeffrey, Salancik, Gerald R., and Leblebici, Husseyin. (1976). The effect of uncertainty on the use of social influence in organizational decision making. *Administrative Science Quarterly* 21: 227–245.

Pfeffer, Jeffrey, and Salancik, Gerald R. (1978). *The External Control of Organizations: A Resource Dependence Perspective*. New York: Harper & Row.

Pinner, F. (1962). The crises of the state universities: Analysis and remedies. In N. Sanford (ed.) *The American College*. New York: Wiley.

Pondy, Louis R. (1983). Personal correspondence. Class lecture University of Illinois at Urbana-Champaign, Fall.

Rabi, I. I. (1956). Scientist and humanist: Can the minds meet? *Atlantic Monthly* 197 (1, Jan.): 64–67.

Salancik, Gerald R. (1977). Commitment and the control of organizational behavior and belief. In B. M. Staw and G. R. Salancik (eds.), *New Directions in Organizational Behavior*. Chicago: St. Clair Press.

Salancik, Gerald R., and Pfeffer, Jeffrey (1974). The bases of power in organizational decision making: The case of a university. *Administrative Science Quarterly* 19: 453–473.

Salancik, Gerald R., Staw, Barry M., and Pondy, Louis R. (1980). Administrative turnover as a response to unmanaged organizational interdependence. *Academy of Management Journal* 23: 422–437.

Schein, Edgar. (1978). *Career Dynamics*. Reading, MA: Addison Wesley.

Snow, C. P. (1959). *Two Cultures and the Scientific Revolution*. New York: Cambridge University Press.

Trilling, Lionel. (1962). Science, literature, and culture. *Commentary* 33(6, June): 461–477.

Trow, Martin. (1975). *Teachers and Students: Aspects of American Higher Education*. New York: McGraw-Hill.

Weick, Karl. (1976). Educational organizations as loosely coupled systems. *Administrative Science Quarterly* 21: 1–19.

APPENDIX
CONSTRUCTION OF INDICES USED TO TEST THE MODEL

The indices used to test the proposed model were constructed in four stages. First, we reviewed the Carnegie study faculty questionnaire for items which seemed consistent with the model's conceptual elements. Next, the identified items were factor-analyzed (using the SPSS program with varimax rotation) to confirm the appropriateness of our selections. Items which did not load cleanly onto a single factor (rotated factor loadings < .40) were not used. The 15 variables which survived were analyzed a second time to ensure that the

**TABLE A1. Factor Loadings for Variables Used for Indices
in the Proposed Model**

	Rotated factor loadings			
	1	2	3	4
IDEOL. Politics				
Forced busing	.648			
White racism causes riots	.619			
Vietnam stance	.555			
Characterize yourself politically	.751			
IDEOL. AmHiEd				
PH.D's not scholars		.420		
No meaning in science		.636		
Grad. Ed. doing good job		−.523		
IDEOL. AttAdm				
Need fewer administrators				.453
Faculty on governing board				.488
Trustees only raise money				.611
DEPT. Participation				
Dept. autocratic/democratic			−.773	
Opportunity to influence			.579	
Decisions made by vote			.595	

factors would correspond to the indices desired. The results of this analysis are reported in Table A1.

Four factors with eigenvalues greater than 1.0 were extracted from the initial factor solution and rotated using the orthogonal varimax procedure. As shown in Table A1, the rotated factors correspond to the four components in our model: IDEOL. Politics; IDEOL. AmHiEd; IDEOL. AttAdm; and DEPT. Participation. All variables comprising a single index loaded most highly onto the same factor. Their factor loadings ranged from an acceptable .42 up to .77. The median loading was .60.

A similar four-step procedure was used to confirm the appropriateness of the items selected for the satisfaction indices. Because the indices were composed of fewer items (general satisfaction with the university and satisfaction with the administration were measured with a single item, while indices for satisfaction with teaching, research, and the collegial environment were composed of just two or three items), we could not use an eigenvalue of 1.0 as the cutoff for the number of factors to extract for rotation. Instead, we specified four factors which correspond with the number of satisfaction indices created.

TABLE A2. Factor Loadings for Variables Used for Satisfaction Indices

	Rotated factor loadings			
Satisfaction with	1	2	3	4
Collegiality				
Intellectual environment	.555			
Relations with faculty	.885			
Faculty-student relations	.627			
Research				
Nonmonetary resources		.736		
Research funds available		.732		
Teaching				
Teaching load			.524	
Faculty-student ratio			.764	
General				
University in general				.582
Administration				.473

When four factors were extracted, the varimax rotation successfully confirmed the desired dimensions (see Table A2). Each satisfaction item in a given index fell cleanly onto a single factor, with the exception of our two single-item measures, which loaded onto a single factor. Factor loadings ranged from .47 to .89, with a median loading of .63.

When the two factors whose eigenvalues were greater than 1.0 were rotated (again using the varimax procedure), the general satisfaction rating aligned itself with the satisfaction-with-colleagues items, while the satisfaction-with-teaching and research-support items loaded cleanly onto the second. Satisfaction with administration was split evenly between these two factors (which one might label satisfaction with "general" versus "work-related" issues).

The Influence of College on Moral Development

Larry Nucci

and

Ernest T. Pascarella
University of Illinois at Chicago

Does college have a significant impact on a student's moral judgment and behavior? From a social scientist's perspective, the answer to this question may be quite complex and not entirely satisfactory. There is little doubt, however, that at its very inception American higher education had a clearly defined perception of its central role in developing young men who would both think and act morally (Rudolph, 1956; Sloan, 1979, 1980). Indeed, as suggested by Morrill (1980) and Rudolph (1962), 19th-century American higher education had a strongly entrenched tradition of moral philosophy which was manifest in a major portion of the collegiate curriculum.

In addition to what Rudolph (1962, p. 140) describes as an "impressive arsenal of weapons for making men out of boys" (e.g., religious revivals, dedicated and underpaid professors, unheated dormitory rooms), the religiously based liberal arts college of the early 1800s often included courses on ethics and values as part of the core curriculum (McBee, 1980). The culmination was a capstone course in moral philosophy, usually taught by the college president and required of all senior students. This course, transplanted largely from the residential universities of 18th-century England and Scotland, was designed to integrate the students' entire collegiate experience and send them into the larger world not only wiser, but also sensitive to their moral and ethical responsibilities (Sloan, 1979). Thus, the academic curriculum and the entire campus environment clearly viewed the formation of student character as a central mission of the collegiate experience. Consistent with the classical tradition, the liberal arts college believed, as did Plato, "that education makes good men and that good men act nobly" (Adler, 1952).

In the second half of the 18th century, the establishment of state-supported, public institutions under the Morrill Act, the rise of research universities, and the fragmentation of knowledge which accompanied the evaluation of academic disciplines contributed to major structural and curricular changes in American higher education. Direct curricular approaches to the development of student character and moral sensitivity became less evident, and faculty became more concerned with the logic, language, and literature of their own disciplines than with broader questions of human values and morality (Morrill, 1980).

Despite these fundamental changes, however, the tradition of liberal education and its attendant concerns with developing the whole individual still hold a prominent place in the ethos of American higher education (e.g., Chickering, 1969; Heath, 1968; Sanford, 1967; Trow, 1976; Winter, McClelland, and Stewart, 1981). We expect much from our colleges and universities in terms of their influence on student development. There continues to be a presumption that the college experience, and liberal education in particular, contributes not only to cognitive development, but also to an expansion of the student's world view and the capacity to apply reasoning and intellect to interpersonal, political, and social as well as to purely academic questions (Averill, 1983; Gamson, 1984). Given this expectation, it is not unreasonable to ask what the accumulated evidence suggests with regard to the impact of college on student moral development.

MORAL DEVELOPMENT THEORY

For the past 25 years, moral development research has been dominated by the theory of moral growth presented by Lawrence Kohlberg. Our review of literature on college effects upon moral development will thus reflect the preeminence of Kohlbergian theory. During the past decade, however, a number of serious challenges and alternatives to the standard Kohlberg position have been offered. These have led both to the establishment of competing cognitive-development accounts of moral development, and to important revisions in the Kohlberg model itself. Since applied research, almost by definition, lags behind changes in the basic disciplines, most of these shifts in moral development theory have not as yet been reflected in reports concerning moral growth in the college years. In this section, therefore, we wish to present an overview of the current formulation of the Kohlberg model particularly as it pertains to changes in persons of college age. We will also present some of the more important challenges to the model and will provide a framework from which to evaluate and interpret existing data pertaining to college students' moral development.

KOHLBERG'S THEORY OF MORAL DEVELOPMENT

The focus of Kohlberg's theory is on the development of moral judgment. While it is also Kohlberg's purpose to begin to provide an account of moral behavior, his theory reflects an understanding that at the core of moral action is the element of choice and intention (Frankena, 1963).[1] In the standard formulation of the theory, development is described as proceeding through six stages embedded within three levels. (A general description of each stage is provided in Table 1.) At each point in development, the central feature of moral reasoning is said to be a concern for justice or fairness. At the earlier stages, however, justice is confounded with nonmoral considerations such as prudence or convention. In addition, the child's conceptions of justice are egocentric and thus inherently biased and narrow in perspective. Only at the most advanced stages of moral development is morality structured entirely by universalizable principles of justice. Accordingly, Kohlberg has defined the course of moral development as entailing (1) the progressive differentiation of morality as justice from nonmoral concerns such as authority, law, and punishment and (2) the extension and integration of justice concepts which become progressively nonegocentric (objective and universal) in application.

In the most recent formulations of the theory (Kohlberg, 1984), the focus has been on efforts to define the stages in terms of their "sociomoral" perspective. At Level I (Stages 1 and 2), persons are said to reason from a concrete individual perspective. At this level, moral reasoning is based on the person's concerns for his or her own interests and for those of others the individual might care about. Concerns for law at this level primarily focus on their effects upon the self (e.g., breaking the law might lead to punishment). At Level II (Stages 3 and 4), moral reasoning shifts to a member-of-society perspective in which concerns for the needs of individuals are subordinated to the needs of the social group. Moral judgments are based on concerns to maintain the social order and to meet the expectations of others. Law is seen from an "insider's" perspective as necessary to protect and maintain the group as a whole. This maintenance of the system orientation is replaced at Level III (Stages 5 and 6) by a prior-to-society perspective. The basis of this postconventional or "principled" morality is a differentiation of the legal-societal point of view from a moral point of view rooted in a deontological conception of justice. At this third level, morality is seen as a set of universal principles that would be held by any rational moral individual. They are thus first principles and hence exist prior to societal codification. This is in a sense an "outsider's" perspective in that it permits the individual (1) to judge the moral worth of a society or its practices, and (2) to rationally commit himself or herself to a society (Kohlberg, 1984, p. 175).

Though there is no direct correspondence between age and developmental stage, research to date would place most college-age people in the conventional level of moral reasoning. If college contributes significantly to moral development beyond general age-typical experience, it should be evidenced (1) by a general upward shift in moral stage among persons who attend college, and (2) by a greater proportion of postconventional reasoners among college graduates than among either entering freshmen or same-age peers in the general population.

TABLE 1. The Six Moral Stages

Level and Stage	Content of Stage		Social Perspective of Stage
	What Is Right	Reasons for Doing Right	
LEVEL I – PRECONVENTIONAL Stage 1 – Heteronomous Morality	To avoid breaking rules backed by punishment, obedience for its own sake, and avoiding physical damage to persons and property.	Avoidance of punishment, and the superior power of authorities.	Egocentric point of view. Doesn't consider the interests of others or recognize that they differ from the actor's, doesn't relate two points of view. Actions are considered physically rather than in terms of psychological interests of others. Confusion of authority's perspective with one's own.
Stage 2–Individualism, Instrumental Purpose, and Exchange	Following rules only when it is to someone's immediate interest; acting to meet one's own interests and needs and letting others do the same. Right is also what's fair, what's an equal exchange, a deal, an agreement.	To serve one's own needs or interests in a world where you have to recognize that other people have their interests, too.	Concrete individualistic perspective. Aware that everybody has his own interest to pursue and these conflict, so that right is relative (in the concrete individualistic sense).
LEVEL II – CONVENTIONAL Stage 3 – Mutual Interpersonal Expectations, Relationships, and Interpersonal Conformity	Living up to what is expected by people close to you or what people generally expect of people in your role as son, brother, friend, etc. "Being good" is important and means having good motives, showing concern about others. It also means keeping mutual relationships, such as trust, loyalty, respect and gratitude.	The need to be a good person in your own eyes and those of others. Your caring for others. Belief in the Golden Rule. Desire to maintain rules and authority which support stereotypical good behavior.	Perspective of the individual in relationships with other individuals. Aware of shared feelings, agreements, and expectations which take primacy over individual interests. Relates points of view through the concrete Golden Rule, putting yourself in the other guy's shoes. Does not yet consider generalized system perspective.

Table 1 (continued)

Stage	What is Right	Reasons for Doing Right	Social Perspective of Stage
Stage 4 - System and Conscience	Fulfilling the actual duties to which you have agreed. Laws are to be upheld except in extreme cases where they conflict with other fixed social duties. Right is also contributing to society, the group, or institution.	To keep the institution going as a whole, to avoid the breakdown in the system "if everyone did it," or the imperative of conscience to meet one's defined obligations. (Easily confused with Stage 3 belief in rules and authority.)	Differentiates societal point of view from interpersonal agreement or motives. Takes the point of view of the system that defines roles and rules. Considers individual relations in terms of place in the system.
LEVEL III - POST-CONVENTIONAL, or PRINCIPLED Stage 5 - Social Contract or Utility and Individual Rights	Being aware that people hold a variety of values and opinions, that most values and rules are relative to your group. These relative rules should usually be upheld, however, in the interest of impartiality and because they are the social contract. Some nonrelative values and rights like life and liberty, however, must be upheld in any society and regardless of majority opinion.	A sense of obligation to law because of one's social contract to make and abide by laws for the welfare of all and for the protection of all people's rights. A feeling of contractual commitment, freely entered upon, to family, friendship, trust, and work obligations. Concern that laws and duties be based on rational calculation of overall utility, "the greatest good for the greatest number."	Prior-to-society perspective. Perspective of a rational individual aware of values and rights prior to social attachments and contracts. Integrates perspectives by formal mechanisms of agreement, contract, objective impartiality, and due process. Considers moral and legal points of view; recognizes that they sometimes conflict and finds it difficult to integrate them.
Stage 6 - Universal Ethical Principles	Following self-chosen ethical principles. Particular laws or social agreements are usually valid because they rest on such principles. When laws violate these principles, one acts in accordance with the principle. Principles are universal principles of justice: the equality of human rights and respect for the dignity of human beings as individual persons.	The belief as a rational person in the validity of universal moral principles, and a sense of personal commitment to them.	Perspective of a moral point of view from which social arrangements derive. Perspective is that of any rational individual recognizing the nature of morality or the fact that persons are ends in themselves and must be treated as such.

Note: Adapted from Kohlberg (1976).

In an early longitudinal study (Kramer, 1968) employing data from Kohlberg's original subjects, the expected shift from conventional to postconventional (principled) reasoning among college students was found to be preceded by an apparent regression to Stage 2 relativism. When first reported, this finding posed a significant problem for Kohlberg's theory since it appeared to violate the basic assumptions of a hierarchical stage sequence. In subsequent analyses, however, the apparent Stage 2 reasoning was recognized as something considerably more complex and different from the reasoning provided by 10-year-olds and other "true" Stage 2 adults. The reasoning of the relativistic college students seemed instead to reflect a transitional period in which the Stage 4 societal basis for morality, coupled with a view of societal systems as incommensurate, led to a relativistic stance (Kohlberg, 1973; Turiel, 1974). This relativism was seen as an initial and unstable reflection on earlier conceptions of society as a basis for morality, leading eventually to a prior-to-society postconventional perspective.

Moral relativism among college students is given considerable attention in two other models of moral growth which we will address in this chapter, those offered by William Perry and by Elliot Turiel. It should be noted that Kohlberg and his colleagues have recently reappraised their interpretations of relativistic thinking to define relativism as a transitional metaethical position that can appear with differing levels of sophistication at points of stage change anywhere in the developmental sequence (Colby et al., 1983).

Revisions in the Kohlberg Model

As we mentioned earlier, there have been a number of recent substantive revisions in the Kohlberg model. Some of these, such as the reinterpretation of relativistic thinking and the definition of moral stages in terms of sociomoral perspective, have already been described. Most of the changes in the model have resulted from analyses of data generated for a 20-year longitudinal study of moral development (Colby et al., 1983), and from efforts by Kohlberg and his colleagues to devise a reliable measure of moral growth (Colby et al., 1982). These changes are presented in detail in Kohlberg (1984). For our purposes we will focus on only two additional revisions here. The first of these pertains to distinctions Kohlberg makes between A and B substages. The second concerns the current theoretical status of Stage 6.

A and B Substages

Kohlberg's theory may be seen as an extension of Piaget's (1932) account of moral development. Piaget had defined moral growth in terms of a shift in middle childhood from a heteronomous morality based on rules and authority to an autonomous morality based on justice and reciprocity. Kohlberg's (1958) stage description maintained the shift from morality based on convention and authority to one based on justice. However, in Kohlberg's analysis, the process of differentiating moral (justice) from nonmoral (rule and authority) bases for moral judgment was seen as more gradual and only fully realized in persons reaching the principled stages of moral development (Kohlberg, 1971).

One outcome of the recent attempts to generate a reliable scoring system has been a reassessment of autonomous and heteronomous thinking throughout the course of development. This analysis led Kohlberg (1984) to propose an A and B substage for each moral stage with the exception of Stage 6. The A substage reflects a heteronomous orientation toward rules and authority; the B substage, on the other hand, reflects an autonomous emphasis on justice and welfare considerations. According to Kohlberg, the B substage is the more advanced, or equilibrated, form reasoning at a given stage. However, individuals, when shifting from one stage to the next, may maintain their A or B substage status. While subjects may exhibit B substage reasoning at early points in development (e.g., Stage 2), it should not be confused with fully articulated principled moral reasoning. We will take this issue up in a moment when we discuss the current view of Stage 6. Kohlberg (1984) maintains that subjects employing B substage reasoning are more apt to engage in moral actions they believe to be just. In essence, Kohlberg is now claiming an intuitive basis for moral (justice) decision making at all levels of development.

The Status of Stage 6

Stage 6 no longer appears as an identifiable form of moral reasoning in current scoring systems and has been dropped from the model as an empirically demonstrated developmental stage (Kohlberg, 1984). This is so because, according to current scoring criteria, very few persons have been found whose statements would be classified as evidencing Stage 6 moral reasoning. Statements which under earlier scoring systems would have been considered Stage 6 are now frequently coded as intuitive justice reasoning at lower stages. For example, many of the protocols coded as Stage 6 in Kohlberg's (1958) original work have now been recoded as Stage 4, Substage B. For reasoning to now be classified as Stage 6, the person must evidence "a clearly formulated moral principle of justice and respect for persons that provides a rationale for the primacy of this principle" (Kohlberg, 1984, p. 271). At this point, Stage 6 remains a theoretical construct with an epistemological status not unlike the predictions made by astronomers or physicists which result from the logical extension of existing data and theory.

Challenges to Kohlberg's Model

The changes in scoring procedure and corollary revisions in the theory have in some measure been a response to criticisms. Some of these criticisms, such as the ones directed at the psychometric properties of the scoring system (Kurtines and Greif, 1974), have been successfully addressed. Other areas of controversy remain. One critic, in fact, has suggested that the recent reformulations may signal the beginning of the epicycle stage of the theory (Shweder, Mahapatra, and Miller, in press). While we are not endorsing so harsh a judgment of Kohlberg's work, we do wish to acknowledge some of the more salient areas of controversy concerning his model.

Stages or Incremental Changes?

Kohlberg (1984) has attempted to define moral development in terms of what he refers to as "hard" Piagetian stages. In recent years, however, questions have been raised with regard not only to Kohlberg's description of moral stages, but to Piaget's stage concept itself (Flavell, 1982; Gelman and Baillargeon, 1983). With specific reference to Kohlberg, the criticisms have centered on claims that the stages of moral reasoning constitute "structured wholes" (Kohlberg, 1984). Critics have noted that (1) development in the moral domain is gradual rather than abrupt as one would expect on the basis of stage theory (Rest, 1983a; Fischer, 1983), and (2) individuals' moral judgments shift from one stage to another as a function of the issue being addressed (Fischer, 1983). Most notable stage inconsistencies have been reported between responses to standard Kohlberg dilemmas and issues pertaining to sexuality (Gilligan et al., 1971; Stein, 1973) and abortion (Gilligan, 1982). With respect to inconsistencies in moral stage, James Rest (1983a), a researcher generally sympathetic to the Kohlberg view, has concluded that moral judgments tend to contain elements from several stages, and that development should be defined quantitatively, in terms of how much reasoning of a given type is employed, rather than qualitatively, in terms of a particular stage.

Kohlberg and his colleagues (Colby et al., 1983) have responded to these criticisms by disclaiming the extreme view of structured wholes attributed to them. Their position is that a person's moral judgments can be best described in terms of a dominant stage and, at most, one adjacent stage during periods of transition. They attribute Rest's (1983a) claims of greater stage mixture to an artifact in his measurement procedure which relies on recognition of and preference for moral statements, rather than the production of moral judgments. We will take this subject up again when we discuss measurement issues. Finally, Kohlberg and his colleagues accept as consistent with a "dominant stage" model the notion that shifts from one stage to another may occur over time. They note, however, that while change is not saltatory, it is less gradual within individuals than would be suggested by the group average trends cited by their critics.

Is There a Separate "Women's" Morality?

Carol Gilligan (1982) has recently suggested that Kohlberg's theory, which is based on a rights and justice orientation to morality, underestimates or ignores a second moral orientation based on caring. She has argued further that the justice ethic is more characteristic of the reasoning of men and boys, while a caring ethic typifies the judgments of women and girls. As a result, Kohlberg's system, she claims, tends to mischaracterize and undervalue the reasoning expressed by this other, "feminine" voice. In early studies using Kohlberg's system, men were usually scored as Stage 4 while women tended to be scored as Stage 3.

Gilligan's position was stated with considerable eloquence and found a sympathetic audience among many women who felt she had captured their moral position. Recent reviews of the research (Walker, 1984) and subsequent studies (Pratt, Golding, and Hunter, 1983; Thoma, 1984; Walker, 1985) directly examining Gilligan's hypotheses have failed, however, to sustain the claim of gender differences in moral judgment. Reported differences between men's and women's moral judgment scores as measured with the Kohlberg system vanished when controlled for subject education and occupational level. What is more, the subjects of both sexes at a range of ages tended to exhibit both justice and caring orientations (Pratt et al., 1983; Walker, 1985). Nonetheless, Kohlberg (1984) has acknowledged that Gilligan has drawn attention to a moral dimension not readily tapped by his standard interview, and one which deserves greater attention.

Is the Kohlberg Theory Culturally Biased?

A basic premise of cognitive-developmental theory is that developmental stages hold universally for persons with normal biological capacities. In recent years several researchers (Shweder et al., in press; Simpson, 1974; Sullivan, 1977) have questioned the cross-cultural universality of Kohlberg stages. These criticisms have focused on (1) the postenlightenment philosophical premises of the theory and (2) findings that relatively few non-Western subjects display postconventional reasoning. From the perspective of these critics, Kohlberg's philosophical stance has generated a theory biased against traditional societies whose moral systems are based on duty rather than on an individual rights perspective.

The arguments presented on both sides are very rich and are beyond the scope of this chapter. The interested reader is referred to sources already mentioned, plus Snarey (1985), Spiro (1985), Turiel (1983), and Turiel, Killen, and Helwig (in press). In brief, Kohlberg (1984) has reminded his critics that it is a logical fallacy (the genetic fallacy) to reject a theory as invalid on the basis of the sociocultural origins of the theorist, on the sociohistorical underpinnings of the theory. Its validity is instead to be determined empirically. With respect to the empirical status of Kohlberg's claims for cross-cultural universality, the issue seems to be one of reading the glass as half empty or as half full. From Kohlberg's perspective, the incidence of Stage 5 reasoning cross-culturally is sufficient to warrant support of the theory. In short, postconventional reasoning of some form has been observed among the urban population in each society studied, while the general sequence of stages up to Stage 4 has been observed among villagers (Snarey, 1985). The lack of Stage 5 reasoning among villagers is interpreted by Kohlberg as reflecting the range of opportunities for disequilibrating social interaction rather than a limitation in the theory.

Morality and Convention: Are They Distinct Domains?

Kohlberg's analysis placed justice at the center of moral judgment, but in keeping with the Kantian and Piagetian roots of his theory, he suggested that morality as justice remains confounded with considerations of authority and convention until the latter stages of development. Only at the level of principled morality, according to Kohlberg (1971), are a person's judgments truly moral (i.e., based on justice). Over the past decade, however, a considerable body of data has been gathered which supports a counterproposal, namely, that morality as justice constitutes a conceptual and developmental system distinct from concepts of convention and social organization (Turiel, 1978, 1983; Turiel et al., in press). According to this view, an objective, justice-based morality is available to very young children and remains distinguishable from the person's concepts of authority and convention throughout the life span. Because this proposal has important implications for how we might interpret the college-age shift from ''conventional'' to ''postconventional'' morality reported in research conducted in the Kohlberg tradition, our discussion of the distinct domains model of moral development will be extended.

Turiel and his colleagues distinguish social convention and morality in the following way (Turiel, 1983). Conventions (such as mode of dress or forms of address) are behavioral uniformities determined by the social system in which they are formed. While necessary for social coordination, they are not intrinsically prescriptive, in that different forms of a given convention could achieve the same social organizational goal. Conventions are thus context-dependent, and their content may vary as a function of the social system. Concepts about social convention are structured by underlying conceptions of social systems. In contrast with convention, moral considerations stem from factors intrinsic to actions, for example, consequences resulting from acts such as harm to others, violations of rights, and effects on the general welfare. While morality also applies to social systems, the individual's moral prescriptions are determined by factors inherent in social relationships, as opposed to a particular form of social, cultural, or religious structure. Moral concepts are structured by underlying conceptualizations of justice and beneficence. It has been proposed that there are patterns of social interaction that correspond to the definitions of morality and convention just outlined, and that, from those interactions, individuals (including very young children) construct their moral and social conventional knowledge systems (Nucci and Turiel, 1978; Nucci, 1985; Turiel, 1983).

Research in support of the distinct domains model is contained in over 25 published studies reviewed in detail by Nucci (1982), Turiel (1983), and Turiel et al. (in press). In brief, that research has shown the following:

1. Moral transgressions (e.g., hitting and hurting, stealing personal property, slander) are viewed as wrong irrespective of the presence of governing rules, while conventional acts (addressing teachers by first names, women wearing pants, premarital sex between adults) are viewed as wrong only if they are in violation of an existing rule or standard.

2. Individuals view conventional standards to be culturally relative and alterable, while moral prescriptions are viewed as universal and unchangeable.

3. Individuals tend to view moral transgressions as more serious than violations of convention, and as deserving of more severe punishment.

4. Prosocial moral acts tend to be viewed as better or more positive than adherence to conventions.

5. The forms of social interaction in the context of moral events differ qualitatively from interactions in the context of conventions. Specifically, it was found that children's and adults' responses to events in the moral domain focus on features intrinsic to the acts (e.g., harm, justice), while responses in the context of conventions focus on aspects of the social order (e.g., rules, regulations, normative expectations).

The general pattern of results has been obtained for subjects ranging in age from 3 to 25 years, sustaining the claim that morality and convention emerge as distinct domains early in childhood. In addition, several studies have replicated the basic findings with subjects in other cultures (Hong Kong—Song, Smetana, and Kim, 1985; Indonesia—Carey and Ford, 1983; Nigeria—Hollos, Leis and Turiel, 1986; U.S. Virgin Islands—Nucci, Turiel, and Encarnacion-Gawrych, 1983). Studies examining age-related changes within domains have revealed that the development of justice concepts and social conventional concepts follow distinct developmental patterns. Unfortunately, with respect to the moral domain, systematic research has been conducted only with young children. The sequence of changes observed in children's distributive justice reasoning shows that with development, children form increased understandings of benevolence, equality, and reciprocity (Damon, 1977, 1980; Enright, Franklin, and Manheim, 1980). A more complete picture has been obtained of developmental changes in the conventional domain. As can be seen in Table 2, the development of social conventional concepts reflects the person's underlying conceptions of social organization and moves toward an understanding of convention as constitutive of social systems and as important for the coordination of social interactions.

Recent evaluations by the Kohlberg camp of the distinct domains model of social development have been muted (Kohlberg, 1984). Earlier, more critical

TABLE 2. Major Changes in Social Conventional Concepts

	Approximate ages
Convention as descriptive of social uniformity.	6–7
Convention viewed as descriptive of uniformities in behavior. Convention is not conceived as part of structure of function of social interaction. Conventional uniformities are descriptive of what is assumed to exist. Convention maintained to avoid violation of empirical uniformities.	
Negation of convention as descriptive of social uniformity.	8–9
Empirical uniformity not a sufficient basis for maintaining conventions. Conventional acts regarded as arbitrary. Convention is not conceived as part of structure of function of social interaction.	
Convention as affirmation of rule system; early concrete conception of social system.	10–11
Convention seen as arbitrary and changeable. Adherence to convention based on concrete rules and authoritative expectations. Conception of conventional acts not coordinated with conception of rule.	
Negation of convention as part of rule system.	12–13
Convention now seen as arbitrary and changeable regardless of rule. Evaluation of rule pertaining to conventional act is coordinated with evaluation of the act. Conventions are ''nothing but'' social expectations.	
Convention as mediated by social system.	14–16
The emergence of systematic concepts of social structure. Convention as normative regulation in system with uniformity, fixed roles, and static hierarchical oraganization.	
Negation of convention as social standards.	17–18
Convention regarded as codified societal standards. Uniformity in convention is not considered to serve the function of maintaining social system. Conventions are ''nothing but'' societal standards that exist through habitual use.	
Convention as coordination of social interactions.	18–25
Conventions as uniformities that are functional in coordinating social interactions. Shared knowledge, in the form of conventions, among members of social groups facilitate interaction and operation of the system.	

Note. Adapted from Turiel (1978).

responses (Rest, 1983a) focused on two issues. The first question raised was whether the moral-conventional distinction would be obtained in other (especially non-Western) cultures. While this is still an issue subject to debate (Shweder et al., in press), the cross-cultural research we reported earlier indicates that the distinction between morality and convention is not simply a Western phenomenon. The second question raised was whether one could ever truly extricate morality from convention. This criticism notes that there are many issues that are not exclusively moral or conventional. For example, class or caste systems are ostensibly maintained through social convention. Yet, their existence results in members of a class having access to goods and privileges denied members of another class. Such inequalities in distribution are ostensibly a matter of morality. James Rest (1983a) concluded that the existence of many such events rendered the distinction between morality and convention invalid. Rest's argument, however, ignores the considerable amount of evidence suggesting that individuals distinguish between prototypical moral and conventional events and commits a logical error by assuming that instances of category overlap invalidate class distinctions. Using Rest's argument, the existence of homosexuals, bisexuals, transvestites, transsexuals, and hermaphrodites would invalidate the categories male and female. We would hold that Rest's dismissal of the proposed distinction between morality and convention was premature and that it was based on an incomplete understanding of the model.

The existence of analytically distinct structures of social knowledge does not preclude their conjoining or coordination in reasoning about social events. This would be particularly the case in the context of multifaceted situations. Turiel (1983) has suggested that such multifaceted situations take at least three forms: (1) those in which conventional concerns for social organization and coordination entail injustices (as in a caste system); (2) second-order events in which violation of a convention results in "psychological harm" to persons who adhere to the convention (e.g., failure of a young white man to address an older black man by the title "Mister"); and (3) ambiguously multidimensional events, such as abortion, in which significant discrepancies exist in their domain attribution by different people. Reasoning about multifaceted events entails the coordination (or failure of coordination) of both the moral and the conventional features considered. In research on subjects' reasoning about multifaceted events (Smetana, 1982; Turiel and Smetana, 1984), three modes of domain relations emerged: (1) a predominant emphasis on one domain, with subordination of the other; (2) conflict between the two, with inconsistencies and the absence of resolution of reconciliation of the two components; and (3) coordination of the two components, so that the two are taken into account in the solution to the problem.

The picture of social reasoning that emerges from the distinct domains model just outlined both clarifies the nature of morality and makes it apparent that our current views of moral development and moral judgment are incomplete. A comprehensive analysis of moral development would entail (1) an analysis of the development of justice concepts throughout the life span; (2) an analysis of domain coordinations that would take into account the forms of domain relations outlined above; and (3) the structure of those relations in the context of differential development within domains. From this perspective, the Kohlberg model may be seen as a first approximation of an analysis of the development of domain coordinations.

MEASURING MORAL GROWTH

Notwithstanding controversies surrounding the Kohlberg model, researchers have attempted to assess the impact of college on students' moral stage. This impact has been assessed in three ways: through the use of the standard Kohlberg interview (MJI); with a paper-and-pencil measure devised by James Rest (1983b), called the Defining Issues Test (DIT); and finally by a related index proposed by William Perry, called the Reflective Judgment Interview (RJI), specifically designed to measure intellectual and ethical development in the college years. In this section, we will present a brief description of each instrument and a discussion of the psychometric properties of each before turning to a review of the literature on college effects on moral development.

Moral Judgment Interview (MJI)

The moral judgment interview now in use (Colby et al., 1982) has undergone progressive revision and development over the past 25 years. There are three parallel forms of the interview. Each form consists of three hypothetical moral dilemmas followed by a series of standardized questions designed to elicit justifications for the subject's moral judgments. While the interview format is standardized, the interviewer adjusts probe questions in response to the subject's statements. This component of the interview is adapted from Piaget's clinical method and is intended to permit the subject to elaborate or clarify responses. Scoring of the interview follows a standardized four-tier classification system designed to permit an analysis of the structure of the subject's reasoning divorced from any dilemma-specific content. The current scoring system, known as Standard Issue Scoring, yields either a global interview score in terms of dominant and minor stages or a continuous "moral maturity" score (MMS), which is a weighted average of the total scored responses to the interview.

The current scoring system was generated in part to counter earlier criticisms (Kurtines and Grief, 1974) of the psychometric properties of the Kohlberg interview. While the current system does not break with the basic premises of the original Kohlberg (1958) model, the revisions entailed by the new scoring system are such that direct comparisons of data scored prior to 1978 (when current stage definitions first appeared) with data from subsequent studies should not be undertaken. The information pertaining to the reliability and validity of Standard Issue Scoring is presented in detail by Colby and colleagues (1983). In brief, they report test-retest correlations ranging from .96 to .99. Interrater reliability coefficients for the three parallel forms of the interview ranged from .92 to .98. The reliability for alternate forms of the interview ranged from .84 to .95. The validity of the test was assessed in terms of two theoretical constructs: the invariance of the stage sequence and the "structured wholeness" of stages, or internal consistency. Internal consistency, using Cronbach's α, for the three interview forms, ranged from .92 to .96. With regard to the invariant sequence hypothesis, longitudinal data gathered at 3- to 4-year intervals over a 20-year period showed that 56 of 58 subjects demonstrated upward movement with no subject skipping any stages. Perhaps more impressive are data indicating that of the 195 comparisons, only 6% showed backward shifts between two testings, well within the limits of measurement error.

Defining Issues Test (DIT)

While the MJI may be properly considered the best device for assessing the moral judgment of individuals, the most widely used instrument in research on moral development is the Defining Issues Test (DIT) developed by James Rest (1979c). The popularity of the DIT stems from its ease of administration relative to the MJI. The DIT is a paper-and-pencil test that can be group-administered and quickly and objectively scored. The DIT, like the MJI, asks subjects to respond to moral dilemmas. There are six moral dilemmas in the DIT, three of which were taken from Kohlberg's 1958 interview. Accompanying each dilemma are 12 issue statements which represent ways in which subjects at Stages 2 through 6 might respond. The subject is asked to indicate on a five-point scale how important each issue statement is in making a decision regarding the dilemma. On the basis of subject responses, several scores are produced. The most widely used is the P index, which is a measure of the relative importance subjects give to postconventional (principled) Stage 5 or 6 justifications. The higher the P index, presumably the more developed the subject.

The psychometric characteristics of the DIT are quite good for subjects fluent in English with at least an eighth-grade reading level. As reported in Rest (1979c), test-retest reliability averages .81, and internal consistency averages .78. Validity of the DIT has been assessed in two ways: (1) through longitudinal studies and (2) through correlations with the Kohlberg interview. Longitudinal studies showed a strong relationship between age and DIT score. In three longitudinal studies in which subjects were assessed at two- and four-year intervals, 66% of the subjects moved upward and 7% moved downward.

Correlations between the DIT and the Kohlberg interviews show a modest relation between the two measures (correlations range from .65 to .75 with heterogeneous samples). Though the correlations are respectable, the two indices tend to give somewhat different estimates of subjects' moral level, with the DIT tending to generate somewhat higher scores. This is to be expected since the Kohlberg interview is a production measure requiring subjects to generate their own moral judgments while the DIT is a recognition-preference measure.

Reflective Judgment Interview (RJI)

The Reflective Judgment Interview (RJI) has evolved out of William Perry's (1968) highly influential study of global changes in college students' orientations toward knowledge and authority in establishing a personal intellectual or ethical stance. Perry suggested that these changes follow a sequence of nine positions that fall roughly within three phases. The first, dualistic phase is characterized by a tendency to dichotomize phenomena into "good versus bad," "right versus wrong," the "expert" and the "ignorant." For the dualist, there are authorities who have the answers, and if one learns these from them, one will attain the truth. This dualism is gradually replaced by a relativistic recognition that "experts" disagree. Their disagreement, however, invalidates the truth of their positions. Now anyone's claim has equal validity. In the world of ethics, anyone's morality is as valid as the next person's. Eventually this relativism is supplanted by a realization that commitments based on warranted assumptions can and must be made in the face of uncertainty. In ethics, the absolutism of the dualist has given way to the universalism of the Socratic scholar.

Kohlberg (1984) has recognized the parallels between Perry's scheme and his own distinction between conventional and postconventional morality. He has also acknowledged the similarity between the relativism described by Perry and the postconventional relativism of the college students described in longitudinal studies of moral growth (Kramer, 1968; Colby et al., 1983). Kohlberg (1984), however, draws a distinction between what he calls "hard" stages, which define intellectual operations, and "soft" stages, which define more general world views. In the first category, he would place Piaget's stages of intellectual development and his stages of morality. In the latter category, Kohlberg would place Loevinger's stages of ego development and Perry's description of the intellectual and ethical growth of college students. Kohlberg's distinction is in line with Perry's (1970) own view, which saw his effort as one of drawing general trends and transformations rather than strict stages.

Growth within the Perry scheme is assessed through the Reflective Judgment Interview. The interview, like the MJI and DIT, evokes student responses to a series of dilemmas. The four dilemmas which comprise the RJI concern issues of science, history, religion, and current events. Following each dilemma are two opposing position statements. Subjects are asked to select and defend one of the positions. The interviewer, through a series of standardized probes, attempts to elicit the subject's justifications for supporting the chosen position. Interviews are coded in terms of the subject's openness to opposing positions and to the use of evidence and authority in support of the subject's point of view.

While the RJI has enjoyed considerable use as a research tool (Brabeck, 1983), the current status of the instrument is not unlike that of the Kohlberg interview prior to 1978. Though respectable interrater reliabilities (.53–.96) have been obtained for the RJI and a modest correlation between RJI and DIT scores have been reported (.48–.61, King, Kitchener, and Wood, 1985), a definitive procedure for scoring the RJI and attendant psychometric data is as yet unavailable. Ongoing projects by Patricia King at Bowling Green State University and Karen Strohm Kitchener at the University of Denver hold out the promise for such a standardized instrument in the near future.

COLLEGE EFFECTS ON
MORAL DEVELOPMENT: THE RESEARCH

In this section, we will present a review of the research conducted to date. The organizing structure for this literature review was adapted from Pascarella (1985a). The review will address four basic questions.

1. *What evidence exists that moral development increases during college?* All subsequent questions we might ask concerning the impact of college hinge on this most fundamental one. Unless there is some reason to believe that student moral judgment develops during the college years, questions such as those about the impact of different collegiate experiences or environments become largely irrelevant.

2. *What evidence exists that differentiated changes in moral development occur as the result of differential exposure to postsecondary education?* This question is more specific than the initial question in that it is concerned not only with change, but also with the extent to which change can be attributed to college attendance.

3. *What evidence exists that different postsecondary institutions differentially influence student moral development?* This question is essentially asking if discernible differences in moral development during college are attributable to the type of institution attended.

4. *What evidence exists that differential change in student moral development is attributable to different college experiences within the same institution?* This question is concerned with identifying different subenvironments and/or curricular and noncurricular experiences within an institution that may differentially influence student moral development.

Evidence Pertaining to Changes
in Moral Development During College

It is unlikely that increased sensitivity to moral issues and moral responsibility develops in isolation from other cognitive and affective changes in students which coincide with college attendance. Rather, moral development is perhaps most appropriately seen as an integral part of an interconnected, and often mutually reinforcing, network of developmental trends characterizing changes that tend to occur in college students. There is a rather substantial and growing body of research which documents these changes (e.g., Astin, 1977; Astin and Panos, 1969; Bowen, 1977; Feldman and Newcomb, 1969; Pascarella, 1985a; Spaeth and Greeley, 1970; Withey, 1971). In terms of the larger context in which individual moral development occurs, two areas of change during college seem particularly salient: cognitive development and change in personality and value orientations.

There is a substantial body of evidence to suggest that students make statistically reliable gains, not only in general and specific knowledge during college (e.g., Bowen, 1977; Dumont and Troelstrup, 1981; Lenning, Munday, and Maxey, 1969), but also in the ability to think critically, flexibly, and abstractly (e.g., Eisert and Tomlinson-Keasey, 1978; Kahlili and Hood, 1983; Keeley, Brown and Kreutzer, 1982; Lehmann, 1963; Mentkowski and Strait, 1983; Winter, McClelland, and Stewart, 1981). Similarly, there is abundant evidence to suggest a clear link between college attendance and a general liberalization of personality and values. In the vast majority of studies conducted, upper classmen, as compared to freshmen, tend to be less authoritarian or dogmatic and more open and flexible in their thinking processes; more autonomous and independent of authority imposed through social institutions; more tolerant and understanding of others; and more interpersonally aware and skilled (Chickering, 1974; Chickering and McCormick, 1973; Clark et al., 1972; Feldman and Newcomb, 1969; Heath, 1968; Lehmann and Dressel, 1962, 1963; Pace, 1974; Spaeth and Greeley, 1970; Trent and Medsker, 1968; Withey, 1971).

Given such development in the cognitive/intellectual and the personal/value orientations of college students, it seems reasonable to hypothesize that changes in moral judgment might also accompany the experience of college. The evidence to support this hypothesis is impressive, not only in terms of the sheer number of studies conducted, but also in terms of the extensive diversity of samples employed and the different instruments used to assess moral judgment. Since the Defining Issues Test (Rest, 1975, 1979a) is a group-administered paper-and-pencil measure designed to measure Kohlberg's (1958) stage theory of moral development, it is not surprising that it is the most frequently employed instrument in cross-sectional as well as longitudinal studies.

With few exceptions (e.g., White, 1973), the cross-sectional studies employing the DIT show clear and statistically reliable age-education trends in moral judgment. The DIT index typically used in these studies is the P index, which is a measure of the relative importance given to principled moral considerations (Stages 5 and 6) in making a moral decision (Rest, 1979c). Rest (1976, 1979a,b) and Rest, Davison, and Robbins (1978) synthesized data from over 50 published and unpublished cross-sectional studies in the United States using the DIT. These represented 5,714 subjects and 136 different samples. When the P scores were aggregated and averaged across samples, Rest found that average P scores tended to increase about 10 points at each level of education as a student progressed from junior high (average $P = 21.9\%$), to senior high ($P = 31.8\%$), to college ($P = 42.3\%$), to graduate or professional school ($P = 53.3\%$). Grouping the samples by these age-education categories accounted for about 38% of the variation in P scores. Similar results have been reported in other cross-sectional studies with the DIT (e.g., Cohen, 1982; Martin, Shafto, and Van Deinse, 1977; Mentkowski and Strait, 1983; Yussen, 1976).

The strong age-education trends in DIT P scores are not confined to American samples. Recently, Moon (1985) reviewed and synthesized a number of studies of moral judgment development using foreign samples: from Hong Kong (Hau, 1983); Korea (Park and Johnson, 1983); Iceland (Thornlidsson, 1978); the Philippines (Villanueva, 1982); and Australia (Watson, 1983). As with the American samples, nearly all the studies show clear developmental trends in principled thinking. Subjects who were older and who had completed higher levels of formal education (through college) tended to attribute more importance to principled moral considerations on the DIT than subjects who were younger and less well educated. Thus, the pronounced developmental trends in principled thinking as measured by the P score of the DIT appear to be reasonably independent of national setting.

While longitudinal studies following the same cohort of subjects over time are less numerous than cross-sectional investigations, there is, nevertheless, considerable evidence to suggest that students tend to have significantly higher DIT P scores as end-of-year freshmen or upperclassmen than they did as entering freshmen. Moreover, exposure to postsecondary education appears to be linked with marked increases in principled thinking, even when subjects are followed beyond the typical four-year period of college.

Whiteley (1982) found modest, but statistically significant, increases in P scores during the freshman year for three successive cohorts of students. The average P-score increase for all three classes was 4.08 points. Shaver (1985) followed a single cohort of students over a four-year period from freshman to senior year and found a significant average P-score increase of 10.85 points. Two cohorts of entering freshmen were followed during their sophomore through senior years by Mentkowski and Strait (1983). Significant freshman-to-sophomore and sophomore-to-senior *P*-score increases were found for the combined sample. The total freshman-to-senior *P*-score increase was 9.7 points, although the freshman-to-sophomore increase (7.37 points) was substantially larger than the sophomore-to-senior gain (2.33 points).

Rest and Thoma (1985) and Deemer (1985) report on research which followed three cohorts of high school graduates over 6 and 10 years, respectively. For students who had completed at least three years of college, the 6-year increase in *P* score was 14 points. This compared with a 1.5 point increase for those with 2 years of college or less. Similarly, when followed up after 10 years, Deemer reports that students with at least some college had an average *P*-score increase of approximately 11 points.

The only evidence inconsistent with the trend of increases in *P* scores during college was reported by McGeorge (1976). McGeorge found positive but nonsignificant gains in *P* score over a two-year period for samples of New Zealand Teachers College students.

While the Defining Issues Test is a group-administered paper-and-pencil instrument, other approaches have employed interview methods to assess level or stage of moral development. These are primarily structured-interview instruments designed to assess the stage theories of Kohlberg (1958, 1964) using the Moral Judgment Interview (e.g., Colby et al., 1978; Kohlberg, 1981), and of Perry (1970), using the Reflective Judgment Interview (e.g., Brabeck, 1983; King, 1977; Kitchener, 1977; Schmidt and Davison, 1981).

Research using the MJI has shown a positive association between level of formal education and moral development with both cross-sectional (Lei, 1981; Lei and Cheng, 1984; Mentkowski and Strait, 1983; Whitla, 1978) and longitudinal (Colby, Kohlberg, Gibbs, and Lieberman, 1983) data. Lei and Cheng found that Taiwanese college students had higher average scores on the MJI than did secondary-school students, and that graduate students had higher scores than college students. The difference between college and high school was 3 1/2 times as large as the difference between graduate and college students. Further, while 70% of the graduate students and 34.8% of the college students were functioning at the higher, or more principled, stages or moral maturity (Kohlberg's Stages 4 and 4/5), only 17.1% of the secondary-school students were at these stages. Mentkowski and Strait (1983) found that graduating seniors at an American institution had significantly higher moral maturity scores on the MJI than did entering freshmen. Compared to freshmen, there was a noticeably lower proportion of seniors in the preconventional stages of Kohlberg's scheme, and there were proportionately more in the postconventional stages.

Similar results have been reported by Whitla (1978) with a multi-institutional sample. Using a paper-and-pencil adaptation of the MJI, Whitla found that seniors at a private college and a state college showed significantly higher levels of moral maturity than did freshmen. At a public junior college, sophomores scored significantly higher than freshmen. In all cases, the freshmen and upperclass cohorts were matched on entering academic ability (SAT scores) and high-school rank, though not on entering MJI scores.

Colby et al. (1983) conducted a 20-year longitudinal study of moral development in a sample of men from two suburban Chicago schools (one predominantly upper middle class, and the other predominantly lower middle and working class). The correlations between moral judgment stage and level of formal education at four different follow-ups of the sample (ages 24–36) ranged from .54 to .77, all statistically significant. Similar findings are reported in a recent longitudinal study by Lind (1985, 1986). Lind's sample was made up of German university students coming from various fields of study. They were tested in the first and third year of college with the MJT, an instrument constructed to assess both affective and cognitive aspects of moral judgment behavior. Over a two-year period, there was a modest, but statistically reliable, average gain in the group's capacity to judge social dilemmas by moral principles.

Less convincing evidence of gains in moral maturity during college is presented by Mentkowski and Strait (1983). Following two cohorts of entering students through their senior year, they found an overall small but nonsignificant gain in moral maturity from freshman to senior year. From freshman to sophomore year, however, the change in moral maturity score was negative, while from sophomore to senior year, the change was positive.

Research employing the RJI to assess stage development within the structure of Perry's (1970) model of intellectual and ethical development provides evidence quite consistent with that yielded by the DIT and the MJI. With few exceptions (e.g., Glatfelder, 1982), both the cross-sectional and the longitudinal evidence has consistently shown that RJI scores have a marked, positive association with level of formal education. Not only do college students generally have higher RJI scores than high school students, and graduate students higher scores than undergraduate students, but students appear to significantly increase their RJI scores during college (e.g., Brabeck, 1980; King, 1977; King et al., 1983; Kitchener, 1977; Kitchener and King, 1981; Lawson, 1980; Mines, 1980; Schmidt, 1985; Strange, 1978; Welfel, 1982; Welfel and Davison, 1986). Detailed and cogent reviews of this research are presented in Brabeck (1983) and Schmidt and Davison (1983).

Clearly, the overwhelming body of evidence collected with the DIT, the MJI, and the RJI suggests that extent of principled moral reasoning is positively associated with level of formal education, and that students generally make statistically reliable gains in principled moral reasoning during college. Simply showing that such trends and changes are coincident with college attendance, however, is quite different from demonstrating that they occur as the result of college attendance. A number of factors potentially confound the association between moral reasoning and college attendance reported in a large portion of the investigations reviewed above.

In cross-sectional designs (e.g., comparing samples of high school students, college students, and graduate students), a major confounding factor is age. Since amount of formal education obviously varies with age, one might question whether the development of moral reasoning is due to one's educational experience or is simply a function of growing older. Similarly, there may be other confounding factors, such as subject intelligence or socioeconomic status. Clearly, both of these factors are positively related to college attendance (e.g., Wolfle, 1980, 1983), and there is evidence that both have a modest positive association with level of principled moral judgment (e.g., Colby et al., 1983; Coder, 1975). Consequently, the finding that college students tend to have higher levels of principled moral judgment than high school students may not represent an effect of college. Rather, it may be largely due to the fact that college students represent a more selective population of intelligence and social status than do high school students. In the same way, changing institutional recruiting standards over time, as well as the natural attrition of less intellectually capable students from freshman to senior year, may produce a somewhat more selective population of seniors than the population of freshmen to whom they are compared. Thus, differences in moral judgment between freshmen and seniors could be a consequence of comparing samples from differentially selective populations instead of a result attributable to the collegiate experience.

While longitudinal designs control for many of these threats to the internal validity of the findings by comparing a cohort with itself over time, the attrition of subjects from the study may yield a sample which is less variable and which is unrepresentative of the population. Moreover, longitudinal studies without a control group of similar individuals who do not attend college are still potentially confounded by the age factor. Without such a control group, it is extremely difficult to disaggregate the gains in moral judgment due to the experience of college from those due to normal cognitive-moral maturation in young adults.

Attributing Growth in Moral
Judgment to Postsecondary Education

Determining if differential gains in moral judgment are attributable to differences in exposure to postsecondary education is a reasonably complex matter. Cross-sectional studies (e.g., comparing high school seniors and college seniors) typically attempt to control for the influence of potentially confounding variables such as age or intelligence. Similarly, longitudinal studies (e.g., assessing gains in the same cohort of students from freshman to senior year) typically attempt to include a control group of subjects who do not attend college or who have less than four years' exposure to postsecondary education. Because it is nearly impossible to control individual differences among subjects by random assignment to different levels of exposure to college, these longitudinal studies typically rely on various forms of statistical control (e.g., partial correlation, multiple regression, analysis of covariance) to conditionally identify the unique influence of college.

A number of cross-sectional studies employing the DIT have attempted to determine the extent to which higher levels of principled moral reasoning are attributable to levels of formal education by comparing the strength of the association between DIT P score and education with the corresponding association between P score and age. In nearly all these studies, level of formal education had a substantially stronger association with P score than did age. Coder (1975), for example, studied 87 adults (ages 24–50) in a religious education program and found a slightly negative ($r = -.10$) correlation between P score and age. The correlation between P score and level of formal education achieved by each subject, however, was substantial ($r = .25$) and statistically significant. Crowder (1976), in a study of 70 adults (ages 18–59), reported findings almost exactly replicating those of Coder. Age correlated $-.05$ with P score, whereas level of formal education and P score were correlated .25. Consistently similar results have been reported with American samples (Dortzbach, 1975; Mentkowski and Strait, 1983), a Chinese sample (Hau, 1983), and an Australian sample (Watson, 1983).

In terms of determining the effects of college on moral reasoning, as measured by the DIT, the most significant longitudinal study is probably that reported by Rest and Thoma (1985). Thirty-nine subjects were tested with the DIT in high school and at two-year intervals over a six-year period following graduation from high school. When subjects were divided into ''low-education'' (two years or less of college) and ''high-education'' groups (three years or more of college), the groups showed increasingly divergent developmental pathways in terms of principled moral judgment. The high-education group showed increasing gains after high school, while the low-education group showed a leveling off. At graduation from high school, the low-education group had a P score of 33, while the high-education group had a P score of 37 (a difference of only 4 points). Six years later, however, the P score for the low-education group was 34.5, while the high-education group had a P score of 51 (a difference between groups of 16.5 points). When analysis of covariance solved by multiple regression was used to control for group differences in P score at high school graduation, the high-education group still had a significantly higher adjusted P score after six years than the low-education group. Years of college education accounted for a significant increase in the explained variance in P scores of 14% above and beyond that due to P score at high school graduation. Such evidence is quite consistent with Rest's (1979a,b) contention that principled moral judgment tends to increase with exposure to additional levels of formal education beyond high school. For individuals not exposed to educational environments beyond high school, however, it tends to plateau or level off.

Generally confirmatory results are reported in a more limited longitudinal study by Kitchener et al. (1984). Samples of high school juniors, college juniors, and doctoral-level graduate students were matched on gender, hometown size, and Scholastic Aptitude Test scores. They completed the DIT in 1977 and were followed up two years later in 1979. The college undergraduates and graduate students both showed significant increases in P scores, with the gains for the latter group being somewhat more pronounced. In contrast, the high school students did not show P score increases over the two-year period. Analysis of covariance, controlling for verbal ability (as measured by the Concept Mastery Test), indicated that the group and time effects on P scores persisted.

Evidence concerning the effects of college on moral reasoning using Kohlberg's MJI or the RJI operationalizing Perry's model is not as consistent as that derived from the DIT. In a cross-sectional investigation using the MJI, Mentkowski and Strait (1983) employed analysis of covariance to statistically remove the confounding influence of student age and found that differences in moral maturity scores between college freshmen and seniors at a single institution were nonsignificant. More positive evidence, however, is reported in Colby et al. (1983) 20-year longitudinal study of 58 males. The study included an initial testing with the MJI during high school and five follow-ups (using three parallel forms of the MJI) over the 20-year period. With initial intelligence (based on school records) and socioeconomic status (based on parents' occupation and education) controlled statistically, the partial correlation between level of formal education and the MJI mental maturity score was .26 (significant at $P < .05$). No partial correlations were computed controlling for high-school moral-maturity score.

A number of studies have employed the RJI in attempts to identify the unique influence of college on moral judgment within Perry's scheme. The results of this research have been mixed. Strange (1978) sought to determine if scores on the RJI were more a function of extent of exposure to college than of age or normal maturation. The research design employed a sex-balanced sample of liberal arts college students in four groups: traditionally-aged freshmen (age = 18); non-traditionally-aged freshmen (age = 22); traditionally aged seniors (age = 22); and non-traditionally-aged seniors (age = 26). Seniors were found to have significantly higher reflective judgment scores than freshmen across both the traditional and nontraditional age groups. Conversely, students who were four years apart in age but who were at the same stage in their collegiate careers (i.e., freshmen or seniors) did not differ significantly in reflective judgment. Despite the absence of a control group, Strange's results appear to suggest that degree of exposure to undergraduate education may be more important than simple maturation in the development of moral judgment— at least, as measured by the RJI.

More recent research with the RJI has yielded somewhat less convincing results with respect to the unique influence of college on reflective judgment. Lawson (1980) presents evidence with graduate students to suggest that age is a more salient factor than extent of exposure to postsecondary education in accounting for differences in reflective judgment. The difference in RJI scores between two graduate-student groups that differed in both age and education was essentially the same as the difference between two nonstudent groups that were the same in education and that differed only in age.

Findings by Schmidt (1985) suggest that age and education in combination account for education-related differences in reflective judgment. Average RJI scores for a group of non-traditional-age freshmen (age = 21; RJI = 3.47) were less than those of traditional-age juniors (age = 21; RJI = 3.54), but greater than those of traditional-age freshmen (age = 18; RJI = 3.36). Statistical contrasts, however, indicated that although juniors scored significantly higher than combined traditional and nontraditional freshmen (age and education confounded), they did not score significantly higher than the nontraditional freshmen alone (age held constant). On the other hand, age had no unique influence when extent of college exposure was held constant (i.e., there was a nonsignificant contrast between 18- and 21-year-old freshmen).

The confidence with which one can attribute higher levels of moral judgment to the collegiate experience depends, to some extent then, on the specific instrument used to assess moral judgement. Studies employing Rest's Defining Issues Test have been quite consistent in indicating that higher levels of principled moral judgment or reasoning are a direct effect of exposure to postsecondary education. Those investigations using interview instruments to assess moral judgment (i.e., the MJI and the RJI) have been less consistent in their findings. Despite these differences associated with the measurement instrument employed, there is sufficient evidence in the total body of research to suggest that college has a unique, positive effect on growth in principled moral judgment.

Such a conclusion is quite consistent with the findings of Hyman and Wright (1979), who studied 38 samples of approximately 44,000 adults (ages 25–72) from national surveys conducted between 1949 and 1975. Controlling for background factors such as age, race, sex, religion, ethnicity, social-class origin, and residential origin, Hyman and Wright investigated contrasting values of groups with differing amounts of education. Their findings suggest that the profile most pronounced among individuals who have gone to college includes valuing civil liberties for all groups; due process of law; freedom from the constraints of arbitrary laws in personal and social, as well as economic and political spheres; measures to reduce pain, injury, suffering, or deprivation; and humanitarian conduct toward others, as opposed to social mores or manners. Similar conclusions about the effects of liberal education in particular on student values are reported by Heath (1976).

Thus, it would appear that the body of evidence suggesting a unique impact of college on principled moral judgment is congruent with evidence from national samples indicating that a humanization of values is positively associated with the collegiate experience. Clearly, however, it should be pointed out that any attribution of collegiate effects on principled moral reasoning, or on the broader context of humanitarian values in which it may be embedded, must be tempered by the fact that all studies reviewed in the section are, at best, quasi-experimental in design. Consequently, any causal attributions are tenuous and conditional. Moreover, due to the correlational or quasi-experimental nature of the evidence, it is difficult to determine the magnitude of the unique influence of college.

Evidence Pertaining to the Differential Effects of Different Postsecondary Institutions on Moral Judgment

There is a small but growing body of research to suggest that different types of postsecondary institutions have discernibly different effects on student outcomes in such areas as intellectual development, personality development, values, and occupational attainment (e.g., Jacob, 1957; Chickering, 1974; Chickering and McCormick, 1973; Smart and Pascarella, 1986; Winter, McClelland and Stewart, 1981). It seems reasonable, therefore, to hypothesize that different types of postsecondary institutions might have differential effects on the development of student moral judgment. Our literature review, however, found no studies which directly addressed this issue. What evidence does exist can be considered only preliminary and suggestive in nature.

Rest (1979a) has compiled what is probably the most comprehensive data set focusing on the level of college students' moral judgment. His data consist of a composite sample of nearly 2,500 students from various colleges and universities across the country. Across all samples, Rest reports an average DIT P score of 41.6. The lowest P scores were from colleges in the southeastern United States. The two college samples from Georgia and Virginia had average DIT P scores of 24.5 and 34.0, respectively. These were the two lowest averages in the combined college sample. Rest speculates that the particularly low scores from these two southern samples could reflect a conservative intellectual milieu which functions to inhibit moral judgment development. Such a conclusion is consistent with findings reported by Cady (1982) and Ernsberger (1976) in studies of the level of moral judgment development among clergy. Alternatively, however, such findings could simply reflect differential selection and recruitment procedures rather than the unique effect of the college experience. That is, a conservative intellectual milieu may tend to attract individuals with initially lower levels of moral reasoning to begin with, rather than having a particularly inhibiting influence on moral reasoning development. Of course, it is possible that there is some contextual influence associated with being in an institutional environment dominated by peers with predominantly low levels of moral reasoning (Burstein, 1980; Firebaugh, 1980). Finally, it is quite possible, if not likely, that the low scores obtained by these conservative religious students is an artifact of the methodology. Conservative religious subjects are likely to give high weights to statements on the DIT pertaining to obedience to law and authority. As a result, they would obtain low DIT scores. From the distinct domains perspective (Turiel, 1983) discussed earlier, however, such responses may not be indicative so much of these subjects' moral level as of their views of conventionality. Since the DIT is not a pure measure of moral (just, beneficent) thinking, the responses obtained from these subjects may reflect a subordination of justice to conventional or religious considerations in the context of the test. Thus, the level of moral (just, beneficent) thinking of these subjects may be underestimated.

To further investigate the hypothesis of differences among postsecondary institutions in level of students' moral judgment development, we conducted a secondary analysis of Rest's (1979a) data on the DIT *P* scores of college students. From information on the sample characteristics supplied by Rest, we grouped institutions into six basic categories: (1) public research-oriented universities (those in the top 100 institutions in federally funded research for fiscal year 1983 as ranked by the National Science Foundation); (2) public comprehensive universities (not in the top 100 research universities); (3) private universities; (4) private liberal arts colleges; (5) church-affiliated liberal arts colleges; and (6) two-year colleges. We then conducted a six-group analysis of covariance with DIT *P* scores as the dependent measure, and with the year of enrollment of each institutional sample (i.e., freshman, sophomore, junior, or senior) as the covariate. Each separate institutional sample was considered a single data point.

The results of our analysis indicated that year of student enrollment accounted for a significant portion of the variance in DIT *P* scores (22.0%, $p < .001$), year in college being positively associated with *P* scores. When we controlled statistically for differences in year of enrollment across the various samples, institutional type was also associated with a significant increase in the variance in *P* scores (R^2 increase = 31.26%, $p < .001$). The adjusted *P* scores for institutional type appeared to cluster in three general groups. The lowest three were, in ascending order, public comprehensive universities (*P* score = 38.97); private universities (*P* score = 40.16); and private liberal arts colleges (*P* score = 40.48). Somewhat higher were two-year colleges (*P* score = 43.16) and public research universities (P score $=$ 43.46). Highest of all were church-affiliated liberal arts colleges (P score $=$ 50.49).

Whether such differences are representative of national trends is, of course, quite problematic. It is difficult to determine the degree of national representativeness in Rest's data, in terms of both the total sample and the extent to which the different types of institutions in his sample are isomorphic with the parent populations from which they were drawn. Even if Rest's institutional samples were, in fact, quite representative of parent populations, our analyses may simply be reflecting differential recruiting trends rather than some unique effect of institutional type on the stimulation of student moral development. For these reasons, we are hesitant about attempting substantive interpretations of our analyses of Rest's data.

What is clearly suggested by our analyses, however, is the possibility that different institutional environments may have differential effects on the development of moral reasoning in college students. Whether such effects are adequately captured by the types of groupings we made in our analyses (e.g., public research universities, public comprehensive universities, and church-related liberal arts colleges) is questionable. It is likely that there are substantial differences in the press of the academic, social, and cultural environments of institutions within the same category. Thus, identifying the true causal influences of differences in student moral reasoning associated with institutional characteristics may entail analyses which describe how the experience of college differs among institutions.

Evidence Pertaining to Differences
in Principled Moral Judgment
Attributable to Different
Experiences Within the Same Institution

There is sufficient evidence to suggest that, while there is substantial variation among institutions, colleges and universities tend not to be monolithic organizations with a single or homogeneous set of environmental stimuli impinging equally on all students. (Abbott and Penn, 1979; Berdie, 1967; Hartnett and Centra, 1977; Lacy, 1978; Pascarella, 1976; Phelan, 1979; Weidman, 1979). Instead, students tend to be members of different subenvironments (e.g., peer groups, academic majors, extracurricular activities, residential groupings, work experiences) that may have differing, and sometimes conflicting, impacts on development during college. Thus, there may be specific types of experiences during college which are particularly salient in terms of their impact on growth in principled moral judgment.

Kohlberg's (1969) own theoretical conception of how development occurs in moral judgment would suggest that the most important experiences have the following general characteristics: (1) exposure to divergent perspectives and cognitive moral conflict (e.g., experiences and interpersonal interactions which challenge the individual's own rules for social cooperation and conduct); (2) exposure to the next highest stage of moral reasoning; (3) active participation in and concern about group decision-making, as well as concern about moral decisions in group discussions, classrooms, and meetings; (4) a general moral atmosphere of fairness and sense of community; and (5) social role-taking opportunities which stimulate cognitive-structural development (Selman, 1976). Evidence reported by Maul (1980) suggests that a secondary-school environment purposefully structured to enhance such student experiences had a positive influence on student moral judgment. With academic aptitude and grade level controlled statistically, years of exposure to the school had partial correlations of .44 with the P score of the DIT and .69 with the MJI.

College Experiences

A small but growing body of research has addressed the issue of the specific types of collegiate experiences which are systematically associated with moral judgment.[2] These investigations have taken several forms. One has been the large longitudinal survey as exemplified by the work of Barnett (1982), Biggs, Schomberg, and Brown (1977), Biggs and Barnett (1981), Schomberg (1978), and Spickelmier (1983). Since these scholars appear to have been analyzing the same large-sample, longitudinal data set, the studies will be reviewed in chronological order.

Biggs et al. (1977) examined the relationship between precollege experiences and the level of moral judgment of 767 freshmen at the University of Minnesota. Moral judgment was assessed with the P score of the DIT administered during December of the freshman year. Using a detailed checklist of precollege experiences, the authors found that students with the highest freshman-year P scores (compared to those with the lowest P scores) reported that they had read greater numbers of prominent authors and books; were better acquainted with topics in the physical and social sciences and mathematics; were better informed about nationally prominent individuals and issues; and were more knowledgeable about artists, sculptors, and composers. In short, level of freshman year moral judgment was positively associated with an academic, literary, and culturally enriched precollege environment.

Using the same sample as Biggs et al. (1977), Schomberg (1978) assessed students' involvement and success in experiences with an expanded checklist of 10 scales. The findings suggest that freshmen with initially higher principled moral judgment tended to have higher average scores for the following types of freshman year experiences: academic/conceptual; study; artistic literary; intercultural; social issues; and cultural affairs. Thus, freshman students who were initially high in moral judgment (compared to those with relatively lower freshman *P* scores) were better read, more knowledgeable about and involved in academic experiences, and more socially and culturally active throughout their freshman year.

The picture emerging from these two studies is one suggesting self-selection of collegiate experiences which function to enhance or accentuate initial levels of development (Feldman and Newcomb, 1969). Compared to their classmates, students who enter college with relatively high levels of principled moral judgment tend to come from precollege environments that are likewise richer in terms or academic, intellectual, literary, and cultural experiences. In turn, these same students tend to engage in freshman year experiences which are more likely to reflect a similar set of intellectual, cultural, artistic, and social interests. Whether these experiences are causally related to moral judgment development or whether they merely covary with the true causal influence, however, cannot be clearly discerned from the designs of the studies.

The Minnesota sample was followed up in its junior year by Biggs and Barnett (1981) in an effort to determine the differential impact of various college experiences on student moral judgment. Students with initially lowest quartile and initially highest quartile freshman-year DIT scores were the comparison groups. When multiple regression was used to control for other predictors, junior-year DIT scores for the initially low group were significantly associated only with their causal attribution beliefs concerning personal responsibility. For the initially high DIT score group, junior-year DIT scores were best predicted by freshman-year scores and participation in extracurricular activities (e.g., residence hall groups, sports clubs, political action groups, music groups), which had a significant negative partial regression coefficient with junior-year moral reasoning. Thus, junior-year level of moral reasoning was negatively associated with "traditional" or "collegiate" extracurricular involvement. There were significant zero-order correlations between level of acquaintance with contemporary social and political issues (e.g., environment, civil rights, drug abuse, international affairs) and junior-year moral reasoning for both the low ($r = .20$) and the high ($r = .29$) groups. These correlations became nonsignificant, however, when other influences (e.g., freshman-year moral reasoning scores) were taken into account.

Barnett (1982) reanalyzed the Minnesota data for 128 seniors and found that seniors who were in the highest quarter in freshman moral judgment (as measured by the DIT) also tended to be significantly more involved socially, politically, academically, and culturally through their college years than did seniors initially in the bottom quarter in freshman moral judgment. These findings are quite similar to those for freshmen reported by Schomberg (1978). Conversely, seniors from the lowest freshman group tended to show greater involvement in traditional campus and religious experiences during the four years of college than did seniors in the initially high moral reasoning group as freshmen. However, when Barnett classified individuals by their dominant pattern of freshman to senior change in moral judgment (upward, downward, or no change), no significant differences on the experience measures were indicated among groups.

It seems reasonably clear from this sequential program of research on the Minnesota data that level of moral reasoning (at least as assessed by the Defining Issues Test) is positively associated with extent of involvement in social, political, cultural, and intellectual/academic experiences during college. Moreover, moral reasoning appears to be negatively associated with involvement in traditional campus extracurricular activities and religious experiences. With the possible exception of the negative association with traditional extracurricular activities, however, there is little in the evidence from the Minnesota data to suggest that involvement in such experiences has a causal influence on the development of moral reasoning during college. As an alternative hypothesis, such involvement during college may simply reflect the coincidental intellectual, social, and cultural interests of students who enter postsecondary education with a relatively mature level of moral judgment.

Evidence presented by Kraack (1985), as reviewed by Barnett and Volker (1985), would tend to support the latter hypothesis, although the investigation was somewhat different in focus from the research conducted on the Minnesota sample. Kraack conducted a longitudinal study of change in moral reasoning from the beginning of the freshman year to the end of the sophomore year at Marquette University. Students completed the DIT at both times as well as an instrument assessing their degree of campus involvement. They were also rated on involvement and leadership by university professional staff. When Kraack controlled statistically for initial student differences, no significant relationships were found between moral judgment development and work participation, involvement in noncampus activities, extent of involvement and participation in campus activities and groups (e.g. political, religious, athletic, cocurricular, publications), or level of leadership.

A somewhat different approach to the study of the specific college or life experiences influencing the development of moral reasoning has involved several researchers (Rest, 1975, 1985; Spickelmier, 1983; Volker, 1979; Whiteley, 1980; Whiteley et al., 1985). These investigators have relied, to a large extent, on subjects' retrospective perceptions of experiences and individuals who have significantly influenced their moral development. Rest (1975, 1985) conducted a longitudinal study of a group of young adults which began when they were in high school and followed them every two years for four years. At the first testing (two years after high school), the subjects were asked to reflect upon their experience of the previous two years and to speculate about what had influenced their moral reasoning. Responses were grouped into six categories: (1) formal instruction, reading, or study which led to expanded knowledge of world events and affairs; (2) new "real-world" responsibilities (e.g., job, marriage, managing money); (3) maturation or sense of "just growing-up"; (4) new social contacts, new friends, and an expanded worldview; (5) religious experience and/or instruction; and (6) direct involvement in community or world affairs, political involvement, or assumption of leadership roles. Rest found that those subjects who cited the first two kinds of experiences (i.e., formal instruction or new "real-world" responsibilities) as influencing their moral development showed greater gains in DIT *P* scores than did subjects not citing those experiences.

A similar study of New Zealand college students by McGeorge (1976) failed to replicate Rest's (1975) findings, and a second follow-up of the same sample four years after high school yielded somewhat inconsistent findings (Rest, 1985). Subjects' responses about particularly influential experiences during the preceding four years were grouped in 18 categories, including the 6 from the first follow-up. There was little consistency, however, with the findings of the first follow-up, and no specific experience was cited as influential by a majority of subjects. Rest points out that developmental theory in no way guarantees that one particular type of life experience will be the preeminent cause of development in moral judgment. Rather, it may be the case that different events or experiences have different influences on different people. The absence of a predominant theme across his findings would appear to be consistent with this notion of the conditional, rather than general, effects of "life experiences" on moral judgment.

In what appears to be a further follow-up using Rest's data, Spickelmier (1983) conducted retrospective interviews with 24 students two years after their expected graduation from college. The interviews were then distilled into eight experimental categories. Consistent with the earlier findings of Barnett (1982), Biggs and Barnett (1981), and Schomberg (1978), Spickelmier found that students scoring highest on DIT *P* scores as freshmen, seniors, and two years after college were also judged from the retrospective interviews to have experienced a strong educational orientation during college. (A strong educational orientation indicated a strong commitment to accomplishing educational or academic objectives rather than just having a good time in college.) Two years after college, *P* scores were significantly and positively associated with college academic success, informed tolerance toward diversity, and an academic postcollege environment.

Of course, such associations are potentially confounded by differential subject selection. Thus, associations between *P*-score gain patterns and college experiences may be more informative. Here Spickelmier reports that, compared to other students interviewed, students showing the greatest upward gain pattern in *P* scores more often reported that they became more interested in academics during college and that they broke with their secondary-school friends when they went to college. Unfortunately, the statistical reliability of these associations was not established, nor do there appear to be any statistical controls for the possibly confounding effects of freshman-year differences in DIT P scores.

Volker (1979), Whiteley (1980), and Whiteley et al. (1985) conducted a series of studies which generally drew on students enrolled in a residential/academic intervention designed to influence student character (Whiteley, 1982). The intervention, known as the Sierra Project, was carried out in a large public university (University of California at Irvine). Volker (1979) sampled undergraduates from the Sierra Project and from a small midwestern liberal arts college. A 72-item checklist (Moral Reasoning Experience Checklist) was employed to collect student self-reports of college or other experiences they judged to be salient in their development. For both samples, only a few experiences were rated as highly salient to the individual and also significantly and positively associated with DIT P scores. They were (1) attending a course which presented material from different perspectives; (2) learning to adjust to the lifestyles of roommates; (3) work experience which exposed the individual to persons of more mature thinking; and (4) campaigning in state, local, or national politics.

Whiteley (1980) and Whiteley et al. (1985) asked senior students who had participated in the Sierra Project to retrospectively identify those college experiences which most significantly influenced their moral development during the freshman year and for all four years of college. In terms of the freshman year, the majority of students mentioned experiences involving their immediate peer group that dealt with exposure to different perspectives, exposure to more mature thinking (i.e., sophomore staff in the residence unit), a relationship with a person of the opposite sex, or personal spiritual experiences. In terms of the influence of their total undergraduate experience, four general themes were identified from student responses. These were the importance of a sense of community, exposure to diversity, the significance of interpersonal relationships, and the development of autonomy. The specific activities or experiences indicated as having the most important influence on moral development were living away from home, assuming additional responsibility for oneself, discussing values and morals, and getting to know different people on campus.

Students were also asked to identify those groups who had most significantly influenced their moral growth during college. These were close friends or peers, the staff of the Sierra Project, and parents or an intimate partner. The importance of interactions with faculty appeared to have a variable influence, being important for some students but not others. Both the Whiteley (1980) and the Whiteley et al. (1985) studies appear to rely solely on the validity of students' retrospective perceptions of those experiences and individuals having the most salient influence on moral reasoning. They do not attempt to estimate the association between those experiences or individuals recalled as most salient and actual measures of moral development.

Although there are clearly design and measurement problems with the Volker

(1979), Whiteley (1980), and Whiteley et al. (1985) studies, they nevertheless provide at least modest support for several of Kohlberg's notions concerning salient influences on moral development. In particular, all three studies report evidence to suggest the importance of exposure to divergent perspectives (e.g., living away from home, roommates, peers) and cognitive moral conflict (e.g., courses presenting material from different perspectives, discussion of morals and values) as influences on moral reasoning. In this sense, their findings are consistent with those of Rest (1975). Similarly, all three studies indicate the importance of exposure to more advanced stages of moral reasoning (i.e., work-related experiences or interactions with upperclass residential staff in freshman dormitories). Finally, there is some evidence to support the notion of social role-taking (e.g., assuming new personal responsibilities and work experiences, adjusting to the lifestyle of roommates) as an important influence on growth in moral reasoning. Rest (1975) also reports evidence to suggest the salience of new "real-world" responsibilities in the development of moral reasoning.

Differences in Moral Reasoning
by Academic Major or Residence Arrangement

There is a small body of inquiry into the association between academic major or concentration and measures of moral reasoning. The evidence from this research, however, is inconsistent. Schomberg (1975), for example, found that engineers tended to have higher levels of moral reasoning (as measured by the DIT) than did either liberal arts or agriculture majors. Gallia (1976), however, found that humanities undergraduates had more developed DIT scores than science majors even when other individual student differences were taken into account. The study of New Zealand college students by McGeorge (1976) reported significant differences by academic major, with English, language, math, and science students tending to have higher DIT P scores than either social science or physical education majors. It is difficult to discern a pattern in these results, and the waters become even more muddied by the fact that Bransford (1973), Dispoto (1974, 1977), and Whitla (1978) found no clear pattern in DIT scores among various academic majors.

Similar conflicting results have been reported in studies investigating differences in reflective judgment among academic majors. Kitchener (1977), for example, noted a trend for liberal arts majors to have higher scores on the RJI than did scientific or technical majors. Welfel (1982) and Welfel and Davison (1986), however, found no significant differences among engineering, humanities, and social science majors in terms of changes in RJI scores from freshman to senior year.

In addition to the small body of studies which have focused on differences in moral reasoning among academic majors, one investigation was uncovered which considered differences associated with residential or social arrangement. Marlowe and Auvenshine (1982) traced changes in DIT *P* scores over a nine-month period for freshmen in a liberal arts college. They were specifically interested in whether or not fraternity-affiliated freshmen differed from nonfraternity freshmen in terms of changes in *P* score over the freshman year. Their findings, however, indicated no reliable differences in moral reasoning between the two groups.

Effects of Moral Education Interventions on Moral Reasoning

Perhaps the most promising line of research with respect to the influence of specific college experiences on student moral judgment comes from the literature on moral education. Rather than simply attempting to assess the specific college experiences associated with moral judgment, this research has generally attempted to fashion curricular or course interventions with the major goal of enhancing growth in moral judgment. Most of the studies reporting the results of these interventions have employed the DIT as the measure of moral development. Schlaefli, Rest, and Thoma (1985) conducted a meta-analytic review of 55 such studies, all using the DIT. The review was not limited just to college students, but also included junior and senior high school students, as well as adults. Various types of interventions were included in the review (e.g., group discussion of moral dilemmas, psychological development programs, social studies and humanities courses), and the length of the intervention was also considered. Because of the comprehensive nature of this review, a detailed discussion of its methodology and results is warranted.

As described by Schlaefli et al. (1985, pp. 342–343), the types of interventions were as follows:

1. *Dilemma Discussion:*

    Programs that emphasize peer discussion of controversial moral dilemmas according to the suggestions of Kohlberg (e.g., Blatt and Kohlberg, 1975). Frequently the reports of the programs cite Galbraith and Jones (1976) as the specific guide for their ''Kohlbergian'' programs. These guides give specific suggestions for setting up the group discussion, selecting dilemmas for the stimulus material and the role of the teacher as discussion leader. . . . Presumably the effective condition for facilitating development in this type of treatment is providing concentrated practice in moral problem solving, stimulated by peer give-and-take (challenging one another's thinking, reexamining assumptions, exposure to different points of view, building lines of argument and responding to counter-argument).

2. *Personality Development:*

    Programs that emphasize personal psychological development and involve some experimental activity and intense self-reflection. Initiated by Mosher and

Sprinthall (1971), these programs are intended to promote personality and social development in general, of which moral development is a major strand. The programs involve subjects in diverse kinds of activities (e.g., cross-age teaching, empathy training, communication skill training, cooperation simulation games, volunteer service work, keeping logs about one's personal thoughts and feelings), but the activities all have the objective of promoting reflection about the self and self in relation to others. What one learns about oneself in these concrete activities is blended with learning the general theories of developmental psychology through assigned readings and class discussions. Frequently, one of the theories that subjects encounter is Kohlberg's theory of moral judgment development.

3. *Academic Course:*

Programs that emphasize the academic content of humanities, social studies, literature, or contemporary issues. These programs do not focus as much as the previous two grouping of programs on extended practice in moral problem solving or personal development activities. While value issues are discussed and related to real life events, emphasis is placed on learning bodies of information and the basic tenets of academic discipline. The contents of these programs are varied (criminal justice and U.S. law, great books, various topics in Social Studies).

4. *Short Term:*

In this last group are programs where duration was short-term—only three weeks or less. These programs are characterized not by type of activity in the intervention, but by the shortness of the intervention.

Using a procedure developed by Glass (1977), Schlaefli et al. computed an effect size for each treatment and control group, which was defined as the difference between the mean of the pretest and posttest DIT score divided by the weighted average standard deviation within the groups of the study. Thus, the effect size is analogous to a standardized score or Z score. Each effect size was subsequently weighted to reflect relative sample size within the total sample of experimental and control group subjects representing all studies. Thus, an intervention with 40 subjects was weighted twice as heavily in the aggregate results as one with 20 subjects. The principle findings from the review indicated that dilemma discussion and psychological development programs produce the strongest effects, that treatments longer than three weeks are more effective than short-term treatments (i.e., less than three weeks in duration), and that programs with adults (24 years old or older) produce larger effect sizes than programs with younger subjects. Significant effect sizes, however, were obtained for aggregate moral-education interventions with all groups, including college students. The overall effect size for college students across all types of moral education interventions was .28. This can be considered a posttest improvement of slightly more than 11% over the pretest and was significant at $p < .05$. Conversely, the effect size for all control groups was .19, which failed to reach statistical significance at $p < .05$.

Although the results suggest small but statistically reliable positive effects of moral education interventions on the moral judgment of college students, Schlaefli et al. did not disaggregate the effects of different types of interventions for different subsamples (e.g., college students, junior high, adult). To address this issue, we reanalyzed the data specifically for the college student sample. Data from an additional study by Straub and Rodgers (1978) were included in our reanalysis since they were apparently not included in the original Schlaefli et al. review. The inclusion of this additional study had a negligible influence on the results. Using information on each study and an identical weighting procedure, we conducted a 4 (type of intervention) by 2 (randomized versus nonrandomized design) analysis of variance with effect size as the dependent measure. Only the experimental conditions were considered, and due to unequal cell sizes, a least-squares solution was employed.

When we controlled for type of intervention, there was no significant difference between the effect size of the studies with random assignment of subjects to treatments (effect size $= .34$) and those without random assignment (effect size $= .26$). Thus, the strength of the study design was generally unassociated with the magnitude of the results for college students. This finding was quite consistent with the overall findings of Schlaefli et al.'s review.

When we controlled for randomized versus nonrandomized design, there was a significant ($p < .05$) difference in effect size across the four types of interventions. The most effective in stimulating growth in college students' moral judgment were dilemma discussion (effect size $= .51$) and personality development (effect size $= .41$). Academic courses were somewhat less effective (effect size $= .17$), and by the far the least effective were short-term interventions (effect size $= .03$). Again, these results, for college students in particular, closely parallel the results obtained by Schlaefli et al. when adults and students from all levels of formal education were pooled.

Clearly the small sample sizes and the attendant instability of effect sizes based on so few cases must be considered when considering the results of our reanalysis of Schaefli et al.'s data for college students. Nevertheless, the findings do suggest that purposefully designed curricular or course interventions can have positive, if modest, effects on the development of moral judgment during college. In terms of research studies using the DIT, moral education interventions employing dilemma discussion and those emphasizing personality development appear to be the most influential.

While the body of research focusing on the influence of educational interventions on moral judgment as measured by the DIT is by far the most extensive, there is a small body of studies which looks at the relationship between educational interventions and other measures of moral judgment. Boyd

(1980) evaluated the effects of a course intervention for college sophomores designed to stimulate development in moral judgment by integrating material from an introductory philosophy course in ethics with perspectives on late adolescent moral development taken from Kohlberg's theory. Students could chose whether or not to take the course, thus introducing the possibilities of selection bias and the interaction of selection and change as potential threats to the internal validity of the study. To counter this, Boyd used an elaborate matching procedure to achieve a reasonably equivalent control group of students not receiving the intervention. The control group was chosen, as far as possible, from the same recruitment pool as those students in the course and was matched on grade level, age, sex, and degree of prior exposure to Kohlberg's theory. The experimental and control groups did not differ significantly on preintervention moral maturity scores from the MJI. An immediate postintervention assessment showed significantly greater change toward postconventional stages of moral reasoning by the experimentals than by the controls. A nine-month delayed posttest showed similar differences, which, however, failed to reach statistical significance.

Similar results are reported by Page and Bode (1982). They had freshman and sophomore students in three sections of an ethics class (experimental group) and one section of an introductory psychology course (control group) complete the Ethical Reasoning Inventory (ERI) at the beginning and end of a 10-week academic quarter. The ERI is a paper-and-pencil measure of Kohlberg's stages of moral reasoning that employs the six Kohlbergian dilemmas and prototypical statements representing Stages 1–5. (It correlates .54 with the MJI and .57 with the DIT.) The experimental ethics course focused on the rational evaluation and justification of traditional normative ethical theories. Important historical ethical theories (e.g., utilitarianism, Kantianism) were examined as examples of various types of ethical theories, and reasons were given for accepting or rejecting them. In order to avoid contamination of the results through increased familiarity with dilemmas or Kohlberg's theory, no discussion of Kohlberg's stages of moral development or any of the ERI dilemmas was undertaken in the course. Here Bode and Page differed in design from the earlier study by Boyd (1980), which did introduce the experimental group to Kohlberg's theory.

Since students were not randomly assigned to experimental and control conditions, Page and Bode had the internal validity problems inherent in a nonequivalent control-group design. Fortunately, however, the experimental and control groups were almost identical in terms of pretest scores on the ERI. At the end of the 10-week quarter, the students in the experimental ethics course showed greater average gain in ERI scores from pretest to posttest than did the control group.

Faust and Arbuthnot (1978) took a somewhat different tack from either Boyd (1980) or Page and Bode (1982). They were interested in the effects of moral education intervention on college students, but in addition, they anticipated that the effectiveness of such a program would depend to some extent on the students' stage of Piagetian cognitive development. To test this hypothesis, they conducted an experiment that included students who were enrolled in a five-week moral education program and a control group not in the program. The moral education program was based on Blatt and Kohlberg (1975) and stressed exposure to intensive moral argument and discussion. The dependent measure was Form A of a standardized Kohlberg questionnaire. The results indicated an overall significant effect on moral reasoning development which favored the moral education program. The magnitude of the effect, however, varied for students at different Piagetian reasoning stages. For those functioning primarily at the concrete stage, the advantage of the moral education program was .11. This compared to an advantage of .34 for the moral education program for those students who were at a more advanced Piagetian stage (i.e., formal reasoning). Such results suggest the possibility that not all college students may benefit equally from Kohlbergian moral education programs based on moral argument and discussion. Rather, Piagetian stage of cognitive development may function to set a ceiling on development in moral reasoning and, consequently, on the benefits derived from Kohlbergian moral education interventions.

Finally, there is also a small body of research which evaluates specific curricular experiences designed to facilitate development along Perry's (1970) scheme of intellectual and moral development. Stephenson and Hunt (1977) report the results of a course-based intervention based on cognitive-developmental instruction. Similar to Kohlberg's notions about the types of experiences which stimulate development in moral judgment, cognitive-developmental instruction assumes that development occurs as the result of cognitive conflict or dissonance which forces students to alter the constructs they have typically employed to reason about certain situations (Widick, Knefelkamp, and Parker, 1975). The experimental intervention was a freshman social science course which focused on human identity as addressed in literature and psychology (readings were from authors such as Edward Albee, James Baldwin, Arthur Miller, and Sylvia Plath). The instructional approach was intended to stimulate movement of dualistic students toward the relativistic stage of Perry's continuum. Consequently, the instructional approach emphasized challenges to the students' values and cognitive constructs within a supportive teaching paradigm. The control groups were students in a humanities and an English class which focused on essentially similar course content, but without the cognitive-developmental approach to instruction.

Because students self-selected themselves into both the experimental and the control conditions, the results are possibly confounded by various forms of selection bias and/or the interaction of selection and change. Despite these limitations, the findings indicated greater upward stage movement on the Perry scheme by the students receiving developmental instruction (mean change = +.85 stage) than the control groups (mean change = .25 stage).

Similar results have been reported by Knefelkamp (1974), Widick et al. (1975), and Widick and Simpson (1978). These studies found that cognitive-developmental course instruction matched to the student's initial stage on the Perry scheme (either dualistic or relativistic) was associated with substantial pre- to posttreatment upward change on the Perry scheme. In one study, cognitive-developmental instruction matched with primarily dualistic and primarily rela- tivistic students resulted in pre- to postcourse gains for both groups of slightly more than three quarters of a stage in the Perry scheme. The absence of a control group, however, makes it difficult to disaggregate change due to the intervention from that due to maturational influences. In a second study, 63% of an experimental history-course section receiving cognitive-developmental instruc- tion matched to the dualistic stage exhibited stage progress on the Perry continuum. This percentage was somewhat larger than the average for the control groups (51.5%), two sections of the same course taught in a more traditional manner. It is unclear from the description of this study, however, if students could choose the instructional approach or if some type of random assignment (individuals or intact groups) was possible. The latter, of course, provides for greater certainty in making inferences about the factors causally linked to the results.

CONCLUSIONS AND DIRECTIONS FOR FUTURE RESEARCH

This final section is organized around the four basic questions addressed in the beginning of the chapter. It uses a brief summary of findings as a point of departure for suggesting salient areas for future research on the impact of college on student moral development.

Changes in Moral Judgment During College

The majority of research on the influence of college on student moral judgment has focused on changes that occur during college. There is sufficient evidence from a large number of cross-sectional and longitudinal studies employing differing measures of levels of moral judgment to conclude that exposure to college is linked with statistically reliable increases in the sophistication with which students reason about moral issues. Not only do upperclassmen (i.e., juniors and seniors) tend to show more sophisiticated moral judgment than lowerclassmen (i.e., freshmen and sophomores), but it also is the case that students tend to make discernible, nonchance gains in moral judgment during college. The higher one's formal educational attainment beyond secondary school, the more pronounced these increases in moral reasoning sophistication appear to be. Moreover, this general link between level of postsecondary educational attainment and moral reasoning or judgment is not confined to samples of American college students. Similar trends have been found in a number of cross-national investigations, which included samples from countries such as Hong Kong, Korea, Iceland, the Philippine Islands, Australia, and Germany.

This pervasive association between the level of postsecondary educational attainment and level of sophistication in judging moral issues is perhaps the strongest generalization we can make from the existing body of evidence concerning the impact of college on student moral development. At the same time, however, such a correlational link, no matter how consistently found, is not the equivalent of establishing a causal link between college and moral development. Most of the studies on which this conclusion is based are confounded by such factors as subject age, differential institutional selectivity over time, or the absence of a reasonably similar control group of students who do not attend college. Thus, although what we have learned from research of this genre is valuable, we may have reached a point of diminishing returns in terms of what additional knowledge is to be learned from further inquiry of this kind. Knowing, as we do, that there is a positive association between college and students' moral judgment, we need to address additional significant questions.

Attributing Development in
Moral Judgment to Postsecondary Education

There is sufficient evidence to suggest that extent of exposure to postsecondary education may have a statistically reliable and unique influence on the development of sophistication in students' moral judgment. The degree of certainty with which such attributional statements can be made, however, varies to some extent with the instrument used to assess moral judgment. The largest and most consistent body of evidence is drawn from studies employing the DIT. Both cross-sectional studies, which statistically control for age, and longitudinal studies, which apply statistical controls for initial differences between college and noncollege groups, suggest that extent of exposure to college uniquely influences the development of growth in principled moral judgment (DIT P scores). Indeed, the rather consistent evidence from DIT studies would lead one to conclude (as did Rest, 1979a,b) that principled moral reasoning tends to increase with exposure to additional levels of formal education beyond secondary school and tends to plateau for individuals who do not go to college.

The evidence from cross-sectional studies employing the MJI or the RJI are less consistent. Holding age constant, some studies have indicated a unique effect due to postsecondary education, while others have not. Still other evidence has suggested the joint contribution of age and extent of exposure to college as the underlying cause of growth in moral judgment. Longitudinal evidence with a control group of noncollege subjects has been more positive. With initial level of intelligence held constant statistically, level of formal education was shown to have a significant partial association with the moral maturity score of the MJI.

Of the studies reviewed in relation to the issue of the causal impact of college on moral development, the soundest methodologically were longitudinal ones done with control groups of subjects who either did not attend college or varied in their degree of exposure to postsecondary educational environments. Since it is obviously impossible to randomly assign individuals to different levels of exposure to postsecondary education, these studies, by necessity, relied on statistical controls (e.g., partial correlation, regression analysis, analysis of covariance) to remove the potentially confounding influence of initial differences among subjects (e.g., initial level of moral judgment, intelligence). Strictly speaking, of course, causal inferences cannot be made with the same level of certitude from such correlational or quasi-experimental data as they can from randomized experiments. Even with extensive statistical controls, one cannot be sure that all confounding influences are taken into account. Rather than the collegiate experience itself, individual differences among students related to their likelihood of attending college may be the true causal influences underlying differential change in moral judgment.

This interaction of selection and change (or motivation) is a potentially important threat to the internal validity of even the most carefully conducted longitudinal studies of the effect of college on moral judgment (e.g., Rest and Thoma, 1985; Colby et al., 1983). Despite this limitation, however, the body of research represented by these studies is an important contribution to our knowledge about the potential impact of college attendance. In the absence of conditions which permit the random assignment of individuals to different levels of exposure to college, quasi-experimental designs with appropriate and comprehensive statistical controls are our most valid available means of estimating the unique impact of college.

Although the overall body of evidence does suggest that college may have a unique, positive influence on the development of moral judgment, it is not clear that the influence is the same for all students. Investigations which seek to determine if the nature of the impact of college on moral development is general (i.e., the same for all students) or conditional (i.e., different in magnitude for different kinds of students) are an important direction for future research. Attributes such as age, socioeconomic status, gender, ethnicity, intelligence, level of Piagetian reasoning (i.e., formal or concrete), and stage of moral judgment upon leaving secondary school may be worth considering in terms of their moderating the impact of college on change in moral judgment.

Differences Among Postsecondary Institutions in Their Effects on Moral Judgment

No systematic research has addressed the issue of differences among institutions in the magnitude of their impact on student moral judgment. Our own analysis of an existing data base from Rest (1979a) suggests that such differences may exist. However, the institutional variables represented in the data base are insufficient to draw more than the most tentative conclusions. This is clearly an area in need of much additional inquiry. Hopefully, such inquiry will take into account differences in the characteristics of students who attend different types of institutions. Unless this is done, of course, it will be easy to mistake the results of differential students recruitment and enrollment patterns among colleges for the effects of different college environments. Investigations which clearly exemplify the importance of controlling for initial differences among the student bodies enrolled in different institutions are found in the work of Astin (1968, 1977) and Wolfle (1983).

If one is to study the impact of different institutional environments on the development of student moral judgment, a significant related issue is the specificity with which the characteristics of different institutional environments are assessed. Previous research has indicated that structural characteristics or traditional measures of institutional quality (e.g., academic selectivity of the student body, student-faculty ratio, library size, money spent per student, faculty salaries) have few direct influences on student development (e.g., Astin, 1968, 1977; Nichols, 1964; Pascarella, 1985a), although they may have modest indirect effects (e.g., Lacy, 1978; Pascarella, 1985b). Thus, it is likely that the most informative research on the impact of differential college environments on the development of moral judgment will consider differences among institutions on more specific intellectual, interpersonal, and social-psychological influences. Different institutions may, in fact, vary in terms of their impact on the moral development of students. This knowledge will be of limited value, however, unless we come to a clearer understanding of the unique intellectual, social, and ethical contexts of those institutions which, to borrow from Philip Jacob (1957), have a "particular potency" in fostering growth in student moral judgment.

Effects of Differential Experiences Within the Same Institution on Moral Judgment

The literature pertaining to the influence of different college experiences on student moral judgment offers few consistent findings upon which to form sound generalizations. Nevertheless we offer some very tentative and suggestive conclusions. There is modest support for what, according to Kohlberg's (1969) theories, are salient experiences in the fostering of growth in moral judgment. Collegiate experiences in which an individual is exposed to divergent perspectives (e.g., living away from home, interacting with roommates) or is confronted with cognitive moral conflict (e.g., courses presenting issues from different perspectives) were reported by students as having a salient influence on their moral development. Also consistent with Kohlberg's expectations, students indicated the importance of interacting with upperclassmen in residential facilities (i.e., exposure to more advanced stages of moral reasoning) and assuming new personal responsibilities (i.e., social role-taking).

A number of these experiences form a major part of the intellectual and interpersonal socialization process confronting the vast majority of students in residential colleges and universities. One might therefore conclude that the impact of college on moral judgment is of the Gestalt variety, with no specific experience or set of experiences being clearly the most salient. This conclusion is supported by the fact that few, if any, specific collegiate experiences or activities were found to be significantly related to measures of moral judgment across studies.

Of course, such a conclusion may need to be tempered by the fact that little or no research has focused on how individual student differences might interact with specific collegiate experiences to influence moral development. The critical question may not be what dimensions of the college experience are most important in fostering growth in moral reasoning for all students. Instead, *what may be most important to learn is what different collegiate experiences or involvements are most important for what kinds of students under what kinds of conditions*. The investigation of such conditional effects on the development of moral judgment is likely to yield a body of evidence with greater complexity than the study of general effects. Such complexity, however, may be necessary to validly model reality.

Little consistent evidence exists to suggest that broad curricular categorizations are significantly associated with differences in the development of moral judgment. Certain curricular or course interventions with college students, however, do appear to foster increased sophistication in judging moral issues (as measured by the DIT). Based on our reanalysis of the Schlaefli et al. (1985) data, the most consistently effective interventions are those emphasizing moral dilemma discussion or personality development, and the least effective are short-term interventions of under three weeks' duration. Different academic course interventions appear to be positively associated with gains in moral stage development on the Perry scheme, although certain design problems limit the results of these studies. Clearly the weight of evidence suggests that the academic program of an institution may be a powerful mechanism for fostering student growth in moral judgment. This is perhaps not too surprising, given the link between cognitive or intellectual development and sophistication in judging moral issues (Rest, 1979a). Once again, however, the important issue for future research may be less one of estimating general effects than one of estimating the conditional effects of different academic experiences. Evidence does exist to suggest that the magnitude of the effect of academic interventions designed to facilitate sophistication in moral reasoning depends to some extent on the student's prior level of cognitive development. There may, of course, be other student attributes which interact with various academic interventions.

Student self-reports of the experiences during college which were important influences on their moral development have suggested the salience of interactions with peers, upperclassmen, and roomates. Because much of this interaction occurs in university residence facilities, one might hypothesize the nature of the residence experience as a potentially important influence on growth in student moral judgment. Almost no research has addressed this issue, even though residence arrangement and the quality of residence life have been shown to influence a wide range of student outcomes (Astin, 1973; Chickering, 1969). Clearly, the influence of living on campus versus commuting to college, as well as the influence of different residential arrangements on campus, are important areas for future inquiry.

College Experience and Moral Behavior

The focus of our chapter has been on college effects on the development of moral judgment. A final and significant area for future research, however, has to do with understanding the complex pattern of interrelationships and influences among the collegiate experience, growth in moral judgment, and moral behavior. Clearly there is sufficient evidence in the research literature we have reviewed to suggest that college does positively influence growth in principled moral judgment. As also indicated (see Note 1), there is impressive evidence to suggest positive systematic links between moral judgment scores and what would be considered moral behavior (e.g., resistance to cheating, helping others in need, and civil disobedience) among college students. What is less clear, however, is the link between college and moral behavior. Does the collegiate experience increase the likelihood of principled behavior as well as principled moral judgment?

From the existing evidence, we would suggest that there may be at least the presence of an indirect link or effect between college and moral behavior. Postsecondary education would appear to foster a growth in moral judgment which, in certain situations, may enhance the likelihood of moral action. Thus, the major influence of postsecondary education on moral behavior may be transmitted largely through its impact on the development of moral reasoning. Of course, this hypothesized indirect effect is largely an extrapolation from independent bodies of correlational evidence. While it has a certain logical and intuitive appeal, it obviously requires fuller and more comprehensive verification.

Acknowledgments. An earlier version of this paper was presented at the 1986 meeting of the American Educational Research Association, San Francisco. We wish to thank James Rest for generously sharing his raw data with us and John Whiteley for kindly sending us numerous prepublication copies of his work. Thanks are also due to Richard Johnson, Vice Chancellor for Academic Affairs at the University of Illinois, for a summer research appointment which supported the second author's work on the chapter. Finally, since both authors contributed equally to the chapter, we have chosen to list our names in alphabetical order.

NOTES

1. The relation between moral judgment and action is complex, and a full account of the issues involved is beyond the scope of this chapter. A definitive review of the relations between Kohlberg's moral stage and behavior can be found in Blasi (1980). Other comprehensive discussions of the issue can be found in Blasi (1983), Kohlberg (1984), Rest (1983a,b), Turiel and Smetana (1984), and Turiel (1983).

   While inconsistencies between reasoning and behavior have been found in some studies, we would concur with Blasi (1980) that "the empirical literature supports the hypothesis of a significant relationship between moral thinking and moral behavior" (p. 10). Research focusing specifically on the relations between moral judgment stage and behavior in college students has reported significant positive relations between moral judgment score and resistance to cheating (Dunivant, 1975; Leming, 1979; Malinowski, 1978; Malinowski and Smith, 1985; Schwartz et al., 1969), helping behavior (Andreason, 1975; McNamee, 1972, 1978; Staub, 1974), resistance to authority in the Milgram paradigm (Kohlberg & Candee, 1984), and civil disobedience (Haan, 1975; Haan, Smith, & Block, 1968).

2. A significant part of this section draws on excellent review by Barnett and Volker (1985). Their review, however, focuses on a broader view of life experiences than those occurring during college.

REFERENCES

Abbot, K., and Penn, R. (1979). Value preferences in dissimilar campus living groups. *Journal of College Student Personnel* 20: 122–128.

Adler, M. (1952). *The Great Ideas: A Synopticon of Great Books of the Western World* Vol. 1. Chicago, IL: Encyclopedia Britannica.

Andreason, A. (1975). The effects of social responsibility, moral judgment, and conformity on helping behavior. Unpublished doctoral dissertation, Brigham Young University, Provo, UT.

Astin, A. (1968). Undergraduate achievement and institutional excellence. *Science* 161: 661–668.

Astin, A. (1973). The impact of dormitory living on students. *Educational Record* 54: 204–210.

Astin, A. (1977). *Four Critical Years: Effects of College on Beliefs, Attitudes, and Knowledge.* San Francisco: Jossey-Bass.

Astin, A., and Panos, R. (1969). *The Educational and Vocational Development of College Students.* Washington, DC: American Council on Education.

Averill, L. (1983). *Learning to Be Human: A Vision for the Liberal Arts.* Port Washington, NY: Associated Faculty Press.

Barnett, R. (1982). Change in moral judgement and college experience. Unpublished master's thesis, University of Minnesota.

Barnett, R., and Volker, J. (1985). Moral judgements and life experiences. Unpublished manuscript, University of Minnesota.

Berdie, R. (1967). A university is a many faceted thing. *Personnel and Guidance Journal* 45: 768–775.

Biggs, D., and Barnett, R. (1981). Moral judgement development of college students. *Research in Higher Education* 14: 91–102.

Biggs, D., Schomberg, S., and Brown, J. (1977). Moral judgement development of freshmen and their precollege experiences. *Research in Higher Education* 7: 329–339.

Blasi, A. (1980). Bridging moral cognition and moral action: A critical review of the literature. *Psychological Bulletin* 88: 1–45.

Blasi, A. (1983). Moral cognition and moral action: A theoretical perspective. *Developmental Review* 3: 178–210.

Blatt, M., and Kohlberg, L. (1975). The effects of classroom moral discussion upon children's level of moral judgement. *Journal of Moral Education* 4: 129–161.

Bowen, H. (1977). *Investment in Learning: The Individual and Social Value of American Higher Education.* San Francisco: Jossey-Bass.

Boyd, D. (1976). Education toward principled moral judgement: An analysis of an experimental course in undergraduate moral education applying Lawerence Kohlberg's theory of moral development. Unpublished doctoral dissertation, Harvard University, Cambridge.

Boyd, D. (1980). The condition of sophomoritis and its educational cure. *Journal of Moral Education* 10: 24–39.

Brabeck, M. (1980). The relationship between critical thinking skills and the development of reflective judgement. Unpublished doctoral dissertation, University of Minnesota.

Brabeck, M. (1983). Critical thinking skills and reflective judgement development: Redefining the aims of higher education. *Journal of Applied Developmental Psychology* 4: 23–34.

Bransford, C. (1973). Moral development in college students. Unpublished manuscript, St. Olaf College, Northfield, MN.

Burstein, L. (1980). The analysis of multilevel data in educational research and evaluation. In D. Berliner (Ed.), *Review of Research in Education,* Vol. 8. Washington, DC: American Educational Research Association.

Cady, M. (1982). Assessment of moral development among clergy. Unpublished honors thesis, Augsburg College, Minneapolis, MN.

Carey, N., and Ford, M. (1983). Domains of social and self-regulation: An Indonesian study. Paper presented at the meeting of the American Psychological Association, Los Angeles.

Chickering, A. (1969). *Education and Identity.* San Francisco: Jossey-Bass.

Chickering, A. (1974). The impact of various college environments on personality development. *Journal of the American College Health Association* 23: 82–93.

Chickering, A., and McCormick, J. (1973). Personality development and the college experience. *Research in Higher Education* 1: 43–70.

Clark, B., Heist, D., McConnell, M., Trow, M., and Yonge, G. (1972). *Students and Colleges: Interaction and Change.* Berkeley: Center for Research and Development in Higher Education, University of California.

Coder, R. (1975). Moral judgment in adults. Unpublished doctoral dissertation, University of Minnesota.

Cohen, E. (1982). Using the Defining Issues Test to assess stage of moral development among sorority and fraternity members. *Journal of College Student Personnel* 23: 324–328.

Colby, A., Kohlberg, L., Gibbs, J., Candee, D., Speicher-Dubin, B. Kauffman, K., Hewer, A., and Power, C. (1982). *The Measurement of Moral Judgment: A Manual and Its Results*. New York: Cambridge University Press.

Colby, A., Kohlberg, L., Gibbs, J., Candee, D., Speicher-Dubin, B., and Power, C. (1978). *Assessing Moral Judgment Stages: A Manual*. Cambridge, MA: Moral Education Research Foundation.

Colby, A., Kohlberg, L., Gibbs, J., and Lieberman, M. (1983). A longitudinal study of moral judgement. *Society for Research on Child Development Monograph* 48 (1–2, Serial No. 200).

Crowder, J. (1976). The Defining Issues Test and correlates of moral judgement. Unpublished master's thesis, University of Maryland.

Damon, N. (1977). *The Social World of the Child*. San Francisco: Jossey-Bass.

Damon, W. (1980). Patterns of change in children's social reasoning: A two-year longitudinal study. *Child Development* 51: 1010–1017.

Deemer, D. (1985). Research in moral development. Paper presented at the annual meeting of the American Educational Research Association, Chicago.

Dispoto, R. (1974). Socio-moral reasoning and environmental activity, emotionality and knowledge. Unpublished doctoral dissertation, Rutgers University, New Brunswick, NJ.

Dispoto, R. (1977). Moral valuing and environmental variables. *Journal of Research in Science Teaching* 14: 273–280.

Dortzbach, J. (1975). Moral judgement and perceived locus of control: A cross-sectional developmental study of adults, aged 25–74. Unpublished doctoral dissertation, University of Oregon.

Dumont, R., and Troelstrup, R. (1981). Measures and predictors of educational growth with four years of college. *Research in Higher Education* 14: 31–47.

Dunivant, N. (1975). Moral judgment, psychological development, situational characteristics and moral behavior: A medicational interactionist model. Unpublished doctoral dissertation, University of Texas at Austin.

Eisert, D., and Tomlinson-Keasey, C. (1978). Cognitive and interpersonal growth during the college freshman year: A structural analysis. *Perceptual and Motor Skills* 46: 995–1005.

Enright, R., Franklin, L., and Manheim, L. (1980). On children's distributive justice reasoning: A standardized and objective scale. *Developmental Psychology* 16: 193–202.

Ernsberger, D. (1976). Intrinsic-extrinsic religious identification and level of moral development. Unpublished doctoral dissertation, University of Texas.

Faust, D., and Arbuthnot, J. (1978). Relationship between moral and Piagetian reasoning and the effectiveness of moral education. *Developmental Psychology* 14: 435–436.

Feldman, K., and Newcomb, T. (1969). *The Impact of College on Students*. San Francisco: Jossey–Bass.

Firebaugh, G. (1980). Assessing group effects: A comparison of two methods. In E. Borgatta and D. Jackson (eds.), *Aggregate Data Analysis and Interpretation*. Beverly Hills, CA: Sage.

Fischer, K. (1983). Illuminating the process of moral development. Commentary on A.

Colby, L. Kohlberg, J. Gibbs, and M. Lieberman, A longitudinal study of moral judgment. *Monographs of the Society for Research in Child Development* 48 (1–2, Serial No. 200).

Flavell, J. H. (1982). Structures, stages and sequences in cognitive development. In A. Collins (Ed.), *Minnesota Symposium on Child Psychology,* Vol. 15. Hillsdale, NJ: Erlbaum.

Frankena, W. K. (1963). *Ethics.* Englewood Cliffs, NJ: Prentice-Hall.

Froming, W. J., and McColgan, E. B. (1979). Comparing the Defining Issues Test and the Moral Dilemma Interview. *Developmental Psychology* 15: 658–659.

Galbraith, R., and Jones, T. (1976). *Moral Reasoning: A Teaching Handbook for Adopting Kohlberg to the Classroom.* Minneapolis: Greenhaven Press.

Gallia, T. (1976). Moral reasoning in college science and humanities students: Summary of a pilot study. Unpublished manuscript, Glassboro State College, Glassboro, NJ.

Gamson, Z. (1984). *Liberating Education.* San Francisco: Jossey-Bass.

Gelman, R., and Baillargeon, R. (1983). A review of some Piagetian concepts. In J. H. Flavell and E. M. Markman (eds.), *Manual of Child Psychology: Vol. 3. Cognitive Development.* New York: Wiley.

Gilligan, C. (1982). *In a Different Voice: Psychological Theory and Women's Development.* Cambridge: Harvard University Press.

Gilligan, C., Kohlberg, L., Lerner, J., and BeLenky, M. (1971). Moral reasoning about sexual dilemmas: A developmental approach. *Technical report of the Commission on Obscenity and Pornography,* Vol. 1 (No. 52560010). Washington, DC: U. S. Government Printing Office.

Glass, G. (1977). Integrating findings: The meta-analysis of research. *Review of research in education* 5: 351–379.

Glatfelder, M. (1982). Identity development, intellectual development, and their relationship in re-entry women students. Unpublished doctoral dissertation, University of Minnesota.

Haan, N. (1975). Hypothetical and actual moral reasoning in a situation of civil disobedience. *Journal of Personality and Social Psychology* 32: 255–270.

Hahn, J., Smith, M., and Block, J. (1968). Moral reasoning of young adults: Political-social behavior, family background, and personality correlates. *Journal of Personality and Social Psychology* 10: 183–201.

Hartnett, R., and Centra, J. (1977). The effects of academic departments on student learning. *Journal of Higher Education* 48: 491–507.

Hau, K. (1983). A cross-cultural study of a moral judgment test (The D.I.T.). Unpublished master's thesis, Chinese University, Hong Kong.

Heath, D. (1968). *Growing Up in College: Liberal Education and Maturity.* San Francisco: Jossey-Bass.

Heath, D. (1976). What the enduring effects of higher education tell us about a liberal education. *Journal of Higher Education* 47: 173–190.

Hollos, M., Leis, P. E., and Turiel, E. (1986). Social reasoning in Ijo children and adolescents in Nigerian communities. *Journal of Cross-Cultural Psychology* 17: 352–374.

Hyman, H., and Wright, C. (1979). *Education's Lasting Influence on Values.* Chicago: University of Chicago Press.

Jacob, P. (1957). *Changing Values in College: An Exploratory Study of the Impact of College Teaching.* New York: Harper.

Kagan, J., ed. (in press). *The Emergence of Moral Concepts in Young Children.* Chicago: University of Chicago Press.

Keeley, S., Browne, M., and Kreutzer, J. (1982). A comparison of freshmen and seniors on general and specific essay tests of critical thinking. *Research in Higher Education* 17: 139–154.

Khalili, H., and Hood, A. (1983). A longitudinal study of change in conceptual level in college. *Journal of College Student Personnel* 24: 389–394.

King, P. (1977). The development of reflective judgement and formal operational thinking in adolescents and young adults. Unpublished doctoral dissertation, University of Minnesota.

King, P., Kitchener, K., Davison, M., Parker, C., and Wood, P. (1983). The justification of beliefs in young adults. *Human Development* 26: 106–111.

King, P. M., Kitchener, K. S., and Wood, P. K. (1985). The development of intellect and character: A longitudinal-sequential study of intellectual and moral development in young adults. *Moral Education Forum* 10: 1–14.

Kitchener, K. (1977). Intellectual development in late adolescents and young adults: Reflective judgement and verbal reasoning. Unpublished doctoral dissertation, University of Minnesota.

Kitchener, K., and King, P. (1981). Reflective judgement: Concepts of justification and their relationship to age and education. *Journal of Applied Developmental Psychology* 2: 89–116.

Kitchener, K., et al. (1984). A longitudinal study of moral and ego development in young adults. *Journal of Youth and Adolescence* 13: 197–211.

Knefelkamp, L. (1974). Developmental instruction: Fostering intellectual and personal growth. Unpublished doctoral dissertation, University of Minnesota.

Kohlberg, L. (1958). The development of modes of moral thinking and choice in years ten to sixteen. Unpublished doctoral dissertation, University of Chicago.

Kohlberg, L. (1964). Development of moral character and moral ideology. In M. Hoffman (Ed.), *Review of Child Development Research*, Vol. 9. New York: Russell Sage Foundation.

Kohlberg, L. (1969). Stage and sequence: The cognitive-developmental approach to socialization. In D. Goslund (Ed.), *Handbook of Socialization Theory and Research*. Chicago: Rand McNally.

Kohlberg, L. (1971). From is to ought: How to commit the naturalistic fallacy and get away with it in the study of moral development. In T. Mischel (Ed.), *Cognitive Development and Epistemology*. New York: Academic Press.

Kohlberg, L. (1973). Continuities in childhood and adult moral development revisited. In P. B. Baltes and K. W. Schare (eds.), *Life-Span Developmental Psychology: Personality and Socialization*. New York: Academic Press.

Kohlberg, L. (1976). Moral stages and moralization: The cognitive-developmental approach. In T. Lickona (Ed.), *Moral Development and Behavior: Theory Research and Social Issues*. New York: Holt, Rinehart & Winston.

Kohlberg, L. (1981). *The Meaning and Measurement of Moral Development*. Worcester, MA: Clark University Press, 1981.

Kohlberg, L. (1984). *Essays on Moral Development. Vol. 2: The Psychology of Moral Development*. San Francisco: Harper & Row.

Kohlberg, L., and Candee, D. (1984). The relationship of moral judgment to moral action. In W. Kurtines and J. Gewirtz (Eds.), *Morality, Moral Behavior, and Moral Development*. New York: Wiley-Interscience.

Kraack, T. (1985). The relation of moral development to involvement and leadership experiences. Unpublished doctoral dissertation, University of Minnesota.

Kramer, R. (1968). Moral development in young adulthood. Unpublished doctoral dissertation, University of Chicago.

Kurtines, W., and Greif, E. (1974). The development of moral thought: Review and evaluation of Kohlberg's approach. *Psychological Bulletin* 81: 453–470.

Lacy, W. (1978). Interpersonal relationships as mediators of structural effects: College student socialization in a traditional and an experimental university environment. *Sociology of Education* 51: 201–211.

Lawson, J. (1980). The relationship between graduate education and the development of reflective judgment: A function of age or educational experience? Unpublished doctoral dissertation, University of Minnesota.

Lehmann, I. (1963). Changes in critical thinking, attitudes and values from freshman to senior years. *Journal of Educational Psychology* 54: 305–315.

Lehmann, I., and Dressel, P. (1962). *Critical Thinking, Attitudes and Values in Higher Education.* East Lansing: Michigan State University.

Lehmann, I., and Dressel, P. (1963). *Changes in Critical Thinking Ability, Attitudes and Values Associated with College Attendance.* East Lansing: Michigan State University.

Lei, T. (1981). The development of moral, political and legal reasoning in Chinese societies. Unpublished master's thesis, University of Minnesota.

Lei, T., and Cheng, S. (1984). An empirical study of Kohlberg's theory and scoring system of moral judgement in Chinese society. Unpublished manuscript, Harvard University, Center for Moral Education, Cambridge.

Leming, J. (1979). The relationship between principled moral reasoning and cheating behavior under threat and nonthreat situations. Paper presented at the American Educational Research Association, San Francisco.

Lenning, O., Munday, L., and Maxey, J. (1969). Student educational growth during the first two years of college. *College and University* 44: 145–153.

Lind, G. (1985). Moral competence and education in democratic society. In G. Zecha and P. Weigartner (eds.), *Conscience: An Interdisciplinary View.* Dordrecht, The Netherlands: Reidel.

Lind, G. (1986). Growth and regression in cognitive-moral development. In C. Harding (Ed.), *Moral Dilemmas: Philosophical and Psychological Issues in the Development of Moral Reasoning.* Chicago: Precedent.

Malinowski, C. (1978). Moral judgment resistance to the temptation to cheat. Paper presented at the American Psychological Association Convention, Toronto.

Malinowski, C., and Smith, C. (1985). Moral reasoning and moral conduct: An investigation prompted by Kohlberg's theory. *Journal of Personality and Social Psychology* 49: 1016–1021.

Marlowe, A., and Auvenshine, C. (1982). Greek membership: Its impact on the moral development of college freshmen. *Journal of College Student Personnel* 23:53–57.

Martin, R., Shafto, M., and Van Deinse, W. (1977). The reliability, validity and design of the Defining Issues Test. *Developmental Psychology* 13: 460–468.

Maul, J. (1980). A high school with intensive education: Moral atmosphere and moral reasoning. *Journal of Moral Education* 10: 9–17.

McBee, M. (1980). The values development dilemma. In M. McBee (ed.), *Rethinking College Responsibilities for Values.* San Francisco: Jossey-Bass.

McGeorge, C. (1976). Some correlates of principled moral thinking in young adults. *Journal of Moral Education* 5: 265–273.

McNamee, S. (1972). Moral behavior, moral development and needs in students and political activists. Unpublished doctoral dissertation, Case Western Reserve University, Cleveland.

McNamee, S. (1978). Moral behavior, moral development and motivation. *Journal of Moral Education* 7: 27–32.

Mentkowski, M., and Strait, M. (1983). A longitudinal study of student change in cognitive development and generic abilities in an outcome-centered liberal arts curriculum. Paper presented at the annual meeting of the American Educational Research Association, Montreal.

Milgram, S. (1963). Behavioral study of obedience. *Journal of Abnormal and Social Psychology* 67: 371–378.

Milgram, S. (1974). *Obediance to Authority: An Experimental View*. New York: Harper & Row.

Mines, R. (1980). Levels of intellectual development and associated critical thinking skills in young adults. Unpublished doctoral dissertation, University of Iowa.

Moon, Y. (1985). A review of cross-cultural studies on moral judgment development using the defining issues test. Paper presented at the annual meeting of the American Educational Research Association, Chicago.

Morrill, R. (1980). *Teaching Values in College*. San Francisco: Jossey-Bass.

Mosher, R., and Sprinthall, N. (1971). Psychological education: A means to promote personal development through adolescence. *The Counseling Psychologist* 2: 3–82.

Nichols, R. (1964). Effects of various college characteristics on student aptitude test scores. *Journal of Educational Psychology* 55: 45–54.

Nucci, L. (1982). Conceptual development in the moral and conventional domains: Implications for values education. *Review of Educational Research* 52: 93–122.

Nucci, L. (1985). Social conflict and the development of children's moral and conventional concepts. In M. Berkowitz (Ed.), *Peer Conflict and Psychological Growth*. New Directions for Child Development, No. 29. San Francisco: Jossey-Bass.

Nucci, L., and Turiel, E. (1978). Social interactions and development of social concepts in preschool children. *Child Development* 49: 400–407.

Nucci, L., Turiel, E., and Encarnacion-Gawrych, G. (1983). Children's social interactions and social concepts: Analyses of morality and convention in the Virgin Islands. *Journal of Cross-Cultural Psychology* 14: 469–487.

Pace, C. R. (1974). The Demise of Diversity: A Comparative Profile of Eight Types of Institutions. Berkeley, CA: The Carnegie Commission on Higher Education.

Page, R., and Bode, J. (1982). Inducing changes in moral reasoning. *Journal of Psychology* 112: 113–119.

Park, J., and Johnson, R. (1983). Moral development in rural and urban Korea. Unpublished manuscript, Hankook University of Foreign Studies, Seoul, Korea.

Pascarella, E. (1976). Perceptions of the college environment by students in different academic majors in two colleges of arts and science. *Research in Higher Education* 4: 165–176.

Pascarella, E. (1985a). College environmental influences on learning and cognitive development: A critical review and synthesis. In J. Smart (ed.), *Higher Education: Handbook of Theory and Research*, Vol. I, pp. 1–62. New York: Agathon Press.

Pascarella, E. (1985b). Student affective development within the college environment. *Journal of Higher Education* 56: 640–663.

Perry, W. (1968). *Forms of Intellectual and Ethical Development in the College Years*. New York: Holt, Rinehart & Winston.

Phelan, W. (1979). Undergraduate orientations toward scientific and scholarly careers. *American Educational Research Journal* 16: 411–422.

Piaget, J. (1932, 1948). *The Moral Judgment of the Child*. Glencoe, IL: Free Press.

Pratt, M., Golding, G., and Hunter, W. (1983). The character and consistency of moral judgment in young mature, and older adults. Paper presented at the biennial meetings of the Society for Research in Child Development, Detroit.

Pratt, M., Golding, G., Hunter, W., and Sampson, R. (1985a). Principles and prototypes: Do women and men think differently about moral issues. Paper presented at the biennial meetings of the Society for Research in Child Development, Toronto, Canada.

Pratt, M., Golding, G., Hunter, W., and Norris, J. (1985b). Age and sex differences over the life-span in moral judgment: Getting the big picture. Paper presented at the biennial meetings of the Society for Research in Child Development, Toronto, Canada.

Rest, J. (1975). Longitudinal study of the Defining Issues Test: A strategy for analyzing developmental change. *Developmental Psychology* 11: 738–748.

Rest, J. (1976). *Moral Judgement Related to Sample Characteristics*. Technical Report No. 2. Minneapolis: University of Minnesota.

Rest, J., (1979a). *Development in Judging Moral Issues*. Minneapolis: University of Minnesota Press.

Rest, J. (1979b). *The impact of higher education on moral judgement development*. Technical Report No. 5. Minneapolis: Minnesota Moral Research Projects.

Rest, J. (1979c). *Revised Manual for the Defining Issues Test*. Minneapolis: Moral Research Projects.

Rest, J. R. (1980). Development in moral judgment research. *Developmental Psychology* 16: 251–256.

Rest, J. (1983a). Morality. In P. Mussen (ed.), *Carmichael's Manual of Child Psychology*. New York: Wiley.

Rest, J. R. (1983b). Morality. In J. H. Flavell and E. M. Markman (eds.), *Handbook of Child Psychology. Vol. 3: Cognitive Development* (4th ed.). New York: Wiley.

Rest, J. (1985). Moral development in young adults. Unpublished manuscript, University of Minnesota.

Rest, J., Davison, M., and Robbins, S. (1978). Age trends in judging moral issues: A review of cross-sectional longitudinal, and sequential studies of the Defining Issues Test. *Child Development* 49: 263–279.

Rest, J., and Thoma, S. (1985). Relation of moral judgement development to formal education. *Developmental Psychology* 21: 709–714.

Rudolph, F. (1956). *Mark Hopkins and the Log: Williams College, 1836–1872*. New Haven, CT: Yale University Press.

Rudolph, F. (1962). *The American College and University*. New York: Vintage Books.

Sanford, N. (1967). *Where Colleges Fail*. San Francisco: Jossey-Bass.

Schlaefli, A., Rest, J., and Thoma, S. (1985). Does moral education improve moral judgement? A meta-analysis of intervention studies using the Defining Issues Test. *Review of Educational Research* 55: 319–352.

Schmidt, J. (1985). Older and wiser? A longitudinal study of the impact of college on intellectual development. *Journal of College Student Personnel* 26: 338–394.

Schmidt, J., and Davison, M. (1981). Does college matter? Reflective judgment: How students tackle the tough questions. *Moral Education Forum* 6: 2–14.

Schmidt, J., and Davison, M. (1983). Helping students think. *Personnel and Guidance Journal* 61: 563–569.

Schomberg, S. (1975). Some personality correlates of moral maturity among community college students. Unpublished manuscript, University of Minnesota.

Schomberg, S. (1978). Moral judgement development and its association with freshman year experiences. Unpublished doctoral dissertation, University of Minnesota.

Schwartz, S., Feldman, K., Brown, M., and Heingartner, A. (1969). Some personality correlates of conduct in two situations of moral conflict. *Journal of Personality* 37: 41–57.

Scott, S. (1975). Impact of residence hall living on college student development. *Journal of College Student Personnel* 16: 214–219.

Selman, R. (1976). Social-cognitive understanding: A guide to educational and clinical practice. In T. Lickona (ed.), *Moral Development and Behavior*. New York: Holt, Rinehart & Winston.

Shaver, D. (1985). A longitudinal study of moral development at a conservative, religious liberal arts college. *Journal of College Student Personnel* 26: 400–404.

Shweder, R. A., Mahapatra, M., and Miller, J. G. (in press). Culture and moral development. In Kagan, ed. *The Emergence of Moral Concepts in Young Children*.

Simpson, E. L. (1974). Moral development research: A case study of scientific cultural bias. *Human Development* 17: 81–106.

Sloan, D. (1979). *The Teaching of Ethics in the American Undergraduate Curriculum, 1876–1976*. Hastings Center Report, (9), 21–41.

Sloan, D. (1980). The teaching of ethics in American undergraduate curriculum, 1876–1976. In D. Callahan and S. Bok (eds.), *The Teaching of Ethics*. New York: Plenum Press.

Smart, J., and Pascarella, E. (1986). Socioeconomic achievements of former college students. *Journal of Higher Education* 57: 529–549.

Smetana, J. G. (1982). *Concepts of Self and Morality: Women's Reasoning about Abortion*. New York: Praeger.

Snarey, J. (1985). The cross-cultural universality of social-moral development: A critical review of Kohlbergian research. *Psychological Bulletin* 97(2): 202–232.

Song, M., Smetana, J. G., and Kim, S. (1985). Korean children's conceptions of moral and conventional transgressions. Paper presented at the biennial meeting of the Society for Research in Child Development, Toronto, Canada.

Spaeth, J., and Greeley, A. (1970). *Recent Alumni and Higher Education*. New York: McGraw-Hill.

Spickelmier, J. (1983). College experience and moral judgement development. Unpublished doctoral dissertation, University of Minnesota.

Spiro, M. (1985). Cultural relativism and the future of anthropology. Unpublished manuscript, La Jolla, CA.

Staub, E. (1974). Helping a distressed person: Social, personality and stimulus determinants. In L. Berkowitz (Ed.), *Advances in Experimental Social Psychology*, Vol. 7. New York: Academic Press.

Stein, J. L. (1973). Adolescent's reasoning about moral and sexual dilemmas: A longitudinal study. Unpublished doctoral dissertation, Harvard University, Cambridge.

Stephenson, B., and Hunt, C. (1977). Intellectual and ethical development: A dualistic curriculum intervention for college students. *Counseling Psychologist* 6: 39–42.

Strange, C. (1978). Intellectual development, motive for education and learning styles during the college years: A comparison of adult and traditional age college students. Unpublished doctoral dissertation, University of Iowa.

Straub, C., and Rodgers, R. (1978). Fostering moral development in college women. *Journal of College Student Personnel* 19: 430–436.

Sullivan, E. V. (1977). A study of Kohlberg's structural theory of moral development: A critique of liberal social science ideology. *Human Development* 20: 352–376.

Thoma, S. (1984). Estimating gender differences in the comprehension and preference of moral issues. Unpublished manuscript, University of Minnesota.

Thornlidsson, T. (1978). Social organization, role-taking, elaborated language and moral judgement in an Icelandic setting. Unpublished doctoral dissertation, University of Iowa.

Trent, J., and Medsker, L. (1968). *Beyond High School: A Psychosocial Study of 10,000 High School Graduates*. San Francisco: Jossey-Bass.

Trow, M. (1976). Higher education and moral development. *AAUP Bulletin* 62: 20–27.

Turiel, E. (1974). Conflict and transition in adolescent moral development. *Child Development* 45: 14–29.

Turiel, E. (1978). The development of concepts of social structure: social convention. In J. Glick and A. Clarke-Steward (eds.), *The Development of Social Understanding*. New York: Gardner Press.

Turiel, E. (1983). *The Development of Social Knowledge: Morality and Convention*. Cambridge: Cambridge University Press.

Turiel, E., Killen, M., and Helwig, C. (in press). Morality: its structure, functions and vagaries. In Kagan, ed., *The Emergence of Moral Concepts in Young Children*.

Turiel, E., and Smetana, J. (1984). Social knowledge and action: The coordination of domains. In J. L. Gewirtz and W. M. Kurtines (eds.), *Morality, Moral Development and Moral Behavior*. New York: Wiley.

Villanueva, E. (1982). Validation of a moral judgement instrument for Filipino students. Unpublished doctoral dissertation, University of the Phillippines, Quezon City.

Volker, J. (1979). *Moral Reasoning and College Experience*. Project Report No. 4. Minneapolis: Higher Education and Cognitive-Social Development Project, University of Minnesota.

Walker, L. J. (1984). Sex defferences in the development of moral reasoning: A critical review. *Child Development* 55: 677–691.

Walker, L. J. (1985). Sex differences in morality and what they mean. Paper presented at the annual conference of the Association for Moral Education, Toronto, Canada.

Walker, L. J. (1986). Sex differences in the development of moral reasoning: A rejoinder to Baumrind. *Child Development* 57: 522–526.

Watson, W. (1983). A study of factors effecting the development of moral judgement. Unpublished manuscript, Monash Chirering, Clayton, Victoria, Australia.

Weidman, J. (1979). Nonintellective undergraduate socialization in academic departments. *Journal of Higher Education* 50: 48–62.

Welfel, E. (1982). How students make judgements: Do educational level and academic major make a difference? *Journal of College Student Personnel* 23: 490–497.

Welfel, E., and Davison, M. (1986). The development of reflective judgment in the college years: A four-year longitudinal study. *Journal of College Student Personnel* 27: 209–216.

White, C. (1973). Moral judgement in college students: The development of an objective measure and its relationship to life experience dimension. Unpublished doctoral dissertation, University of Georgia.

Whiteley, J. (1980). A development intervention in higher education. In V. Erickson and J. Whiteley (eds.), *Developmental Counseling and Teaching*. Monterey, CA: Brooks/Cole.

Whiteley, J. (1982). *Character Development in College Students*. Vol. 1. Schenectady, NY: Character Research Press.

Whiteley, J., Bertin, B., Ferrant, E., and Yokota, N. (1985). Influences on character development during the college years: The retrospective view of recent undergraduates.

In J. Whiteley (ed.), *Character Development in College Students,* Vol. 2. Schenectady, NY: Character Research Press.

Whitla, D. (1978). Value Added: Measuring the Impact of Undergraduate Education. Cambridge: Office of Instructional Research and Evaluation, Harvard University.

Widick, C., Knefelkamp, L., and Parker, C. (1975). The counselor as developmental instructor. *Counselor Education and Supervision* 14: 286–296.

Widick, C., and Simpson, D. (1978). Developmental concepts in college instruction. In C. Parker (ed.), *Encouraging Development in College Students.* Minneapolis: University of Minnesota Press.

Williams, D., and Reilly, R. (1972). The impact of residence halls on students. *Journal of College Student Personnel* 13: 402–410.

Winter, D., McClelland, D., and Stewart, A. (1981). *A New Case for the Liberal Arts: Assessing Institutional Goals and Student Development.* San Francisco: Jossey-Bass.

Withey, S. (1971). *A Degree and What Else? Correlates and Consequences of a College Education.* New York: McGraw-Hill.

Wolfle, L. (1980). The enduring effects of education verbal skills. *Sociology of Education* 53: 104–114.

Wolfle, L. (1983). Effects of higher education on ability for blacks and whites. *Research in Higher Education* 19: 3–10.

Yussen, S. (1976). Moral reasoning from the perspective of others. *Child Development* 47: 551–555.

An Analysis of
Student Academic Rights

D. Parker Young
and
Martha C. Braswell
University of Georgia

During the decade of the 1970s, consumerism came to the campus and with it a flood of legal challenges to academic decisions when students felt that they had been treated arbitrarily or capriciously. Since that time, there has been no diminishing of court cases in the academic arena as students continue to challenge decisions ranging from admissions to graduation.

In order to analyze the legal parameters regarding student academic affairs in higher education, recent court decisions must be studied since these rulings constitute the most significant source of law affecting higher education. Although constitutions, statutes, and administrative policies are important sources of law, familiarity with these sources will not provide a complete description of the state of the law regarding student rights. An awareness of recent court decisions and the literature interpreting those decisions is an absolute must.

The influence of court decisions in the 1980s is profound. We live in a litigious society in which almost all vital questions are taken to our judicial courts for resolution. Few administrative decisions are accepted at any level in higher education without question. As a general rule, many of these decisions are appealed to the appropriate court and sometimes even to the U.S. Supreme Court.

The proliferation of court cases in higher education began in the 1960s. The trend in the decisions has now changed somewhat. Those decisions of the 1960s and early 1970s sought to ensure a respect for individual rights on campus; today's suits, however, are largely concerned with alleged arbitrary academic decisions and with liability. Educators' legal responsibilities are inescapable as they are now held legally accountable for all of their actions and decisions and for the consequences thereof (Kaplin, 1985). That is not to say that they are personally liable for acts within the scope of their authority. In most cases, educators are subject to "qualified immunity" to personal liability (Forch, 1983; *Wood* v. *Strickland*, 1975). Even academic freedom has no special privileges insofar as legal responsibilities are concerned. The courts have not been clear in interpreting "academic freedom" as a constitutionally protected right, although it has been characterized as a special concern of the First Amendment (Katz, 1983; *Keyishian* v. *Board of Regents*, 1967).

Courts have been deferential to the judgment of academicians and generally have upheld the decisions of faculty and administrators (Young, 1977; Mass, 1980; Kaplin, 1985). The courts have been reluctant to embark upon courses of judicial action which would require continuing supervision of the official conduct of public officers. In refusing to review a teacher's academic assessment of a student's work, the court's restraint is based on a "confidence that school authorities are able to discharge their academic duties with fairness and with competence. It is born alike of the necessity for shielding the courts from an incalculable new potential for lawsuits, testing every Latin grade and every selection for the safety patrol." This restraint also "protects every teacher from the cost and agony of litigation by pupils and their parents who would rely upon the legal process rather than the learning process." It also "protects every school system . . . from an added and unbearable burden of continuous legal turmoil" (*Woodruff* v. *Georgia State University*, 1983, p. 699).

This restraint by the courts has protected academic autonomy and recognized academic freedom. The courts have also recognized the beneficial student-faculty relationship and the fear that exists that judicial intervention could cause deterioration of that relationship. From this, it is apparent that if academicians do not abuse their discretion in dealing with students, they need not fear judicial intervention. Intervention comes when evidence exists of arbitrary or negligent treatment of students or the denial of their protected rights. However, judicial deference to academic judgment does not insulate academics from litigation, for students are increasingly challenging academic decisions. Because of increases in the number of court decisions dealing with academic matters, the judiciary is becoming more willing to evaluate academic decisions under circumstances in which earlier courts deferred to academic judgment.

PUBLIC AND PRIVATE DIFFERENCES

Prior to an analysis of the legal parameters of student academic rights in higher education, it is appropriate to look at the legal differences between public and private institutions of higher education. The most basic difference between public and private colleges and universities is their responsibilities under the Fourteenth Amendment to the U.S. Constitution. That amendment prohibits the state from depriving a citizen of his or her legally guaranteed rights. These rights are secured by the Bill of Rights, the first ten amendments to the Constitution, and by federal and state statutes. The government is prohibited from depriving citizens of rights embodied in those amendments. Simply put, the Fourteenth Amendment declares that no state shall deprive any citizen of life, liberty, or property without due process of law or equal protection of the laws. Since public universities are creations of the state, they must fall under the prohibitions of the Fourteenth Amendment and respect all of the constitutional rights of students as set forth by the courts.

Except in a few special circumstances, the Fourteenth Amendment does not refer to or place a restriction upon private action. Therefore, private citizens and private institutions of higher education are not bound by the prohibitions in the amendment. The private institution is not in a constitutional relationship with its students unless it is in some way acting on behalf of the state (Young, 1977; Haskell, 1982). However, it is rare that private institutions are found to be engaged in "state action."

Courts are frequently asked to determine whether a particular private institution is engaged in "state action." In making that determination, courts sift and weigh the facts and circumstances surrounding the particular institution's involvement with the state. Generally, state action is not involved in controversies arising from private actions unless it can be shown that the private institution is so entwined with the state that the state action concept would apply. The mere receipt of public funds by a private institution or the enjoyment of a tax exemption are both insufficient by themselves to justify a finding of state action (*Williams* v. *Howard University*, 1976). Also, the public function of "educating persons" has been rejected as constituting state action on the part of a private institution (*Grossner* v. *Trustees of Columbia University*, 1968). If it is found that the private institution is entwined with the state to a great degree, such as involvement with the governance of the institution or a contractual relationship with the state (there are also many other factors in conjunction with each other to be considered, such as receipt of public funds and tax exemptions), it may be declared to be engaged in "state action," which would trigger constitutional guarantees for its students (Kaplin, 1985).

The relationship between the student and the public university is contractual as well as constitutional. The relationship between the student and the private university is primarily contractual unless the institution is engaged in state action. It then must respect the constitutional rights of its students. The resulting relationship would then be the same as with the public institutions.

A contractual relationship exists when a student enters either a public or private institution by his or her own free will and agrees to abide by certain rules and regulations set down by the institution. In return, the institution agrees to grant a degree to the student if he or she meets and fulfills all of the requirements set forth in writing (usually in the college catalog). It is assumed that the administration will decide when the rules are broken, and the procedures and the discipline itself will only have to fall within the purview of not being arbitrary, unreasonable, or outside the legal limits of the discretion allowed to administrators of institutions of higher education. If the student fails to meet the required standards, she or he can be dismissed, and if the institution fails to adhere to its own regulations and standards, the student may seek judicial relief (Young, 1977). Institutions have been given latitude in interpreting or changing their regulations. The terms of the student-institution contract, implications of school catalogs, and the extent of authority maintained by the institution are still developing (Kaplin, 1985).

LEGAL RELATIONSHIP BETWEEN THE COLLEGE AND THE STUDENT IN THE ACADEMIC ARENA

Institutions must be aware today of the basic constitutional rights that all students share as citizens. Students have, as a general rule, the same legal rights and responsibilities as adults. Thus, the legal parameters regarding students and all of their campus activities must be understood.

Prior to 1961, the relationship between the student and the institution was one in which the institution stood *in loco parentis* to the student. That concept placed the student under the jurisdiction of the institution, which was able to stand in place of the parent. This allowed the institution to regulate the student in any manner it chose up to the limit that the parent could.

Since the *Dixon* case in 1961, the doctrine of *in loco parentis* has been replaced with a relationship which might best be described as constitutional. This means that students are citizens and do not shed any of their constitutional rights when they enroll in an institution. On the other hand, students do not gain any special privileges upon enrollment. Under the law, states must treat people equally. Since the public institution is an arm of the state, it must abide by constitutional parameters and respect all of the constitutional rights of students. Any restriction or regulation of those rights must be justified in light of the legitimate aims and purposes of the institution.

In addition to the constitutional rights which students inherently have as citizens, they also enjoy certain other rights which are the result of laws enacted by Congress and the state legislatures. These statutory rights are applicable to students enrolled in any institution, public or private, which is subject to the legislation, either specifically or through the receipt of federal or state funds. The primary federal statutory rights of college students are those found in Title IX of the Education Amendments of 1972, Section 504 of the Rehabilitation Act of 1973, and the Family Educational Rights and Privacy Act of 1974. Each statute is similar in prohibiting discrimination but addresses a different group of beneficiaries.

Title IX of the Education Amendments of 1972, 20 U.S.C. secs. 1681 et seq., states that ''No person in the United States shall, on the basis of sex, be excluded from participation in, be denied the benefits of, or be subjected to discrimination under any education program or activity receiving Federal financial assistance.'' Tax-exempt social fraternities and sororities are excluded from coverage. ''Educational institutions may not discriminate on the basis of sex in admissions and recruitment (with certain exceptions) (see Section 4.2.4.2); in awarding financial assistance (Section 4.3.3); in athletics programs (Section 4.11.2); or in the employment of faculty and staff members (Section 3.3.2.3) or students (see 45 C.R.F. sec. 86.38)'' (Kaplin, 1978, p. 409). The application of Title IX is to both public and private higher education and, therefore, has a broader reach than the ''equal protection'' clause of the First Amendment. The definitive case filed under Title IX is *Cannon* v. *University of Chicago* (1979). The court declared, ''While the statute provides for judicial review of agency action, it does not authorize a private right of action against the University'' (p. 1259). In other words, the action must be brought by a federal regulatory agency on behalf of an aggrieved individual or group.

Section 504 of the Rehabilitation Act of 1973 parallels Title IX by stating that ''no otherwise handicapped individual in the United States, as defined in Section 7(6) 29 USCS 706(6) shall solely by reason of his handicap, be excluded from the participation in, be denied the benefits of, or be subjected to discrimination under any program or activity receiving Federal financial assistance.'' A handicapped person is defined as any person who (1) has a physical or mental impairment which substantially limits one or more major life activities; (2) has a record of such impairment; or (3) is regarded as having such an impairment. A ''qualified'' handicapped person who meets academic and technical standards for admission or participation in an educational program by a fund recipient cannot be discriminated against.

The Family Educational Rights and Privacy Act of 1974, popularly known as the Buckley Amendment, ensures that only appropriate ''school officials'' with a legitimate ''educational interest'' may see student files without the consent of the student. The legislation also provides students with access to all information placed in their official files. Students have the right to an informal hearing regarding information in their files, and if they do not receive satisfaction at the hearing, they may insert explanatory material in their files. The legislation does not grant students the right to contest grades, although they may request a hearing to contest whether the grade assigned by the professor has been correctly recorded. For example, in *State ex. rel. Mecurio* v. *Board of Regents* (1983), the court ruled that a failing grade does not have to be expunged from a student's record because some of the examination papers of the student were missing. Secondary evidence of the missing document was given by witnesses under oath and was subjected to cross-examination validating the grade of the missing document.

The regulations implementing this legislation do allow for student waivers under certain circumstances. The regulations are fairly specific in outlining just what institutions must do in order to comply. Persons who have made application for admission to an institution but who have not been accepted are not covered by the law. Also, students who apply for admission to different departments within the institution are not covered. Although much has been written concerning the Buckley Amendment, there has not been a multitude of court cases regarding the legislation. It may be that the legislation has not caused the degree of problems originally feared by higher education officials.

As in constitutional due process, Title IX and the Buckley Amendment contain regulations for the process of suspension or dismissal of a student. Institutions with fair and reasonable policies for "exhaustion of remedies" may forestall litigation by the student (Kaplin, 1985).

In addition to the constitutional and statutory rights that students possess, they also have certain contractual rights. The basic elements of a contract are present by virtue of (1) an offer by the university for students to attend and partake of its curriculum and services; (2) an acceptance by the student of that offer; and (3) consideration (money) tendered by the student (*Williams* v. *Howard University*, 1976, pp. 660–661). In its various publications, the university outlines its rules, regulations, and requirements, as well as the services offered. Upon payment of all fees by the student, a contract has been entered into which requires that both parties respect the terms of that agreement. Students may also enter into contracts for such things as housing and meal plans.

In academic affairs, a contractual relationship exists between the student and the institution. The basic provisions of the college catalog, recruiting brochures, various bulletins, and student handbooks become part of the contract. These include such provisions as tuition, fees, refund policy, program, and graduation requirements. The courts have supported the contractual relationship between a student and a university in academic matters and have noted that the terms of that contract may be implied from a student handbook or other statements of academic policy (see *Ikpeazu* v. *University of Nebraska*, 1985; *Kraft* v. *W. Alanson White Psychiatric Foundation*, 1985). The institution also sets forth certain requirements for passing courses and for successful completion of programs and graduation. The student who fails to meet the required standards can be dismissed. But if the institution fails to respect its own regulations, then the student may seek judicial relief. This contractual relationship is true for both the public and the private institution.

A case illustration of the contractual nature of college catalogs is found in the *University of Texas Health Science Center at Houston* v. *Babb* (1982). A nursing student was dismissed from her program for having low grades. The student had entered the institution in January 1979 under the terms of a catalog which required all students who fell below a 2.0 grade-point average to be placed on probation, but the recorded grade for repeated courses would be the last one obtained. The catalog also specified that students would be held to the requirements of the catalog under which they had entered, and that they had six years to complete degree requirements. In the Fall 1979 term, the student was officially notified that she was failing a twelve-hour course and was advised to withdraw from the program and seek readmission for the January term. She was given "WF's" for her fall courses and was readmitted in January. Subsequently, the student made a "C" in all the courses she had previously made "WF's" in. However, the new catalog for 1979–1981 contained a new regulation which provided for the dismissal of students who had more than two "D's." The student received two "D's" and was expelled from the program on the basis of the new regulation.

The court held that while the university has the right to modify its standards, it expressly promised students that they could continue through the program under the catalog in effect when they entered. The students had been guaranteed six years to complete the program. Thus, any rule changes could not be applied retroactively. This underscores the freedom of the institution to modify or change its requirements, but not in an arbitrary or capricious manner.

Institutions should be very conscious of the obligations which might be created by unequivocal statements or representations in recruiting brochures, catalogs, and other publications. Certain disclaimers should be included in these publications, as well as a statement to the effect that rules, regulations, requirements, and so on are subject to change from time to time. In *Idrees* v. *American University of the Caribbean* (1982), a laboratory technician at Beth Israel Medical Center in New York resigned his position in order to enroll in the American University of the Caribbean (AUC) Medical School, British West Indies, when he was not allowed an education leave. One month later, he withdrew from AUC and accused them of fraudulent misrepresentation. Among the items misrepresented were various library materials, audiovisual aids, laboratory facilities that included microscopes, slides, and skeletons, all of which did not exist. Furthermore, a photograph of the Montserrat Hospital was used in an advertisement calculated to give a prospective student the impression that students would use the facilities of the hospital, when in fact no students were able to use any of the facilities of the hospital. The court found that AUC had materially misrepresented the facilities and faculty of its school. It further declared that the university had a duty to inform its students of major changes which could affect their decision to attend its school. The representations made by AUC were material to the student's decision to attend the school, and AUC's failure to correct that representation constituted recklessness, if not actual concealment.

Although the courts have recognized that colleges and universities do have a substantial amount of discretion regarding requirements for admission, academic programs, and graduation, the institution should be careful not to abuse that discretion. Some students have been awarded monetary damages where institutions have promised job placement or preparation for finding a job and have not fulfilled the promise (see *Dizick* v. *Umpqua Community College*, 1979, and *Delta School of Business, Etc.* v. *Shropshire*, 1981).

Under normal circumstances, the requirements outlined in the catalog become effective when the student enters the institution and are controlling until the student graduates. Modifications or changes can be made if conditions warrant. Allowing students the option of meeting the requirements of the catalog in effect at the time of their admission or of adhering to the new regulations is a viable option for both institution and students. However, most institutions' catalogs state that the ultimate responsibility for knowing degree requirements rests with the student.

STUDENT RIGHTS IN
ACADEMIC DISCIPLINARY PROCEEDINGS

Students may be dismissed from an institution for academic or disciplinary reasons. In the case of an academic dismissal, the student has no absolute right to the due process guarantees of notice and hearing as he or she would have in a disciplinary dismissal case (Young, 1977; Henderson and Isenberg, 1983). The basis of this interpretation rests with *Board of Curators of the University of Missouri* v. *Horowitz* (1978), where the court held that no hearing was required for academic dismissal. However, the court implied that an informal hearing would be appropriate. The informal hearing would provide an opportunity for the student to explain why the academic dismissal should not be imposed (Marx, 1984). The student bears the heavy burden of proof if he or she charges the institution with arbitrary, capricious, or bad faith effort (Henderson and Isenberg, 1983).

In *Horowitz*, the student claimed that she was "stigmatized" by her academic dismissal and should have been afforded a due process hearing. She was a medical student at the University of Missouri-Kansas City School of Medicine who was dismissed near the end of her program of study for deficiencies in clinical competence, peer and patient relations, and personal hygiene, and with lack of ability to accept criticism. No hearing was afforded before the Council on Evaluation, the Coordinating Committee, or the dean during the dismissal procedure, nor was she informed of the time or place of any of their meetings. She claimed that the stigma of dismissal would prevent her from continuing her medical education and would damage her chances of obtaining employment in a medically related field.

The U.S. Court of Appeals held that where the dismissal of a student for academic and personal deficiencies results in that student's being "stigmatized" in such a way that he or she will be unable to continue the pursuit of education and employment in that field, such dismissal affects a liberty interest in such a manner that the due process clause of the federal Constitution requires a hearing as a condition precedent to dismissal. The U.S. Supreme Court overturned that decision upon appeal.

The Supreme Court declared that it was not necessary to decide whether the student's dismissal deprived her of a liberty interest in pursuing a medical career or any other interest constitutionally protected against deprivation without procedural due process. It stated, "Assuming the existence of a liberty or property interest, [the student] has been awarded at least as much due process as the Fourteenth Amendment requires. The school fully informed [her] of the faculty's dissatisfaction with her clinical progress and the danger that this posed to timely graduation and continued enrollment. The ultimate decision to dismiss [the student] was careful and deliberate. These procedures were sufficient under the Due Process Clause of the Fourteenth Amendment" (pp. 84–85). The Court noted the difference between the failure of a student to meet academic standards and the violation by a student of valid rules of conduct and ruled that this difference calls for far less stringent procedural requirements in the case of an academic dismissal:

> The decision to dismiss [the student] rested on the academic judgment of school officials that she did not have the necessary clinical ability to perform adequately as a medical doctor and was making insufficient progress toward that goal. Such a judgment is by its nature more subjective and evaluative than the typical factual questions presented in the average disciplinary decision. Like the decision of an individual professor as to the proper grade for a student in his course, the determination whether to dismiss a student for academic reasons requires an expert evaluation of cumulative information and is not readily adapted to the procedural tools of judicial or administrative decisionmaking. (pp. 89–90)

Therefore the Court ruled that

> Under such circumstances, we decline to ignore the historic judgment of educators and thereby formalize the academic dismissal process by requiring a hearing. The educational process is not by nature adversarial; instead it centers around a continuing relationship between faculty and students, "one in which the teacher must occupy many roles—educator, advisor, friend, and, at times, parent-substitute". . . . This is especially true as one advances through the system, and the instruction becomes both more individualized and more specialized. . . . We decline to further enlarge the judicial presence in the academic community and thereby risk deterioration of many beneficial aspects of the faculty-student relationship. (p. 90)

The U.S. Court of Appeals had expressly failed to reach the question of substantive due process, and the student urged that the case be remanded to that court for consideration of a claim of arbitrary and capricious treatment. The U.S. Supreme Court did not find it necessary to issue a ruling as to whether Horowitz had been deprived of a liberty or property interest. It noted that a number of lower courts had implied that academic dismissals from state colleges and universities can be enjoined if "shown to be clearly arbitrary or capricious." However, the Court declared that even assuming that courts can review an academic decision under such a standard, it agreed with the district court that no showing of arbitrariness or capriciousness had been made in this case.

It can be assumed from the Supreme Court decision that due process requires "careful and deliberate" decision making with notification to the student of standing. By the Court's ruling, it is imperative that cases be categorized as either academic or disciplinary, a sometimes difficult process.

In a disciplinary dismissal, a student must be afforded a procedural due process hearing. Procedures for a disciplinary dismissal were established in *Dixon* v. *Alabama State Board of Education* (1961), where the court determined that a student must be notified of the charges against him or her, and that a rudimentary hearing must be provided where he or she can rebut those charges (pp. 156–157).

Since the *Dixon* case, students enrolled in a public institution or in a private institution which is engaged in state action have a constitutional right to due process prior to any long-term suspensions. (See also *Goss* v. *Lopez*, 1975.) Most institutions have structured and published in catalogs constitutional procedures for disciplinary dismissal (Golden, 1982). There are two types of due process: procedural and substantive. *Procedural due process* refers to the procedures and methods used in seeing that laws and rules are carried out and enforced. *Substantive due process* examines more than just procedure in considering whether the purpose or the implementation of the law or regulation is fair, reasonable, and just (Young, 1977). The courts do not precisely define due process; rather, they define it by the gradual process of "judicial inclusion and exclusion" on a case-by-case basis (*Davidson* v. *New Orleans*, 1877).

Due process requires some degree of specificity of rules and regulations but not the specificity of the criminal code. The degree of specificity required is that which will allow a student to adequately prepare a defense against the charge (*Soglin* v. *Kauffman*, 1969; *White* v. *Knowlton*, 1973). For example, the term *misconduct* has been judged by the courts to be too vague. For prolonged suspension or expulsion, an institution's action may not be based solely on "misconduct" without reference to some preexisting rule for adequate guidance. However, in *Esteban* v. *Central Missouri State College* (1969), the court stated,

> We see little basically or constitutionally wrong with flexibility and reasonable breadth, rather than meticulous specificity, in college regulations relating to conduct. Certainly these regulations are not to be compared with the criminal statute. They are codes of general conduct which those qualified and experienced in the field have characterized not as punishment but as part of the educational process itself and as preferably to be expressed in general rather than in specific terms. (p. 1077)

Procedural due process requires that students in public institutions be given a written notice of the specific charges against them, the time and place of the hearing, the evidence which will be presented against them, and the possible action to be taken against them if the charges are supported. The notice should be provided to the student in enough time prior to the hearing to allow the student to prepare a defense. An accused student cannot frustrate the notice process by failing to keep the institution informed of a change of address if the institution requires notification and by the subsequent failure to actually receive the notice. College officials are required only to employ their best efforts and nothing more in attempting to give written notice to a student. It should be pointed out that although private institutions are not required to meet the same constitutional standards as public schools, most private colleges and universities afford more due process than is required of public institutions (Young, 1977; Kaplin, 1985).

Student disciplinary proceedings have been held to be civil and not criminal proceedings and, therefore, do not necessarily require all of the judicial safeguards and rights accorded to criminal proceedings (*Dixon*, 1961; *Wright* v. *Texas Southern University*, 1968). The hearing itself should provide the student an opportunity to present his or her defense and to present witnesses in support of the student's case. There is no general absolute requirement at this time that the student be warned against self-incrimination or be permitted to cross-examine witnesses. Also, rules of evidence which apply in criminal proceedings are not applicable. There is also no requirement that the hearing be open to the public or to members of the college community. In fact, an open hearing would violate the Buckley Amendment unless the student agreed to a public hearing. The student is entitled to appeal the decision. The hearing is intended to be not a full-blown adversary proceeding but simply a fair and ample opportunity for both sides to present the facts (*Cloud* v. *Trustee of Boston University*, 1983).

Procedural due process does not guarantee students the absolute right to be represented by counsel in disciplinary cases. Institutions may allow students to be represented by legal counsel or other advisers, but this is the prerogative of the institution. This is not to say, however, that in a specific case it might be determined that in order for a student to receive a fair hearing, he or she must be allowed legal counsel. There is simply no absolute right to counsel in all cases since it must be remembered that campus proceedings are civil and not criminal (*French* v. *Bashful*, 1969). If, however, the institution proceeds through counsel in the campus hearing, then the student does have the same right to be represented. Also, if a student is charged with a serious crime off-campus as well as on-campus, the student should be allowed to have her or his attorney at the hearing in order to advise the student.

Two recent cases concerning right to counsel in the academic arena are *University of Houston* v. *Sabeti* (1984) and *Hall* v. *Medical College of Ohio at Toledo* (1984). In the first case, the student who initiated this suit claimed that he had been expelled for plagiarism in violation of his right to due process.

Specifically, he claimed that his counsel at the hearing was allowed only to advise him and was not permitted to address the hearing board nor question witnesses. His initial hearing was held before the engineering department, which found him guilty and recommended expulsion since this was his second academic dishonesty offense. His second hearing was conducted by the college honesty board, and it was here that his counsel, a law student, was not permitted to speak, argue, or question witnesses. The student directed his questions to the hearing officer, who asked them of the witnesses; however, not all questions the student presented were asked of the witnesses. The university was not represented by counsel.

In overturning the lower court's decision and finding for the university, the district court noted that college students do not forfeit their constitutional rights by attending a university; however, due process is a flexible concept. The university gained no advantage in refusing to permit the participation of counsel, and none of the factors favoring representation through counsel were present: "(1) the proceeding was not criminal; (2) the government did not proceed through counsel; (3) the student was mature and educated; (4) the student's knowledge of the events enabled him to develop the facts adequately; and (5) the other aspects of the hearing, taken as a whole, were fair" (p. 689).

The second case, *Hall*, involved a medical student who was dismissed for allegedly consulting an old examination while taking another. He was afforded a hearing and an administrative appeal. At the hearing, he was allowed to testify on his own behalf, to present his own witnesses, and to cross-examine witnesses. He was not allowed an attorney. A copy of the hearing panel's report and a transcript of the hearing were made available to the student. The student alleged that his due process rights had been violated by the college since he was not allowed to be represented by an attorney.

The court upheld the university, noting that aside from the question of the attorney, the college could not have furnished more complete procedural safeguards. The hearing was not a courtroom trial, and therefore, "right to counsel" had no basis. The court noted that there was clear evidence that the student had improperly consulted an old examination while he was taking an examination, and that therefore, the college had good cause for expelling the student. His expulsion was caused not by whatever due process violation might have occurred when he was denied the assistance of legal counsel at his disciplinary hearing, but by his academic dishonesty.

It should be underscored that the court found no "clearly established" right of a student to be represented by counsel at a disciplinary hearing and admonished that it was not speaking to the issue of whether such a right should exist in this kind of disciplinary hearing. Therefore, the court refused to remand the case to the district court on the merits of that question. It should be pointed out that in most of the court cases involving student disciplinary proceedings, the students have been given the right to counsel. However, no court has declared that student disciplinary cases can in any way be held to be criminal proceedings, and therefore, the right to counsel is not inherent in the due process requirements for such cases.

An interim suspension may not be based upon a presumption of guilt. Rather, an interim suspension should logically be based upon facts which show that the student's continued presence on the campus constitutes a danger to ongoing campus functions, to property, to the student herself or himself, or to others. Students who are suspended on an interim basis must be accorded a preliminary hearing unless it can be shown that it is impossible or unreasonably difficult to provide it. In any event, at the earliest possible time, the student must be provided an opportunity to show why his or her continued presence on campus does not constitute a danger to campus functions, to others, to himself, or herself, or to property.

Although a student has no absolute right to the due process guarantee of notice and hearing in an academic dismissal, he or she does have the right to be advised of academic deficiencies prior to termination. This advice can be given in any form, such as notice that the student is being placed on academic probation (*Horowitz*, 1978). As mentioned earlier, when decisions and/or actions by a college or university would stigmatize a student and cause future injury, that student may be justified in receiving a due process hearing. In cases of this type, the student should be given an opportunity to defend her or his conduct and to explain it in what she or he deems the proper context.

Several recent cases illustrate the fact that courts do not require the same type of due process procedures for academic dismissals as are required in disciplinary actions. In certain cases, the courts have characterized cheating as a matter of discipline rather than as an academic matter. In *Moresco* v. *Clark* (1984), a student was suspended for two separate incidents of plagiarism. According to the university's rules for disciplinary action, the student was confronted by the accusing professor and was asked to sign a memo. A grievance hearing was held where the student was found guilty, but she was not provided the findings in accordance with the rules of the university. Also, the New York State Administrative Procedure Act requires state agencies conducting adjudicatory proceedings to provide rules for appeal; to make a complete record of hearings, including the evidence presented, the findings of fact, and the reasons for the decision; and to provide a copy to the parties. The Supreme Court, Apellate Division, of New York overturned the lower court's decision, declaring that the statute in question did not apply to the proceedings that led to the student's dismissal. Quoting from *Dixon*, the court held that the student had been afforded all the necessary due process required in a disciplinary case. The court also held that the lower court had erred in finding that the student should have been provided with a written record of the proceedings and a right to counsel: "Such mandates would be counterproductive to the balance struck here between the rights of the student and the university. To do so would place on the university system an onerous fiscal and administrative burden'' (p. 845).

In accordance with this case, state institutions may or may not be subject to state procedural acts. Due consideration should be given to such provisions, although the primary source of due process is the federal Constitution.

In another case where the institution disregarded its own rules and regulations as set forth in its handbooks or brochures, the court found that the student had a contractual right to due process. In *Corso* v. *Creighton University* (1984), a Creighton University medical student was accused of cheating on his first-year final examinations. He was informed of the accusation by a letter and was told that a special committee would investigate the matter and make a recommendation to the dean of the School of Medicine. It was recommended that the student be expelled.

The student was given copies of the evidence against him but was denied his request to personally appear before the executive committee. The dean of the School of Medicine then conducted his own personal investigation, including interviews with twenty to twenty-five medical students. The accused student denied that he had cheated. However, most of the other students implicated him. Based upon all of the evidence, the dean expelled the student.

Creighton's Student Handbook created two distinct procedural formats for student discipline: one for ''academic and academic-related'' offenses and the other for ''nonacademic'' offenses (p. 531). It then delegated full authority for academic disciplinary matters to the deans of the particular schools. Nonacademic offenses, however, were handled by officials who were representatives of the university as a whole and by the University Committee on Student Discipline. The handbook also elaborated the procedures to be followed by the University Committee in the adjudication of disciplinary matters (*Note 3*, p. 531).

In addition, the handbook also provided that ''In all cases where misconduct may result in serious penalties, all procedural safeguards are observed and the student has the privilege of a hearing before the University Committee on Student Discipline.'' Based upon that provision, the student claimed that he had a contractual right to a due process hearing before the committee on student discipline. The medical school regarded the matter as an academic disciplinary matter and thus placed full authority in the dean of the medical school (pp. 531–532).

The court ruled that cheating on exams is clearly an academic matter, and that in this case, the lying was directly related to the alleged cheating. It further ruled that the school was not engaged in state action, so the relationship between the student and the school was one of contract, with the student handbook containing the provisions of that contract in this instance. The court further stated that the clear meaning of the contract was to place plenary authority in the academic deans to adjudicate academic disciplinary offenses except as to those cases that will result in the imposition of a serious penalty. In the cases where a serious penalty may follow, such as expulsion, the student is to be provided the procedural safeguard of a fair hearing before the university committee and the right to appeal the committee's findings to the president of the university. Since this was the case, the student had a contractual right to a procedural due process hearing before the University Committee on Student Discipline (p. 533).

Courts have also upheld implied contracts when an institution has consistently or traditionally practiced certain procedures. However, in the absence of arbitrary or capricious treatment, the courts continue to adhere to the institution's decision, as is illustrated in the case *Regents of University of Michigan* v. *Ewing* (1985). Here, the lower court found for a medical student who had been expelled from the medical program at the University of Michigan. He had repeated academic difficulties and was advised that any future deficiencies would lead to dismissal. When the student failed the first part of a licensing examination, the college concluded that the student did not have the right to retake the exam and dismissed the student. The student appealed on the grounds that the university, by a pattern of practice as well as a statement in a promotional pamphlet, led a qualified student to believe that he would be allowed to retake the licensing examination. The court pointed out that the U.S. Supreme Court has held that property interests which are created and defined by existing rules, understandings, or agreements may give rise to constitutional protections. It ruled that there is an implied understanding when one is admitted to a college or university that he will not be arbitrarily dismissed. The court noted that medical students were routinely given a second opportunity to pass that particular examination. Further, the court noted that a university promotional pamphlet entitled "On Becoming a Doctor" stated that a qualified student would be given a second chance to take the examination and that this had been the consistent practice of the university.

The U.S. Supreme Court overturned the lower court's decision, pointing out that it assumed the existence of a constitutionally protectable property right in the student's continued enrollment. Thus the question was whether the university had acted arbitrarily in dropping the student from the program without permitting a reexamination. The Court pointed out that the student's claim must be that the university misjudged his fitness to remain a student. In ruling that the student had not been denied any substantive due process right as a result of the decision to dismiss him from the program, the Court reasoned that the record unmistakably demonstrated that the faculty's decision was made conscientiously and with careful deliberation, based on an evaluation of the entirety of the student's academic career. The Court declared that "Considerations of profound importance counsel restrained judicial review of the substance of academic decision" (p. 513). It also declared its concern for "a reluctance to trench on the prerogatives of state and local educational institutions and our responsibility to safeguard their academic freedom, 'a special concern of the First Amendment'" (p. 514).

Rules and regulations structured and published in handbooks and so on must be consistently followed. For example, in *Morrison* v. *University of Oregon Health Sciences* (1984), a dental student was dismissed for "lack of professional skills development and lack of adequate clinical performance." He brought suit seeking review of his dismissal and was granted one before the Academic Dismissal Hearing Committee. The student handbook specified that the committee would "review and evaluate only the evidence and information presented at the hearing" (p. 441). In addition, Oregon statutes provide that in a contested case hearing, only evidence which is part of the record will be considered in the determination of the case.

When the committee went into closed session, a faculty member who was not on the committee engaged the committee in a verbal interchange, making statements about the student which were not in the original record of the hearing. The committee upheld the dismissal. The student alleged that consideration of such comments violated his rights under both the student handbook rules and the Oregon statutes.

The court found that the committee considered matters in closed session that were not on the record in violation of the student handbook's rules and the Oregon statutes. It stated, "We find that the committee erred materially in discussing matters not in the record, particularly when such discussion included a nonmember of the committee. The entire purpose of a hearing is undermined when relevant factual information is discussed and considered for the first time in a closed session without the opportunity for objection or response" (pp. 443–444).

The court supported the findings of the committee, but was critical of the way in which they had arrived at their decision. Had the procedures been followed, the institution would have been successful in defending its decision.

In another case with similar facts, *Clayton* v. *Trustees of Princeton University* (1985), a student had been accused and found guilty by the university honor committee of cheating during a lab practical exam. The university was held to a standard requiring it to follow its own rules. The court first noted several New Jersey state court decisions regarding any judicial review of disciplinary actions of private associations. It concluded that judicial intrusion into disciplinary procedures of private associations should be confined to procedures that are fundamentally unfair.

In holding that the procedures used by Princeton had been fundamentally fair, the court declared that the procedures were adequate to safeguard a student from being unfairly convicted of cheating. It noted, however, that the hearing afforded the student was not the equivalent of a trial before a judicial tribunal, but that it was an impartial, fair proceeding with basic due process protections. Simply stated, the court declared that the student "got a fair shake."

In summary the court concluded, "Princeton places great reliance in the Honor Code and attaches considerable sanctity to it. It does not behoove this court to tell any private institution how they should handle alleged cheating as long as the dictates of fundamental fairness are met. Clayton knew about the Honor Code when he arrived, and he was found to have violated it. If the Code needs correction, it is for Princeton to correct, and not this court'' (p. 440).

The use of honor codes by institutions has been upheld by the courts as long as students are fully informed of their contents. In *Patterson* v. *Hunt* (1984), three first-year dental students accused of cheating on a pathology exam were suspended for breaching the honor code, an agreement they had signed upon entering dental school. The university has an honor code about which each student is informed upon entering the school. The accused students were each informed of its existence and had signed a document agreeing to abide by the conditions set forth in the code. In addition to prohibiting cheating or assisting others to cheat, the code states that students who suspect others of cheating must issue a warning to the individual through or with the knowledge of an honor council member. Two students had used an answer key during an exam, and a third student had known of the occurrence. The students were asked to appear before the honor council, where they were questioned separately and were not allowed to discuss the proceedings. All three were found guilty and were suspended by the dean. The court, in finding for the college, noted that because the students had entered a guilty plea they had waived their rights to object to due process violations. It was also noted that, although previous honor code violations had been dealt with differently, each violation must be approached and evaluated in light of the specific facts of each case.

It should be noted that in the use of honor codes, selective enforcement is not a constitutional violation as long as that selectivity is not based on some unjustifiable standard like race or religion. The Supreme Court praised professional schools for using honor codes that upheld violations with some type of punishment.

Decisions made by educators, even ones which result in disenrollment, will not be overturned by the courts in the absence of any clearly capricious or arbitrary treatment by the institution. One such case occurred where a second-year cadet at the Maritime College was disenrolled after it was determined that he was not "suited for the regimented life of the college." In *Sabin* v. *State University of New York Maritime College at Fort Schuyler* (1983), the student, who had been charged with vandalism and possession of drug-related paraphernalia, had been accorded a hearing based on college rules. He was represented by an attorney and was allowed to challenge evidence, present his own proof, and cross-examine witnesses. The student had a good academic record but had accumulated a large number of demerits, and evidence of a lack of sobriety was recorded. The student was allowed the opportunity to discuss the case with the commandant, who disenrolled him at the end of the interview.

The court noted that the student had received a hearing in full accordance with the college's rules, and that there was nothing to support the idea that the student's previous disenrollment had affected the college's judgment. The court further found that there was no capricious or arbitrary behavior on the part of the college and that disenrollment was not unfair punishment.

When a student has been afforded due process and a favorable decision has been rendered for that student, the institution must abide by that decision. Courts have held that for an institution to do otherwise would be an illusion of due process. In reality, such action by the institution would be arbitrary and capricious. *Jones* v. *Board of Governors of University of North Carolina* (1983) involved a student in the School of Nursing at the University of North Carolina at Charlotte. While taking an exam, the student had asked the professor for clarification of two questions. After the test was concluded, she told some other students that the professor had told her the answer to two questions. Five days later, the student was called in to see the dean of the Nursing School, who informed her that several students had accused her of cheating on the examination. She was given the choice of taking an "F" in the course or being prosecuted in the student court. Upon choosing the student court, the procedures regarding the student's hearing did not follow the full panoply of procedural due process. Formal notice of the hearing was not given until the day of the hearing. She was not provided notice of the identity of her accusers, the nature of the evidence against her, or the specifics of the charges.

Under university rules, neither party was entitled to an attorney; however, the dean appeared at the hearing and acted as "attorney for the prosecution" and, according to the student, "intimidated" the student justices. The student court found her guilty and imposed, as a sanction, a grade of "F" for the course, as well as disciplinary probation for a semester. No record was made of the hearing.

The student then retained counsel and filed a written appeal with the chancellor of the university. She was granted a new hearing before the chancellor's hearing panel. They deliberated a day before finding the student not guilty, as charged.

The attorney for the College of Nursing then appealed to the chancellor, arguing for the student's guilt and urging that the "advice" of the hearing panel be "considered of little use or consequence." The chancellor then directed that the vice-chancellor for academic affairs review the case and render a decision. The vice-chancellor concluded that the student was guilty and reinstated the original penalty recommended by the student court.

The student brought suit seeking a temporary restraining order to compel her reinstatement as a student in good standing under university rules. She alleged that the chancellor had arbitrarily disregarded university rules, had rendered her procedurally fair hearing before the hearing panel meaningless, and had thus denied her due process of law.

The court noted in the district court's decision that the actions by the university were such that it appeared that due process had been conducted but that, in substance, the university had acted arbitrarily. In finding for the student, the court stated that its role is not to proscribe the procedures that must be followed in all cases of student discipline, but to determine whether the procedures afforded in this case were constitutionally adequate. It concluded that the student had demonstrated probable success on the merits, in alleging that she had been denied due process.

The courts continually view questions of dismissal of students in light of the conduct of the institution—whether arbitrary, capricious, or in bad faith. When conduct of the institution proves to be out of the bounds of consistent and fair practices, the courts rarely hesitate to find for the student, but they tend to avoid any decisions that involve academic standards or degrees of discipline. The standards of academics and the discipline of the institutions are respected by the courts as the responsibilities of that institution without question (*Wood* v. *Strickland*, 1975).

Increasingly, the federal courts have viewed alleged cheating and plagiarism in the same light as disciplinary situations and are beginning to require that students be afforded due process in these cases. Alleged cheating and plagiarism reflect upon the student's good name, reputation, and integrity. Therefore, the student has a liberty interest, in addition to a possible property interest, which would trigger due process guarantees.

Courts generally will respect institutions' procedures for handling academic affairs cases, as well as their decisions resolving these cases. When colleges have not adhered to the conclusions of hearings in academic disciplinary cases, the courts have intervened in accordance with a ''liberty'' interest. Again, the threat to the student's good name, reputation, honor, or integrity requires due process when questions of cheating are involved.

A recent case illustrates the fact that instructors cannot refuse to change a grade where the student has prevailed in a due process hearing. In addition, a ''liberty'' interest exists where a student's good name and reputation are concerned. In *Lightsey* v. *King* (1983), a student at the U.S. Merchant Marine Academy was charged by an instructor with cheating on an examination and was given a grade of zero. As a result of the zero, he failed the course and was therefore rendered ineligible for the Third Mates Licensing Examination offered by the U.S. Coast Guard.

The instructor reported the alleged cheating to the academy's honor board. After a hearing by the honor board, the student was found to be ''not guilty.'' The instructor then refused to change the grade of zero, and this refusal was supported by the administration of the academy. The instructor and the administration claimed that ''grades'' are delegated to the faculty and reviewable only by the administration. The student alleged that his due process rights had been violated by the refusal to change the grade after the honor board had found him ''not guilty'' of cheating.

The court found that the refusal by the institution to change the zero grade was a violation of the student's due process rights when the student had been found "not guilty" at a due process hearing. It noted that "despite the artful semantics of the defendants," this was not a case of discretionary grading but a disciplinary matter (p. 648). It further noted that the academy had not determined the matter to be an "academic" matter involving "grades" until the honor board had cleared the student of the charge of cheating. The court declared that had the academy claimed that the matter was an "academic" one from the outset and applied its "academic" procedures fairly, rationally, and in good faith, then the court would not have presumed to question the academy's judgment (p. 648).

The court reasoned that whether or not the student had a "property" interest at stake, he certainly had a "liberty" interest. This was so because the student's good name, reputation, honor, or integrity was at stake because of what the government was doing to him. Therefore, he must be given appropriate due process.

In ruling that the student's due process rights had been violated, the court declared that "The procedural requirements of due process presuppose that the results of those required procedures will be respected" (p. 649). It further pointed out that there is no difference between failing to provide a due process hearing and providing one but ignoring the outcome. Once the honor board found the student "not guilty," the academy was bound by its regulations to respect that verdict. A failure to do so constituted arbitrary and capricious action.

This case underscores the fact that an institution must carry out the procedures and regulations it creates for itself. To afford students due process and not to abide by the results of a valid due process hearing leaves students with an empty right.

An illustration of the court's attitude toward disciplinary proceedings as distinguished from criminal proceedings can be found in *Jaska* v. *Regents of University of Michigan* (1984). In this case, a student was accused of cheating on his statistics final examination. The statistics professor had received an anonymous telephone call from a student who said that he had seen the accused student switch exam cover sheets and submit his cover sheet with a classmate's exam. The professor's inspection of the exams revealed that the student's cover sheet was attached to another student's exam. A copy of the charges was presented to the student, and he met several times with the Assistant Dean of Student Academic Affairs. He was given a *Manual of Procedure for the Academic Judiciary* and was afforded a hearing before a four-member panel consisting of two students and two professors. The panel unanimously found the student guilty of cheating and recommended a two-semester suspension. The student wrote a letter to the Academic Judiciary Appeal Board seeking leniency. He confessed his cheating, and the appeal board then reduced his penalty to a one-semester suspension.

The student brought action, alleging that the proceedings against him had been fundamentally unfair and that he had been denied procedural due process in violation of the Fourteenth Amendment. Specifically, he charged that the *Manual* had not been followed, that no representative for him had been present at the hearing, that no transcript of the hearing had been provided, that he had not been permitted to confront the anonymous accuser, and that no detailed explanation of the reasons for finding him guilty had been given.

The court noted that the student was entitled to the protection of the Fourteenth Amendment. However, the court pointed out that a school disciplinary proceeding is not a criminal trial and that a student accused of cheating is not entitled to all of the procedural safeguards afforded criminal defendants. Further, noncompliance with the *Manual* simply did not rise to the level of a constitutional deprivation (p. 1251). However, courts are split on the issue of a representative at hearings. In this case, the court concluded that the student did not have a constitutional right to be represented either by counsel or by any representative at his suspension hearing. Nor was there any requirement for a transcript or recording of the hearing. Further, the real accuser, the court said, was the professor and not the anonymous person. Again, there is no constitutional right to confront or cross-examine in school disciplinary proceedings.

In a summary statement, the court declared that since the student

> was threatened with the loss of a protected interest, he was entitled to the protection of the Due Process Clause. The Due Process Clause requires that the plaintiff be given adequate notice of the charges against him, and a meaningful opportunity to be heard. The specific procedures required in any given circumstances depend on the nature of the interests affected, the risk of an erroneous deprivation of that interest through the procedures used, and the burdens on the state of additional or substitute procedures. Balancing these factors in this case, I conclude that plaintiff has been afforded his due process rights (p. 1254).

A two-step inquiry outlined by the U.S. Supreme Court suggests that first, a determination must be made regarding whether due process applies within the Fourteenth Amendment's protection of liberty and property interests (*Board of Regents* v. *Roth*, 1972). Second, if due process applies, then a determination must be made as to what process is due (*Morrissey* v. *Brewer*, 1972).

The real question is how much process is due under the circumstances (Golden, 1982). In a recent case, *Nash* v. *Auburn University* (1985), the court concluded that two students who were charged with academic dishonesty did indeed have both a "property" and a "liberty" interest in pursuing their education. In that case, the two students in Auburn University's College of Veterinary Medicine were charged with giving or receiving assistance or communications during an anatomy examination. They were given several days to prepare a defense to be presented before the Student Board of Ethical

Relations. At that hearing, they were accompanied by an attorney who was allowed to counsel and advise them during the hearings but was not allowed to participate directly in the hearings. The students were not allowed to directly cross-examine witnesses; rather, they were allowed to direct questions to the witnesses through the student chancellor of the board. The board unanimously found the students guilty and recommended that they be suspended for one year. The students appealed that decision to the dean, who referred the case to the college's Faculty Committee on Admission and Standards for a recommendation. The students presented both oral and written statements to the committee, which voted unanimously to uphold the decision of the student board. Ultimately the president of the university affirmed those decisions.

The students brought action alleging that they had been denied both procedural and substantive due process rights. They claimed that the hearings had been flawed and that the decision to suspend them was arbitrary and capricious action not supported by substantial evidence.

The Court found that the students had not been denied any procedural due process rights. It conceded that the students did have both a property and a liberty interest but agreed that there is no set procedure to be followed in due process. Accused students must be afforded some kind of notice and some kind of hearing at which they have a fair and reasonable opportunity to defend themselves. There is no absolute right to have an attorney present their case, according to the courts, and no absolute right to cross-examine witnesses. The court affirmed that there was reasonable evidence to support the suspension. The degree of due process required depends on the specific facts of each case. However, conscientious academic administrators will follow the procedures outlined in catalogs, handbooks, and so on, to ensure sufficient process would be given the student.

There has been little litigation in the area of degree rescission. In a 1723 case of England's King's Bench, *Rex* v. *Cambridge University*, the court declared that an academic degree is "a great office, a dignity and a freehold. And it is a place for life" (Stevens, 1985).

In a recent case concerning degree rescission, *Crook* v. *Baker* (1984), Crook was accused of having used false and fabricated research data for his degree. He was given a hearing before the Ad Hoc Disciplinary Committee in order to defend himself. The hearing did not follow the procedural requirements of a trial-type proceeding. The results of the Ad Hoc Disciplinary Committee were reported to the executive board of the graduate school, which unanimously recommended to the regents that Crook's degree be rescinded. The board of regents allowed the holder's attorney to present a fifteen-minute argument on behalf of the holder, after which they voted to rescind the degree. The holder brought suit, alleging that he had both a property interest and a liberty interest in his degree.

The court ruled that the holder of a degree has a legitimate claim of entitlement to his degree. It pointed out that this entitlement is grounded in the university's stated requirements for the degree and its certification, through its faculty; that the holder had satisfied those requirements; that the governing board had agreed to award the degree; and that the degree had actually been conferred. In summary, the court declared "That legitimate claim of entitlement gives rise to a lifetime property interest in the degree" (p. 1554). The court outlined the following procedural safeguards which a university must follow before proceeding to rescind a degree, assuming that the university did have the authority to rescind:

1. Adequate notice of the charges and evidence against him, given sufficiently in advance of the hearing to allow for adequate preparation of a defense;
2. An effective opportunity to be heard and present evidence;
3. The opportunity to be meaningfully represented by counsel, and to have that counsel fully participate in all proceedings;
4. An effective opportunity to confront and cross-examine all adverse witnesses;
5. The opportunity to present evidence to the decision maker;
6. A decision based solely on the evidence adduced at the hearing; and
7. An impartial decision maker. (p. 1558)

The lawful mission and goals of each institution of higher learning should determine the nature of student discipline. This discipline may be viewed as a part of the learning process—the instruction of the students. It may be viewed as a guidance function which attempts to lead the student in the proper direction dictated by the institution's purposes. It may also be viewed as completely divorced from the academic process, with no relationship to or bearing on the instruction of students. Only when the case of permanent expulsion or extended suspension arises, do student disciplinary proceedings even approach a resemblance of criminal proceedings, and even here they simply determine that the student is no longer acceptable in the institution. Student disciplinary cases do not in any way actually parallel criminal proceedings, even in expulsion cases. There is no imprisonment, fine, or loss of any freedom guaranteed under the U.S. Constitution. The only determination made has been that the student's continued attendance at the institution and the implementation of the goals of the institution are at odds, and that those goals can be best served by the removal of the student from the institution. This is the most extreme case in student discipline.

For cases which involve reprimands, probation, and other lesser disciplinary measures, it has been said that this is merely an extension of the teaching process carried on through guidance and counseling implementation in some instances. However, there are those who would refute this position and who would hold that student discipline in any degree has absolutely no relation to the teaching process and should be viewed as completely separate from that function. Arguments can be offered which try to show that discipline is not one of the most important or effective means of controlling conduct.

In the most severe of discipline cases, the student may suffer irreparable harm to his or her future. Since such cases become a part of their records, students may be refused admission to another institution and may be harmed socially and economically. For these reasons, administrative proceedings should be as fair and as reasonable as the lawful purposes of the institution will allow. The very nature of higher education dictates that this be so. However, when the preoccupation with the student offender and his or her rights becomes so great as to interfere with the overall purpose of the institution, there must be a weighing of the individual right against the purposes and the good of all concerned. There should be no real conflict here if the purposes are wholesome and if the administrative procedures are fair.

In the *General Order on Judicial Standards of Procedure and Substance in Review of Student Discipline in Tax-Supported Institutions of Higher Education*, 45 F.R.D. 133, 145 (W.D. Mo., 1968), the court stated:

> In the field of discipline, scholastic and behavioral, an institution may establish any standards reasonably relevant to the lawful missions, processes, and functions of the institution. It is not a lawful mission, process, or function of [a public] institution to prohibit the exercise of a right guaranteed by the Constitution or a law of the United States to a member of the academic community in the circumstances. Therefore, such prohibitions are not reasonably relevant to any lawful mission, process or function of [a public] institution.
>
> Standards so established may apply to student behavior on and off the campus when relevant to any lawful mission, process, or function of the institution. By such standards of student conduct the institution may prohibit any action or omission which impairs, interferes with, or obstructs the missions, processes, and functions of the institution.
>
> Standards so established may require scholastic attainments higher than the average of the population and may require superior ethical and moral behavior. In establishing standards of behavior, the institution is not limited to the standards or the forms of criminal laws. (p. 145)

While the student has the responsibility of adhering to the standards of the institution and of following the proper channels and procedures, the administration also has the responsibility to see that the standards are consistent with the lawful purposes of the institution. By creating and adhering to fair standards, the institution maintains its integrity and fulfills its purposes.

ADMISSIONS

The area of college and university admissions has been subject to an ever-increasing degree of judicial challenge and scrutiny. Several reasons have been advanced for this recent judicial activity.

The emphasis on civil rights developed in the 1960s, initially applied to student discipline, has been broadened to include admissions issues as well.

Students are now applying standards developed in the disciplinary arena to admissions criteria and procedures. The notion of students as consumers of education has also had its spin-off effect on admissions programs when students spend a great deal of time and money preparing for graduate training only to be rejected by the institution of their choice. This rejection, coupled with the increased importance of graduate training for professional careers, has led these unsuccessful candidates to question the criteria established for admission and the processes and procedures used to evaluate candidates.

Colleges and universities have the inherent right to determine admissions criteria, but once established, these standards must be applied equally. The increasing intrusion of the federal government has made the task of the admissions committees even more difficult in recent years. The proliferation of federal laws and regulations, designed to protect individual rights, has created a number of complex issues which are being litigated with increased frequency.

The standards established must comply with the requirements imposed by other relationships. For example, private institutions have a contractual relationship with students. Once the admission standards are established and advertised, the students must be evaluated in accord with the announced criteria. Furthermore, private institutions which can be shown to be acting under "color of state law" and public institutions must also conform to the U.S. Constitution. In this respect, institutions must be careful not to violate equal protection guarantees. At the same time, the admission standards of public or private institutions which are recipients of federal financial assistance must comply with a variety of federal statutes, each designed to prohibit discrimination in educational programs and activities. Sometimes it is difficult to know if admissions standards which comply with one requirement are in violation of another.

In the absence of arbitrariness, capriciousness, or bad faith, college and university officials have broad discretionary power to determine the fitness of applicants to enter academic programs. The courts have pointed out that institutions are not limited to considering objective criteria for admission and that subjective criteria may be utilized also (*Arizona Board of Regents* v. *Wilson*, 1975). However, whatever criteria are employed must not be utilized in a discriminatory manner.

The courts have upheld the institution's right to refuse entrance or to expel a student who is already enrolled if false information has been given at the time of admission. In *Martin* v. *Helstad* (1983), an applicant for admission to the University of Wisconsin Law School completed the application form but failed to disclose his 1978 conviction and incarceration for aiding and abetting interstate transportation of forged securities. The form specifically requested information regarding criminal conduct, and the applicant did disclose that he was a former legal offender but that he had received a full pardon in 1971 from the governor of Wisconsin.

The applicant was accepted for admission, but the law school later learned of his 1978 conviction and incarceration when personnel from the Milan Correctional Institution and members of the U.S. Bureau of Prisons in Madison called the law school in order to coordinate his parole release with the orientation program for new students at the law school. He was advised to submit additional information regarding his conviction and incarceration. In response to this request, he submitted a letter. However, his admission was then revoked based upon his failure to make a full and truthful disclosure of material information which was specifically requested and which was relevant in making decisions for admission to law school and to the bar. He was told by letter of this decision and of why the information he had submitted was insufficient to support the failure to disclose the information on the application.

The applicant brought action, alleging that he had been denied due process. The court stated that an offer of admission to a law school and the subsequent acceptance of that offer creates a mutually explicit understanding that the accepted applicant will be admitted. The court concluded that "While an accepted applicant has only a slight property interest in admission prior to matriculation, I conclude that there is a sufficient interest so as to require some procedural due process in the factual determination of nondisclosure when that determination is the basis for rescinding an acceptance" (p. 1482).

Although the court held that due process was required, it further ruled that the applicant in this case had been afforded adequate notice and an ample opportunity to explain his prior nondisclosure. It declared that in the particular circumstances of this case, where the factual question was sharply focused and extremely narrow, and the law school had before it all the pertinent information, the school officials were not required to provide the applicant an opportunity to appear in person.

The court summarized that "Because I am convinced that the risk of an erroneous determination of the nondisclosure issue was negligible, and because additional procedural safeguards would contribute little in the way of increased fairness or reliability of the underlying determination, I conclude that the procedural due process afforded plaintiff in this case was constitutionally sufficient" (p. 1485).

The court reaffirmed that academic institutions are accorded great deference in their freedom to determine who may be admitted to study at their institutions. As long as admissions standards remain within constitutionally permissible parameters, it is exclusively within the province of higher educational institutions to establish criteria for admissions.

A second case illustrating false information in the admissions process is found in *North* v. *West Virginia Board of Regents* (1985). A medical student was expelled for providing false information on his admissions application. The information North provided that was false included his grade-point average, courses taken, degrees, date of birth, and marital status. He alleged that his expulsion was unjustified because there was no applicable rule prohibiting him from making false statements since he was not a student at the time he made application. However, the court, in finding for the university, said that "academic administrators must be given wide discretion to determine dismissals. As long as the conduct of educators is not high-handed, arbitrary or capricious, educators should be left alone to do their job without interference from the judiciary which has neither the expertise nor the insight to evaluate those decisions" (pp. 146–147).

Although the courts afford much discretion in the admissions standards of higher educational institutions, administrators must adhere to three limitations. First, admission policies cannot be arbitrary or capricious. Second, published guidelines must be honored. Finally, race, sex, age, handicap, or citizenship cannot be unjustifiably considered in admissions policies. As long as these criteria are adhered to, the institution has the discretion to make determinations in admissions, which includes rejection based on false admission statements.

ACADEMIC ADVISING

Academic advising occurs under the umbrella of academic affairs, which involves a contractual relationship. Frequent updating of the legal decisions in academics is a must for advisers, since they are on the front line of the college or university in dealing with students. Often the success or failure of the student's education and growth is influenced greatly by the advising function.

Institutions should be conscious of an adviser's obligations, which might be created by unequivocal statements regarding adviser's responsibilities. These usually appear in an adviser's handbook and other publications readily available to the student. An increasing emphasis on quality advising to enhance retention brings added responsibilities to the adviser. Scheduling, registration procedures, degree and program requirements, referral services, and possibly career counseling are examples of information and procedures the adviser is expected to know. Thus, if institutions promise such services from their advising system, they should ensure that their advisers will be able to deliver these services. Where advisers fail to perform their contractual obligation, liability could be present.

Most college catalogs state that the ultimate responsibility for knowing degree requirements rests with the student. These statements normally would protect advisers if they commit an advising error. Generally, the adviser is not going to be held personally liable for erroneous advising in the absence of gross negligence, irresponsible behavior, or arbitrary or capricious treatment of the student (Young, 1982b). An accurate record of advising sessions would help solve any disputes over the content of previous advising and would also serve as a legitimate protection against claims of erroneous advising. Since advisers maintain educational records (records of advisees' grades and other academic information), they must understand the provisions of the Family Educational Rights and Privacy Act.

In *Wilson* v. *Illinois Benedictine College* (1983), Craig Wilson, a senior accounting major at Illinois Benedictine College, a private institution, was notified during his final semester that he would not be graduated because of his failure to obtain a grade of "C" or better in two economics courses. The college bulletin stated that a student must earn a "C" average for 120 semester hours of work and "Only courses in which a student has received a 'C' or better may be applied to the major. Repetition may be required if the student received a 'D' in a course in his or her major, and specific departmental regulations so require." The bulletin also stated that "since students are responsible for their own academic programs, and for meeting the requirements of their major department, it is recommended that they meet with their faculty advisors for counseling, at least once each semester" (p. 905).

Wilson had received two "D's" in required economics courses. He received grade reports each term, and copies of these reports were also contained in his advising file. His adviser, however, stated that he was unaware of Wilson's deficiencies until the student contacted him. The adviser thus never discussed the consequences of the "D's," although he met with Wilson each semester. The student was offered several options for repeating the courses, but Wilson rejected them and sought an injunction requiring the college to graduate him.

The court, in finding for the college, agreed that the relationship between the college and the student was contractual based on terms of the contract as presented in the institution's catalog. It further stated that the catalog was not ambiguous in its statement that the responsibility for meeting the requirements of a student's academic program rested with the student. Wilson never consulted the bulletin nor inquired about the consequences of his low grades. There was no obligation for the college to notify the student of a deficiency, nor was the student required to meet with his adviser. This was merely a recommendation, not an obligation.

The court did not hold the adviser responsible for any omission of warnings due to the printed statement of the catalog. The importance of written policies, especially in advisement, cannot be emphasized enough.

LIABILITY

Consumerism abounds throughout the country today and has also come to the campus. The ultimate in consumerism on today's campuses is liability, as evidenced by two recent cases, *Eiseman* v. *State* (1985), and *Life Chiropracter College, Inc.* v. *Fuchs* (1985).

In *Eiseman*, a conditionally released prisoner, Larry Campbell, who was attending the State University College at Buffalo under a special program for the economically and educationally disadvantaged, raped and murdered Rhonda Eiseman in an off-campus apartment. He also murdered Thomas Tunney, another student, and stabbed a nonstudent acquaintance during the same episode.

In his application for admission to the program, Campbell had listed different prisons for his present and former addresses. He had discussed his background with a college counselor, who had made no attempt to check on the prisoner's emotional or personal background. Eiseman's parents brought suit against the state for damages on the basis that the college had failed to inquire into Campbell's background and suitability for admission and the prison's failure to warn the college of Campbell's mental illness and drug abuse.

The court, in finding for the Eisemans, pointed out that once the college had begun a program which would be open to convicted felons, it had a duty to establish criteria to screen applicants to determine if they posed a risk to the college community. Quoting from the *Palsgraf* formulation, the court noted that "the risk reasonably to be perceived defines the duty to be obeyed" (p. 965) (see *Palsgraf* v. *Long Island Railroad Company*, 1928). Thus, the college was "negligent in admitting Campbell without any attempt to determine the nature of the risk he might present. Moreover, the College breached both a statutory and an assumed duty to its students in administering the SEEK program without adequate study, safeguards or inquiry, thereby creating an unreasonable risk of harm to the College community including Rhona Eiseman" (p. 963).

The court was very clear in pointing out that this reasoning and analysis applied only to the special circumstances of this case—where a college is enrolling persons from penal institutions. The requirement to screen such applicants does not generalize to the entire college population. The court said that the admission of a convicted felon gave rise to an inference by others that he was just another student, and that it was thus predictable that students would interact with him, neglect to take precautions, and invite him into their homes and apartments.

In the *Fuchs* case, a student was accused of falsifying grade change forms. He was given a hearing at which several instructors testified that they had not signed the grade change forms. The student was given the rudiments of due process at a student judiciary committee hearing. As a result of the hearing, the student was suspended for three quarters.

The court held that there was no evidence that the suspension had been administered in an arbitrary or capricious manner. The student had alleged fraud by claiming that the school bulletin provided that he would be allowed to finish his education. He also alleged that he had been slandered by statements made during the course of the hearing.

The court ruled that the college was not guilty of fraud. The allegation by the student that the college bulletin had led the student to believe that he would be allowed to finish his education was not upheld. The court further held that there was no allegation of conduct by the college that could be considered so "humiliating, terrifying, or insulting as to give rise to a cause of action for intentional inflection of emotional distress" (p. 49). Finally, the court held that the student had not been slandered by any statement at the hearing.

CONCLUSIONS

All colleges and universities have rules and regulations relating to students. In general, the extent to which institutions may subject students to certain rules and regulations depends upon the legal relationship between the student and the college. These rules and regulations must be adhered to and, even in adherence, frequently lead to litigation regarding academic matters.

The voluntary application of the spirit and principles of due process to academic affairs can reduce the incentives for legalism and reliance upon the courts by students when they feel aggrieved. With clearly defined grievance procedures in place, courts will generally decline to intervene until a student exhausts this administrative remedy. Institutions or individual departments or divisions should outline procedures that students must follow in registering grievances. The following suggested procedures should be construed not as specific prescriptions to cover every case, but as guidelines:

1. Students should be given catalogs, handbooks, and other pertinent publications to inform them of the rules and regulations governing their college career.
2. Students should be given a syllabus on the first day of class and should be informed of the ground rules for attendance, tardiness, and so on.
3. In the course syllabus, the student should be informed of the instructor's regulations, the grading process (whether objective or subjective), the assignment procedures, class participation, attitude, and any other criteria pertinent to successful completion of the course.
4. Every student should be given the ground rules about plagiarism, footnotes, and other research processes.
5. There should be published guidelines for the prosecution of cheating, guaranteeing due process similar to the disciplinary process.
6. There should be an appeals procedure for any academic decision. The burden of proof would rest upon the apellant.

Implementation and promulgation of these recommendations would guarantee that the institution would develop and maintain a responsible attitude toward students, and that students would understand more clearly their responsibilities in the educational process. The channeling of complaints through an appeals procedure would formalize a fair and reasonable process which does not exist on many campuses today.

Arrival of consumerism on the campus and the lowered age of majority have probably been major factors in the increase of cases involving academic affairs. Consumerism on-campus today considers whether or not an institution delivers to the student the product it claims to deliver in its various publications, as well as in oral presentations. As legal adults, students must accept more responsibility for their actions on-campus and thus may also have a greater inclination to press charges against the institution when they believe they have received arbitrary or capricious treatment. This does not mean that all students might file a court suit when they reach the age of majority, but since they must accept the responsibilities of that status, they will most likely be more jealous of their rights. An understanding of the legal parameters will ensure a responsible attitude toward students and will protect their rights as well as those of the institution. The courts have consistently refused to intervene in academic matters unless there is a clear case of arbitrariness, capriciousness, or unfairness to a student. The rationale underlying this principle is simply that the courts are not qualified to pass judgment on a student's attainment of academic competence and will thus leave those decisions to responsible institutional officials. The courts have declared that, in the absence of such arbitrary and capricious treatment of students, college instructors and officials have absolute authority to determine whether or not a student should be penalized or dismissed for academic incompetence, and that they will leave such decisions to those responsible on-campus.

The courts continue to outline the rights of students and their institutions in the academic arena. Litigation in this area is on the rise, and the judiciary is more frequently involved in reviewing academic decisions. Many of the regulations, laws, and judicial decisions involving academic matters have been brought on because institutions have ignored the fact that students do not leave their constitutional or other rights when they enter the campus gates (*Tinker* v. *Des Moines Independent Community School District*, 1969). Students today are older and more consumer-oriented. They will not permit the time, money, and effort they have invested in their education to be sacrificed to arbitrary treatment. Institutions have no choice but to stay abreast of recent developments in case law as well as in statutory law. Although some litigation is inevitable, only well-informed administrators can deter necessary litigation.

REFERENCES

The Family Educational Rights and Privacy Act of 1974.
Forch, Paul J. (1983). Academic discretion and the constitution: The fundamentals for public higher education. *University of Richmond Law Review* 17: 699–719.
Golden, Edward J. (1982). College student dismissals and the Eldridge factors: What process is due? *Journal of College and University Law* 8(4): 495–509.
Haskell, Paul G. (1982). The university as trustee. *Georgia Law Review* 17(1): 1–32.
Henderson, Donald H., and Isenberg, Barry P. (1983). The law and academic evaluation and dismissal in higher education. *The Cumberland Law Review* 13: 475–497.

Kaplin, William A. (1985). *The Law of Higher Education* (2nd ed.). San Francisco: Jossey-Bass. (Idem, 1st edition, 1978.)

Katz, Katheryn D. (1983). The First Amendment's protection of expressive activity in the university classroom: A constitutional myth. *University of California, Davis Law Review* 16: 857–932.

Long, Nicholas Trott. (1985). The standard of proof in student disciplinary cases. *The Journal of College and University Law* 12(1): 71–81.

Marx, Charles A. (1984). Horowitz: A defense point of view. *Journal of Law and Education* 13(1): 51–58.

Mass, Michael A. (1980). Due process rights of students: Limitations on *Goss v. Lopez*— A retreat out of the thicket. *Journal of Law and Education* 9: 449–462.

Rehabilitation Act of 1973; Section 504; Section 7(6) 29 USCS 706(6).

Stevens, George E. (1985). Rescending a college degree: Ungowning and the law. *American Business Law Journal* 23(3): 467–477.

Title IX of the Education Amendments of 1972, 20 U.S.C. secs. 1681, Section 4.2.4.2); Section 4.3.3); Section 4.11.2); Section 3.3.2.3); 45 C.R.F. sec. 86.38.

Young, D. Parker (1970). *The Legal Aspects of Student Dissent and Discipline in Higher Education*. Athens, GA: Institute of Higher Education.

Young, D. Parker (1977). *The Yearbook of Higher Education Law*. Topeka, KA: National Organization on Legal Problems of Education.

Young, D. Parker. (1982a). Academic Affairs. *The College Student and the Courts* 5(2): 284.

Young, D. Parker. (1982b). Legal issues regarding academic advising. *NACADA Journal* 2(2): 41–46.

Young, D. Parker, and Gehring, Donald D., eds. (1983a). Tort Liability. *The College Student and the Courts* 10(2): 508.

Young, D. Parker, and Gehring, Donald D., eds. (1983b). Academic Affairs. *The College Student and the Courts* 10(3): 520.

Young, D. Parker, and Gehring, Donald D., eds. (1983c). Academic Affairs. *The College Student and the Courts* 10(4): 531–533, 537–538.

Young, D. Parker, and Gehring, Donald D., eds. (1983d). Admission. *The College Student and the Courts* 11(1): 550.

Young, D. Parker, and Gehring, Donald D., eds. (1983e). Academic Affairs. *The College Student and the Courts* 11(2): 557–558.

Young, D. Parker, and Gehring, Donald D., eds. (1983f). Notice and Hearing. *The College Student and the Courts* 11(3): 572–574.

Young, D. Parker, and Gehring, Donald D., eds. (1984a). Academic Affairs/Due Process. *The College Student and the Courts* 11(4): 583–586.

Young, D. Parker, and Gehring, Donald D., eds. (1984b). Academic Affairs. *The College Student and the Courts* 12(1): 594.

Young, D. Parker, and Gehring, Donald D., eds. (1985a). Right to Counsel. *The College Student and the Courts* 12(2): 605–607.

Young, D. Parker, and Gehring, Donald D., eds. (1985b). Academic Affairs. *The College Student and the Courts* 13(1): 643–646.

Young, D. Parker, and Gehring, Donald D., eds. (1986). Academic affairs. *The College Student and the Courts* 13(2): 654–655.

CASES

Arizona Board of Regents v. *Wilson*. (1975), 539 P.2d 943.

Bd. of Curators of Univ. of Missouri v. *Horowitz*. (1978), 435 U.S. 78, 98 S.Ct. 948.

Board of Regents v. *Roth.* (1972), 408 U.S. 564.

Cannon v. *University of Chicago.* (1979), 441 U.S. 677.

Clayton v. *Trustees of Princeton University.* (1985), 608 F.Supp. 413.

Cloud v. *Trustee of Boston University.* (1983), 720 F.2d 721.

Corso v. *Creighton University.* (1984), 731 F.2d 529.

Crook v. *Baker.* (1984), 584 F.Supp. 1531.

Davidson v. *New Orleans.* (1877), 96 U.S. 97.

Delta School of Business, Etc. v. *Shropshire.* (1981), 399 So.2d 1212.

Dixon v. *Alabama State Board of Education.* (1961), 294 F.2d. 150.

Dizick v. *Umpqua Community College.* (1979), 599 P.2d 444.

Eiseman v. *State.* (1985). 489 N.Y.S. 2d 957.

Esteban v. *Central Missouri State College.* (1969), 415 F.2d 1077.

French v. *Bashful.* (1969), 303 F.Supp 1333.

General Order on Judicial Standards of Procedure and Substance in Review of Student Discipline in Tax-Supported Institutions of Higher Ed. (1968), 45 F.R.D. 133, 145.

Goss v. *Lopez.* (1975), 419 U.S. 565, 95 S.Ct. 729.

Grossner v. *Trustees of Columbia University.* (1968), 287 F. Supp. 535.

Hall v. *Medical College of Ohio at Toledo.* (1984), 742 F.2d 299.

Idrees v. *American University of the Caribbean.* (1982), 546 F.Supp. 1342.

Ikpeazu v. *University of Nebraska.* (1985), 775 F.2d 250.

Jaska v. *Regents of University of Michigan.* (1984), 597 F.Supp. 1245.

Jones v. *Board of Governors of University of North Carolina.* (1983), 704 F.2d 713.

Keyishian v. *Board of Regents.* (1967), 385 U.S. 589.

Kraft v. *W. Alanson White Psychiatric Foundation* (1985), 498 A. 2d 1145.

Life Chiropractic College, Inc. v. *Fuchs.* (1985), 337 S.E.2d 45.

Lightsey v. *King.* (1983), 567 F.Supp. 645.

Martin v. *Helstad.* (1983), 578 F.Supp. 1473.

Moresco v. *Clark.* (1984), 475 N.Y.S.2d 843.

Morrison v. *University of Oregon Health Sciences.* (1984), 685 P.2d 439.

Morrissey v. *Brewer.* (1972), 408 U.S. 471.

Nash v. *Auburn University.* (1985), 621 F. Supp. 748.

North v. *West Virginia Board of Regents.* (1985), 332 S.E.2d 141.

Palsgraf v. *Long Island Railroad Company.* (1928), 248 N.Y. 339, 162 N.E. 99.

Patterson v. *Hunt.* (1984), 682 S.W.2d 508.

Regents of the University of Michigan v. *Ewing.* (1985), 106 S.Ct. 507, 54 L.W. 4055.

Rex v. *Cambridge University.* (1723), 92 Eng. Rep. 818.

Sabin v. *State University of New York Maritime College at Fort Schuyler.* (1983), 460 N.Y.S.2d 332.

Soglin v. *Kauffman.* (1969), 418 F.2d 163.

State ex rel. Mecurio v. *Board of Regents.* (1983), 329 N.W.2d 87.

Tinker v. *Des Moines Independent Community School District.* (1969), 393 U.S. 503, 89 S.Ct. 733.

University of Houston v. *Sabeti.* (1984), 676 S.W.2d 685.

University of Texas Health Science Center at Houston v. *Babb.* (1982), 646 S.W.2d 502.

White v. *Knowlton.* (1973), 361 F.Supp 445.

Williams v. *Howard University.* (1976), 528 F.2d 658.

Wilson v. *Illinois Benedictine College.* (1983), 445 N.E.2d 901.

Wood v. *Strickland.* (1975), 420 U.S. 308.

Woodruff v. *Georgia State University.* (1983), 304 S.E.2d 697.

Wright v. *Texas Southern University.* (1968), 392 F.2d 728.

The Expansion of Higher Education Enrollments in Agrarian and Developing Areas of the Third World

William Edgar Maxwell
University of Southern California

During the past fifteen years a lively debate has emerged in the research literature over the issue of what has caused the worldwide explosion of university enrollments, particularly in the Third World. The dialogue has had some of the stuff of good academic drama, including astonishing research findings, ideological overtones, standing-room-only panel sessions at national meetings, coteries of enthusiastic graduate students, a controversy carried out in a great stream of articles and books, and traffic in language such as revolution, "diploma disease," and charges of "facile epiphenomenalism."

In addition to clashes between ideologies and theories, there has also been a general mystification of research methods. Some of this includes the long-standing communication difficulties between area studies specialists and quantitative researchers, reflecting differing levels of skill and interest in languages, cultures, and statistical methods. The old chestnut charging the total irrelevance of statistics to any complex educational phenomenon has occasionally been dragged out of the fire and hurled as an epithet. Yet, apparently due to the arcane, inner-circle qualities of the recent statistical methods, particularly regression equations, the reaction of the field has been generally deferential to even extremely unusual statistical findings which challenge mainstream views. The literature on the topic is notably lacking in its scrutiny of the methods with which evidence has been amassed on the main ideas (for an important exception, see Craig, 1981b).

The controversy has not been perceived by the protagonists as much related to methods or ideologies, however, but rather as a debate between new and old ideas about which factors best explain the phenomenal growth of higher education. Many of these ideas have been summarized in several stimulating theoretical reviews focused primarily upon primary and secondary levels of education (Archer, 1982; Craig, 1981a; Meyer et al., 1977). The common wisdom is that national features—such as political relations, religion, and especially economics—have produced most of the variations in enrollment expansion between societies (Ben-David, 1963; Meyer, 1971). Against this view, a spate of recent research has produced evidence from global studies of about a hundred nations, on which it is argued that national characteristics do not explain post-World War II enrollments. Instead, it is proposed, a world revolution in education has flared out across the globe, and the force fanning the flames of expansion is the capitalist world economy dominated by the United States (Meyer and Hannon, 1979). Set against both of these views is a recent interpretation which argues for the independent effect of educational systems on their own enrollments (Archer, 1982). And, finally, a fourth view damns all of the foregoing as missing the point of the importance of the academic virtues of imagination and free inquiry and recommends that the elites remove the mandate for large enrollments and vocational training from the university and return the groves of academe to the unencumbered gifts of the mind.

The debate has implications far beyond theoretical questions. These implications concern such policy questions, for example, as: Are international forces on national markets and politicians so great that the overall numbers of enrollments in the Third World are beyond the control of domestic forces and political policy? If national and education elements do have some leverage over enrollments, over which enrollments do which levers operate? And, as Dore (1976) has asked, what are the consequences for the academic community?

This is rather heady stuff. It treats of globe-encircling trends among peoples, it deals with policies in high places, and it entails the ancient academic pieties. This review must follow a less exalted path, plodding along the trail and details of the ideas and evidence involved. Before commencing this journey, we may review briefly recent general trends in research on Third World higher education.

AN OVERVIEW OF RECENT COMPARATIVE HIGHER EDUCATION RESEARCH ON THE THIRD WORLD

Though research on a potentially large number of societies is relevant for this review, there are definite demarcations on the research and topics to be examined. With some exceptions, this review covers the literature published since 1970 on the expansion of enrollments in the Third World societies of Africa, Asia, and Latin America, past or present. As Altbach (1970a) has stated, before 1970 "research of a more analytical nature [was] almost entirely lacking" (p. 11).[1] Altbach and Kelly (1974, 1985; Altbach, 1970a, 1976, 1979) have compiled a series of broad bibliographies and overview essays for comparative higher education studies of Third World nations. General reviews and the history of the field of comparative higher education have also been carefully and recently documented elsewhere (Altbach, 1979; Altbach, Kelly, and Kelly, 1981; Ramirez and Meyer, 1980).

It is only recently that the Third World expansion of enrollments and the causes of this expansion have become major topics for scholarly investigation. In earlier years, the emphasis of research was more on the effects of expansion than on expansion itself. Thus expansion was seen as a secondary concern in relation to such issues as economic development, student politics, the brain drain, social development, dependency, the production and distribution of knowledge, and the development of academic quality in the Third World.

A backdrop for the growth of research on the comparative higher education of Third World nations was the midcentury American participation in three major Asian wars and a phenomenal expansion of business activity with the countries along the rim of the Pacific and Indian oceans. In the early 1960s, several studies of the economic development effects of higher education were initiated (McClelland, 1966; Harbison and Myers 1964; Peaslee, 1969). At the same time, a large group of scholars, with some coordination from the Harvard University Center for International Affairs, began research on student politics in agrarian nations (Altbach, 1968a, 1970b, 1981a; Arnove, 1971, 1977; Beckett and O'Connell, 1977; Chan, Rosen, and Unger, 1980; Emmerson, 1968; Hanna and Hanna, 1975; Liebman, Walker, and Glazer, 1972; Lipset, 1968; Lipset and Altbach, 1970; Nakata, 1975; Prizzia and Sinsawasdi, 1974; Rosen, 1981, 1982). A review and update of this area of research has just recently appeared (Altbach, 1984). Another major area of research on students has concerned the international migrations of students between the higher education systems of various countries, particularly from the Third World to the industrial and powerful nations (Agarwal and Winkler, 1985; Altbach, Kelly, and Lulat, 1985; Barber, Altbach, and Myers, 1984; Burn, 1980; Lulat and Altbach, 1985; Myers, 1972; Spaulding and Flack, 1976).

Skepticism over investment in and the social development impact of higher education also began to mount in the late 1960s (Ward, 1974), resulting in two different ideological interpretations and research directions. In the first of these directions, Western observers committed to the premises of modernization, and usually also to capitalism, expanded research on the social development activities of universities (Thompson and Fogel, 1976) and on the capital benefits to individuals investing in higher education (Psacharopoulos, 1973, 1980, 1982). A second direction emerged in studies undertaken by some Third World and, more recently, Western scholars. These analysts rejected the assumption that development was occurring, or could occur, in their societies. With imperialism theories revised under the new banners of dependency, neocolonialism, and world systems analysis, these theorists contended that institutions such as universities were part of a world system of domination of agrarian and underdeveloped societies (Altbach, 1971, 1977, 1981b; Altbach and Kelly,

1978, 1984; Amin, 1975; Arnove, 1980; Berman, 1979; Foley, 1984; Frank, 1965; Kraus, Maxwell, and Vanneman, 1979; Wallerstein, 1974). A related area of study has investigated the worldwide production and distribution of knowledge as a facet of imperialism (Altbach, 1975, in press; Altbach and Rathgeber, 1980; Eisemon, 1981, 1982; Spitzberg, 1980).

A recent development has been the growth of collections of international census data, which has permitted a variety of global statistical analyses, particularly multiple-regression equations, concerning the relations between societies and higher education (Chenery and Syrquin, 1975; Meyer, 1971; Meyer and Hannan, 1979; Sica and Prechel, 1981).

Finally, a few recent studies have criticized almost all of these foregoing research traditions for their emphasis on economic development outcomes, charging that a preoccupation with vocational training and mobility in Third World societies has led to the overexpansion of enrollments where the intellectual climate is one of testing and sorting of students rather than a celebration of academic imagination and a quest for knowledge (Court, 1980; Dore, 1976).

Ideology and Analysis

The reader will note in the preceding chronology of research the frequently close interplay between values and hypotheses, for both the ideological right and left, which is characteristic of the social sciences. Both sides of the argument tend, however, to take a Western materialist and liberal emphasis by focusing on economic development and social equality. The main theme projected by this emphasis is manifested in the general research question: What are and what can be the effects of higher education and national development upon each other? This question is sometimes rephrased, though much less often, to also address the development of political freedom for both Third World persons and Third World nations.

Against this first theme, a second chord is heard from scholars who resent the intrusion of the concerns of the marketplace and economic development activities into the academy. This point of view is generally disturbed by any government interference with academic freedom, from the right or the left, and seems especially concerned over government and mass pressures on the universities to be especially concerned with national development research. This approach is taken not only by some Western observers but is found also among some scholars in the Third World. Thompson and Fogel (1976) note that in one small sample, it was apparent among leaders of some Asian universities. A research question which represents this view can be stated as: Under what conditions can higher education be independent to pursue free intellectual inquiry, imagination, and the development of students' critical and imaginative faculties?[2]

THEORIES AND HYPOTHESES

Given the diversity of the world's cultures and resources, theories of the expansion of higher education have been remarkable for their tendency to posit only one or a few factors as explaining increases in enrollments in the various nations of the globe. The resulting images of undergraduate students are one-dimensional, lacking the vivid colors and contrasts between the colleges of different countries. When the several theories are taken together, a more elaborate and probably more adequate picture of students and societies comes into view.

Capitalism, Technical Functionalism, and Modernization

Industrialism and other forms of modern economic growth are seen by functional theory as requiring job skills of an increasing range and complexity. Increases in economic production cause a growing demand for leaders and employees with higher education. Human capital theories hypothesize that job seekers enroll in colleges to acquire the skills that they believe will lead to the highest wages offered by employers using the most advanced technologies (Brubacher and Rudy, 1976; Collins, 1971; Harbison and Myers, 1964; Psacharopoulos, 1982; Trow, 1972). Dominant groups in a nation also allocate tax monies and private wealth to higher education to promote the increasingly sophisticated skills necessary for the economy.

Two variants of the human capital perspective are the screening and signaling theories. The first of these criticizes the capitalist hypothesis that higher education provides economically productive training, contending instead that the function of higher education is in sorting and selecting—that is, "screening"—potential employees for employers (Dore, 1976, p. 28). The second theory explains that occupationally ambitious persons crowd into colleges to acquire the diplomas that will "signal" to employers their potential productivity and compliance with the employer's directions (Spence, 1974).

Cultural Imperialism

One version of imperialism theory asserts that the world's people do not hold the traditional capitalist view that economic growth precedes enrollment expansion. They believe instead that educational growth precedes economic development. In this interpretation, the independent variable is a worldwide cultural system which includes beliefs in the economic and political efficacy of universities (Meyer et al., 1977, pp. 246, 255). The hypothesis proposes that the world system diffuses these beliefs among dependent societies. Both dependent elites and the masses then see education as legitimating their claims for privileged positions within the modern sector of the nation. The rulers of dependent nations expand enrollments in the belief that higher education promotes economic growth and also the development of their domestic and international political power. The masses swell enrollments and press politicians to provide even more seats for students with the idea that this will bring about their upward social mobility.

Meyer and his colleagues have added an unusual assumption to cultural imperialism theory which maintains that national state and societal processes have little effect on the current growth of the universities. The influential conditions are to be found instead in the world system and in the populations engaged in the educational systems, relatively independent of other national economic, political, and demographic features.

Political and Economic Imperialism

More conventional imperialism theories analyze the political economy of the relations between the ruling groups in metropolitan and dependent societies (Altbach and Kelly, 1978, 1984). A curious feature of both modernization and imperialism discussions is that the same general theoretical framework is used to derive diametrically opposed hypotheses, often without recognition of the implicit discrepancy. Thus, two different outcomes of imperialism are predicated on the political economy of dependency: the dependent rulers hypothesis asserts the restriction of enrollments, and the indoctrination hypothesis asserts the expansion of enrollments.

According to the indoctrination hypothesis, Altbach (1971), Arnove (1980), and Foley (1984) explain that foreign powers encourage the expansion of enrollments in a curriculum attuned to foreign interests. The socialization of large numbers of students in such a curriculum facilitates the growth of state control over the nation's peoples and the training of a labor force for participation in work geared to an international capitalist economy.

The dependent rulers hypothesis explains that those who govern dependent societies maintain power through their foreign linkages. Consequently, they have less need for powers based on mobilization of the indigenous masses and are less inclined to invest their resources in educational expansion to promote national integration as a means of political strength (Meyer et al., 1977, p. 243; Sica and Prechel, 1981). The implications for enrollments are the opposite from that predicted under both the legitimation and indoctrination hypotheses. That is, the greater the dependency, the less likely is a society to expand higher education.

Status and Political Conflict

Conflict theories assume that dominant groups in modern societies attempt to monopolize control of access to universities which are maintained as gateways to elite positions (Archer, 1979, 1982; Ben-David, 1963; Collins, 1971, 1977, 1979, 1981). Several types of controlling groups are possible, including dominant status groups, political groups, and those situations where a ruling group is dominant in spheres of both culture and politics. The general conflict hypothesis proposes that to the extent that dominant groups are successful in linking educational credentials with privileged positions, other groups compete to enroll their young in higher education. From these premises, two hypotheses have been drawn: First, the greater the degree of centralization of status or political power in a society, the less likely are university enrollments to expand, and second, the fewer the number of middle-class mobility channels, the greater the struggle to expand university enrollments (Ben-David, 1963; Turner, 1959).

Ben-David (1963) also proposes that domination of higher education by an elite status group tends to maintain a university curriculum in which enrollments are permitted only in those fields associated with the group's elite culture. This narrowness of the curriculum, when combined with a weak middle class offering minimal alternative mobility channels, has led to an explosion of enrollments in the few university fields of study offered in many Third World societies.

A view theoretically similar to the conflict perspective suggests that enrollments are likely to be increased by the members of groups threatened by downward social mobility (Allmendinger, 1975). Craig and Spear (1982a) observe that a sense of either economic or social deprivation leads members of some groups to enter universities disproportionately.

Though not all of the above views have been drawn from or applied to Third World settings, most are based in part on an early period of development of modern universities. Thus each appears to be applicable to currently developing or agrarian societies.

RECENT EVIDENCE
ABOUT THE GROWTH OF HIGHER EDUCATION

Universities have been expanding at an astounding rate in the Third World. In the context of worldwide movements for national independence and economic change among the poorer countries of the world, higher education has been a leading flag carried by those marching toward goals of personal freedom and self-development. The rate of growth of postsecondary education has been rapid since World War II, picking up speed especially during the period of 1950–1975. Meyer et al. (1977, pp. 244, 245, 247) summarize this tremendous growth as universal around the globe, reporting that in no country did higher education decline during 1950–1970. They describe much of this expansion as proceeding in a pattern that can be approximated by the S-shaped curve that is used to portray the adoption of innovations in diffusion research (Rogers, 1962, 1983). The histories of higher education in individual nations and regions have actually been more complex and varied than indicated by the foregoing generalizations. For example, there were important instances of declines in the numbers of students and gross enrollment ratios in some countries. Before discussing these variations in enrollment expansion, it is necessary to digress briefly to review the notion of gross enrollment ratios as a concept for the analysis of expansion.

Enrollment ratios facilitate the comparison of enrollments over time and between nations whose populations vary, and they augment the portrayal of enrollments provided by the simple numbers of students. The ratio is the number of students enrolled in higher education at a given time in relation to some approximately corresponding age group in the total population of the society.[3] Thus, for example, the 42,667 students in Sri Lanka higher education in 1980, in relation to the 1,509,785 twenty- to twenty-four-year-olds in that year, can be represented by a gross enrollment ratio of 2.8. An interesting alternative to this kind of ratio has been used by Meyer (1971), in which the higher education enrollments are expressed as a percentage of secondary enrollments. The estimation of higher education enrollment ratios has improved in recent decades but is still subject to a variety of important errors (Coombs, 1985, pp. 73–80).

The general contours of enrollment expansion since the last world war are displayed in Table 1. During this period, the annual number of Third World higher education students climbed from less than a million to over fifteen million by 1980. During the twenty-five years following 1950, the gross enrollment ratio doubled approximately every decade. The overall pattern is unmistakably great and continuing growth. The overwhelming qualities of these statistics has obscured for some observers, however, the fact that the trends are not universal. There are important differences between regions. The rates of growth have recently slowed in Asia and have increased in Latin America. The S curve of innovation diffusion research, while it may or may not become apparent after a much longer period, is not visible in the enrollment ratios of all regions during recent decades.

Though most individual nations manifest a history of sustained enrollment

TABLE 1. Higher Education Gross Enrollment Ratios by Region, 1950–1980[a]

Region	Year		
	1960	1970	1980
Africa	0.7	1.6	3.2
Asia	2.9	5.8	8.1
Latin America	3.0	6.3	14.3

[a]Adapted from UNESCO, *Statistical Yearbook*, pp. II 34–35. Copyright 1983 by United Nations Educational, Scientific and Cultural Organization. By permission.

growth, the exceptions are noteworthy. China, with a major proportion of Asia's college students, has had a dramatic roller-coaster history of great leaps, declines, and revolutions in admissions and enrollments. Between political liberation in 1949 and 1957, the number of entering students in Chinese higher education doubled. In the next three years, admissions tripled and then lost a equal amount in one year. From 1961 to 1966, admissions grew rapidly again, though not nearly as fast as before. Then, in 1966, the Cultural Revolution closed the universities entirely for four years. A slower rate of growth prevailed between 1970 and 1976. In the next two years, the entrance rate doubled. In 1979, the entrance rate dropped about 30% and has since commenced to rise again. Between 1949 and 1982, the total enrollments increased about 1,000% (Henze, 1984, pp. 101, 117). These changes in admission rates, the establishment and disestablishment of new colleges, and other factors produced an enrollments trend that declined three times between 1946 and 1983, including a drop from 962,000 students in 1960 to 48,000 students in 1970.

In the context of wars, student political activism, economic depression, and political revolutions, several Third World nations have experienced fluctuating higher education enrollment ratios during the years since 1970.[4] For most nations, a decline has been small and temporary, followed by a resumption of growth. For others, such as Iran, the decline has been sharp, and enrollments have not yet returned to previous levels. Finally, even among nations with uninterrupted histories of growth, there seem to be several patterns which differ in the rate of expansion.

RECENT EVIDENCE
ABOUT THE SOURCES OF EXPANSION

Capitalist and Political Modernization

The evidence begins with the modern capitalist view of the impact of economic development on enrollment expansion. By the end of the 1960s, modernization research, as well as other viewpoints, had demonstrated a strong correlation between economic growth and the numbers of college students in the industrial nations (Ben-David, 1963; Machlup, 1970; Harbison and Myers, 1964; McClelland, 1966; Peaslee, 1969).

More recently, with the birth of many new nations and the growing effectiveness of United Nations data collection, there has been a growth in the pool of quantitative data about a larger number of developing as well as industrial societies (notwithstanding the questionable validity of some of the data). With samples including as many as 139 nations, Chenery and Syrquin (1975, p. 30), Harbison and Myers (1964), Meyer (1971), Meyer, Hannan, Rubinson, and Thomas (1979), and Sica and Prechel (1981) have demonstrated very strong correlations between national economic activity and enrollments. These correlations are displayed in Table 2. Though each of the samples of nations used in these analyses included the industrial societies, as did the preceding, the great majority of the cases used in these recent samples are Third World nations.

The correlations between economics and higher education enrollment listed in Table 2 are very substantial. The points in time examined cover the period of approximately 1950–1975. The magnitudes of the correlations are relatively similar for the several studies, though Harbison and Myers found a somewhat stronger correlation in the middle of the period. Our confidence in these measures as a group is increased by the fact that two different measures of economic activity, per capita gross national product (GNP) and per capita use of electricity, produced similar results.

Despite the growing weight of this evidence, these data still consist primarily of correlations at one point in time and, with Peaslee's (1969) and Sica and Prechel's (1981, p. 396) findings, some evidence of correlations over time. The question must be raised as to what are the links in the chain, the intervening variables, by which economic growth and industrialization affect enrollments.

TABLE 2. Correlations Between National Economic Level and Enrollments Ratios

Study	Political economy of nations in sample	Number of nations in sample	Measure of economics (and time measured)	Measure of enroll-ments (and time measured)	Type of correla-tion statistic	Statistical correlation between economics and enrollments
1. Harbison and Myers (1964)	Most kinds, industrial and poor	75	Per capita GNP, 1957	Higher enrollments/ population ratio, 1960	Pearson correlation	.74
2. Meyer (1971)	Most kinds, industrial and poor	139	Per capita, GNP, 1957	Higher/ secondary enrollments ratio, 1964	Tau beta	.44
3. Meyer et al. (1979a)	Most kinds, industrial and poor	87	Log per capita GNP, 1950	Higher enrollments/ population ratio, 1950	Pearson correlation	.64
4. Sica and Prechel (1981)	Non-Commu-nist, indus-trial and poor	50	Per capita kilowatt hours	Higher enrollments/ population ratio 1960–1975	Pearson correlation	.65

The modernization hypotheses explain the linkage as follows: Economic expansion involves an increase in the number of positions requiring highly skilled persons (Altbach and Gopinathan, 1982, p. 28). Since it is possible to provide at least some important portion of this training within postsecondary education, colleges expand at the behest both of modernizing elites and the ambitious persons who wish to acquire job training for upward social mobility.

Unfortunately, little research has been conducted in agrarian nations on the variables which link and intervene between economic growth and enrollment expansion. Kaneko's (1984) study of the educational credentials of the Asian labor force suggests, as have earlier studies, that there is some positive correlation between university enrollments and economic development. However, Kaneko also found that, after controlling for per capita GNP, nations with lower rates of industrialization were those with the highest proportions of university graduates among their professional and technical employees. The most rapid industrialization was not associated with high numbers of university graduates when the effects of per capita GNP were held constant between countries.

Another possible avenue of linkage between economics and enrollments lies in the greater potential of richer nations to invest in higher education. By this line of reasoning, the greater the level of economic development, the greater the investment in colleges, thus resulting in greater enrollments. Garms (1968) and Chenery and Syrquin (1975) demonstrated that gross national product is substantially related to the level of national educational expenditure. This hypothesis was examined by Meyer (1971) using a measure of the proportion of the gross national product expended on education. Meyer introduced per capita GNP as a control variable for the correlation between tertiary enrollments and the educational expenditure ratio. The resulting correlations showed little or no relationship for poor societies. Thus expenditures may not be a major means by which economic development affects enrollment expansion.[5]

Political Modernization

Other findings by Meyer (1971) may be interpreted to suggest that it is not primarily economics but instead political factors and the age of a higher education system itself that may be the chief variables related to enrollment expansion. From Black's (1967) comparative historical study, Meyer borrows a measure which he calls political modernization and defines as the degree to which (and the recency with which) modernizing elites control a country (Meyer and Hannan, 1979, p. 53). Meyer's (1971, p. 38) multivariate analysis of the effects of political modernization and per capita GNP on enrollments indicates no appreciable enrollment differences for the different economic levels but very large variations for the two political categories. This analysis can be seen in

Table 3. These findings provide relatively substantial evidence that in agrarian and developing nations, something in addition to, or even in place of, economic production strongly shapes the growth of enrollments. The absence of economic effects is not explained by most of the other lines of research. This would seem to be a very important finding, and yet it has been ignored by subsequent research. The research literature has not compared the relative effects of political and economic variables, nor has it considered the possibility that controlling for political variables might demonstrate a spurious relationship between economics and enrollments.

Closer inspection of Black's original political variable indicates that Meyer's dichotomy is not primarily a general measure of elite political activity. Actually it is mainly a dichotomy which compares a category comprised largely of recently independent African nations with all other agrarian nations. Thus the factor involved seems possibly related to two clusters of phenomena: African cultural and political features, including the distinctive earlier formation of African nations within the grasp of colonialism, and the amount of time since independence from colonial domination. The latter is likely to be related to the age of a nation's university system.

The impact on enrollments of time since independence and of economics has been explicitly examined by Meyer (1971, p. 41) in a multivariate analysis of former colonies distinguished by when they gained their independence, either before 1914 or since 1945. The results are quite striking and are displayed in Table 4. The effect of higher per capita GNP is slight, while the effect of time since independence is very strong. Comparing the effects of the two variables of GNP and date of independence, the likelihood of a country having higher enrollments is four to seven times greater with a longer period since indepen-

TABLE 3. Percentage of Nations High on Higher/Secondary Enrollment Ratio in Relation to Political Modernization and Per Capita Gross National Product[a]

Political modernization	Per capita GNP[b]	
	Low	Medium
High	50% (12)	50% (28)
Low	6% (31)	0% (6)

[a]Adapted from "Economic and political effects on National Educational Enrollment Patterns," by J. W. Meyer, *Comparative Education Review* 15: 38. Copyright 1971 by the Comparative and International Education Society. By permission.
[b]Numbers in parentheses are numbers of cases on which all entries are based.

dence than it is with a higher level of per capita GNP. Some caution is warranted with these data because the research report does not specify the nations in the samples, and thus it is difficult to determine what variables may be confounding the resulting analysis.[6]

Among Third World countries, then, the impact of politics may have been considerably more decisive for university enrollments than was economics for at least a part of this century prior to 1970. The effect of economics is unclear and possibly rather weak for at least some periods. This is in great contrast to the research comparing agrarian and industrial countries, where the economics of the latter may have more strongly promoted the expansion of higher education enrollments. That is, the differences in economic growth between the agrarian and industrial societies are correlated with great differences in enrollment rates. As we have seen, the correlation between economics and enrollments disappears among poor nations when control variables for political and timing factors are introduced. In the comparison of the poor and the industrial nations, despite the introduction of control variables for politics, the correlation with economics remains (Meyer, 1971). Why is there such an interaction between per capita GNP and certain political variables? This is another puzzle that has not yet been pursued in the literature. Part of the answer may lie in the greater variation in per capita GNP among industrial nations compared with poor nations. Whatever the reason, this interaction indicates the risk in the prevailing practice of using global samples for generalizations about enrollments in both industrial and agrarian societies. The analyses should be conducted separately for each of the several types of societies.

We certainly must also examine what it is about the duration of time since national elites have taken greater control over domestic institutions that is so

TABLE 4. Percentage of Nations High on Higher/Secondary Enrollment Ratio in Relation to Recency of Independence from Colonialism and Per Capita Gross National Product[a]

	Per capita GNP[b]	
Independence	Low	Medium
Before 1914	89% (9)	94% (18)
Since 1945	39% (31)	50% (10)

[a]Adapted from "Economic and political effects on National Educational Enrollment Patterns," by J. W. Meyer, *Comparative Education Review* 15: 41. Copyright 1971 by the Comparative and International Education Society. By permission.
[b]Numbers in parentheses are numbers of cases on which all entries are based.

much related to enrollments. Full discussion of this question must wait until taking up the hypotheses of conflict theory in a later section of this chapter.

Critique of Modernization Research

Several lines of reasoning and of evidence suggest that the strong correlations between economics and enrollments should be treated as very tentative evidence: the criticisms of Berg (1970), Collins (1971), and Dore (1976) of the necessity for university vocational training, the lack of evidence as to what is the linkage between economics and enrollments, and such findings as Kaneko's unexpected datum regarding the modest educational credentials of professionals in some industrializing nations.

Thus far, the evidence consists largely of quantitative measures of a few kinds of gross national economic productivity and various aggregate enrollment measures. Missing are studies of such linking factors as employer personnel policies and processes and prospective employee educational calculations. Without evidence about the mechanisms which link economics and enrollments, there has not been much progress toward resolution of the competing hypotheses of human capital, screening, and signaling theories. Nor is it clear how much screening processes focus on productive abilities or compliance with status norms (Collins, 1979).

Another limitation of most of this evidence has been the tendency to mix industrial and poor nations in the same sample. To answer questions about the impact of economics upon the enrollments in agrarian and developing nations, research must examine samples focused on the Third World.

One-factor explanations have been overly stressed in the economic research. Other factors, particularly politics, also have important impacts on enrollments and should be included in the study of economic effects. It is also possible that some economic effects interact with other independent variables. For example, in a subsequent section of this chapter, we will observe Meyer's (1971, p. 40) evidence that economics has more effect in less centralized political systems in the Third World.

Imperialism: Dependency,
Neocolonialism, and World Systems

Some of the more astonishing and recently influential studies of enrollment expansion have appeared in the dependency research. Particularly unusual is the observation by Meyer et al. (1977) that characteristics of individual nations have no apparent effect on enrollments. For example, they report finding that in the period after World War II, there were no effects on the expansion of higher education from the increasing wealth of nations, no impact of political changes, and no consequences from varying levels of taxation or massive urbanization.

The principal dynamics of dependency analysis concern the domination of agrarian and underdeveloped nations by a world capitalist system through the cooperation of ruling groups in both the rich and the poor societies. This point of view criticizes modernization research for assuming that development is a function of national features and for failing to acknowledge that the dominant capitalist powers tend to exploit the resources and productivity of agrarian societies so thoroughly as to hold them indefinitely in a state of underdevelopment. The restriction (or expansion) of university enrollments in Third World nations is analyzed as a factor contributing to the maintenance of foreign domination or as a by-product of this domination.

Imperialism as Restriction of Enrollments: The Dependent Rulers Hypothesis

The Stanford World System Studies

A group of researchers originally based at Stanford University, and led by John Meyer, has been notably creative and productive in developing a series of quantitative global studies of enrollment expansion. These researchers proposed to test several hypotheses about the effect of national and international social structural characteristics on enrollment expansion. The national characteristics were selected on the basis of various modernization theories, and the choice of the international factors was based on dependency theory. Their guiding hypothesis from dependency theory asserted that Third World ruling groups, whose political power comes from foreign nations, have little need for extensive enrollment expansion as a means of indigenous political mobilization and strength. Eleven measures corresponding to national characteristics and three measures of world system factors were selected for study. These fourteen measures are listed in Table 5. Each of these fourteen measures was entered as an independent variable into its own separate multiple-regression equation *after* an independent composite variable comprising measures of 1955 secondary and higher education enrollments and population growth was entered into the equation. The dominant components of this latter composite variable were the measures of the 1955 enrollment levels.[7] For each of the regression equations, the dependent variable was the amount of expansion in the higher education enrollment ratio over the period 1955–1970.[8]

The right-hand column of Table 5 lists the standardized regression coefficients for the relationship of each of the national and international characteristics to the 1955–1970 expansion. All of these coefficients are small. The precise coefficients for the relations between 1955 enrollments and 1955–1970 expansion were not disclosed by the researchers but were reported as uniformly positive and statistically significant.

TABLE 5. Regression Analyses of the 1955–1970 Expansion in National Higher/Secondary Enrollment Ratios: Independent Variables, Standardized Regression Coefficients[a]

Equation	n	1955 Enrollments held constant[c]	Log of GNP/ capita 1955	Other national variables[b]	Coefficient
1.	84	positive		Log GNP/capita, 1955	.13
2.	69	positive		Log KWH/capita, 1955	.24*
3.	89	positive		% Non ag. male labor force	.02
4.	84	positive	positive[d]	Urbanization	−.02
5.	41	positive	negative[e]	Formal political rep., 1951–1955	.25
6.	43	positive	positive[d]	Polit. particip., 1957–1962	.20
7.	81	positive	positive[d]	Political modernization	.09
8.	44	positive	positive[d]	Government revenue/GDP	.02
9.	48	positive	positive[d]	Cabinet size, 1950	.03
10.	84	positive	positive[d]	State centralization	−.03
11.	84	positive	positive[d]	Ethnolinguistic fractionalization	−.05
12.	56	positive	positive[d]	Colonial independence pre-1945 or 1945–1957	−.12
13.	84	positive	positive[d]	Colonial independence before or after 1957	−.11
14.	64	positive	positive[d]	Export partner concentration, 1955	−.07

[a]Adapted from "The world educational revolution, 1950–1970," by J. W. Meyer et al., *Sociology of Education*, 50: 250. Copyright 1977 by the American Sociological Association. By permission.

[b]The dependent variable for each of the regression equations is the 1955–1970 growth of the higher education enrollment ratios calculated as the difference in the percentage of the appropriate age group enrolled in 1955 and 1970.

[c]In this equation (and each of the other regression equations) this variable is based on the 1955 enrollments equation specified in Note 7. Meyer et al. describe their procedure as treating the 1955 enrollments equation and its coefficients "as fixed entering them in their entirety as [a] single term" in this regression equation. The researchers do not report the magnitude of the coefficient of this 1955 enrollments variable for this equation but do report that it is positive and statistically significant. This variable is described as entered into the equation in such a fashion that it is "held constant . . . to see if" the national variable in this equation "can contribute to the explanation of educational expansion over and above that which is self-generating" (Meyer et al., 1977, pp. 249, 250).

[d]The researchers do not report the magnitude of the coefficient for this variable but do report that it is positive and statistically insignificant.

[e]The researchers do not report the magnitude of the coefficient for this variable but do report that it is negative and statistically insignificant.

*$p < .05$.

These findings were interpreted by Meyer et al. to mean that national structural characteristics, and especially, measures of national economic, political, and social modernization actually account for very little expansion in education (1977, p. 242). "Rather, between 1950 and 1970, education has expanded everywhere as a function of the available population to be educated and of the level of education existing in 1950" (ibid., p. 255).

The evidence considered by these researchers is thus not primarily focused on dependency variables, even though their theories are focused on dependency. Their reasoning is that if national characteristics do not explain enrollment expansion, then the explanation must be based on some other factors, such as dependency. The researchers then proceed to conclude their analysis with interesting speculations about the impact of international cultural dependency.

Despite the interpretations drawn by these researchers, the regression equations did not actually examine any hypotheses about the magnitude of the total effects of national characteristics on enrollment expansion. These equations do suggest that each of the national characteristics variables is less strongly correlated with the 1955–1970 enrollment expansion than is the variable of the 1955 level of enrollments. However, this certainly *does not* mean that the national factors had no effect on the subsequent changes in enrollments. Given that it is known from Meyer and Hannan (1979) and other studies that many of these national factors are strongly correlated with enrollment levels and enrollment expansion, the regression evidence further suggests that the variation in each of the national factors that is correlated with 1955–1970 enrollment expansion is also correlated with 1955 enrollment levels. That is, national factors and 1955 enrollment levels "share" a correlational relationship with 1955–1970 enrollment expansion. Finally, the regression coefficients suggest that the national factors measured *may* not have any independent relationship with (that is, any independent "effect" on) enrollment expansion beyond that which is shared with 1955 enrollment levels. This latter interpretation, however, is beclouded by the possibility that substantial "multicollinearity" between the two independent variables has underestimated the magnitude of the independent relations between the national factors and the 1955–1970 enrollment expansion.

The research design was mismatched, then, with the theories of national factors which it purported to test. The crux of the inappropriate analysis has to do with the researchers' assumptions about the variance and effects shared by the independent variables. The research procedure implicitly and implausibly *assumed* that all of the shared correlation of the independent variables with the dependent variable, enrollment expansion, was to be attributed only to the independent variable of the 1955 enrollment level and not at all to the various national factors. This is an arbitrary, undiscussed, and not very credible assumption, for which evidence is lacking in the researchers' report. In addition, the design used by Meyer and colleagues *assumed* that all effects of national factors, if there are any such effects, are independently related to enrollment expansions and are not correlated with or transmitted through 1955 enrollment levels.

An alternative and theoretically more plausible research design for some of the national factors hypotheses would assume that 1955 enrollment levels served as an intervening variable, and thus that the effects of some national factors on enrollments at Time 2 are at least partially mediated through their effects on Time 1 enrollments.[9] For example, a major petroleum find in the 1940s might have led to increased national wealth in a given nation by 1950, thereby facilitating both increased funds for college classroom construction and family financial support for children, with the result of increased higher education enrollments in 1955 (Time 1), which, with continuing financial affluence, facilitated increasing supplies of school and college teachers and classrooms for even more enrollment expansion over the 1955–1970 period (Time 2).

These criticisms aside, the work of Meyer, Ramirez, Rubinson, and their other colleagues has been especially important for its stimulating, creative view of the possibilities of large-scale historical and comparative analysis of changes in higher education in the Third World.[10]

An especially interesting finding by Meyer et al. (1977) concerns the strong relation between the levels of secondary and tertiary enrollments in the 1950s and the subsequent growth of tertiary enrollments. What is responsible in the Third World for such a large correlation? Though Meyer et al. provide several suggestions, and other researchers (e.g., Archer, 1979, 1982) have recently examined the impact of educational factors on enrollments in European societies, there has been little study of the effect of these elements in educational systems in the Third World. Some of the correlation between secondary and tertiary enrollments is attributable to the former level of enrollments supplying students to the latter level. It may also be due to the tendency for secondary schools to be major employers of the graduates of higher education. There may also be important causal relations between urbanization and secondary and tertiary enrollments.

Other Political Dependency Studies

The available evidence from other dependency studies of enrollments indicates a few weak to moderate effects of the world system on enrollments, but without much of a clear pattern. Sica and Prechel (1981), in a carefully designed and documented global analysis of a sample of industrial and agrarian nations, report that only one of three dependency measures was even weakly related to enrollments in the predicted direction. Investigating the hypothesis that political dependency restricts enrollments, they found the level of exports to be slightly negatively related to enrollments, but they found no enrollment effects from either domestic capital formation or external public debt.

Kraus et al. (1979) found some correlation between enrollments in three Asian nations and economic dependency, but the relationship was neither straightforward nor consistent over time. These researchers also found evidence that ruling bureaucrats of all three nations had similar group interests in usually restricting university enrollments regardless of the degree of economic and political dependency of their nations. The latter finding suggests that enrollment policies in Asia may be relatively less affected by world system influences than possibly in, say, Latin America or Africa, which have been so much more dominated by the world system in this century and which were the primary regions of inspiration for recent dependency theories.

Coombs (1985) attributes much of the slowing of enrollments in the 1970s to worldwide financial shortages, an explanation that highlights world system effects on enrollments. It is not clear how this fits with notions of political dependency. The hypothesis implies that when Third World national ruling groups receive less foreign economic support, they might then turn to enrollment expansion as a domestic source of political power. Coombs's interpretation of the 1970s economic downturn does not support such a hypothesis and seems to support instead the economic modernization hypothesis of enrollment changes whereby enrollment expansion or decline is a direct function of economic growth.

Imperialism as Expansion of Enrollments: The Indoctrination Hypothesis

Altbach (1971, 1975, 1977, 1981b, in press), Altbach and Rathgeber (1980), Berman (1979), Carnoy (1974a,b), Eisemon (1981, 1982), Foley (1984), Mazrui (1975), and Zachariah (1985) have demonstrated that Western forces have extensively influenced, even dominated, the university curriculum, the general learning environment, and the training of professors in many Third World countries at various times. In all of these studies, there is the implication that expansion of enrollments in a capitalist or foreign curriculum promotes foreign metropolitan interests.

Arnove (1980, pp. 48–54) more explicitly states that the expansion and extension of education in the Third World occurs as part of the international competition between societies. Thereby "previously isolated or excluded individuals can be mobilized for multiple purposes: nation building, the opening of national markets, the fulfillment of economic plans." The secondary school enrollments in Jamaica are similarly interpreted as having been expanded to "develop a controlled well-disciplined work force . . . and to hold from the market the growing proportion of youth who could not be employed within the context of Jamaica's dependent capitalist economy."

Despite abundant evidence of foreign penetration of curricula in the Third World, these dependency studies have not provided much evidence, pro or con, about imperialist effects on the expansion of higher education enrollments. Several other studies have produced findings which fail to detect a relationship between dependency and expanding enrollments. The modest amount of evidence from Sica and Prechel's research tends to discomfirm the dependency hypothesis of enrollment expansion. Kraus et al. (1979) found that, regardless of the extent of foreign domination, Asian ruling bureaucrats seek to limit high education enrollments. Kopf's (1984) study of Orientalist Englishmen of the East India Company in nineteenth-century India concludes that even the cultural objectives and effects of the foreigners can never be assumed merely from reference to the dominant economic interests of their foreign nation.

Possible dependency effects may be seen in the graphs produced by Meyer et al. (1977, p. 254), in which they plot the expansion of enrollments over 1950–1970 for different groups of countries classified by date of independence. The researchers report finding no differences in relation to independence from colonial rule. Inspection of their graph, however, suggests that poor countries independent before 1956 expanded enrollments at a faster rate than did poor countries gaining independence during 1956–1970. These are essentially the same data that Meyer (1971) earlier reported as manifesting a relationship between date of independence and enrollment rates. Whether these are an indication of the effect of international colonialism, a reflection of regional differences as suggested in earlier remarks above, or the result of some other factors cannot be seen in these data because of the absence of designations of the countries involved.

Imperialism as Expansion of Enrollments: The Legitimation Hypothesis

Meyer et al. (1977) proposed that the world cultural system diffuses beliefs in the economic and political efficacy of education to the elites and masses of Third World nations and that higher education enrollments consequently increase. Both elites and masses then promote and seek education to demonstrate their legitimate participation in and access to positions within the privileged sectors of society. The hypothesis implies convergence throughout the Third World on a similar expansionary course. Meyer et al. (1977) document such convergence for many developing societies during 1950–1970, though they omit discussion of instances of enrollment decline and divergence which actually occurred during this period. Coombs (1985) also notes that enrollments during the period 1950–1970 expanded at a faster rate and more similarly throughout the world than during the 1970s. With respect to the explanation of the causes of the 1950–1970 enrollment expansion in terms of worldwide processes of legitimation, thus far this hypothesis has not been systematically researched, and the evidence for it is anecdotal.

Critique of Dependency Research

Imperialism studies have been useful in several kinds of analysis, including indictments and explanation, and as agendas for the future. Our concern here is with their fruitfulness for explanations.

The evidence for the relationship of enrollments to various dependency hypotheses is mixed and, thus far, rather weak. This may be due especially to the new and very incomplete scope of research recently conducted on these hypotheses. In several studies where the evidence has not supported the theory, the discussion and conclusions have still tended to treat the theory as if it is generally irrefutable. Thus, for example, when little evidence was found to support the specific hypothesis that political and economic dependency slows the growth of enrollments, some researchers revised the hypothesis to propose the opposite effect, despite the lack of any relevant evidence (Meyer et al., 1977). Other researchers retained their original hypothesis but, after finding few supporting results from regression equations, simply rejected the method and proposed that other methods—for example, qualitative techniques—would be more likely to produce the evidence that would support the hypothesis (Sica and Prechel, 1981, p. 400).

Though some of these proposals for revising dependency hypotheses and research methods are very reasonable, this posture of so little criticism of one's own theory is not very productive. This seems like yet one more point of view, as with modernization theory, that is held so strongly that even in the face of disconfirming evidence, its supporters decline to discuss the possibility that any major assumptions of the theory may be doubtful and to specify which of the assumptions have been put into question by their evidence.

A sound theoretical approach to research design for both modernization and dependency hypotheses would imply that the historical analysis of enrollments would select variables, categories within variables, and cases as dictated by theory rather than merely by the convenience of available UNESCO and handbook compilations of cases, variables, and arbitrary data intervals. For example, if one proposes to examine the effects of government higher education modernization policies, then it is appropriate to identify the particular years in which these policies change, include measures which reflect these policies, and to include cases which manifest the full range of possible variations on the independent variable. The case of China illustrates some of the relevant considerations. China was not included in the higher education statistics tables of many editions of the UNESCO handbooks, nor in many of the recent multiple-regression studies of enrollments. If one were to use data points only at the conventional five- or ten-year points at the beginning and middle of decades, rather than observations as dictated by theoretical considerations, one could miss the fact that Chinese universities were closed and had no enrollments for the years 1966–1969. The conclusion by Meyer et al. (1977) that national political factors had little effect on higher education enrollments during the period since the last world war seems generally untenable in the face of the evidence from several of the Asian nations with which I am acquainted. When applied to China, such a conclusion appears farfetched.

The soaring enrollments of some poor and unindustrialized societies appear as if a sorcerer's apprentice has lost control of the unleashed forces of university expansion. The initial establishment and expansion of Third World enrollments in Western forms and curricula of higher education may indeed serve imperialist purposes. However, how much expansion serves neocolonial interests? And what explains the tendency in some Third World nations for expansion to proceed to the point of effecting a drain on economic resources, stagnation, unemployment, and political instability? Possibly the dialectical notion of contradictions offers some analytical possibilities here.

It may also be that one reason that imperialism research has had so little to say about enrollment expansion rates is that the high expansion rates of some Third World societies are inimical to metropolitan interests and that imperialism theories are, of course, not unlimited in their capacity to account for the domestic processes within a society. We turn in the next section to consider theories which examine domestic processes in relation to the intentions and resources of the primary actors, the students and their families and other national groups, all of which may be affected in varying degree by foreign powers as posited by imperialism theory, but which may also be considerably independent of international forces.

Conflict Research

Conflict and human capital theories both emphasize the strong interest of individuals in swelling the enrollments of higher education. Individuals of flesh and blood, with independent and personal desires, have been ignored in the modernization and dependency research, which emphasizes aggregate and group elements such as the GNP, educational expenditures, and international economic domination. Each of the persons in the Third World has her or his own reasons and desires for seeking, or avoiding, advanced training and credentials. These reasons are mainly the money, prestige, and superior working conditions of the best jobs available (Dore, 1976, p. 3; Ringer, 1979, p. 51). For the majority who do not obtain the best jobs, human capital research has demonstrated that university degrees are still a good investment for individuals toward obtaining modern employment and better income than one could earn without the degree (Psacharopoulos, 1980, 1982, p. 148).

In contrast to capitalist theories, conflict theories assume that individuals are relatively successful in banding together to monopolize money, prestige, and pleasant work. If one group manages to monopolize most of the attractive middle-rank jobs in a society and restricts the number of job entry channels to only educational routes, it is hypothesized that great pressure to expand enrollments will rapidly develop. Variations between societies in the enrollment rates are affected by several aspects of social monopolies, including the number of alternative mobility channels, status group domination of the universities, political centralization, shifts in the resources of groups, and the succession of dominant groups.

In previously colonized agrarian societies where independence has only recently been wrested away from foreign interests, there has been a tendency for the ruling bureaucrats to expand the civil bureaucracy and to place most of the desirable modern jobs within it. Government bureaucracies typically use one main explicit criterion for selection of personnel: educational credentials, with the best jobs reserved for university graduates (Kraus et al., 1979). The result of the government monopoly of modern jobs is what Dore (1976) calls the "late development effect" in contemporary agrarian countries. This hypothesis asserts that the later development starts, the faster the growth of school enrollments. Increasingly rapid enrollment expansion is caused by widespread ambition for social mobility where only one main channel exists as an outlet for this dammed-up reservoir of aspirations. Dore's (1976, pp. 71, 76, 78) evidence comparing enrollments in early and "late" settings covers very few societies and is uncorrected for several confounding variables. Nevertheless, his comparisons are striking. Annual university enrollment expansion in Kenya over 1965–1970 was 31%. In Sri Lanka, a society which struggled free of colonialism earlier, the annual expansion rate for the same period was 0%. In a comparison of possibly more comparable development periods for secondary-school enrollments, the annual expansion rate for Japan over 1900–1910 was 8% and for Kenya, during 1960–1970, the annual rate was 20%.

The preoccupation of students with the few but dazzlingly attractive top government jobs may be responsible for a curious finding in some large samples of fourteen-year-olds drawn from a sample of only six nations. Saha (1982, p. 258) found that students from the less wealthy countries of India, Hungary, and Chile are more likely to have high occupational aspirations than are students in the United States, England, and Australia.[11]

Social monopolies thus appear to provide important points of comparison between higher education systems. The preceding review has suggested that the number of alternative channels of mobility into the modern labor force is one such point of comparison. Where a civilian government monopolizes the modern jobs, enrollments are likely to expand. Ben-David (1963) contends that in other societies in which alternative social mobility channels emerge before the rise of higher education manages to monopolize all of the routes into the labor market, the expansion of enrollments is likely to be less. For example, Dore (1976, p. 73) describes Hong Kong society as having few government jobs until recently but as supporting a variety of mobility channels into business circles for which university credentials were not necessary.

Conflict theory suggests two other dimensions of competition relevant for higher-education-based monopolies: the centralization of power within the realm of prestige and culture and the centralization of political power. Centralization of either kind tends to be associated with limited enrollments.[12]

In societies where one group's culture dominates the universities and is the standard of selection in the educational system, the typical result is a restriction of university enrollments (Ben-David, 1963; Dore, 1976, p. 78; Turner, 1959). In other societies where cultural forces compete more readily, several groups may successfully press to expand the enrollments in higher education in their struggle over access to resources (Collins, 1971, 1977, 1979; Meyer and Rubinson, 1975, p. 156). Levy (1982, pp. 114–117; 1985) notes that increasing status competition in Spanish American nations between the elite and upper-middle status groups, on one side, and the middle and lower-middle groups, on the other side, has been responsible for much of the establishment and expansion of private universities in this century. A similar increase in the establishment and enrollment expansion of private colleges in the early modernization of Japan is attributed by Amano (1969, 1979) to the competition between samurai, rural landlord, and other status groups.

Ben-David (1963) notes also that domination by one status group is associated with the restriction of the curriculum to those areas of culture and professional activity characteristic of this elite. In some Third World countries lacking other professional training courses in the university or alternative mobility channels outside the educational system, the result has been severe overcrowding in the limited number of the academic fields of study permitted by the elites.

States characterized by the centralization of political power are likely to exert control over higher education and to limit university enrollments (Ben-David and Zloczower, 1962; Dore, 1976, p. 78; Kraus et al., 1979; Meyer and Rubinson, 1975, pp. 150, 153). Maxwell (1975, pp. 472–473) found that the highly centralized political power of the ruling group in Thailand prior to the 1970s enabled the elites to narrowly restrict university enrollments. Similarly, Dore reports that Tanzanian higher education has been limited in its expansion by the centralized power of government bureaucrats. Unlike the Spanish American nations, the strong central government of Brazil exercises greater control over the public universities and their admissions processes (Haar, 1976, pp. 182–183) and has restricted their expansion of enrollments (Levy, 1982, pp. 110–111).

In contrast to the above examples of centralized nations, a few case studies of politically divided systems indicate a more rapid growth in the numbers of universities and students. The political division of Germany in the early nineteenth century is interpreted by Ben-David and Zloczower (1962) as permitting the competition between provincial powers in the establishment of new universities. Levy (1982, p. 107) credits political decentralization in Latin America as a condition which permitted the creation and expansion of private universities in this century.

The specific hypothesis that democratic traditions affect access to enrollments can be seen as related to these notions of the centralization of power. Dore (1976, pp. 78–79) contends that in less politically centralized agrarian nations with strong democratic processes, the competition between political parties provides an arena for the struggle between groups over social resources that is especially likely to enlarge admissions into universities. The increases in the numbers of colleges and enrollments in the agrarian nineteenth-century United States are attributed by Brubacher and Rudy (1976, p. 59) primarily to democratic politics and the absence of a high degree of national centralization of culture and government.

Scholars have not yet undertaken comparative research on several Third World societies that systematically extends or discredits the above findings.[13] Thus our evidence of the significance of centralization is primarily dependent upon the foregoing case studies. Two possibly relevant but highly inferential and contradictory pieces of evidence from wider samples of countries are available in Meyer's earlier (1971, p. 36, 40) global statistical studies.

The first piece of evidence from Meyer's data compares the higher education enrollments for two types of governments, representational and mobilizational. The former are those governments using democratic representational forms to some degree, and the latter are politically mobilized for national social change, typically for economic development (two thirds of the nations in this category are Communist). From this definition of categories, one might infer that the mobilizational systems are the more politically centralized of the nations. The findings are displayed in Table 6.[14] It can be seen in this table that of the mobilizational governments, in both the very low and low per capita GNP societies, about one third have high rates of postsecondary enrollments. Of the representational governments in very-low-income societies, only 17% (in clearer terms, only one of six low-income representational societies) have a high rate of enrollments. About half, 47%, of the representational governments in low-income societies have high enrollment rates.

There are many cautions which one might raise about the data in Table 6 beyond the usual concerns over crude global statistical measures, samples, and the like: First, Meyer excluded from this sample all of the cases not high on either representation or mobilizational qualities and noted that these excluded countries tended to be the less "modernized" nations. It is unclear whether the excluded group involved a number of politically centralized traditional regimes. The second caution concerns the very small number of cases in this sample, a mere total of thirty-eight nations. Though such a number is much larger than the

TABLE 6. Percentage of Nations High on Higher/Secondary Enrollment Ratio in Relation to Political System and Per Capita Gross National Product[a]

Political system	Per capita GNP[b]	
	Very low	Low
Representational	17% (6)	47% (15)
Mobilizational	36% (11)	33% (6)

[a]Adapted from "Economic and political effects on National Educational Enrollment Patterns," by J. W. Meyer, *Comparative Education Review* 15: 40. Copyright 1971 by the Comparative and International Education Society. By permission.
[b]Numbers in parentheses are numbers of cases on which all entries are based.

few countries involved in the case studies reviewed above, it is a very small number for percentage comparisons of table cells with information about only the three measures involved. With these caveats, what implications are suggested by these data? The mobilizational, and presumably politically centralized, governments do not have a noticeably lower rate of enrollments. With this small sample of cases, which primarily compare somewhat democratic polities with Communist and socialist governments, the conflict hypothesis finds no support. It may even be that some types of centralized governments, particularly socialist states, tend to have higher enrollment rates than do other types of centralized nations in the Third World. It is likely that there is more than one type of centralized government.

One will recall that in our earlier discussion of modernization theory, we observed only a small relationship among poor countries between economic development and enrollments. These data in Table 6 may suggest an interaction between the variables of the political system and per capita GNP, so that a relationship in poor countries between per capita GNP and enrollments is likely to occur only in the countries using at least some of the processes of democracy.

The second piece of evidence from Meyer's (1971) global analysis concerns a concept labeled as the extractive power of the central government and based on a measure of an expenditure ratio, the total expenditures of the central government calculated as a proportion of the gross national product. It is possible that this ratio reflects the power of the central government to enforce taxes and may also reflect the state's power emanating from its ability to buy resources.[15] If the assumption is made that the ratio is an indicator of the centralization of power, then the conflict hypothesis would predict that the larger the expenditure ratio, the smaller the enrollment rate. This conflict hypothesis of an inverse correlation is precisely what Meyer reports that he found between the expenditure ratio and the enrollment rate.

Declining status or the threat of downward social mobility involves status conflict that sometimes pushes individuals toward postsecondary credentials (Craig and Spear, 1982a, pp. 151–153). This seems to be the case particularly for groups which formerly enjoyed high or middle levels of prestige. For example, demographic changes occasionally intersect with status conflict as a major force to push persons either down the status ladder or into new avenues such as higher education. Allmendinger (1975) analyzed the process by which an insufficient agricultural inheritance, as a result of the ratio of the burgeoning population to the limited supply of land, led farmer's children in nineteenth-century New England to seek new kinds of livelihood. These sons of the soil sought to avoid both landless rural poverty and social descent into the ranks of urban wage labor. Many of them turned instead to the rural colleges being established in the region and were a major force for the expansion of institutions and enrollments for that period.

Political conflict and change which reduces the status and resources of a group may also lead to increased enrollments from that group. The Japanese samurai, which were suddenly without a claim upon positions in the modernizing government of the Meiji Restoration, found themselves competing with several other groups for access to the new order. Amano (1969, 1979) observes that sons of the samurai groups were an important source of enrollments in the new universities, comprising a majority of the early graduates from the top-ranking national universities.

Educational Systems

There has been little theorizing about the enrollment-expanding tendencies of the actors themselves within educational systems of the Third World (however, for universities in industrial nations, see Archer, 1979, 1982; Ben-David and Zloczower, 1962; Craig, 1984; Pempel, 1973; Ringer, 1979). One of the most interesting findings of Meyer et al. (1977) is the large correlation between the 1955 enrollment levels and subsequent enrollment expansion. It is seems likely that several features of an educational system themselves, and their societal correlates, directly influence later growth of the system.

For example, a given stratum of universities can be seen as constituting a monopoly of attractive jobs, for which there may be more eager applicants among graduates than there are job openings. Would-be professors unable to obtain a job in these most desirable organizations are then likely to cooperate with other status groups in establishing and expanding other zones and institutions of the higher educational system.

Professors at the top-ranked universities may then experience a conflicting set of interests. On the one hand, their prestige and resources inhere in their links with the dominant groups to whom they supply graduates, and from whom they receive crucial resources. It is in their interest to protect the monopoly of educational credentials of this alliance. On the other hand, these professors also have potential clientele among the professors and officials in the lower-ranking organizations of higher education as places for the employment of some of their academic graduates and as sources of various forms of lucrative and interesting part-time employment.

The resulting mix of academic interests and pressures from the several levels within the higher education system tends both to restrict and to expand enrollments. It is in the interplay of these various educational system forces with groups and individuals in the larger society that changes in enrollments come about.

Summary of Conflict Research

The discussion has focused mainly on the advantages of educational credentials which might be described as pulling persons to them (Craig and Spear, 1982a, p. 139). People are drawn into colleges by the prospect of higher-paying and more prestigious jobs, which, in contemporary agrarian and developing societies, are frequently located in the government sector. As a result, enrollments have increased at a faster rate than economic growth in recent decades. Despite this credential inflation, attending higher education is still a good investment risk for the individual in most Third World societies. Added to these forces of attraction are conditions such as declining status, which push some persons into higher education.

Several structural features of societies affect the direction in which ambitious persons are channeled and the extent to which enrollments enlarge. These features include the number of alternative mobility channels, status group domination of the universities, political centralization, shifts in the resources of groups, and the succession of dominant groups.

Critique of Conflict Research

The conflict perspective is among the more vague of the theories which have been applied to enrollment phenomena. Few of its main concepts are clearly defined, its concepts resist quantification, and like dependency theories, it tends toward irrefutability. Proponents are able, after the fact, to explain almost any turn of events with the theory. Case studies often apply the hypotheses on an *ad hoc* basis after the data are collected.

For example, how does one define the concept of mobility channels sufficiently so that one could count the number of such channels in each of several different societies? Are all channels equal? Is the size of the channel an issue?

Are some smaller than others, and if so, how is this difference in size to be defined and measured? The definition and measurement of political centralization are difficult enough (Meyer, Boli-Bennett, and Chase-Dunn, 1975), while discussions of the definition of status centralization are rare, and those that exist are diffuse. The possibility that centralized socialist states have different enrollment policies from traditional centralized states implies that conflict theory could be further developed to conceive of the possible variations in a dominant group's interests and purposes, its bases of power, and its alliances with and relations to other groups.

The theory is also not well elaborated concerning the constituent factors. For example, what are the links or variables that intervene between centralization and the restriction of enrollments? What are the factors that intervene between the number of mobility channels, the aspirations of young people, and entry on various vocational ladders?

Notwithstanding all of these shortcomings, this approach is promising for its sensitivity to variation in local cultures and thus for its susceptibility to comparative analysis (conversely, this may be part of the source of its vague quality), and for its potential synthesis with the other perspectives (e.g., cf. Collins, 1971).

METHODS FOR FURTHER RESEARCH

Expansion is the consequence of several, sometimes lengthy chains of events. Only the historians, mainly in studying the agrarian past of now industrialized nations, have used methods which have enabled them to look at all or most of the links in these chains. Statistical analyses of bivariate correlations or multiple regressions have often omitted all of the intervening links in the chain of variables. Usually, this short chain view of enrollment expansion has been used as a step in a preliminary and exploratory phase of research on the topic. The research has advanced far enough now so that it can profitably use methods that permit a view of the full length of the process. Particularly useful would be historical case studies of expansion during this century in a few Third World countries. For quantitative studies of several societies, statistical methods that link several variables are necessary. For example, something akin to path analysis would be promising.

Recent comparative research has concentrated on global or regional sets of national enrollment statistics. These methods have necessarily omitted all behavior of students other than their enrollment rates; unexamined are their motives, their job searching, and their images of the educational and occupational systems (an interesting exception is Saha, 1982). Omitted also are the more complex aspects of national and educational systems, including historical, cultural, political, and academic features. For these two sets of neglected elements, two kinds of methods are especially proposed: qualitative and questionnaire studies of student attitudes and comparative studies of a few societies.

In only a few qualitative reports such as Allmendinger's (1975) do the students become persons with complex sets of attitudes, feelings, and personal strategies for enrolling in higher education. So many questionnaire surveys of Third World students have been collected in the past two decades that secondary analysis of the corresponding computer data sets probably could be profitably undertaken, as, for example, Saha (1982) has done with the International Educational Attainment Studies. These questionnaires would be somewhat limited by their preoccupation with Western categories of observation. To move beyond these latter categories, ethnographic and historical studies could seek to use the students' own categories of perception to enhance our breadth of understanding and also to inform subsequent statistical analyses.

Comparative studies of extended time periods in a few agrarian and developing societies which are particularly comparable in relation to a specific research question will permit better causal analyses of the various elements bearing on enrollments. Levy (1982, 1985, 1986), for example, has studied university expansion of several nations within the Latin American region. Others have examined higher education within three or more Asian societies (Kaneko, 1984; Kraus et al., 1979). Focus on a few societies will allow time enough to include a broad range of evidence, including, for example, the development over time of the relevant processes, the policy documents and resource struggles of dominant national and international groups, and qualitative and statistical materials concerning student motives, perceptions, and admissions and enrollment behavior.

Regression equations, which have been used so often in the analysis of enrollment rates, could be handled in a more balanced and informative manner. Few, if any, of the researchers have demonstrated that their equations for one set of societies can be replicated with the same variables and approximately the same coefficients for a comparable set of nations (for a near attempt at such replication, see Sica and Prechel, 1981). The available evidence, including that from other methods, suggests that many of the recently estimated equations probably could not be replicated. This is particularly a problem in research where the equations have so many independent variables and thus are potentially less stable. Another regression technique noted earlier, the entering of several independent variables characterized by shared variance and multicollinearity, requires theoretical clarification and alternative methods to be meaningful (cf. Meyer and Hannan, 1979). Generally, with any technique using estimates as unstable as regression coefficients, it would be wise to compare several types of evidence and analytic methods. Qualitative historical materials, percentages, and scattergrams would leaven nicely many of the current reports of regression analysis.

The future literature of research on this topic could be much improved with respect to the publication and editorial standards for the discussion of the research and analytic methods used. Possibly a major reason that there has been so little criticism and improvement of inappropriate research designs has been that the readers simply haven't been able to decipher the cryptic published reports of methods and findings. The interpretation of various techniques and statistics requires a complete accompanying statement of relevant evidence and methods. For example, if an analysis is made of a sample of many countries around the globe, a full list of these societies is necessary for the reader to judge the meaning of the findings. Another example concerns regression equations: their interpretation necessitates the reporting of the relevant zero-order correlations, the range of values, the means and standard deviations, the standardized regression coefficients, and the standard errors (for two studies that happily go far toward meeting these criteria for reports, see Saha, 1982; Sica and Prechel, 1981).

THEORETICAL DIRECTIONS FOR FURTHER RESEARCH

One of the conditions which beclouds this field of inquiry is the set of biased and focused interests common to contemporary social science. The proponents of various social values appear to be essentially uninterested in the linkage of enrollments with social values and elements other than their own. Whatever the apparently objective facade which prefaces their reports, the researchers as advocates seem to focus on questions narrowly related to their social goals: What advantages accrue to those who swell university enrollments? How can university enrollments be used to promote international economic growth? How is enrollment expansion a result of national or international inequalities and conflict? How is expansion related to the quality of academic imagination and the satisfactions of the faculty's work? Our study would probably be more penetrating if we simply asked: What are the several conditions which lead to the expansion or contraction of enrollments?

Even though a broad understanding eludes us at present, the research is substantial and certainly interesting enough to tempt one to feel that we are on the verge of understanding why enrollments have expanded in various ways and in different countries and times. Recent research has extended around the globe and back through history. Several plausible hypotheses, supported by at least some evidence, have been identified.

There seems to be a complex web of interrelations between the many variables involved, and possibly much circularity of influence, so that the direction of effects flows back and forth. Nevertheless, some phenomena stand out as more forceful and as more independent of the others. There is considerable evidence for the independent effects of both domestic economics and politics. When these two factors are compared, tentative evidence suggests that political variables are the stronger of the two in poor agrarian societies.

The relative impact of politics and economics may be largely a reflection of greater range and variation in political relations than in economic structure among agrarian societies, though the published reports have not clarified the relative range of values and standard deviation of these variables. (The lack of clarity in publications about the relative characteristics of these variables is yet another area for greater editorial standards.) To merely use the term *politics* is to be very vague. Vaguely is, however, the manner in which too many of the studies have treated political variables. Terms such as *political modernization, bureaucratic modernization, westernization, centralization, mobilizational,* and *representational* are used, especially in quantitative global studies, with little or no theoretical or operational definition. Regardless of the quality of definition, most of the preceding list of factors are purported to be measures of political variables and have been found to be highly related to enrollments even when the level of national economic production is statistically controlled. While their meaning is currently unclear, these findings suggest potentially fruitful areas for clarification and analysis.

Frequently mentioned but not systematically examined are the processes of political and status domination and competition that affect university expansion. There is no tradition of research on the Third World that has compared the enrollment rates of systematic samples of democratic and of nonsocialist centralized nations. Another example of a puzzling finding warranting further research concerns the relations between political centralization, government educational expenditures, and enrollment rates.

Though thus far without much evidence from published enrollments research, dependency and population change appear to be strong independent variables. World system and dependency phenomena affect the universities in so many ways that it is reasonable to continue exploring possible linkages with enrollments. Few researchers other than Allmendinger (1975) have carefully examined the force of population growth in relation to the supply of land and subgroups. The rapid population growth occurring in many poor agrarian societies is forcing many persons off the farmlands. This factor looms in the background as a specter of potentially great impact. Urbanization and urban migration are likely to be correlated with enrollment expansion.

Earlier it was noted that various methods used by researchers have precluded the possibility of their finding evidence about the multiple long chains of factors affecting enrollments. This choice of methods stems in part from their overly simplistic theoretical images of a single short chain of only one or a few factors producing expansion. These factors are also conceived of as if they are above history, having the same impact at the origin of the universities as at later points in their expansion (Archer, 1982, p. 5). Some dependency theorists reject national elements as explanations of recent expansion and emphasize instead world system domination (Meyer et al., 1977). Many economists have analyzed university enrollments as if they are simply reflections of labor market demand without a mediating political life of their own (Chenery and Syrquin, 1975; Harbison and Myers, 1964; McClelland, 1966; Peaslee, 1969). And in reply, some sociologists emphasizing the autonomy of universities have dismissed such ingredients as money and politics as accounting for no more than a small proportion of the differences in historical expansion (Archer, 1982, pp. 3–4). Three analytical strategies would improve theorizing about expansion:

1. Identifying the variation of impact of a factor at different points over time;
2. Conceiving of several chains of elements as influencing expansion;
3. And identifying the sequence of elements or variables intervening between enrollments and autonomous elements.

Intervening between the relatively autonomous independent variables and enrollments are a variety of elements, including urbanization, the modernization of the labor force, educational expenditures, secondary enrollments, university processes, and other educational phenomena. For example, though its effect has been discounted in some of the global quantitative studies (Meyer, 1971; Meyer et al., 1977), urbanization has long been considered one of the chief factors promoting social mobility (Lipset and Bendix, 1966) and is often related to the establishment of secondary schools which feed into higher education. It may be that much of the effect of political and economic development on enrollments occurs through the growth of urban populations participating in the bureaucratized labor force; sending their children to the better secondary schools, which are clustered in the cities; and seeking for these children higher education, which will enable them to enter desirable jobs in the cities. This is an abbreviated statement of a hypothetical example of the chains of events which were postulated earlier as affecting enrollments.

Any speculations for further research could note that the main variable of expansion can also be defined much more broadly. Most of the research has been concerned only with total numbers of student enrollments or, occasionally, with the numbers of institutions. The numbers of enrollments could also be considered with respect to full- or part-time enrollment, the gender of the students (cf. Ramirez and Weiss, 1979), age, class and status origins, field of study (Psacharopoulos, 1980, 1982), career objectives, and type of institution. In addition to numbers of students, expansion involves also the size, number, and kinds of institutions, the kinds of curriculum (Ben-David, 1963), and the number of faculty.

While most studies of the past decade recognize that some combination of the above hypotheses would best explain international differences in expansion rates, few theoretical syntheses have appeared (Craig and Spear, 1982b). A provocative exception is Perrone's (1978, cited in Craig, 1981a, p. 156) analysis proposing that different theories explain enrollment expansion for the different classes in the United States, for example, the human capital hypothesis for the managerial class and the screening hypothesis for the urban working class.

CONCLUSIONS

Beyond the broad hypotheses suggested above for further research, it is premature to list generalizations about Third World enrollments expansion. In conclusion, we can instead relate recent enrollment research to comparative higher education studies generally and to American higher educational practices and problems.

A Subfield of Comparative Higher Education

The status of research on the expansion of Third World higher education can be summarized by contrasting it with comparative studies on other topics. A strength of enrollments research has been its use, more than with some other topics, of theories explicitly aimed at comparing several or even many societies. This research has frequently used explicitly cross-national theories such as dependency, modernization, and status and political conflict theories. While a relative strength, since its theoretical accomplishments have been modest at best, this intentional comparative emphasis is much needed in a field which calls itself comparative higher education when, in fact, it is mainly a collection of interesting but relatively isolated case studies.

This strength of comparative and theoretical emphasis is related to a weakness of much of the research on the topic: the neglect of the full history and features of expansion in specific societies. An exception is Wyatt's (1969) history of the elaborate web of political and cultural processes surrounding educational policy and enrollment changes in nineteenth-century Siam. Another example of this overly abstract tendency is that most of the research has stressed aggregate characteristics of the society without much attention to such primary actors as the students. Other fields of comparative higher education have better grasped the student point of view, particularly some of the case studies of student political activism in the Third World (Altbach, 1968a; Arnove, 1971; DiBona, 1967; Hanna and Hanna, 1975). Thus it is suggested that enrollments research could now benefit from comparative historical studies of several nations, with both qualitative and quantitative evidence, such as have appeared in the studies of the production and distribution of knowledge by Ben-David (1971) and Eisemon (1981).

There has been more study of the causes of enrollment expansion than of its effects. This is curious because some of the phenomena possibly affected have been of great interest to comparative educators and also to policymakers. These matters include economic development, political activism, institutional autonomy, and knowledge production and publication. Third World nations have heavily invested in expanding higher education, assuming economic and social development dividends without much clear evidence of these effects. Recently several commentators have raised doubts about the economic benefits of large enrollments in the Third World (Collins, 1971; Dore, 1976; Meyer and Hannan, 1979; Thompson and Fogel, 1976; Ward, 1974), yet the issue has received scanty analysis. There has been little research on the hypothesis advanced by Altbach (1968b, pp. 39, 54; 1984, p. 641) and others that large enrollments have promoted student political activism in the Third World. The autonomy of universities *vis-à-vis* politicians, merchants, and citizens has been frequently studied (Court, 1980; Dore, 1976; Levy, 1980), but without much clear evidence of a relationship to enrollments, despite the potential links with student activism and also government expenditures. The production and distribution of knowledge is receiving increasing study (Altbach and Rathgeber, 1980; Eisemon, 1981, 1982; Spitzberg, 1980) in comparative higher education, but with little evidence about the potential competition for scarce funds in the Third World between enrollments and the production and publication of ideas.

Third World Enrollments
and American Universities

In recent years, North American campuses have become hosts to very large numbers of students from the Third World. The expansion of enrollments in developing nations seems likely to be related to these waves of international students in American higher education. The precise nature of this relationship is not clear, however. Cross-sectional evidence concerning international migrations from Asian societies in 1978 has been analyzed by Cummings (1984, p. 250) as having virtually no relationship to the size of enrollments. If there is a relationship between enrollments and student migrations, it is probably more complicated than can be observed at only one point in time. For example, the number of American students migrating to German universities in the nineteenth century became large only after the expansion of the enrollments and employment opportunities on American campuses, and then it later tapered off as American institutions became large and prosperous enough to become leading centers of research. Possibly a curvilinear pattern over time characterizes the student migrations of many Third World societies. The pattern and timing of foreign migration in relation to domestic enrollments may also be different for undergraduate and graduate students. Research on this relationship will help us understand the future flows of international students which have become so important to the graduate research programs in American higher education.

Throughout this century, American academics have also been directly involved in promoting the establishment and expansion of university enrollments in the Third World. American professors have served as advisers or directly as teachers in expanding programs, and American universities have been involved in many large-scale development projects in Africa, Asia, Latin America, and Oceania. The sponsors of such involvement have been many and varied, including religions, Third World governments, foundations, corporations, victorious armies, and individuals. Some of these academic programs supported in the Third World have been quite exclusive, but most of them have tended to be expansionist in character and, whatever the actual outcomes, are seen by the participating Americans as democratic in effect. Few of these efforts have been carried out with sure evidence as to the effect of enrollment expansion. Though the number of these activities has markedly slowed in recent years, there are still many such exchanges between America and the Third World. These programs offer us an excellent opportunity to study the nature of expansion as well as its benefits and penalties.

Acknowledgments. For their thoughtful comments on an earlier draft I am grateful to William Cummings and Daniel Levy.

NOTES

1. Two journals which focus most upon comparative higher education in the Third World, *Minerva* and *Higher Education*, began publication as recently as the 1960s. Leading articles in the field are also published in the *Comparative Education Review* and various social science journals.
2. Having characterized the field as highly and naturally ideological in its premises, this reviewer can hardly claim objectivity himself. My concerns are more with the development of the freedom and skills of individuals in the agrarian and urban masses than with the development of national states, gross national products, and universities teaching the culture of an urban elite. However, the majority of the recent research on universities is not concerned with the relations between universities and the masses of urban and rural persons with low incomes. Consequently, the availability of materials will dictate much of the direction of this review. As to the interpretation of the main factors affecting the universities and national populations, my approach will be eclectic: most of the major viewpoints seem to me to reasonably explain at least some important phenomena.
3. The national statistics compiled by UNESCO designate the corresponding population age group as 20 to 24. This is a fairly reasonable, yet somewhat arbitrary estimate since the official age group varies a bit between nations.
4. It is likely that some of the fluctuations recorded in the UNESCO statistical reports represent the enumeration and reporting errors of countries.
5. The number of cases involved in this analysis is modest, so this finding should be considered with some caution.
6. The researcher makes no mention of any attempts to control for related and possibly confounding variables. One is tempted to wonder if the variable of time since

independence (pre-1913 versus post-1945) is in reality a dichotomy comprised mainly of Latin American and African nations.

7. The actual composite measure entered as an indicator of 1955 enrollments was a value predicted by a regression equation which the researchers defined as indicating the self-generating "expansion which is built into the educational system itself." The equation used was as follows:

$$t_{70} - t_{50} = a + bt_{55}(1 - t_{55}) + s_{55}(1 - t_{55}) + pop_{70}/pop_{55} + 1/pop_{70}$$

where

t_{70}	=	tertiary enrollments as a proportion of the tertiary age-group population in 1970
t_{50}	=	tertiary enrollments as a proportion of the tertiary age-group population in 1950
t_{55}	=	tertiary enrollments as a proportion of the tertiary age-group population in 1955
s_{55}	=	secondary enrollments as a proportion of the secondary age-group population in 1955
pop_{70}	=	total population in 1970
pop_{55}	=	total population in 1955

The particular form of this equation was based on a model of two types of diffusion in human populations, including contagion and diffusion from a constant source.

8. In the equations for the eleven noneconomic independent variables, the variable for the logarithm of per capita GNP in 1955 was also entered as an independent variable.

9. Another alternative hypothesis may be that some national factors acted as intervening variables for the effect of Time 1 enrollments on Time 2 enrollments.

10. A number of new researchers have been directly influenced by their work, though too many of the latter have used an atheoretical approach to research design.

11. The regression coefficient for this relationship even increased when the effect of parental status was statistically controlled. The standardized regression coefficient estimates of the total direct and indirect effects equal 0.21.

12. This is another theory in which many of the linking variables have yet to be elaborated—in this case, the variables linking centralization of prestige and culture and universities.

13. Meyer et al. (1977) did include measures of political centralization in their regression analyses of a global sample of nations. Unfortunately, because their findings concerning national political structures are simply an artifact of their longitudinal regression equations, which attributed all of the shared variance to earlier enrollments as explained above, these findings can not be used to address the issue.

14. Meyer does not distinguish between industrialized and agrarian societies in his sample. So I have elected to include in Table 6 only the poorer societies from his sample, specifically those with a per capita GNP in 1957 of less than $351. Low-income countries are those with an annual per capita GNP of $111 to $350, and very-low-income countries are those where the figure was less than $111. The rate of enrollments is measured as the ratio of higher to secondary education enrollments.

15. While Meyer does not specify for which levels of enrollments this finding applies,

his remarks imply that it holds for each level, including higher education. Meyer does not indicate the number or the type of countries involved in his analysis but describes it as a "limited number," presumably substantially less than his total sample of 141 nations. This may mean that the proportion of Third World societies in this sample is less than in his larger sample because of the better availability of government financial data in the industrial nations. Nevertheless, Meyer reports having analyzed the enrollment effect of the ratio for each of his GNP categories of nations. Thus, it is assumed that computations were made for low- and very-low-income countries, the samples of interest for our purposes here. The rate of enrollments is measured as the ratio of higher to secondary education enrollments.

REFERENCES

Agarwal, V., and Winkler, D. (1985). Foreign demand for United States higher education: A study of developing countries in the eastern hemisphere. *Economic Development and Cultural Change* 33: 623–644.

Allmendinger, D. F. (1975). *Paupers and Scholars: The Transformation of Student Life in Nineteenth-Century New England*. New York: St. Martin's.

Altbach, P. G. (1984). Student politics in the third world. *Higher Education* 13: 635–655.

Altbach, P. G. (1981a). *Student Politics: Perspectives for the Eighties*. Menuchen, NJ: Scarecrow.

Altbach, P. G. (1981b). The university as center and periphery. *Teachers College Record* 82: 601–621.

Altbach, P. G. (1979). *Comparative Higher Education: Research Trends and Bibliography*. London: Mansell.

Altbach, P. G. (1977). Servitude of the mind? Education, dependency, and neocolonialism. *Teachers College Record* 79: 187–204.

Altbach, P. G., ed. (1976). *Comparative Higher Education Abroad: Bibliography and Analysis*. New York: Praeger.

Altbach, P. G. (1975). Literary colonialism: Books in the Third World. *Harvard Educational Review* 45: 226–236.

Altbach, P. G. (1971). Neocolonialism and education. *Teachers College Record* 72: 543–558.

Altbach, P. G. (1970a). *Higher Education in Developing Countries: A Select Bibliography*. Cambridge: Harvard University Center for International Affairs.

Altbach, P. G., ed. (1970b). *The Student Revolution: A Global Analysis*. Bombay: Lalvani.

Altbach, P. G. (1968a). *Turmoil and Transition: Higher Education and Student Politics in India*. New York: Basic Books.

Altbach, P. G. (1968b). Student politics and higher education in India. In P. G. Altbach (Ed.), *Turmoil and Transition: Higher Education and Student Politics in India*. New York: Basic Books.

Altbach, P. G. (in press). *Publishing and Knowledge Distribution in International Perspective*. Albany: State University of New York Press.

Altbach, P. G., and Gopinathan, S. (1982). The dilemma of success: Higher education in advanced developing countries. In P. G. Altbach (ed.), *Higher Education in the Third World*, pp. 25–44. Singapore: Maruzen Asia.

Altbach, P. G., and Kelly, D. H. (1985). *Higher Education in International Perspective*. London: Mansell.

Altbach, P., and Kelly, D. H. (1974). *Higher Education in Developing Countries, 1969–1974: A Selected Bibliography.* New York: Praeger.

Altbach, P. G., Kelly, D. H., and Lulat, Y. (1985). *Research on Foreign Students and International Study: An Overview and Bibliography.* New York: Praeger.

Altbach, P. G., and Kelly, G. P., eds. (1984). *Education and the Colonial Experience* (rev. ed.). New Brunswick, NJ: Transaction.

Altbach, P. G., and Kelly, G. P., eds. (1978). *Education and Colonialism.* New York: Longman.

Altbach, P. G., Kelly, G. P., and Kelly, D. H. (1981). *International Bibliography of Comparative Education.* New York: Praeger.

Altbach, P. G., and Rathgeber, E. (1980). *Publishing in the Third World: Trend Report and Bibliography.* New York: Praeger.

Amano, I. (1979). Continuity and change in the structure of Japanese higher education. In W. K. Cummings, I. Amano, and K. Kitamura (eds.), *Changes in the Japanese University: A Comparative Perspective.* New York: Praeger.

Amano, I. (1969). Higher education and social mobility in modern Japan. *Journal of Educational Sociology* 24: 77–92.

Amin, Samir. (1975). What education for what development? *Prospectus: Quarterly Review of Education* 5: 48–52.

Archer, M. S., ed. (1982). *The Sociology of Educational Expansion.* Beverly Hills, CA: Sage.

Archer, M. S. (1982). Introduction: Theorizing about the expansion of educational systems. In Archer, *Sociology of Educational Expansion,* pp. 3–64.

Archer, M. S. (1979). *The Social Origins of Educational Systems.* London: Mansell.

Arnove, R. (1980). Comparative education and world systems analysis. *Comparative Education Review* 24: 48–62.

Arnove, R. (1977). Students in Venezuelan politics, 1958–1974. In D. J. Myers and J. D. Martz (eds.), *Venezuela: Is Democracy Institutionalized?* New York: Praeger.

Arnove, R. (1971). *Student Alienation: A Venezuelan Study.* New York: Praeger.

Barber, E., Altbach, P. G., and Myers, R. (1984). *Bridges to Knowledge: Foreign Students in Comparative Perspective.* Chicago: University of Chicago Press.

Beckett, P., and O'Connell J. O. (1977). *Education and Power in Nigeria: A Study of University Students.* London: Houghton & Stoughton.

Ben-David, J. (1963). The growth of the professions and the class system. *Current Sociology* 12: 256–277.

Ben-David, J. (1971). *The Scientist's Role in Society: A Comparative Study.* Englewood Cliffs, NJ: Prentice-Hall.

Ben-David, J., and Zloczower, A. (1962). Universities and academic systems in modern societies. *European Journal of Sociology* 3: 45–84.

Berg, I. (1970). *Education and Jobs.* New York: Praeger.

Berman, E. H. (1979). Foundations, United States foreign policy, and African education, 1945–1975. *Harvard Educational Review* 49: 145–179.

Black, C. E. (1967). *The Dynamics of Modernization.* New York: Harper & Row.

Brubacher, J. S., and Rudy, W. (1976). *Higher Education in Transition.* New York: Harper & Row.

Burn, B. (1980). *Expanding the International Dimension of Higher Education.* San Francisco: Jossey-Bass.

Carnoy, M. (1974a). *Education and Cultural Imperialism.* New York: McKay.

Carnoy, M. (1974b). Review of *The World Education Crisis as Systems Analysis. Harvard Educational Review* 44: 178–187.

Chan, A., Rosen, S., and Unger, J. (1980). Students and class warfare: The social roots of the Red Guard conflict in Guangzhou. *The China Quarterly* 83. 397–446.

Chenery, H., and Syrquin, M. (1975). *Patterns of Development: 1950–1970*. New York: Oxford University Press.

Collins, R. (1981). *Sociology Since Midcentury*. New York: Academic Press.

Collins, R. (1979). *The Credential Society*. New York: Academic Press.

Collins, R. (1977). Some comparative principles of educational stratification. *Harvard Educational Review* 47: 1–27.

Collins, R. (1971). Functional and conflict theories of educational stratification. *American Sociological Review* 36: 1002–1019.

Coombs, P. H. (1985). *The World Crisis in Education: The View from the Eighties*. New York: Oxford University Press.

Court, D. (1980). The development ideal in higher education: The experience of Kenya and Tanzania. *Higher Education* 9: 657–680.

Craig, J. E. (1984). *Scholarship and Nation Building: The Universities of Strasbourg and Alsatian Society, 1870–1939*. Chicago: University of Chicago Press.

Craig, J. E. (1981a). The expansion of education. *Review of Research in Education* 9: 151–213.

Craig, J. E. (1981b). On the development of educational systems. *American Journal of Education* 89: 189–211.

Craig, J. E., and Spear, N. (1982a). Explaining educational expansion: An agenda for historical and comparative research. In Archer, *Sociology of Educational Expansion*, pp. 133–157.

Craig, J. E., and Spear, N. (1982b). Rational actors, group processes, and the development of educational systems. In Archer, *Sociology of Educational Expansion*, pp. 65–90.

Cummings, W. (1984). Going overseas for higher education: the Asian experience. *Comparative Education Review* 28: 241–257.

DiBona, J. (1967). Indiscipline and student leadership in an Indian university. In S. M. Lipset (ed.), *Student Politics*, pp. 372–393. New York: Basic Books.

Dore, R. (1976). *The Diploma Disease*. Berkeley: University of California Press.

Eisemon, T. O. (1982). *The Science Profession in the Third World: Studies from India and Kenya*. New York: Praeger.

Eisemon, T. O. (1981). Scientific life in Indian and African Universities: A comparative study of peripherality in science. *Comparative Education Review* 25: 164–182.

Emmerson, D. R. (ed.). (1968). *Politics in Developing Nations*. New York: Praeger.

Foley, D. (1984). Colonialism and schooling in the Philippines, 1898–1970. In Altbach and Kelly, *Education and the Colonial Experience*, pp. 33–53.

Frank, A. G. (1965). *Capitalism and Underdevelopment in Latin America*. New York: Monthly Review Press.

Garms, W. (1968). A multivariate analysis of the correlates of educational effort by nations. *Comparative Education Review* 12: 281–299.

Haar, J. (1976). *The Politics of Education in Brazil*. New York: Praeger.

Hanna, W. J., and Hanna, J. L., eds. (1975). *University Students and African Politics*. New York: Africana.

Harbison, F., and Myers, C. (1964). *Education, Manpower and Economic Growth*. New York: McGraw-Hill.

Henze, J. (1984). Higher education: The tension between quality and equality. In R. Hayhoe (ed.), *Contemporary Chinese Education*, Armonk, N.Y.: Sharpe.

Kaneko, M. (1984). Education and labor force composition in Southeast and East Asian development. *The Developing Economies* 22: 47–68.

Kopf, D. (1984). Orientalism and the Indian educated elite. In Altbach and Kelly, *Education and the Colonial Experience*, pp. 117–135. New Brunswick, NJ: Transaction.

Kraus, R., Maxwell, W., and Vanneman, R. (1979). The interests of bureaucrats: Implications of the Asian experience for recent theories of development. *American Journal of Sociology* 85: 135–155.

Levy, D. C. (1986). *Higher Education and the State in Latin America*. Chicago: University of Chicago Press.

Levy, D. C. (1985). Latin America's private universities: How successful are they? *Comparative Education Review* 29: 440–459.

Levy, D. C. (1982). The rise of private universities in Latin America and the United States. In Archer, *Sociology of Educational Expansion*, pp. 93–132.

Levy, D. C. (1980). *University and Government in Mexico: Anatomy of an Authoritarian System*. New York: Praeger.

Liebman, A., Walker, K., and Glazer, M. (1972). *Latin American University Students: A Six-Nation Study*. Cambridge: Harvard University Press.

Lipset, S. M., ed. (1968). *Student Politics*. New York: Basic Books.

Lipset, S. M., and Altbach, P. G. (eds.). (1970). *Students in Revolt*. Boston: Beacon.

Lipset, S. M., and Bendix, R. (1966). *Social Mobility in Industrial Society*. Berkeley: University of California Press.

Lulat, Y. G.-M., and Altbach, P. G. (1985). International students in comparative perspective: Toward a political economy of international study. In J. C. Smart (ed.), *Higher Education: Handbook of Theory and Research*, Vol. I, pp. 439–494. New York: Agathon Press.

Machlup, F. (1970). *Education and Economic Growth*. Lincoln, Neb.: University of Nebraska Press.

Maxwell, W. (1975). Modernization and mobility into the patrimonial medical elite in Thailand. *American Journal of Sociology* 81: 465–490.

Mazrui, A. A. (1975). The African university as a multinational corporation: Problems of penetration and dependency. *Harvard Educational Review* 45: 191–210.

McClelland, D. (1966). Does education accelerate economic growth? *Economic Development and Cultural Change* 14: 257–78.

Meyer, J. W. (1971). Economic and political effects on national educational enrollment patterns. *Comparative Education Review* 15: 28–43.

Meyer, J. W., Boli-Bennett, J., and Chase-Dunn, C. (1975). Convergence and divergence in development. *Annual Review of Sociology* 1: 223–246.

Meyer, J. W., and Hannan, M., eds. (1979). *National Development and the World System: Educational, Economic and Political Change*. Chicago: University of Chicago Press.

Meyer, J. W., Hannan, M. T., Rubinson, R., and Thomas, G. M. (1979a). National economic development, 1950–1970: Social and political factors. In Meyer and Hannan, *National Development and the World System*, pp. 85–116.

Meyer, J. W., Tyack, E., Nagal, J., and Gordon, A. (1979b). Public education as nation-building in America: Enrollments and bureaucratization in the American states, 1870–1930. *American Journal of Sociology* 85: 591–613.

Meyer, J. W., Ramirez, F. O., Robinson, R., and Boli-Bennett, J. (1977). The world educational revolution, 1950–1970. *Sociology of Education* 50: 242–258.

Meyer, J. W., and Rubinson, R. (1975). Education and political development. *Review of Research in Education* 3: 134–162.

Myers, R. G. (1972). *Education and Emigration: Study Abroad and The Migration of Human Resources*. New York: McKay.

Nakata, Thinapan. (1975). *The Problems of Democracy in Thailand: A Study of Political Culture and Socialization of College Students*. Bangkok: Praepittaya.

Peaslee, A. L. (1969). Education's role in development. *Economic Development and Cultural Change* 17: 293–318.

Pempel, T. J. (1973). The politics of enrollment expansion in Japanese universities. Journal of Asian Studies 33: 67–86.

Prizzia, R., and Sinsawasdi, N. (1974). *Thailand: Student Activism and Political Change*. Bangkok: Allied.

Psacharopoulos, G. (1982). The economics of higher education in developing countries. *Comparative Education Review* 26: 139–159.

Psacharopoulos, G. (1980). *Higher Education in Developing Countries: A Cost-Benefit Analysis*. Washington, DC: World Bank, Staff Paper No. 440.

Psacharopoulos, G. (1973). *Returns to Education: An International Comparison*. Amsterdam: Elsevier.

Ramirez, F. O., and Meyer, J. W. (1980). Comparative education: The social construction of the modern world system. *Annual Review of Sociology* 6: 369–399.

Ramirez, F. O., and Weiss, J. (1979). The political incorporation of women. In Meyer and Hannan, *National Development and the World System*, pp. 238–249.

Ringer, F. K. (1979). *Education and Society in Modern Europe*. Bloomington and London: Indiana University Press.

Rogers, E. M. (1983). *Diffusion of Innovations*. New York: Free Press.

Rogers, E. M. (1962). *Diffusion of Innovations*. New York: Free Press.

Rosen, S. (1982). *Red Guard Factionalism and the Cultural Revolution in Guangzhou (Canton)*. Boulder, CO: Westview.

Rosen, S. (1981). *The Role of Sent-Down Youth in the Chinese Cultural Revolution: The Case of Guangzhou*. Berkeley: Center for Chinese Studies, University of California, Research Monograph No. 19.

Rudolph, S. H., and Rudolph, L. I. (1972). *Education and Politics in India*. Cambridge: Harvard University Press.

Saha, L. (1982). National development and the revolution of rising expectations: Determinants of career orientations among secondary school students in comparative perspective. In Archer, *Sociology of Educational Expansion*, pp. 241–264.

Sica, A., and Prechel, H. (1981). National political-economic dependency in the global economy and educational development. *Comparative Education Review* 25: 384–402.

Spaulding, S., and Flack, M. J. (1976). *The World's Students in the United States: A Review and Evaluation of Research on Foreign Students*. New York: Praeger.

Spence, A. (1974). *Market Signaling: Informational Transfer in Hiring and Related Screening Processes*. Cambridge: Harvard University Press.

Spitzberg, I. J. (1980). *Universities and the International Distribution of Knowledge*. New York: Praeger.

Thompson, K., and Fogel, B. (1976). *Higher Education and Social Change*. New York: Praeger.

Trow, M. (1972). The expansion and transformation of higher education. *International Review of Higher Education* 18: 61–83.

Turner, R. (1959). Sponsored and contest mobility and the school system. *American Sociological Review* 25: 855–867.

Wallerstein, I. (1974). The rise and future demise of the world capitalist system: Concepts for comparative analysis. *Comparative Studies in Society and History* 16: 387–415.

Ward, F. C., ed. (1974). *Education and Development Reconsidered*. New York: Praeger.

Wyatt, D. K. (1969). *The Politics of Reform in Thailand: Education in the Reign of King Chulalongkorn*. New Haven, CT: Yale University Press.

Zachariah, M. (1985). Lumps of clay and growing plants: Dominant metaphors of the role of education in the Third World, 1950–1980. *Comparative Education Review* 29: 1–21.

The Organization and Provision
of Continuing Professional Education:
A Critical Review and Synthesis

Ronald M. Cervero
University of Georgia
and
William H. Young
Northern Illinois University

From the earliest days of the organization of professional groups, their leaders have assumed that the practitioner should be engaged in learning throughout the life span. Many methods, such as books, meetings, discussion with colleagues, and supervised practice, were accepted ways of accomplishing this learning. Rather suddenly, however, in the mid-1960s there began an explosive growth in the provision of formal continuing education programs. Nobody has yet been able to estimate how many billions of dollars are spent each year to provide these programs, but the amount is sizable. As a result, organized, comprehensive continuing education programs are evident in business, law, medicine, pharmacy, veterinary medicine, counseling, nursing-home administration, nursing, the military, public school education, religion, and many other professions. In fact, many professions (Kenny, 1985) have a system of accreditation for providers of continuing education.

This growth of continuing professional education (CPE) has led to an increasing recognition of its importance as a distinct area of practice and study. There are a number of books (Houle, 1980; Stern, 1983b; Cervero and Scanlan, 1985), as well as journals (*The Journal of Continuing Education in Nursing, Mobius: A Journal for Continuing Education Professionals in Health Sciences and Health Policy,* and the *Journal of Continuing Social Work Education*), devoted exclusively to CPE in specific professions. Another sign of the importance of CPE is the entry of foundations into this field. The Kellogg Foundation, for example, has identified CPE as one of its major focuses. Also, the way in which professional associations organize themselves reflects an increasing awareness of CPE. For example, two of the major associations of continuing educators (the National University Continuing Education Association and the American Association for Adult and Continuing Education) have specialized divisions devoted to CPE. Finally, there is a trend for continuing professional educators in specific occupations to form interest groups within the national professional association (e.g., the American Nurses' Association) or to form their own associations (e.g., the Society of Medical College Directors of Continuing Medical Education, and the Society for the Advancement of Continuing Education in Ministry).

With this explosion of formal CPE programs, the building of systems of CPE within each profession is seen as a desirable next step (Houle, 1980; Stern, 1983b). A prominent scholar puts it this way:

> The plans to establish basic educational programs for those entering the professions were thought in the first quarter of this century to be visionary, but they have now been realized at levels far beyond those of the original dreams. Continuing education will follow the same pattern of growth; what we hardly dare prophesy today will be seen by later generations as efforts to achieve a manifest necessity. (Houle, 1980, p. 302)

Two major issues are being considered as the planning and delivery of professionwide systems of CPE are being discussed. The first is the extent to which the "central aim . . . will focus on raising the optimum level of performance of all practitioners" (Houle, 1983, p. 257). The second, which is the focus of this chapter, is the extent to which the providers of CPE will work in an interdependent fashion.

There is little doubt that interdependence among providers is emerging as one of the major issues in CPE. One of the central themes of two recent books (Alford, 1980; Stern, 1983b) is the need for more collaboration among providers of CPE. While the reasons for the emergence of this issue are complex, two fundamental ones may be discerned. First, CPE itself has been seen increasingly as an important segment of professional education and as a potentially unlimited educational market. These realizations have caused many professions to see the potential of a system of continuing education. At present, however, the provision of CPE in most professions can be characterized by organizations offering CPE with little regard for what other providers are doing. It is not surprising, then, that the two questions addressed most often are "Who should provide what?" and "Should providers be encouraged to compete or collaborate?"

The second reason for the prominence of provider interdependence as an issue is that it is also an issue at other levels of professional education. Thus, as leaders within a profession begin to conceptualize a system of CPE, they look to the many models and examples in their own experience based on preservice professional training. Two examples from medicine are illustrative: (1) Universities and community hospitals have had formal collaborative arrangements for some time; and (2) professional specialty associations virtually dictate the content of the university curriculum in their specialties because they control the certification examinations. There are many collaborative institutional arrangements already in place as the professions seek to create systems of CPE.

The role that higher education should play in these interdependent systems of CPE is a point of great concern. Those continuing educators in colleges and universities feel that higher education should be an important provider because of its central role in the preservice preparation of professionals. Yet, for a variety of reasons, these educators believe that higher education has "consented to be led by professional societies" (Stern, 1980, p. 22). One of the most important of these reasons is that higher education lacks a set of coherent policies about CPE (Berlin, 1983; Stern, 1980).

Given the variety of providers of CPE, the essential question raised in the literature is the extent to which institutions will work collaboratively or competitively. Implicit in Stern's (1983a) description of the current situation as a "disorderly market" is the assumption that CPE should be provided in more collaboratively. While this issue will be worked out separately within each profession (Houle, 1980), the processes underlying interinstitutional collaboration are similar. In fact, interinstitutional collaboration has been an important area of study among scholars for some time (Schermerhorn, 1975), and its theories can profitably be applied to the field of CPE.

Because the issue of collaboration among providers of CPE is just emerging, the literature is much more prescriptive and descriptive than analytical. There is relatively little research and even less theory related to the topic. Given the state of the literature base, we believe that this chapter can usefully serve two purposes: (1) to critically review the literature on the topic of interdependence among providers of CPE; and (2) to synthesize this material into a framework that would guide further research on the topic. The remainder of this chapter is divided into four major sections. First, the major providers of CPE are described and analyzed. Next follows a critical review of the literature on interdependence among providers of CPE. Third, we present a framework that should guide further research on this topic. In the last section, we discuss the implications of the framework for research and practice in CPE.

PROVIDERS OF
CONTINUING PROFESSIONAL EDUCATION

In summarizing the contributions of a variety of experts, Houle (1983) offered the following description of CPE:

> At a minimum, continuing professional education appears to be a complex of instructional systems, many of them heavily didactic, in which people who know something teach it to those who do not know it. The central aim of such teaching, which is offered by many providers, is to keep professionals up to date in their practice. (p. 254)

While the providers of these instructional systems are as varied as they are pervasive, there exists no national repository of statistics that describes the number of providers, the number of participants, or the amount of money spent for CPE (Stern, 1983b; Arnstein, 1983; Suleiman, 1983). Where data are available, the estimates vary so wildly that one cannot trust any one estimate. Thus, in trying to determine who are the major providers of CPE, we must follow Stern's (1983b) advice that until statistics do become available "the experience of 'old hands' . . . will be a major resource" (p. 134).

There is a general concensus in the literature that the four major providers are universities and professional schools, professional associations, employing agencies, and independent providers (Berlin, 1983; Cross, 1981; Houle, 1980; Lynton, 1983; National University Continuing Education Association—NUCEA, 1984; Nowlen and Stern, 1981). Other types of providers that are described in the literature are government (Lynton, 1983), foundations (NUCEA, 1984), autonomous groups such as teachers' centers (Houle, 1980), and purveyors of professional supplies and equipment (Houle, 1980). Within each of the types of providers listed above, many forms and subtypes can be identified.

It is impossible to estimate which of these types of providers is most or least prominent in terms of number of offerings or participants. Arnstein (1983) notes that while there are reasonably well-established rules for counting participants in continuing higher education, "these rules do not extend to continuing education when offered by business and professional societies" (p. 238). Thus, there is no common metric nor a national collecting agency for data on CPE. Also, the relative importance of each type of provider varies with the individual profession. Whereas universities are major providers in medicine and engineering (Derbyshire, 1983; Griffith, 1983), they are second to professional associations in the field of certified public accountancy (Cruse, 1983) and provide virtually no CPE in the field of real estate (Bloom, 1983). Thus, even if we could know how much CPE is offered by each type of provider, it is likely that the estimates would vary by profession. In the next sections, we offer brief descriptions of the four major types of providers and assessments of their relative strengths and weaknesses in terms of ability to deliver CPE.

Universities and Professional Schools

Houle (1980) offers a succinct summary of this type of provider: "Professional schools collectively offer a massive offering of opportunities for continuing education. . . . There are many kinds and levels of such schools; some are free-standing and others are parts of larger entities, often universities" (p. 175). A recent development is the sponsorship of these schools by corporations, such as Arthur D. Little and Rand. Eurich (1985) has identified 18 such "corporate colleges."

There is a great deal of variance in the patterns by which higher education organizes the delivery of CPE. The primary difference is whether CPE is coordinated into a single university function (centralized administration) or is administered separately by individual professional schools (decentralized administration). An extreme example of the latter approach is that in 1977, a major university had 38 separate administrative units responsible for the provision of continuing education (Houle, 1980, p. 181). The decentralized approach is favored by those who insist that the programming function can be performed only by individuals trained in the specific profession. Another reason that this is a desirable option for professional schools is that CPE generates revenue, which can be used to fund other projects. The centralized approach, however, is becoming a more viable option because it can provide programming in a more efficient manner. Houle (1980, pp. 182–183) notes that general extension divisions are building up staffs of competent programmers with advanced degrees in adult education. In addition, these divisions may have substantial physical resources, such as residential centers, audiovisual materials, and computer-assisted instruction. It seems inefficient for several professional schools at the same university to establish duplicative staffs and facilities.

As a provider of CPE, higher education has a number of strengths. Because of its research orientation, the university is the primary source of knowledge for most professions. It is most appropriate, then, that the faculty members who developed this new knowledge should teach it to practitioners through CPE (Smutz, Crowe, and Lindsay, 1986). Universities have a great deal of experience with lengthy and complex forms of instruction, as delivered in preservice training (Queeny, 1984) and provide certification for the successful completion of such instruction (Cruse, 1983; Houle, 1980). Unlike other providers which generally deliver relatively discrete forms of instruction over a short time period, the university is more capable of offering continuous and lengthy types of learning experiences that lead to continuing education credits. Unlike most other providers, universities have a large resident staff whose full-time responsibility is instruction (Houle, 1980; Suleiman, 1983). With the decline of the school-age population, many of these faculty members have insufficient numbers of preservice students and thus are able to turn their energies to CPE.

Another strength is that these institutions ordinarily have more abundant and readily available physical facilities than other providers (Bloom, 1983; Houle, 1980). These include housing, libraries, meeting rooms, state-of-the-art equipment, and food service. Furthermore, the problems faced by professionals are often complex and require solutions that are interdisciplinary in nature. For example, members of several professional groups (i.e., physicians, attorneys, ministry, and counselors) may be involved in a decision to remove life support systems from a patient. The university is in an excellent position to provide these solutions through CPE because of its comprehensive nature (Smutz, Crowe, and

Lindsay, 1986). Particularly where programming is done by the centralized approach, an individual professional such as a social worker might attend a program that has instructors from medicine and law as well as social work.

Last, and perhaps most important, is the overall perception of universities as having a natural credibility with their potential audience in terms of integrity and identity (Cross, 1981; Cruse, 1983; Suleiman, 1983). In other words, "Quality is higher education's most important attribute" (Cross, 1981, p. 7). This characteristic, which is a function of several of the strengths described above, is noted even by those who believe that higher education is losing its place as a major provider of CPE (Stern, 1980; Berlin, 1983).

Higher education also has a number of weaknesses as a provider of CPE. The weakness having the most comprehensive effects is that because CPE is not a primary function of higher education institutions, substantial and reliable funding is not generally available (Sneed, 1972). Primarily as a result of the lack of a funding base, "The university as an institution has no independent policy and no independent set of practical guidelines in continuing professional education" (Stern, 1980, p. 22). Thus, the CPE efforts at any one institution are often uneven because they rely upon an enthusiastic committee member, the ability of the programming staff to convince faculty to teach above their normal teaching load, or the presence of grant monies to support special programming. In addition, universities generally do not have the ability to link what is taught to practice (NUCEA, 1984; Sneed, 1972). Even the continuing education representatives of higher education recognize that universities do not return to the work settings of professionals and thus cannot provide reinforcement of what is taught as well as other providers can (NUCEA, 1984). Several other weaknesses have been cited by a prominent leader among the independent providers of CPE: Suleiman (1983) notes that universities are generally limited to their own faculty and facilities; are generally insensitive to instructional quality; have only limited ideas about how to price their product; lack proper marketing expertise; have internal organizational characteristics that are not conducive to developing, marketing, and administering programs; and tend to be rooted in traditional approaches to fields of knowledge.

Professional Associations

The way that professional associations think about and deliver CPE varies considerably, depending on the number of its members, its scope of purpose, and the size and structure of its staff. In many cases, however, the educational program would be defined as "having to do with the accreditation of professional schools or other training programs, the issuance of publications, the sponsorship of conventions and conferences, and the operation of special training programs, such as courses, conferences, workshops, and other activities clearly defined as instructional'' (Houle, 1980, p. 172). A study done in 1977 showed that nearly all associations provided some form of continuing education for their members, but only one third sponsored certificate, licensure, or degree programs (Hohmann, 1980).

One of the major strengths of associations in the provision of CPE is their ability to secure a wide array of talent, especially from among their membership. Other providers are usually limited to members of their own staffs. In contrast, associations include among their membership many, if not most, of the professionals in the field, who can bring a variety of points of view to the educational programming (Houle, 1980; Sulieman, 1983). Additionally, because of ''an association's breadth of service and continuity of coverage, its educational program has a special capacity to deliver discrete and not necessarily sequential messages'' (Houle, 1980, p. 174). Associations generally sponsor conferences, which build on this strength, as opposed to programs that require depth of coverage over a relatively long duration. Associations also have direct access to professionals who are seeking CPE and are generally familiar with their learning needs (Cruse, 1983; Suleiman, 1983). Finally, in comparison to private enterprises, associations enjoy a nonprofit status and thus have certain financial advantages, such as reduced postage expenses.

A major weakness of professional associations in the provision of CPE is the organizational placement of the continuing education function (Hohmann, 1980; Houle, 1980). The educational function is typically divided into separate divisions or committees responsible for publications, conventions, and ''the educational program.'' The effect of this practice is that the education division has responsibility for only a few specific programs (e.g., short courses and telelectures) and must constantly compete for internal resources with other association divisions (e.g., conferences) that have greater public relations value. A second weakness stems from the role of association staff in carrying out the CPE function. Staff members usually cannot take the leadership in programming because they are viewed as subordinate to volunteer committees of association members. Although they would like to take a more substantive role in programming, staff are often viewed as simply ''seminar schedulers'' (Hohmann, 1980, p. 88). Also, directors of education generally carry other major association responsibilities which compete for time that could be devoted to program development (Hohmann, 1980). Finally, Suleiman (1983) notes that associations typically lack marketing expertise and have only a limited idea about how to price their product.

Employment Settings

Employers such as hospitals, social agencies, business firms, and governments offer a tremendous amount of continuing education to their employees. While estimates of the money spent by employers on the educational function vary, a commonly accepted figure is $60 billion annually (Eurich, 1985, p. 6), which may be compared to $55 billion spent by all higher education institutions in 1981–1982. Although not all of this money is spent on the education of professionals, a reasonable hypothesis is that more CPE is offered by employers than by higher education. Shelton and Craig (1983) cite evidence that indicates at least half of the continuing education in health care is provided by employers in contrast with other providers, and that "most management education is done by employers and by the training industry" (p. 154). The central task of CPE in employment settings is to improve participants' performance with respect to the mission of the agency. The measure of success is the extent to which the problem which gave rise to an educational program has been remedied (Houle, 1980; Kost, 1980; Shelton and Craig, 1983).

Without a doubt, the greatest strength of providing CPE within employment settings is the employers' ability to directly assess "specific inadequacies of personal or collective service" (Houle, 1980, p. 186). Unlike any other provider, professionals' performance problems can be directly assessed on a regular basis and can be used to determine both the need for an educational program and the extent to which the program has made a difference on the job. Other strengths from the employer's viewpoint are the relative convenience of scheduling and the cost-effectiveness of providing in-house CPE when there are large numbers of employees (Shelton and Craig, 1983). The consequences of the fact that education is secondary to the main purpose of the business is a major weakness of employer-provided CPE. This means that the education function often suffers from a lack of regular and substantial support from the parent body, particularly in difficult financial situations (Houle, 1980).

Independent Providers

The providers in this category represent a wide range of institutions and constitute a growing segment of the field (Suleiman, 1983). Some of these providers are operated for profit and others are nonprofit; some are cooperative self-help ventures; and some are philanthropic organizations (Houle, 1980, p. 188). Research organizations (e.g., SRI), consulting firms (e.g., Arthur D. Little), accounting firms, and manufacturers/suppliers (e.g., IBM) use seminars and conferences to gain exposure to customers and client groups. Publishers are also moving into CPE as another way to serve well-defined audiences to whom they currently provide print materials. There are also the "privates" (Suleiman, 1983, p. 140), institutions which are organized on a free-standing basis and which treat the CPE field as a business.

The greatest advantage that the independent providers have is in program development. Suleiman (1983) argues that they can respond quickly to learners' needs "with good instruction free from problems of faculty involvement, committee approvals, and other political considerations" (p. 138). Most private organizations offer programs nationally. This enables them to amortize development costs over more offerings. Because of their flexibility, independent providers have pioneered new formats and methods of instruction that have subsequently been adopted by larger and better established providers of CPE (Houle, 1980, p. 189).

The independent providers' major weakness is that they lack an image of quality and thus are less credible to their audiences until they demonstrate otherwise. Sponsorship by manufacturers is generally suspect until it is clear that they are not simply using an educational format to promote their own products. The lack of an image of quality is a problem partly because CPE is an easy-entry field and many independent providers have exploited professionals' desire to learn or need to meet recertification requirements with programs that promised more than was delivered (Houle, 1980, p. 189).

INTERDEPENDENCE IN CPE: A CRITICAL REVIEW

As described in the previous section, there are multiple providers within the field of CPE. Since these several major providers are often serving the same audiences, a major issue has arisen regarding "Who should do what?" (Houle, 1980, p. 192). This has become a highly charged issue because CPE, often a highly visible activity, can promote an organization. Also, CPE produces substantial revenue, which is often used to subsidize other functions of an organization.

The CPE field has been characterized by the higher education establishment as a confused and disorderly marketplace (NUCEA, 1984) "in which many groups and individuals hawk their wares under the confused scrutiny of a mixed bag of controllers and preservers of order" (Stern, 1983a, p. 5). Implicit in this description of the field as disorderly is a prescription to make it more orderly. To bring about this order, some have explicitly recognized the need for a system of CPE. The Kellogg Foundation, one of the leaders in the field, has argued that with entry-level preparation programs well in place, CPE should become the "new frontier" in professional education: "The center of attention must now turn to the soaring edifice" of CPE (Mawby, 1985, p. 3). However, those who work in the field realize that the articulation of an orderly and comprehensive system of CPE within any profession will be a difficult undertaking (Smutz et al., 1986).

The way to approach the question of "Who should do what?" has often been identified as a choice in which providers should be encouraged to compete or collaborate with each other (Cervero, 1984; Houle, 1980; Smutz et al., 1986). In discussing the provision of CPE in science and engineering, Hazzard (1977) asked the question: "Is it best just to let the free market operate with supply responding to demand in the many ways already extant? Or should there be more bureaucratic ways of response?" (p. 190). The leaders of the continuing education establishment in higher education have focused their attention on how functional collaborative relationships between the major providers could be achieved (NUCEA, 1984). Others proclaim the virtues of competition as producing higher quality education (Bloom, 1983; Kost, 1980; Griffith, 1983). Their argument is "Let the various providers do what seems best and the test of the market place will prevail" (Houle, 1980, p. 194).

What, in reality, is the extent of competition and collaboration in CPE? There is a small, but increasing, amount of information with which to answer this question. A great deal of our knowledge comes from anecdotal reports and eyewitness accounts. Much of the literature is prescriptive, describing relationships among providers most often as competitive, although collaboration is to be preferred. In summarizing the chapters in his book that deal with this issue, Stern (1983a) says, "Each author describes interactions among providers, occasionally as cooperative, more frequently as competitive. But from these chapters emerge some natural linkages which point to the advantages of more formal collaboration in the next decade" (p. 39). In an earlier work, Stern (1980) argued that the field of continuing education is in an undefined, transitional stage between competition and collaboration. Stern notes that the context in which the issue is being discussed is not which pattern of relationships would produce the highest quality program. Rather, "the important question is that of polity" (p. 16), which means "turf" in less polite language.

One of the problems that plagues the literature on this topic is the lack of clarity about the phenomenon being discussed. Nowhere is a definition of competition among providers given, although most writers appear to assume that it means the opposite of cooperation. The presence of a relationship among providers has been described by many terms, such as *cooperation* (Beder, 1984c), *collaboration* (Cervero, 1984), *partnerships* (Nowlen and Stern, 1981), *exchange* (Valentine, 1984), and *interdependence* (Fingeret, 1984). Like Schermerhorn (1975), we believe that the lowest common denominator among these concepts is organizational interdependency. Litwak and Hylton (1962) consider two or more organizations interdependent if they take each other into account in pursuing individual goals. Thus, a continuum can be conceptualized in which there are high degrees of interdependence at one end (e.g., collaborative relationships) and low degrees at the other end (e.g., competitive relationships). Weaver (1979) describes some of the components of high degrees of interdependency: "Collaboration is not . . . a matter of goodwill, but an agreed upon distribution of power, status, and authority . . . the nature of shared governance relationships will vary in kind and difficulty according to the degree to which vested interests conflict or coincide" (p. 24).

The literature on organizational interdependence is very extensive, and we will draw upon this literature primarily in developing a framework for research in a later section of this chapter. The literature reviewed in this section will focus on that published in the field of continuing professional education. The references can be categorized into three types: those that deal with organizational interdependence in a prescriptive, a descriptive, and an analytical fashion. Most of the literature is in the first category and addresses the question of whether there should be more or less interdependence. In the second area are institutional descriptions and other forms of descriptive information about the extent of interdependent relationships in CPE. Finally, there is a small but growing body of research about why CPE providers seek to develop interdependent relationships. The references in this section are covered in greater depth because we believe this to be the most important area for future research.

The Prescriptive Literature

The normative question of whether interdependence among providers of CPE should be encouraged or discouraged has been discussed in the context of many professions, including teaching (Ferver, 1981), engineering (Bruce, Siebert, Smullin, and Fano, 1982), and medicine (Derbyshire, 1983). There appears to be only a small amount of support for encouraging competitive relationships, even though it is the most common mode of operation at the present time. The literature overwhelmingly supports greater interdependence among providers of CPE.

Almost all those who support competition among providers base their argument on the "free market" system of the economy, wherein only the highest-quality (Bloom, 1983; Kost, 1980), best-managed (Stern, 1983a), and most effectively delivered (Griffith, 1983) programs would survive. Kost (1980) presents the most direct argument for competition when he says, "Competition is needed to drive up the quality of such programs or to replace them in the marketplace. Competition is also needed to produce more innovative approaches in curriculum planning, program development, instruction, and program delivery" (p. 42). In contrast to these positive assessments of competition, Curran (1983) argues that professional associations in banking should reduce interdependent relationships with universities because of previous negative experiences in which the latter have taken control of program content and delivery. Even among those promoting competition, no one believes that this should be the only principle governing relationships among providers. For example, Kost (1980) and Bloom (1983) see the need for the coexistence of competitive and cooperative relationships.

The most common form of the argument for greater interdependence promotes its desirability without being specific about the ends it serves or the form it should take (Berlin, 1983; NUCEA, 1984; Ryor, Shanker, and Sandefeur, 1979; Stern, 1980). Berlin (1983) provides some insight in support of interdependent relationships as a general good: "Cooperative or collaborative arrangements have a beguiling appeal, sustained at least in part by the rhetoric of the idea and its apparent political correctness" (p. 127). Others are more specific about the form that interdependence should take. Several authors propose developing a superordinate body to coordinate the provision of CPE. Eurich (1985) proposes a "strategic council for educational development" to coordinate the programs offered by the multiple providers. Lynton (1983) suggests forming "human resource councils" to perform this function. Bruce et al. (1982) propose a council that "insures speedy development of lifelong cooperative education by aggressively promoting and supporting collaborative efforts by industry and engineering schools" (p. 46). Finally, several authors have suggested that interdependent relationships can help to achieve a specific end, such as worker development (Shelton and Craig, 1983), improved performance of practitioners (Houston and Freiberg, 1979), and improved patient care (Derbyshire, 1983).

In discussing the reasons that interdependence among providers should be encouraged, a number of authors have identified benefits that each provider should expect as a result. By collaborating with employers and associations, higher education improves their access to potential students (Lynton, 1981; Smutz et al., 1986) and their ability to identify learning needs (Smutz et al., 1986). Professional associations improve their access to faculty, obtain the use of better facilities, and decrease their program development costs by collaborating with higher education (Smutz et al., 1986). Employers can provide education in a more cost-effective manner by buying what they need from higher education than by providing it themselves. Furthermore, they also guarantee their employees regular access to new knowledge (Lynton, 1981). It is both difficult and expensive for employers to duplicate the structure and service of a tax-supported higher education system. By collaborating with associations and higher education, an independent provider can share their aura of quality as well as their nonprofit privileges for mailings (Suleiman, 1983).

There are also problems associated with the development of interdependent relationships. Several authors have noted that efforts to develop relationships between providers are likely to fail if their only basis is that such relationships are good (Eurich, 1985; Lynton, 1981). For most collaborations to be successful, they should be in specific areas that are congenial to the needs and capabilities of both providers.

A number of deterrents to the formation of interdependent relationships between higher education and other providers have been noted. Smutz et al. (1986) explain that there are deep-seated value differences between higher education and other providers. Whereas higher education is primarily concerned with individual development even in its CPE endeavors, other providers use CPE primarily to develop revenue for their agencies. Employers criticize universities for being too inflexible in the time, place, and format of their offerings. Moreover, universities provide CPE that is both too narrowly focused on the cognitive domain and too theoretical. Finally, universities do not know how to teach adults properly (Lynton, 1981).

The Descriptive Literature

Several studies have used national samples to answer the question about the extent to which providers form collaborative relationships with one another (Knox, 1982; Nowlen and Stern, 1981; Younghouse, 1983). In addition to these systematic studies, hundreds of examples of particular collaborations are described in the literature. Except for scattered anecdotal reports, no research has been undertaken to answer the question of how much programming is done on a collaborative versus a competitive basis. One exception is that Cervero (1984) found that the CPE programming unit at the University of Illinois cosponsors 70% of its programs with other organizations. Although this figure may be high when compared with other providers, both the national surveys and the institutional descriptions suggest that interdependent relationships are formed with much higher frequency than the non-data-based literature indicates.

A national study of all accredited medical schools in the United States found that approximately 70% cosponsor ongoing continuing medical education programs with community hospitals (Younghouse, 1983). Some of the consequences of these collaborative arrangements for the medical schools, as reported by continuing education deans and directors, were that they (1) fulfilled part of the medical schools' missions and goals; (2) increased the medical schools' image and visibility; (3) provided visibility to new medical school faculty; and (4) increased referrals to the medical schools' teaching hospitals and clinics.

Knox (1982) conducted a national study of university-based CPE programming units in five fields: medicine, pharmacy, social work, education, and law. He found that while small programs seemed unconcerned about working with other providers, large offices depended on effective relationships with other providers to maintain the size and diversity of their efforts. They did this by cosponsoring programs that would have had smaller attendance if provided independently. Knox also found that while these university units collaborated with other types of providers, they tended not to form relationships with other university units:

> In each of the five fields there were many examples of cosponsorship and other forms of collaboration between the office and associations and employers. . . . Most of the CPE offices in medical schools had established relationships with cooperating hospitals, which included provision of CPE, opportunities for internships and residencies for medical students and sources of patient referrals for teaching and research. The

most noteworthy examples of collaboration illustrated the importance of mutual benefits. There were few examples of sustained collaboration with other professional schools in the same field, in part illustrating the lack of complementarity on which sustained cooperation usually depends. (p. 122)

A 1979 study of association and university collaboration efforts included 110 professional associations and 136 universities (Nowlen and Stern, 1981). This study found that 48% of the associations and 85% of the universities had undertaken collaborative programming. For universities, the chief benefits of collaboration were strengthened awareness of university capabilities (88%), the collegiality generated (88%), improvement in the quality of the association program (85%), and as a result of this experience, an interest expressed by one or more additional professional groups in exploring cooperation with the university (83%). On the other side, the associations believed that they had benefited more from the relationship financially than had the universities. Additionally, the associations perceived that the chief benefits were an improved association program (90%), a greater awareness of university capabilities (79%), improved professional competence (70%), and the generation of collegiality between association and university personnel at various levels (70%).

This study also found major problems encountered in these collaborations. Among the associations, 48% reported "turf" definition problems (i.e., who was responsible for what); 25% said that university business procedures were inadequate; and 10% said that faculty behaved unprofessionally. Of the universities, 43% encountered "turf" definition problems; 36% had difficulty with dorm accommodations; and 26% found costs higher than expected.

In addition to these comprehensive studies of collaboration, there is no shortage of descriptions of particular collaborative programs. Several examples come from the fields of teaching (Ferver, 1981; Davies and Aquino, 1975), medicine (Manning et al., 1979), and accounting (Cruse, 1983). Eurich (1985) also provides several examples of collaborative programs between universities and employers. Seattle University's School of Engineering, with assistance from Boeing, has started a new master's degree for software engineering to accommodate Boeing's employees as well as other students. Together with 12 leading corporations, 15 universities from the Association for Media-Based Continuing Education for Engineers have developed the National Technological University (NTU). This university operates by satellite to reach engineers in corporate classrooms for advanced professional work leading to NTU's master of science degree (Eurich, 1985, p. 17). Cross (1981) describes four models of university and industry cooperation and gives several examples within each. These models lie on a continuum ranging from industry's control over what is taught and how, to higher education's control over these traditional functions.

A final example of collaborative programs is the Continuing Professional Education Development Project. This was begun in 1980 as a five-year research and development effort funded by the W. K. Kellogg Foundation, The Pennsylvania State University, and 14 participating professional associations (Lindsay, Queeny, and Smutz, 1981). A major goal of the project was to establish collaborative relationships between the university and the professional associations for the purpose of strengthening the development and implementation of CPE programs. Collaboration was implemented by developing a "profession team" for each of the five selected professional groups (accounting, architecture, clinical dietetics, clinical psychology, and gerontological nursing). Each team included representatives from national and state professional associations, regulatory agencies, Penn State University faculty members from appropriate academic departments, and project staff members.

The Analytical Literature

In this section, we move beyond the descriptive literature to theoretical and empirical studies of the factors associated with the extent to which providers engage in interdependent relationships and the dynamics and outcomes of these relationships. Although there has been a great deal of work on these questions in the general literature on organizations (Aiken and Hage, 1968; Molnar, 1978; Mulford, 1984; Schermerhorn, 1975; Schmidt and Kochan, 1977; Whetten and Leung, 1979), the literature related to CPE agencies is very sparse. This section uses the literature to answer three questions: (1) why CPE providers enter into varying levels of interdependent relationships; (2) how the providers behave in creating these relationships; and (3) what are the outcomes of these relationships.

Factors Associated
with CPE Provider Interdependence

The major analytical question that has been addressed in the literature is why providers do and do not develop interdependent relationships with each other. The two lines of inquiry on this question are reviewed here. One is the conceptual underpinnings for the CPE Development Project at Penn State (Lindsay et al., 1981). Although there are published results for some of the professional teams (Lindsay, Crowe, and Jacobs 1986), there are not yet any overall findings on why providers develop interdependent relationships. The second line of inquiry is focused on an environmental interaction model developed by Beder (1978; 1979; 1984a). In these studies, he examines interagency cooperation in continuing education.

Continuing Professional Education Development Project. Lindsay, et al. (1981) used the organizational literature to identify five key elements that guided their creation of collaborative arrangements between universities and professional associations. We describe briefly three of these elements and their implementation as part of the project. The first is the form of interaction that interorganizational relations can take. This ranges from *ad hoc* assistance (cooperation) to working together jointly and continuously on a project (collaboration). The project staff chose collaboration as the form of interorganizational relationship they wanted to establish. This level of conscious reflection on desired form of collaborative relationships is certainly unique in the CPE literature.

The second element guiding the creation of the collaborative relationships was the necessary climate and preconditions. The conceptual perspective taken by the project is that organizations should be seen as open systems that constantly interact with their environments to obtain energy and other inputs that can be translated into products. In systems terms, for the university and associations to find cause to move together, an environmental disturbance must occur. For universities, this disturbance is the resource scarcity caused by the diminishing pool of undergraduates and diminishing tax-based support by federal and state governments. For the professions, the disturbance is the general notion of accountability, which is evidenced by increasing attacks on the professions.

The third and final element is the basis for the interaction. The occurrence of interaction requires motivators that make interaction potentially attractive as well as specific determinants which make the interaction compelling. One motivator for both providers is the common goal of helping professionals become more competent. Another motivator is resource scarcity. For the university, this might mean insufficient numbers of participants for their CPE programs; for the associations, lack of staff to deliver these programs. However, these are necessary but not sufficient conditions for interaction to occur. Domain consensus and resource complementarity are two determinants that would make collaboration compelling. For example, some professional associations are interested in ensuring the competency of their members but are not interested in providing programs and do not have the staff to develop such programs. These associations are more likely to seek cooperative relationships with universities than associations that are interested in and capable of developing their own programs.

A Model for Agency Development. Beder has developed a conceptual model of agency development for the field of continuing education (Beder, 1978) based on the open system perspective (Katz and Kahn, 1971; Evan, 1971; Yuchtman and Seashore, 1967). This model was used as the basis of a book (Beder, 1984c) in which two of the authors used it to analyze interdependent relationships among providers of CPE (Cervero, 1984; Fingeret, 1984). In this section, we briefly describe the model, the two studies related to CPE, and the conclusions drawn by Beder based on this line of research.

In Beder's model (1978, 1984a), interorganizational cooperation is a strategy for obtaining necessary resources from the environment. These are used in the process of program development. The development of more and better programs increases the provider's visibility and prestige, thus improving its chances of acquiring additional resources for future development. The resources are divided into tangible ones, such as money, learners, staff, and information, and intangible ones, such as power and domain. Tangible resources are raw materials without which providers could not operate. These are garnered generally through open negotiation with other institutions in the environment. Yet tangible resources are transitory: participants enter and leave the system at will; information is useful only as it pertains to specific programs; and revenue from continuing education is generally used to support new and innovative projects within the institution. The importance of tangible resources is gauged by the extent to which they increase the provider's intangible resources, which are lasting and, which, once obtained, further the agency's position among its competitors. A provider must secure the greatest number of intangible resources possible to ensure its long-term survival. The guiding principle for establishing cooperative relationships is reciprocity of benefits, specifically tangible and intangible resources. Cooperation works best when each provider benefits by trading something of lesser value for what it gains.

Cervero (1984) used Beder's model to study the CPE program of the University of Illinois at Chicago. He concluded that, for this provider,

> interorganizational collaboration in program development is not consummated because it is theoretically or politically "correct." Rather, these relationships are a key strategy in the agency's immediate and long-term program development efforts. For the short-term (that is, developing 1,500 annual programs), the linkages provide information about participants' needs and interests, an available pool of learners, and conveniently located facilities. In the long run, the intangible resources gained from the linkages—power, prestige, domain—provide a secure foundation for the growth of the agency. (p. 36)

This provider engaged in a substantial amount of interagency collaboration, evidenced by the fact that 70% of its programs were cosponsored with other CPE providers. Consistent with Beder's model, five factors were associated with this relatively high level of collaborative activity. First, the type of instruction is nonroutine and relatively expensive in that a large majority of programs are either one-time events resulting from the latest advances in a field or ones that may be offered more often but for specialized, limited audiences. Given the low frequency with which any one program is conducted, the costs per program are great and cannot be amortized over many offerings. Consequently, the provider seeks to reduce the risk by collaborating with, for example, a professional association. The risk of program failure is reduced because (1) information about its members needs and interests is likely to be accurate and specific; (2) the association expends staff time and other resources in collecting the information, expenses that the university may not have; and (3) the cosponsorship further legitimizes the program, which helps to increase the number of participants.

A second reason for the university's high level of collaboration is that the mandate for establishing interorganizational relationships is listed among the goals of the agency. A third factor is the extraordinary scope of the agency's domain, in that any agency that has an interest in health care is a potential linkage partner. The fourth is the agency's great need to secure an uninterrupted flow of resources from the environment. The principle behind creating a large and diverse number of linkages is that the university increases its autonomy by reducing its dependency on any one other provider. By becoming part of an interdependent network of CPE providers, both tangible and intangible resources flow to the agency on a constant basis. Finally, the university is in a very dynamic environment that has many other institutions that are potential partners, a situation that is conducive to a high level of collaboration.

Fingeret (1984) analyzed an interorganizational collaboration between a large university and a nuclear power company that ultimately failed. The goal of the cooperative venture was to develop a new training program which would provide the nuclear power plant operators with the background necessary to respond in emergency situations. She analyzed the project as a loosely coupled interorganizational system in which both agencies sought resources from their external environment.

She found that the university's federal research support was being cut back; thus, it had to seek new funding sources that would be used to help attract graduate students and eventually to stabilize its flow of resources. She states that "Potential cooperative efforts must be viewed within this framework. Costs and benefits are calculated in terms of future, as well as present, resource acquisition" (p. 55). Thus, the university actively discourages cooperative efforts that are perceived as taking away resources from research or graduate education or that contribute only to service or undergraduate education. The utility originally entered the cooperative relationship under a mandate from the Nuclear Regulatory Commission. However, as the project progressed, the mandate became less strong, and some of the basic differences between the two providers became more prominent. Fingeret argued that these basic differences caused the utility to become dissatisfied with the project.

In the final chapter of his book, Beder (1984b) explains why collaborative relationships succeed and fail. One reason for success is reciprocity. Both providers must tangibly benefit by exchanging less valued resources for more valued resources. The second reason is that collaborations are more likely to succeed when organizations' boundaries are more permeable. Beder describes this phenomenon as system openness. A third reason for successful collaborations is the presence of an atmosphere of genuine trust and commitment. Beder suggests that trust and commitment derive from the style and personality of the key actors and the differences in organizational culture. The final factor is organizational structural incompatibility, in which the operations of collaborating partners become disrupted. To prevent this from occurring, providers that collaborate effectively generally adopt fluid and flexible structures that can adapt well to those of their partners.

Processes of CPE Provider Interdependence

The previous section discussed why high degrees of interdependence occur or do not occur. We now turn our focus to the dynamics of interorganizational relationships, the ''how'' question. In the general organizational literature, this question has been approached from a variety of perspectives (Mulford, 1984). However, only one of these possible research topics has been reported in the CPE literature. This research focuses on the role that ''boundary spanners'' play in interorganizational relationships (Smutz, 1985; Smutz and Toombs, 1985). These authors argue that providers may attempt to structure the decision-making process leading to interorganizational relationships in ways that are consistent with the protection of their own interests. Boundary spanners are individuals who cross their organizations' boundaries to link with other organizations in the environment (Aldrich and Herker, 1977). Because they represent the link between the organization and its environment, boundary spanners play an important role when organizations are considering the formation of interorganizational relationships. Thus, organizations can potentially affect the amount of attention these potential relationships receive by strategically selecting individuals for the boundary-spanning function.

The major question of the Penn State project was whether organizations with particular characteristics select particular types of individuals to serve as boundary spanners. Two types of organizations were found: domain-protecting and domain-expanding (Smutz and Toombs, 1985). Domain-protecting providers, which were primarily nonacademic institutions, entered the project primarily to determine if the new ways of developing CPE programs being investigated posed any threat to their current operations. Domain-expanding providers expected to expand their involvement in continuing education and participated in the project to find ways ''of forming partnerships with organizations already involved in continuing education'' (Smutz and Toombs, 1985, p. 30) that might make their entrance into the field more effective. These two types of providers appoint different types of individuals to the boundary-spanning role:

> Domain protecting organizations tend to select individuals who perceive themselves as having high expertise in continuing education and who have considerable expertise in the field, but who have low level positions in the organization, who do not communicate frequently with the organization, and who have limited influence. In contrast, the domain expanding organizations tend to appoint individuals with little

perceived expertise in continuing education and limited past involvement in the field, but who have high level positions, who communicate frequently with the parent organization, and who are influential. (Smutz and Toombs, 1985, p. 31)

The authors conclude that providers do strategically select boundary spanners depending on their interests. For domain-protecting organizations, the boundary spanners perform an oversight function. On the other hand, the boundary spanners of domain-expanding providers serve a developmental function.

Outcomes of CPE Provider Interdependence

The previous two sections examined the literature related to the conditions that contribute to the formation of interorganizational relationships and to the dynamics of these processes. Although there has been only a small amount of research in these two areas, there has been no systematic study on the outcomes of interdependent relationships, such as the amount and quality of provision of CPE or the extent to which more effective learning occurs among participants. Younghouse (1983) suggests that "Longitudinal research could be undertaken to test behavioral changes in the participating physicians as a result of medical school/community hospital CME programming linkages" (p. 97). In a recent study of factors leading to the termination of three consortia of higher education institutions, Offerman (1985) found that the consortia failed in spite of benefits to the adult learners such as improved scheduling. Thus, while we know something about why providers seek out varying degrees of interdependent relationships, we know virtually nothing about their outcomes. At present, the effectiveness of various types of relationships have simply not been documented through research.

INTERDEPENDENCE IN CPE: A RESEARCH FRAMEWORK

Collaboration has generally been seen as a desirable strategy for action in CPE and one that is worth encouraging. However, in order to effectively stimulate or facilitate interagency collaboration, it is necessary to understand its system of determinants. The growing literature that deals with this phenomenon is more prescriptive than analytical, and it does not provide a "knowledge base for effective action" (Reid, 1964, p. 418). While Beder's model provides some insight into the topic, its focus is more on agency development than on the determinants of interdependent relationships. Although Lindsay et al. (1981) offer useful observations on the question, they have explicitly stated that their work is not a theory or a model. Thus, we have a great deal of anecdotal information and pieces of research that impinge on the question: "Under what conditions do CPE providers enter into what degrees of interdependent relationships with other CPE providers?"

This question in a more general form has guided much research in the literature on organizations and has been integrated in a series of researchable propositions (Schermerhorn, 1975). We borrow heavily from these propositions as well as their supporting literature in developing our own framework because we believe that CPE providers behave as does any other organization when it comes to interorganizational relationships. By building a framework that is grounded in this more general literature, we hope to provide a solid foundation for decision making and research in CPE.

A fundamental assumption of the framework is that providers *decide* to engage in interdependent relationships with one another. As summarized by Schermerhorn (1975):

> The applicability of this decision frame of reference is supported in the literature, and its key insight is the recognition of individuals as mediators of the organizations' interorganizational roles. Theoretically, the phenomenon may be viewed in terms of a scenario depicting an organizational decision-maker influencing organizational behavior under constraints imposed by the organizational and environmental contexts. (p. 852)

The logic of our framework is that certain motivating conditions exist that create a need for cooperation in a decision maker. The decision maker's need, however, is necessary but not sufficient to create action. The need must be developed into demand by one or more of a series of determinants before the decision maker can act. The framework specifies three conditions (motivators) under which CPE providers come to consider high degrees of interdependence as a possible action strategy and three conditions (determinants) under which it becomes a preferred action strategy. The unit of analysis for the framework is a decision maker's (either an individual's or a group's) action strategy with regard to a specific CPE program. This implies that if decision makers are planning several programs at the same time, they could use several different action strategies.

The Dependent Variable: Interdependence

The concept of interdependence has a fairly standard definition in the organizational literature. We use Litwak and Rothman's (1970): "By interdependence we mean that two or more organizations must take each other into account in order to achieve their individual goals . . . that the acts of one organization affect those of another in an immediate way" (p. 147). We propose a continuum of organizational interdependence in CPE along which six qualitatively different orientations can be identified. Although finer distinctions may be identified within the six, the continuum is intended to include all possible ways in which two or more providers can interact with one another. We wish to highlight the assumption that this is a descriptive, rather than a prescriptive, framework. We do not assume that greater interdependence is a more highly valued or successful orientation than less interdependence. The orientations or possible action strategies are listed in order from those which involve the least to the greatest degree of interdependence:

1. *Monopoly.* In this orientation, a provider is the only one of its type (e.g., a university or a professional association) in a service area or is the only one that can program in a certain content area. This kind of situation can occur because of circumstance or tradition or can be mandated by a higher authority, such as a board of higher education. In this orientation, the least common of the six, one provider need not take any other provider into account in planning a CPE program.

2. *Parallelism.* Cross (1981) suggests that CPE providers

> can run parallel operations. In the beginning, the relationship between collegiate institutions and other providers of education services was essentially parallel. . . . Each went along its well-defined paths. Many educators still act as though parallelism still predominates. Plodding along their own paths, they pretty much keep to themselves, quite unaware of travelers on other pathways. (p. 2)

Occasionally, a provider finds that others are offering the same kind of programs but generally continues on the assumption that the market is large enough for more than one provider. In this strategy, there is almost no interdependence, and what does occur results from chance encounters among providers.

3. *Competition.* Many cite competition as a possible action strategy for CPE providers (Beder, 1984a; Cross, 1981). In this orientation, two or more providers offer CPE programs on a specific topic with full knowledge that others are doing the same. Where there is a substantial number of potential participants, neither provider will suffer program cancellations or loss of prestige. However, in many cases, there is a limited number of participants, and conflict between the two providers results. While the providers are not working together to achieve mutual goals, the acts of one organization can obviously affect the other in an immediate way.

4. *Cooperation.* Lindsay et al. (1981) have made useful distinctions among points 4, 5, and 6 on the continuum by drawing from the organizational literature. *Cooperation* refers to the strategy where providers assist each other on an *ad hoc* basis (Whetten, 1981). One provider, for example, may offer a mailing list or a list of potential speakers to another. This represents a greater degree of interdependence than points 1 through 3 because the two providers are working together, although on a limited basis, in offering a CPE program. Our own experience suggests that this is a common form of interaction among CPE providers, although its incidence has never been researched.

5. *Coordination.* In this orientation, providers consistently ensure that their

activities take into account those of others (Hall et al., 1974). The coordination of educational services can occur by mandate from a higher authority, by interorganizational agreements, or by what Cross (1981) defines as a second form of parallelism:

> It is the model in which each provider performs a unique function within well-defined boundaries. . . . In the jargon of the trade, this is known as seeking the "market niche" which means simply that providers who are potentially competitive will seek the unique service where competition is weak or non-existent. . . . Parallelism can be maintained only through conscious and sustained effort and by careful definition of non-overlapping functions. (p. 3)

This strategy requires a high degree of interdependence among providers. The only major difference between this orientation and collaboration is that in the latter, the providers work together on a single program.

6. *Collaboration.* Collaboration refers to providers' "working together jointly and continuously on a particular project towards a specific goal" (Lindsay et al., 1981, p. 5). When people speak of high degrees of interdependence, this is the form of interaction that they usually have in mind. The most common example of this form is cosponsorship of a program by two or more providers. However, there is a great deal of variation in the nature of the agreements between providers, depending on their degree of formality and the organizational level at which they are negotiated (Lindsay et al., 1981; Marrett, 1971). Thus, collaborations may be bound together by informal agreements or legal contracts.

The Independent Variables:
Motivators and Determinants

In this section, we describe three conditions that motivate decision makers to view high degrees of interdependence as a possible organizational strategy and three conditions that make this form of interaction compelling, thus translating it into a desirable strategy.

Motivators

Motivating conditions influencing interorganizational interdependence derive from the benefits potentially associated with such activities (Schermerhorn, 1975).

1. Providers will seek out or be receptive to interorganizational cooperation when faced with situations of resource scarcity or performance distress (Schermerhorn, 1975, p. 848). This is well supported in the general organizational literature (Mulford, 1984; Schermerhorn, 1975) and is consistent with theory and research in continuing education (Beder, 1978; Darkenwald, 1983;

Lindsay et al., 1981). Schermerhorn says that providers may be favorably predisposed toward cooperative relationships where there is a need to gain access to otherwise unavailable resources, to free internal resources for alternative uses, or to employ existing resources more efficiently.

2. Providers will seek out or be receptive to interorganizational cooperation when "cooperation" per se takes on a positive value (Schermerhorn, 1975, p. 848). This positive valuing may arise from internal organizational conditions or from suprasystem norms. This is the factor that Beder (1984a) terms "goal orientation" and that was found by Cervero (1984) and Fingeret (1984) to influence the extent of interdependence among providers.

3. Providers will seek out or be receptive to interorganizational cooperation when a powerful extraorganizational force demands this activity (Schermerhorn, 1975, p. 849). Such demands may stem from governments or third-party organizations such as insurance companies. Fingeret (1984) found this to be a powerful motivator when the Nuclear Regulatory Commission forced utility companies to cooperate with universities in training their engineering employees.

Determinants

1. To the extent that providers' boundaries are open and permeable *vis-à-vis* the external environment, they are more likely to employ interorganizational cooperation as a strategy (Schermerhorn, 1975, p. 850). Beder (1984b) also found this to be a major determinant of cooperation. Furthermore, the Penn State project (Smutz, 1985; Smutz and Toombs, 1985) provides strong empirical evidence for this proposition in its study of boundary spanners.

2. Under conditions where two or more providers experience and recognize some mutual need or purpose, and where organizational domains are not sensitive issues, they are more likely to employ interorganizational cooperation as a strategy (Schermerhorn, 1975, p. 851). For this to occur, two conditions need to be met. The providers' domains or official goals must be complementary rather than similar. Schermerhorn explains: "Since official goals relate an organization to specific input and output domains, goal similarity at this level might well imply competition as opposed to cooperation" (p. 851). As an example of this principle, Cervero (1984) and Knox (1982) both found that universities generally do not collaborate with each other even when they have extensive relationships with other types of providers. Schermerhorn (1975) continues:

> Given that domains are not a sensitive issue, however, divergent operating goals would seem to offer little basis for cooperative relations. Thus, interorganizational cooperation appears more likely in situations where organizational domains are not sensitive issues (complementary official goals) and where mutual performance objectives are perceived (common operative goals). (p. 851)

3. To the extent that physical opportunity for interorganizational cooperative activity exists within the provider and/or its external environment, it is more likely to use interorganizational cooperation as a strategy (Schermerhorn, 1975, p. 852). The geographical proximity of potential partners was found by Cervero (1984) and Beder (1984b) to be an important correlate of cooperation among continuing education providers. An important determinant at the intra-organizational level is a provider's internal capacity to build and support cooperative activities. Schermerhorn suggests that the relevant factors for this determinant include a provider's existing level of cooperative activity, the availability of slack resources to build and explore cooperative ventures, and the ability to mobilize these resources for application to interorganizational cooperation.

Some Preliminary Hypotheses

Several hypotheses could test our fundamental proposition that the motivators are a necessary but not sufficient condition to engage in highly interdependent relationships. First, if none of the three motivating conditions are present, a CPE provider would have no interest in highly interdependent relationships. Thus, the provider would most likely engage in the strategies that we termed *monopoly, parallelism,* or *competition.* Second, if at least one of the motivating conditions is present but none of the determinants are, a CPE provider might see the possibility of highly interdependent relationships but would not receive that extra push to view them as a preferred action strategy. Thus, the decision maker would most likely engage in one of the first three strategies. Third, with at least one motivator and one determinant, a CPE provider would seek out or be receptive to highly interdependent relationships and would most likely engage in Strategy 4 (cooperation), 5 (coordination), or 6 (collaboration). As part of this hypothesis, as more motivators and determinants are present the likelihood of entering highly interdependent relationships increases. As a final note, we would draw attention to the fact that the relationships between the independent and dependent variables of the framework are statistical rather than deterministic. Although providers' forming highly interdependent relationships when no motivators or determinants are present is unlikely, it is possible.

CONCLUSIONS AND IMPLICATIONS

The organization and provision of continuing education for the professions may be characterized in the following ways. Within each profession, four major types of institutions are providing almost all of the continuing education opportunities. Depending on the profession, higher education, professional associations, employing agencies, and independent providers offer differing amounts of continuing education. Although higher education remains an important provider, its stature, if anything, is decreasing according to two of its most astute observers (Berlin, 1983; Stern, 1983a). Although the most common mode of operation is for providers to work independently, there is an increasing interest in and frequency of highly interdependent relationships among providers. It must be noted, however, that this characterization is based on personal observations, anecdotal reports, and fragmentary empirical reports rather than on systematic research studies. Thus, while this seems a reasonable description based on our limited data, we have no way of knowing how closely it represents the true state of affairs.

A number of authors (e.g., Houle, 1980; Stern, 1983a) have suggested that in the future, CPE will be organized in a much more interdependent fashion, similar to the way in which much preservice training is currently organized. The literature overwhelmingly supports the view that these systems of CPE should be based on the principle of collaboration, rather than competition, among providers. However, to date, the literature on interdependent relationships has been more promotional than analytical, more polemical than critical, and more hortatory than descriptive. Of all the literature, we believe that the approaches taken by Beder (1984c) and the Penn State project (Lindsay et al., 1981; Smutz and Toombs, 1985) offer the greatest promise. The most crucial insight common to both approaches is that CPE providers behave as does any other organization when seeking interorganizational relationships. This makes it possible to use the vast amount of literature on organizations in general to understand the conditions under which CPE providers will seek out and be receptive to cooperative relationships. Unless the perspectives from this literature are used to understand the issue, efforts to stimulate or facilitate greater degrees of interdependence among providers are not likely to be very effective.

We have proposed a framework that can be used by decision makers and researchers to approach the practice of interorganizational relationships in a systematic way. The framework is not empirically testable in its current form. Each of the six independent variables as well as the dependent variable of interdependence needs to be operationalized regardless of whether a statistical or nonstatistical approach (e.g., a case study) is employed as the research method. Although each of the motivators and determinants has been demonstrated to affect the extent of interdependent relationships, they would all need to be tested for their applicability to CPE providers. A second research effort should use degrees of interdependence as the independent variable in studies that examine its effectiveness in terms of the adequacy and quality of CPE programs.

Finally, we would like to address the possible future of interorganizational relationships in CPE. One question is to what extent any future systems of CPE will be characterized by highly interdependent relationships among providers. While there is not an answer, we propose a way to think about the question. The number of interdependent relationships will be determined primarily by the extent to which decision makers for CPE providers perceive that the three motivators and three determinants are impinging upon their activities. We cannot predict the future without empirical information regarding their perceptions. Yet, those interested in this question need to consider these factors in order to arrive at a reasonable estimate.

The second question regarding interorganizational relationships in CPE is normative: Should future systems of CPE be characterized by greater degrees of interdependent relationships among providers? We believe that it is unreasonable to take a position on this question because we lack evidence that cooperative relationships lead to desirable outcomes such as higher-quality, more accessible, and more effective CPE programs. We support the view expressed by others (Beder, 1984a; Eurich, 1985; Lynton, 1981) that cooperation is not inherently a better way of organizing continuing education than is competition. It is simply a means to an end, and once the ends are defined and the relationships established, we would know whether greater degrees of interdependence are worth promoting.

REFERENCES

Aiken, M., and Hage, J. (1968). Organizational interdependence and intraorganizational structure. *American Sociological Review* 63: 912–930.

Aldrich, H. E., and Herker, D. (1977). Boundary spanning roles and organizational structure. *Academy of Management Review* 2: 217–230.

Alford, H. J. (1980). *Power and Conflict in Continuing Education*. Belmont, CA: Wadsworth.

Arnstein, G. E. (1983). The federal interest. In M. R. Stern (ed.), *Power and Conflict in Continuing Professional Education*. Belmont, CA: Wadsworth.

Beder, H. W. (1978). An environmental interaction model for agency development in adult education. *Adult Education* 28(3): 176–190.

Beder, H. W. (1979). The relationship of community and sponsor support to selected aspects of adult education agency functioning. *Adult Education* 29(2): 96–107.

Beder, H. W. (1984a). Interorganizational cooperation: Why and how. In H. W. Beder (ed.), *Realizing the Potential of Interorganizational Cooperation*. San Francisco: Jossey-Bass.

Beder, H. W. (1984b). Principles for successful cooperation. In H. W. Beder (ed.), *Realizing the Potential of Interorganizational Cooperation*. San Francisco: Jossey-Bass.

Beder, H. W., ed. (1984c). *Realizing the Potential of Interorganizational Cooperation*. San Francisco: Jossey-Bass.

Berlin, L. S. (1983). The university and continuing professional education: A contrary view. In M. R. Stern (ed.), *Power and Conflict in Continuing Professional Education*. Belmont, CA: Wadsworth.

Bloom, G. F. (1983). The real estate professional. In M. R. Stern (ed.), *Power and Conflict in Continuing Professional Education*. Belmont, CA: Wadsworth.

Bruce, J. D., Siebert, W. M., Smullin, L. D., and Fano, R. M. (1982). *Lifelong Cooperative Education*. Cambridge, MA: Massachusetts Institute of Technology.

Cervero, R. M. (1984). Collaboration in university continuing professional education. In H. W. Beder (ed.), *Realizing the Potential of Interorganizational Cooperation.* San Francisco: Jossey-Bass.

Cervero, R. M. and Scanlan, C. L. (eds.). (1985). *Problems and Prospects in Continuing Professional Education.* San Francisco: Jossey-Bass.

Cross, K. P. (1981). New frontiers for higher education: Business and the professions. In American Association for Higher Education (ed.), *Partnerships with Business and the Professions.* Washington, DC.

Cruse, R. B. (1983). The accounting profession. In M. R. Stern (ed.), *Power and Conflict in Continuing Professional Education.* Belmont, CA: Wadsworth.

Curran, J. R. (1983). The professions in banking. In M. R. Stern (ed.), *Power and Conflict in Continuing Professional Education.* Belmont, CA: Wadsworth.

Darkenwald, G. G. (1983). Perspectives of business and industry on cooperative programming with educational institutions. *Adult Education Quarterly* 33(4): 230–243.

Davies, H. M., and Aquino, J. T. (1975). Collaboration in continuing professional development. *Journal of Teacher Education* 26(3): 274–277.

Derbyshire, R. C. (1983). The medical profession. In M. R. Stern (ed.), *Power and Conflict in Continuing Professional Education.* Belmont, CA: Wadsworth.

Eurich, N. P. (1985). *Corporate Classrooms: The Learning Business.* Princeton, NJ: The Carnegie Foundation for the Advancement of Teaching.

Evan, W. (1971). The organization set: Towards a theory of interorganizational relations. In J. Maurer (ed.), *Readings in Organizational Theory: Open Systems Approaches.* New York: Random House.

Ferver, J. C. (1981). Introduction to coordinating SCDE programs. *Journal of Research and Development in Education* 15(1): 22–72.

Fingeret, A. (1984). Who's in control? A case study of university-industry collaboration. In H. W. Beder (ed.), *Realizing the Potential of Interorganizational Cooperation.* San Francisco: Jossey-Bass.

Griffith, D. E. (1983). Professional continuing education in engineering. In M. R. Stern (ed.), *Power and Conflict in Continuing Professional Education.* Belmont, CA: Wadsworth.

Hall, R., Clark, J., Giordano, P., Johnson, P., and Van Roekel, M. (1974). Interorganizational relationships. Paper presented at the 8th World Conference of Sociology, International Sociological Association.

Hazzard, G. W. (1977). Continuing education for scientists and engineers. In National Science Foundation, *Continuing Education in Science and Engineering.* Washington, DC.

Hohmann, L. (1980). Professional continuing education. In H. J. Alford (ed.), *Power and Conflict in Continuing Education.* Belmont, CA: Wadsworth.

Hohmann, L. (1985). Interorganizational collaboration in continuing professional education. In R. M. Cervero and C. L. Scanlan (eds.), *Problems and Prospects in Continuing Professional Education.* San Francisco: Jossey-Bass.

Houle, C. O. (1980). *Continuing Learning in the Professions.* San Francisco: Jossey-Bass.

Houle, C. O. (1983). Possible futures. In M. R. Stern (ed.), *Power and Conflict in Continuing Professional Education.* Belmont, CA: Wadsworth.

Houston, R. W., and Freiberg, J. H. (1979). Perpetual motion, blindman's bluff, and inservice education. *Journal of Teacher Education* 30(1): 7–8.

Katz, D., and Kahn, R. (1971). Open systems theory. In J. Maurer (ed.), *Readings in Organizational Theory: Open-Systems Approaches.* New York: Random House.

Kenny, W. R. (1985). Program planning and accreditation. In R. M. Cervero and C. L. Scanlan (eds.), *Problems and Prospects in Continuing Professional Education*. San Francisco: Jossey-Bass.

Knox, A. B. (1982). Organizational dynamics in university continuing professional education. *Adult Education* 32(3): 117–129.

Kost, R. J. (1980). Competition and innovation in continuing education. In H. J. Alford (ed.), *Power and Conflict in Continuing Education*. Belmont, CA: Wadsworth.

Lindsay, C. A., Crowe, M. B., and Jacobs, D. F. (1986). Continuing professional education for clinical psychology: A practice oriented model. In B. Edelstein and E. Beiler (eds.), *Evaluation and Accountability in Clinical Training*. New York: Plenum Press.

Lindsay, C. A., Queeny, D. S., and Smutz, W. D. (1981). A model and process for university/professional association collaboration. Paper presented at the National Conference on Higher Education of the American Association for Higher Education, Washington, DC.

Litwak, E., and Hylton, L. (1962). Interorganizational analysis: A hypothesis on coordinating agencies. *Administrative Science Quarterly* 6: 395–420.

Litwak, E., and Rothman, J. (1970). Towards the theory and practice of coordination between formal organizations. In W. R. Rosengren and M. Lefton (eds.), *Organizations and Clients*. Columbus, OH: Charles E. Merrill.

Lynton, E. A. (1981). A role for colleges in corporate training and development. In American Association for Higher Education (ed.), *Partnerships with Business and the Professions*. Washington, DC.

Lynton, E. A. (1983). Higher education's role in fostering employee education. *Educational Record* 64(4): 18–25.

Manning, P. R., Covell, D. G., Mussell, B., Thomas C. J., Bee, R. S., and Denson, T. A. (1979). Continuing medical education: Linking the community hospital and the medical school. *Journal of Medical Education* 54(June): 461–466.

Marrett, C. (1971). On the specification of interorganizational dimensions. *Sociology and Social Research* 56: 83–97.

Mawby, R. G. (1985). Chairman's message: Lifelong learning and the professional. In The Kellogg Foundation, *1985 Annual Report*. Battle Creek, MI.

Molnar, J. (1978). Comparative organizational properties and interorganizational interdependence. *Sociology and Social Research* 63: 24–48.

Mulford, C. L. (1984). *Interorganizational Relations: Implications for Community Development*. New York: Human Sciences Press.

National University Continuing Education Association. (1984). *The Role of Colleges and Universities in Continuing Professional Education*. Washington, DC.

Nowlen, P. N., and Stern, M. R. (1981). Partnerships in continuing education for professionals. In American Association for Higher Education (ed.), *Partnerships with Business and the Professions*. Washington, DC.

Offerman, M. J. (1985). Factors leading to the termination of three consortia of higher education institutions: A case study. Unpublished doctoral dissertation, Northern Illinois University, DeKalb.

Queeny, D. S. (1984). The role of the university in continuing professional education. *Educational Record* 65(3): 13–17.

Reid, W. (1964). Interagency coordination in delinquency prevention and control. *Social Service Review* 38: 418–428.

Ryor, J., Shanker, A., and Sandefeur, J. T. (1979). Three perspectives on inservice education. *Journal of Teacher Education* 30(1): 13–29.

Schermerhorn, J. R. (1975). Determinants of interorganizational cooperation. *Academy of Management Journal* 18(4): 846–856.

Schmidt, S., and Kochan, T. (1977). Interorganizational relationships: Patterns and motivations. *Administrative Science Quarterly* 22: 220–234.

Shelton, H. R., and Craig, R. L. (1983). Continuing professional development: The employer's perspective. In M. R. Stern (ed.), *Power and Conflict in Continuing Professional Education*. Belmont, CA: Wadsworth.

Smutz, W. D. (1985). Differential performance of formal boundary spanners in the formation of university/professional association interorganizational relationships. Paper presented at the Annual Meeting of the Association for the Study of Higher Education, Chicago.

Smutz, W. D., Crowe, M. B., and Lindsay, C. A. (1986). Emerging perspectives on continuing professional education. In J. C. Smart (ed.), *Higher Education: Handbook of Theory and Research*, Vol. II. New York: Agathon Press.

Smutz, W. D., and Toombs, W. (1985). Forming university/professional association collaborative relationships: The strategic selection of boundary spanners. Paper presented at the 1985 conference of the American Educational Research Association, Chicago.

Sneed, J. T. (1972). Continuing education in the professions. *The Journal of Higher Education* 43(3): 223–238.

Stern, M. R. (1980). Universities in continuing education. In H. J. Alford (ed.), *Power and Conflict in Continuing Education*. Belmont, CA: Wadsworth.

Stern, M. R. (1983a). A disorderly market. In M. R. Stern (ed.), *Power and Conflict in Continuing Professional Education*. Belmont, CA: Wadsworth.

Stern, M. R., ed. (1983b). *Power and Conflict in Continuing Professional Education*. Belmont, CA: Wadsworth.

Suleiman, A. (1983). Private enterprise: The independent provider. In M. R. Stern (ed.), *Power and Conflict in Continuing Professional Education*. Belmont, CA: Wadsworth.

Valentine, T. (1984). The consequences of mismanaged interagency collaborations. In H. W. Beder (ed.), *Realizing the Potential of Interorganizational Cooperation*. San Francisco: Jossey-Bass.

Weaver, J. F. (1979). Collaboration: Why is sharing the turf so difficult? *Journal of Teacher Education* 30(1): 24–25.

Whetten, D. (1981). Interorganizational relations: A review of the field. *Journal of Higher Education* 52: 1–28.

Whetten, D., and Leung, T. (1979). The instrumental value of interorganizational relations: Antecedents and consequences of linkage formation. *Academy of Management Journal* 22: 325–344.

Younghouse, R. H. (1983). A national study of cosponsored continuing medical education category one programming activities between medical schools and community hospitals. Unpublished doctoral dissertation, University of Illinois at Urbana-Champaign.

Yuchtman, E., and Seashore, S. (1967). A system resource approach to organizational effectiveness. *American Sociological Review* 32: 891–903.

Author Index

*Names in parentheses identify the senior author for "et al." references.

433

Subject Index